JUNIOR

Active Maths 1

Complete Course for 2014 Exam

Michael Keating, Derek Mulvany and James O'Loughlin

Special Advisors:
Oliver Murphy and Colin Townsend

Editor: Priscilla O'Connor, Sarah Reece

Designer: Liz White

Layout: Compuscript

Illustrations: Compuscript, Denis M. Baker, Rory O'Neill

ISBN: 978-1-84741-928-6

© Michael Keating, Derek Mulvany, James O'Loughlin and Colin Townsend, 2011

Folens Publishers, Hibernian Industrial Estate, Greenhills Road, Tallaght, Dublin 24, Ireland

> **CIC**
>
> Note: The material highlighted in the Table of Contents is the Common Introductory Course (CIC) as suggested by the NCCA and the Project Maths team.
>
> The Common Introductory Course is the minimum course to be covered by all learners at the start of junior cycle. Once the introductory course has been completed, teachers can decide which topics to extend or explore to a greater depth, depending on the progress being made by the class group. The order in which topics are taught is left to the discretion of the teacher.

Acknowledgements

The authors would like especially to thank Jim McElroy for his work on the written solutions and his invaluable advice.

Thanks also to Priscilla O'Connor, Folens Publishers, for all her hard work, enthusiasm and patience throughout the year.

The authors and publisher wish to thank the following for permission to reproduce photographs: Alamy, Corbis, Getty, iStockphoto, Moviestore Collection, Photocall Ireland, Science Photo Library, Sportsfile, Thinkstock.

Photo of triathletes from US Navy website (http://www.navy.mil/view_single.asp?id=48780). The following photos were obtained from Wikimedia Commons: White House, Washington, DC (http://upload.wikimedia. org/wikipedia/commons/5/57/White_House_06.02.08.jpg); Giant's Causeway, Co. Antrim (http://commons. wikimedia.org/wiki/File:Giants_Causeway_cellules_polygonales.JPG); Mercedes-Benz CLK DTM C209 by M. Trischler [CC-BY-SA-2.5 (www.creativecommons.org/licenses/by-sa/2.5)] (http://commons.wikimedia. org/wiki/File:Mercedes_CLK_DTM_C209.jpg); 2009 Ford Focus by Ford Motor Company from USA [CC-BY-2.0 (www.creativecommons.org/licenses/by/2.0)] (http://commons.wikimedia.org/wiki/File:2009_Ford_Focus_ Coupe_2.jpg); Volkswagen Golf VI by Thomas Doerfer [CC-BY-3.0 (www.creativecommons.org/licenses/by/3.0)] (http://commons.wikimedia.org/wiki/File:Opel_Astra_G_front.JPG).

The authors and publisher wish to thank Bord Gáis Energy for permission to reproduce sample bills.

Contents

Introduction

Active Maths 1 is a comprehensive new three-year textbook covering the complete Junior Certificate Ordinary Level course, including Strands 1–4 of the Project Maths syllabus and Strand 5 of the existing syllabus. On completing *Active Maths 1*, Higher Level students can continue the Junior Certificate Higher Level course with *Active Maths 2* (to be published in 2012).

Active Maths 1 reflects the much greater emphasis in the new syllabus on:

- understanding mathematical concepts;
- relating mathematics to everyday experience;
- developing problem-solving skills.

A separate free Activity Book provides a wealth of activities designed to develop students' understanding of each topic in a hands-on way.

Active Maths 1 is co-authored by experienced maths teachers and has been class-tested in Project Maths pilot schools. Teachers using this book will find that they have the new syllabus fully covered. Their students will be ready for the new style of exam question, in which they must apply their mathematical knowledge to solve familiar and unfamiliar problems drawn from daily life.

Students who use *Active Maths 1* will love its approach to mathematics: guided activity-based student learning with a clear emphasis on understanding as opposed to rote learning. *Active Maths 1* is packed with student-friendly features:

- Simple language is used throughout the book.
- Full colour is used throughout to enhance students' understanding.
- Learning Outcomes from the new syllabus are stated at the beginning of each chapter.
- Each chapter includes a You Should Remember section so that students can check they are fully prepared before starting the chapter.
- A list of Key Words at the start of each chapter helps students to consolidate learning.
- Key Words are set apart in Definition boxes to reinforce the importance of understanding their meaning.
- Clear and concise Worked Examples show students how to set out their answers, including step-by-step instructions with excellent diagrams to explain constructions.
- Essential formulae are set apart in Formula boxes.
- Note boxes give useful information and engaging insights.
- The textbook is linked throughout with the Activity Book to introduce topics and emphasise key Learning Outcomes.
- Comprehensive graded exercises on each topic range from the basics to more challenging questions.
- End-of-chapter revision exercises allow students to reinforce their understanding of the topics covered in each chapter.
- Context questions are included throughout.
- Answers to exercises are given at the end of the book.
- Additional teacher resources, including digital material, are provided online at www.folensonline.ie.

Active Maths 1 allows teachers to meet the challenge of the new syllabus for Junior Certificate, and encourages students to discover for themselves that mathematics can be enjoyable and relevant to everyday life.

NB: Constructions in this book are numbered according to the NCCA syllabus for Project Maths at Junior Certificate Ordinary Level.

chapter 1

Sets

Learning Outcomes

In this chapter you will learn:

- How to define a set
- About set notation
- How to describe a set
- How to construct a Venn diagram
- About union and intersection of sets
- About the universal set
- About the complement of a set
- About set difference
- How to solve problems using sets

The branch of mathematics known as set theory was developed at the end of the nineteenth century by the German mathematician Georg Cantor.

Georg Cantor (1845–1918)

A **set** is a collection of well-defined objects. The objects in the set are called **elements**.

1.1 SET NOTATION

The **elements** of a **set** are always placed within a set of curly (or chain) brackets. We use a capital letter to label a set. For example, the set of natural numbers less than 6 could be written as follows:

$$A = \{1, 2, 3, 4, 5\}$$

The symbol $\in$ stands for 'is an element of' and the symbol $\notin$ stands for 'is not an element of'. For example, $2 \in \{1, 2, 3, 4\}$ and $5 \notin \{1, 2, 3, 4\}$.

$\in$ 'is an element of'
$\notin$ 'is not an element of'

The number of elements in a set Q is denoted by #Q. For example, if Q = {8, 9, 10,11}, then #Q = 4.

The **number of elements** in a set is called the **cardinal number** of the set. # means 'number of elements'.

Describing a Set

There are two ways of describing the elements of a set.

(a) **The List Method**

All elements of the set are listed inside curly brackets. For example:

{2, 4, 6, 8, 10}

■ The order in which you list elements is not important.

■ An element may appear once only in a set.

(b) **The Rule Method**

The elements of the set are described using words. For example:

{Even numbers between 1 and 11}

Worked Example 1.1

(i) Use the list method to describe the set P of prime numbers between 30 and 50.

(ii) Use the rule method to describe the following set: O ={11, 13, 15, 17, 19}.

Solution

(i) P = {31, 37, 41, 43, 47}

(ii) O = {Odd numbers between 10 and 20}

Equal Sets

Two sets are said to be equal if they have the same elements. For example, the following sets are equal:

A = {1, 4, 9, 16} and B = {16, 4, 9, 1}. We write A = B.

If two sets are not equal, we write A ≠ B.

The Null Set

If a set has no elements, then it is called the **null set**, or the **empty set**.

Symbol ∅ or { }

For example, the set of square numbers between 17 and 24 is an empty set or a null set, as there are no square numbers between 17 and 24. We use the symbol ∅ or { } to denote the null set.

Worked Example 1.2

Insert the correct symbol in the blank space.

   (i) 2 _____ {1, 3, 5, 7}

  (ii) 4 _____ {1, 4, 9, 16}

 (iii) {1, 2, 3} _____ {2, 3, 5}

 (iv) {11, 13, 17} _____ {17, 13, 11}

Solution

   (i) 2 ∉ {1, 3, 5, 7}

  (ii) 4 ∈ {1, 4, 9, 16}

 (iii) {1, 2, 3} ≠ {2, 3, 5}

 (iv) {11, 13, 17} = {17, 13, 11}

Exercise 1.1

1. List the elements of each of these sets:

   (i) {The positive whole numbers less than 9}

  (ii) {The even numbers between 9 and 15}

 (iii) {The whole numbers between 4 and 10}

 (iv) {The odd whole numbers greater than 1 and less than 8}

2. List the elements of each of these sets:

   (i) {The first five prime numbers}

  (ii) {The divisors of 28}

 (iii) {The multiples of 5 that are less than 46}

 (iv) {The divisors of 36 that are also prime numbers}

3. List the elements of each of these sets:

   (i) {The square numbers between 0 and 97}

  (ii) {The factors of 12}

 (iii) {The proper fractions that can be made from the integers 2, 3 and 4}

 (iv) {The largest whole number less than 100}

4. List the elements of each of these sets:

   (i) {The prime numbers between 24 and 28}

  (ii) {The even whole numbers between 29 and 35}

 (iii) {The square numbers between 40 and 48}

 (iv) {The whole numbers between 1 and 2}

5. A = {2, 4, 6, 8} and B = {8, 6, 4, 2}. Is A = B? Explain your answer.

6. X = {2, 3, 5, 7, 9} and Y = {2, 3, 5, 7, 11}. Is X = Y? Explain your answer.

7. State whether the following statements are true or false. Explain your answers.

   (i) 3 ∈ {1, 3, 5, 9}

  (ii) 10 ∈ {The factors of 24}

 (iii) 15 ∉ {The first five prime numbers}

 (iv) 4 ∈ {The common factors of 16 and 24}

  (v) {2, 4, 6, 8} = {4, 2, 8, 6}

8. A = {1, 3, 5, 7, 9, 11},
B = {2, 4, 6, 8, 10, 12} and
C = {2, 3, 5, 7, 11, 13}.
State whether the following statements are
true or false. If they are false, explain why.

(i)   A = B

(ii) C is the set of odd numbers between 1
and 14.

(iii) 7 ∉ B

(iv) 2^2 ∈ B

(v)   A new set D is formed by adding 1 to
each element of the set A.
D = B.

9. List the elements of the following sets:

(i)   {The set of all rectangles in the diagram}

(ii) {The set of all triangles in the diagram}

(iii) {The set of all squares in the diagram}

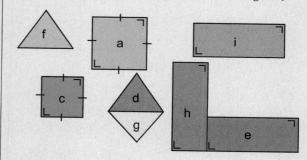

10. X = {1, 3, 5, 7}   Y = {2, 4, 6, 8, 10}

Find: (i) #X   (ii) #Y   (iii) #X + #Y   (iv) #Y − #X   (v) 2(#X) + 3(#Y)

1.2 SUBSETS

If all of the elements of a set A are also in a set B, then we
say that A is a **subset** of B. The symbol for subset is ⊂.

If A = {1, 2}
and B = {1, 2, 3}, then A ⊂ B.

If A is a subset of B and A contains all
the elements of B, then A is an **improper
subset** of B. If A is a subset of B but A
does not contain all the elements of B,
then A is a **proper subset** of B.

The null set is an improper subset
of itself and a proper subset of
all non-empty sets.

If a set has *n* elements, then it will have 2^n subsets.

For example, a set with three elements will have 2^3 = 8 subsets.

Worked Example 1.3

A = {1, 2, 3}

(i)   How many subsets does the set A have?

(ii) List all the subsets of A.

Solution

(i)   A has 2^3 = 8 subsets.

(ii) ∅, {1}, {2}, {3}, {1, 2}, {1, 3}, {2, 3}, {1, 2, 3}

ACTIVITY 1.2

Exercise 1.2

1. Write the following statements in set notation, using the symbols ∈, ∉, ⊂, ⊄.

   (i) 2 is an element of A.

   (ii) {3, 4} is a subset of Y.

   (iii) 7 is not an element of B.

   (iv) {1, 2} is not a subset of {3, 4, 5}.

2. Write the following statements in set notation:

   (i) p is an element of A.

   (ii) X is a subset of Y.

   (iii) q is not an element of B.

   (iv) M is not a subset of N.

3. A = {1, 2, 3, 4, 5, 6}, B = {2, 4, 6, 8} and C = {1, 3, 5, 7}.

   (i) Write down a proper subset of A.

   (ii) Write down an improper subset of B.

   (iii) Is {1, 9} a subset of C? Explain.

4. A = {10, 11, 12, 13, 14, 15, 16, 17} and B = {11, 13, 15, 17}.

   Say whether the following statements are true or false.

   (i) 12 ∈ A

   (ii) 14 ∉ B

   (iii) 13 ∉ B

   (iv) {10, 16} ⊂ A

   (v) A ⊄ B

   (vi) B ⊂ A

5. How many subsets does each of the following sets have?

   (i) {10, 20, 30}

   (ii) {31, 37, 41, 43}

   (iii) {0, 1}

   (iv) {1}

   (v) { }

6. N = {The whole numbers which are greater than 5 and less than 8}.

   (i) List the elements of N.

   (ii) Write down and count all the subsets of N.

   (iii) Divide the subsets into proper and improper subsets.

7. A = {The odd numbers between 4 and 10}.

   (i) List the elements of A.

   (ii) List the eight subsets of A.

8. Copy and complete the table below by filling in the gaps. Use the symbols in the right-hand column.

3 _____ {The even natural numbers}	⊄
{1, 2} _____ {2, 3, 4, 5}	⊂
15 _____ {The multiples of 5}	∈
{2, 4} _____ {The even numbers}	∉

9. State whether the following statements are true or false. Correct any false statements.

   (i) The set of all isosceles triangles is a subset of the set of all triangles.

   (ii) The set of all rectangles is a subset of the set of all four-sided figures.

   (iii) The set of all rectangles is a subset of the set of all squares.

   (iv) The set of all integers is a subset of the set of all natural numbers.

   (v) The set of all integers is a subset of the set of all rational numbers.

10. P = {1, 2, 3, 4, 5, 6, 7}. Say whether or not the following are subsets of P.

   (i) {1, 3, 5, 7}

   (ii) {2, 4, 6, 8}

   (iii) {1}

   (iv) { }

   (v) {7, 3, 1}

1.3 VENN DIAGRAMS, UNION AND INTERSECTION

Venn Diagrams

In 1880 John Venn, an English mathematician, invented a way of representing sets in diagram form. The diagrams are called **Venn diagrams** and are made of overlapping circles.

The Venn diagram shown represents the set A = {1, 2, 3, 4}.

John Venn (1834–1923)

Union and Intersection

> The union of two sets is the set of elements contained in both sets. The union of the two sets A and B is written as A ∪ B.

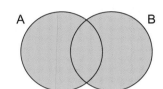

> The intersection of two sets is the set of elements that are common to both sets. The intersection of the two sets A and B is written as A ∩ B.

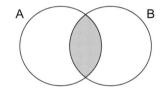

Commutative Properties of Sets

> A ∪ B = B ∪ A, for every set A and B.
> We say that **union is a commutative operation**.

> A ∩ B = B ∩ A, for every set A and B.
> We say that **intersection is a commutative operation**.

ACTIVITY 1.3

Worked Example 1.4

X = {2, 3, 4, 5, 6}

Y = {5, 6, 7, 8, 9}

(i) Represent the sets X and Y on a Venn diagram.

(ii) List the elements of X ∪ Y.

(iii) List the elements of X ∩ Y.

Solution

(i)

X
2•
3•
4•
5•
6•
7•
8•
9•
Y

(ii) X ∪ Y = {2, 3, 4, 5, 6, 7, 8, 9}

(iii) X ∩ Y = {5, 6}

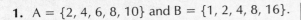

Exercise 1.3

1. A = {2, 4, 6, 8, 10} and B = {1, 2, 4, 8, 16}.

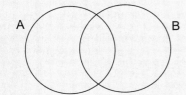

   (i)   Copy and complete the Venn diagram.

   (ii) List the elements of A ∪ B.

   (iii) List the elements of A ∩ B.

   (iv) What is #(A ∪ B)?

   (v)   What is #(A ∩ B)?

2. R = {1, 3, 5, 7, 9} and
   S = { 2, 3, 5, 7, 11}.

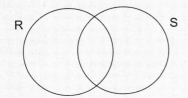

   (i)   Copy and complete the Venn diagram.

   (ii) List the elements of R ∪ S.

   (iii) List the elements of R ∩ S.

   (iv) What is #R?   (vi) What is #(R ∩ S)?

   (v)   What is #S?   (vii) What is #(R ∪ S)?

3. P = {5, 10, 15, 20, 25, 30} and
   Q = {10, 20, 30, 40}.

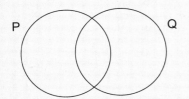

   (i)   Copy and complete the Venn
         diagram.

   (ii) List the elements of P ∪ Q.

   (iii) List the elements of P ∩ Q.

   (iv) What is #(P ∪ Q)?

   (v)   What is #(P ∩ Q)?

4. A = {3, 6, 9, 12, 15} and B = {3, 9, 27, 81}.

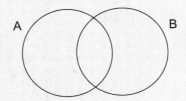

   (i)   Copy and complete the Venn diagram.

   (ii) List the elements of A ∪ B.

   (iii) List the elements of A ∩ B.

5. X = {10, 100, 1,000, 10,000} and
   Y = {1, 2, 3, 4}.

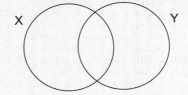

   (i)   Copy and complete the Venn diagram.

   (ii) List the elements of X ∪ Y.

   (iii) List the elements of X ∩ Y.

6. E = {1, 4, 9, 16} and F = {1, 4, 16, 64}.

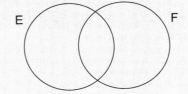

   (i)   Copy and complete the Venn diagram.

   (ii) List the elements of E ∪ F.

   (iii) List the elements of E ∩ F.

7. R = {3, 5, 11} and S = {1, 2, 3}.

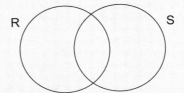

   (i)   Copy and complete the Venn diagram.

   (ii) List the elements of R ∪ S.

   (iii) List the elements of R ∩ S.

8. M = {1, 2, 3, 4, 5, 6} and N = {3, 4}.

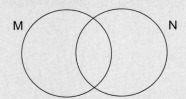

M   N

(i) Copy and complete the Venn diagram.

(ii) List the elements of M ∪ N.

(iii) List the elements of M ∩ N.

(iv) Write down #(M ∪ N).

(v) Write down #N.

9. D = {Whole numbers between 4 and 9} and
   E = {Even numbers between 1 and 15}.

   (i) List the elements of D and E.

   (ii) Show the sets D and E on a Venn diagram.

   (iii) List the elements of D ∪ E.

   (iv) List the elements of D ∩ E.

   (v) What is #D?

   (vi) What is #D ∩ E?

10. P = {1, 2, 3, 4, 5, 6} and Q = {1, 3, 5, 7}.

    (i) Illustrate P and Q on a Venn diagram.

    (ii) List the elements of P ∪ Q.

    (iii) List the elements of P ∩ Q.

1.4 THE UNIVERSAL SET

In a Venn diagram, the universal set is represented by a rectangle. The letter U is used to denote the universal set.

The **universal set** is the set that contains all elements. Every set is a subset of the universal set.

Worked Example 1.5

Represent the following sets on a Venn diagram.

U = {1, 2, 3, 4, 5, 6, 7}

A = {2, 3, 4}

B = {4, 5, 6}

Solution

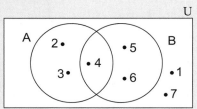

Complement of a Set

The **complement** of a set A is the set of elements in the universal set U that are **not** elements of A.

The complement of a set A is denoted by A'.

In the given diagram, A' is the region coloured yellow.

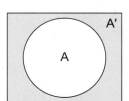

Note: A' can also be written as A^C.

Worked Example 1.6

U = {1, 2, 3, 4, 5, 6, 7, 8}

A = {2, 3, 4}

B = {4, 5, 6}

(i) Represent the sets on a Venn diagram.

(ii) List the elements of (A ∪ B)′.

Solution

(i)

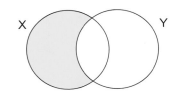

(ii) (A ∪ B)′ is the set of elements in the universal set that are not in A ∪ B.

∴(A ∪ B)′ = {1, 7, 8}

Set Difference

X \ Y is the set of elements that are in X but not in Y.

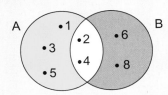

Worked Example 1.7

A = {1, 2, 3, 4, 5} and B = {2, 4, 6, 8}.

Represent A and B on a Venn diagram.

List the elements of:

(i) A \ B

(ii) B \ A

Solution

(i) A \ B is the region shaded yellow.
A \ B = {1, 3, 5}.

(ii) B \ A is the region shaded green.
B \ A = {6, 8}.

ACTIVITY 1.4

1. U = {1, 3, 5, 7, 9, 11, 13, 15} and
   X = {3, 7, 11, 13}.

   (i) Copy and complete the Venn diagram
       below.

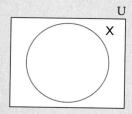

   (ii) List the elements of X′.

2. U = {1, 2, 3, 4, 5, 6, 7, 8, 9, 10},
   A = {2, 3, 7} and B = {2, 4, 6, 8, 10}.

   (a) Copy and complete the Venn diagram
       below.

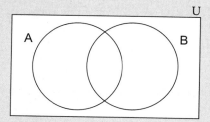

   (b) List the elements of:

       (i) A′   (ii) B′   (iii) A \ B   (iv) B \ A

   (c) Is A \ B = B \ A? Explain.

   (d) Find:

       (i) #A   (ii) #B   (iii) #(A ∪ B)
       (iv) #U   (v) #(A ∪ B) + #A′

3. U = {1, 2, 3, 4, 5, 6, 7, 8, 9, 10, 11, 12},
   P = {2, 4, 6, 8, 10, 12} and Q = {3, 6, 9, 12}.

   (a) Copy and complete the Venn diagram below.

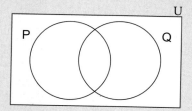

   (b) List the elements of:

       (i) P′   (ii) Q′   (iii) P \ Q   (iv) Q \ P

(c) Find:

    (i) #P   (ii) #Q   (iii) #P′
    (iv) #Q′   (v) #(P \ Q) (vi) #(Q \ P)

4. U = {1, 2, 3, 4, 5, 6, 7, 8, 9, 10}.

   M = {2, 4, 6, 8, 10}.

   N = {3, 4, 5, 6}.

   Represent the sets on a Venn diagram.

   List the elements of:

   (i) (M ∪ N)′   (iii) M \ N

   (ii) (M ∩ N)′   (iv) N \ M

5. X = {2, 3, 5} and Y = {1, 2, 3, 4}.

   List the elements in the sets:

   (i) X \ Y   (iii) (X \ Y) ∪ (Y \ X)

   (ii) Y \ X   (iv) (X ∪ Y) \ (X ∩ Y)

6. A = {1, 2, 3, 4} and B = {2, 3, 4, 5, 6}.

   List the elements of:

   (i) A \ B   (v) (A ∪ B) \ (A ∩ B)

   (ii) B \ A   (vi) (A ∪ B)′

   (iii) A ∪ B   (vii) (A ∩ B)′

   (iv) A ∩ B   (viii) (A \ B)′

7. Name the shaded region in each of the
   following Venn diagrams:

   (a)

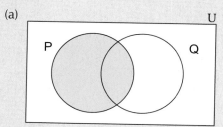

   (b)

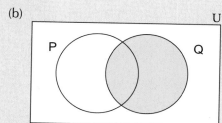

(c)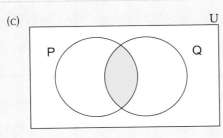

(d)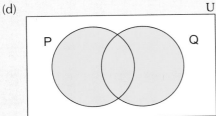

(e)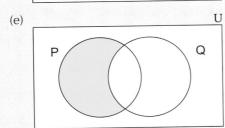

(f)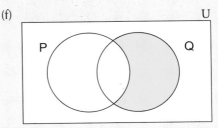

(g)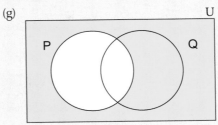

(h)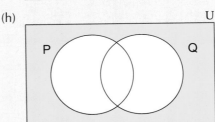

1.5 PROBLEM-SOLVING USING SETS

Sometimes we use Venn diagrams to show the number of elements, rather than the elements themselves.

Worked Example 1.8

Students in a First Year class were asked if they liked Maths or Science. The results are shown in the Venn diagram.
Explain what each number in the diagram represents.

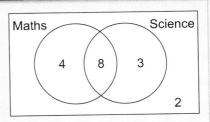

Solution

From the Venn diagram, we can see that eight students like Maths and Science, four students like Maths but not Science, three students like Science but not Maths, and two students like neither Maths nor Science.

Worked Example 1.9

There are 30 people in a class. Fifteen study French and 18 study German. Six students study both French and German. Illustrate the information on a Venn diagram.

How many students study:

(i)   Neither French nor German

(ii) French but not German

(iii) One language only

Solution

6 goes in the middle.

French only = 15 − 6 = 9 students.

German only = 18 − 6 = 12 students.

9 + 6 + 12 = 27

30 − 27 = 3 students

∴ 3 students study neither language.

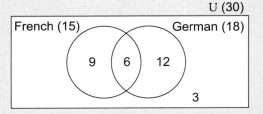

(i) 3 students   (ii) 9 students

(iii) 9 + 12 = 21 students

Exercise 1.5

1. In a survey of 100 teenagers, it was found that 60 watched *The X Factor*, 50 watched *EastEnders* and 15 watched both.

   (i) Represent the information on a Venn diagram.

   (ii) How many teenagers watched neither *EastEnders* nor *The X Factor*?

2. In the Venn diagram, M is the set of students in a class who own a mobile phone, and I is the set of students who own an iPod. #M = 25. Copy and complete the Venn diagram.

   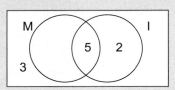

   (a) How many students are in the class?

   (b) How many students owned:

      (i) A mobile phone

      (ii) A mobile phone or an iPod

      (iii) Neither a mobile phone nor an iPod

      (iv) A mobile phone but not an iPod

      (v) An iPod but not a mobile phone

3. A class of 28 students was given a test. Two questions were asked. The results were as follows: 10 students answered both questions correctly, 8 students answered only Question 1 correctly and 4 students answered neither question correctly.

   (i) Represent the information on a Venn diagram.

   (ii) Find the number of students who answered only Question 2 correctly.

4. In a class of 28 students, 23 play hockey, 12 play tennis and 9 play both games.

   (i) Represent this information on a Venn diagram.

   (ii) How many of these students play neither of these sports?

   (iii) How many play hockey but not tennis?

5. An observational study was carried out of people who used the coffee machine in a supermarket. Of those surveyed, 140 had bought a scone, 100 had bought a bar, 10 had bought a bar and a scone, and 30 had bought neither a bar nor a scone.

   (i) Represent this information on a Venn diagram.

   (ii) How many people were surveyed?

   (iii) How many people bought a scone but not a bar?

6. A group of 100 students were asked whether they liked pop music or classical music.

   ■ 77 said they liked pop music.

   ■ 42 said they liked classical music.

   ■ 5 students said they did not like any type of music.

   (i) Represent this information on a Venn diagram.

   (ii) How many liked both types of music?

   (iii) How many liked pop music but not classical music?

   (iv) How many liked pop or classical but not both types of music?

7. A survey of 20 people was carried out in a computer shop. According to the survey, 10 people owned a desktop computer and 8 owned a laptop, while 6 people had neither a desktop nor a laptop.

   (i) Represent the information on a Venn diagram.

   (ii) How many of the sample had both a laptop and a desktop?

8. In a survey, 500 people were asked which foreign language they could speak, French or German. They answered as follows: 200 people said they spoke neither, 50 said they spoke both, and 150 said they spoke French only. Using a Venn diagram, find each of the following:

   (i) The number of people who spoke German

   (ii) The number of people who spoke German only

9. John surveys a random sample of 50 students in his school. He wants to know how many students play soccer and basketball. His survey reveals that 30 play soccer, 25 play basketball and 8 play neither.

   (i) Represent the information on a Venn diagram.

   (ii) How many students play both sports?

10. A group of 70 people were asked whether they liked comedy or science fiction films. 60 said they liked comedy, and 2 said they liked neither comedy nor science fiction.

   (i) How many people liked science fiction only?

   (ii) What is the maximum number that could have liked both comedy and science fiction?

 ## Revision Exercises

1. A = {11, 13, 15, 17, 19, 21},
   B = {12, 14, 16, 18, 20, 22},
   and C = {11, 13, 17, 19}. State whether the following statements are true or false. If they are false, explain why.

   (i) A = B

   (ii) C is the set of all odd numbers between 10 and 20.

   (iii) $17 \notin B$

   (iv) $2^2 \in B$

   (v) A new set E is formed by adding 1 to each element of the set A. E = B.

2. The Venn diagram shows the sets U, X and Y.

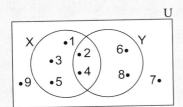

   List the elements of the following sets:

   (i) X   (iv) X ∪ Y   (vii) X \ Y

   (ii) Y   (v) X ∩ Y   (viii) Y \ X

   (iii) U   (vi) X′   (ix) (X ∩ Y)′

3. X = {12, 14, 16, 18, 20, 22, 24, 26} and
   Y = {21, 23, 25, 27}.

   State whether or not these statements are true:

   (i) $12 \in X$ (iv) $\{12, 16\} \subset X$

   (ii) $14 \notin Y$ (v) $X \not\subset Y$

   (iii) $13 \notin Y$ (vi) $X \subset Y$

4. D = {Whole numbers between 6 and 10},
   E = {Even numbers between 5 and 17}.

   (i) List the elements of D and E.

   (ii) Show the sets D and E on a Venn diagram.

   (iii) List the elements of D ∪ E.

   (iv) List the elements of D ∩ E.

5. U = {Whole numbers between 0 and 15}.

   O = {Odd numbers between 0 and 15}.

   P = {Prime numbers between 0 and 15}.

   Represent the sets on a Venn diagram.

   List the elements of:

   (i) O ∪ P   (v) O′   (ix) (O ∪ P)′

   (ii) O ∩ P   (vi) P′   (x) P′ ∩ O′

   (iii) O \ P   (vii) O′ ∪ P′

   (iv) P \ O   (viii) (O ∩ P)′

6. Name the shaded region in each of the following Venn diagrams:

(i)

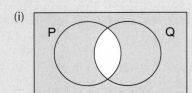

(ii)

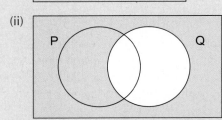

(iii)

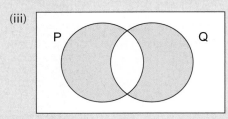

7. A = {3, 4, 7, 13}, B = {2, 4, 6} and C = {2, 3, 4, 7}.

List the elements of the following sets:

(i) A \ C   (iv) A ∪ C

(ii) B ∪ C   (v) (A ∪ C) \ (A ∩ C)

(iii) A ∩ B   (vi) C \ A

8. (a) Copy the Venn diagram six times and shade the following sets:

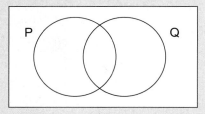

(i) P ∪ Q   (iii) (P \ Q)'   (v) (P ∪ Q)'
(ii) P ∩ Q   (iv) (Q \ P)'   (vi) (P ∩ Q)'

(b) If P = {a, b, c}, Q = {c, d, e} and U = {a, b, c, d, e, f},
find: (i) #P   (iv) #(P ∩ Q)'
      (ii) #P'   (v) #(P \ Q)
      (iii) #(P ∩ Q)   (vi) #(Q \ P)

9. A class of 30 First Year students were surveyed about the types of books they liked to read.

■ 15 liked reading both fictional and factual books.

■ 4 liked reading factual but not fictional books.

■ 2 students said that they did not enjoy reading.

(i) Represent this information on a Venn diagram.

How many students read:

(ii) Fiction but not factual books

(iii) Factual books

(iv) Either factual or fiction but not both

10. First Year classes were surveyed to see whether they wanted to visit the National History Museum or the National Gallery. They could choose the museum, the gallery, both or neither. The results of the survey are shown in the diagram.

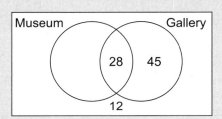

If 96 students were surveyed, how many wanted to go to:

(i) The gallery

(ii) The museum

(iii) Both the gallery and the museum

(iv) Neither the gallery nor the museum

11. Katie did a survey of 100 coffee drinkers and asked whether they liked cream or sugar in their coffee. Thirty-six people said they liked cream in their coffee, 55 said they liked sugar, and 20 said they liked both.

(i) Represent the information on a Venn diagram.

(ii) How many people did not like either cream or sugar?

(iii) How many people liked cream but not sugar?

(iv) How many people liked sugar but not cream?

chapter 2

Natural Numbers

Learning Outcomes

In this chapter you will learn:

➲ How to define a natural number

➲ How to add and subtract natural numbers

➲ How to use a numberline to do addition and subtraction

➲ About factors and multiples

➲ About prime numbers

➲ How to find the LCM and the HCF of a set of natural numbers

➲ How to multiply and divide natural numbers

➲ How to use area models to multiply large numbers

➲ How to use skip counting to multiply numbers

➲ About the commutative, associative and distributive properties

➲ About order of operations

In mathematics, the **natural numbers** are the ordinary counting numbers. The set of natural numbers is an **infinite** set. This means that the set is never-ending. The letter *N* is used to label the set of natural numbers.

$$N = \{1, 2, 3, 4...\}$$

The natural numbers are often represented on a numberline as follows:

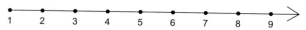

The arrow on the numberline shows that we continue taking whole numbers in the indicated direction only.

2.1 ADDITION AND SUBTRACTION

Addition and subtraction are known as **operations**. If you add two natural numbers together, then you are carrying out the operation of addition on two natural numbers.

Adding natural numbers is finding their sum or total.

Subtracting natural numbers is finding the difference between the two numbers or taking one from the other.

YOU SHOULD REMEMBER...

- How to sum or add two numbers
- How to take one number from another number

KEY WORDS

- Natural number
- Numberline
- Factor
- Multiple
- Prime number
- LCM
- HCF
- Skip counting
- Commutative, associative and distributive properties
- BIMDAS

- For example, the **sum** of the numbers 8 and 12 is $8 + 12 = 20$.

- For example, the **difference** between 12 and 8 is $12 - 8 = 4$.

Worked Example 2.1

Calculate each of the following without using a calculator.

(i) $241 + 345$

(ii) $112 + 211$

(iii) $484 - 213$

Solution

(i) $\begin{array}{r} 241 \\ +\ 345 \\ \hline = 586 \end{array}$

(ii) $\begin{array}{r} 112 \\ +\ 211 \\ \hline = 323 \end{array}$

(iii) $\begin{array}{r} 484 \\ -\ 213 \\ \hline = 271 \end{array}$

Worked Example 2.2

Use a numberline to do the following calculations:

(i) $35 + 4 - 5$

(ii) $19 - 2 + 5$

Solution

(i)

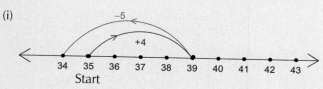

Answer = 34

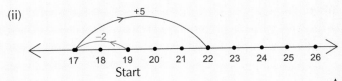

(ii)

+5

−2

17 18 19 20 21 22 23 24 25 26

Start

Answer = 22

ACTIVITY 2.1

- Subtraction is the **inverse operation** to addition.
- Addition is the **inverse operation** to subtraction.

For example:

- 7 **added** to 3 gives a result of 10: 7 + 3 = 10.
- 7 **subtracted** from 10 gives 3: 10 − 7 = 3.

An inverse operation reverses the effect of another operation.

The subtraction reverses the operation of addition.

 Exercise 2.1

1. Copy this numberline and use it to do the following additions and subtractions.

1 2 3 4 5 6 7 8 9 10 11 12 13 14 15 16 17 18 19 20 21 22 23 24 25 26 27 28 29 30

(i) 1 + 2	(v) 29 − 3	(ix) 21 + 6	(xiii) 15 + 4	(xvii) 25 + 2 − 6
(ii) 3 + 4	(vi) 26 − 2	(x) 7 + 5	(xiv) 29 − 5	(xviii) 17 − 3 + 4
(iii) 9 + 5	(vii) 23 − 4	(xi) 27 − 8	(xv) 24 − 7	(xix) 16 − 5 − 3
(iv) 13 + 2	(viii) 14 − 5	(xii) 8 + 7	(xvi) 30 − 8	(xx) 22 + 6 + 2

2. Calculate, without the use of a calculator, the value of each of the following:

   (i) 365 + 332

   (ii) 743 + 67

   (iii) 9,784 + 5,200

   (iv) 6,437 + 5,412

   (v) 23,800 + 9,785

   (vi) 200,000 + 35,098

   Now check your answers with a calculator.

3. Calculate each of the following without using a calculator:

   (i) 365 − 332

   (ii) 743 − 67

   (iii) 9,784 − 5,200

   (iv) 6,437 − 5,412

   (v) 23,800 − 9,785

   (vi) 200,000 − 35,098

   Now check your answers with a calculator.

4. In this number wheel, opposite numbers add to 72. Write down the numbers represented by the letters W, X, Y and Z.

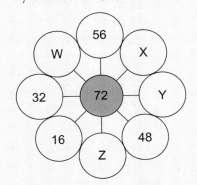

5. The sale prices of four cars manufactured by Mercedes-Benz, Volkswagen, Ford and Toyota are shown below.

Ford €16,250

Toyota €29,950

Volkswagen €26,996

Mercedes-Benz €36,500

(i) What is the total cost of the four cars?

(ii) How much more expensive is the Mercedes-Benz than the Toyota?

(iii) What is the difference in price between the most expensive car and the least expensive car?

(iv) The dealer has decided to reduce the price of all four cars to the nearest thousand euro below the present price. What is the reduction in the total cost of the four cars?

6. On each side of the shapes shown, the numbers in the two circles add to give the number in the square between them. Copy and complete the shapes.

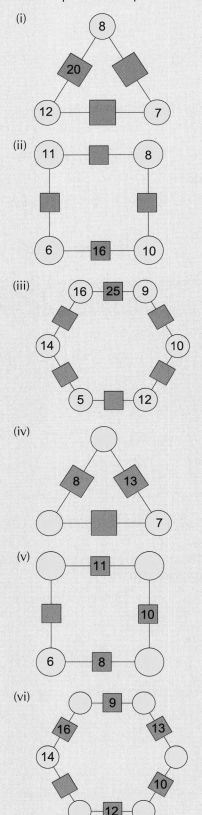

7. Copy and complete the following number pyramids. The missing values are found by adding the values from the two blocks below.

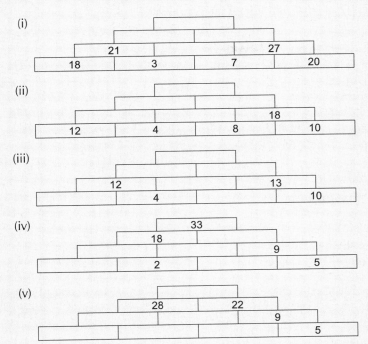

(i)

| | 21 | | 27 | |
| 18 | 3 | 7 | 20 |

(ii)

| | | | 18 | |
| 12 | 4 | 8 | 10 |

(iii)

| | 12 | | 13 | |
| | 4 | | 10 | |

(iv)

	33	
18		9	
	2		5	

(v)

	28	22	
		9	
			5	

8. Thomas feels that subtraction is easier if you are subtracting multiples of 10. He changes all the questions so that the number he is subtracting is a multiple of 10. For example:

$$68 - 29 = 68 - 30 + 1$$
$$= 38 + 1$$
$$= 39$$

What number goes in each circle? Answer all the questions using Thomas' method (no calculator allowed).

(i) $25 - 19 = 25 - 20 + \bigcirc = \bigcirc$

(ii) $44 - 17 = 44 - 20 + \bigcirc = \bigcirc$

(iii) $87 - 28 = 87 - 30 + \bigcirc = \bigcirc$

(iv) $57 - 29 = 57 - 30 + \bigcirc = \bigcirc$

(v) $147 - 98 = 147 - 100 + \bigcirc = \bigcirc$

(vi) $764 - 79 = 764 - 80 + \bigcirc = \bigcirc$

9. More of Thomas' homework. Fill in the boxes (no calculator allowed).

(i) $715 - 57 = 715 - \boxed{} + 3 = \boxed{}$

(ii) $115 - 88 = 115 - \boxed{} + 2 = \boxed{}$

(iii) $964 - 69 = 964 - \boxed{} + 1 = \boxed{}$

(iv) $644 - 29 = 644 - \boxed{} + 1 = \boxed{}$

(v) $776 - 73 = 776 - \boxed{} + 7 = \boxed{}$

(vi) $533 - 21 = 533 - \boxed{} + 9 = \boxed{}$

10. Now, try these (no calculator allowed).

(i) $55 - 19 = 55 - \boxed{} + \bigcirc = \boxed{}$

(ii) $61 - 28 = 61 - \boxed{} + \bigcirc = \boxed{}$

(iii) $48 - 37 = 48 - \boxed{} + \bigcirc = \boxed{}$

(iv) $67 - 49 = 67 - \boxed{} + \bigcirc = \boxed{}$

(v) $81 - 57 = 81 - \boxed{} + \bigcirc = \boxed{}$

(vi) $73 - 18 = 73 - \boxed{} + \bigcirc = \boxed{}$

2.2 FACTORS AND MULTIPLES

In this section we will explore factors and multiples and the difference between them.

Factors

A **factor** of a natural number is any natural number that divides evenly into the given natural number.

For example, all the factors of 12 are {1, 2, 3, 4, 6, 12}.

As you can see, 1 is a factor of 12, and 12 is a factor of 12.

- 1 is a factor of every natural number.
- Every natural number is a factor of itself.

Every factor is part of a pair. The number 12 has three factor pairs:

$1 \times 12 = 12$
$2 \times 6 = 12$
$3 \times 4 = 12$

$\Rightarrow$ Factor pairs are: 1 and 12
                      2 and 6
                      3 and 4

 Worked Example 2.3

(i) List the factors of 20.
(ii) Find their sum.

Solution

(i) $20 = 1 \times 20$
    or 2×10
    or 4×5
Therefore, the factors of 20 are {1, 2, 4, 5, 10, 20}.

(ii) Sum $= 1 + 2 + 4 + 5 + 10 + 20 = 42$.

 Worked Example 2.4

List the pairs of factors of 30.

Solution

$1 \times 30, 2 \times 15, 3 \times 10, 5 \times 6$

Indices (Powers)

If five 2's are multiplied together, i.e. $2 \times 2 \times 2 \times 2 \times 2$, it can be written as 2^5 (pronounced '2 to the power of 5').

Similarly, $3 \times 3 \times 3 \times 3 \times 3 \times 3 = 3^6$ ('3 to the power of 6').

In these examples, the ^{5} and ^{6} are called **indices** or **powers**.

The singular of indices is **index**.

As you can see, 2 is a factor of 2^5, and 3 is a factor of 3^6.

In general, 2 is always a factor of 2^n. 3 is always a factor of 3^n.

Prime Numbers

> Prime numbers are natural numbers that have two factors only.

- 5 is a prime number, as it has only two factors: 1 and 5.
- 2 is the only even prime number. Its two factors are 1 and 2.
- 11 is the first two-digit prime. Its only two factors are 1 and 11.
- 1 is **not** a prime, as it has only one factor: itself.
- 0 is not a prime, as it has an infinite number of factors.

 The Ancient Greek mathematician Euclid proved that the number of primes is infinite. The proof is contained in his famous book *The Elements*, which he wrote about 300 BC.

> Whole numbers that are not prime are called composite numbers.

ACTIVITY 2.2

In Activity 2.2, you will discover how to find primes.

Worked Example 2.5

List the first four prime numbers.

Solution

{2, 3, 5, 7}

Highest Common Factor (HCF)

> The highest common factor (HCF) of two numbers is the highest number that can divide into both of these numbers.

Worked Example 2.6

Find the HCF of 60 and 42.

Solution

②	60
2	30
③	15
5	5
	1

②	42
③	21
7	7
	1

$60 = 2^2 \times 3 \times 5$

$42 = 2 \times 3 \times 7$

- 2 is a common factor of 60 and 42, but 2^2 is not.
- 3 is a common factor.
- There are no other common factors.

∴ HCF = 2 × 3

HCF = 6

ACTIVITY 2.3

Multiples

A **multiple** of a natural number is a number into which the natural number divides, leaving no remainder.

The multiples of 6 are {6, 12, 18, 24, 30, 36...}.

As you can see, it is an **infinite** set, i.e. it goes on forever.

Worked Example 2.7

List the first six multiples of 4.

Solution

$1 \times 4 = 4$
$2 \times 4 = 8$
$3 \times 4 = 12$
$4 \times 4 = 16$
$5 \times 4 = 20$
$6 \times 4 = 24$
{4, 8, 12, 16, 20, 24}

Lowest Common Multiple (LCM)

The **lowest common multiple (LCM)** of two numbers is the smallest multiple that both numbers share.

The LCM of 3 and 4 is 12, as 12 is the smallest number that both 3 and 4 divide evenly into.

Worked Example 2.8

What is the LCM of 4 and 5?

Solution

Find the multiples of 4:

$4 \times 1 = 4$
$4 \times 2 = 8$
$4 \times 3 = 12$
⋮

The multiples of 4 are {4, 8, 12, 16, 20, 24...}.

Find the multiples of 5:

$5 \times 1 = 5$
$5 \times 2 = 10$
$5 \times 3 = 15$
⋮

The multiples of 5 are {5, 10, 15, 20, 25, 30...}.

The LCM of 4 and 5 is 20, as it is the smallest multiple that both numbers share.

The Greeks discovered more than 2,000 years ago that every composite number could be written as a unique product of prime numbers. For example,

$$24 = 2 \times 2 \times 2 \times 3 = 2^3 \times 3$$
$$36 = 2 \times 2 \times 3 \times 3 = 2^2 \times 3^2$$

This fact is useful for finding LCMs.

ACTIVITY 2.4

Worked Example 2.9

(i) Write 60 as the product of its prime factors.

(ii) Write 42 as the product of its prime factors.

(iii) Hence, find the LCM of 60 and 42.

Solution

(i)

$$\begin{array}{c|c} 2 & 60 \\ 2 & 30 \\ 3 & 15 \\ 5 & 5 \\ & 1 \end{array}$$

$60 = 2 \times 2 \times 3 \times 5$

$\Rightarrow 60 = \boxed{2^2} \times \boxed{3} \times \boxed{5}$

(ii)

$$\begin{array}{c|c} 2 & 42 \\ 3 & 21 \\ 7 & 7 \\ & 1 \end{array}$$

$42 = 2 \times 3 \times \boxed{7}$

(iii)
- 2^2 is the bigger of the factors 2 and 2^2.
- 3 is a common factor of both 60 and 42.
- 5 and 7 are the non-common factors.

$\therefore$ LCM $= 2^2 \times 3 \times 5 \times 7$

LCM $= 420$

This gives us a method of writing the prime factors and also of showing that each number is a product of primes.

Exercise 2.2

1. Write down all the factors of each of the following natural numbers:

   (i) 25   (iii) 27   (v) 86   (vii) 89
   (ii) 24   (iv) 12   (vi) 38   (viii) 42

2. List the first **five** multiples of each of the following natural numbers:

   (i) 3   (iii) 7   (v) 10   (vii) 15
   (ii) 5   (iv) 6   (vi) 12   (viii) 16

3. For each of the following natural numbers, write down (a) all its factors, (b) the sum of its factors and (c) the product of its factors.

   (i) 4   (iii) 9   (v) 18   (vii) 16
   (ii) 8   (iv) 24   (vi) 20   (viii) 28

4. Find the HCF of each of the following:

   (i) 8 and 10   (vi) 45 and 60
   (ii) 20 and 25   (vii) 6, 9 and 15
   (iii) 12 and 16   (viii) 15, 25 and 35
   (iv) 27 and 18   (ix) 6, 8 and 12
   (v) 12 and 14   (x) 8, 9 and 10

5. Find the LCM of each of the following:

   (i) 4 and 6   (vi) 16 and 20
   (ii) 8 and 12   (vii) 2, 3 and 4
   (iii) 10 and 12   (viii) 2, 4 and 10
   (iv) 9 and 15   (ix) 8, 10 and 12
   (v) 15 and 18   (x) 12, 15 and 18

6. Answer the following questions, with the help of the Sieve of Eratosthenes from **Activity 2.2.**

   (i) Write down all the prime numbers between 20 and 30.

   (ii) Is the following statement true?

   'There are fewer prime numbers between 51 and 100 than there are between 1 and 50.'

   Justify your answer.

   (iii) Twin primes are pairs of consecutive primes separated only by an even number. For example, 17 and 19 are twin primes.

   List all the twin primes between 1 and 100.

   (iv) The Goldbach conjecture states: 'Every even number greater than 2 is the sum of two prime numbers.'

   For example, 56 is an even number and we can write it as $3 + 53$.

   Show that all the even numbers between 90 and 100 can be written as the sum of two prime numbers.

   (v) Write 56 as the sum of two prime numbers in **two** different ways.

   (vi) Find the smallest **five** consecutive composite numbers.

7. Find the HCF and the LCM of each of the following by writing each number as a product of prime numbers.

   (i) 136 and 102   (v) 123 and 615
   (ii) 117 and 130   (vi) 69 and 123
   (iii) 58 and 174   (vii) 102 and 170
   (iv) 60 and 765   (viii) 368 and 621

8. Write down the following:

   (i) A natural number between 25 and 27

   (ii) A prime number between 50 and 60

   (iii) A factor of 91

   (iv) A multiple of 8

   (v) The HCF of 10 and 12

   (vi) The LCM of 4 and 6

   (vii) A square number between 60 and 70

9. At a birthday party, 124 packets of crisps, 279 fun-size bars and 155 cocktail sausages were eaten. Each person at the party ate the same number of bars. Also, each person ate the same number of cocktail sausages and received the same amount of crisps.

   (i) How many attended the party? Explain your answer.

   (ii) How many cocktail sausages did each person eat?

10. A group of girls bought 72 multi-coloured bracelets, 144 red-and-brown bracelets and 216 pink-and-yellow bracelets. If each girl buys the same number of each type, then what is the largest possible number of girls in the group?

11. Ronan has a piece of paper that measures 168 mm by 196 mm. He wants to cut the entire sheet into squares so that the squares are as large as possible. What is the length of a side of each square?

12. 294 red balls, 252 pink balls and 210 blue balls are distributed equally among some students (i.e. each student gets equal numbers of each colour). What is the largest possible number of students in the group?

13. A gardener has a garden measuring 84 m by 56 m. He wishes to divide up the garden into the largest possible square plots so that the plots completely cover the garden. Show on a diagram how to do this.

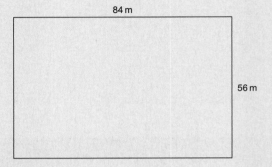

84 m

56 m

14. Alice, Bob and Carl are jumping up a large flight of stairs. Alice jumps two steps at a time, Bob jumps four steps at a time, while Carl jumps five steps at a time. On which step will all three land together for the first time?

15. The bells of St Killian's ring every 15 minutes. The bells of St Trinian's ring every 25 minutes. If they ring together at 9.00 a.m. one morning, when will they next ring together?

16. John looks out to sea and sees two lighthouses flash at the same time. One lighthouse flashes every 20 seconds, and the other flashes every 30 seconds. How long will John have to wait before the lighthouses flash together again?

17. A group of teenagers can be subdivided into smaller groups of either 5, 12 or 17. What is the minimum number of teenagers for which this is possible?

2.3 MULTIPLICATION AND DIVISION

As with addition and subtraction, multiplication and division are also known as **operations**. If you multiply two natural numbers together, then you are carrying out the operation of multiplication on two natural numbers.

If we wish to find the area of a rectangle we multiply the length of the rectangle by the width of the rectangle. Therefore, we can look at the multiplication of two natural numbers as finding an area. In Worked Examples 2.10 and 2.11, we will use area models to multiply large natural numbers.

Worked Example 2.10

Using an area model, evaluate 38×27.

Solution

Step 1

Draw a rectangle measuring 38 units by 27 units.

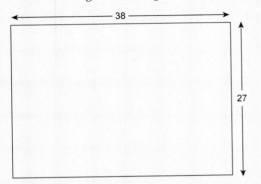

Step 2

- Divide the side of length 38 into two parts of size 30 and 8. (30 is a multiple of 10, and multiplication by 10 or any of its multiples is easy.)

- Divide the side of length 27 into two parts of size 20 and 7.

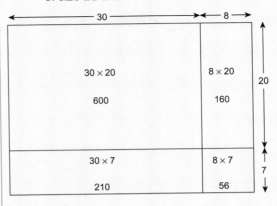

Step 3

Calculate the area of all the rectangles within the larger rectangle:

$38 \times 27 =$ sum of the areas of the small rectangles

$= 600 + 160 + 210 + 56$

$= 1{,}026$

Worked Example 2.11

Using an area model, evaluate 56×35.

Solution

Step 1

Draw a rectangle measuring 56 units by 35 units.

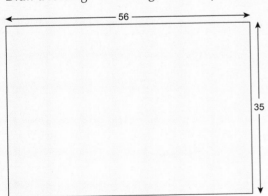

Step 2

- Divide the side of length 56 into two parts of size 50 and 6. (50 is a multiple of 10, and multiplication by 10 or any of its multiples is easy.)

- Divide the side of length 35 into two parts of size 30 and 5.

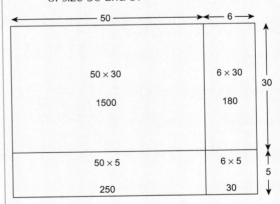

Step 3

Calculate the area of all the rectangles within the larger rectangle:

$56 \times 35 =$ sum of the areas of the small rectangles

$= 1{,}500 + 180 + 250 + 30$

$= 1{,}960$

Worked Example 2.12

We can also use area models to do division.

Use an area model to evaluate $187 \div 11$.

We know that the area of the rectangle in the model is 187 and the height of the rectangle is 11.

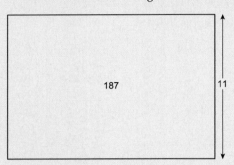

We begin by dividing the rectangle into two smaller rectangles as follows:

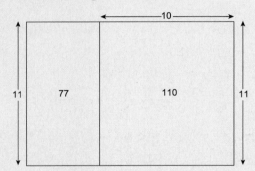

We know that $11 \times 10 = 110$.

Subtracting 110 from 187 gives 77.

The height of the smaller rectangle is 11. Therefore the width is 7, as $11 \times 7 = 77$.

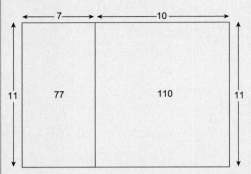

The width of the larger rectangle is $10 + 7 = 17$.

Therefore, $187 \div 11 = 17$.

Worked Example 2.13

Using a numberline, evaluate the following products by skip counting:

(i) 4×3 (ii) 13×2

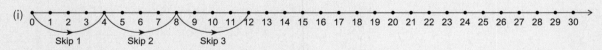

$4 \times 3 = 12$

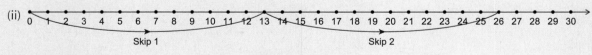

$13 \times 2 = 26$

- ■ Multiplication is the **inverse operation** to division.
- ■ Division is the **inverse operation** to multiplication.

For example:

- ■ 8 **divided** by 2 is 4: $8 \div 2 = 4$.
- ■ 4 **multiplied** by 2 gives 8: $4 \times 2 = 8$.

Multiplication reverses the operation of division.

Exercise 2.3

1. Evaluate:

   (i) 5×6 (iii) 6×11 (v) $(10)(2)$ (vii) $16 \div 8$ (ix) $50 \div 5$

   (ii) $(4)(5)$ (iv) 12×3 (vi) $12 \div 4$ (viii) $25 \div 5$ (x) $100 \div 2$

2. Copy and complete the following multiplication tables:

(i)

×	1	2	3	4	5
1					
2			6		
3					
4					20

(iii)

×	1	3	5	7	9
1					
3					
5					
7			35		63

(ii)

×	2	4	6	8	10
2					
4			24		
6					
8				64	

(iv)

×	1	3			9
2					
		15			
7			42		
	8			64	
					90

3. Copy the numberline shown below. Evaluate the following products by skip counting.

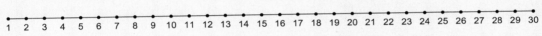

   (i) 5×3 (iii) 8×3 (v) 10×3 (vii) 7×4 (ix) 6×5

   (ii) 3×5 (iv) 3×8 (vi) 3×10 (viii) 4×7 (x) 5×6

4. Multiply the following pairs of numbers by completing the area models.

   (i) 89×68

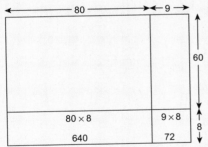

   (ii) 59×76

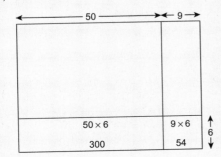

(iii) 93×27

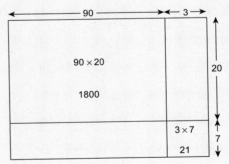

(iv) 86×24

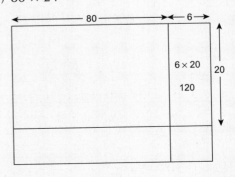

(v) 186 × 25

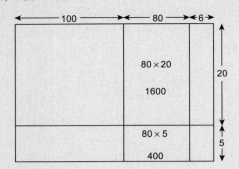

5. Find the following products by constructing a suitable area model.

   (i) 98 × 56   (v) 27 × 19

   (ii) 62 × 29   (vi) 123 × 64

   (iii) 45 × 73   (vii) 769 × 42

   (iv) 34 × 81   (viii) 112 × 234

6. What number goes in each box?

   (i) (132 ÷ 2) ÷ 2 = 132 ÷ ☐ = ☐

   (ii) (144 ÷ 4) ÷ 3 = 144 ÷ ☐ = ☐

   (iii) (180 ÷ 5) ÷ 6 = 180 ÷ ☐ = ☐

   (iv) (140 ÷ 2) ÷ 5 = 140 ÷ ☐ = ☐

   (v) (336 ÷ 4) ÷ 7 = 336 ÷ ☐ = ☐

7. On each side of the shape, the numbers in the two circles multiply to give the number in the square between them. Copy the shapes and fill in the blank circles and squares.

   (i)

   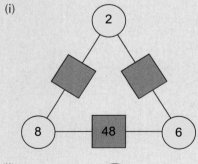

   (ii)

   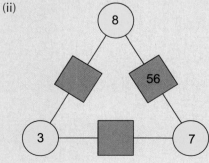

(iii)

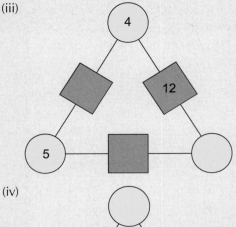

(iv)

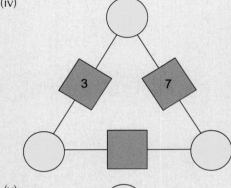

(v)

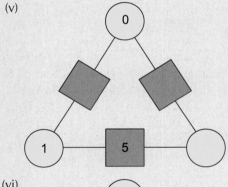

(vi)

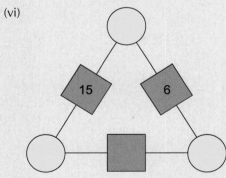

8. Cheryl knows that 512 ÷ 8 = 64. Using this fact, she finds the value of each of the following. What answers did she get?

   Explain your reasoning.

   (i) 512 ÷ 64   (iv) 512 ÷ 4

   (ii) 512 ÷ 16   (v) 256 ÷ 8

   (iii) 512 ÷ 32

9. Jim knows that $324 \div 36 = 9$. He uses this fact to find the value of each of the following. What answers did he get? Explain your reasoning.

(i) $324 \div 9$ (iii) $648 \div 36$

(ii) $324 \div 18$ (iv) $324 \div 108$

10. Given that $420 \div 14 = 30$, find the value of each of the following:

(i) $420 \div 30$ (iv) $210 \div 14$

(ii) $840 \div 14$ (v) $420 \div 15$

(iii) $420 \div 7$

11. Find the value of each of the following:

(i) 2^2 (iv) 5^2

(ii) 2^3 (v) 4^3

(iii) 3^2

12. There are 60 M&M's in a bag. How many will Alice, Bob and Cal get each, if the sweets are shared equally?

13. Xavier has eight times as many songs on his iPod as Yvonne. If Yvonne has 88 songs on her iPod, how many does Xavier have?

14. Nuts are packed in 55 g bags. How many bags can be made from a container containing 1,320 g of nuts?

15. John has a computer with a 20 GB hard drive. His friend Paul has a computer with a 120 GB hard drive. How many times bigger is Paul's hard drive?

16. Megan can pick 80 berries in five minutes. How many can she pick in one minute?

17. A blocklayer can lay 160 blocks in an eight-hour day. How many blocks would she lay in five eight-hour days?

18. How many pages can you type in 90 minutes if you can type one page every three minutes?

19. Eight million tourists visited Ireland in 2009. If the number of visitors remains stable, how many tourists will visit during the next three years?

20. Cineplex Cinemas are charging €7 to see *The Chronicles of Narnia*. If the cinema holds 150 people, how much is collected at the box office on a night when the cinema is full?

21. Chris bought two DVD's at the same price. He also bought a book for €12. If Chris spent €32 in total, how much did one DVD cost?

22. Eimear is 17 and her younger brother Tadhg is 9. The sum of their ages is 26. In how many years will the sum of their ages be double what it is now?

2.4 COMMUTATIVE, ASSOCIATIVE AND DISTRIBUTIVE PROPERTIES

There are three basic properties (laws) that we use with the operations of addition, subtraction, multiplication and division.

Commutative Property

Addition and multiplication are **commutative** operations on the natural numbers.

$$3 + 4 = 4 + 3$$
$$3 \times 4 = 4 \times 3$$

> An operation is commutative if a change in the order of the numbers does not change the result.

However, subtraction and division are **not** commutative operations on the natural numbers.

$$8 - 2 \neq 2 - 8$$
$$8 \div 2 \neq 2 \div 8$$

Associative Property

Addition and multiplication are **associative** operations on the natural numbers.

$$(3 + 4) + 5 = 3 + (4 + 5)$$
$$(3 \times 4) \times 5 = 3 \times (4 \times 5)$$

Subtraction and division are **not** associative operations on the natural numbers.

$$(8 - 4) - 2 \neq 8 - (4 - 2)$$
$$(8 \div 4) \div 2 \neq 8 \div (4 \div 2)$$

> An operation is associative if a change in grouping does not change the result.

Distributive Property

This property means that:

$$5(4 + 3) = (5 \times 4) + (5 \times 3)$$
as $\quad 5(4 + 3) = 5(7) = 35$
and $\quad (5 \times 4) + (5 \times 3) = 20 + 15 = 35$

Also, $\quad 5(4 - 3) = 5(4) - 5(3)$
$$5(1) = 20 - 15$$
$$5 = 5$$

> The distributive property says that multiplication distributes over addition and subtraction.

Worked Example 2.14

Use the commutative, distributive and associative properties to simplify and, hence, evaluate the following:

(i) $(48 + 8) + 92$ (ii) $84 + (456 + 16)$ (iii) $16 \times 44 + 16 \times 56$

Solution

(i) $(48 + 8) + 92 = 48 + (8 + 92)$ (Associative property)

$\qquad = 48 + 100$ (Adding on a hundred is easier)

$\qquad = 148$

(ii) $84 + (456 + 16) = 84 + (16 + 456)$ (Commutative property)

$\qquad = (84 + 16) + 456$ (Associative property)

$\qquad = 100 + 456$ (Adding on a hundred is easier)

$\qquad = 556$

(iii) $16 \times 44 + 16 \times 56 = 16(44 + 56)$ (Distributive property)

$\qquad = 16(100)$ (Multiplication by 100 is easier)

$\qquad = 1,600$

Exercise 2.4

1. What properties (commutative, associative, distributive) are illustrated in the following equations?

(i) $3 + 4 = 4 + 3$ (v) $(7 \times 8) \times 9 = 7 \times (8 \times 9)$

(ii) $3 + (4 + 7) = (3 + 4) + 7$ (vi) $19(10 + 11) = 19(10) + 19(11)$

(iii) $5 \times 4 = 4 \times 5$ (vii) $2(5 - 2) = 2(5) - 2(2)$

(iv) $6(2 + 8) = 6(2) + 6(8)$ (viii) $(5 \times 6) \times 12 = 5 \times (6 \times 12)$

2. Use the associative property of addition to help you evaluate the following sums (no calculators allowed):

(i) (48 + 9) + 91

(ii) (62 + 81) + 19

(iii) 77 + (23 + 86)

(iv) 56 + (44 + 925)

(v) (763 + 95) + 5

3. Use the associative property of addition to help you evaluate the following sums (again, no calculators):

(i) (19 + 36) + 4

(ii) 25 + (15 + 19)

(iii) 179 + (1 + 12)

(iv) (48 + 21) + 79

(v) 85 + (5 + 10)

4. Using the commutative property on the numbers inside brackets, and then the associative property, do the following sums (no calculators allowed):

(i) 86 + (456 + 14)

(ii) (25 + 654) + 75

(iii) 2 + (757 + 98)

(iv) (66 + 479) + 34

(v) 69 + (84 + 31)

5. Using the commutative property on the numbers inside brackets, and then the associative property, do the following sums (no calculators allowed):

(i) 14 + (724 + 986)

(ii) 492 + (612 + 8)

(iii) (18 + 546) + 682

(iv) (4 + 123) + 996

(v) 193 + (542 + 17)

6. Use the distributive property to evaluate the following (no calculators allowed):

(i) $16 \times 44 + 16 \times 56$

(ii) $984 \times 86 + 984 \times 14$

(iii) $765 \times 95 + 765 \times 5$

(iv) $567 \times 69 + 567 \times 31$

(v) $294 \times 67 + 294 \times 33$

7. Use the distributive property to evaluate the following (no calculators allowed):

(i) $716 \times 45 + 716 \times 55$

(ii) $183 \times 96 + 183 \times 4$

(iii) $965 \times 85 + 965 \times 15$

(iv) $567 \times 79 + 567 \times 21$

(v) $394 \times 57 + 394 \times 43$

2.5 ORDER OF OPERATIONS

In maths, the order of operations is the order in which things are done. It is important to have order, otherwise answers will differ.

For example, is $2 + 3 \times 4 = 5 \times 4 = 20$?
or $= 2 + 12 = 14$?

BIMDAS

We can use the guide shown to help us remember the order in which operations are carried out.

These letters stand for **B**rackets, **I**ndex, **M**ultiplication, **D**ivision, **A**ddition and **S**ubtraction. We start at the top of the triangle and work down. Therefore, Brackets come first, then Indices (powers), Multiplication/Division and finally Addition/Subtraction.

For MD and AS read left to right.

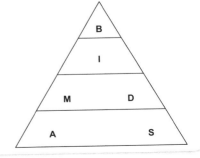

Worked Example 2.15

Find the value of each of the following:

(i) $3 + 4 \times 5$ (ii) $(3 + 5)^2 - 8 \div 4 + 6 \times 4$ (iii) $\dfrac{15 \div 3 + 7 - 2}{6 + 3 - 4}$

Solution

(i) $3 + 4 \times 5$

$= 3 + 20$ (Multiplication)

$= 23$ (Addition)

(ii) $(3 + 5)^2 - 8 \div 4 + 6 \times 4$

$= 8^2 - 8 \div 4 + 6 \times 4$ (Brackets)

$= 64 - 8 \div 4 + 6 \times 4$ (Indices)

$= 64 - 2 + 24$ (Multiplication/Division)

$= 86$ (Addition/Subtraction)

(iii) $\dfrac{15 \div 3 + 7 - 2}{6 + 3 - 4}$

$= \dfrac{5 + 7 - 2}{6 + 3 - 4}$ (Division)

$= \dfrac{10}{5}$ (Addition/Subtraction – need to simplify before dividing)

$= 2$

 Exercise 2.5

1. Calculate each of the following:

(i) $3 + 3$ (iv) $3 \div 3$

(ii) $3 - 3$ (v) 3^3

(iii) 3×3

2. Calculate each of the following:

(i) $2^2 + 3^2$ (iii) $3^2 + 4^2$

(ii) $2^3 + 3^2$ (iv) $1^2 + 1^{10}$

3. Calculate each of the following:

(i) $1^2 \times 3^2$ (iii) $5^3 \div 5^2$

(ii) $5^2 \times 2^2$ (iv) $4^3 - 2^2$

4. Calculate each of the following:

(i) $2(7 - 2)$

(ii) $5(3 + 4) + 3(2 + 5)$

(iii) $3(7 - 4)^2 + 5(5 - 2)^3$

(iv) $2(5 - 2)^2 - 3(4 - 3)^{10}$

5. Calculate each of the following:

(i) $45 \div (3 + 2)$ (v) $98 \div (3 + 4)^2$

(ii) $5 \times 4 + 24 \div 8$ (vi) $12 \times 3 + 24 \div 2^2$

(iii) $5(6) + 2(6) + 7(6)$ (vii) $3(4)^2 + 2(4) + 10$

(iv) $50 \div 10 + 2$ (viii) $(50 \div 10 + 2)^2$

6. Calculate each of the following:

(i) $3(5 - 2)^2 - 3(4 \div 2)^2 + 5(3)^3$

(ii) $2(3)^3 + 5(6 - 2)^2 - 10 \div 2$

(iii) $5(7 + 2)^2 + 3(3 \times 2)^2 + 12(1)^{49}$

(iv) $6(1{,}112 \div 1{,}112)^{50} + 7 \times 3 - 27$

7. Calculate each of the following:

(i) $\dfrac{2 \times 4 + 3}{(6 + 5)}$

(ii) $\dfrac{(4 + 8) \div 3}{12 - 6}$

(iii) $\dfrac{3(5 - 2)^2 - 3(4 \div 2)^2 + 5(3)^3}{(5 - 2)^2 + 1}$

(iv) $\dfrac{7(6 - 2)^2 + 3(10 \div 2)^2 + 3}{(8 - 3)^2 - 6}$

NATURAL NUMBERS

1. (a) On each side of the shape shown, the numbers in the two circles add to give the number in the square between them. Copy and complete the shape.

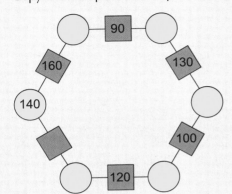

(b) John and Jim get in an elevator on the 12th floor. The elevator goes down three floors and Jim gets out. Then the elevator goes down five more floors and John gets out. On what floor does John get out of the elevator? Explain your answer.

2. (a) Fill in the blank circles and squares without using a calculator.

   (i) $994 - 69 = 994 - \square + 1 = \bigcirc$

   (ii) $776 - 67 = 776 - \square + 3 = \bigcirc$

   (b) Yvonne challenges Tanya to a 100 m race. Yvonne runs 5 m for every 4 m that Tanya runs. How far will Tanya have run when Yvonne crosses the finish line?

3. (a) (i) Write down all the factors of 6.

   Show that the sum of all the factors of 6 is equal to 2×6.

   (ii) A natural number is a perfect number if it is equal to the sum of its factors (excluding the number itself). Six is the smallest perfect number.
   $(6 = 1 + 2 + 3)$

   Show that 28 is also a perfect number.

   (b) A large box of chocolates and a small box of chocolates cost €18.

   If the large box costs €4 more than the small box, then what is the price of the small box of chocolates?

4. (a) {2, 3, 4, 10, 11, 12, 13, 19, 22}

   (i) Write down the prime numbers given in the list.

   (ii) Find the sum of all these prime numbers.

   (iii) Write down all the composite (non-prime) numbers from the list.

   (iv) Find the sum of these composite numbers.

   (v) What do you notice about this sum?

   (b) Bill has €8,000 in €50 notes and €6,000 in €20 notes. How many notes does Bill have?

5. (a) Find the HCF and the LCM of each of the following:

   (i) 12 and 16   (iii) 204 and 228

   (ii) 70 and 105   (iv) 117 and 130

   (b) A cinema has 13 rows of seats. The rows are numbered from 1 to 13. Odd-numbered rows have 18 seats. Even-numbered rows have 20 seats. How many seats are in the cinema?

6. (a) Copy and complete the pyramid shown below. The missing values are found by multiplying the values from the two blocks below.

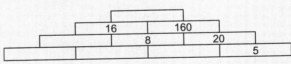

   (b) Two natural numbers sum to 11. What is the greatest possible value of the product of these numbers? (Hint: construct a table with possible values.)

7. Calculate each of the following:

   (i) $12 \times 2 - 6 + 2^3$

   (ii) $10 \div 2 + 2^2 \times 3 - 7$

   (iii) $\dfrac{2^4 \times 2 - 30}{(6 \times 4) \div 12}$

   (iv) $\dfrac{19 + 3^4}{3^3 - (4 - 2)}$

8. (a) Use the commutative, associative and distributive properties to evaluate the following:

    (i) $(59 + 37) + 3$

    (ii) $(35 + 534) + 65$

    (iii) $865 \times 85 + 865 \times 15$

(b) If $X = 2$ and $Y = 8$, which one of the following is not a natural number?

    (i) $X + Y$ (ii) $Y - X$ (iii) $(X)(Y)$ (iv) $X \div Y$ (v) Y^X

9. (a) Evaluate each of the following:

    (i) $\dfrac{2^2(3 + 5)}{(1 + 1)^3}$

    (ii) $3 + (5 - 2)^2 + 15 + 8 \div 2$

(b) The floor of a rectangular room is covered with square tiles. The room is 12 tiles long and six tiles wide. How many tiles touch the wall of the room?

10. In a basketball competition, each competitor shoots ten balls.
The balls are numbered from 1 to 10.
Competitors begin shooting with the ball numbered 1 and work their way through to ball number 10.
If a competitor scores a basket, then she gets points equal to the number on the ball with which she scores (i.e. if she scores with the ball on which the number 8 is written, she will get 8 points).

  (i) What is the maximum score a competitor can achieve?

  (ii) List all the possible ways in which a competitor can get 7 points.

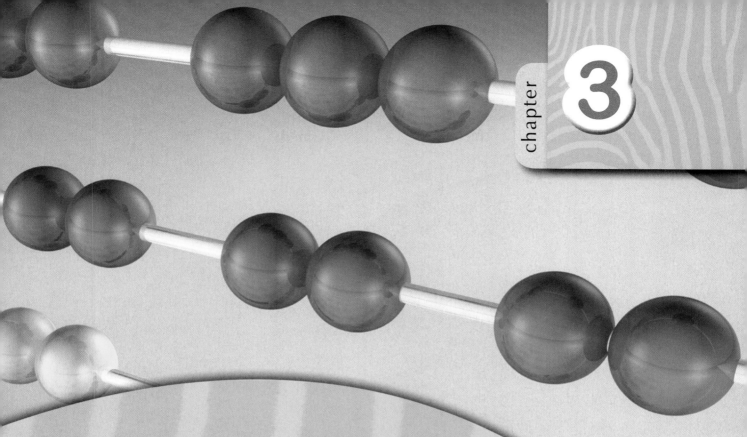

chapter 3

The Fundamental Principle of Counting

Learning Outcomes

In this chapter you will learn to:

➲ List all possible outcomes of an experiment using:

➲ Systematic listing

➲ Two-way tables

➲ Tree diagrams

➲ Apply the Fundamental Principle of Counting

3.1 OUTCOMES

In mathematics and in everyday life, it is important to be able to list all the possible outcomes that can occur in real-life situations or in experiments.

YOU SHOULD REMEMBER...

- How to list outcomes in an ordered way

- Different methods of listing outcomes

Worked Example 3.1

A team plays a hockey match. What are the possible outcomes of the match for the team?

Solution

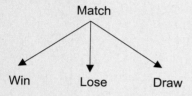

The possible outcomes are Win, Lose or Draw.

KEY WORDS

- **Sample space**
- **Systematic listing**
- **Two-way table**
- **Tree diagram**
- **Fundamental Principle of Counting**

Worked Example 3.2

A swimmer wins a medal in a race. List all the possible outcomes (medals) she could receive.

Solution

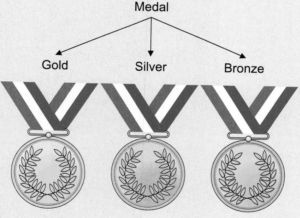

The possible outcomes are Gold, Silver or Bronze.

3.2 LISTING OUTCOMES

When listing outcomes or **sample spaces**, three main methods can be used.

A: Systematic Listing

This method involves writing down all the possible outcomes in a logical order.

The list or set of all possible outcomes is referred to as the sample space.

Worked Example 3.3

A six-sided die is thrown. List all the possible outcomes.

Solution

This is a normal six-sided **die**.

Here are the possible outcomes of rolling one die:

List all the possible outcomes of rolling one die:

{1, 2, 3, 4, 5, 6}

 ACTIVITIES 3.1, 3.2, 3.3, 3.4

Worked Example 3.4

Emma has decided that she will buy a top and a pair of trousers. She has a choice of a pink, green or yellow top and grey or blue trousers. List all the possible colours of clothes that she could wear.

Solution

It helps if we use letters or numbers to show all the different outcomes.

Emma could pick pink (P) *or* green (G) *or* yellow (Y) as the colour of her top.

She could then pick either grey (GY) *or* blue (B) as the colour of her trousers.

The list of all possible outcomes would be:

- Pink and grey (P, GY)
- Pink and blue (P, B)
- Green and grey (G, GY)
- Green and blue (G, B)
- Yellow and grey (Y, GY)
- Yellow and blue (Y, B)

Six outcomes in total are possible.

Worked Example 3.5

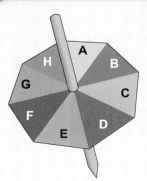

A spinner has eight equal sectors labelled A to H.
When it is spun, what are all the possible outcomes?

Solution

The outcomes are A, B, C, D, E, F, G, H.

 ACTIVITIES 3.5, 3.6, 3.7, 3.8

B: Two-Way Tables

If there are many possible outcomes, listing them all systematically can take a long time.

Two-way tables are a convenient way of showing all possible outcomes.

Worked Example 3.6

Sharon has decided that she will buy a top and a pair of trousers. She has a choice of a pink, green or yellow top and white or blue trousers. List all the possible colours of clothes that she could wear.

Solution

We put the outcomes of Sharon's choice of tops on the side of the table and the outcomes of her choice of trousers on the top of the table.

		Trousers	
		White (W)	Blue (B)
Top	Pink (P)		
	Green (G)		
	Yellow (Y)		

← Intersection of Pink and White

We then look at the intersection of Pink and White in the table. In this box we fill in Pink and White (P, W). The outcome in this box is that Sharon has chosen a pink top and white trousers.

		Trousers	
		White (W)	Blue (B)
Top	Pink (P)	P, W	
	Green (G)		
	Yellow (Y)		

We then fill in the rest of the table:

		Trousers	
		White (W)	Blue (B)
Top	Pink (P)	P, W	P, B
	Green (G)	G, W	G, B
	Yellow (Y)	Y, W	Y, B

ACTIVITIES 3.9, 3.10, 3.11

It is now a simple matter of using the table to list all the outcomes: (1) pink and white, (2) pink and blue, (3) green and white, (4) green and blue, (5) yellow and white and, finally, (6) yellow and blue.

C: Tree Diagrams

A tree diagram is another method of listing outcomes. Its name comes from the fact that, when completed, the diagram looks like the branches of a tree.

> The tree diagram method is useful when listing the outcomes of **two or more events**. For example, rolling a die once is called an event.

Worked Example 3.7

A coin is flipped twice. Use a tree diagram to show all the outcomes.

Solution

Head is written as H, and tail is written as T.

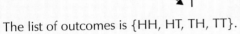

| 1st flip | 2nd flip | Outcome |

- H → H : HH
- H → T : HT
- T → H : TH
- T → T : TT

The list of outcomes is {HH, HT, TH, TT}.

Worked Example 3.8

A spinner coloured black, white and grey is spun twice. List all the possible outcomes.

Solution

When the spinner is spun once, the outcomes (black, white and grey) could be drawn on the tree diagram as follows:

1st Spin

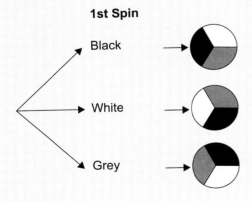

- Black →
- White →
- Grey →

FUNDAMENTAL PRINCIPLE OF COUNTING

The spinner was then spun a second time.

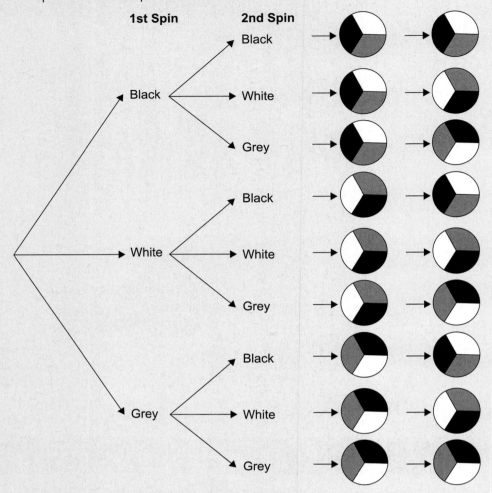

If we follow each branch, we can fill in all the outcomes.

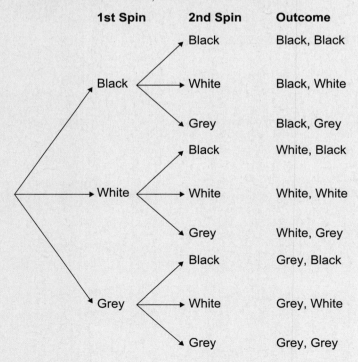

1st Spin	2nd Spin	Outcome
	Black	Black, Black
Black	White	Black, White
	Grey	Black, Grey
	Black	White, Black
White	White	White, White
	Grey	White, Grey
	Black	Grey, Black
Grey	White	Grey, White
	Grey	Grey, Grey

We can then list all the outcomes:

Black, Black		Black, White		Black, Grey	
White, Black		White, White		White, Grey	
Grey, Black		Grey, White		Grey, Grey	

ACTIVITIES 3.12, 3.13

'Mathematics is made of 50 per cent formulas, 50 per cent proofs, and 50 per cent imagination.'

Anonymous

Exercise 3.1

In the following questions, use the most appropriate method unless stated otherwise.

Methods	Systematic listing	Two-way tables	Tree diagrams

1. A spinner with five equal sectors numbered 10 to 14 is spun once.
   What are all the possible outcomes?

2. Bag A contains red, purple and orange marbles.
   Bag B contains yellow and blue marbles.

   Bag A   Bag B

   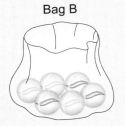

   One marble from each bag is chosen.
   What are the possible outcomes?

3. Francis flips a coin and rolls a die.
   List all the possible outcomes.
   How many outcomes are possible?

4. A restaurant has three choices for the main meal (vegetarian, steak or fish) and two choices for the dessert menu (custard or pudding).
   What are all the possible outcomes if a customer chooses a main course and a dessert?

5. A coloured spinner like the one shown below is spun three times:

   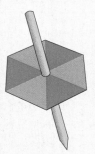

   Use a tree diagram to list all the possible outcomes.

6. Avril wishes to buy a new car. She has a choice of four different models (estate, saloon, hatchback or coupé), and she can have each model in three different colours (silver, electric blue or red). How many different outcomes are there?
   Show how you got your answer.

7. There are three runners in a race, A, B, and C. List all the possible outcomes of how they finish (no dead heats).

   (Hint: A, B, C means A first, B second, C third.)

8. A student answers three 'Yes' or 'No' questions. Use a tree diagram to show all the possible outcomes.

9. A fair spinner numbered from 1 to 3 is spun, and a die is thrown. The score from each is added together.

   (i) Draw a two-way table to show all the outcomes.
   (ii) How many of these outcomes are greater than 8?
   (iii) How many of these outcomes are less than 2?

10. Two dice are thrown and the scores are added together. Complete the table below to show all the outcomes. (Some have been filled in for you.)

		Second Die					
		1	2	3	4	5	6
First Die	1		1 + 2 = 3				
	2			2 + 3 = 5			
	3						
	4						
	5						
	6	6 + 1 = 7					6 + 6 = 12

   (i) How many outcomes are there?
   (ii) How many outcomes add up to a total of 6?
   (iii) List how many ways the score of 10 can be obtained.
   (iv) What is the lowest score possible?

11. Two fair four-sided spinners numbered from 1 to 4 are spun. A score is obtained by multiplying the number the first spinner lands on by the number the second spinner lands on. For example, if the first spinner shows 3 and the second spinner shows 2, that gives a score of 6 (3 × 2).

   (i) Construct a two-way table of possible results.
   (ii) Which is the more likely result – an odd or even number?
   (iii) What fraction of the scores are even?
   (iv) What percentage of the scores are odd?

12. A survey is carried out in a class to determine whether students like a particular subject. The results are as follows:

Boy	Yes	Girl	No	Girl	Yes
Girl	No	Girl	Yes	Girl	Yes
Boy	No	Girl	Yes	Girl	Yes
Boy	No	Boy	Yes	Boy	Yes
Girl	Yes	Boy	No	Boy	No
Girl	Yes	Boy	Yes	Boy	No

(i) Find the number of students in the class.

(ii) Give **one** reason why the survey divided the class into boys and girls.

(iii) Fill in the following two-way table to show all the results of the survey.

	Yes	**No**
Boy		
Girl		

(iv) What fraction of the class liked this subject?

(v) What fraction of boys liked the subject?

3.3 THE FUNDAMENTAL PRINCIPLE OF COUNTING

The fundamental principle of counting is a quick and easy way to determine the number of outcomes of two or more events.

Worked Example 3.9

A six-sided die is rolled and a coin is flipped. How many different outcomes are possible?

FORMULA

Fundamental Principle of Counting If one event has m possible outcomes and a second event has n possible outcomes, then the total number of possible outcomes is $m \times n$.

Solution

The **number of outcomes** for the first event – the die being rolled – is 6 (1, 2, 3, 4, 5, 6).

The **number of outcomes** for the second event – the coin being flipped – is 2 (heads, tails).

The total possible number of outcomes is $6 \times 2 = 12$.

Remember that it is the **number of outcomes** that we multiply each time.

Worked Example 3.10

A hotel has five different types of rooms available, each of which has a shower *or* a bath.
How many different types of rooms can a guest have?

Solution

Different types of rooms – 5 possible outcomes

Shower or bath – 2 possible outcomes

ACTIVITIES 3.14, 3.15

The guest has a choice of 5 × 2 = 10 different rooms.

Worked Example 3.11

A teacher puts labels on the desks in an exam hall. Each desk is labelled with a vowel followed by a digit
(for example, E7). How many different ways can the desks be labelled?

Solution

Vowels – 5 (a, e , i, o, u)

Digits – 10 (0, 1, 2, 3, 4, 5, 6, 7, 8, 9)

The total number of desks that can be labelled is 5 × 10 = 50 desks.

Worked Example 3.12

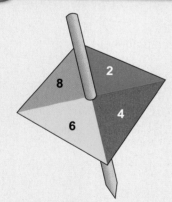

A spinner numbered 2, 4, 6, 8 is spun three times.
How many different outcomes are possible?

Solution

The number of outcomes for the first event is 4 (2, 4, 6, 8).

The number of outcomes for the second event is 4 (2, 4, 6, 8).

The number of outcomes for the third event is also 4 (2, 4, 6, 8).

The total possible number of outcomes is 4 × 4 × 4 = 64.

We could check our answer by trying to list all the different outcomes
but it would take a long time!

Worked Example 3.13

A customer wishes to place an order in a pizzeria and is given the following
choices for a meal:

Starter	Pizza	Drink	Dessert
Potato wedges	Margherita	Cola	Ice cream
Garlic bread	Ham & pineapple	Juice	Apple tart
Chicken wings	Pepperoni	Water	
Ciabatta			

If the customer chooses a starter, a pizza, a drink and a dessert, how many
different meals can be ordered?

Solution

Starter – 4 possible outcomes

Pizza – 3 possible outcomes

Drink – 3 possible outcomes

Dessert – 2 possible outcomes

The total number of different meals that can be ordered is 4 × 3 × 3 × 2 = 72.

ACTIVITY 3.16

Exercise 3.2

1. A cafe has six types of coffee in three sizes. How many different choices of coffee are possible?

2. A new car comes in five different colours and four different engine sizes. How many different options are available?

3. A decorator can choose to paint the door of a room in two colours, the walls in five colours and the ceiling in three colours. How many possible ways can she paint the room?

4. Kellie is trying on a dress which comes in three different sizes and seven different colours. How many different dresses can Kellie try on?

5. What is the total number of possible outcomes if a student has a choice of three pens and five copy books?

6. Evan is preparing to go out. He has five different tee-shirts and two different pairs of jeans. Ignoring the rest of his clothes, how many different ways can he dress?

7. The North Island of a country has ports E, F, G and H. The south Island has ports Q, W, P, R, T and Y.

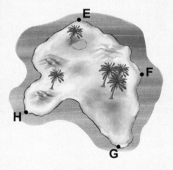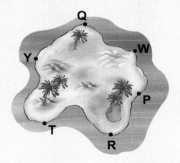

   If a person wants to sail from the North Island to the South Island, how many different routes are possible?

8. In a restaurant there are four choices for the main course (steak, burger, fish or pasta) and three for dessert (jelly, fruit or cake). How many different two-course meals can you eat at this restaurant?

9. In a restaurant there are four choices for the starter, six choices for the main course and five choices for dessert. How many possible three-course meals are there?

10. Éabha has ten tops, three skirts and five pairs of shoes. If we ignore the rest of her clothes, in how many different ways can she dress for the evening?

11. How many outcomes are there if a card is drawn from a pack of cards and a coin is flipped?

12. A coin is flipped two times. How many outcomes are possible?

13. Andrew wants to rent three DVDs. He decides that he wants to rent a horror film, a comedy and an action film. He has a choice of ten horror, five comedy and seven action films. How many different choices of films are possible?

14. A car insurance company classifies its drivers by their age (under 30 years old, between 30 and 40 years old and over 40 years old), gender (male or female) and address (city or countryside). What is the total number of classifications?

15. A lock has a three-digit code, for example 123. How many codes are possible:

　(i)　If a digit can be used only once?

　(ii)　If a digit can be used more than once?

16. A license plate is being designed. It is decided that it will have a letter followed by two digits, for example D 89.

　(i)　How many different license plates are possible?

　(ii)　It is then decided that the digit zero will not be used. How many different license plates are now possible?

17. A test consists of two sections:

　(i)　Section A has four questions and each question has three parts.

　(ii)　Section B has three questions and each question has two parts.

All questions must be answered.

How many parts must a student answer to complete the test?

18. How many three-letter codes can be made using the letters of the English alphabet if no letter can be used more than once (e.g. TPN but not TTN)?

 ## Revision Exercises

1. A poster can be made in three sizes: large, medium or small. They can be in black and white or in colour and they can have a glossy or a matt finish.

　(i)　Draw a tree diagram to show all the different posters that can be made.

It is decided that the posters will only be made in black and white due to the cost.

　(ii)　Find the number of different posters that can now be made.

2. A €1 coin and a €2 coin are flipped. An outcome of heads or tails is recorded. List all the possible outcomes:

　(i)　Systematically

　(ii)　Using a two-way table

　(iii)　Using a tree diagram

Use the Fundamental Principle of Counting to check your answers.

　(iv)　Which of the three methods for listing the outcomes did you prefer? Explain why.

3. These two spinners are spun:

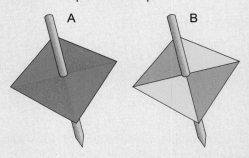

　(i)　Draw a two-way table to show all the possible outcomes.

　(ii)　How many outcomes are possible?

A third spinner is added, and all three spinners are spun again.

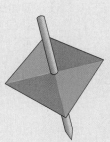

　(iii)　Draw a tree diagram to show all the possible outcomes.

　(iv)　How many outcomes are now possible?

4. A factory produces a range of sheds as follows:

- The shed can be large or small.
- The shed can be pine, oak or maple.
- The shed can have a flat or sloped roof.

   (i) Use a tree diagram to show all the possible sheds that can be made.

The factory then decides to make sheds at a medium size as well, but to stop making sheds with flat roofs.

   (ii) How many different sheds can the factory now produce?

5. A pupil must choose one subject out of each of the following subject groups:

Group A	Group B	Group C
French	History	Maths
Spanish	Geography	
German	Business	
	Economics	

   (i) List all the possible subject choices using the most appropriate method.

   (ii) There is only one choice in Group C. What term is used when we have only one choice?

   (iii) How many subject choices are possible if Applied Maths is added to Group B?

6. In a car racing game, you start by choosing which continent you will race on (America, Europe, Africa, Asia or Australia) and at which level of difficulty (Beginner, Medium, Expert and Insane).

   (i) Draw a two-way table to list all the different races possible.

   (ii) Andy decides that he wants to have a 'Beginner' race on a continent beginning with the letter 'A'.
   How many different races can Andy have?

7. An eight-sided die numbered 1 to 8 is rolled and a coin is flipped.

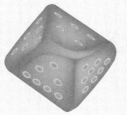 

   (i) How many different outcomes are possible?

   (ii) Draw a two-way table to list all the possible outcomes.

   (iii) How many of these outcomes result in an even number and a head?

On closer inspection, it is discovered that there is a fault with the die. The die has the numbers 1, 2, 3, 4, 5, 6, 7 and 7 on its faces.

   (iv) How many different outcomes are now possible?

8. A coin is flipped two times. Each flip results in a head or a tail.

   (i) Draw a tree diagram to show all the possible outcomes.

   (ii) Using the same tree diagram, show all the possible outcomes if the coin is flipped three times.

   (iii) Using the same tree diagram, show all the possible outcomes if the coin is flipped four times.

   (iv) What difficulty do you encounter when you use this method of determining the number of outcomes?

   (v) A coin is flipped six times. Find the total number of outcomes possible.

FUNDAMENTAL PRINCIPLE OF COUNTING

9. Two spinners as shown are spun. Their scores are added together. If the sum of the scores is even, the letter E is used to record the outcome, and if it is odd, the letter O is used.

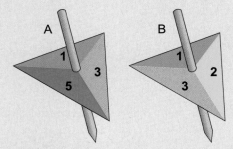

(a) Copy and complete the two-way table to show all the outcomes.

First spinner	Second spinner		
	1	2	3
1			E
3			
5		O	

 (i) How many scores are even?

 (ii) How many scores are odd?

(b) Two students play a game. Student A wins if the score is even, and Student B wins if the score is odd.

 (i) Which player should win the most games?

 (ii) Is this a fair game? Give a reason for your answer.

10. A six-sided die is rolled once, and a coin is flipped once.

 (i) Use the Fundamental Principle of Counting to calculate the number of possible outcomes.

 (ii) Draw a two-way table to show all possible outcomes.

 (iii) If the die is rolled twice and the coin flipped twice, how many different outcomes are possible?

 (iv) The die is rolled six times and the coin is flipped six times. How many different outcomes are now possible?

chapter 4

Integers

Learning Outcomes

In this chapter you will learn:

- ➲ How to represent integers on the numberline
- ➲ How to add and subtract integers
- ➲ How to multiply and divide integers
- ➲ About order of operations

4.1 INTEGERS

In Chapter 2 we met with the **natural numbers**. The natural numbers are also called the **positive whole numbers**. We can solve many real-life problems using just the natural numbers.

Rex has €100 in his bank account and he withdraws €60. What is the balance in his account?

The balance is €100 − €60 = €40. Here, we have used the natural numbers 100, 60 and 40 to solve the problem.

Negative Numbers

Jeff has €100 in his bank account and he withdraws €120 from the bank. What is the balance in his account?

If Jeff had €100 and he withdraws €120, then he must owe the bank €20, but how do we represent a debt of €20? To represent a debt of €20, we must introduce a new set of numbers called **negative numbers**. Negative numbers are preceded by a minus sign. A debt of €20 is represented as the negative number −€20.

YOU SHOULD REMEMBER...

- How to construct a numberline

- How to use the numberline to add and subtract natural numbers

KEY WORDS

- **Integer**

- **Negative number**

- **Zero**

- **Positive number**

- **Sum**

- **Product**

Worked Example 4.1

Anna has a balance of €200 in her bank account. She needs €250 to buy a new phone. She goes to her bank and withdraws €250. What is the balance in her bank account?

Solution

If her balance was €200 and she withdrew €250, then she owes the bank €50. Therefore, the balance in her account is now −€50.

Zero

If Eimear has €50 in her Credit Union account and she decides to withdraw €50, what is left in her account? It is obvious that there is nothing left in her account. We use the number 0 to represent nothing.

> The **integers** are made up of:
> - Zero
> - All the positive whole numbers
> - All the negative whole numbers

Mathematicians use the letter **Z** to represent the integers:

$$Z = \{..., -6, -5, -4, -3, -2, -1, 0, 1, 2, 3, 4, 5, 6, 7, ...\}$$

Z stands for *Zahlen*, which is German for 'numbers'.

'God made integers; all else is the work of man.'

Leopold Kronecker (1823–1891)

The Numberline

We already met with the numberline in Chapter 2. We must now extend the numberline to accommodate the integers.

Here are some importants things to remember about integers on the numberline:

- An integer a is **less than** an integer b if a is to the **left** of b on the numberline:
- An integer x is **greater than** an integer y if x is to the **right** of y on the numberline.
- Sometimes we say that 6 is the opposite of –6, or that –12 is the opposite of 12. Every integer except zero has an **opposite**.

Two integers are opposite if they are the same distance from zero on the numberline.

A positive integer is a whole number greater than zero.

A negative integer is a whole number less than zero.

 **ACTIVITY** 4.1

 Exercise 4.1

1. For each of the following numberlines, find the values of A, B, C and D.

(i)

| –7 | –6 | D | –4 | –3 | B | –1 | 0 | 1 | 2 | A | 4 | 5 | C | 7 |

(ii)

| –7 | –6 | –5 | D | –3 | –2 | –1 | B | 1 | A | 3 | 4 | 5 | 6 | C |

(iii)

| –7 | C | –5 | –4 | –3 | –2 | A | 0 | 1 | 2 | 3 | B | D | 6 | 7 |

2. Copy the numberline, and on it highlight the numbers shown in the box.

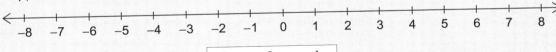

–2	0	1
5	3	–7
2	6	–3

3. Write the following sets of numbers in order of size, beginning with the smallest.

   (i) {0, 9, –20, 12, –16}   (iii) {16, 29, –14, 0, 12}

   (ii) {29, –2, –18, 25, –21}   (iv) {140, –146, 271, –47, –106}

4. Put the following numbers in order of size, beginning with the largest.

   (i) {–9999, –1000, 1000, 9999}   (iii) {–970, 4530, –4880, –9840, 8530, –4370}

   (ii) {0, 101, –101, –8, 8}   (iv) {–10, 100, –100, 1000, –1000}

5. Copy the numberline, and on it circle the numbers given in the table.

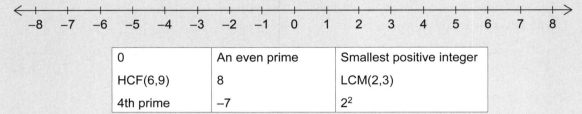

0	An even prime	Smallest positive integer
HCF(6,9)	8	LCM(2,3)
4th prime	–7	2^2

6. Match the items in column A with those in column B.

A	B
The temperature when –3°C cools by 1°C	0
The temperature when –3°C warms by 1°C	1
The smallest prime number	–2
The largest negative integer	–1
The smallest positive integer	2
Zero	8
LCM(2,8)	–4

7. On 21 July 1983, the temperature at the South Pole was –89°C. It was the coldest temperature ever recorded there. On 5 January 1974, the temperature at the Pole was +15°C. This was the warmest temperature ever recorded in the region. What is the difference between the coldest and the warmest temperatures ever recorded at the South Pole?

8. Draw a numberline to help you find the temperature that is midway between –5°C and 7°C.

9. Insert the correct symbol, i.e. < (less than) **or** > (greater than), between the following pairs of integers:

   (i) –3   2   (iii) 5   4   (v) 2   –2   (vii) 0   4   (ix) –3   –2

   (ii) 5   –5   (iv) 2   –3   (vi) –5   –3   (viii) –4   0   (x) 8   –5

10. John is on floor level –4 in the basement of a large hotel. He wishes to get to his room, which is on the ninth floor.

    (i) Use a numberline to show John's current location and the location of his room.

    (ii) John gets into the elevator and presses the button for level 9. How many levels will the elevator pass through before reaching level 9?

11. John played nine holes of golf. The table shows how far above or below par he was for each hole.

Hole number	1	2	3	4	5	6	7	8	9
Above/below par	+2	+1	–1	+2	–2	+3	–1	+2	+4

Find out how far above or below par John was at the end of the nine holes.

4.2 ADDITION AND SUBTRACTION OF INTEGERS

A numberline can be used as an aid for adding and subtracting integers.

Worked Example 4.2

Use a numberline to calculate the following:

   (i) −6 + 4   (ii) 5 − 7   (iii) −2 − 5

> Add: Move Right
> Subtract: Move Left

Solution

(i)

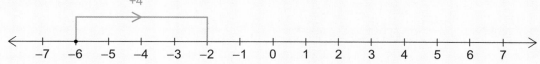

Start at −6 and move 4 units to the right to give an answer of −2.

−6 + 4 = −2

(ii)

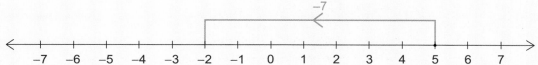

Start at 5 and move 7 units to the left to give an answer of −2.

5 − 7 = −2

(iii)

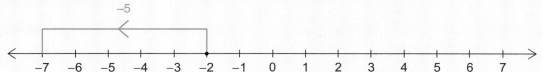

Start at −2 and move 5 units to the left to give an answer of −7.

−2 − 5 = −7

In Activity 4.2, you derived the following rules for addition of integers:

> **Rule 1**
>
> When the signs are the same, add the numbers and keep their sign.
>
> **Rule 2**
>
> When the signs are different, take the smaller number from the bigger number (in absolute terms), and keep the sign of the bigger number.

INTEGERS

Worked Example 4.3

Evaluate:	Solution
(i) $2 + 5$	(i) $2 + 5 = 7$ (Rule 1) $\qquad$ (iv) $-5 - 2 - 3 + 8 = -7 - 3 + 8$ (Rule 1)
(ii) $2 - 5$	(ii) $2 - 5 = -3$ (Rule 2) $\qquad\qquad\qquad\qquad = -10 + 8$ (Rule 1)
(iii) $5 - 2 + 4$	(iii) $5 - 2 + 4 = 3 + 4$ (Rule 2) $\qquad\qquad\qquad = -2$ (Rule 2)
(iv) $-5 - 2 - 3 + 8$	$\qquad\qquad\qquad = 7$ (Rule 1)

Exercise 4.2

1.

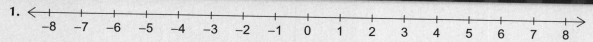

Use the numberline above to calculate each of the following:

(i) $-4 + 3$ $\qquad$ (iii) $5 - 6$ $\qquad$ (v) $-4 + 5$ $\qquad$ (vii) $-3 - 2$ $\qquad$ (x) $1 - 4$

(ii) $2 + 4$ $\qquad$ (iv) $-2 - 3$ $\qquad$ (vi) $-5 + 3$ $\qquad$ (viii) $4 - 6$ $\qquad$ (ix) $-5 + 5$

2. Copy and complete the following number pyramids. Each number is found by adding the numbers from the two blocks below.

(i)

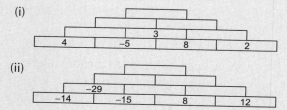

(iii)

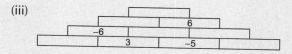

(ii)

(with values -29, -14, -15, 8, 12)

3. Evaluate each of the following:

(i) $3 - 2$ $\qquad$ (iii) $5 - 8$ $\qquad$ (v) $-7 - 4$ $\qquad$ (vii) $5 - 1$ $\qquad$ (ix) $-5 - 1$

(ii) $8 - 4$ $\qquad$ (iv) $7 - 12$ $\qquad$ (vi) $-3 - 8$ $\qquad$ (viii) $1 - 5$ $\qquad$ (x) $-1 - 5$

4. Copy and complete the following number pyramids. Each number is found by adding the numbers from the two blocks below.

(i)

(ii)

(iii)

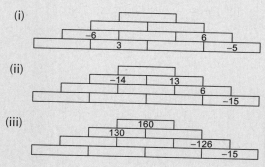

5. In this number wheel the opposite numbers add up to -3.

Write down the values of P, Q, R and S.

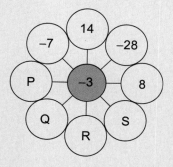

6. Evaluate each of the following:

(i) $3 - 2 + 1$ $\quad$ (iii) $5 - 6 - 2 + 3$ $\quad$ (v) $-7 - 4 - 3 - 4$ $\quad$ (vii) $5 - 5 - 4 + 4$ $\quad$ (ix) $-2 + 5 - 8 + 3$

(ii) $3 - 8 - 2$ $\quad$ (iv) $8 - 2 + 1 - 5$ $\quad$ (vi) $-5 - 2 + 5 + 8$ $\quad$ (viii) $-5 - 8 - 3 + 2$ $\quad$ (x) $8 - 7 + 7 - 8$

7. In this number wheel, the opposite numbers add up to –6.

Write down the values of J, K, L and M.

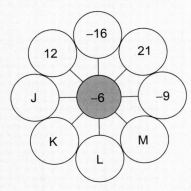

8. Copy and complete these calculations, writing the correct number in each box.

(i) $5 + 23 = \boxed{}$

(ii) $3 - 22 = \boxed{}$

(iii) $7 - \boxed{} = 5$

(iv) $-7 - 5 = \boxed{}$

(v) $\boxed{} - 12 = -9$

(vi) $-15 - \boxed{} = -25$

(vii) $12 - \boxed{} + 8 = 15$

(viii) $-3 - 5 - \boxed{} + 12 = 2$

(ix) $2 = 5 - 3 + \boxed{}$

(x) $15 = 8 - 7 + \boxed{}$

9. On Sunday evening, Gemma has €500 in her bank account. Each day of the following week, Gemma visits her bank.

(i) On Monday, she withdraws €300 from her account.

(ii) On Tuesday, she lodges €100 to her account.

(iii) On Thursday, she withdraws a further €700.

(iv) On Friday morning, she lodges €100.

What is the balance in Gemma's bank account on Friday evening?

10. There are 10 questions on a multiple choice test. A correct answer is worth 5 marks. An incorrect answer incurs a penalty of –2 marks, and an unanswered question is worth 1 mark.

Alice, Bob and Kylie take the test.

(i) Alice answers five questions correctly, leaves two unanswered and gets the rest wrong.

(ii) Bob answers six questions correctly and answers one incorrectly. He leaves the rest unanswered.

(iii) Kylie answers four questions incorrectly and leaves one unanswered. She gets the rest correct.

How many marks did Alice, Bob and Kylie get on the test?

11. Study the following cards. You can put them in different orders, such as 657 or 567.

(i) What is the largest number you can make using all of the cards?

(ii) What is the smallest number you can make using two cards?

12. On 1 January, Keith has a balance of –€1500 in his bank account. His bank manager has advised him to clear his debt by the end of the month. During January the following transactions take place between Keith and the bank:

(i) On 4 January, he lodges €400.

(ii) On 10 January, he lodges a further €100.

(iii) On 20 January, he withdraws €200.

(iv) On 24 January, he pays off half of what he now owes.

(v) On 28 January, he withdraws a further €100.

Does Keith manage to clear his debt by the end of the month?

Show clearly how you arrived at your answer.

4.3 MULTIPLICATION AND DIVISION OF INTEGERS

Multiplication of Integers

We are already familiar with multiplication of natural numbers. We now want to extend the idea to the integers.

Positive × Negative

If we multiply a positive integer by a negative integer, what is the result?

Consider the following practical problem. If John owes €10 to Keith, €10 to Niamh and €10 to Cheryl, then what does John owe in total? He owes €30. Therefore, $3 \times -10 = -30$.

> A positive integer multiplied by a negative integer gives a negative integer.
>
> $(+)(-) = (-)$

Worked Example 4.4

Evaluate the following:

(i) 6×-12

(ii) 5×-11

(iii) 2×-30

Solution

(i) $6 \times -12 = -72$

(ii) $5 \times -11 = -55$

(iii) $2 \times -30 = -60$

Negative × Positive

How do we evaluate -3×10? Remember the commutative property of multiplication from Chapter 2? It also applies to integers. Therefore, $-3 \times 10 = 10 \times -3 = -30$.

For example, if Tiernan owes €3 to 10 people (-3×10), this is the equivalent of stating that 10 people are owed €3 by Tiernan (10×-3).

> A negative integer multiplied by a positive integer gives a negative integer.
>
> $(-)(+) = -$

Worked Example 4.5

Evaluate the following:

(i) $(-5)(7)$

(ii) $(-12)(4)$

(iii) $(-8)(9)$

Solution

(i) $(-5)(7) = -35$

(ii) $(-12)(4) = -48$

(iii) $(-8)(9) = -72$

Negative × Negative

What is $(-3)(-5)$? To answer this questions, we will use **number decomposition**.
Consider the product 23×35. We will consider three different decompositions: D1, D2 and D3.

D1

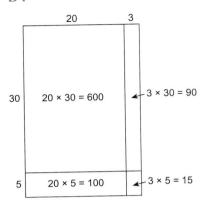

$$23 \times 35 = 600 + 100 + 90 + 15$$
$$= 805$$

D2

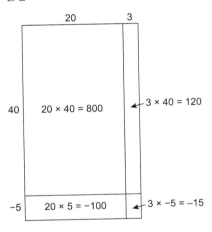

$$23 \times 35 = 800 + 120 - 100 - 15$$
$$= 920 - 115$$
$$= 805$$

This shows that negative numbers can be used in decomposition.

D3

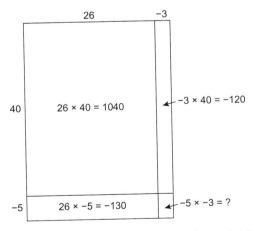

We now sum the areas we know:
$$1{,}040 - 130 - 120 = 1{,}040 - 250$$
$$= 790$$

We know that all areas must sum to 805.
Therefore, $-5 \times -3 = 805 - 790$
$$= 15$$

A negative integer multiplied by a negative integer gives a positive integer.

$$(-)(-) = +$$

This leads us to the rule of signs for multiplication.

Rules for Multiplication

(i)   positive × positive = positive

(ii) positive × negative = negative

(iii) negative × positive = negative

(iv) negative × negative = positive

INTEGERS

Worked Example 4.6

Evaluate the following:

    (i) -6×-12

    (ii) -5×-11

    (iii) $-2 \times -30 \times -2$

Solution

    (i) $-6 \times -12 = 72$

    (ii) $-5 \times -11 = 55$

    (iii) $-2 \times -30 = 60$

       $\therefore -2 \times -30 \times -2 = 60 \times -2$

                 $= -120$

ACTIVITY 4.3

Worked Example 4.7

Evaluate the following:

    (i) 2^3 (ii) $(-5)^2$ (iii) $(-3)^3$ (iv) $(-4)^4$ (v) $(-2)^5$

Solution

    (i) $2^3 = 2 \times 2 \times 2 = 8$

    (ii) $(-5)^2 = -5 \times -5 = 25$

    (iii) $(-3)^3 = -3 \times -3 \times -3$

              $= 9 \times -3$

       $\therefore (-3)^3 = -27$

    (iv) $(-4)^4 = -4 \times -4 \times -4 \times -4$

                $= 16 \times -4 \times -4$

                $= -64 \times -4$

       $\therefore (-4)^4 = 256$

    (v) $(-2)^5 = -2 \times -2 \times -2 \times -2 \times -2$

                $= 4 \times -2 \times -2 \times -2$

                $= -8 \times -2 \times -2$

                $= 16 \times -2$

       $\therefore (-2)^5 = -32$

> In general, a negative integer raised to an even power gives a positive answer, and a negative integer raised to an odd power gives a negative answer.

Division of Integers

The operations of division and multiplication are closely linked.

- $2 \times 4 = 8$ implies that 2 and 4 are factors of 8. In fact, $8 \div 4 = 2$ **and** $8 \div 2 = 4$.
- $2 \times -4 = -8$, means that 2 and -4 are factors of -8. So, $-8 \div 2 = -4$ **and** $-8 \div -4 = 2$.
- Also, $-2 \times -4 = 8$ implies that $8 \div -4 = -2$, and that $8 \div -2 = -4$.

These simple calculations give us the **rule of signs** for division (which are similar to multiplication).

Rules for Division

    (i)   positive $\div$ positive = positive   (iii)   negative $\div$ positive = negative

    (ii)   positive $\div$ negative = negative   (iv)   negative $\div$ negative = positive

Exercise 4.3

1. Copy and complete the multiplication tables.

(i)

×	3	5	8
−9			
−6			
−2			

(ii)

×	0	1	3	4
−4				
−3				
−2				
−1				

2. Copy and complete the multiplication tables.

(i)

×	−10	−7	−4
−8			
−5			
−1			

(ii)

×	10	100	1,000
−20			
−10			
−1			

3. Evaluate the following (no calculators allowed):

(i) (5)(6)

(ii) (−5)(6)

(iii) (5)(−6)

(iv) (−5)(−6)

(v) (10)(4)

(vi) (−2)(16)

(vii) (7)(−8)

(viii) (−15)(−6)

(ix) (−5)(6)(−3)

(x) (−15)(−2)(−5)

4. Evaluate the following (no calculators):

(i) $15 \div 3$

(ii) $-24 \div 6$

(iii) $-39 \div -13$

(iv) $21 \div -7$

(v) $16 \div 4$

(vi) $-99 \div -33$

(vii) $-66 \div 11$

(viii) $144 \div -12$

(ix) $-16 \div -8$

(x) $5^3 \div -5$

5. Evaluate the following (no calculators):

(i) (25)(3)

(ii) (−12)(8)

(iii) (6)(−7)

(iv) (−11)(−4)

(v) $15 \div -3$

(vi) $-18 \div -6$

(vii) $-72 \div -8$

(viii) $18 - 19$

(ix) $25 - 14$

(x) $-105 - 17$

6. Match the items in column A with those in column B.

A	B
The product of a positive integer and a negative integer	0
Your lucky number multiplied by zero	−x
The product of two negative integers	Negative integer
The number of students in your class multiplied by 1	13
The sum of this integer and x is zero.	Positive integer
The opposite of −4	The number of students in your class
13 divided by 1	4

7. The numbers in the circles are multiplied to give the numbers in the squares. Fill in the missing values.

(i)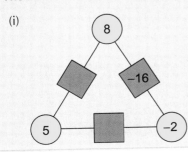

(ii)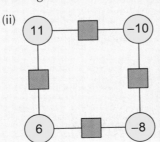

(iii)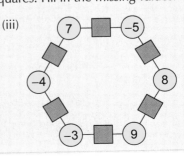

8. The numbers in the circles are multiplied to give the numbers in the squares. Fill in the missing values.

(i)

(ii)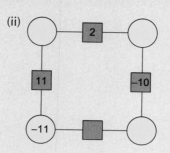

(iii)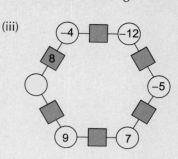

9. Copy and complete the following number pyramids. Each number is found by finding the product of the numbers from the two blocks below. (Note: To find the product of two numbers, multiply them.)

(i)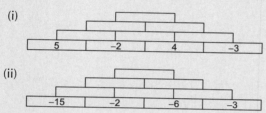

(iii)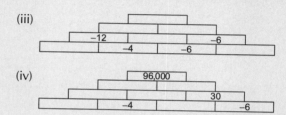

(ii)

(iv)

10. Calculate the following (no calculators):

(i) $(2)^2$ (iii) $(4)^2$ (v) $(1)^3$ (vii) $(3)^3$ (ix) $(6)^2$ (xi) $(10)^3$

(ii) $(3)^2$ (iv) $(1)^2$ (vi) $(2)^3$ (viii) $(5)^2$ (x) $(4)^3$ (xii) $(5)^3$

11. (i) $(-2)^2$ (iii) $(-4)^2$ (v) $(-2)^4$ (vii) $(-6)^2$ (ix) $(-2)^5$

     (ii) $(-3)^2$ (iv) $(-2)^3$ (vi) $(-3)^3$ (viii) $(-2)^1$ (x) $(-2)^6$

4.4 ORDER OF OPERATIONS

We have already met with order of operations in Chapter 2. The order of operations on the set of integers is the same as the order of operations on the natural numbers.

We will once again use the BIMDAS method to sort out the order of operations.

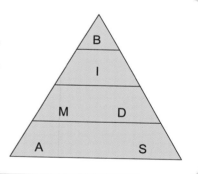

Worked Example 4.8

Evaluate:

$3 \times (4 - 2) + 5 \times (2 - 6)$

Solution

$3 \times (4 - 2) + 5 \times (2 - 6) = 3 \times 2 + 5 \times (-4)$ (Brackets)

$= 6 - 20$ (Multiplication)

$= -14$ (Addition)

Worked Example 4.9

Evaluate:

$3(6 - 8)^3 + 125 \div (2 + 3)^2$

Solution

$3(6 - 8)^3 + 125 \div (2 + 3)^2 = 3(-2)^3 + 125 \div (5)^2$ (Brackets)

$= 3(-8) + 125 \div (25)$ (Indices)

$= -24 + 5$ (Multiplication/Division)

$= -19$ (Addition/Subtraction)

Exercise 4.4

1. Calculate each of the following:

   (i) $2 \times 3 + 3 \times (-4)$

   (ii) $4 \times 5 + 2 \times (-3)$

   (iii) $3 \times (-2) + 5 \times 4$

   (iv) $3 \times (-2) + 5 \times (-3)$

2. Calculate each of the following:

   (i) $3 + 4 \times 2 + 6 \times 3$

   (ii) $5 + 3 \times (-2) - 8$

   (iii) $5 \times 1 + 4 \times 0 - 3 \times 5$

   (iv) $8 - 3 \times 2 + 7$

3. Calculate each of the following:

   (i) $2 \times (3 + 4) + 5 \times (3 - 2)$

   (ii) $2 \times (5 - 8) + 3 \times (7 - 11)$

   (iii) $5 \times (2 - 3) + 6 \times (4 - 1)$

   (iv) $5 \times (2 - 8) + 3 \times (1 - 6)$

4. Calculate each of the following:

   (i) $5(3 - 2)^2 + 4(3 - 2) + 5$

   (ii) $3(6 - 2)^2 + 2(5 - 4) + 7$

   (iii) $2(8 - 4)^2 + 3(8 - 4) + (8 - 4)$

   (iv) $2(2)^3 + 2(2)^2 + 2(2)$

5. Calculate each of the following:

   (i) $3 + (-3)$ (iv) $3 \div (-3)$

   (ii) $3 - (-3)$ (v) $(-3)^2$

   (iii) $3 \times (-3)$ (vi) $(-3)^3$

6. Calculate each of the following:

   (i) $(-4)^2 + (3)^2$ (iii) $(-5)^2 - (-5)^2$

   (ii) $(-2)^3 - (5)^2$ (iv) $(7)^2 - (-3)^2$

7. Calculate each of the following:

   (i) $1^2 \times (-3)^2$ (iii) $(-5)^3 \div 5^2$

   (ii) $(-5)^2 \times 2^2$ (iv) $4^3 - (-2)^2$

8. Calculate each of the following:

   (i) $2(-7 - 2)$

   (ii) $5(3 - 4) - 3(2 - 5)$

   (iii) $3(-7 + 4)^2 - 5(5 - 2)^3$

   (iv) $2(4 - 2)^2 - 3(-4 + 3)^{10}$

9. Calculate each of the following:

   (i) $49 \div (-3 - 4)^2$

   (ii) $-5(4)^2 - 2(4) - 20$

   (iii) $-12 \times 3 - 24 \div (-2)^2$

   (iv) $(3 - 50 \div 5)^2$

10. Calculate each of the following:

   (i) $4(-5 - 2)^2 - 3(-4 \div 2)^2 + 6(-3)^3$

   (ii) $5(-3)^3 + 5(6 - 3)^2 - 10 \div 2$

   (iii) $-5(-7 + 2)^2 - 3(-3 \times 2)^2 + 12(-1)^{49}$

   (iv) $6(-1002 \div 1002)^{50} + 8 \times 3 - 20$

Revision Exercises

1. Calculate each of the following:

(i) 5 – 8

(ii) 7 – 4

(iii) 15 – 18

(iv) 5 + 4 – 9

(v) 3 + 5 – 9

(vi) 7 – 4 – 4

2. Calculate each of the following:

(i) 5 + (–5)

(ii) 9 + (–9)

(iii) 9 – (–9)

(iv) 11 – (–11)

(v) 2 + 7 – (–4)

(vi) –3 – 7 + 4

3. Calculate each of the following:

(i) 5 + (5 + 3)

(ii) 8 – (2 + 3)

(iii) 9 + (5 + 4) – (2 + 3)

(iv) (5 + 2) – (3 + 4) – (1 + 5)

(v) 5 – (2 + 4) + (3 – 2) – (5 – 4)

(vi) 10 + 2 × 7

(vii) 100 – 3 × 2

(viii) $5 + 3 \times 4^2$

4. Copy the numberline, and on it represent the numbers shown in the box.

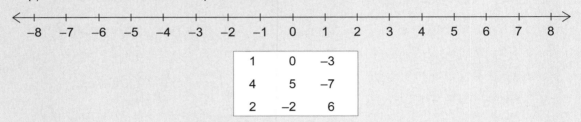

1	0	–3
4	5	–7
2	–2	6

5. What are the values of A, B, C and D on the numberline shown below?

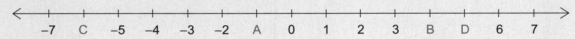

6. Order the following sets of numbers, beginning with the smallest.

(i) {–24, –20, –28, –29}   (ii) {24, 20, 28, 29}   (iii) {24, –20, 28, –29}   (iv) {–24, 20, –28, 29}

7.

(i) Write out all the positive and negative three-digit integers that can be made from the digits shown in the cards above. Each digit may be used only once in a number. For example, –556 is not allowed. (There are six positive and six negative integers.)

(ii) Put the 12 numbers in order, starting with the smallest.

8. The opposite numbers in the number wheel **add up** to –9.

Find the values of A, B, C and D.

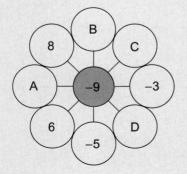

9. The opposite numbers in the number wheel **multiply** to give –24.

Find the values of P, Q, R and S.

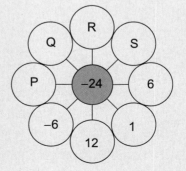

10. The opposite numbers in the number wheel **multiply** to give 28.

Find the values of W, X, Y and Z.

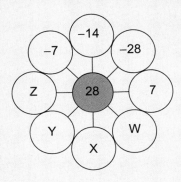

11. Copy and complete these calculations:

(i) $3 \times 4 = \boxed{}$

(ii) $4 \div -2 = \boxed{}$

(iii) $3 + 7 = \boxed{}$

(iv) $10 \div \boxed{} = -5$

(v) $-10 \div \boxed{} = 2$

(vi) $(3 + \boxed{})^2 - 9 = 40$

(vii) $\boxed{} + (-3 - 2)^3 = -120$

(viii) $3^3 + (24 - (\boxed{})) = 0$

(ix) $5^2 + (24 - (\boxed{})) = 0$

12. Insert < (less than) **or** > (greater than) between each of the following pairs of integers.

(i)   5   3   (iii) −5   −3

(ii) −5   3   (iv)   5   −3

13. Complete the following multiplication table:

×	−8	−2		3	5
−20					
			−30	−45	
−10					
−4					
−2					

14. The temperature is −19°C. The temperature goes up 2°C every hour. What will the temperature be:

(i)   After 6 hours

(ii) After 12 hours

15. A diver was at −65 metres. A shark was 8 metres below him.

The diver rose 16 metres and the shark rose 12 metres. How far apart are the diver and the shark now?

16. The table shows the recorded highest and lowest temperatures in five cities during one year.

	City				
	Dublin	**New York**	**London**	**Athens**	**Beijing**
Highest temperature	28°C	29°C	30°C	35°C	32°C
Lowest temperature	−4°C	−8°C	−5°C	6°C	−10°C

(i)   Which city had the highest temperature?

(ii) Which city had the lowest temperature?

(iii) Which city had the largest difference in temperature and by how many degrees?

(iv) Which city had the smallest difference in temperature and by how many degrees?

17. On Sunday evening, Jerry has a balance of −€500 in his account.
During the following week, these transactions take place between Jerry and the bank:

(a) On Monday, Jerry lodges €300.

(b) On Wednesday, Jerry withdraws €100.

(c) On Friday, Jerry lodges €200.

What is the balance in Jerry's account on Friday evening?

Rational Numbers

Learning Outcomes

In this chapter you will learn:

- ⊃ How to define a rational number
- ⊃ About equivalent fractions
- ⊃ How to add and subtract fractions
- ⊃ How to multiply and divide fractions
- ⊃ About ratio and proportion

5.1 RATIONAL NUMBERS OR FRACTIONS

In Chapter 4, we saw the need to extend our numbers from natural numbers to integers. We now need to explore the **rational numbers** or **fractions**, as there are real-life problems that we cannot solve with integers alone.

A mother has three apples that she wants to divide evenly between her two children. How does she divide the apples?

She can give one apple to each child and then divide the other apple into two equal parts. She gives one part to one child and the second part to the other child. One part out of two is represented by the number $\frac{1}{2}$. This number is not an integer, but it is made up of two integers, 1 and 2. We call such numbers rational numbers.

The letter Q is used to represent the set of rational numbers:

$Q = \{$Any number which can be written in the form $\frac{a}{b}$, where $a, b \in Z, b \neq 0\}$

Fractions are most often used to represent parts of the whole. There are two parts to every fraction, the **numerator** (the top) and the **denominator** (the bottom). In the fraction $\frac{3}{4}$, the top number, 3, is the numerator and the bottom number, 4, is the denominator.

3 Numerator
4 Denominator

$\frac{3}{4}$

Different Types of Fractions

When we use fractions, it is important to remember the difference between **proper fractions**, **improper fractions** and **mixed numbers**.

Fractions that represent part of the whole are called proper fractions.

Fractions that represent more than the whole are called improper fractions.

For example, $\frac{1}{2}$ is a proper fraction.

For example, $\frac{8}{5}$ is an improper fraction.

A number that is made up of an integer and a proper fraction is called a mixed number.

For example, $2\frac{2}{3}$ is a mixed number.

Equivalent Fractions

Consider once again the division of the three apples between two children. What if the apple had been divided into four equal parts? How many parts would each child get? Each child would get two out of the four parts. So, $\frac{2}{4} = \frac{1}{2}$.

We call $\frac{2}{4}$ and $\frac{1}{2}$ **equivalent fractions**. This is shown in the two fraction strips.

$\frac{1}{2}$

$\frac{2}{4}$

Worked Example 5.1

Which fraction is bigger, $\frac{2}{5}$ or $\frac{5}{12}$?

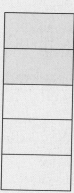
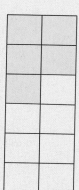

Solution

Step 1

Find a common denominator. This means that we must find an equivalent fraction for $\frac{2}{5}$ and $\frac{5}{12}$ such that both equivalent fractions have the same denominator.

The lowest common denominator will be the LCM of 5 and 12, which is 60.

Step 2

$$\frac{2}{5} = \frac{24}{60} \text{ and } \frac{5}{12} = \frac{25}{60}$$

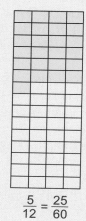

$$\frac{2}{5} = \frac{24}{60} \qquad \frac{5}{12} = \frac{25}{60}$$

$$\frac{25}{60} > \frac{24}{60}$$

Therefore, $\frac{5}{12} > \frac{2}{5}$.

Worked Example 5.2

Write $2\frac{1}{2}$ as an improper fraction.

Solution

$$2\frac{1}{2} = 2 + \frac{1}{2}$$
$$= \frac{4}{2} + \frac{1}{2}$$
$$\therefore 2\frac{1}{2} = \frac{5}{2}$$

Exercise 5.1

1. What fraction of each of the following shapes is coloured?

(i)
(ii)
(iii)

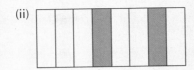

(iv)
(v)
(vi)

2. For each pair of diagrams, state whether the shaded fractions are equivalent.

(i)
(ii)

3. Rewrite each of the following and fill in the blanks to make equivalent fractions.

(i) $\dfrac{1}{2} = \dfrac{}{6}$ (vi) $\dfrac{17}{5} = \dfrac{}{20}$

(ii) $\dfrac{3}{4} = \dfrac{}{8}$ (vii) $\dfrac{3}{8} = \dfrac{}{16} = \dfrac{}{32} = \dfrac{}{128}$

(iii) $\dfrac{8}{7} = \dfrac{}{49}$ (viii) $\dfrac{36}{12} = \dfrac{}{6} = \dfrac{}{4} = \dfrac{}{2}$

(iv) $\dfrac{10}{11} = \dfrac{}{33}$ (ix) $\dfrac{100}{200} = \dfrac{}{20} = \dfrac{}{10} = \dfrac{}{2}$

(v) $\dfrac{6}{5} = \dfrac{}{15}$ (x) $\dfrac{50}{100} = \dfrac{}{50} = \dfrac{}{20} = \dfrac{}{2}$

4. Change each of the following mixed numbers into improper fractions.

(i) $4\dfrac{1}{2}$ (iv) $5\dfrac{2}{3}$ (vii) $8\dfrac{5}{6}$

(ii) $1\dfrac{3}{5}$ (v) $6\dfrac{7}{8}$ (viii) $9\dfrac{3}{11}$

(iii) $4\dfrac{3}{8}$ (vi) $7\dfrac{3}{13}$ (ix) $14\dfrac{5}{8}$

5. Change each of the following improper fractions into mixed numbers.

(i) $\dfrac{4}{3}$ (iv) $\dfrac{23}{21}$ (vii) $\dfrac{18}{4}$

(ii) $\dfrac{9}{5}$ (v) $\dfrac{17}{2}$ (viii) $\dfrac{15}{4}$

(iii) $\dfrac{10}{7}$ (vi) $\dfrac{15}{6}$ (ix) $\dfrac{5}{3}$

6. A group of students are doing a survey on the types of books in their homes. Nicole says that $\dfrac{2}{3}$ of the books in her house are biographies. Seán says that $\dfrac{1}{3}$ of the books in his house are biographies. Nicole then states that there are more biographies in her house.

Is Nicole correct? Explain your answer.

7. Arrange each of the following groups of fractions in order of size, putting the smallest first.

(i) $\left\{\dfrac{2}{3}, \dfrac{5}{6}, \dfrac{1}{2}, \dfrac{3}{15}\right\}$ (iii) $\left\{\dfrac{20}{30}, \dfrac{3}{4}, \dfrac{11}{15}, \dfrac{7}{10}\right\}$

(ii) $\left\{\dfrac{5}{6}, \dfrac{5}{12}, \dfrac{1}{2}, \dfrac{1}{24}\right\}$ (iv) $\left\{\dfrac{13}{40}, \dfrac{2}{5}, \dfrac{3}{8}, \dfrac{7}{20}\right\}$

8. Arrange each of the following groups of fractions in order of size, putting the largest first.

(i) $\left\{\dfrac{13}{25}, \dfrac{1}{2}, \dfrac{23}{50}, \dfrac{12}{25}\right\}$ (iii) $\left\{\dfrac{3}{10}, \dfrac{1}{5}, \dfrac{7}{20}, \dfrac{1}{4}\right\}$

(ii) $\left\{\dfrac{1}{2}, \dfrac{2}{3}, \dfrac{1}{4}, \dfrac{21}{30}\right\}$ (iv) $\left\{\dfrac{37}{50}, \dfrac{77}{100}, \dfrac{3}{4}, \dfrac{19}{25}\right\}$

9. Consider the two fractions, $\dfrac{1}{6}$ and $\dfrac{1}{7}$.

(i) Which is the bigger of the two fractions? Explain your answer.

(ii) Fill in the blanks:

$\dfrac{1}{6} = \dfrac{}{84}$ and $\dfrac{1}{7} = \dfrac{}{84}$

(iii) Name a fraction between $\frac{1}{6}$ and $\frac{1}{7}$.

(iv) Find two other fractions between $\frac{1}{6}$ and $\frac{1}{7}$.

10. Consider the two fractions $\frac{1}{8}$ and $\frac{1}{9}$.

  (i) Which is the bigger of the two fractions? Explain your answer.

  (ii) Fill in the blanks:

$$\frac{1}{8} = \frac{}{144} \text{ and } \frac{1}{9} = \frac{}{144}$$

  (iii) Name a fraction between $\frac{1}{8}$ and $\frac{1}{9}$.

  (iv) Find six other fractions between $\frac{1}{8}$ and $\frac{1}{9}$.

11. Is $\frac{7}{10}$ closer to $\frac{3}{4}$ or $\frac{2}{3}$? Explain your answer.

12. State what fraction of the figures below is shaded and what fraction is not shaded.

(i)  (ii)

(iii) (iv)

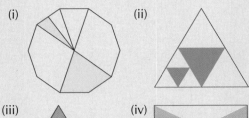

5.2 ADDING AND SUBTRACTING FRACTIONS

Alice, Bob and Conor are each given a bar of chocolate. Alice eats $\frac{1}{6}$ of her bar, Bob eats $\frac{2}{6}$ of his bar, while Conor eats $\frac{5}{6}$ of his bar. In total, how many bars have all three eaten?

$$\frac{1}{6} + \frac{2}{6} + \frac{5}{6} = \frac{8}{6}$$

The answer is $\frac{8}{6}$ or $1\frac{2}{6} = 1\frac{1}{3}$ bars.

Why was this question easy to answer? Because **all three bars were divided into the same number of parts**. This is the key to adding and subtracting fractions.

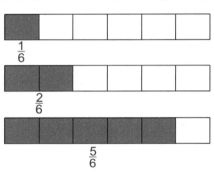

Worked Example 5.3

Tom and John are building a wall. At the end of the week, John counts the number of blocks he has laid. He declares that he has built $\frac{1}{2}$ the wall in one week. Tom counts the number of blocks he has laid and says that he has built $\frac{1}{3}$ of the wall. Using fraction strips to model your answer, find what fraction of the wall has been completed in the week.

Solution

We need to add the fractions $\frac{1}{3}$ and $\frac{1}{2}$. We can model the problem as follows:

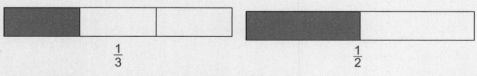

As both strips are not divided into the same number of parts, we cannot add the fractions. How should we divide the strips?

The number of parts must be divisible by 2 and must also be divisible by 3.

There are infinitely many numbers that are both divisible by 2 and by 3, but the number that suits us is the smallest number that is divisible both by 2 and by 3.

What number is this? It is the LCM of 2 and 3, which is 6. Therefore, divide both strips into six parts.

It is now clear that $\frac{1}{3} + \frac{1}{2}$

$$= \frac{2}{6} + \frac{3}{6}$$

$$= \frac{5}{6}$$

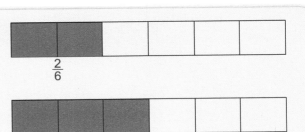

$\frac{2}{6}$

$\frac{3}{6}$

So, $\frac{5}{6}$ of the wall is built at the end of the week.

Worked Example 5.4

Julie has been working on her science project. As she has completed all the practical work, she now has $\frac{3}{4}$ of the project to do. She will complete $\frac{1}{8}$ of the project over her mid-term break. Using fraction strips, find the fraction of the project that will be unfinished after the mid-term break.

Solution

The fraction that is unfinished is $\frac{3}{4} - \frac{1}{8}$.

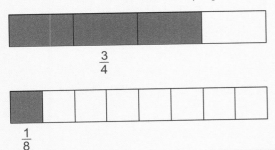

$\frac{3}{4}$

$\frac{1}{8}$

Now divide both strips into eight parts, as 8 is the LCM of 4 and 8.

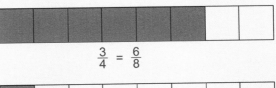

$\frac{3}{4} = \frac{6}{8}$

$\frac{1}{8}$

Therefore:

$$\frac{3}{4} - \frac{1}{8}$$

$$= \frac{6}{8} - \frac{1}{8}$$

$$= \frac{5}{8}$$

Worked Example 5.5

Evaluate each of the following:

(i) $\frac{3}{5} + \frac{2}{9}$ (ii) $10\frac{4}{5} + 6\frac{3}{4}$ (iii) $\frac{5}{6} - \frac{3}{8}$

Solution

(i) **Step 1** Find the LCM of 5 and 9:

LCM (5, 9) = 45

Step 2 Write $\frac{3}{5}$ and $\frac{2}{9}$ as fractions with denominator 45:

$$\frac{3}{5} + \frac{2}{9} = \frac{27}{45} + \frac{10}{45}$$

Step 3 Add the fractions:

$$\frac{27}{45} + \frac{10}{45} = \frac{37}{45}$$

$$\therefore \frac{3}{5} + \frac{2}{9} = \frac{37}{45}$$

(ii) **Step 1** Add the whole numbers:

$$10 + 6 = 16$$

Step 2 Add the fractions:

$$\frac{4}{5} + \frac{3}{4}$$

$$= \frac{16}{20} + \frac{15}{20}$$

$$= \frac{31}{20}$$

$$= 1\frac{11}{20}$$

Step 3 Add the result from Step 1 to the result for Step 2:

$$16 + 1\frac{11}{20} = 17\frac{11}{20}$$

(iii) $\frac{5}{6} - \frac{3}{8} = \frac{20}{24} - \frac{9}{24}$

$$= \frac{11}{24}$$

ACTIVITY 5.2

RATIONAL NUMBERS

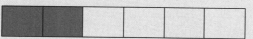

Exercise 5.2

1. The diagram shows that $\frac{1}{3} = \frac{2}{6}$.

Draw diagrams to show that:

(i) $\frac{1}{2} = \frac{2}{4}$ (iv) $\frac{3}{5} = \frac{9}{15}$

(ii) $\frac{2}{3} = \frac{4}{6}$ (v) $\frac{2}{5} = \frac{4}{10}$

(iii) $\frac{3}{4} = \frac{9}{12}$ (vi) $\frac{3}{4} = \frac{6}{8}$

2. Use fraction strips to evaluate each of the following:

(i) $\frac{1}{2} + \frac{2}{5}$ (iv) $\frac{5}{8} + \frac{3}{4}$

(ii) $\frac{3}{4} + \frac{3}{16}$ (v) $\frac{2}{7} + \frac{3}{14}$

(iii) $\frac{2}{3} + \frac{1}{2}$ (vi) $\frac{1}{4} + \frac{1}{3}$

3. Use fraction strips to evaluate each of the following:

(i) $\frac{1}{3} - \frac{1}{6}$ (iii) $\frac{3}{5} - \frac{2}{15}$ (v) $\frac{2}{5} - \frac{3}{10}$

(ii) $\frac{3}{4} - \frac{1}{2}$ (iv) $\frac{7}{8} - \frac{3}{4}$ (vi) $\frac{5}{6} - \frac{2}{3}$

4. Alice and Bob are filling two identical tanks with water.

The water from both tanks will be poured into a third tank which is identical to the other two tanks.

Alice has filled $\frac{1}{4}$ of her tank and Bob has filled $\frac{2}{3}$ of his tank. They need to find out if they have put enough water in the tanks. Alice puts 12 equally spaced markings on the side of each tank.

(i) Why did Alice choose to put 12 markings on the side of the tanks?

(ii) If the water from both tanks is poured into the third tank, what fraction of the third tank will be full?

5. Without using a calculator, express each of the following as a single fraction:

(i) $\frac{1}{4} + \frac{3}{8}$ (vi) $\frac{5}{8} + \frac{7}{12}$

(ii) $\frac{2}{5} + \frac{1}{6}$ (vii) $\frac{3}{7} + \frac{3}{8}$

(iii) $\frac{2}{9} + \frac{5}{12}$ (viii) $\frac{9}{10} + \frac{13}{20}$

(iv) $\frac{3}{5} + \frac{3}{4}$ (ix) $\frac{3}{20} + \frac{19}{50}$

(v) $\frac{3}{7} + \frac{4}{9}$ (x) $\frac{5}{32} + \frac{7}{64}$

6. Without using a calculator, express each of the following as a single fraction:

(i) $\frac{1}{2} + \frac{1}{4} + \frac{1}{8}$ (vi) $\frac{2}{3} + \frac{1}{4} + \frac{1}{2}$

(ii) $\frac{3}{5} + \frac{7}{10} + \frac{2}{20}$ (vii) $\frac{3}{4} + \frac{1}{2} + \frac{1}{3}$

(iii) $\frac{1}{3} + \frac{2}{9} + \frac{1}{27}$ (viii) $\frac{2}{5} + \frac{1}{6} + \frac{2}{3}$

(iv) $\frac{3}{4} + \frac{1}{8} + \frac{5}{12}$ (ix) $\frac{5}{12} + \frac{3}{4} + \frac{1}{5}$

(v) $\frac{1}{9} + \frac{7}{18} + \frac{1}{36}$ (x) $\frac{3}{2} + \frac{5}{6} + \frac{4}{5}$

7. Without using a calculator, do the following subtractions:

(i) $\frac{1}{2} - \frac{3}{8}$ (vi) $\frac{3}{4} - \frac{1}{2}$

(ii) $\frac{5}{6} - \frac{2}{5}$ (vii) $\frac{1}{2} - \frac{1}{3}$

(iii) $\frac{4}{13} - \frac{3}{10}$ (viii) $\frac{1}{12} - \frac{1}{15}$

(iv) $\frac{2}{15} - \frac{1}{8}$ (ix) $\frac{4}{5} - \frac{2}{7}$

(v) $\frac{6}{11} - \frac{2}{9}$ (x) $\frac{7}{9} - \frac{1}{3}$

8. Without using a calculator, evaluate each of the following:

(i) $2\frac{1}{2} + 3\frac{1}{4}$ (vi) $4\frac{3}{5} - 2\frac{5}{6}$

(ii) $5\frac{3}{4} - 3\frac{1}{8}$ (vii) $11\frac{1}{4} + 3\frac{1}{6} - 4\frac{7}{8}$

(iii) $5\frac{1}{6} + 6\frac{3}{8}$ (viii) $3\frac{3}{4} + 5\frac{4}{5} - 4\frac{11}{20} - \frac{7}{10}$

(iv) $9\frac{7}{8} - 3\frac{7}{12}$ (ix) $100 - \frac{7}{8} - \frac{7}{16}$

(v) $3\frac{1}{2} - 1\frac{3}{4}$ (x) $50 - \frac{1}{2} + \frac{3}{4}$

9. Complete these number wheels. Opposite wheels add up to the number in the centre.

(i)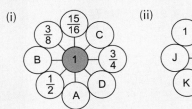

(ii)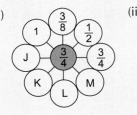

(iii)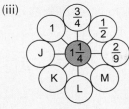

(iv)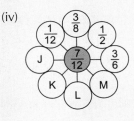

10. John spends $\frac{2}{5}$ of his pocket money on phone credit and $\frac{1}{4}$ on fizzy drinks. He saves the rest.

   (i) What fraction of his pocket money does John save?

   (ii) If John received €30 in pocket money, how much would he save?

11. In October 2010, a RED C opinion poll asked the question, 'If there was a general election tomorrow, to which party or independent candidate would you give your first preference vote?' The table below gives the result of the poll. All respondents gave an answer.

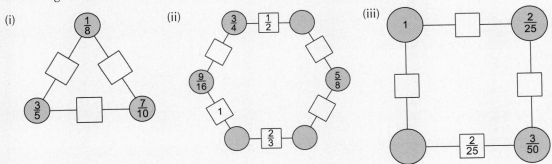

Party	Fianna Fáil	Fine Gael	Labour	Independent	Greens	Sinn Féin	Don't know
Fraction	$\frac{7}{50}$	$\frac{8}{25}$	$\frac{27}{100}$	$\frac{1}{10}$		$\frac{9}{100}$	$\frac{1}{25}$

   (i) What fraction of those sampled would give their first preference to the Green Party?

   (ii) Which party has the greatest support?

   (iii) Which party has the least support?

12. In the following diagrams, the value in the square is equal to the sum of the values in the two connecting circles. Find the value in each blank square and each blank circle.

(i)

(ii)

(iii)

13. Sebastian is training for a 10 km road race. On Monday of last week, he ran $4\frac{2}{5}$ km. On Thursday he ran $5\frac{3}{8}$ km and on Sunday he ran $5\frac{1}{2}$ km. How many kilometres did Sebastian run last week?

5.3 MULTIPLYING FRACTIONS

What are we doing when we multiply two fractions together?

For example, what does $\frac{4}{5} \times \frac{2}{3}$ mean? $\frac{4}{5} \times \frac{2}{3}$ actually means 'Find $\frac{4}{5}$ of $\frac{2}{3}$'.

Let us use fraction strips to find $\frac{4}{5}$ of $\frac{2}{3}$.

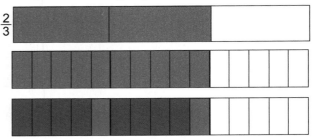

Now divide each third into five parts. The whole is now divided into 15 parts.

We need $\frac{4}{5}$ of each red third, so shade four out of five parts in each red third.

Eight out of 15 parts are shaded, so $\frac{4}{5} \times \frac{2}{3} = \frac{8}{15}$.

Worked Example 5.6

Evaluate the following:

(i) $\frac{1}{5} \times \frac{2}{3}$ (ii) $\frac{3}{5} \times \frac{3}{4}$

Solution

(i) $\frac{1}{5} \times \frac{2}{3} = \frac{1}{5}$ of $\frac{2}{3}$

From the fraction strip, we see that $\frac{1}{5} \times \frac{2}{3} = \frac{2}{15}$.

You have probably noticed that we can also get the result we are looking for by multiplying the numerators together and then the denominators:

$$\frac{1}{5} \times \frac{2}{3} = \frac{1 \times 2}{5 \times 3}$$
$$= \frac{2}{15}$$

(ii) $\frac{3}{5} \times \frac{3}{4}$

$= \frac{3 \times 3}{5 \times 4} \left(\frac{\text{Numerator} \times \text{Numerator}}{\text{Denominator} \times \text{Denominator}} \right)$

$= \frac{9}{20}$

Worked Example 5.7

Evaluate the following:

(i) $2\frac{1}{4} \times 3\frac{1}{5}$

(ii) $3\frac{1}{3} \times 2$

Note: When multiplying mixed numbers, first change to improper fractions.

Solution

(i) $2\frac{1}{4} \times 3\frac{1}{5} = \frac{9}{4} \times \frac{16}{5}$

$= \frac{9 \times \overset{4}{\cancel{16}}}{\underset{1}{\cancel{4}} \times 5}$

$= \frac{36}{5}$

$\therefore 2\frac{1}{4} \times 3\frac{1}{5} = 7\frac{1}{5}$

(ii) $3\frac{1}{3} \times 2 = \frac{10}{3} \times \frac{2}{1}$

$= \frac{10 \times 2}{3 \times 1}$

$= \frac{20}{3}$

$\therefore 3\frac{1}{3} \times 2 = 6\frac{2}{3}$

Exercise 5.3

1. Use fraction strips to do the following multiplications:

   (i) $\frac{1}{4} \times \frac{1}{2}$ (iii) $\frac{2}{5} \times \frac{2}{3}$

   (ii) $\frac{3}{4} \times \frac{1}{3}$ (iv) $\frac{1}{4} \times \frac{3}{5}$

2. Use fraction strips to do the following multiplications:

   (i) $\frac{3}{4} \times \frac{1}{5}$ (iii) $\frac{1}{3} \times \frac{2}{5}$

   (ii) $\frac{2}{5} \times \frac{3}{4}$ (iv) $\frac{1}{6} \times \frac{1}{2}$

3. Use fraction strips to do the following multiplications:

   (i) $\frac{1}{3} \times \frac{2}{3}$ (iii) $\frac{2}{5} \times \frac{3}{5}$

   (ii) $\frac{1}{4} \times \frac{3}{4}$ (iv) $\frac{1}{6} \times \frac{5}{6}$

4. Express each of the following as a single fraction in its simplest form:

   (i) $\frac{1}{5} \times \frac{2}{3}$ (vi) $\frac{3}{7} \times \frac{7}{15}$

   (ii) $\frac{1}{2} \times \frac{1}{3}$ (vii) $\frac{2}{3} \times \frac{1}{4}$

   (iii) $\frac{5}{6} \times \frac{1}{4}$ (viii) $\frac{1}{2} \times \frac{3}{5}$

   (iv) $\frac{4}{5} \times \frac{4}{9}$ (ix) $\frac{7}{8} \times \frac{2}{9}$

   (v) $\frac{3}{5} \times \frac{3}{4}$ (x) $\frac{5}{12} \times \frac{6}{25}$

5. (i) $1\frac{1}{2} \times 4\frac{2}{3}$ (vi) $9\frac{2}{3} \times 1\frac{1}{4}$

   (ii) $5\frac{1}{4} \times 1\frac{3}{7}$ (vii) $2\frac{2}{5} \times 7\frac{1}{2}$

   (iii) $3\frac{1}{2} \times 8\frac{1}{4}$ (viii) $6\frac{1}{4} \times \frac{2}{5}$

   (iv) $2\frac{1}{2} \times 5$ (ix) $1\frac{3}{4} \times 2$

   (v) $1\frac{1}{8} \times 4$ (x) $3 \times 6\frac{1}{5}$

6. The distributive property also applies to rational numbers. Verify that:

   (i) $\frac{3}{4}\left(\frac{2}{5} + \frac{3}{5}\right) = \frac{3}{4}\left(\frac{2}{5}\right) + \frac{3}{4}\left(\frac{3}{5}\right)$

   (ii) $\frac{3}{8}\left(\frac{1}{3} + \frac{1}{6}\right) = \frac{3}{8}\left(\frac{1}{3}\right) + \frac{3}{8}\left(\frac{1}{6}\right)$

   (iii) $\frac{1}{3}\left(\frac{1}{4} + \frac{3}{4}\right) = \frac{1}{3}\left(\frac{1}{4}\right) + \frac{1}{3}\left(\frac{3}{4}\right)$

   (iv) $\frac{2}{3}\left(\frac{1}{5} + \frac{5}{8}\right) = \frac{2}{3}\left(\frac{1}{5}\right) + \frac{2}{3}\left(\frac{5}{8}\right)$

7. Louise has planted 96 shrubs. The garden centre guaranteed her that at least $\frac{7}{8}$ of the shrubs would survive. What is the minimum number of shrubs that should survive?

8. A property developer buys just enough land to build 88 houses. Each house will be built on a site of area $\frac{7}{16}$ hectare. What is the area, in hectares, of the land purchased by the property developer?

9. John tiled $\frac{4}{5}$ of a bathroom wall. The next day he grouted $\frac{3}{4}$ of the tiled section. Use a fraction strip to find the fraction of the bathroom wall that had the tiles grouted.

10. Mark spent $\frac{1}{4}$ of his income on rent and $\frac{2}{5}$ of what was left on food. What fraction of his income was left after buying the food?

11. Which is larger, $\frac{3}{4}$ of $2\frac{1}{2}$ or $\frac{2}{5}$ of $6\frac{1}{2}$?

12. Express each of the following as a fraction in its simplest form:

   (i) $\frac{1}{2} \times \left(-\frac{1}{3}\right)$ (v) $2\frac{1}{2} \times -5$

   (ii) $\left(-\frac{3}{5}\right) \times \frac{3}{4}$ (vi) $-4\frac{1}{2} \times 7\frac{1}{2}$

   (iii) $\left(-\frac{1}{2}\right) \times \left(-\frac{5}{4}\right)$ (vii) $-1\frac{1}{2} \times 4\frac{2}{3}$

   (iv) $-2\frac{2}{5} \times \left(-\frac{3}{4}\right)$ (viii) $\frac{1}{8} \times \frac{1}{3} \times \left(-\frac{5}{6}\right)$

5.4 DIVIDING FRACTIONS

Fiona has invited 15 of her friends to her house to watch a DVD. She has ordered four pizzas and decides that each friend will get $\frac{2}{9}$ of a pizza. Will she have enough pizza for everybody?

Once again, we can model this problem using fraction strips. We will need four strips, as there are four 'whole' pizzas.

Each fraction strip is divided into nine equal parts. We need to know how many $\frac{2}{9}$ are in four. Therefore, we shade every two parts of the strip.

There are eight blocks shaded ▨▨ = 8 servings.

There are eight blocks shaded ▨▨ = 8 servings.

We put the spare blocks together:

☐☐☐☐ = 2 servings.

Total number of servings
= 8 + 8 + 2 = 18 servings.

Fiona and 15 friends = 16 servings.

Therefore, Fiona has enough for everybody.

 ACTIVITY 5.4

Worked Example 5.8

Evaluate the following:

(i) $\frac{5}{6} \div \frac{1}{4}$ (ii) $3\frac{1}{2} \div 2\frac{1}{3}$

Solution

In Activity 5.4, you learned a method of dividing fractions. There are two steps in the method.

Step 1 Find the reciprocal of the fraction by which you are dividing.

Step 2 Multiply this reciprocal by the other fraction.

The **reciprocal** of a fraction is found by turning the fraction upside down.

For example, the reciprocal of $\frac{11}{12}$ is $\frac{12}{11}$.

(i) $\frac{5}{6} \div \frac{1}{4} = \frac{5}{6} \times \frac{4}{1}$

$= \frac{20}{6}$

$= \frac{10}{3}$

$\therefore \frac{5}{6} \div \frac{1}{4} = 3\frac{1}{3}$

(ii) $3\frac{1}{2} \div 2\frac{1}{3} = \frac{7}{2} \div \frac{7}{3}$ (Write as improper fractions)

$= \frac{7}{2} \times \frac{3}{7} \left(\text{Reciprocal of } \frac{7}{3} \text{ is } \frac{3}{7}\right)$

$= \frac{3}{2}$

$\therefore 3\frac{1}{2} \div 2\frac{1}{3} = 1\frac{1}{2}$

Exercise 5.4

1. Use fraction strips to do the following divisions:

   (i) $2 \div \frac{2}{5}$ (iii) $4 \div \frac{2}{11}$

   (ii) $5 \div \frac{5}{8}$ (iv) $3 \div \frac{3}{7}$

2. Use fraction strips to do the following divisions:

   (i) $5 \div \frac{5}{6}$ (iii) $3 \div \frac{3}{8}$

   (ii) $5 \div \frac{5}{8}$ (iv) $4 \div \frac{2}{3}$

3. Use fraction strips to do the following divisions:

   (i) $3 \div \frac{3}{5}$ (iii) $2 \div \frac{2}{9}$

   (ii) $3 \div \frac{3}{10}$ (iv) $6 \div \frac{6}{5}$

4. Use fraction strips to do the following divisions:

   (i) $2 \div \frac{1}{2}$ (iii) $5 \div 2\frac{1}{2}$

   (ii) $3 \div 1\frac{1}{2}$ (iv) $7 \div 3\frac{1}{2}$

5. Simplify each of the following and write the answer as a single fraction in its simplest form:

(i) $\frac{1}{6} \div \frac{2}{3}$ (iv) $\frac{6}{25} \div \frac{9}{10}$ (vii) $\frac{2}{5} \div \frac{1}{10}$

(ii) $\frac{1}{4} \div \frac{2}{3}$ (v) $\frac{7}{8} \div \frac{3}{4}$ (viii) $\frac{1}{2} \div \frac{3}{8}$

(iii) $\frac{3}{5} \div \frac{1}{4}$ (vi) $\frac{1}{9} \div \frac{1}{3}$ (ix) $\frac{4}{5} \div \frac{1}{7}$

6. Evaluate each of the following:

(i) $3\frac{1}{9} \div 2\frac{1}{3}$ (iv) $4\frac{4}{5} \div 1\frac{1}{7}$ (vii) $5\frac{2}{5} \div 4\frac{3}{27}$

(ii) $12\frac{2}{5} \div 3\frac{1}{10}$ (v) $2\frac{1}{2} \div \frac{1}{4}$ (viii) $7\frac{1}{8} \div \frac{19}{16}$

(iii) $28\frac{1}{2} \div 2\frac{3}{8}$ (vi) $4\frac{1}{3} \div \frac{13}{5}$ (ix) $1\frac{3}{4} \div \frac{7}{12}$

7. Usain Bolt, the fastest man on earth, has a stride length of $2\frac{4}{5}$ m when he is at full stride. How many strides would Usain take to cover 70 m if his stride length is $2\frac{4}{5}$ m?

8. How many strips of ribbon, each $2\frac{1}{2}$ cm long, can be cut from a roll of ribbon $32\frac{1}{2}$ cm long?

9. A ball-bearing weighs $1\frac{1}{4}$ grams. How many ball-bearings weigh a total of 35 grams?

10. John consumes $\frac{3}{4}$ kg of sugar every week.

(i) How much sugar will he consume in 52 weeks?

(ii) How long does he take to eat 30 kg?

11. Caoimhe has bought 12 bars of chocolate. How many pieces will she have if she breaks the bars into:

(i) Halves

(ii) Quarters

(iii) Thirds

5.5 RATIO AND PROPORTION

Ratio is used to compare the sizes of two or more quantities. A ratio of 2 : 1 means two parts of one quantity for every one part of the other quantity.

In the picture on the right, for every two red paperclips, there is one blue paperclip. This is easily seen when we take the paperclips and lay them out as follows:

In each group, there is a total of three paperclips – two red and one blue.

Therefore, $\frac{2}{3}$ of the paperclips are red and $\frac{1}{3}$ are blue.

Worked Example 5.9

John and Tony divided €250 between them in the ratio 1 : 4. How much did each receive?

Solution

1 : 4 means that for every €1 John received, Tony received €4. Therefore, for every €5, John received €1 and Tony received €4. So, John gets $\frac{1}{5}$ of the €250 and Tony gets $\frac{4}{5}$.

John: $\frac{1}{5} \times €250 = €50$ Tony: $\frac{4}{5} \times €250 = €200$

Worked Example 5.10

Máire, Shaun and Donal have shared a prize in a local Lotto. Máire invested €5 in the draw, Shaun invested €4 and Donal paid €3. They decide to split the winnings in the ratio of their investments. If Shaun gets €108, how much is the prize?

Solution

Add the individual investments: €5 + €4 + €3 = €12.

We know that for every €12 of the prize, Máire gets €5, Shaun gets €4 and Donal gets €3.

So Shaun gets $\frac{4}{12}$ or $\frac{1}{3}$ of the prize.

If $\frac{1}{3}$ of the prize is €108, then $\frac{3}{3}$ or the whole prize is €108 × 3 = €324.

Worked Example 5.11

Express the ratio $\frac{1}{2} : \frac{1}{7}$ as a whole number ratio.

Solution

The common denominator is 14. We can multiply both sides of the ratio by 14.

$$\frac{1}{2} : \frac{1}{7}$$
$$14 \times \frac{1}{2} : 14 \times \frac{1}{7}$$
$$7 : 2$$

It is common practice to write ratios as whole numbers.

Exercise 5.5

1. An artist mixes three parts yellow paint with one part red paint to get the shade of orange she wants.

   (i) What is the ratio of red paint to yellow paint?

   (ii) Copy and complete the given table to find the amount of colour needed to make different quantities of orange paint.

Yellow	3		6		9		15
Red	1	5		8		12	

2. Write each of the following ratios in its simplest form:

   (i) 4 : 20   (iv) 25 : 100   (vii) 8 : 4 : 2   (x) 30 : 15 : 5

   (ii) 5 : 25   (v) 18 : 12   (viii) 12 : 18 : 30   (xi) 35 : 45 : 30

   (iii) 20 : 30   (vi) 51 : 6   (ix) 12 : 4 : 2   (xii) 24 : 12 : 60

3. Express each of the following in its simplest whole number form:

   (i) $\frac{1}{4} : \frac{1}{2}$ (iii) $\frac{1}{6} : \frac{1}{5}$ (v) $2 : \frac{1}{5} : \frac{1}{10}$ (vii) $1\frac{1}{3} : 3\frac{2}{3}$ (ix) $4\frac{1}{2} : 7\frac{1}{2}$

   (ii) $\frac{1}{5} : \frac{1}{3}$ (iv) $\frac{1}{2} : \frac{1}{4} : \frac{1}{6}$ (vi) $3\frac{1}{2} : 4\frac{1}{2}$ (viii) $1\frac{1}{4} : 1\frac{3}{4}$ (x) $\frac{1}{3} : \frac{1}{4} : \frac{1}{5}$

RATIONAL NUMBERS

4. Express each of the following in its simplest form:

    (i)   20 cent as a ratio of €5

    (ii) 10 cm as a ratio of 3 m

    (iii) 300 g as a ratio of 2 kg

    (iv) 2 km as a ratio of 50 cm

    (v) 10 seconds as a ratio of 6 hours

    (vi) €10 as a ratio of 50 cent

    (vii) 3 mm as a ratio of 65 cm

    (viii) 3 kg as a ratio of 200 g

    (ix) 3 minutes as a ratio of 2 days

5. A plank of wood 6 m long is cut in the ratio 1 : 5. Find the length in centimetres of the longer piece.

6. Divide 60 g of cereal between two brothers so that one gets twice as much as the other.

7. Fernando and Wayne are two professional footballers. They decide to take part in a penalty competition to raise money for their favourite charities. €45,000 is raised.

It is decided to divide the money in the ratio of penalties scored. Fernando scores five penalties and Wayne scores four penalties.

How much does Wayne's charity get?

8. The ratio of red counters to blue counters in a bag is 3 : 5. There are 48 counters in the bag.

    (i) How many blue counters are in the bag?

    (ii) What is the probability of drawing a red counter from the bag?

9. The ratio of soft sweets to hard sweets in a bag is 5 : 3. There are 15 hard sweets in the bag. How many sweets in total are in the bag?

10. John, a hotel owner, buys concentrated orange juice that needs to be mixed with water in the ratio concentrate : water = 1 : 6.

    (i) One morning, 70 litres of orange juice is mixed. How many litres of concentrate was needed for this?

    (ii) How many litres of juice will John get from 5 litres of concentrate?

11. Danny lives in New York. Every Christmas, he sends $500 to his two nieces. The money is divided in the ratio of their ages. Monica, the elder of the nieces, was 6 years old in 2004 and Naomi was 4 years old.

    (i) How much did each get in 2004?

    (ii) How much did each get in 2009?

5.6 ORDER OF OPERATIONS

The order of operations on the set of rational numbers is the same as the order of operations on the set of integers.

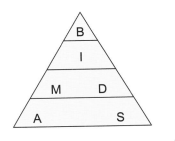

Evaluate:

(i) $\frac{1}{2} \times \frac{5}{8} + 3 \times \frac{2}{5} - \left(\frac{1}{4}\right)^2$ (ii) $\frac{2}{5} - \frac{3}{4} \times \frac{3}{10} + \left(\frac{2}{5}\right)^2$

Solution

(i) $\frac{1}{2} \times \frac{5}{8} + 3 \times \frac{2}{5} - \left(\frac{1}{4}\right)^2$

$= \frac{1}{2} \times \frac{5}{8} + \frac{3}{1} \times \frac{2}{5} - \frac{1}{16}$ (Indices)

$= \frac{5}{16} + \frac{6}{5} - \frac{1}{16}$ (Multiplication)

$= \frac{25}{80} + \frac{96}{80} - \frac{5}{80}$

$= \frac{121}{80} - \frac{5}{80}$ (Addition)

$= \frac{116}{80}$ (Subtraction)

$= \frac{29}{20}$

$= 1\frac{9}{20}$

(ii) $\frac{2}{5} - \frac{3}{4} \times \frac{3}{10} + \left(\frac{2}{5}\right)^2$

$= \frac{2}{5} - \frac{3}{4} \times \frac{3}{10} + \frac{4}{25}$ (Indices)

$= \frac{2}{5} - \frac{9}{40} + \frac{4}{25}$ (Multiplication)

$= \frac{80}{200} - \frac{45}{200} + \frac{32}{200}$

$= \frac{35}{200} + \frac{32}{200}$ (Addition)

$= \frac{67}{200}$

Exercise 5.6

1. Evaluate each of the following:

   (i) $\frac{1}{2} \times \frac{1}{4} - \frac{1}{3}$ (iii) $\frac{1}{5} \times \frac{3}{5} + \frac{1}{8}$

   (ii) $\frac{1}{3} + \frac{3}{4} \times \frac{3}{8}$ (iv) $\frac{1}{2} \times \frac{3}{4} - \frac{1}{8}$

2. Write as a single fraction:

   (i) $\frac{1}{2} + \frac{1}{4} - \frac{1}{8}$ (iii) $\frac{3}{8} - \left(\frac{1}{2} - \frac{1}{4}\right)$

   (ii) $\frac{3}{5} - \left(\frac{1}{10} + \frac{1}{15}\right)$ (iv) $\frac{4}{5} - \left(\frac{1}{25} + \frac{3}{10}\right)$

3. Evaluate the following:

   (i) $\frac{1}{2} \times \frac{1}{4} + \frac{1}{3} \times \frac{1}{6}$ (iii) $\frac{1}{4} \times \frac{2}{5} - \frac{1}{2} \times \frac{7}{10}$

   (ii) $\frac{1}{5} \times \frac{3}{10} + \frac{1}{2} \times \frac{3}{8}$ (iv) $\frac{3}{4} \times \frac{1}{8} - \frac{1}{10} \times \frac{3}{10}$

4. Calculate:

   (i) $\frac{1}{4} \times \frac{2}{9} - \left(\frac{5}{6}\right)^2$ (iii) $\frac{1}{4} \times \frac{1}{4} - \left(\frac{1}{4}\right)^2$

   (ii) $\frac{1}{2} \times \frac{5}{8} - \left(\frac{3}{4}\right)^2$ (iv) $\frac{3}{8} \times \frac{2}{5} - \left(\frac{3}{4}\right)^2$

5. Evaluate:

   (i) $\frac{1}{5} \times \frac{3}{2} + \frac{1}{2} \times \frac{1}{4} - \left(\frac{1}{3}\right)^2$

   (ii) $\frac{3}{5} \times \frac{4}{9} - \frac{1}{4} \times \frac{1}{2} + \left(\frac{3}{5}\right)^2$

   (iii) $\frac{1}{9} \times \frac{1}{2} + \frac{1}{3} \times \frac{1}{4} - \left(\frac{1}{5}\right)^2$

   (iv) $\frac{3}{4} \times \frac{2}{9} - \frac{1}{4} \times \frac{2}{5} + \left(\frac{1}{10}\right)^2$

6. Calculate the following:

   (i) $(2)^2 + \frac{3}{4} \div \frac{1}{2} + \frac{1}{9} \div \frac{4}{3}$

   (ii) $\frac{1}{2} \div \frac{1}{4} + \left(\frac{1}{4}\right)^2 + \frac{1}{6} \div \frac{1}{3}$

   (iii) $\frac{3}{5} \times \frac{15}{27} + \frac{5}{6} \div \frac{2}{3} - \left(\frac{1}{2}\right)^2$

   (iv) $\frac{1}{2} \div \frac{1}{8} - \left(\frac{1}{3}\right)^2 + \frac{1}{6} \div \frac{1}{3}$

7. Write as a single fraction:

   (i) $\left(\frac{1}{2} + \frac{1}{3}\right)^2 - \frac{1}{2} \times \frac{1}{8}$ (iii) $\left(\frac{1}{2} + \frac{1}{4}\right)^2 - \left(\frac{1}{8}\right)^2$

   (ii) $\left(\frac{1}{5} + \frac{3}{10}\right)^2 - \left(\frac{1}{10}\right)^2$ (iv) $\left(\frac{3}{4} + \frac{2}{5}\right)^2 - \frac{1}{2} \div \frac{1}{4}$

1. Evaluate:

   (i) $\frac{1}{2} + \frac{3}{10}$ (iii) $\frac{1}{3} + \frac{4}{9}$

   (ii) $\frac{1}{3} + \frac{1}{6}$ (iv) $\frac{3}{8} + \frac{1}{4}$

2. Calculate:

   (i) $\frac{3}{7} + \frac{5}{14}$ (iii) $\frac{7}{8} - \frac{1}{4}$

   (ii) $\frac{1}{10} - \frac{1}{5}$ (iv) $\frac{9}{10} - \frac{1}{2}$

3. Evaluate:

   (i) $\frac{1}{2} + \frac{1}{4} + \frac{3}{8}$ (iii) $\frac{14}{15} - \frac{1}{5} + \frac{1}{3}$

   (ii) $\frac{3}{5} + \frac{2}{5} + \frac{1}{10}$ (iv) $\frac{3}{4} + \frac{1}{8} - \frac{1}{4}$

4. Write as single fraction:

   (i) $\frac{1}{2} \times \frac{1}{4} + \frac{3}{8}$ (iii) $\frac{1}{3} \times \frac{1}{6} + \frac{1}{10} \div \frac{3}{5}$

   (ii) $\frac{1}{2} \div \frac{1}{4} + \frac{5}{8}$ (iv) $\frac{1}{2} \times \frac{1}{8} + \frac{1}{4} \div \frac{1}{2}$

5. Write as a single fraction:

   (i) $\left(\frac{1}{2} + \frac{1}{4}\right)^2 - \frac{1}{8}$

   (ii) $\left(\frac{1}{5} - \frac{1}{10}\right)^2 + \left(\frac{1}{2} + \frac{1}{4}\right)^2$

   (iii) $\left(\frac{1}{4} + \frac{1}{8}\right) \times 2 - \left(\frac{1}{4} - \frac{1}{8}\right) \times 3$

   (iv) $\left(\frac{3}{4} + \frac{1}{8}\right) \times \frac{1}{2} - \left(\frac{3}{4} - \frac{1}{8}\right) \times \frac{1}{4}$

6. (a) Write down five fractions that are equivalent to $\frac{2}{3}$.

   (b) Arrange the following fractions in order of size, putting the smallest first.

   $\frac{4}{9}, \frac{1}{3}, \frac{7}{20}, \frac{2}{5}, \frac{3}{10}$

   (c) Is $\frac{9}{10}$ closer to $\frac{19}{20}$ or $\frac{37}{40}$?

   Explain your answer.

7. (i) Change the following improper fractions to mixed numbers:

   $\frac{5}{4}, \frac{19}{3}, \frac{16}{7}, \frac{6}{5}$

   (ii) Find four fractions between $\frac{1}{5}$ and $\frac{1}{6}$.

   (iii) A waiter pours out two glasses of juice in the ratio 4 : 5. The larger glass contains 150 ml of juice. How much does the smaller glass contain?

8. (a) Use fraction strips to evaluate each of the following:

   (i) $\frac{1}{4} - \frac{1}{6}$ (iii) $\frac{5}{8} + \frac{3}{4}$

   (ii) $\frac{2}{5} - \frac{1}{3}$ (iv) $\frac{1}{5} \times \frac{2}{3}$

   (b) Express each of the following as a single fraction:

   (i) $\frac{2}{5} + \frac{3}{8}$ (iii) $2\frac{1}{2} + 3\frac{1}{3}$

   (ii) $\frac{1}{4} + \frac{9}{16}$ (iv) $3\frac{1}{7} + 2\frac{3}{5}$

   (c) Put the correct sign, < or >, between each pair of fractions:

   (i) $\frac{5}{18} \square \frac{2}{3}$ (iii) $\frac{11}{15} \square \frac{7}{10}$

   (ii) $\frac{5}{20} \square \frac{17}{30}$ (iv) $\frac{3}{7} \square \frac{4}{9}$

9. In Annette's class, eight pupils wear glasses and 12 do not wear glasses.

   (i) How many pupil's are in Annette's class?

   (ii) What fraction wear glasses?

10. At a meeting 24 parents voted in favour of and 36 voted against sending pupils on a school tour.

    (i) How many people voted?

    (ii) What fraction voted for sending the pupils on the tour?

    (iii) What fraction voted against sending them?

11. (i) Find the value of $\frac{1}{5} + \frac{1}{2}$ and, hence, the value of $\frac{1}{5} + \frac{1}{2} - \frac{1}{10}$.

    (ii) If $3\frac{3}{4}$ cm is increased by $\frac{1}{2}$ cm, what is the new measurement?

    (iii) Orla drank half a carton of milk on Monday. The next day, she drank half of the milk that was left in the carton. What fraction of the original milk is now left?

12. (a) Use fraction strips to do the following multiplications:

    (i) $\frac{1}{4} \times \frac{2}{3}$ (iii) $\frac{2}{5} \times \frac{3}{5}$

    (ii) $\frac{1}{4} \times \frac{2}{5}$ (iv) $\frac{1}{7} \times \frac{5}{6}$

    (b) Evaluate $3\frac{1}{5} \times 2\frac{1}{2} \times 4\frac{3}{4}$.

(c) A property developer buys two adjoining fields. One field has an area of $35\frac{1}{2}$ acres, while the other field has an area of $7\frac{7}{8}$ acres. He joins the two fields.

    (i) Find the total area of the two fields.

    (ii) He then divides the area up into five sites of equal area. Find the area of each site.

13. (a) Use fraction strips to do the following divisions:

    (i) $10 \div \frac{5}{8}$

    (ii) $6 \div \frac{3}{10}$

    (iii) $4 \div \frac{2}{9}$

    (iv) $2 \div \frac{2}{5}$

(b) Evaluate:

$$\frac{1\frac{2}{5} \div \frac{3}{8}}{\frac{5}{8} \div \frac{1}{4}}$$

(c) A drum in a washing machine revolves once every $1\frac{1}{2}$ seconds. How many times does it revolve in a minute?

14. Evaluate each of the following, giving your answer in the simplest form:

(i) $\dfrac{\frac{3}{4} + \frac{5}{8}}{\frac{5}{8} - \frac{1}{4}}$

(ii) $\left(2\frac{5}{8} - 1\frac{1}{2}\right)\left(1\frac{7}{8} + 3\frac{1}{4}\right)$

(iii) $\dfrac{1\frac{3}{4} - \frac{7}{8}}{2\frac{1}{2} - 1\frac{1}{6}}$

15. Solve these problems:

(a) Kathleen has 2,500 shares in her local credit union. If she sells $\frac{1}{4}$ of her shares, how many shares will she have left?

(b) Students were asked how they travelled to school each day. $\frac{1}{2}$ said they travelled by bus, $\frac{2}{5}$ said they walked, and the rest travelled by car.
What fraction of the students travelled by car?

(c) A lotto machine contains balls of four different colours. $\frac{1}{3}$ of the balls are black, $\frac{2}{9}$ are white, six are yellow and two are red.
How many balls are:

(i) Black

(ii) White

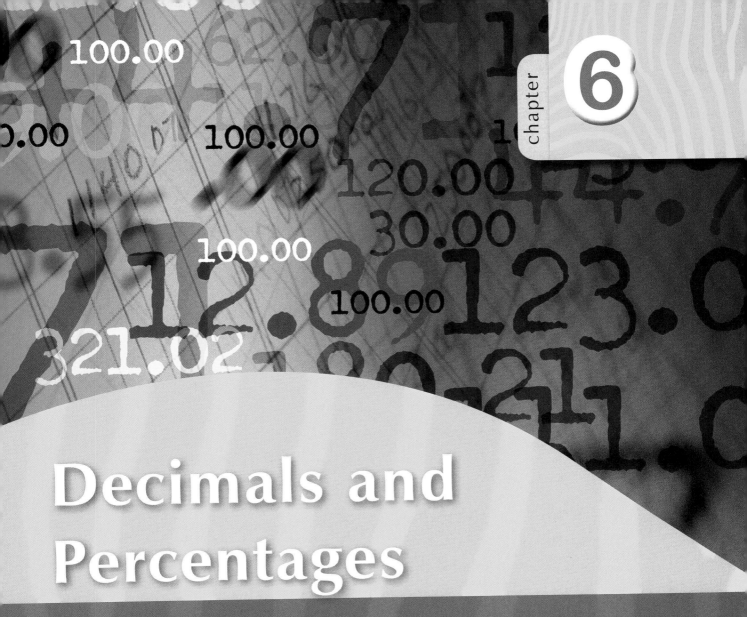

chapter

6

Decimals and Percentages

Learning Outcomes

In this chapter you will learn:

- About place value
- How to convert fractions to decimals
- About rounding
- About operations with decimals
- About estimation
- About percentages
- About percentage increase and percentage decrease

Decimals and percentages are other ways in which we can represent fractions. In fact, every fraction can be written as either a decimal or a percentage. However, not all decimals can be written as fractions.

6.1 DECIMALS

We can write a decimal as a fraction by breaking it into parts. We start with the whole part of the number, then tenths, hundredths, and so on. For example, a number such as 5.3456 is really

$$5 + \frac{3}{10} + \frac{4}{100} + \frac{5}{1,000} + \frac{6}{10,000} = 5\frac{3,456}{10,000}$$

The **decimal point** is a dot that separates the whole part of the number from the rest of the number.

ACTIVITY 6.1

Place Value

The value of a digit in a decimal number depends on its position in the number – its **place value**.

The value of each digit in the number 1,234.56789 is given in the table below:

Digit	1	2	3	4	•	5	6	7	8	9
	$1 \times 1,000$	2×100	3×10	4×1		$5 \times \frac{1}{10}$	$6 \times \frac{1}{100}$	$7 \times \frac{1}{1,000}$	$8 \times \frac{1}{10,000}$	$9 \times \frac{1}{100,000}$
Value	1,000	200	30	4		$\frac{5}{10}$	$\frac{6}{100}$	$\frac{7}{1,000}$	$\frac{8}{10,000}$	$\frac{9}{100,000}$

YOU SHOULD REMEMBER...

- How to add fractions
- How to apply BIMDAS (order of operations)

KEY WORDS

- Decimal
- Recurring decimal
- Terminating decimal
- Percentage
- Rounding
- Significant figures

Worked Example 6.1

What is the value of 7 in each of the following numbers?

   (i) 2.742   (ii) 16.3742   (iii) 26.8971

Solution

  (i) $2.742 = 2 + \frac{7}{10} + \frac{4}{100} + \frac{2}{1,000}$. Therefore, the value of 7 is $\frac{7}{10}$.

  (ii) $16.3742 = 16 + \frac{3}{10} + \frac{7}{100} + \frac{4}{1,000} + \frac{2}{10,000}$. So, the value of 7 is $\frac{7}{100}$

  (iii) $26.8971 = 26 + \frac{8}{10} + \frac{9}{100} + \frac{7}{1,000} + \frac{1}{10,000}$. Hence, the value of 7 is $\frac{7}{1,000}$.

Worked Example 6.2

Write the following decimals as fractions in their simplest form:

   (i) 0.2   (ii) 0.03   (iii) 0.0005

Solution

  (i) $0.2 = 2 \times \frac{1}{10}$

        $= \frac{2}{10}$

        $= \frac{1}{5}$

  (ii) $0.03 = 0 \times \frac{1}{10} + 3 \times \frac{1}{100}$

         $= 0 + \frac{3}{100}$

         $= \frac{3}{100}$

(iii) $0.0005 = 0 \times \frac{1}{10} + 0 \times \frac{1}{100} + 0 \times \frac{1}{1,000} + 5 \times \frac{1}{10,000}$

$= \frac{5}{10,000}$

$= \frac{1}{2,000}$

6.2 FRACTIONS AND DECIMALS

Many fractions can easily be converted to decimals. For example, $\frac{2}{5} = \frac{4}{10} = 0.4$.

Worked Example 6.3

Write the following fractions as decimals:

(i) $\frac{3}{10}$ (ii) $\frac{7}{100}$ (iii) $\frac{9}{1,000}$ (iv) $\frac{243}{1,000}$

Solution

(i) $\frac{3}{10} = 3 \times \frac{1}{10}$

$= 0.3$

(ii) $\frac{7}{100} = 0 \times \frac{1}{10} + 7 \times \frac{1}{100}$

$= 0.07$

(iii) $\frac{9}{1,000} = 0 \times \frac{1}{10} + 0 \times \frac{1}{100} + 9 \times \frac{1}{1,000}$

$= 0.009$

(iv) $\frac{243}{1,000} = 2 \times \frac{1}{10} + 4 \times \frac{1}{100} + 3 \times \frac{1}{1,000}$

$= 0.243$

Worked Example 6.4

Convert the following fractions to decimals:

(i) $\frac{3}{4}$ (ii) $\frac{7}{20}$ (iii) $\frac{3}{500}$

Solution

(i) Multiply the numerator and the denominator by 25: $\frac{3}{4} \times \frac{25}{25} = \frac{75}{100} = 0.75$

(ii) Multiply the numerator and denominator by 5: $\frac{7}{20} \times \frac{5}{5} = \frac{35}{100} = 0.35$

(iii) Multiply the numerator and denominator by 2: $\frac{3}{500} \times \frac{2}{2} = \frac{6}{1,000} = 0.006$

Worked Example 6.5

Use your calculator to convert the following:

(i) $\frac{5}{32}$ (ii) $\frac{17}{125}$ (iii) $\frac{29}{80}$

Solution

(i) $\frac{5}{32}$

The answer 0.15625 is displayed.

(ii) $\frac{17}{125}$

The answer 0.136 is displayed.

(iii) $\frac{29}{80}$

The answer 0.3625 is displayed.

Exercise 6.1

1. Write the following sums as decimals:

(i) $3 + \dfrac{1}{10} + \dfrac{4}{100} + \dfrac{6}{1,000}$

(ii) $76 + \dfrac{2}{10} + \dfrac{1}{100} + \dfrac{5}{1,000}$

(iii) $35 + \dfrac{6}{10} + \dfrac{5}{100} + \dfrac{1}{1,000}$

(iv) $14 + \dfrac{6}{10} + \dfrac{7}{100} + \dfrac{8}{1,000}$

2. Write the following sums as decimals:

(i) $2 + \dfrac{6}{10} + \dfrac{7}{100} + \dfrac{5}{1,000}$

(ii) $1 + \dfrac{7}{10} + \dfrac{5}{100} + \dfrac{8}{1,000}$

(iii) $8 + \dfrac{5}{10} + \dfrac{6}{100} + \dfrac{7}{1,000}$

(iv) $765 + \dfrac{3}{10}$

3. What is the value of the digit 2 in each of the following?

(i) 3.248   (iv) 7.289

(ii) 5.4267   (v) 7.6293

(iii) 7.3421   (vi) 30.56782

4. What is the value of 9 in each of the following?

(i) 3.09   (iv) 4.2349

(ii) 5.269   (v) 5.976

(iii) 7.901   (vi) 8.29

5. Write the following decimals as fractions:

(i) 0.8   (iv) 0.001   (vii) 0.24

(ii) 0.3   (v) 2.5   (viii) 0.213

(iii) 0.09   (vi) 1.05   (ix) 0.175

6. Write the following fractions as decimals:

(i) $\dfrac{1}{2}$ (vi) $\dfrac{7}{20}$ (xi) $\dfrac{1}{25}$

(ii) $\dfrac{9}{50}$ (vii) $\dfrac{8}{5}$ (xii) $\dfrac{11}{25}$

(iii) $\dfrac{11}{500}$ (viii) $-3\dfrac{19}{50}$ (xiii) $7\dfrac{1}{20}$

(iv) $\dfrac{4}{5}$ (ix) $\dfrac{7}{200}$ (xiv) $12\dfrac{3}{100}$

(v) $-\dfrac{1}{200}$ (x) $\dfrac{11}{4}$ (xv) $\dfrac{317}{10}$

7. Use your calculator to convert the following fractions to decimals:

(i) $\dfrac{17}{400}$ (vi) $\dfrac{49}{800}$

(ii) $\dfrac{11}{1,280}$ (viii) $\dfrac{179}{3,200}$

(iii) $\dfrac{33}{1,250}$ (vii) $\dfrac{67}{1,600}$

(iv) $\dfrac{17}{50}$ (ix) $\dfrac{1,601}{2,000}$

(v) $\dfrac{5}{1,024}$ (x) $\dfrac{1,603}{2,048}$

8. Use your calculator to convert the following fractions to decimals:

(i) $\dfrac{171}{250}$ (vi) $\dfrac{23}{50}$

(ii) $\dfrac{75}{1,024}$ (vii) $\dfrac{37}{1,250}$

(iii) $\dfrac{69}{800}$ (viii) $\dfrac{53}{8,000}$

(iv) $\dfrac{27}{1,600}$ (ix) $\dfrac{5}{1,280}$

(v) $\dfrac{3}{1,000}$ (x) $\dfrac{5}{10,000}$

Terminating Decimals

A decimal such as 0.1489 is called a **terminating decimal**.
It is called 'terminating' because it terminates (or ends) after four decimal places.

A fraction (excluding whole numbers) is a terminating decimal if the denominator's prime factors are only 2 and/or 5.

> A decimal with a fixed number of digits after the decimal point is called a terminating decimal.

Worked Example 6.6

By finding the prime factors of 400 and 800, show that the fractions $\frac{97}{400}$ and $\frac{179}{800}$ terminate.

Solution

2	400
2	200
2	100
2	50
5	25
5	5
	1

2	800
2	400
2	200
2	100
2	50
5	25
5	5
	1

Since the prime factors of 400 and 800 are only 2 and 5, the fractions $\frac{97}{400}$ and $\frac{179}{800}$ terminate.

A calculator gives $\frac{97}{400} = 0.2425$ and $\frac{179}{800} = 0.22375$.

$400 = 2^4 \times 5^2$ $800 = 2^5 \times 5^2$

Recurring Decimals

A decimal such as 0.484848..., which contains infinitely many digits and where the digits form a pattern, is called a **recurring** or **repeating decimal**.

> Any fraction whose prime factors are not only 2 and/or 5 is a recurring decimal. A decimal that does not recur is called a terminating decimal.

- Examples of fractions that are recurring decimals are $\frac{1}{3}$, $\frac{2}{9}$ and $\frac{5}{13}$.

All fractions are either recurring decimals or terminating decimals.

The **dot notation** is often used to represent a recurring decimal. For example, 0.424242... can be written as $0.\dot{4}\dot{2}$. The dots go over the first digit of the block to be repeated and the last digit of the block to be repeated. For example, $0.2\dot{1}7\dot{3} = 0.2173173173...$

 Worked Example 6.7

Find the prime factors of 50 and 9 and, hence, decide whether the fractions $\frac{3}{50}$ and $\frac{1}{9}$ recur or terminate.

Solution

$50 = 5^2 \times 2$. As the only prime factors are 2 and 5, the fraction $\frac{3}{50}$ will terminate.

Checking on the calculator reveals that $\frac{3}{50} = 0.06$.

$9 = 3^2$. As the prime factors are not 2 and/or 5, the fraction $\frac{1}{9}$ will recur.

Checking on the calculator reveals $\frac{1}{9} = 0.11111...$ (or $0.\dot{1}$).

 Exercise 6.2

1. Write down the first 10 decimal places of:

   (a) (i) $0.\dot{7}$ (ii) $0.7\dot{1}$ (iii) $0.\dot{7}\dot{1}$ (iv) $0.7\dot{1}\dot{5}$ (v) $0.\dot{7}1\dot{5}$

   (b) (i) $0.\dot{3}$ (ii) $0.\dot{3}\dot{4}$ (iii) $0.\dot{3}4\dot{7}$ (iv) $0.34\dot{7}$ (v) $0.3\dot{4}\dot{7}$

   (c) (i) $3.6\dot{2}$ (ii) $3.\dot{6}\dot{2}$ (iii) $3.62\dot{4}$ (iv) $3.6\dot{2}\dot{4}$ (v) $3.\dot{6}2\dot{4}$

2. Write the following recurring decimals using dot notation:

    (i) 0.5555...   (vi) 9.4131313...

    (ii) 0.353535...   (vii) 3.911111...

    (iii) 0.4353535...   (viii) 2.8957957...

    (iv) 0.0172172...   (ix) 3.128128128...

    (v) 0.682682...

3.   (i) Find the prime factors of each of the following numbers:

        40, 2, 5, 50, 65, 400

    (ii) Hence, decide whether the following fractions can be converted into recurring decimals:

$$\frac{3}{40}, \frac{1}{2}, \frac{3}{5}, \frac{6}{50}, \frac{9}{65}, \frac{13}{400}$$

    (iii) Use your calculator to investigate if your answers to part (ii) are correct.

4. Use your calculator to convert $\frac{1}{7}$ to a decimal.

    (i) Write your answer using the dot notation.

    (ii) Using the answers from part (i), and with the aid of a calculator, write the following fractions as recurring decimals:

$$\frac{2}{7}, \frac{3}{7}, \frac{4}{7}, \frac{5}{7}, \frac{6}{7}$$

5. Using a calculator, convert $\frac{1}{6}$ to a recurring decimal.

    (i) Write your answer using the dot notation.

    (ii) Using the answers from part (i), and with the aid of a calculator, write the following fractions as recurring decimals:

$$\frac{1}{3}, \frac{2}{3}, \frac{5}{6}$$

6. Using a calculator, convert $\frac{1}{11}$ to a recurring decimal.

    (i) Write your answer using the dot notation.

    (ii) Using the answers from part (i), and with the aid of a calculator, write the following fractions as recurring decimals:

$$\frac{2}{11}, \frac{5}{11}, \frac{7}{11}, \frac{9}{11}$$

7. Using a calculator, convert $\frac{1}{12}$ to a recurring decimal.

    (i) Write your answer using the dot notation.

    (ii) Using the answers from part (i), and with the aid of a calculator, write the following fractions as recurring decimals:

$$\frac{5}{12}, \frac{7}{12}, \frac{11}{12}$$

6.3 ROUNDING

Whole Numbers

Carrauntoohil in County Kerry is Ireland's highest mountain. It is 1,050 m high. This height can be rounded to 1,000 m, which is an easier number to remember. By rounding to 1,000 m, we can give the height to the nearest thousand.

Worked Example 6.8

Write the following, correct to the nearest whole number:

    (i) 12.56   (ii) 9.48

Solution

    (i) 12.56

        When rounding to the **nearest whole number**, we look at the **first number after the decimal point**.

        ■ If this number is 5 or greater, then we round up to 13.

        ■ If this number is less than 5, then the corrected answer is 12.

As 5 is the first number after the decimal point, 12.56 rounded to the nearest whole number is 13.

Answer = 13

On the numberline above, it is clear that 12.56 is nearer to 13 than to 12.

(ii) 9.48

Here, the first number after the decimal point is 4, which is less than 5. Therefore, the corrected answer is 9.

On the numberline, 9.48 is closer to 9 than to 10.

Answer = 9

Rounding to Decimal Places

In geometry, the number of times the diameter of a circle divides into the circumference is called π. We normally substitute 3.14 for π in these calculations. However, 3.14 is just an approximation:

- There are infinitely many decimal places in π.
- π is 3.141592654 to nine decimal places.
- For simplicity, we often write π as 3.14, i.e. to two decimal places.
- Engineers use 3.1416 as an approximation for π.

% Worked Example 6.9

Write the following, correct to one decimal place:

(i) 2.57   (ii) 39.32

Solution

(i) 2.57

When rounding to **one decimal place,** we look at the **second number after the decimal point**. Again, if this number is 5 or greater, we round up to 2.6. Otherwise, the corrected answer is 2.5. As 7 is the second number after the decimal point, we round up to 2.6.

Answer = 2.6

(ii) 39.32

Here, the second number after the decimal point is 2, which is less than 5. Therefore, the number rounded to one decimal place is 39.3.

Answer = 39.3

Significant Figures

John measures the height of his bedroom door with a metre stick. He concludes that the door is 2 m high. His brother measures the height of the door with a ruler that is graduated in centimetres and finds the height to be 2.14 m.

The **significant figures** of a number are all digits except zeros at the start and end.

John's measurement is correct to one significant figure. His brother's measurement is correct to three significant figures.

- Leading zeros are not significant figures. For example, 0.00078 has two significant figures, 7 and 8.
- Zeros that appear between two non-zero digits **are** significant. For example, 708.45 has five significant figures.

% Worked Example 6.10

Correct the following numbers to two significant figures:

    (i) 3.67765   (ii) 61,343   (iii) 0.00356

Solution

(i) 3.67765

The **first significant figure** in a number is the **first non-zero digit in the number**. In this number, 3 is the first significant digit in the number. We need to correct to two significant figures, so we look at the third significant digit. If this number is 5 or greater, we round up the second digit. The third digit is 7, so the corrected number is 3.7.

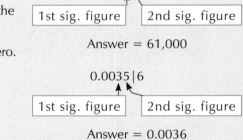

(ii) 61,343

Here, the third digit is 3, which is less than 5. Therefore, the rounded number is 61,000.

Note that all other digits after the rounded digit change to zero.

(iii) 0.00356

The third significant digit is 6. Therefore, the rounded number is 0.0036.

ACTIVITY 6.2

Exercise 6.3

1. Write these numbers correct to two decimal places:

    (i) 5.132   (ii) 3.857   (iii) 12.459   (iv) 1.374   (v) 5.965

2. Write these numbers correct to one decimal place:

    (i) 22.34   (ii) 4.67   (iii) 1.48   (iv) 0.09   (v) 1.75

3. Write these numbers correct to three decimal places:

    (i) 2.2343   (ii) 31.2897   (iii) 0.01675   (iv) 0.0038   (v) 1.3795

4. Write these numbers correct to one significant figure:

    (i) 32.14   (ii) 3.857   (iii) 19,345   (iv) 1,698   (v) 5,965

5. Write these numbers correct to two significant figures:

(i) 0.00985 (iii) 0.0125 (v) 1.000034 (vii) 0.238 (ix) 52.487

(ii) 0.00234 (iv) 0.000000785 (vi) 0.000849 (viii) 52.00285 (x) 967,333

6. Copy and complete the following table:

Number	Number corrected to 1 decimal place	Number corrected to 2 decimal places	Number corrected to 3 decimal places
3.2432	3.2		
5.7652			
81.6545		81.65	
0.0125			
0.0356			0.036

7. Use your calculator to write these fractions as decimals, and then correct the number to two decimal places:

(i) $\frac{2}{3}$ (iii) $\frac{13}{21}$

(ii) $\frac{7}{11}$ (iv) $\frac{3}{7}$

8. (i) Write 4.2 correct to the nearest whole number.

(ii) Write 8.8 correct to the nearest whole number.

(iii) Write 6.4 correct to the nearest whole number.

(iv) Use your answers from parts (i) to (iii) to estimate the value of:
$\frac{4.2 \times 8.8}{6.4}$

(v) Use your calculator to find the exact answer to:
$\frac{4.2 \times 8.8}{6.4}$

9. (i) Write 14.7 correct to the nearest whole number.

(ii) Write 1.2 correct to the nearest whole number.

(iii) Write 2.1 correct to the nearest whole number.

(iv) Use your answers from parts (i) to (iii) to estimate the value of:
$\frac{14.7 \times 1.2}{2.1}$

(v) Use your calculator to find the exact answer to:
$\frac{14.7 \times 1.2}{2.1}$

10. (i) Write 3.78 correct to the nearest whole number.

(ii) Write 8.21 correct to the nearest whole number.

(iii) Write 7.6 correct to the nearest whole number.

(iv) Use your answers from parts (i) to (iii) to estimate the value of:
$\frac{3.78 \times 8.21}{7.6}$

(v) Calculate to four decimal places:
$\frac{3.78 \times 8.21}{7.6}$

11. (i) Write 20.3 correct to the nearest whole number.

(ii) Write 6.93 correct to the nearest whole number.

(iii) Write 2.8 correct to the nearest whole number.

(iv) Write 3.2 correct to the nearest whole number.

(v) Use your answers from parts (i) to (iv) to estimate the value of:
$\frac{20.3 + 6.93}{2.8 \times 3.2}$

(vi) Use your calculator to find the exact answer to:
$\frac{20.3 + 6.93}{2.8 \times 3.2}$

12. (i) Write 4.4 correct to the nearest whole number.

(ii) Write 6.4 correct to the nearest whole number.

(iii) Write 9.1 correct to the nearest whole number.

(iv) Write 2.7 correct to the nearest whole number.

(v) Use your answers from parts (i) to (iv) to estimate the value of:
$$\frac{4.4 \times 6.4}{9.1 + 2.7}$$

(vi) Calculate to one decimal place:
$$\frac{4.4 \times 6.4}{9.1 + 2.7}$$

13. (i) By rounding each number to the nearest whole number, estimate the value of $1.23 + 5.16(2.89)^2$.

(ii) Evaluate $1.23 + 5.16(2.89)^2$ correct to three significant figures.

6.4 PERCENTAGES

A percentage is a special type of fraction. 'Per cent' means 'out of each 100' or 'per 100'.

> The symbol for per cent is %.

- 10% means 10 parts of 100, which is $\frac{10}{100} = 0.1$

- 20% means 20 parts of 100, which is $\frac{20}{100} = 0.2$

% Worked Example 6.11

Express 30% as:

(i) A fraction

(ii) A decimal

Solution

(i) $30\% = \frac{30}{100}$

$= \frac{3}{10}$

Answer $= \frac{3}{10}$

(ii) $30\% = \frac{30}{100}$

$= \frac{3}{10}$

$= 0.3$

Answer $= 0.3$

% Worked Example 6.12

Write 12.5% as:

(i) A fraction

(ii) A decimal

Solution

(i) 12.5% means 12.5 parts of 100, which is:

$$\frac{12.5}{100} = \frac{125}{1,000} = \frac{1}{8}$$

(ii) $\frac{125}{1,000} = 0.125$

 ACTIVITY 6.3

Worked Example 6.13

Use your calculator to convert $\frac{1}{4}$ to: (i) A decimal   (ii) A percentage

Solution

(i)

The answer 0.25 is displayed.

Answer = 0.25.

(ii) From part (i): $\frac{1}{4} = 0.25$

$$= \frac{25}{100}$$

$$= 25\%$$

Another way of converting a fraction to a percentage is to multiply the fraction by 100.

Worked Example 6.14

Sam received 12 marks out of a possible 17 marks in his last Maths test. What percentage did he score? Give the answer correct to two decimal places.

Solution

$\frac{12}{17}$ as a percentage

$$= \left(\frac{12}{17} \times 100\right)\%$$

$$= 70.59\% \text{ (2 d.p.)}$$

Exercise 6.4

1. Change each of the following percentages into a fraction in its simplest form:

   (i) 75%   (iii) 20%   (v) 90%   (vii) 60%   (ix) $33\frac{1}{3}\%$

   (ii) 5%   (iv) 25%   (vi) 38%   (viii) 80%   (x) 12.5%

2. Change each of the following fractions into percentages:

   (i) $\frac{3}{10}$ (iii) $\frac{17}{20}$ (v) $\frac{7}{25}$ (vii) $\frac{11}{20}$ (ix) $\frac{1}{50}$

   (ii) $\frac{4}{5}$ (iv) $\frac{3}{50}$ (vi) $\frac{7}{10}$ (viii) $\frac{11}{25}$ (x) $\frac{1}{4}$

3. Convert each of the following decimals into a percentage:

   (i) 0.12   (iii) 0.3   (v) 0.42   (vii) 0.41   (ix) 0.67

   (ii) 0.25   (iv) 0.69   (vi) 0.145   (viii) 0.51   (x) 0.923

4. Copy and complete the table below by filling in the blank spaces. Write all fractions in their simplest form.

Fraction	$\frac{3}{5}$		$\frac{9}{20}$		$\frac{17}{50}$		$\frac{1}{2}$	
Percentage	60%	30%		40%		20%		
Decimal	0.6			0.25		0.14		0.24

5. Arrange the following in increasing order:

2%, $\frac{1}{30}$, 0.32, $\frac{3}{10}$, 0.03, 5%

6. Arrange the following in decreasing order:

0.29, $\frac{7}{25}$, $\frac{36}{125}$, 30%, 0.27, $\frac{31}{100}$

7. What percentage of each of the following shapes is shaded?

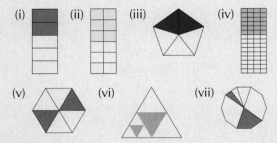

(i) (ii) (iii) (iv)

(v) (vi) (vii)

8. Last week, Marie had tests in five of her subjects. She got:

- 27 out of 30 for History
- 17 out of 20 for CSPE
- 91% for Maths
- 0.85 of the total marks in Science
- 185 out of 200 for English

(i) What percentage did Marie get in each subject?

(ii) In which subject did she score best? Justify your answer.

9. What percentage of 3 hours is 18 minutes?

10. In a survey of shopping habits, six out of 20 of those surveyed said they buy their books on the Internet, ten out of 20 said they buy their books in bookshops, and four out of 20 said they never buy books.

(i) What percentage of those surveyed bought their books on the Internet?

(ii) What percentage never buy books?

11. Albert, Isaac and Leonardo each share a prize in a lottery. Isaac gets 0.2 of the prize. Albert gets $\frac{1}{3}$ of the prize. What percentage of the prize does each get?

Calculating with Percentages

 Worked Example 6.15

Find 20% of 500.

Solution 1

Step 1: Convert 20% to a fraction.

$$20\% = \frac{20}{100}$$
$$= \frac{1}{5}$$

Step 2: Multiply $\frac{1}{5}$ by 500.

$$\frac{1}{5} \times 500 = 100$$

Answer = 100

OR

Solution 2

Step 1: Convert 20% to a decimal.

$$20\% = 0.20$$

Step 2: Multiply 500×0.20

$$500 \times 0.20 = 100$$

Answer = 100

Worked Example 6.16

In 2001, the population of a small village is 150.

In 2011, the population has decreased by 10% on the 2001 figure.

Calculate the population of the village in 2011.

Solution

Method 1

Find 10% of 150:

$150 \times \dfrac{10}{100}$

$= 150 \times \dfrac{1}{10}$

$= 15$

Subtract from 150:

New population is $150 - 15 = 135$

Method 2

The population has fallen by 10%, so it is now 90% of the original population.

Find 90% of 150:

$\dfrac{90}{100} \times 150 = 135$

Worked Example 6.17

An English class lasts for 40 minutes. The teacher shows a DVD for 12 minutes. The rest of the time is taken up by a discussion.

   (i) What percentage of the time is spent watching the DVD?

   (ii) What percentage of the time is taken up by the discussion?

Solution

   (i) Time spent watching DVD

      Fraction $= \dfrac{12}{40} = \dfrac{3}{10}$

      Percentage $= \dfrac{3}{10} \times 100 = 30\%$

   (ii) Percentage of time spent on discussion

      $100\% - 30\% = 70\%$

ACTIVITY 6.4

Worked Example 6.18

A book contains 125 pages. 12% of the pages consists of pictures only. All other pages contain just text.

Use your calculator to find the number of pages containing text only.

Solution

Step 1: If 12% of the book contains pictures only, then $100 - 12 = 88\%$ contains text only.

Step 2: Find 88% of 125.

125 × 88 2ndF %

The answer 110 is displayed.

Answer = 110 pages.

Note: Individual calculators may differ.

Exercise 6.5

1. 47% of all pupils in a class are boys. What percentage of the class are girls?

2. A bag contains red balls and blue balls. If 35% of the balls are blue, then what percentage of the balls are red?

3. Find:

   (i)   25% of 32   (iv) 1% of 70

   (ii) 70% of 340   (v)   4% of 90

   (iii) 12% of 250   (vi) 8% of 225

4. Find 5% of the following:

   (a) 20   (c) 20 km

   (b) 240 kg   (d) €15

5. The femur (thigh-bone) is about 25% of a person's height. James is 1.6 m tall. About how long is his femur?

6. Use your calculator to evaluate the following:

   (i)   55% of 300 m   (vi)   52% of 60 cm

   (ii)   19% of 200 g   (vii) 29% of €1,500

   (iii) 5% of 150 mm   (viii) 51% of 60 g

   (iv)   45% of 100 km   (ix) $33\frac{1}{3}$% of 96 kg

   (v)   12% of 300 m   (x)   15% of €120

7. A charity makes €1,200 selling raffle tickets. 25% of the money is used for prizes and printing. How much of the money goes to the charity?

8. An adult's brain weighs 2% of a person's total weight. What is the approximate weight of the brain of an adult weighing 60 kg?

9. There are 60 members in a squash club, and 36 of them are male.

   (i)   What percentage of the club is male?

   (ii) What percentage of the club is female?

   (iii) In the near future, the club hopes to have the same number of female as male members. If the club restricts the number of male members to 36, then how many more females need to join the club to achieve this target?

10. Copy and complete the following bill:

Soup	€3.50
Roast Beef	€10.00
Ice Cream	€3.00
Coffee	€2.50
SUB-TOTAL	
Service Charge 10%	
TOTAL	

Percentage Increase and Percentage Decrease

Often we have to express an increase or a decrease in a quantity as a percentage increase or decrease. Percentage increases/decreases are calculated using the formula shown:

FORMULA

$$\text{Percentage increase/decrease} = \frac{\text{Increase/decrease}}{\text{Original number}} \times \frac{100}{1}$$

 ## Worked Example 6.19

John spent €11.25 on a calculator last year. His friend Thomas spent €14.50 on the same calculator this year. Find, correct to two decimal places, the percentage increase in the price of the calculator.

Solution

Step 1: Find the increase in the price of the calculator.

Increase: €14.50 − €11.25 = €3.25

Step 2: Write the increase as a fraction of the original cost.

Increase as a fraction: $\dfrac{3.25}{11.25}$

Step 3: Write the fraction as a percentage.

Percentage increase: $\dfrac{3.25}{11.25} \times 100 = 28.89\%$

 Worked Example 6.20

A bookshop has reduced the price of *Harry Potter and the Deathly Hallows* from €10.35 to €8.05. Find, correct to two decimal places, the percentage decrease in the price of the book.

Solution

Step 1: Find the decrease in price.

Decrease: €10.35 – €8.05 = €2.30

Step 2: Write the decrease as a fraction of the original price.

Decrease as a fraction: $\dfrac{2.30}{10.35}$

Step 3: Write the fraction as a percentage.

Percentage decrease: $\dfrac{2.30}{10.35} \times 100 = 22.22\%$

 Exercise 6.6

1. In the year 2000, the population of a town was 5,320. The population has now grown to 5,652. Find the percentage increase in the population, correct to two decimal places.

2. Claire bought a new iPod on eBay for €110. The retail price of the iPod in an electrical shop was €150.

    (i) How much did Claire save by buying on eBay?

    (ii) What percentage saving did Claire get by buying on eBay?

3. John invests €900 in shares. The value of the shares falls by €140.

    (i) How much are John's shares now worth?

    (ii) Find the percentage decrease in the value of the shares.

4. There were 80 hours of sunshine in May. In June, the number of hours of sunshine increased to 120. Find the percentage increase in the hours of sunshine.

5. On 1 January 2007, the minimum wage for a person under 18 was €5.81 an hour. By 1 January 2010, the minimum wage for a person under 18 had increased to €6.06 an hour. Find the percentage increase in the minimum wage, for a person under 18, during the period 2007–2010 (correct to two decimal places).

6. (i) Work out the percentage increase when 260 kg is increased to 300 kg (correct to two decimal places).

    (ii) Work out the percentage decrease when 300 kg is decreased to 260 kg.

    (iii) Explain why your answers to part (i) and part (ii) are different.

7. In a sale, a book has been reduced by 15%. It now costs €15.30. Find the original price of the book.

8. In 2011 Coláiste Chian had 840 pupils. This was an increase of 20% from 2010. How many pupils attended the school in 2010?

9. A sum of money is increased by 10% to give a figure of €22. How much was the original sum?

10. Over a two-month period, the number of viewers of a TV show decreased from 520,000 to 450,000. Find the percentage decrease in viewers correct to the nearest whole number.

11. Aoife and Sinéad take two tests. The results are shown in the table.

	Test A	Test B
Aoife	62	76
Sinéad	50	64

Whose test mark has increased by the greatest percentage? Show clearly how you got your answer.

12. The price of fish and chips increases from €5.60 to €5.90. Calculate the percentage increase in the price (correct to two decimal places).

13. A computer system was priced at €1,000 in January 2009. In June 2009, the computer was priced at €800. At the end of December 2009, the price of the computer had decreased by a further 2.5% on the June price.

Find the overall percentage decrease in the price of the computer in 2009.

14. The number 5.356 is rounded to two decimal places.

   (i) What is the rounded number?

   (ii) What is the difference between the rounded number and 5.356?

   (iii) What is the percentage increase in the original number due to rounding (correct to two decimal places)?

15. The number 4.352 is rounded to two decimal places.

   (i) What is the rounded number?

   (ii) What is the difference between the rounded number and 4.352?

   (iii) What is the percentage decrease in the original number due to rounding (correct to two decimal places)?

16. The table shows the breakdown of seats for the 30th and 31st Dáils.

	Fine Gael	Fianna Fáil	Labour	Green Party	Sinn Féin	Independent	PD's
30th Dáil	51	78	20	6	4	5	2
31st Dáil	76	20	37	0	14	19	0

Find the percentage increase/decrease in the number of seats for each party.

Revision Exercises

1. (a) What is the value of the digit 9 in each of the following:

   (i) 2.9   (iv) 29   (vii) 29,000

   (ii) 2.09   (v) 290   (viii) 2.0009

   (iii) 2.009   (vi) 2,900   (ix) 290,000

   (b) Write the following decimals as percentages:

   (i) 0.9   (iv) 0.8   (vii) 1.2

   (ii) 0.09   (v) 0.82   (viii) 1.25

   (iii) 0.009   (vi) 0.825   (ix) 1.125

   (c) Write the following fractions as decimals:

   (i) $\frac{11}{50}$ (iv) $\frac{3}{25}$ (vii) $\frac{1}{8}$

   (ii) $\frac{13}{20}$ (v) $\frac{13}{25}$ (viii) $\frac{1}{3}$

   (iii) $\frac{17}{25}$ (vi) $\frac{17}{60}$ (ix) $\frac{3}{5}$

2. (a) Use your calculator to convert $\frac{1}{18}$ to a recurring decimal.

   (i) Write your answer using the dot notation.

   (ii) Using your answer from part (i), write the following as recurring decimals:
   $\frac{5}{18}$ and $\frac{7}{18}$

(b) How much do you get if you increase €50 by 15%?

3. (a) Write these numbers correct to one decimal place:

    (i) 2.83   (ii) 5.87   (iii) 29.24

(b) Write the following numbers correct to two significant figures:

    (i) 12.8   (ii) 0.000149   (iii) 64,250

4. (a) Find 30% of 30.

(b) (i) By rounding appropriately, estimate the value of:

$$\frac{3.2 \times 4.5 + 5.1}{18.2 \div 9.4}$$

    (ii) Using your calculator, find the exact answer.

5. (a) Change the following percentages into fractions in their simplest form:

    (i) 35%   (iv) 5%   (vii) 90%

    (ii) 80%   (v) 17%   (viii) 12%

    (iii) 15%   (vi) 26%   (ix) 55%

(b) Change the following fractions into percentages:

    (i) $\frac{3}{10}$ (iv) $\frac{1}{2}$ (vii) $\frac{7}{10}$

    (ii) $\frac{3}{4}$ (v) $\frac{1}{4}$ (viii) $\frac{9}{20}$

    (iii) $\frac{4}{5}$ (vi) $\frac{2}{5}$ (ix) $\frac{11}{25}$

6. (a) The recommended price of a camera is €270. John can order the camera on the Internet and get a discount of 30%. Calculate the Internet price of the calculator.

(b) The price of a newspaper goes up by 5% to €2.52. What was the original price of the newspaper?

7. (a) A jeweller increases the price of a ring by 6%. The new price is €8,957.

What was the price of the ring before the increase?

(b) A coat is normally sold for €350. In a sale, the price is reduced to €205.

What is the percentage reduction (two decimal places)?

8. (a) Write 20% as (i) a fraction and (ii) a decimal.

(b) Add 20% of 180 to 15% of 60.

(c) Last year the number of salmon in a fish farm increased from 30,000 to 45,000. What percentage increase does this represent?

9. Donna bought a bike for €85. She sold it later and made a 20% loss. How much did she sell the bike for?

10. A holiday for two people in August costs €1,200. A holiday to the same destination in September costs 15% less. What is the price of the holiday for two people in September?

11. A bank is offering 4.5% interest per annum on deposits. Leo lodges €800 in the bank. How much will he have after one year?

12.

Blood type	% of population
O	42
A	44
B	10
AB	4

The table above displays the percentages of the population having blood types O, A, B and AB. Four hundred people are chosen at random from the population.

(i) How many would you expect to have type O blood?

(ii) How many would you expect to have type A blood?

(iii) How many would you expect to have either blood type B or blood type AB?

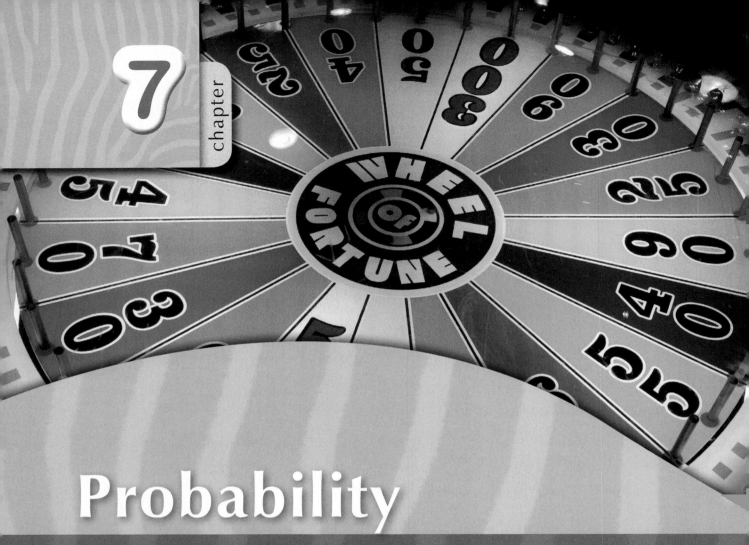

7 chapter

Probability

Learning Outcomes

In this chapter you will learn to:

- ➲ Understand the language used in probability
- ➲ Put probabilities in order on a probability scale
- ➲ Predict and determine probabilities
- ➲ Predict and investigate the frequency of a specific outcome
- ➲ Associate the probability of an event with its long-run, relative frequency
- ➲ Compare expected frequencies and actual frequencies
- ➲ Determine the theoretical probability of an outcome in a probability experiment
- ➲ Use a two-way table and tree diagram to determine probabilities

7.1 INTRODUCING PROBABILITY

What is the chance that you will win the lottery, be hit by lightning or have to pay higher car insurance? All of these questions are linked to the branch of mathematics called probability.

From its earliest beginnings, probability has been used for practical purposes. It was first developed in 17th-century France when a gambler, the Chevalier de Méré, wanted to increase his chances of winning in the casinos of Europe! Ever since then, this branch of mathematics has played an important role in everyday life.

YOU SHOULD REMEMBER...

- How to work with fractions
- How to work with decimals
- How to work with percentages
- Two-way tables
- Tree diagrams

- Spouses of smokers have an approximately **30%** increased risk of lung cancer.

- There is a small probability that Apophis, a near-earth asteroid, will hit the Earth in 2036.

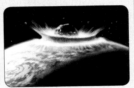

- Young car drivers are 5 times more likely to be involved in collisions than older groups, and young motorcyclists are 20 times more likely.

- There is a 70% chance of rain.

Probability is used to determine the chance of something occurring. We can describe probability by using words or, more commonly, a numerical value.

KEY WORDS

- **Probability scale**
- **Relative frequency**
- **Fairness**
- **Equally likely**
- **Theoretical probability**
- **Expected frequency**
- **Two-way table**
- **Tree diagram**

PROBABILITY

'The most important questions of life are, for the most part, really only problems of probability.'

Pierre-Simon Laplace (1749–1827), French mathematician

7.2 THE LANGUAGE OF PROBABILITY

When you cross a road or make a guess in an exam, you are using probability to determine your chance of success or failure. Probability, or chance, deals with the likelihood that something called an 'event' might occur.

In probability we will encounter many common terms that have special meanings we must be aware of. Here are some important examples.

Examples of **trials** include throwing a die and recording which face it shows, or flipping a coin and noting which side it lands on.

> A trial is the act of doing an experiment in probability.

> We often say 'a dice', but this is not correct. The singular is 'die' and the plural is 'dice'. For example, you roll one die but you roll two dice.

When you roll a die, the possible **outcomes** are 1, 2, 3, 4, 5 or 6. When you flip a coin, the possible outcomes are a head or a tail.

> An outcome is one of the possible results of a trial.

For a die, the **sample space** is {1, 2, 3, 4, 5, 6}. For a coin, it is {head, tail}.

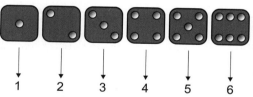

| 1 | 2 | 3 | 4 | 5 | 6 | Head | Tail |

> The set or list of all possible outcomes in a trial is called the sample space.

Rolling a 6 on a die or a flipped coin landing on a tail are **events**.

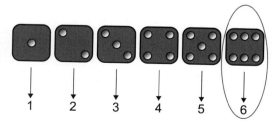

1 2 3 4 5 6

> An event is the occurrence of one or more desirable outcomes.

> Dice made of animal bone have been found and date back to more than 6,000 years ago.

7.3 THE LIKELIHOOD SCALE

The probability of an event can be described using certain words like the ones below:

Impossible   Unlikely   Evens   Likely   Certain

> The terms '50–50' or 'equal chance' are used to describe an event that has an **evens probability** of occurring.

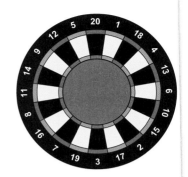

What do you think the chances are that you could hit the red bull's-eye with a single throw of a dart?

We use many different phrases to describe the probability of success or failure. Many sayings that we use in everyday life can be used to describe certain probabilities.

ACTIVITIES 7.1, 7.2

 Exercise 7.1

Describe each of the following as: impossible, unlikely, evens, likely or certain to occur.

1. Class will be given homework in mathematics.

2. A flipped coin will land on a tail.

3. Roll a normal die once and get a 1.

4. The sun will rise tomorrow.

5. Aliens will land in Ireland.

6. School summer holidays will start in December.

7. A coin is flipped three times and lands heads up each time.

8. It will snow in Ireland in January.

9. It will snow in Ireland in July.

10. Roll an even number on a single throw of a **fair** die.

11. Christmas Day will be on a Tuesday this year.

12. The colour of an apple will be purple.

13. The sun will set in the west.

14. It will rain next month.

15. The next Taoiseach of Ireland will be under 25 years of age.

16. A coin is tossed three times and lands heads up at least once.

17. The Irish Sea will disappear tomorrow.

18. The next baby born in Ireland will be a girl.

19. Tuesday will come after Monday.

20. Roll a fair die and get a prime number.

> A fair die is a die in which all the numbers are equally likely to occur.

7.4 THE PROBABILITY SCALE

In mathematics, we need to use a scale that is more precise and less open to different interpretations. The chances of an event occurring can be shown on a **probability scale**. The scale goes from 0 to 1, or 0% to 100%. Probability is a numerical measure of the chance of an event happening.

- A probability of **0 or 0%** means that the event will never happen – **impossible**.
- A probability of **1 or 100%** means that the event will definitely happen – **certain**.
- A probability of a $\frac{1}{2}$, **0.5 or 50%** means that the event has an **even chance** of happening.

A probability can be written as a decimal, fraction or percentage. We usually use fractions, and they should be expressed in their simplest form.

Events that are close to 0 are unlikely to happen, while events that are close to 1 are likely to happen.

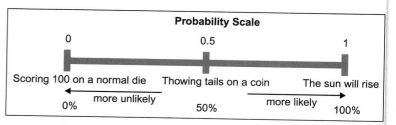

The closer you move to 0, the less likely an event is to occur.

The closer you move to 1, the more likely an event is to occur.

Consider the following table:

Coin	Head	Tail
Probability	$\frac{1}{2}$	$\frac{1}{2}$

We can see that the probabilities add up to 1.

The probabilities of all outcomes for a particular experiment add up to 1.

Worked Example 7.1

For each event below, mark on the probability scale an estimate of its probability:

A: You will draw a red card in a single pick from a complete pack of 52 cards.

B: It will rain for a week without stopping.

C: A baby will be born in Ireland today.

D: Out of a bag of red and yellow marbles, a blue marble is drawn.

Solution

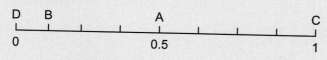

ACTIVITIES 7.3, 7.4, 7.5

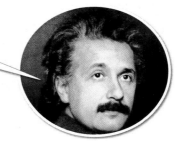

'I, at any rate, am convinced that He [God] does not throw dice.'

Albert Einstein (1879–1955)

Exercise 7.2

1. Draw a probability scale. Mark each event with its letter on the scale:

    A: You will get a 5 or 6 on a single throw of a die.

    B: A coin will land on heads in a single flip.

    C: You went to school today.

    D: Your county will win the Sam Maguire Cup this year.

    E: You will pick a number card from a normal pack of cards.

2. Draw a probability scale. Mark each event with its letter on the scale:

    A: You will pick an odd number when selecting at random a number between 1 and 10.

    B: There will be a heat wave in Spain in August.

    C: A card picked from a pack of cards will be a picture card.

    D: You will catch a cold this year.

    E: You will go to bed tonight.

3. Mark the following events on a probability scale:

    A: You will go to the moon in the next decade.

    B: Throw a fair die and get a 0.

    C: You will roll a 1, 2, 3 or 4 on a single roll of a fair die.

    D: You will grow to be over 2 metres in height.

    E: You are getting older.

4. Mark the probability of each event A, B, C, D, and E on a probability scale:

    A: You will win the National Lottery.

    B: Someone in your family will win the National Lottery.

    C: Someone in your local area will win the National Lottery.

    D: Someone in your county will win the National Lottery.

    E: Someone in your country will win the National Lottery.

5. The probabilities of five events are shown on the probability scale below:

    (a) Which event is impossible?

    (b) Which event is more than likely to occur?

    (c) Which event is unlikely to happen?

    (d) Which event is certain to occur?

    (e) Which event has a 50–50 chance of happening?

6. Liam says that the probability that he will fail his History exam is $\frac{13}{10}$.
Explain what is wrong with this statement.

7. Ann tells her friends that the probability of her getting married is -0.5. Explain what is wrong with this statement.

7.5 RELATIVE FREQUENCY (EXPERIMENTAL PROBABILITY)

Sometimes it can be very difficult to work out the probability of an event. For example, will a football team win their next match? In this case, we can use statistical evidence from observations or experiments to determine the experimental probability or **relative frequency** of an event.

> **Relative frequency** is an estimate of the probability of an event.

The relative frequency of an event is the number of times that an event happens in a trial out of the total number of trials.

FORMULA

$$\text{Relative frequency} = \frac{\text{frequency or number of times the event happens in a trial}}{\text{total number of trials}}$$

Worked Example 7.2

The word 'hazard' is thought to derive from an Arabic word for a die.

A fair die was rolled 100 times. It landed on 1 twenty times.
Find the relative frequency of getting a 1.

Solution

Relative frequency $= \dfrac{\text{number of times a 1 was rolled}}{\text{number of times die was rolled}} = \dfrac{20}{100} = \dfrac{1}{5}$ or 0.2 (or 20%)

Worked Example 7.3

A spinner has three equal sectors: red, green and blue.
It is spun 20 times and the results are tallied as follows:

Result	Tally	Frequency
Red	IIII	4
Green	IIII IIII	9
Blue	IIII II	7

What is the relative frequency of the spinner landing on green?

Solution

Relative frequency $= \dfrac{\text{number of times spinner landed on green}}{\text{number of times spinner was spun}} = \dfrac{9}{20} = 0.45$

It is important to note that increasing the number of times an experiment is repeated generally leads to better estimates of probability.

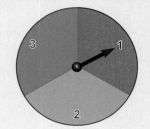

ACTIVITIES 7.6, 7.7, 7.8, 7.9, 7.10

Worked Example 7.4

An experiment is conducted to show how the number of trials improves the accuracy of the relative frequency. Michelle flips a coin and records her results every 10 flips:

10 Flips	Total	Relative frequency
Head	6	0.6
Tail	4	0.4

40 Flips	Total	Relative frequency
Head	18	0.45
Tail	22	0.55

20 Flips	Total	Relative frequency
Head	13	0.65
Tail	7	0.35

50 Flips	Total	Relative frequency
Head	24	0.48
Tail	26	0.52

30 Flips	Total	Relative frequency
Head	13	0.43
Tail	17	0.57

Michelle then plots her results for getting tails as a graph.

Show Michelle's results on a graph and comment on the overall trend.

Solution

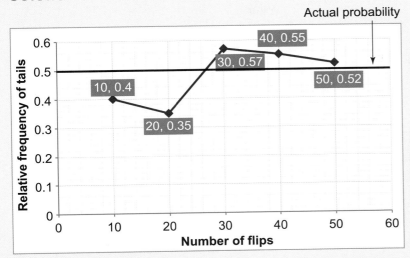

She notices that the more the experiment is repeated, the closer the relative frequency is to the actual probability (in this Worked Example: $\frac{1}{2}$ or 0.5).

In general, the more trials or experiments carried out, the closer the relative frequency will be to the actual probability of an event.

 ACTIVITY 7.11

Exercise 7.3

1. Thirty students are late on a certain school day. A total of 300 students are in school that day. What is the relative frequency of a student being late that day?

2. A die is rolled 75 times. A 3 is rolled 15 times. What is the relative frequency of rolling a 3?

3. A computer store sells 20 computers in one day from a total of 50 computers. What is the relative frequency of the number of computers sold that day?

4. A student does a survey of left-handed students in his class. Five students out of 25 are found to be left-handed. What is the relative frequency of:

   (i) Left-handed students in the class
   (ii) Right-handed students in the class

5. Records show that it rained 20 days in the month of November in the village of Kildalkey. What is the relative frequency that it rained in Kildalkey on a day in November? Express your answer as:

   (i) A fraction
   (ii) A decimal correct to two decimal places

6. In an experiment, it was found that 70 out of 80 students liked a particular brand of cola. What is the relative frequency of a student liking that brand of cola? Express your answer as:

   (i) A fraction
   (ii) A decimal

7. A die is rolled 50 times and the relative frequency for each possible outcome is recorded in the table below:

Number on die	1	2	3	4	5	6
Relative frequency	0.1	0.15	0.2	0.18	0.12	

   (i) Work out the relative frequency of rolling a 6 on the die.
   (ii) Which outcome occurred least often?
   (iii) Which outcome occurred most often?
   (iv) How many times did the die show a 4?

8. A car salesperson records the number of cars sold each day in one week:

Day	Monday	Tuesday	Wednesday	Thursday	Friday
Cars sold	5	2	0	4	9

    (i) Work out the relative frequency of the number of cars sold for each day.

    (ii) The manager decides to hire an extra salesperson for one day per week. What day should the manager pick?

        Explain your answer.

9. The results of tennis matches played by three children are shown in the table:

Child	Games won	Games lost	Games played
Mia	4	0	4
Alex	3	1	4
Seán	8	4	12

    (i) What is the relative frequency of a win for each child?

    (ii) Who, according to their relative frequencies, is the best player?

    (iii) Is this a fair way of picking the best player? Explain.

10. There are 100 cars in a shopping centre car park. Thirty of these cars are blue, 20 are green, and the rest are silver.

    (i) What is the relative frequency of a blue car in the car park?

    (ii) What is the relative frequency of a silver car in the car park?

11. Data is collected on the different types of vehicles that pass through a toll bridge during a one-hour period. The results are as follows:

Type	Frequency
Car	94
Van	27
Coach	34
Lorry	45

    (i) How many vehicles passed through the toll bridge during the hour?

    (ii) What is the relative frequency of a car passing through the toll bridge? Write your answer as a fraction.

    (iii) What is the relative frequency of a van passing through the toll bridge? Write your answer as a decimal.

    (iv) What is the relative frequency of a coach passing through the toll bridge? Write your answer as a percentage.

7.6 RELATIVE FREQUENCY AND FAIRNESS

A die is rolled.

If each outcome from 1 to 6 has the same chance of occurring, then the outcomes can be referred to as being equally likely to occur.

This means that the die is a **fair** or **unbiased** die.

> If all outcomes are equally likely to occur, then the trial or experiment is considered to be fair or unbiased.

Worked Example 7.5

A coin is flipped. How often would you expect it to land on heads if the coin is unbiased?

Solution

There should be an equal chance of each outcome occurring if the coin is fair. As there are only two outcomes – heads or tails – a fair or unbiased coin should land on heads 50% of the time.

Worked Example 7.6

A spinner with sectors labelled A to E is spun, and the results are recorded in the table below:

Letter on spinner	Frequency	Relative frequency
A	10	0.08
B	20	0.16
C	50	0.40
D	30	0.24
E	15	0.12

Is the spinner fair?

Solution

With a spinner of five equal sectors, it would be expected that the relative frequency of each letter would be roughly the same. It is clear from the relative frequencies shown that this is not the case. The spinner lands on C far more often than it lands on any other letter.

Also, the spinner was spun 125 times, which should lead to a more reliable answer than a small number of trials.

We can say with reasonable confidence that all five sectors are not the same size. Therefore the spinner is not fair.

Kerrich's Coin Flips

The English mathematician John Kerrich was working in Denmark when the Second World War broke out. When Germany invaded Denmark, Kerrich was interned in a prison camp. To help pass the time, he carried out an experiment to see if a coin was fair (unbiased). He flipped the coin 10,000 times and recorded his results:

Heads	Tails
5067	4933

He then calculated the relative frequency for both results:

Relative frequency for heads = $\frac{5,067}{10,000} = 0.5067$

Relative frequency for tails = $\frac{4,933}{10,000} = 0.4933$

While not exactly 50–50, the results were so close to the expected values that he concluded that the coin was fair or unbiased.

Exercise 7.4

1. A coin is flipped 500 times and lands on heads 275 times.

   (i) What is the relative frequency of getting a head?

   (ii) Is the coin unbiased?
   Give a reason for your answer.

2. A die is rolled and the number of times it lands on each number is recorded.

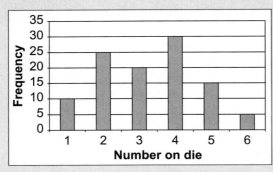

   (i) How many times was the die rolled?
   (ii) Which number appeared most often?
   (iii) Which number appeared least often?
   (iv) In your opinion, is the die fair?
   Give a reason for your answer.

3. The spinner shown is spun.

   (i) What colour would you predict the spinner is more likely to land on?
   Give a reason for your answer.

   (ii) Explain how you would change the colours on the spinner so that each colour is equally likely to occur.

4. A die is rolled 800 times. The number 2 appears 300 times. Is the die unbiased?
   Give a reason for your answer.

> **Loaded dice** are unfair dice that have been altered to give a more predictable outcome.

5. A card is picked at random from a deck of cards. A red card (Heart or Diamond) is picked 550 times out of 1,000.

   (i) Joe argues that this proves the deck of cards is fair. Aoife disagrees. Who do you think is right? Explain your choice.

   (ii) What other experiments could you use to establish whether or not the pack is unbiased?

6. Darragh wishes to investigate if a die is fair or biased. He rolls a die 20 times and lists the results:

Number on die	1	2	3	4	5	6
Times rolled	1	5	6	3	4	1

   (i) What is the relative frequency of each number of the die? Express your answers as decimals.

   (ii) Explain why Darragh believes the die is biased.

   (iii) How could this experiment be made more reliable?

7. A coin is flipped 30 times. The results are shown below:

T	T	H	T	H	T	T	T	H	H
T	T	H	T	H	T	H	T	T	H
H	H	T	T	H	H	T	T	H	H

   (i) How many times did heads appear?

   (ii) What is the relative frequency of getting a head? Give your answer as a fraction.

   (iii) Without using the table, what is the relative frequency of getting a tail?

   (iv) Do you think that the coin is fair? Explain your answer.

8. A die is rolled 600 times, and the results are recorded and shown in the table below:

Number on die	1	2	3	4	5	6
Frequency	93	104	101	97	99	

   (i) How many times was a 6 rolled?

   (ii) Work out the relative frequency for each event to two decimal places.

   (iii) Do you think that the die is biased? Give a reason for your answer.

9. A bag contains a number of marbles coloured red, orange, yellow and blue. A marble is drawn from the bag at random, its colour is noted and it is then returned to the bag. This is done a hundred times and the results are shown in the table below:

Colour of marble	Red	Orange	Yellow	Blue
Relative frequency	0.2	0.5	0.1	0.1

(i) Do you think the number of marbles in each colour is the same? Explain your answer.

(ii) Evan suggests that a mistake was made in calculating the relative frequencies. What evidence is there to support Evan's claim?

10. (a) A spinner is divided into three sections, numbered 1, 2 and 3. The spinner is spun 10,000 times and John lists the results:

Number on spinner	1	2	3
Frequency	3,000	2,500	4,500

(i) What is the relative frequency of each number of the spinner? Express your answers as decimals.

(ii) Do you think the spinner is fair? Explain your answer.

(b) Kerry suggests that it might be better to spin the spinner 20,000 times and then record the relative frequencies.

(iii) Explain why Kerry has suggested this.

(iv) Explain why John might disagree.

7.7 PROBABILITY

If all outcomes are equally likely to occur, then we can calculate the probability of an event happening. This type of probability is sometimes referred to as **theoretical probability**.

Probability is the numerical measure of the chance of an event happening.

 ## Worked Example 7.7

A fair six-sided die is thrown. What is the probability of rolling a 4?

Solution

Each of the outcomes (1, 2, 3, 4, 5, 6) are equally likely to occur.

The total number of outcomes is six.
The event we want to occur is a 4, which occurs just once in the list of outcomes.

∴ The probability of rolling a 4 on a die is $\frac{1}{6}$.

This can also be written as $P(4) = \frac{1}{6}$.

Remember that probability is usually written as a fully simplified fraction or as a decimal.

FORMULA

$$\text{Probability} = \frac{\text{number of desirable outcomes}}{\text{total number of all possible outcomes}}$$

A nice way to remember the formula is:

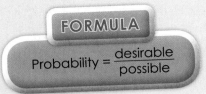

FORMULA

Probability = $\dfrac{\text{desirable}}{\text{possible}}$

 Worked Example 7.8

A bag contains two red, three green and five blue marbles.
A marble is picked at random from the bag.

What is the probability that it is red? Write your answer as a decimal.

Solution

Number of red marbles = 2

Total number of marbles = 2 + 3 + 5 = 10

P(red marble) = $\dfrac{\text{number of red marbles}}{\text{total number of marbles}} = \dfrac{2}{10} = \dfrac{1}{5} = 0.2$

 Worked Example 7.9

Remember that there are four suits (Clubs, Diamonds, Hearts and Spades) in a normal pack of 52 cards. Each suit contains an Ace, a King, a Queen and a Jack, as well as numbered cards from 2 to 10.

A card is drawn at random from a pack of cards. What is the probability of each of the following?

 (i) A red card

 (ii) A Heart

 (iii) A Seven

 (iv) A picture card

Solution

 (i) P(red card) = $\dfrac{\text{number of cards that are red}}{\text{total number of cards in the pack}} = \dfrac{26}{52} = \dfrac{1}{2}$

 (ii) P(Heart) = $\dfrac{\text{number of cards that are Hearts}}{\text{total number of cards in the pack}} = \dfrac{13}{52} = \dfrac{1}{4}$

 (iii) P(Seven) = $\dfrac{\text{number of cards that are Sevens}}{\text{total number of cards in the pack}} = \dfrac{4}{52} = \dfrac{1}{13}$

 (iv) P(picture card) = $\dfrac{\text{number of picture cards}}{\text{total number of cards in the pack}} = \dfrac{12}{52} = \dfrac{3}{13}$

We know that the probabilities of all outcomes for a particular experiment add up to 1.

Let us say that in a certain experiment, the probability of an event is 0.25.

0.25

This means that the probability of the event NOT happening is 1 − 0.25 = 0.75.

0.25

Worked Example 7.10

A fair six-sided die is rolled.

(i) What is the probability that on a single throw the die will land on a 2?

(ii) What is the probability that on a single throw the die will **not** land on a 2?

Solution

There are six possible outcomes: 1, 2, 3, 4, 5, 6.

(i) The probability of rolling a 2 = $\dfrac{\text{Number of 2's on die}}{\text{Total number of outcomes}}$

$$\therefore P(2) = \frac{1}{6}$$

(ii) The probability of not rolling a 2 = $\dfrac{\text{Number of outcomes} \neq 2}{\text{Total number of outcomes}}$

$$P(\text{not } 2) = \frac{5}{6}$$

Alternatively,

If $P(2) = \dfrac{1}{6}$, then

$P(\text{not } 2) = 1 - P(2)$

$= 1 - \dfrac{1}{6}$

$= \dfrac{5}{6}$

> The probability of something not happening = 1 − the probability that it will happen.

 ACTIVITIES 7.14, 7.15, 7.16, 7.17, 7.18, 7.19

Remember, the probability of something **not** happening = 1 − the probability that it **will** happen.

Exercise 7.5

1. A fair six-sided die, numbered 1 to 6, is rolled. What is the probability that the number you get is:

   (i) 2

   (ii) 3

   (iii) 0

   (iv) An even number

   (v) An odd number

   (vi) A number greater than 4

   (vii) 1, 2, 3, 4, 5 or 6

2. A fair spinner with 10 equal sectors numbered 1–10 is spun. What is the probability that it lands on:

   (i) 1

   (ii) 8

   (iii) 11

   (iv) An even number

   (v) An odd number

   (vi) A prime number

3. A card is selected at random from a pack of 52 playing cards. What is the probability that the card selected is:

   (i) A black card

   (ii) A Diamond

   (iii) A Queen

   (iv) The Ace of Spades

   (v) A red King

   (vi) A picture card

Explain why the card had to be picked at random.

> The Dead Man's Hand is a poker hand with two Aces and two Eights. The famous American gunfighter and gambler Wild Bill Hickok (1837–76) supposedly had this hand of cards at the time of his murder.

4. Students in a class are asked to list their favourite type of pet. The results are given in the table below:

Pet	Number
Dog	7
Cat	4
Fish	3
Rodent	4
None	2

A student is picked at random from the class. What is the probability that their favourite pet is:

   (i) A dog

   (ii) A cat

   (iii) A dog **or** a cat

   (iv) A fish

   (v) **Not** a rodent

5. A class consists of 15 boys and 10 girls. A student is chosen at random from the class. What is the probability that the student is:

   (i) A girl   (ii) A boy

6. A letter is selected at random from the word MATHS. What is the probability that the letter selected is:

   (i) A   (iii) A vowel

   (ii) T   (iv) A consonant

7. A number is chosen at random from the following list: 1, 3, 6, 8, 9, 77 and 89. What is the probability of picking:

   (i) An even number

   (ii) An odd number

   (iii) A two-digit number

   (iv) A prime number

   (v) A number divisible by 3

8. A letter is picked at random from the word EXERCISE. What is the probability that the letter is:

   (i) S

   (ii) E

   (iii) A vowel

   (iv) A consonant

   (v) A vowel **or** an S

9. The letters of the words SAMPLE and TREE are written on separate cards and are placed in a bag. A card is picked at random. What is the probability of picking:

   (i) S   (ii) E   (iii) A vowel

10. A bag contains four red marbles and six green marbles. A marble is taken at random from the bag. What is the probability (as a percentage) that this marble will be:

   (i) Red   (ii) Green

11. The fair spinner shown is spun. What is the probability that the spinner lands at:

   (i) Blue

   (ii) Yellow

   (iii) Blue **or** red

12. A sports club has 150 members. Fifty members are adults and the rest are children. A member is selected at random. What is the probability that the member selected is:

   (i) An adult   (ii) A child

13. In a batch of 2,000 computer components, 12 were found to be faulty. If a computer component is chosen at random, what is the probability that it will be faulty?

14. A bag contains 30 marbles: 15 red, 8 silver and the rest blue. A marble is selected at random. What is the probability that the marble will be:

   (i) Red
   (ii) Silver
   (iii) Blue
   (iv) Not red

15. Stephen has a choice of two boxes. Box A contains 10 prizes and five booby prizes. Box B contains four prizes and three booby prizes.

A   B

Which box should Stephen pick to give himself the highest probability of winning a prize?
Show clearly how you got your answer.

16. There are 30 students in a class. This table shows the number who are girls or boys and how many do or do not wear glasses:

	Wears glasses	Does not wear glasses
Girl	7	12
Boy	3	8

A student is picked at random from the class. Find the probability (as a fraction in its simplest form) that this person will be:

   (i) A boy who wears glasses
   (ii) A girl who does not wear glasses
   (iii) A girl
   (iv) A person who wears glasses

17. Helen is going to play a hockey match. She says, 'We can win, lose or draw, so the probability that we will win must be $\frac{1}{3}$.'

Explain why Helen's statement is wrong.

7.8 EXPECTED FREQUENCY

If we know the relative frequency or probability of an event, we can then estimate how many times that event would happen over a certain number of trials. This is called the **expected frequency**.

FORMULA

Expected frequency = number of trials × relative frequency or probability.

Worked Example 7.11

A coin is flipped 500 times. How many times would a head be expected to occur?

Solution

$$P(\text{head}) = \frac{1}{2}$$

The number of times a head would be expected to occur after 500 flips is:

$$500 \times \frac{1}{2} = 250$$

Worked Example 7.12

A student carries out a random survey of 50 people on car ownership in his local area. Forty people respond that they own a car.

(i) Calculate the relative frequency of owning a car.

(ii) Estimate how many of the 3,000 people in the local area own a car.

Solution

(i) The relative frequency of owning a car = $\frac{40}{50} = \frac{4}{5}$ or 0.8.

(ii) The expected frequency of car ownership = $3,000 \times 0.8 = 2,400$ people.

ACTIVITIES 7.20, 7.21, 7.22, 7.23, 7.24

Exercise 7.6

1. A die is thrown 6,000 times. How many times would the die be expected to land on:

   (i) The number 1
   (ii) An even number

2. A card is selected at random from a pack of 52 playing cards and then replaced. This is done 1,040 times. How many times would you expect to get the following cards:

   (i) A red card
   (ii) A King
   (iii) The Queen of Hearts

3. An unfair coin is flipped and the relative frequency with which it lands on a tail is calculated to be 0.35. Estimate the number of times the coin will land on a tail if it is flipped 600 times.

4. Around 90% of people are right-handed. In a survey of 1,500 people, how many would you predict to be left-handed?

5. A survey states that 20% of people are allergic to cats.

   (i) In a school of 550 students, how many would you expect to suffer from this allergy?

   (ii) The survey also states that 50% of people who are allergic to cats are also allergic to dogs. How many students who are allergic to cats are also allergic to dogs?

6. The probability that a player wins on a slot machine is $\frac{1}{9}$. The cost of each game is 50c.

   (i) How many times would a player be expected to win in 45 games?

   (ii) If the slot machine pays out €2 for every win, how much money could the player win in 90 games?

   (iii) Would the player expect to make a profit or a loss in 90 games? How much profit or loss?

7. A factory that makes music discs produces on average one faulty disc for every 50 discs. The factory produces 7,500 discs in an hour.

   (i) How many of these discs would be expected to be faulty?

   (ii) Another factory checks the quality of its discs. Out of 8,000 discs, 100 are found to be faulty. Which factory has the lowest relative frequency of faulty discs?

8. A student makes a list of all the students who go home for lunch in his school in a 10-minute period. As they leave school, he records whether they are a boy (B) or a girl (G). The results are as follows:

B	B	G	B	G	B	B	B	B	G
B	G	B	G	B	G	G	B	G	B
B	G	G	G	G	B	B	B	G	G
B	G	G	G	B	B	B	G	B	G
B	G	G	B	G	B	B	B	B	G

   (i) How many boys left school for lunch in the 10-minute period?
   (ii) How many girls left school for lunch in the 10-minute period?
   (iii) How many out of 100 students leaving for lunch would you expect to be boys?
   (iv) How many out of 300 students leaving for lunch would you expect to be girls?

9. An unfair die is rolled 100 times and lands on a 4 thirty times.

   (i) How many times would it be expected to land on a 4 in 300 rolls?
   (ii) How many times would it be expected to land on a 4 in 600 rolls?
   (iii) How many times on a normal die would it be expected to land on a 4 in 600 rolls?

10. A bag contains 10 marbles. A marble is selected at random from the bag, its colour is noted, and it is then returned to the bag. This experiment is done 50 times. Every 10th time, the relative frequency was worked out. The graph of the results is shown below:

   (i) Find the number of blue marbles picked after 10 selections.
   (ii) Find the number of blue marbles picked after 20 selections.
   (iii) Find the number of blue marbles picked after 30 selections.
   (iv) Find the number of blue marbles picked after 40 selections.
   (v) Find the number of blue marbles picked after 50 selections.
   (vi) How many blue marbles do you think are in the bag? Explain.

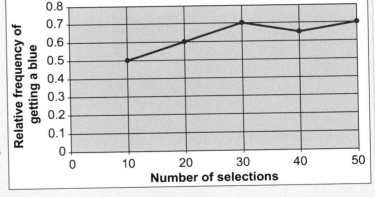

   (vii) If the experiment was performed 1,000 times, how many times would you expect a blue marble to be picked?

7.9 USING COUNTING METHODS TO SOLVE PROBABILITY QUESTIONS

When dealing with more complicated questions involving probability, simply listing the outcomes may be difficult. In this case, we can use **sample space** diagrams to help work out the probabilities. This method is especially useful when dealing with the probability of **combined events**.

> A combined event is where two or more events occur and their outcomes are combined together.

Worked Example 7.13

A fair coin is flipped twice.

    (i) Draw a table of all possible outcomes.

   (ii) Write down the number of possible outcomes.

  (iii) Work out the probability of getting two heads.

  (iv) Work out the probability of getting a head and a tail.

Solution

    (i) Draw a table of all possible outcomes.

First flip / Outcomes of 1st flip	Second flip	
	Outcomes of 2nd flip	
	Head	Tail
Head	HH	HT
Tail	TH	TT

   (ii) Write down the number of possible outcomes:

       From the table, it is evident that there are **four** possible outcomes {HH, HT, TH, TT}.

  (iii) Probability of two heads, i.e. P(H, H)

       Only one outcome gives two heads (coloured red):

First flip / Outcomes of 1st flip	Second flip	
	Outcomes of 2nd flip	
	Head	Tail
Head	HH	HT
Tail	TH	TT

       ∴ The probability of getting two heads = $\dfrac{\text{number of outcomes that have two heads}}{\text{total number of possible outcomes}} = \dfrac{1}{4}$

  (iv) Probability of a head and a tail

       It is important to note that the order is not important. We can have a head on the first flip and a tail on the second, or a head on the second flip and a tail on the first. A total of two outcomes gives a head and tail (coloured red):

First flip / Outcomes of 1st flip	Second flip	
	Outcomes of 2nd flip	
	Head	Tail
Head	HH	HT
Tail	TH	TT

       ∴ The probability of getting a head and a tail

       $= \dfrac{\text{number of outcomes that have a head and a tail}}{\text{total number of possible outcomes}} = \dfrac{2}{4} = \dfrac{1}{2}$

Worked Example 7.14

Two fair dice are thrown and the scores are added together.

Find the probability that the score on the two dice is:

(i) 7

(ii) Even

(iii) Odd

(iv) A prime number

(v) A multiple of 3

Solution

We must first draw a two-way table to show all the outcomes.

- Put the outcomes of the first die along the side.
- Put the outcomes of the second die along the top.
- Find all possible outcomes by adding the two scores, e.g. 6 + 3 = 9.

<table>
<tr><td></td><td colspan="7" align="center">Second die</td></tr>
<tr><td></td><td></td><td>1</td><td>2</td><td>3</td><td>4</td><td>5</td><td>6</td></tr>
<tr><td rowspan="6">First die</td><td>1</td><td>2</td><td>3</td><td>4</td><td>5</td><td>6</td><td>7</td></tr>
<tr><td>2</td><td>3</td><td>4</td><td>5</td><td>6</td><td>7</td><td>8</td></tr>
<tr><td>3</td><td>4</td><td>5</td><td>6</td><td>7</td><td>8</td><td>9</td></tr>
<tr><td>4</td><td>5</td><td>6</td><td>7</td><td>8</td><td>9</td><td>10</td></tr>
<tr><td>5</td><td>6</td><td>7</td><td>8</td><td>9</td><td>10</td><td>11</td></tr>
<tr><td>6</td><td>7</td><td>8</td><td>9</td><td>10</td><td>11</td><td>12</td></tr>
</table>

We then count the total number of possible outcomes, which in this case is 36.

(i) Probability of a score of 7

A total of six outcomes add up to 7 (coloured yellow).

<table>
<tr><td></td><td colspan="7" align="center">Second die</td></tr>
<tr><td></td><td></td><td>1</td><td>2</td><td>3</td><td>4</td><td>5</td><td>6</td></tr>
<tr><td rowspan="6">First die</td><td>1</td><td>2</td><td>3</td><td>4</td><td>5</td><td>6</td><td>7</td></tr>
<tr><td>2</td><td>3</td><td>4</td><td>5</td><td>6</td><td>7</td><td>8</td></tr>
<tr><td>3</td><td>4</td><td>5</td><td>6</td><td>7</td><td>8</td><td>9</td></tr>
<tr><td>4</td><td>5</td><td>6</td><td>7</td><td>8</td><td>9</td><td>10</td></tr>
<tr><td>5</td><td>6</td><td>7</td><td>8</td><td>9</td><td>10</td><td>11</td></tr>
<tr><td>6</td><td>7</td><td>8</td><td>9</td><td>10</td><td>11</td><td>12</td></tr>
</table>

The probability of scoring a $7 = \dfrac{\text{number of outcomes that total 7}}{\text{total number of possible outcomes}} = \dfrac{6}{36} = \dfrac{1}{6}$

(ii) Probability of an even score

A total of 18 outcomes add up to even numbers (coloured red).

		Second die					
		1	2	3	4	5	6
First die	1	2	3	4	5	6	7
	2	3	4	5	6	7	8
	3	4	5	6	7	8	9
	4	5	6	7	8	9	10
	5	6	7	8	9	10	11
	6	7	8	9	10	11	12

The probability of scoring an even number

$$= \frac{\text{number of outcomes that are even numbers}}{\text{total number of possible outcomes}} = \frac{18}{36} = \frac{1}{2}$$

(iii) Probability of an odd score

If 18 outcomes are even and there are 36 possible outcomes, then the number of outcomes that will give us an odd score is 36 − 18 = 18.

The probability of scoring an odd number $= \frac{18}{36} = \frac{1}{2}$

(Alternatively, we could count them in the two-way table.)

(iv) Probability that the score is a prime number

A total number of 15 outcomes add up to a prime number (coloured orange).

		Second die					
		1	2	3	4	5	6
First die	1	2	3	4	5	6	7
	2	3	4	5	6	7	8
	3	4	5	6	7	8	9
	4	5	6	7	8	9	10
	5	6	7	8	9	10	11
	6	7	8	9	10	11	12

The probability of scoring a prime number

$$= \frac{\text{number of outcomes that are prime numbers}}{\text{total number of possible outcomes}} = \frac{15}{36} = \frac{5}{12}$$

The Roman emperor Augustus (63 BC to AD 14) was said to be an avid dice player.

(v) Probability that the score is a multiple of 3

Count the outcomes that are multiples of 3. There are 12 in total (coloured blue).

		Second die					
		1	2	3	4	5	6
First die	1	2	3	4	5	6	7
	2	3	4	5	6	7	8
	3	4	5	6	7	8	9
	4	5	6	7	8	9	10
	5	6	7	8	9	10	11
	6	7	8	9	10	11	12

The probability of scoring a multiple of 3

$$= \frac{\text{number of outcomes that are a multiple of 3}}{\text{total number of possible outcomes}} = \frac{12}{36} = \frac{1}{3}$$

Tree Diagrams

We can also use tree diagrams to help us solve probability questions.

 Worked Example 7.15

A fair coin is flipped twice. Using a tree diagram, determine the probability of getting:

   (i) Two heads   (ii) A tail followed by a head   (iii) A tail and a head

Solution

We first draw a tree diagram to show all our outcomes.

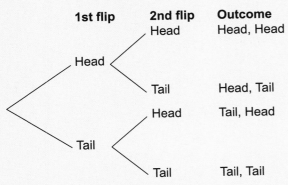

We can count four possible outcomes.

   (i) Probability of getting two heads:

      Two heads as an outcome appear once (Head, Head).

      P(Two heads)

$$= \frac{\text{number of outcomes that have two heads}}{\text{number of possible outcomes}} = \frac{1}{4}$$

   (ii) Probability of a tail followed by a head:

      A tail followed by a head as an outcome appears once

      P(A tail followed by a head)

$$= \frac{\text{number of outcomes that have a tail followed by a head}}{\text{number of possible outcomes}} = \frac{1}{4}$$

   (iii) Probability of a tail and a head:

      Here order is not specified. We can have Tail, Head **or** Head, Tail. There are two desirable outcomes:

      P(A tail and a head)

$$= \frac{\text{number of outcomes that have a tail and a head}}{\text{number of possible outcomes}}$$

$$= \frac{2}{4} = \frac{1}{2}$$

 **ACTIVITIES** 7.25, 7.26, 7.27, 7.28

1. A fair coin is flipped and a spinner with five equal sectors coloured red, green, blue, white and purple is spun.

		Spinner				
		R	G	B	W	P
Coin	H		HG			
	T					TP

(i) Copy and complete the two-way table to show all possible outcomes.

(ii) How many outcomes are possible?

(iii) Find the probability of getting a head and blue.

(iv) Find the probability of getting a tail and white.

(v) Find the probability of getting a head and purple.

2. The fair spinner shown below is spun twice.

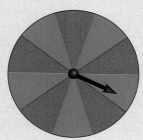

(i) Use a tree diagram to list all the possible outcomes.

(ii) What is the probability of the spinner landing on the blue sector after one spin?

(iii) What is the probability of the spinner landing on the blue sector on both spins?

(iv) What is the probability of the spinner landing on a blue and then a red sector after two spins?

3. A red die and a black die are thrown.

		Black die					
		1	2	3	4	5	6
Red die	1						
	2			(2, 3)			
	3						
	4						
	5					(5, 5)	
	6						

(i) Copy and complete the two-way table to show all the possible outcomes.

(ii) How many outcomes are possible?

Find the probability of getting:

(iii) A 2 on the red die and a 4 on the black die

(iv) A 6 on the red die and a 6 on the black die

(v) An even number on the red die and an odd number on the black die

(vi) Equal scores (i.e. both dice show the same number)

(vii) A score on the red die bigger than the score on the black die

(viii) A difference of 2 between the scores on each die

4. A chef designs the following menu:

(i) Draw a tree diagram to show all the possible menu choices.

A food critic enters the restaurant and decides to pick at random from the menu. Find the probability that the critic picks:

(ii) Soup for starter and beef for the main course

(iii) Garlic bread for the starter and chicken for the main course

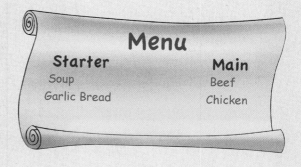

Menu

Starter
Soup
Garlic Bread

Main
Beef
Chicken

5. A four-sided die and a six-sided die are rolled. The outcome for the first die can be A, B, C or D. The outcome for the second die can be 1, 2, 3, 4, 5 or 6. An outcome is listed as shown in the following table:

	Second die					
	1	2	3	4	5	6
A					A5	
B						
C				C4		
D						

First die

(i) Copy and complete the table.

What is the probability that the outcome will be:

(ii) A1

(iii) D5

(iv) A and an even number

(v) C and an odd number

6. Two fair dice, one red and one black, are thrown. The score from the first die is added to the score from the second die.

	Black die					
	1	2	3	4	5	6
1	2					
2						
3						
4						
5					10	
6		8				

Red die

(i) Copy and complete the two-way table to show all the possible outcomes.

What is the probability that the score on the two dice will add up to:

(ii) 5

(iii) 8

(iv) A number divisible by 5

(v) A factor of 6

Which totals are the *least* probable? Give a reason for your answer.

7. A fair spinner coloured red, green and blue is spun twice.

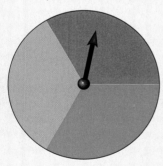

(i) List all the possible outcomes.

Find the probability that:

(ii) The spinner will land on red both times.

(iii) The spinner will land on red and green in any order.

8. A game is played with a spinner labelled X, Y and Z.

The spinner is spun twice, and a point is scored if the spinner lands on the same letter twice.

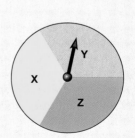

	Second spin		
	X	Y	Z
X	XX		
Y			
Z		ZY	

First spin

(i) Copy and complete the two-way table:

Find the probability that:

(ii) The spinner lands on the same letter twice.

(iii) A point will not be scored on the first turn.

9. Two fair dice are thrown. The score on the second die is subtracted from the score on the first die.

		Second die					
		1	2	3	4	5	6
First die	1	0					
	2	1		−1			
	3					−2	
	4						
	5						
	6						

(i) Copy and complete the two-way table.

Find the probability that the outcome shown is:

(ii) 1

(iii) A negative number

(iv) A positive number

(v) An integer

(vi) A zero

(vii) A number greater than 5

10. A person wins a car in a prize raffle. The car model can be a hatchback or an SUV. The car colour can be red or blue.

(a) Using the tree diagram below, fill in all the possible choices of car.

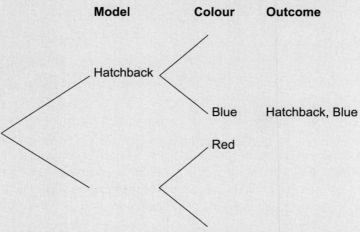

(b) A person picks the colour and model of the car at random. Find the probability that they pick a car that is:

(i) A red hatchback   (ii) A blue SUV   (iii) An SUV   (iv) A red car

 Revision Exercises

1. (a) Fill in the following probabilities on a probability scale.

```
 |    |    |    |    |    |    |    |    |    |    |
 0                       0.5                      1
```

(i) Flipping a coin and getting a head

(ii) That the day after next Saturday will be Sunday

(iii) Choosing a card at random from a deck and getting a heart

(iv) Scoring a total of 13 when adding the scores of two dice

(b) Use the following terms to describe each event and mark each event on a likelihood scale.

Impossible	Unlikely	Evens	Likely	Certain

(i) An event that has a probability of 0.75

(ii) An event that has a probability of 0.2

(iii) An event that has a probability of 1/2

(iv) An event that has a probability of 100%

(v) An event that has a probability of zero

(c) Which event, if any, is more likely to happen? Give a reason for your answer.

   (i) Rolling a fair die and getting a 6 **or** flipping a fair coin and getting a head
   (ii) Rolling a fair die and getting a 1 **or** rolling a fair die and getting a 6
   (iii) Flipping a fair coin and getting a tail **or** rolling a fair die and getting an even number
   (iv) Picking a red card at random from a pack of cards **or** rolling a 1 or 2 on a fair die

2. (a) There are 10 marbles in a box – five red, two green and the rest yellow. A marble is taken at random from the box. Find the probability that the marble is:

   (i) Red   (ii) Green   (iii) Yellow   (iv) Not red   (v) Red or green

   (b) A fair coin is flipped three times and lands on heads each time. What is the probability that it lands on heads on the next throw? Explain your answer.

   (c) A fair coin is flipped and a coloured token (red, blue, green or yellow) is chosen at random. Copy and complete the following two-way table.

		Token			
		Red	Blue	Green	Yellow
Coin	H				HY
	T			TG	

Calculate the probability of getting:

   (i) A head on the coin flip and a red token
   (ii) A tail on the coin flip and a blue token
   (iii) A token that is yellow
   (iv) A tail on the coin flip

3. (a) A piggy bank contains seven 2c coins, three 5c coins, four 10c coins, and two €1 coins.

Tom chooses a coin at random from the bank. Find the probability that the coin chosen is:

   (i) A 5c coin
   (ii) A €1 coin
   (iii) A 2c or 5c coin
   (iv) Not a €1 coin

   (c) Two dice are rolled. If the numbers shown are different, the score from the first die is added to the score from the second die. If the numbers shown are the same, only the score of the first die is recorded.

   (i) Use a two-way table to show all the possible outcomes.
   (ii) What outcome is the most likely to occur?
   (iii) Find the probability of obtaining this score.
   (iv) What is the probability of getting an outcome that is even?

(b) A survey is taken of two First Year classes in a school, SD 1 and SL 1. The survey asks what mode of transport the students use to get to school. The table below shows the results:

	Car	Walk	Cycle	Other
SD 1	5	7	3	3
SL 1	8	3	4	1

   (i) Calculate the number of students in each class.

A student is chosen at random from the two classes. Find the probability that the student travels to the school by:

   (ii) Car
   (iii) Cycling
   (iv) Not walking

A student is chosen at random from class SL 1. Find the probability that the student picked from this class travels to school by:

   (v) Car
   (vi) Cycling

4. (a) A card is drawn at random from a pack of 52 cards. Find the probability that the card is:

    (i) A Spade   (iv) A red card

    (ii) An Ace   (v) The King of Hearts

    (iii) A picture card

If you draw a card randomly from a pack 200 times, how many times would you expect to get a spade?

(b) A coin is flipped 100 times, and the number of times the coin has landed on tails is recorded every 20th flip. The diagram below shows the results:

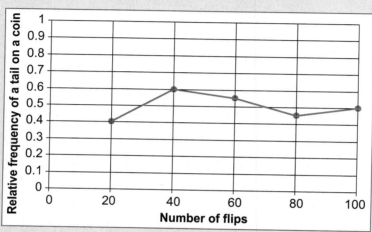

(i) Calculate the number of tails obtained after 40 flips.

(ii) Calculate the number of tails obtained after 80 flips.

(iii) Do you think that the coin is fair? Explain your answer.

(c) Bag A contains two marbles numbered 1 and 2. Bag B contains two marbles numbered 3 and 4.

One marble is removed at random from Bag A and then one marble is removed at random from Bag B. Using a tree diagram, list all the possible outcomes.

Bag A   Bag B

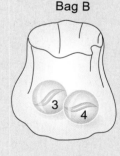

Find the probability that:

    (i) A marble numbered 1 will be drawn from Bag A, and a marble numbered 3 will be drawn from Bag B.

    (ii) A marble numbered 2 will be drawn from Bag A, and a marble of any number will be drawn from Bag B.

    (iii) The number on the marble drawn from each bag will be odd.

    (iv) The number on the marble drawn from each bag will be even.

5. (a) A person (chosen at random) is asked to name the month of their birthday.

    (i) Taking all months as equally likely, find the probability that the person's birthday is in May.

    (ii) If 60 people are stopped at random, how many would you expect to have their birthdays in May?

(b) A student records how many times a coin lands on tails. She records that the coin lands on tails 20 times out of 50 flips.

She uses this result to predict how many times the coin would land on tails if she flipped it 1,000 times.

What is her prediction for this? Show how you got your answer.

(c) Two fair dice are each marked 1, 1, 2, 2, 3, 3.
Copy and complete the two-way table to show all the possible outcomes.

	Second die		
	1	**2**	**3**
1	(1, 1)		
2			
3		(3, 2)	

First die

(i) How many outcomes are possible?

Find the probability of getting:

(ii) A 1 on the first die and a 2 on the second die
(iii) A 3 on the first die and a 3 on the second die
(iv) An even number on the first die and an even number on the second die
(v) Equal scores (i.e. both dice show the same number)
(vi) Different scores (i.e. each die shows a different number)

6. (a) A person is stopped in the street at random and asked on what day of the week they were born. What is the probability that the day on which this person was born was:

(i) A Sunday
(ii) Not a Sunday
(iii) A Saturday or Sunday
(iv) A weekday (Monday to Friday)
(v) A day beginning with the letter T

(b) A student was asked to tally the outcomes when a fair die was rolled 24 times. Which of the following is most likely to be the genuine tally for 24 rolls of the die: Tally A, B or C? Give a reason for your answer.

	#1	#2	#3	#4	#5	#6
Tally A	4	4	4	4	4	4
Tally B	10	6	3	2	1	2
Tally C	5	4	5	4	3	3

7. In a game, two dice are rolled in turn by the players. The table below represents all 36 outcomes. The total on the two dice is recorded.

(a) Complete the table, filling in the totals in each case.

	Second die					
	1	**2**	**3**	**4**	**5**	**6**
1						
2		4				
3						
4						
5				9		
6						12

First die

(b) State if the following statements are true or false:

Statement	True	False
All totals are equally likely.		
A total of 7 is the most likely.		
A total of 5 is as likely as a total of 9.		
You are not very likely to get a total of 12.		
The probability of getting a total of 6 or more is about 50%.		
A total of 13 is impossible.		
You are more likely to get a total under 7 than over 7.		
You get a total of 2 about 3% of the time.		

8. (a) There are 20 students in a class. This table shows the number who are girls or boys and how many are left-handed or right-handed:

	Left-handed	**Right-handed**
Girls	2	10
Boys	3	5

(i) A student is picked at random from the class. Find the probability (as a percentage) that this person will be:

■ A right-handed girl

■ A right-handed boy

■ A girl

■ Left-handed

(ii) A boy is picked at random from the class. Find the probability that he will be left-handed.

(b) All the picture cards (Jack, Queen and King) from a deck of 52 playing cards are removed. Find the probability that a single card picked at random from the remaining cards will be:

(i) An Ace

(ii) A Heart

(iii) A Heart or a Diamond

(iv) A Two of Clubs or a Three of Clubs

9. (a) The tree diagram below shows the possible outcomes when a fair die is rolled twice.

1st Roll	2nd Roll	Outcome

½ — P P, P

½ — N P, N

½ — P N, P

½ — N N, N

P = Prime Number
N = Not a Prime Number

½ P

½ N

(i) Calculate the probability of getting:

■ A prime number on both rolls

■ A number that is not a prime number on both rolls

■ A prime number on the first roll and a non-prime number on the second roll

(ii) If this experiment were carried out 100 times, how many times would you expect to get a prime number on both rolls?

(b) Two girls play a game with two fair spinners as shown.

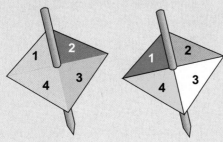

The spinners are spun and the score from each spinner is added together.

If the total score is an even number, Kate wins. If the total score is divisible by 5, Margaret wins.

(i) Draw a two-way table to show all the outcomes.

(ii) Is this game fair? Explain your answer by calculating the probabilities of each player winning the game.

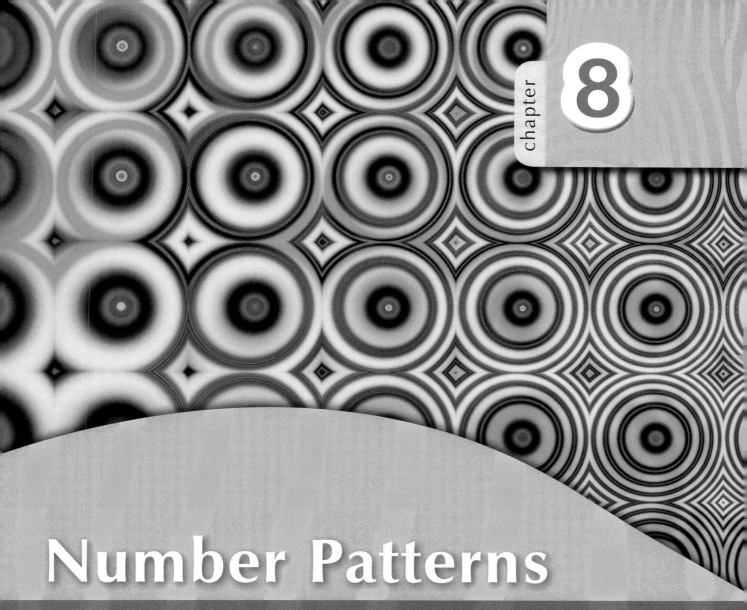

chapter 8

Number Patterns

Learning Outcomes

In this chapter you will learn to:

- ⊃ Use tables to represent a repeating pattern
- ⊃ Generalise and explain patterns and relationships in words and numbers
- ⊃ Write arithmetic expressions for particular terms in a sequence
- ⊃ Find the underlying formula written in words from which the data is derived (linear relations)
- ⊃ Recognise features of linear, quadratic and exponential patterns

8.1 PATTERNS

A pattern is a set of numbers, objects or diagrams that repeat in a predictable manner.

To help predict what will come next in the pattern, we must find the rule that links one number or diagram with the next.

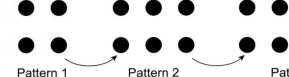

Pattern 1   Pattern 2   Pattern 3

To help us determine what will happen next in a pattern, we can draw a table.

KEY WORDS

■ Pattern
■ Repeating
■ Linear
■ Difference
■ Quadratic
■ Exponential
■ Term
■ General term
■ Starting value

 ACTIVITY 8.1

NUMBER PATTERNS

Worked Example 8.1

A repeating pattern is made up of shaped tiles as shown. The pattern repeats every four tiles.

(i) What shape is the 10th tile?
(ii) What shape is the 27th tile?

(iii) What shape is the 38th tile?
(iv) What shape is the 620th tile?

Solution

We draw a table to help us:

Tile	Shape
1	△
2	△
3	□
4	○
5	△
6	△
7	□
8	○

We can see that the pattern **repeats every four tiles**. This is important to know, as we can now predict what will happen in this pattern.

(i) What shape is the 10th tile?

To find the 10th tile, we can just continue on the table:

5	△
6	△
7	□
8	○
9	△
10	△

The 10th tile is a triangle △.

(ii) What shape is the 27th tile?

We could try to find this by drawing a table, but it could take a long time:

Tile	Shape	Tile	Shape	Tile	Shape	Tile	Shape	Tile	Shape
1	Δ	9	Δ	17	Δ	25	Δ	33	Δ
2	Δ	10	Δ	18	Δ	26	Δ	34	Δ
3	□	11	□	19	□	27	□	35	□
4	○	12	○	20	○	28	○	36	○
5	Δ	13	Δ	21	Δ	29	Δ	37	Δ
6	Δ	14	Δ	22	Δ	30	Δ	38	Δ
7	□	15	□	23	□	31	□	39	□
8	○	16	○	24	○	32	○	40	○

However, we know that the pattern repeats every four tiles.

$27 \div 4 = 6$, with a remainder of 3 (six repeating blocks of four tiles and three extra tiles).

We now look at our original table.

Tile	Shape
1	Δ
2	Δ
3	□
4	○

The third tile is a square □, which corresponds to the 27th tile.

(iii) What shape is the 38th tile?

$38 \div 4 = 9$, with a remainder of 2 (nine repeating blocks of four tiles and two extra tiles).

The second tile is a triangle Δ, which corresponds to the 38th tile.

(iv) What shape is the 620th tile?

$620 \div 4 = 155$, with a remainder of 0 (155 repeating blocks of four tiles).

∴ 620 is a multiple of 4.

If we consider our table, we see that every multiple of 4 will be a circle ○.

The 620th tile is a circle ○.

Worked Example 8.2

A six-block repeating pattern made up of coloured blocks is shown.

If the pattern continued, what colour would each of the following blocks be?

(i) The 42nd block

(ii) The 80th block

(iii) The 1,000th block

Solution

Again, we draw a table:

Block	Colour
1	Blue
2	Green
3	Red
4	Green
5	Red
6	Yellow

The pattern **repeats every six blocks**.

(i) The 42nd block

$42 \div 6 = 7$, with a remainder of 0.

∴ 42 is a multiple of 6.

If we consider our table, we see that every multiple of 6 will be a yellow block.

The 42nd block is yellow.

(ii) The 80th block

$80 \div 6 = 13$, with a remainder of 2.

The second block is green.
∴ the 80th block will be a green block.

(iii) The 1,000th block

$1,000 \div 6 = 166$, with a remainder of 4.

The fourth block is green.
∴ the 1,000th block will be a green block.

Arranging Objects to Create Patterns

Patterns may also involve one or two more objects within a certain diagram.

 Worked Example 8.3

A pattern of discs is shown. How many discs would be needed for the next pattern?

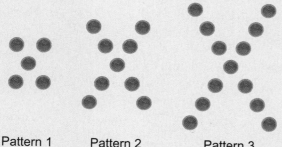

Pattern 1   Pattern 2   Pattern 3

Solution

We draw a table and count the number of discs needed in each pattern:

Pattern	Number of discs
1	5
2	9
3	13

To get from one pattern to the next, we have to add four discs each time.

∴ The next pattern would require $13 + 4 = 17$ discs.

 Exercise 8.1

1. Identify the next shape in each of the following patterns:

   (i)   □ □ ○ ○ □ □   (repeats every four)

   (ii) △ □ △ □ △ □   (repeats every two)

   (iii) ○ ☼ ■ ○ ☼ ■   (repeats every three)

   (iv) ♣ ♣ ♥ ♦ ♣ ♣   (repeats every four)

   (v)   ☺ ☺ △ ☺ ☺ △   (repeats every three)

2. A coloured pattern is shown. In each case, after the last block the pattern repeats. Identify the colours of the next three blocks.

   (i)

   (ii)

(iii)

(iv)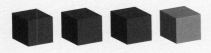

3. A four-block repeating pattern made up of coloured blocks is shown.

    (i) What colour is the 42nd block?

    (ii) What colour is the 80th block?

    (iii) What colour is the 1,000th block?

4. A five-tile repeating pattern made up of shaped tiles is shown.

    (i) What shape is the 10th tile?

    (ii) What shape is the 27th tile?

    (iii) What shape is the 39th tile?

    (iv) What shape is the 620th tile?

5. A six-marble repeating pattern made up of coloured marbles is shown.

    (i) What colour is the 32nd marble?

    (ii) What colour is the 60th marble?

    (iii) How many times does a red marble appear in the first 20 marbles of this pattern?

6. A repeating pattern made up of shaped tiles is shown. The pattern repeats after six tiles.

    (i) What shape is the 10th tile?

    (ii) What shape is the 27th tile?

    (iii) What shape is the 39th tile?

    (iv) How many times does a circle shape appear in the first 50 shapes of this pattern?

7. A repeating pattern is made up of matchsticks.

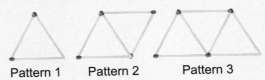

Pattern 1   Pattern 2   Pattern 3

    (i) How many matchsticks will Pattern 4 need?

    (ii) How many matchsticks will Pattern 5 need?

    (iii) Draw Pattern 4 and Pattern 5.

8. A repeating pattern made from blue and red marbles is shown.

Pattern 1   Pattern 2   Pattern 3

    (i) How many blue marbles will Pattern 4 need?

    (ii) How many red marbles will Pattern 5 need?

    (iii) How many marbles in total will Pattern 6 need?

    (iv) Draw Pattern 6.

8.2 LINEAR PATTERNS

6, 10, 14, 18... is an example of a number sequence.

Each number or diagram in a sequence can be called a **term**.

1st Term	2nd Term	3rd Term	4th Term
6	10	14	18

A pattern that is given as an ordered list is called a **sequence**. A pattern of numbers is called a **number sequence**.

 ACTIVITY 8.2

Each term is connected to the next term by a certain rule or difference.

1st Term	6
2nd Term	6 + 4 = 10
3rd Term	10 + 4 = 14
4th Term	14 + 4 = 18
Rule: Add 4	

As the difference between each term is the same, this pattern is **linear**.

In a **linear pattern or sequence**, the difference or change between one term and the next is always the same number. This means that change in a linear sequence is **constant** (same value).

1st Term	2nd Term	3rd Term	4th Term
T_1	T_2	T_3	T_4
6	10	14	18

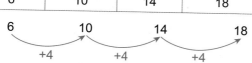

It is called a linear sequence because if we were asked to graph this pattern, it would be a straight line.

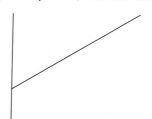

This difference between each term in a linear sequence can be referred to as the **common difference**.

Worked Example 8.4

Find the next three terms in the following sequences.

 (i) 11, 18, 25, 32...

 (ii) 2, –1, –4, –7...

The ... (ellipsis) at the end of a sequence implies that the sequence carries on and does not stop at the last term given.

Solution

(i) Examining the sequence, we can see that to get from any term to the next term we add 7.

The difference is +7.

4th Term T_4	32
5th Term T_5	32 + 7 = 39
6th Term T_6	39 + 7 = 46
7th Term T_7	46 + 7 = 53

(ii) Examining the sequence, we can see that the common difference is –3.

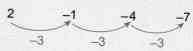

4th Term T_4	–7
5th Term T_5	–7 – 3 = –10
6th Term T_6	–10 – 3 = –13
7th Term T_7	–13 – 3 = –16

Describing Linear Sequences in Words

We may also be asked to describe a linear sequence in words.

Worked Example 8.5

Describe in your own words the following sequence:

7, 10, 13, 16...

Solution

To describe a linear sequence, we have to say where it starts and how to get from one term to the next. The start term is 7 and the common difference between each term is 3.

The rule for this sequence is: 'Start with 7 and add 3 every term.'

Worked Example 8.6

A sequence is described as 'Start with 20 and add 6 every term.' Write down the first four terms.

Solution

Remember that the first term is the number we start with, in this case 20.

T_1	20
T_2	20 + 6 = 26
T_3	26 + 6 = 32
T_4	32 + 6 = 38

∴ Sequence is 20, 26, 32, 38...

Exercise 8.2

1. For each linear sequence, find:

   (a) The start term

   (b) The common difference

   (c) The next three terms

   (i) 5, 11, 17, 23, 29...

   (ii) 8, 13, 18, 23, 28...

   (iii) 16, 18, 20, 22, 24...

   (iv) 6, 25, 44, 63, 82...

   (v) 14, 30, 46, 62, 78...

   (vi) 2, 13, 24, 35, 46...

   (vii) 200, 185, 170, 155, 140...

   (viii) −10, −4, 2, 8, 14...

   (ix) −5, −9, −13, −17, −21...

2. Write down the missing terms in the following sequences:

   (i) 1, 5, 9, ___, 17, 21, ___, 29, 33

   (ii) 18, 21, 24, ___, 30, ___, 36, 39

   (iii) 26, 38, 50, ___, ___, 86, 98, 110

   (iv) 15, 31, 47, 63, ___, ___, 111, ___, 143

   (v) 8, ___, 40, 56, 72, ___, 104, ___, 136

   (vi) −30, −23, ___, −9, ___, 5, 12, ___, 26

   (vii) 15, ___, 19, ___, 23, ___, 27, 29

   (viii) −9, ___, ___, −42, −53, ___, −75, −86, −97

3. Use the following rules to find the first four terms of each sequence:

   (i)   Start at 0, add 2 every term
   (ii) Start at 10, add 4 every term
   (iii) Start at 200, subtract 10 every term
   (iv) Start at –20, add 4 every term
   (v)   Start at –80, subtract 7 every term

4. Describe in your own words each of the following linear sequences:

   (i)   3, 8, 13, 18, 23
   (ii) 26, 22, 18, 14, 10
   (iii) 6, 15, 24, 33, 42
   (iv) 17, 33, 49, 65, 81
   (v)   75, 55, 35, 15, –5

8.3 GENERAL TERM OF A LINEAR SEQUENCE

Consider the sequence 3, 9, 15, 21...; we may need to find a way of describing or finding any term in the sequence.

For example, to find what the 50th term is, it could be difficult if we are asked to use the rule 'Start with 3 and add 6 every term.'

It would be helpful to change this rule into an arithmetic expression that would give us a general rule for every term.

Describing a sequence in this way is called **finding the general term** or T_n (pronounced nth term) of a sequence.

We are using the position of the term, i.e. the term number, to find the rules of the pattern.

> T_n or the general term of a sequence is a formula that can be used to find the value of any term of the sequence.

One approach to finding the general term of a sequence is to consider the **multiples of the common difference** and the **term number**.

Examine the sequence 3, 9, 15, 21, 27.

The common difference of this sequence is **6**.

Term number	Difference × term number	Term value
T_1	6 × 1 = 6	3
T_2	6 × 2 = 12	9
T_3	6 × 3 = 18	15
T_4	6 × 4 = 24	21
T_5	6 × 5 = 30	27

If we subtract 3 from each of the values in the middle column, they will then be equal to the term value.

To get the general term, we use the letter n instead of the term number:

Term number			Term value
T_1	6 × 1 = 6	6 – 3 = 3	3
T_2	6 × 2 = 12	12 – 3 = 9	9
T_3	6 × 3 = 18	18 – 3 = 15	15
T_4	6 × 4 = 24	24 – 3 = 21	21
T_5	6 × 5 = 30	30 – 3 = 27	27

T_n	6 × n = 6n – 3

So, the general term is $T_n = 6n - 3$.

We can now use the general term to find the 50th term:

$$T_{50} = 6(50) - 3 = 300 - 3 = 297$$

 ACTIVITY 8.3

Worked Example 8.7

Find the general term of the following linear sequences and, hence, find the 50th term.

(i) 2, 7, 12, 17...   (ii) 6, 8, 10, 12...   (iii) −7, −4, −1, 2...   (iv) −3, −5, −7, −9...

Solution

(i) 2, 7, 12, 17...

The common difference is **5**.

Term number			Term value
T_1	**5** × 1 = 5	5 − 3 = 2	2
T_2	**5** × 2 = 10	10 − 3 = 7	7
T_n	**5** × n = 5n	5n − 3	

$T_{50} = 5(50) − 3 = 250 − 3 = 247$

(ii) 6, 8, 10, 12...

The common difference is **2**.

Term number			Term value
T_1	**2** × 1 = 2	2 + 4 = 6	6
T_2	**2** × 2 = 4	4 + 4 = 8	8
T_n	**2** × n = 2n	2n + 4	

$T_{50} = 2(50) + 4 = 100 + 4 = 104$

(iii) −7, −4, −1, 2...

The common difference is **+3**.

Term number			Term value
T_1	**3** × 1 = 3	3 − 10 = −7	−7
T_2	**3** × 2 = 6	6 − 10 = −4	−4
T_n	**3** × n = 3n	3n − 10	

$T_{50} = 3(50) − 10 = 150 − 10 = 140$

(iv) −3, −5, −7, −9...

The common difference is **−2**.

Term number			Term value
T_1	**−2** × 1 = −2	−2 − 1 = −3	−3
T_2	**−2** × 2 = −4	−4 − 1 = −5	−5
T_n	**−2** × n = −2n	−2n − 1	

$T_{50} = −2(50) − 1 = −100 − 1 = −101$

Exercise 8.3

1. In each of the following linear sequences, find:

(a) The start term
(b) The common difference
(c) The nth term (general term)
(d) The value of the given term

(i) 14, 18, 22, 26, 30...   Find 10th term.
(ii) 4, 10, 16, 22, 28, 34... Find 12th term.
(iii) 10, 22, 34, 46, 58...   Find 18th term.
(iv) 19, 29, 39, 49, 59...   Find 35th term.
(v) 0, 7, 14, 21, 28...   Find 100th term.

(vi) 75, 84, 93, 102, 111...   Find 27th term.
(vii) 22, 20, 18, 16, 14...   Find 50th term.
(viii) 250, 280, 310, 340, 370... Find 10th term.
(ix) 22, 12, 2, −8, −18...   Find 16th term.
(x) −16, −20, −24, −28, −32   Find 30th term.

2. The nth term (general term) of three linear sequences is given.
   In each case, find the first, second, third and 100th term of the sequence.

(i) $T_n = 2n + 5$ (ii) $T_n = 4n − 2$ (iii) $T_n = −2n + 8$

8.4 NON-LINEAR PATTERNS

Quadratic Patterns

There are also number sequences that are **non-linear**.

For example, 2, 5, 10, 17...

We can see that the first difference between each term is **not** the same.

When we look at the second difference, i.e. the difference between the differences, we may be able to spot a pattern.

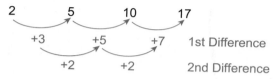

In **non-linear sequences**, the difference changes between each term.

The second difference is the same value each time.

In this case, the pattern is referred to as a **quadratic pattern**.

A quadratic pattern graphed will be a **curve** and **not** a straight line.

When the second difference is constant, you have a **quadratic sequence** (or pattern).

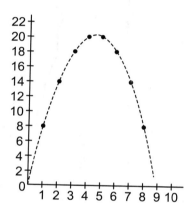

Worked Example 8.8

Find the second difference for each of the following quadratic sequences.

   (i) 6, 1, 0, 3, 10   (ii) 5, 12, 13, 8, −3

Solution

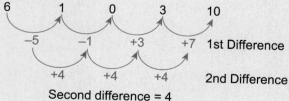

Second difference = 4

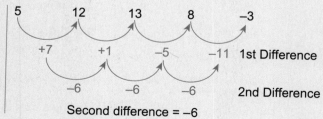

Second difference = −6

As a quadratic pattern can be represented by a quadratic graph, they share the same characteristics.

Every quadratic pattern **eventually** increases or decreases to a certain **maximum** or **minimum** value before it starts to **decrease** or **increase** again.

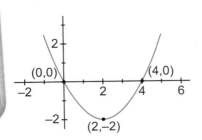

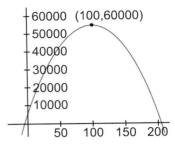

Exponential Patterns

Another example of a non-linear pattern is:

4, 8, 16, 32...

If we draw out a table, we can identify the rule that connects each term to the next:

Patterns that involve doubling, tripling, etc. are referred to as **exponential patterns**.

1st Term	4
2nd Term	$4 \times 2 = 8$
3rd Term	$8 \times 2 = 16$
4th Term	$16 \times 2 = 32$

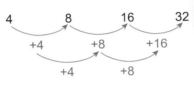

Again, the difference between each term is not the same value.

The second difference will also not be the same value.

Note: Exponential patterns on our course are limited to doubling or tripling.

Exponential patterns may also be graphed. Again, they are **not** straight lines.

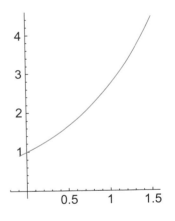

ACTIVITY 8.5

NUMBER PATTERNS

8

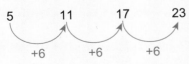

For each sequence, indentify the type of sequence and find the next three terms:

    (i) 5, 11, 17, 23...   (ii) 9, 27, 81, 243...   (iii) 2, 15, 36, 65...

Solution

    (i) 5, 11, 17, 23...

        5   11   17   23

           +6   +6   +6

    The first difference is a constant of $+6$.

    $\therefore$ The sequence is linear.

To find the next three terms it is helpful to use a table:

1st Term	5
2nd Term	$5 + 6 = 11$
3rd Term	$11 + 6 = 17$
4th Term	$17 + 6 = 23$
5th Term	$23 + 6 = 29$
6th Term	$29 + 6 = 35$
7th Term	$35 + 6 = 41$

$\therefore$ The next three terms are 29, 35, 41.

(ii) 9, 27, 81, 243...

This sequence is exponential, as terms are tripled each time.

1st Term	9
2nd Term	9 × 3 = 27
3rd Term	27 × 3 = 81
4th Term	81 × 3 = 243
5th Term	243 × 3 = 729
6th Term	729 × 3 = 2,187
7th Term	2,187 × 3 = 6,561

∴ The next three terms are:
729, 2187, 6561

(iii) 2, 15, 36, 65...

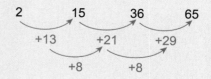

The first difference is not constant, but the second one is.

The second difference is +8.

∴ The sequence is quadratic.

1st Term	2
2nd Term	2 + 13 = 15
3rd Term	15 + 21 = 36
4th Term	36 + 29 = 65
5th Term	65 + 37 = 102
6th Term	102 + 45 = 147
7th Term	147 + 53 = 200

∴ The next three terms are 102, 147, 200.

Exercise 8.4

1. For each quadratic sequence, find:

    (a) The start term   (b) The second difference   (c) The next three terms

    (i) 13, 15, 23, 37...   (iii) 16, 17, 19, 22...   (v) 15, 23, 39, 63...   (vii) 5, 7, 5, −1, −11...
    (ii) 6, 11, 25, 48...   (iv) 12, 14, 17, 21...   (vi) 8, 12, 14, 14, 12...   (viii) 1, −2, −2, 1...

2. For each exponential sequence, find:

    (a) Whether it involves doubling or tripling   (b) The next three terms

    (i) 8, 16, 32, 64, 128, 256...   (iii) 33, 99, 297, 891, 2,673...   (v) −5, −15, −45, −135, −405...
    (ii) 6, 18, 54, 162, 486...   (iv) 13, 26, 52, 104, 208...

3. For each of the following sequences, identify whether it is quadratic or exponential. In each case, give reasons for your answer:

    (i) 1, 6, 15, 28, 45...   (iii) 7, 14, 28, 56, 112...   (v) 4, 1, 1, 4, 10...
    (ii) 12, 16, 23, 33, 46...   (iv) −1, −3, −9, −27, −81...

8.5 PROBLEMS INVOLVING PATTERNS

The rules we have studied for patterns have many uses.

 ## Worked Example 8.10

The height of a plant is measured. The plant is 4 cm tall to start with and every day the plant grows 3 cm. What is the height of the plant after:

(i) Seven days   (ii) 20 days

Solution

Again, we can use a table to represent this data.
The plant grows 3 cm every day.

(i) Height of the plant after seven days

Day	Height (cm)
Day 1	4 + 3 = 7
Day 2	7 + 3 = 10
Day 3	10 + 3 = 13
Day 4	13 + 3 = 16
Day 5	16 + 3 = 19
Day 6	19 + 3 = 22
Day 7	22 + 3 = 25

After seven days, the plant height is 25 cm.

(ii) Height of the plant after 20 days

The plant grows 3 cm every day.

In 20 days it will have grown 20 × 3 = 60 cm.

The plant height was 4 cm to begin with.

Plant height = 60 + 4 = 64 cm

 ## Worked Example 8.11

John has €500 in his savings account. He decides to put €250 into his account every week.

(i) Show in a table the amount in John's savings account per week for four weeks.

(ii) How much money has John saved after 30 weeks?

Solution

(i) The amount in his savings account per week for four weeks

John saves €250 every week

Week	Amount (€)
Week 1	500 + 250 = 750
Week 2	750 + 250 = 1,000
Week 3	1,000 + 250 = 1,250
Week 4	1,250 + 250 = 1,500

(ii) How much money has John saved after 30 weeks?

He saves €250 every week.

In 30 weeks he will have saved
30 × 250 = €7,500.

John already had €500 in his account.

The total amount of money in John's account is €7,500 + €500 = €8,000.

Exercise 8.5

1. A bike is hired for €10 per day. €18 for insurance must also be paid (regardless of the number of days hired).

   Show in a table how much the bike costs to rent for five days.

2. A bus costs €50 to hire and then costs €5 per student. How much would it cost to hire the bus for:

   (i) 10 students

   (ii) 50 students

3. A scientist measures the bacteria in a petri dish. She counts 1,000 bacteria. If the bacteria numbers triple every hour, how many bacteria will there be in five hours?

4. A dry cleaner charges €7 per item of clothing. Find the cost of dry cleaning:

   (i) Five items of clothing

   (ii) 20 items of clothing

5. A bath contains 3 litres of water. A tap fills this bath at a rate of 500 ml per minute.

   (i) How many litres will be in the bath in 10 minutes?

   (ii) If the capacity of the bath is 50 litres, how long will it take for the bath to overflow?

6. Chairs in a restaurant are to be arranged as shown.

   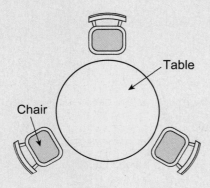
   Table
   Chair

   (i) How many chairs are needed for 10 tables?

   (ii) How many tables are needed for 60 chairs?

7. A pond contains 100 litres of water. Water evaporates from the pond at a rate of 1.5 litres per day. Assuming that no more water enters the pond:

   (i) How many litres will be left in the pond in five days?

   (ii) How many litres will be left in the pond in 15 days?

   (iii) How long will it take for the pond to empty?

8. A repeating pattern is made up of matchsticks.

   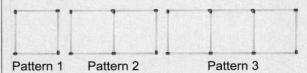
   Pattern 1   Pattern 2   Pattern 3

   (i) How many matchsticks will be needed to make Pattern 4?

   (ii) How many matchsticks will be needed to make Pattern 5?

   (iii) How many matchsticks will be needed to make Pattern 15?

9. Five miles is roughly equivalent to eight kilometres.

   (i) Show in a table, from 0 to 50 miles, the equivalent number of kilometres for every five miles.

   (ii) How many kilometres are there in 200 miles?

10. A mechanic charges €50 to fix a car plus €30 labour costs per hour.

    (i) Show in a table the charge to fix a car per hour up to a maximum of five hours.

    (ii) If a car cost a total of €230 to fix, how long did it take the mechanic to fix the car?

11. Bacteria in contaminated food are counted. The bacteria double in number every hour.

    (i) If there were 10,000 bacteria to begin with, find the number of bacteria in the food after 1, 2, 3, 4, 5 and 6 hours.

    (ii) Give a name to this type of growth.

12. The wind speed, in km/hr, measured at a lighthouse is shown in the table below.

Time	Wind speed (km/hr)
13:00	16
14:00	21
15:00	24
16:00	25
17:00	24
18:00	21

(i) Describe the pattern that this table shows.

(ii) What would be the wind speed at 20:00? Explain your answer (assuming the same pattern).

13. A firework is launched from the roof of an office block. Its height above the roof (in metres) is shown in the table below.

Time (seconds)	Height (m)
0	12
1	39
2	60
3	75
4	84
5	87
6	84
7	75
8	60
9	39

(i) From what height was the firework launched?

(ii) According to the table, how high did the firework go?

Revision Exercises

1. A repeating pattern is made up of pens.

Pattern 1   Pattern 2   Pattern 3

(i) Complete the following table:

Pattern number	Number of pens
1	1
2	4
3	
4	
5	

(ii) Describe the pattern in your own words.

(iii) How many pens will Pattern 4 need?

(iv) How many pens will Pattern 5 need?

(v) How many pens will Pattern 10 need?

2. Consider the following pattern:

Pattern 1   Pattern 2   Pattern 3

If the pattern continues as shown:

(i) Describe the pattern in your own words.

(ii) How many blocks will Pattern 4 need?

(iii) How many blocks will Pattern 6 need?

(iv) How many blocks will Pattern 20 need?

3. A pattern made of pebbles is laid out on a floor.

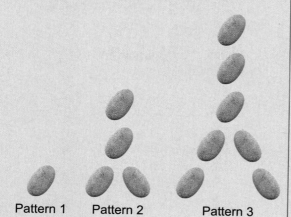

Pattern 1   Pattern 2   Pattern 3

(i) Describe the pattern in your own words.

(ii) How many pebbles will Pattern 4 need?

(iii) How many pebbles will Pattern 8 need?

(iv) How many complete patterns could be made out of 100 pebbles?

4. A repeating pattern made up of coloured blocks is made.

The pattern is Blue, Blue, Red, Orange.

(i) Draw a diagram to show this pattern.

(ii) What colour is the 22nd block?

(iii) What colour is the 35th block?

(iv) What colour is the 100th block?

5. An eight-marble repeating pattern made up of coloured marbles is shown.

(i) What colour is the 14th marble?

(ii) What colour is the 20th marble?

(iii) What colour is the 36th marble?

(iv) What colour is the 600th marble?

6. For each linear sequence, find:

(a) The start term   (b) The common difference   (c) The next three terms

(i) 6, 18, 30, 42, 54...   (iii) 9, 23, 37, 51, 65...   (v) −5, −11, −17, −23, −29...

(ii) 6, 21, 36, 51, 66...   (iv) 13, 28, 43, 58, 73...

7. In each of the following linear sequences, find:

(a) The start term   (c) The nth term (general term)

(b) The common difference   (d) The value of the given term

(i) 12, 26, 40, 54, 68...   Find 12th term.   (iv) 50, 77, 104, 131, 158...   Find 60th term.

(ii) 15, 17, 19, 21, 23...   Find 17th term.   (v) 326, 295, 264, 233, 202...   Find 23rd term.

(iii) 13, 31, 49, 67, 85...   Find 25th term.

8. For each exponential sequence, find:

(a) Whether it involves doubling or tripling

(b) The next three terms

(i) 6, 12, 24, 48, 96...

(ii) 4, 12, 36, 108, 324...

(iii) 10, 20, 40, 80, 160...

(iv) 27, 81, 243, 729, 2,187...

(v) 1.5, 4.5, 13.5, 40.5, 121.5...

9. For each quadratic sequence, find:

(a) The start term

(b) The second difference

(c) The next three terms

(i) 11, 16, 22, 29, 37...

(ii) 0, 6, 20, 42, 72...

(iii) 2, 4, 13, 29, 52...

(iv) 3, 4, 4, 3, 1...

(v) 5, 7, 5, −1, −11...

NUMBER PATTERNS

10. For each sequence:

(a) Identify whether it is linear, quadratic or exponential.

(b) In the case of each linear sequence, find the common first difference.

(c) In the case of each quadratic sequence, find the common second difference.

(d) Write down the start term.

(e) Find the next five terms.

    (i) 3, 7, 15, 27, 43...

    (ii) 5, 10, 20, 40, 80...

    (iii) 14, 31, 48, 65, 82...

    (iv) 15, 16, 19, 24, 31...

    (v) 5, 18, 31, 44, 57...

    (vi) 12, 36, 108, 324, 972...

    (vii) 8, 24, 40, 56, 72...

    (viii) 1, 2, 4, 7, 11...

    (ix) −3, −10, −17, −24, −31...

    (x) −3, −6, −5, 0, 9...

11. A car park has two charging options.

■ Option A: Pay a fee of €10 and then €3 per hour of parking.

■ Option B: €5 per hour of parking.

    (i) Complete the following table:

Hours parked	Cost option A	Cost option B
0		
1		
2		
3		
4		
5		

    (ii) How much would it cost to park for five hours under Option B?

    (iii) How much would it cost to park for eight hours under Option A?

    (iv) If someone wanted to park for 10 hours, which option would be cheaper?

12. Ben and Holly both open savings accounts with €1,000. The table shows how much they lodged into their account over three months.

Month	Ben	Holly
0	1,000	1,000
1	1,250	1,030
2	1,500	1,120
3	1,750	1,270

    (i) If Ben and Holly both continue to save as before, complete the table to show how much they would have saved in six months.

    (ii) What other term could be used instead of 0 months?

    (iii) After 12 months, who had saved the most?

13. A repeating pattern made from pens and red counters is shown.

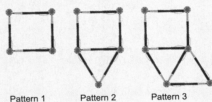

Pattern 1   Pattern 2   Pattern 3

    (i) How many pens and red counters will Pattern 4 need?

    (ii) How many red counters will Pattern 10 need?

    (iii) How many pens in total will patterns 1 to 6 use up?

14. An exponential repeating pattern made of blocks is shown.

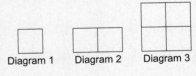

Diagram 1   Diagram 2   Diagram 3

    (i) How many blocks will be needed for Diagram 4?

    (ii) How many blocks will be needed for Diagram 5?

    (iii) How many blocks will be needed for Diagram 10?

If the pattern is quadratic instead of exponential:

    (iv) How many blocks will be needed for Diagram 4?

    (v) How many blocks will be needed for Diagram 5?

Algebra:
An Introduction

Learning Outcomes

In this chapter you will learn to:

- ⊃ Evaluate algebraic expressions
- ⊃ Add and subtract algebraic terms
- ⊃ Multiply algebraic terms
- ⊃ Multiply algebraic expressions

The word 'algebra' comes from the title of a book, *al-Jabr wa'l Muqabala*, written by Muhammad ibn Musa al-Khwarizmi, a Persian mathematician, in the ninth century. It was from this book that the idea and rules of algebra became widespread.

al-Khwarizmi

In his book al-Khwarizmi showed how various mathematical problems may be solved by using algebra. For example, Tom goes to the shops with €20 and buys one CD. If Tom has €8.50 change, how much did the CD cost?

Like many aspects of maths, algebra has certain rules that must be followed. The following sections will introduce you to the basic rules of algebra.

KEY WORDS
- **Variable**
- **Term**
- **Constant**
- **Coefficient**
- **Expression**

9.1 EVALUATING EXPRESSIONS

We can calculate what $11 + 5(2)$ is equal to by using certain mathematical rules.
But what if one of the numbers is unknown or changes?
If we pick the 2 as our variable, we can then write this sum as:

$11 + 5(x)$

x would be the **variable**.

11 would be the **constant**.

$5(x)$ would be an example of a **term**.
This is written as $5x$.

5 is called the **coefficient** of x.

This means that $7y$ would be $7(y)$.
$4xy$ would be $4(x)(y)$.

This also means that $x4$ is the same as $4x$.
However, we normally write it as $4x$.

For us to understand the basic concepts of algebra, we must be able to evaluate or work out various **expressions**.

> A **variable** is a letter (usually x or y) that represents a number. The number may change or be unknown. A **constant** is something that doesn't change value.

> A constant, a variable or a constant multiplied by a variable are all considered **terms**.

> A **coefficient** is a number or symbol multiplied with a variable in an algebraic term.

> An **algebraic expression** is an expression that contains one or more numbers, one or more variables, and one or more arithmetic operations.

x^2 **Worked Example 9.1**

Find the value of $2x - 5$ if: (i) $x = 4$ (ii) $x = -3$

Solution

We rewrite the expression, using brackets to replace the variable and insert (substitute) the given value of x.

(i) When $x = 4$

$2x - 5$

$= 2(4) - 5$

$= 8 - 5$

$= 3$

(ii) When $x = -3$

$2x - 5$

$= 2(-3) - 5$

$= -6 - 5$

$= -11$

x^2 Worked Example 9.2

If $a = 4$ and $b = -2$, find the value of the following expressions:

(i) $3a - 2b + 3$ (ii) $a^2 - b^2$ (iii) $2a^3 - 2b^5$ (iv) $2ab^2$

Solution

Again we rewrite the expression, using brackets to replace the variable, and insert the given value of a and b.

(i) $3a - 2b + 3$

$= 3(4) - 2(-2) + 3$

$= 12 + 4 + 3$

$= 19$

(ii) $a^2 - b^2$

$= (4)^2 - (-2)^2$

$= 16 - (4)$

$= 16 - 4$

$= 12$

(iii) $2a^3 - 2b^5$

$= 2(4)^3 - 2(-2)^5$

$= 2(64) - 2(-32)$

$= 128 + 64$

$= 192$

(iv) $2ab^2$

$= 2(4)(-2)^2$

$= 2(4)(4)$

$= 32$

$2ab^2$ could also be written as $2 \times a \times b \times b$.

 **ACTIVITIES 9.1, 9.2**

Exercise 9.1

1. If $x = 2$ and $y = 1$, find the value of:

(i) $x + y$ (iii) $y - x$ (v) $4x - 2y$ (vii) $3y - 2x$ (ix) $-x - y$

(ii) $x - y$ (iv) $2x + y$ (vi) $x + 7y$ (viii) $3x + 4y$ (x) $-3x - 2y$

2. If $a = 1$, $b = 2$ and $c = 3$, find the value of:

(i) $a + b + c$ (ii) $2a + b$ (iii) $3a - 4b - c$ (iv) $2a - 3b + 4c$ (v) $10a - 7b + 3c$

3. If $x = 5$, $y = 4$ and $z = -2$, find the value of:

(i) $x - y + z$ (ii) $2x - 2y - 2z$ (iii) $6x + 3y + z$ (iv) $3x - 5y - 2z$ (v) $4x + 2y + 10z$

4. If $p = -3$, $q = -1$ and $r = 2$, find the value of:

(i) $4(p + q)$ (ii) $2q + (r - p)$ (iii) $3(r + p) - 2q$ (iv) $-3(p - r) - q$ (v) $\frac{1}{3}p + \frac{1}{4}q - \frac{1}{2}r$

5. If $x = 1$, $y = 2$ and $z = -3$, find the value of:

(i) x^2 (iii) z^3 (v) $3y^2$ (vii) xy (ix) $\frac{1}{3}xyz$

(ii) y^2 (iv) $2x^2$ (vi) $7z^2$ (viii) x^2y (x) $x^2y^3z^2$

6. If $a = 4$, $b = 3$ and $c = 2$, find the value of:

(i) a^2 (iii) $-3c^2$ (v) $a^2 + 3b - 6c$ (vii) $a^3 + a^2 - a$ (ix) $2a^2 - 2b^2 + c^2$

(ii) b^2 (iv) $-a^2$ (vi) $2a^2 + b - c$ (viii) $3a^2 + b^2 - c$ (x) $4a^2 - b^2 - c^2$

7. If $p = -1$, $q = -4$ and $r = -3$, find the value of:

(i) pq (iii) $3rqp$ (v) $2p^2 + q^2$ (vii) $2(p - q)^2$ (ix) $(-3p - r)^{-q}$

(ii) pqr (iv) $3(p - q - r)$ (vi) $(p + r)^3$ (viii) $-rp - r$ (x) $\frac{1}{4}p^2 + \frac{1}{8}q^2 - \frac{1}{3}r^3$

9.2 ADDING AND SUBTRACTING TERMS

Ann goes shopping and buys five apples and four bananas. When she returns home, she adds them to her fruit bowl, which contains three apples and two bananas.

How many apples and bananas does Ann now have?

The answer is eight apples and six bananas.

This problem illustrates a basic rule for adding and subtracting algebraic terms.

First we let a = apples and b = bananas.

This question could then be written as:

$5a + 4b + 3a + 2b$

$= 8a + 6b$

When considering if terms are alike or the same, we must also consider the power of the term. $5x^2 + 6x$ cannot be added, as the terms are not the same. x^2 is not the same as x.

We could, however, add $5x^2 + 4x^2$, which leads us to our next rule.

5 oranges + 4 oranges = 9 oranges

$5x^2 + 4x^2 = 9x^2$

> **Algebra Rule:** We can only add or subtract terms that have the same letter(s) raised to the same power. These are referred to as like terms.

> **Algebra Rule:** When adding or subtracting like terms, the powers of the variables do not change.

x^2 Worked Example 9.3

Simplify each of the following:

    (i) $x + x + x$ (ii) $2y - 4y + 3y$ (iii) $2a^2 + 3a^2 - 6a^2$

> 'Simplify' means to make the expression simpler by adding, subtracting, multiplying or dividing.

Solution

    (i) $x + x + x$ (ii) $2y - 4y + 3y$ (iii) $2a^2 + 3a^2 - 6a^2$

        $= 3x$ $= -2y + 3y$ $= 5a^2 - 6a^2$

                          $= y$ $= -a^2$

x^2 ## Worked Example 9.4

Simplify each of the following:

(i) $4x - 2y + 3x - 5y + 3$ (ii) $5a^2 - 2a - 7 + 4a - 3a^2 + 3$ (iii) $2x^3y^2 - 3x^2y^3 - 4x^3y^2$

Solution

(i) $4x - 2y + 3x - 5y + 3$

> It can sometimes be easier to put the like terms together. This is called grouping the like terms.

$= 4x + 3x - 2y - 5y + 3$

$= 7x - 7y + 3$

(ii) $5a^2 - 2a - 7 + 4a - 3a^2 + 3$

$= 5a^2 - 3a^2 - 2a + 4a - 7 + 3$

$= 2a^2 + 2a - 4$

> For our final answer we usually put the term with the highest power first, the term with the next highest power second and so on.

(iii) $2x^3y^2 - 3x^2y^3 - 4x^3y^2$

$= 2x^3y^2 - 4x^3y^2 - 3x^2y^3$

$= -2x^3y^2 - 3x^2y^3$

> Remember that x^3y^2 is not the same as x^2y^3.

 ACTIVITIES 9.3, 9.4

Exercise 9.2

Simplify each of the following questions:

1. (i) $x + x$ (iii) $2y + 4y$ (v) $4b + 2b$ (vii) $4z + 7z$ (ix) $3x - 3x$
    (ii) $2x - x$ (iv) $2a + a$ (vi) $7x - 3x$ (viii) $8y - 3y$ (x) $10a - 7a$

2. (i) $x + x + x$ (ii) $4a + 5a + 4$ (iii) $7b - 7b + b$ (iv) $2c + 5c - 3c$ (v) $10x + 5x - 6x + 2$

3. (i) $2a + 3b + a$ (iii) $7p - 6q - 4p - q$ (v) $8a - 4b - 3b + 2a$
    (ii) $4x + 2y - 3x - y$ (iv) $-3m + 2n - 4m + 3n + 4$ (vi) $3p + 2q + 7q - 4p$

4. (i) $3ab + 2ab - 4ab$ (iii) $pq - 3pq + 4rq$ (v) $4ba + 2ba - 3bc$
    (ii) $4xy - 3xy + 7xy$ (iv) $-4mn + 10nm - 3nm$ (vi) $2xy - 4yz - 6yz$

5. (i) $4x - 3x + 4y - 2x + 3y + 4y$ (iv) $8m + 2n + 5l - 3l - 2n - 5m$
    (ii) $2a + 3b - c + 3a - 8b + 3c$ (v) $20x - 20y - 30z - 20x + 23y - 30z$
    (iii) $12p + 24q - r - 5q - 12p + r$ (vi) $9a + 12b - 8c + 7c - 4b + 3a$

6. (i) $3ab + 4bd - 2ab + 8bd$ (iv) $4xy + 9 + 2yx - 5x + 2q$
    (ii) $7xy + 7xz - 3xy - 9xz$ (v) $6ab + 2cd - 4ab + dc + a$
    (iii) $-9pq + 6rq - 6pq + 7rq + 8qp$ (vi) $2xy + 3xz - 4xy + 2zx$

7. (i) $x^2 + x^2 + x^2$ (iv) $y^3 + 5y^3 + 2y^3$ (vii) $6h^4 - 2h^4$ (x) $-3m + 2m - 6m^2$

(ii) $a^3 + a^3$ (v) $7a^2 - 5a^2 + a^2$ (viii) $4x^2 + 3x^2 + x$

(iii) $c^2 + 2c^2$ (vi) $-2p^2 - 3p^2 + p^2 + 4p^2$ (ix) $10z + 5z^3 - 6z^3$

8. (i) $5x^2 + 2x + 4x - 4x^2$ (iii) $p^2 - 4p + p^3 - 2p^2 - 5p$ (v) $y^3 - 3y + y^2$

(ii) $b^3 + 2b^2 + b + b^3 - 2b^2 - 3b$ (iv) $-r^2 + 2r + 5 - r^2 + 7r - 6$ (vi) $3r^2 - 8t^2 + r^2 - 2t^2$

9. (i) $p^2 + q^2 + p^2$ (v) $3p^2 - 2q^2 + p^2 - q^2$ (ix) $4x^2y - 2xy^2 - 3x^2y - 2xy^2$

(ii) $2x^2 + 2y^2 + 3x^2 - 4y^2$ (vi) $-r^2 + 2r + 5 - r^2 + 7r - 6$ (x) $-3pq^2 + 2q^2p - 6pq^2 + p^2q$

(iii) $2m^2 - 3n^2 + m^2 - n^2$ (vii) $4 + 4x^2 - 3y^2 + 7 - 6x^2 + 5y^2$

(iv) $a^2 - 3b^2 + 5a^2 - 2b^2$ (viii) $4ab^2 + 3ab^2$

9.3 MULTIPLYING TERMS

When we multiply terms, we encounter another set of rules that it is important to understand.

Algebra Rule: To multiply terms: number × number, variable × variable.

$(5a)(10b) = (5)(10)(a)(b) = 50ab$

$(10x)(20y) = (10)(20)(x)(y) = 200xy$

Special care must be taken when dealing with terms that have powers and share the same letter (variable).

Consider $2^3 \times 2^1 = 2 \times 2 \times 2 \times 2 = 2^4 (2^{3+1})$.

Algebra Rule: When multiplying terms that have the same letter, we add the powers or indices.

$5 \times 5 = 5^2$ **or** $5^1 \times 5^1 = 5^2$ $3 \times 3 \times 3 = 3^3$ **or** $3^1 \times 3^1 \times 3^1 = 3^3$ $7^3 \times 7 = 7^4$ **or** $7^3 \times 7^1 = 7^4$

Therefore:

$a \times a = a^2$

$b^2 \times b = b^3$ **or** $b \times b \times b = b^3$

$y^3 \times y^5 = y^8$ **or** $(y \times y \times y) \times (y \times y \times y \times y \times y) = y^8$

 ACTIVITY 9.5

x^2 Worked Example 9.5

Simplify each of the following:

(i) $(3x)(2)$ (ii) $(4x)(3x)$ (iii) $(3x)(2xy)$

Solution

(i) $(3x)(2)$

$= (3)(2)(x)$

$= 6x$

(ii) $(4x)(3x)$

$= (4)(3)(x)(x)$

$= 12x^2$

(iii) $(3x)(2xy)$

$= (3)(2)(x)(x)(y)$

$= 6x^2y$

x^2 **Worked Example 9.6**

Multiply:

(i) $(2x^2y^3)(4y^2)$ (ii) $(-7x^2)(6y^2z)$ (iii) $(3x^2)(-2y^2)(3x^2)$

Solution

(i) $(2x^2y^3)(4y^2)$

$= (2)(4)(x^2)(y^3)(y^2)$

$= (2)(4)(x)(x)(y)(y)(y)(y)(y)$

$= 8x^2y^5$

(ii) $(-7x^2)(6y^2z)$

$= (-7)(6)(x^2)(y^2)(z)$

$= -42x^2y^2z$

(iii) $(3x^2)(-2y^2)(3x^2)$

$= (3)(-2)(3)(x^2)(y^2)(x^2)$

$= -18x^4y^2$

Exercise 9.3

Simplify each of the following questions:

1. (i) $(4)(5x)$
(ii) $(2y)(8)$
(iii) $(10r)(5)$
(iv) $(-3x)(4)$
(v) $(-5a)(-a)$

2. (i) $(x)(x)$
(ii) $(x)(y)$
(iii) $(x)(x^2)$
(iv) $(-p)(p^3)$
(v) $(p^2)(-p)$

3. (i) $(2x)(4x)$
(ii) $(5y)(2y)$
(iii) $(10y)(3y^2)$
(iv) $(-3x^2)(-4x^3)$
(v) $(-5x^2)(2)$

4. (i) $(x)(xy)$
(ii) $(10x)(5xy)$
(iii) $(7xy)(7xy)$
(iv) $(-4pq)(2pq^2)$
(v) $(-3m)(-3mn)$

5. (i) $(2y)(-4y)(y)$
(ii) $(2x)(3x^2)(4)$
(iii) $(5m)(5m)(2m^2)$
(iv) $(-3a)(4a^2)(-2a)$
(v) $(-2t)(-t)(-4t)$

6. (i) $(3y)(-2y)(x)$
(ii) $(y)(3y^2)(-2)$
(iii) $(3p)(7q^2)(4p)$
(iv) $(8a)(2b^2)(-3a^2)$
(v) $(-4y^2)(-x^2)(-x)$

7. (i) $(4xy)(2x)(3y)$
(ii) $(x)(2xy)(y^2)$
(iii) $(-2m)(-3m^2n)(4mn)$
(iv) $(-4ab)(2ab)(3a^2)$
(v) $(-2p^2q)(pq^2)(p)$

8. (i) $(2ab)^2$
(ii) $(4xy)^2$
(iii) $(-2ab)^2$
(iv) $(3xy^2)^3$
(v) $(-4a^2b)^3$

9.4 MULTIPLYING TERMS WITH BRACKETS 1

We should already understand the use of brackets from BIMDAS. For example, $5(3+1) = 5(4) = 20$.

There is, however, an alternative method that can be used to solve this sum:

$5(3+1) = 5(3) + 5(1)$

> Both numbers inside the bracket are multiplied by +5.

$= 15 + 5 = 20$

Both methods will give the correct answer.

The second method is used to deal with questions involving brackets in algebra.

$5(x + 1)$

> Each inside term is multiplied by the outside term.

$= 5(x) + 5(1)$

> Both numbers inside the bracket are multiplied by +5.

$= 5x + 5$

x^2 Worked Example 9.7

Remove the brackets and simplify:

| The same question may be phrased as expand the brackets and simplify. |

(i) $2(x + 4)$

(ii) $3(4a - 3)$

(iii) $-2(4y - 1)$

(iv) $5(2a - b) - 3(a - 2)$

(v) $2(x + y - 1) - (2x + 2y - 1)$

Solution

(i) $2(x + 4)$

$= 2(x) + 2(4)$

$= 2x + 8$

| The outside term is a positive 2. |

(ii) $3(4a - 3)$

$= 3(4a) + 3(-3)$

$= 12a - 9$

(iii) $-2(4y - 1)$

$= -2(4y) - 2(-1)$

$= -8y + 2$

| The outside term is a negative 2. |

(iv) $5(2a - b) - 3(a - 2)$

$= 5(2a) + 5(-b) - 3(a) - 3(-2)$

$= 10a - 5b - 3a + 6$

To make it easier for us to simplify we group the terms.

$= 10a - 3a - 5b + 6$

We can now add/subtract the like terms.

$= 7a - 5b + 6$

(v) $2(x + y - 1) - (2x + 2y - 1)$

We insert a 1 outside the second bracket to aid in the multiplying.

$= 2(x + y - 1) - 1(2x + 2y - 1)$

$= 2x + 2y - 2 - 2x - 2y + 1$

$= 2x - 2x + 2y - 2y - 2 + 1$

$= -1$

 **ACTIVITY** 9.6

x^2 Worked Example 9.8

Remove the brackets and simplify:

(i) $2(x^2 + 4x + 2) + 4(x^2 + 3x - 2)$

(ii) $3(2y^2 + 4y - 1) - 2(y^2 + 3y - 1)$

Solution

(i) $2(x^2 + 4x + 2) + 4(x^2 + 3x - 2)$

$= 2(x^2) + 2(4x) + 2(2) + 4(x^2) + 4(3x) + 4(-2)$

$= 2x^2 + 8x + 4 + 4x^2 + 12x - 8$

We now group the terms.

$= 2x^2 + 4x^2 + 8x + 12x + 4 - 8$

$= 6x^2 + 20x - 4$

(ii) $3(2y^2 + 4y - 1) - 2(y^2 + 3y - 1)$

$= 3(2y^2) + 3(4y) + 3(-1) - 2(y^2) - 2(3y) - 2(-1)$

$= 6y^2 + 12y - 3 - 2y^2 - 6y + 2$

$= 6y^2 - 2y^2 + 12y - 6y - 3 + 2$

$= 4y^2 + 6y - 1$

9

Exercise 9.4

In each question remove the brackets and simplify:

1. (i) $2(x + 2)$

(ii) $4(x - 3)$

(iii) $3(x + 2)$

(iv) $3(x - 4)$

(v) $8(x - 8)$

2. (i) $4(2y + 3)$

(ii) $9(3y - 1)$

(iii) $-4(2y - 3)$

(iv) $5(7y + 2)$

(v) $-(4y + 5)$

3. (i) $2(2a + b)$

(ii) $4(3a - 2b)$

(iii) $7(11a + 4b)$

(iv) $-3(a - 3b)$

(v) $-4(-b - 7a)$

4. (i) $8(4x + 2y - 3)$

(ii) $6(2x - 3y + 4)$

(iii) $2(3x - 4y - 9)$

(iv) $-3(5x + 6y + 2)$

(v) $-4(7x - 2y - 1)$

5. (i) $7(x^2 + y)$

(ii) $4(x^2 - 7y^2)$

(iii) $-3(x^2 - 2y^2)$

(iv) $5(2x^2 + 4y^2 - 3)$

(v) $-(x^2 - 2y^2 + 7)$

6. (i) $4(x + 2) + 3(x + 1)$

(ii) $3(y + 4) + 5(y - 1)$

(iii) $2(p - 2) - 3(p + 4)$

(iv) $5(q - 3) - 2(x - 5)$

(v) $-4(m - 1) + 2(x - 8)$

7. (i) $4(x + 1) + 2(4x + 2)$

(ii) $3(6x + 2) + 4(3x - 3)$

(iii) $2(y + 3) - 3(8y - 5)$

(iv) $4(2a - 2) - (7a - 12)$

(v) $-3(2b + 2) - 2(2 - 4b)$

8. (i) $4(2x + y - 3) + 3(x + y - 2)$

(ii) $2(3a + b + 5) + 4(a + 2b - 3)$

(iii) $1(m + n - 2) + 2(m - 4n - 6)$

(iv) $5(y - 2z - 2) + (3y - 2z + 1)$

(v) $3(4p - 3q + 5) - 2(3p - 5q - 1)$

(vi) $(2a + 4b + 3) - (4a - 2b)$

(vii) $-(5x - 2y + 2) + 3(2x - 4)$

(viii) $2(-5x - 3y - 4) - (-2y + 2x - 4)$

9. (i) $3(2x^2 + 2x + 2) + 4(x^2 + x + 3)$

(ii) $2(y^2 + 4y - 2) + 3(y^2 + y - 2)$

(iii) $3(p^2 - p + 1) + 2(p^2 + p + 4)$

(iv) $(5a^2 + 3a - 2) - 3(3a^2 + 5a - 3)$

(v) $5(m^2 - 2m - 1) - 4(m^2 - m - 1)$

(vi) $4(b^2 - 5b + 4) - (2b^2 - 2b - 1)$

(vii) $-2(4c^2 + 1) - 3(2c^2 + 2c)$

(viii) $-(3x^2 + 8x - 1) + 4(2x^2 - 2)$

9.5 MULTIPLYING TERMS WITH BRACKETS 2

Sometimes when multiplying out brackets we have to deal with terms whose power or index will change.

$5x(x + 4)$

Again we multiply each inside term by the outside term, in this case $+5x$.

$5x(x) + 5x(4) = 5x^2 + 20x$

x^2 Worked Example 9.9

Remove the brackets and simplify:

(i) $2x(x - 1)$ (ii) $-a(2a^2 - 3a)$ (iii) $2x(x - 3) - 4x(x + 3)$ (iv) $2x(x^2 + x - 1) - 2(x - 1)$

Solution

(i) $2x(x - 1)$
$= 2x(x) + 2x(-1)$
$= 2x^2 - 2x$

(ii) $-a(2a^2 - 3a)$
$= -a(2a^2) - a(-3a)$
$= -2a^3 + 3a^2$

(iii) $2x(x - 3) - 4x(x + 3)$
$= 2x^2 - 6x - 4x^2 - 12x$
$= 2x^2 - 4x^2 - 6x - 12x$
$= -2x^2 - 18x$

(iv) $2x(x^2 + x - 1) - 2(x - 1)$
$= 2x^3 + 2x^2 - 2x - 2x + 2$
$= 2x^3 + 2x^2 - 4x + 2$

ACTIVITY 9.7

Exercise 9.5

In each question remove the brackets and simplify:

1. (i) $2x(x + 3)$
(ii) $3y(y + 4)$
(iii) $5p(p + 2)$
(iv) $3r(r - 2)$
(v) $4a(2a - 3)$

2. (i) $3a(2a^2 + 1)$
(ii) $2p(2p^2 + 2)$
(iii) $b^2(b - 3)$
(iv) $-5y^2(y - 4)$

3. (i) $4x(x^2 - 1)$
(ii) $7a(2a^2 + 4)$
(iii) $2p(3p^2 + 2)$
(iv) $-3y(y^2 - 4)$
(v) $2b(-3 - b^2)$

4. (i) $2a(2a^2 + 1) + a(a^2 + 1)$
(ii) $p(p^2 + 3) + 2p(2p^2 + 3)$
(iii) $x^2(x - 3) + 3(x^3 + 2)$
(iv) $y^2(y - 1) - 2y(3y^2 - 4)$
(v) $x^2(3x - x) - x(x^2 + 2)$

5. (i) $a(a^2 + a + 1) + a(a^2 + 2a + 1)$
(ii) $3x(2x^2 + 2x + 2) + 4x(x^2 + x + 3)$
(iii) $p(2p^2 - 2p + 1) + 2p(p^2 - p - 4)$
(iv) $2y(3y^2 - y - 1) + 3y(y^2 + 4y + 2)$
(v) $5m(m^2 - 2m - 1) - 4m(m^2 - 2m - 1)$
(vi) $4x(2x^2 - 2x + 2) - 4x(x^2 - x - 2)$

(vii) $7y(y^2 - 2y - 1) - 5y(y^2 + y - 3)$
(viii) $2y(2 - 2[y^2 - 4y]) + 3y(y^2 + y - 2)$
(ix) $3x(2x^3 + 2x + 2) - x(x^2 - x - 3)$

6. (i) $3ab(2ab + 2a + b) + 2a(2ab + 2b - a)$
(ii) $4(1 - [2x^2 - x + 1]) + 4(x^3 - 3)$

9.6 MULTIPLYING TWO EXPRESSIONS

Another type of algebra question involves the multiplication of two expressions. For example, $(x + 3)(x - 4)$.

Again we can use numbers to explain the method used.

$(5 + 3)(5 - 4) = (8)(1) = 8$

However:

$5(5 - 4) + 3(5 - 4)$
$= 5(5) + 5(-4) + 3(5) + 3(-4)$
$= 25 - 20 + 15 - 12$
$= 8$

If we apply this method to our algebra question:

$(x + 3)(x - 4) = x(x - 4) + 3(x - 4)$

> First term by second bracket ± second term by second bracket.

$= x(x) + x(-4) + 3(x) + 3(-4)$
$= x^2 - 4x + 3x - 12$
$= x^2 - x - 12$

x^2 Worked Example 9.10

Remove the brackets and simplify:

(i) $(x + 1)(x + 7)$ (ii) $(x + 3)(x - 2)$ (iii) $(y - 1)(y - 3)$

Solution

(i) $(x + 1)(x + 7)$
$= x(x + 7) + 1(x + 7)$

> Check that both brackets use the second expression.

$= x(x) + x(7) + 1(x) + 1(7)$
$= x^2 + 7x + x + 7$
$= x^2 + 8x + 7$

(ii) $(x + 3)(x - 2)$
$= x(x - 2) + 3(x - 2)$
$= x(x) + x(-2) + 3(x) + 3(-2)$
$= x^2 - 2x + 3x - 6$
$= x^2 + x - 6$

(iii) $(y - 1)(y - 3)$
$= y(y - 3) - 1(y - 3)$
$= y(y) + y(-3) - 1(y) - 1(-3)$
$= y^2 - 3y - y + 3$
$= y^2 - 4y + 3$

ACTIVITY 9.8

x^2 Worked Example 9.11

Remove the brackets and simplify:

(i) $(x - 1)(2x - 5)$ (ii) $(2a - 3)(4a + 3)$ (iii) $(2x - 3)^2$

Solution

(i) $(x - 1)(2x - 5)$
$= x(2x - 5) - 1(2x - 5)$
$= 2x^2 - 5x - 2x + 5$
$= 2x^2 - 7x + 5$

(ii) $(2a - 3)(4a + 3)$
$= 2a(4a + 3) - 3(4a + 3)$
$= 8a^2 + 6a - 12a - 9$
$= 8a^2 - 6a - 9$

(iii) $(2x - 3)^2$
$= (2x - 3)(2x - 3)$
$= 2x(2x - 3) - 3(2x - 3)$
$= 4x^2 - 6x - 6x + 9$
$= 4x^2 - 12x + 9$

Exercise 9.6

Multiply each of the following expressions and simplify your answer:

1. (i) $(x + 1)(x + 2)$
(ii) $(a + 3)(a + 4)$
(iii) $(b + 5)(b + 1)$
(iv) $(m + 7)(m + 1)$
(v) $(y + 1)(y + 10)$

2. (i) $(x + 1)(x - 3)$
(ii) $(x - 2)(x + 2)$
(iii) $(a + 2)(a - 3)$
(iv) $(r - 6)(r + 1)$
(v) $(y + 1)(y - 5)$

3. (i) $(y - 2)(y - 4)$
(ii) $(y - 5)(y - 1)$
(iii) $(x - 3)(x - 2)$
(iv) $(p - 1)(p - 3)$
(v) $(a - 2)(a - 2)$

4. (i) $(2a + 2)(a + 1)$ (vi) $(5x - 4)(x + 1)$
(ii) $(4x + 1)(x + 1)$ (vii) $(6y + 1)(2y - 4)$
(iii) $(3x - 2)(2x + 3)$ (viii) $(4x - 3)(2x - 4)$
(iv) $(2b - 3)(4b + 2)$ (ix) $(3 - 2a)(2 - 5a)$
(v) $(2a - 2)(3a - 2)$ (x) $(4 - 2a)(3a - 1)$

5. (i) $(x + 1)^2$ (iv) $(y - 2)^2$
(ii) $(x + 2)^2$ (v) $(2a - 1)^2$
(iii) $(y - 4)^2$ (vi) $(5a - 2)^2$

6. (i) $(x + 2)(x + 1) + (x + 3)(x + 2)$
(ii) $(y + 3)(y - 1) + (y - 2)(y - 2)$
(iii) $(a - 4)(a - 2) - (a + 1)(a - 4)$

ALGEBRA: AN INTRODUCTION

1. (a) If $x = 5$, find the value of:

   (i) $2x + 7$ (iv) $x - 9$

   (ii) $5x - 1$ (v) $11 - 2x$

   (iii) $x + 3$ (vi) x^2

(b) If $a = 3$ and $b = -7$, find the value of:

   (i) $a + b$ (iv) $2a - 3b$

   (ii) $a - b$ (v) $1 - (a + b)$

   (iii) $2a + 3b$ (vi) $a^2 + 2ab + b^2$

(c) If $a = 3$, $b = -5$ and $c = -1$, evaluate the following:

   (i) $a + b + c$

   (ii) $a - b - c$

   (iii) $3a + 5b - 10c$

   (iv) $a + 2(b - c)$

   (v) $ab + c$

   (vi) $a - 2bc$

   (vii) ab^2

   (viii) a^2b

   (ix) $a + b(c + 4)^2$

   (x) $10abc - 3abc - 7abc$

2. (a) If $y = 6$, find the value of:

   (i) $8y$ (iv) $10y - 2y$

   (ii) $6y + 2y$ (v) $9y - y$

   (iii) $y + 7y$ (vi) $y^2 + 2y + 2$

(b) If $a = 3$, $b = 4$ and $c = -5$, evaluate:

   (i) $a + b + c$ (iii) $\dfrac{a^2 + b^2}{c^2}$

   (ii) $a - b - c$ (iv) $\sqrt{2ab - 8c}$

(c) If $x = 4$ and $y = -2$, insert the correct symbol ($<$, $>$ or $=$) between each pair of brackets.

   (i) $(x + y)$ $(x - y)$

   (ii) $(4x + x)$ $(5x)$

   (iii) $(10y - 3y)$ $(7y)$

   (iv) (xy^2) (x^2y)

   (v) $(x^2 + y^2)$ $(x + y)^2$

   (vi) $(2x^2)$ $(2x)^2$

   (vii) $(3xy)$ $(5xy - 2xy)$

   (viii) $\left(\dfrac{x}{y}\right)$ $\left(\dfrac{y}{x}\right)$

3. (a) Simplify each of the following:

   (i) $2a + 5a$

   (ii) $a + 2a + 3a$

   (iii) $9a^2 + 3a^2$

   (iv) $-x - x$

   (v) $2x - x - x$

(b) Simplify each of the following:

   (i) $2a + 3b + 9c + 7a - b - 11c$

   (ii) $3x^2 - x - 3 + 7x^2 + 5x - 8$

   (iii) $3y^3 + 3x^2 - 2y^2 + 3x^2 + 3x - 2y + 4$

(c) Simplify each of the following:

   (i) $3x^2 + 4x - 7 + x^2 - 8x - 1$

   (ii) $11ab - xy - xy - ab - x^2$

   (iii) $2a - b - 2c - a + b - c$

   (iv) $5x^2 + 7x^3 - 4x^2 - x^3 - 4x^3 - x^3$

   (v) $\dfrac{1}{2}x + 7y + 3x - \dfrac{1}{2}y - \dfrac{3}{4}x - y$

4. (a) Multiply each of the following:

   (i) $a^5 \times a^4$ (vi) $(2x)(3x)(4x)$

   (ii) $(3y)(4y)$ (vii) $(7y)(-2y^2)(5y^3)$

   (iii) $(3x)(5x)$ (viii) $(-4x)^2$

   (iv) $(9p)(-2p)$ (ix) $(-2x)^3$

   (v) $(-3t)(-4t)$ (x) $(2a^2)^3$

(b) If $a = 2$ and $b = 5$, insert the correct symbol ($<$, $>$ or $=$) between each pair of brackets.

   (i) (ab^2) (ab^2)

   (ii) $(ab)^3$ (a^3b^3)

   (iii) $(a + b)^2$ $(a^2 + b^2)$

   (iv) $(2a^2b)^2$ $(2a^4b^2)$

   (v) $(b - a)^3$ $(b^3 - a^3)$

(c) Simplify each of the following (if possible):

    (i) $2ab + 3ab$

    (ii) $(2ab)(3ab)$

    (iii) $2ab - 3ab$

    (iv) $3x + 4y$

    (v) $(3x)(4y)$

    (vi) $3x - 4y$

    (vii) $3x^2y + 5x^2y$

    (viii) $(3x^2y)(5x^2y)$

    (ix) $3x^2y - 5x^2y$

    (x) $4x^2 + 5x$

    (xi) $(4x^2) + (5x)$

    (xii) $4x^2 - 5x$

    (xiii) $5y^3 + y^3$

    (xiv) $(5y^3)(y^3)$

    (xv) $5y^3 - y^3$

5. (a) Remove the brackets:

    (i) $3(2a + 4b)$

    (ii) $4(5x - 2y)$

    (iii) $7(3a + b)$

    (iv) $10(6a - 5b + c)$

    (v) $2(10a + 9b + c)$

(b) Remove the brackets and simplify:

    (i) $2(3p + 2q) + 5(3p + q)$

    (ii) $4(3x - 2y) + 3(x - y)$

    (iii) $7(a - 2b) - 6(a - 4b)$

    (iv) $2(p + 3q) - 5(p - 2q)$

    (v) $2(5m - 4n) - (3m - 7n)$

(c) Remove the brackets and simplify:

    (i) $2(x^2 - 4x + 5) - 3(x^2 + x - 3)$

    (ii) $4(2x^2 + 5x - 1) - (8x^2 - 2x + 7)$

    (iii) $2(6x^2 - 5x + 7) - 3x(4x - 2)$

    (iv) $5x(x - 3) - 2(x^2 - x - 1)$

    (v) $x^2(x - 1) + x(x - 1) + (x - 1)$

6. (a) If $A = x^2 - x - 1$ and $B = 2x^2 + 3x - 4$, write these in terms of x:

    (i) $A + B$

    (ii) $A - B$

    (iii) $2A - B$

(b) $p = 4k - 3t$, $q = 5k - t$ and $r = k - 9t$. Write these in terms of k and t:

    (i) $p + q + r$

    (ii) $2p + q - 5r$

    (iii) $4p - 3q - r$

(c) Expand the brackets:

    (i) $2x(x^2 + 1)$ (iv) $2x(x^2 + 7)$

    (ii) $3a(a^2 - 5)$ (v) $3x(x^2 - 9)$

    (iii) $y(y^2 - 7)$ (vi) $10a(a^2 - 8)$

7. (a) Expand the brackets and simplify:

    (i) $(a + 10)(a + 2)$

    (ii) $(x + 3)(x + 10)$

    (iii) $(y + 2)(y + 6)$

    (iv) $(a + 1)(a + 5)$

    (v) $(x - 3)(x + 5)$

(b) Expand the brackets and simplify:

    (i) $(2x - 1)(3x + 4)$

    (ii) $(3x + 2)(2x - 5)$

    (iii) $(3x - 1)(4x - 1)$

    (iv) $(5p - 1)(4p - 3)$

    (v) $(2a - b)(3a - 4b)$

(c) Expand the brackets and simplify:

    (i) $(2b + 7)^2$

    (ii) $(x + 12)^2$

    (iii) $(5t - 4)^2$

    (iv) $2(x - 6)^2$

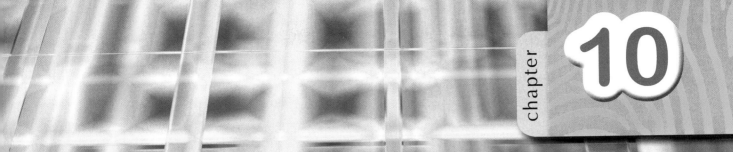

chapter 10

Algebra: Solving Linear Equations

Learning Outcomes

In this chapter you will learn to:

⮕ Solve first-degree equations in one variable (coefficients elements of Z)

10.1 SOLVING EQUATIONS 1

Al-Khwarizmi's book *al-Jabr wa'l Muqabala* explains a set of rules that can be used to find the value of an unknown variable in a question.

If $3x + 2 = 20$, what is the value of x?

This is referred to as 'solving'.

> This chapter will explain how to solve linear equations in one variable, i.e. there will be one unknown and its power will be 1. These are also called first-degree equations.

> An **equation** is when a term or expression is equal (=) to some value.

KEY WORDS

- **Equation**
- **Balance**
- **Equal sign**

One of the most basic equations is one where we only have one term equal to a certain value.

$5x = 10$

This means that 5 times $x = 10$ (or $x + x + x + x + x = 10$).

So 5 times a certain number is equal to 10.

To find the value of that number we divide 10 by 5.

$\therefore x = 2$

ACTIVITY 10.1

x^2 Worked Example 10.1

Solve for x in each of the following equations:

   (i) $2x = 8$ (iv) $20 = 4x$

   (ii) $3x = 9$ (v) $-5x = 30$

   (iii) $20x = 100$ (vi) $4x = -8$

Solution

   (i) $2x = 8$

      We want to find the value of one x, but we have the value of two x's.

      So we divide both sides of the equation by 2.

> The **equal sign** divides an equation into two sides – left and right.

> **Algebra Rule:** What you do to one side of the equation you must do to the other side as well. This is called **balancing** the equation.

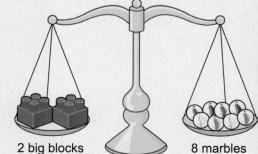

2 big blocks   8 marbles

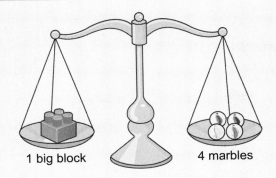

1 big block   4 marbles

$$\frac{2x}{2} = \frac{8}{2}$$
$$x = 4$$

(ii) $3x = 9$

If 3 times x gives us 9, then the inverse operation 9 ÷ 3 should give us x.

$$\frac{3x}{3} = \frac{9}{3}$$
$$x = 3$$

Algebra Rule: We divide both sides of the equation by the number in front of the x (variable).

(iii) $20x = 100$
$$\frac{20x}{20} = \frac{100}{20}$$
$$x = 5$$

If needed, we can check to see if our answer is correct. 20 × 5 is equal to 100 ∴ we know our answer is right.

(iv) $20 = 4x$

The equation is written in the opposite direction. The rules, however, still apply.

$$\frac{20}{4} = \frac{4x}{4}$$
$$5 = x$$

This is more commonly written as $x = 5$.

If A = B, then B = A.

(v) $-5x = 30$

Note that the number in front of the x is −5.

$$\frac{-5x}{-5} = \frac{30}{-5}$$

A negative divided by a negative is a positive.

$$x = -6$$

(vi) $4x = -8$
$$\frac{4x}{4} = \frac{-8}{4}$$

A negative divided by a positive is a negative.

$$x = -2$$

 **ACTIVITY 10.2**

 ## Exercise 10.1

Solve each of the following equations:

1. (i) $2x = 10$
(ii) $5x = 50$
(iii) $3a = 15$
(iv) $4b = 32$
(v) $30c = 30$

2. (i) $4x = -20$
(ii) $2x = -18$
(iii) $-7a = 49$
(iv) $-6p = 48$
(v) $-9x = 72$

3. (i) $-2x = -8$
(ii) $-3x = -9$
(iii) $-20x = -60$
(iv) $-4x = -64$
(v) $-x = -5$

4. (i) $16 = 8x$
(ii) $5x = 0$
(iii) $-150 = 50x$
(iv) $-20 = 5a$
(v) $0 = -3x$

10.2 SOLVING EQUATIONS 2

Once we have learned how to solve basic equations, we can then move on to equations that require more than one step to solve them.

The first of these types is where we have an extra term either side of the equal sign, for example, $3x + 1 = 22$.

We know that once we have $3x = $ a number, we can solve for x.

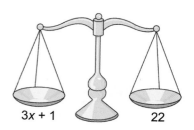

$3x + 1$ 22

Therefore, we must remove the $+ 1$ from the left-hand side of the equation.

To do this, we subtract 1 from the left-hand side of the equation:

$3x + 1 - 1$

Following the rules we learned in the previous section, we must always balance an equation. If we subtract 1 from the left-hand side, we must also subtract 1 from the right-hand side:

$3x + 1 - 1 = 22 - 1$

$3x = 21$

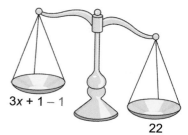

$3x + 1 - 1$

22

Once we have the equation in this form, we can then solve for x:

$\dfrac{3x}{3} = \dfrac{21}{3}$

$x = 7$

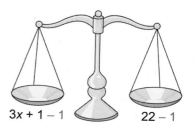

$3x + 1 - 1$ $22 - 1$

x^2 Worked Example 10.2

Solve for x in each of the following equations:

   (i) $2x + 3 = 15$ (ii) $5x - 4 = 16$ (iii) $3x - 3 = -12$

Solution

(i) $2x + 3 = 15$

$2x + 3 - 3 = 15 - 3$

$2x = 12$

$\dfrac{2x}{2} = \dfrac{12}{2}$

$\therefore x = 6$

(ii) $5x - 4 = 16$

> The opposite of subtracting 4 is adding 4, so we add 4 to both sides.

$5x - 4 + 4 = 16 + 4$

$5x = 20$

$\dfrac{5x}{5} = \dfrac{20}{5}$

$\therefore x = 4$

(iii) $3x - 3 = -12$

$3x - 3 + 3 = -12 + 3$

$3x = -9$

$\dfrac{3x}{3} = \dfrac{-9}{3}$

$\therefore x = -3$

x^2 Worked Example 10.3

Solve for x in each of the following equations:

   (i) $-4x + 3 = 35$ (ii) $4x = 12 - 2x$ (iii) $30 = 3x + 9$

ACTIVE MATHS 1

Solution

(i) $-4x + 3 = 35$

$-4x + 3 - 3 = 35 - 3$

$-4x = 32$

$\dfrac{-4x}{-4} = \dfrac{32}{-4}$

$\therefore x = -8$

(ii) $4x = 12 - 2x$

> The opposite of subtracting 2x is adding 2x, so we add 2x to both sides.

$4x + 2x = 12 - 2x + 2x$

$6x = 12$

$\dfrac{6x}{6} = \dfrac{12}{6}$

$\therefore x = 2$

(iii) $30 = 3x + 9$

> Remember that $30 = 3x + 9$ is the same as $3x + 9 = 30$. However, we can solve with the x on the right-hand side.

$30 - 9 = 3x + 9 - 9$

$21 = 3x$

$\dfrac{21}{3} = \dfrac{3x}{3}$

$\therefore 7 = x \quad$ or $\quad x = 7$

Exercise 10.2

Solve each of the following equations:

1. (i) $3x + 12 = 21$

(ii) $2a + 1 = 5$

(iii) $6b + 9 = 27$

(iv) $4p - 8 = 16$

(v) $3x - 3 = 21$

(vi) $2x - 10 = 2$

(vii) $9q - 9 = 36$

(viii) $5r - 4 = 26$

(ix) $5y + 8 = 8$

(x) $4x - 7 = 17$

2. (i) $4a - 4 = 20$

(ii) $2b + 15 = 9$

(iii) $3c + 4 = -20$

(iv) $3d - 3 = -9$

(v) $-3x - 8 = -11$

(vi) $4y - 1 = -13$

(vii) $-2z + 4 = -12$

(viii) $-2p - 8 = -2$

(ix) $-7 - 5q = 3$

(x) $2 - 5r = -8$

3. (i) $4x = 3 + 3x$

(ii) $6x = 16 - 2x$

(iii) $-2x = 3x + 5$

(iv) $4y = 2y + 12$

(v) $3y = -12 - y$

(vi) $-8p = 4 - 4p$

(vii) $-3q = 7 + 4q$

(viii) $10 = 4x + 18$

(ix) $4x = 9x$

(x) $3 = 2y + 3$

10.3 SOLVING EQUATIONS 3

Another type of equation is one where there are numerous steps required to balance the equation.

x^2 Worked Example 10.4

Solve the following equation:

$6x + 1 = 4x + 7$

Solution

> Remember that what we do to one side of the equation we must do to the other.

We must decide which side the x's will be on. This is usually the left-hand side. This means that the numbers will be on the right-hand side.

We can now begin solving the equation by first eliminating the constant on the left-hand side.

To do this, we must subtract 1 from both sides:

$$6x + 1 - 1 = 4x + 7 - 1$$

$$6x = 4x + 6$$

There are now no constants on the left-hand side. To continue, we must ensure that we get rid of the x's on the right-hand side. To do this we now subtract $4x$ from both sides:

$$6x - 4x = 4x - 4x + 6$$

$$2x = 6$$

Once we have the equation in this form, we can then solve for x:

$$\frac{2x}{2} = \frac{6}{2}$$

$$\therefore x = 3$$

x^2 Worked Example 10.5

Solve each of the following equations:

(i) $4x + 1 = 2x + 11$

(ii) $5y - 4 = 2y - 25$

Solution A

(i) $4x + 1 = 2x + 11$

$$4x + 1 - 1 = 2x + 11 - 1$$

$$4x = 2x + 10$$

$$4x - 2x = 2x - 2x + 10$$

$$2x = 10$$

$$\frac{2x}{2} = \frac{10}{2}$$

$$\therefore x = 5$$

(ii) $5y - 4 = 2y - 25$

$$5y - 4 + 4 = 2y - 25 + 4$$

$$5y = 2y - 21$$

$$5y - 2y = 2y - 2y - 21$$

$$3y = -21$$

$$\frac{3y}{3} = \frac{-21}{3}$$

$$\therefore y = -7$$

There is a shortcut that may be used to speed up the balancing of an equation. With this shortcut we refer to terms being 'brought over' or 'crossing' the equal sign. It is very important that we fully understand balancing before we try this shortcut.

Solution B

(i) $4x + 1 = 2x + 11$

> 1 is to be moved to the right-hand side. It 'crosses over' the equal sign, so it must pay a toll. The toll is that it must change sign, from +1 to −1.

$$4x = 2x + 11 - 1$$

$$4x = 2x + 10$$

> 2x is to be moved to the left-hand side. Its toll is that it must change sign, from +2x to −2x.

$$4x - 2x = 10$$

$$2x = 10$$

$$\frac{2x}{2} = \frac{10}{2}$$

$$\therefore x = 5$$

(ii) $5y - 4 = 2y - 25$

$$5y = 2y - 25 + 4$$

$$5y = 2y - 21$$

$$5y - 2y = -21$$

$$3y = -21$$

$$\frac{3y}{3} = \frac{-21}{3}$$

$$\therefore y = -7$$

x^2 Worked Example 10.6

Solve $3x + 25 = 7x - 3$.

Solution

$3x + 25 = 7x - 3$

$3x = 7x - 3 - 25$

$3x = 7x - 28$

> This equation would be easier to solve if we put the x's on the right-hand side.

$28 = 7x - 3x$

$28 = 4x$

$\dfrac{28}{4} = \dfrac{4x}{4}$

$7 = x \qquad x = 7$

Exercise 10.3

Solve each of the following equations:

1. $4x + 5 = 3x + 6$
2. $5x + 8 = 4x + 10$
3. $2x + 6 = x + 12$
4. $10x + 3 = 7x + 9$
5. $7x - 2 = 3x + 18$
6. $4y + 1 = -2y + 13$
7. $6y - 7 = 4y - 9$
8. $9y - 2 = 7y + 4$

9. $-y - 8 = 6 - 2y$
10. $-3y + 2 = -8y + 7$
11. $3a - 5 = -9 - a$
12. $5x + 8 = 4x + 10$
13. $4a - 1 = -19 - 2a$
14. $-3a + 2 = -a + 6$
15. $6a - 4 = 5a - 8$
16. $3b - 16 = -2b + 14$

17. $2b + 1 = 5b + 10$
18. $-8 + 3b = 5b + 8$
19. $10 + 2x = -6x - 38$
20. $-4 - 2b = -5b - 25$
21. $4x + 3 = 2x + 9$
22. $5x - 3 = 2x + 15$
23. $12x + 4 = 8x - 12$
24. $5x + 2x - 1 = -10 - 2x$

10.4 SOLVING EQUATIONS: BRACKETS

The final section of this chapter deals with solving equations that involve brackets.

Again, all the algebra rules that we have learned so far may be used.

x^2 Worked Example 10.7

Solve for x in each of the following equations:

(i) $4(x + 2) = 3(x + 2)$ (ii) $2(x - 2) = 3(2x + 4)$

Solution

(i) $4(x + 2) = 3(x + 2)$

> Multiply out the brackets.

$4x + 8 = 3x + 6$

$4x - 3x = 6 - 8$

$\therefore x = -2$

(ii) $2(x - 2) = 3(2x + 4)$

$2x - 4 = 6x + 12$

$-4 - 12 = 6x - 2x$

$-16 = 4x$

$\dfrac{-16}{4} = \dfrac{4x}{4}$

$\therefore -4 = x \qquad x = -4$

x^2 **Worked Example 10.8**

Solve for y:

(i) $3(y + 4) - 5(y - 1) = 9y - 5$

(ii) $2(2 - y) = y + 3 - 8(y - 2)$

Solution

(i) $3(y + 4) - 5(y - 1) = 9y - 5$

$3y + 12 - 5y + 5 = 9y - 5$

> We can simplify the left-hand side of the equation even further before we start to balance the equation. This is called 'tidying up'.

$3y - 5y + 12 + 5 = 9y - 5$

$-2y + 17 = 9y - 5$

$17 + 5 = 9y + 2y$

$22 = 11y$

$\dfrac{22}{11} = \dfrac{11y}{11}$

$\therefore 2 = y$

$y = 2$

(ii) $2(2 - y) = y + 3 - 8(y - 2)$

$4 - 2y = y + 3 - 8y + 16$

> We tidy up the right-hand side.

$4 - 2y = -7y + 19$

$-2y + 7y = 19 - 4$

$5y = 15$

$\dfrac{5y}{5} = \dfrac{15}{5}$

$\therefore y = 3$

Exercise 10.4

Solve each of the following equations:

1. (i) $3(x - 2) = 6$

(ii) $5(x + 4) = 25$

(iii) $4(x - 4) = 12$

(iv) $4(x - 1) = 2(3x - 7)$

(v) $5(3x + 4) = 4(x - 6)$

(vi) $4(x - 1) = 3(x - 5)$

(vii) $-(x - 2) = 2(2x - 4)$

(viii) $18(x + 1) = 9(3x + 3)$

(ix) $2(5x - 10) = 4(2x - 5)$

(x) $-(x - 1) + 2(4x + 3) = 0$

2. (i) $4(x + 3) = 5 + 3(x + 2)$

(ii) $2(2x + 1) - 7 = 3(x + 2)$

(iii) $6(x - 1) + 2(x + 5) = 28$

(iv) $-3(x - 4) = 3(2x - 3) + 12$

(v) $-2(2x - 4) = 15 - 3(2x - 1)$

(vi) $3(x - 6) + 15 = 4(x - 1) + 4$

(vii) $9 - 2(x - 2) = 5(2x - 1) + 18$

(viii) $-2(5x - 2) + 6 = -2(3x + 1) + 16$

(ix) $5(2x - 6) + 9 = 2(2x - 3) + 4x - 23$

(x) $-(3x + 5) + 1 - 4(x - 2) + 5x - 2 = 0$

3. (i) $4(x - 3) = 20$

(ii) $4(x - 3) = 3(2x - 6)$

(iii) $7(2x - 1) = 5(x - 14)$

(iv) $8(2x - 3) = 2(3x - 2)$

(v) $-3(4x - 8) = -2(x + 3)$

(vi) $3(2x - 1) - 5 = 2(2x + 3) + 4$

4. (i) $2(x + 1) + 3(x + 2) = 3(2x + 4)$

(ii) $4(3x - 3) = 2(x + 4) + 3(x - 2)$

(iii) $(2x - 5) - 2(2x - 3) + 3(2x + 1) = 0$

(iv) $-3(x - 1) + 5 = 2(x + 1) - 3(5x - 1) + 13$

(v) $5(2x + 3) + 4(7x - 5) - 2(x - 1) = -39$

Revision Exercises

Solve each of the following equations:

1. (a)   (i) $4x + 2 = 14$

       (ii) $2x + 1 = 11$

       (iii) $10x + 9 = 99$

       (iv) $7x - 1 = 20$

       (v) $9x - 3 = 33$

   (b)   (i) $5x + 4 = 2x + 25$

       (ii) $9x + 2 = 2x + 30$

       (iii) $6x + 3 = x + 18$

       (iv) $3x + 10 = x + 18$

       (v) $x + 15 = 4x + 3$

   (c)   (i) $7x - 11 = 39 - 3x$

       (ii) $3 + 5x = 33 - x$

       (iii) $22 - 5x = 4 - 2x$

       (iv) $31 - 7x = 3 - 3x$

       (v) $2 - x = x - 12$

2. (a)   (i) $x - 5 = 14$

       (ii) $4x + 5 = 49$

       (iii) $6a - 2 = 40$

       (iv) $10y - 3 = 107$

       (v) $2p + 1 = 63$

   (b)   (i) $29 + x = 7x + 5$

       (ii) $3x - 1 = x + 5$

       (iii) $5x - 4 = x + 16$

       (iv) $7x - 12 = 2x + 3$

       (v) $3x + 11 = 11x - 5$

   (c)   (i) $3 - 2x = x - 30$

       (ii) $19 - x = 28 - 4x$

       (iii) $4(x - 1) = 5(x - 2)$

       (iv) $7x + 3(2 + x) = 12x$

       (v) $5(1 - x) = 1 - 4x$

3. (a)   (i) $2t - 21 = 39$

       (ii) $5x + 4 = 459$

       (iii) $4k - 13 = 411$

       (iv) $7x + 17 = 360$

       (v) $25n + 48 = 823$

   (b)   (i) $5x - 14 = x + 30$

       (ii) $7x = 5x + 12$

       (iii) $2y + 30 = 8y$

       (iv) $11k - 24 = 3k$

       (v) $3x - 11 = -2x + 9$

   (c)   (i) $11 - (1 - x) = 2x + 1$

       (ii) $5x - 2(3 + x) = 2(x + 2)$

       (iii) $100 - 9(x - 1) = x - 1$

       (iv) $3(x + 4) - 5(x - 1) = 9x - 5$

       (v) $3(x - 5) - 2(1 - x) = 3 - 3(4 - x)$

Geometry I

Learning Outcomes

In this chapter you will learn to:

- ➲ Understand the basic concepts of geometry and geometry notation
  - ➲ The plane
  - ➲ Points on the plane
  - ➲ Lines, line segments and rays (half-lines)
  - ➲ Length of line segments
  - ➲ Collinear points
- ➲ Recognise angles in terms of rotation

- ➲ Understand angle notation
- ➲ Identify different types of angles
- ➲ Estimate and then measure angles accurately
- ➲ Recognise and understand the terms *perpendicular, parallel, vertical* and *horizontal lines*
- ➲ Understand what an axiom is and use axioms to solve problems

11.1 GEOMETRY

Geometry comes from the Greek word γεωμετριτα or *geometria*, which means 'earth measurement' (*geo* = earth, *metria* = measure). It is one of the oldest branches of mathematics. Geometry investigates the properties and measurement of lines, angles, two-dimensional and three-dimensional shapes.

The Parthenon was built in Athens, Greece, in the fifth century BC. It is a famous example of how geometrical rules were applied to architecture.

Surveyors, engineers and designers of computer games – all these careers and many more require an understanding of geometry.

KEY WORDS

- **Plane**
- **Point**
- **Line**
- **Line segment**
- **Ray**
- **Angle**
- **Parallel**
- **Perpendicular**
- **Axiom**

Euclid was a brilliant Greek mathematician who is often called the 'Father of Geometry'. He is famous for his book *The Elements*, which he wrote about 300 BC. It is one of the oldest mathematics textbooks still in existence. Many of our ideas on geometry come from Euclid, and even after 2,000 years, many of his ideas still hold true.

11.2 BASIC CONCEPTS

Euclid

The Plane

A **plane** is a flat, two-dimensional surface. 'Two-dimensional' means that it has length and width, but it has no thickness. A plane stretches on to infinity, that is, it goes on forever. Points and lines are drawn on a plane.

Points on the Plane

A **point** is a location or position on a plane. It has no dimensions. It is denoted by a capital letter and a dot.

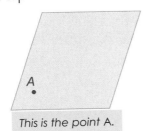

A

This is the point A.

If points lie on the same plane, they are said to be coplanar.

Lines, Line Segments and Rays

A **line** is a straight line that goes on forever in both directions – it has **no endpoints**. A line can be named by any two points on the line or by a lowercase letter. It has an infinite number of points on it.

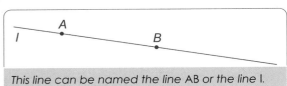

This line can be named the line AB or the line l.

A **line segment** is part of a straight line. It has **two endpoints** and can be measured.

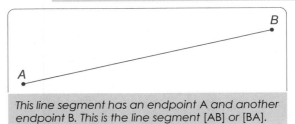

This line segment has an endpoint A and another endpoint B. This is the line segment [AB] or [BA].

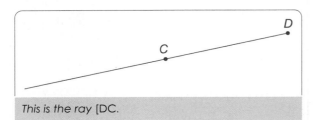

This is the ray [CD. Note that there is only one bracket to denote where the ray's endpoint is.

A **ray** is part of a line that has **one endpoint**. The other end goes on to infinity. It is sometimes called a **half-line**.

The point where two or more lines, line segments or rays meet or cross is called the **point of intersection**.

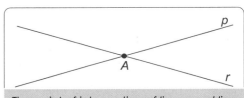

This is the ray [DC.

The point of intersection of line p and line r is point A.

Length of a Line Segment

We can use a ruler to measure a line segment.

A ———————— 6 cm ———————— B

In this case, the length of the line segment [AB] is equal to 6 cm. This is written as $|AB| = 6$ cm.

Collinear Points

A, B and C are all on the same line, which means that they are **collinear**.

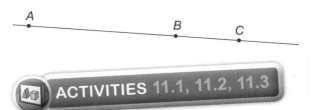

Points that lie on the same line are called **collinear points**.

ACTIVITIES 11.1, 11.2, 11.3

11.3 ANGLES

Recognise Angles in Terms of Rotation

An angle is a measure of rotation. When two rays meet at a point called the **vertex**, they make an angle. The two rays that make up the angle are sometimes called the **arms** of the angle.

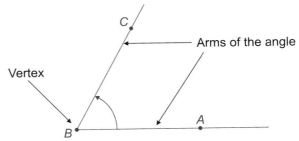

The measure or size of the angle is how much one ray rotates or turns around the vertex.

Most angles you encounter will be measured in degrees.

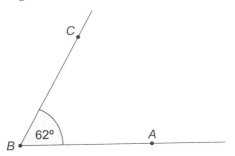

It is not the length of the arms that determines the size of the angle but the rotation of the arms of the angle.

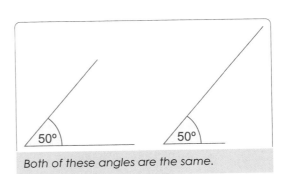

Both of these angles are the same.

Understand Angle Notation

We can use many different ways to label an angle. We normally use three points to name an angle. **The vertex is always the centre letter.**

This is the angle *ABC*. The angle could also be named as the angle *CBA*, or it could be called simply the angle *B* because the vertex of the angle is at the point *B*.

We could also call it the angle 1 or even the angle α.

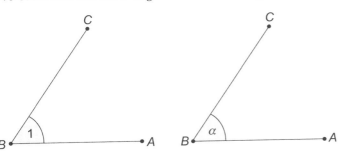

Identify Different Types of Angles

Angles can be divided into many different types.

An **acute angle** is an angle that is less than 90°. It gets its name from the fact that the angle looks sharp or 'acute'.

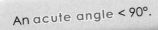

An acute angle < 90°.

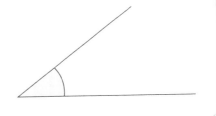

A **right angle** is an angle of exactly 90°. It also gets a special symbol that shows that the angle is 90°.

> A right angle = 90°.

An **obtuse angle** is an angle that is greater than 90° but less than 180°. This angle looks blunt or 'obtuse'.

> An obtuse angle > 90° but < 180°.

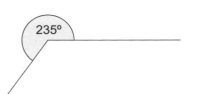

A **straight angle** is an angle of 180°. The two arms of the angle make a straight line.

> A straight angle = 180°.

180°

A **reflex angle** is an angle greater than 180° but less than 360°.

> A reflex angle > 180° but < 360°.

235°

A **full angle** is an angle where the one arm of the angle has completed one full rotation. It has completed a full turn of 360°, the same as a circle.

> A full angle = 360°.

360°

An **ordinary angle** is any angle that is less than 180°.

> An ordinary angle < 180°.

A **null angle** is any angle where the arms coincide with one another. A null angle measures 0°.

> A null angle = 0°.

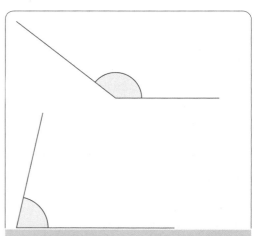

Both of these angles are ordinary angles.

Two angles are **supplementary** if they add up to 180°. These two angles are supplementary.

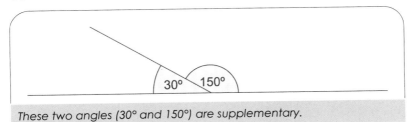

These two angles (30° and 150°) are supplementary.

Supplementary angles don't have to be beside each other.

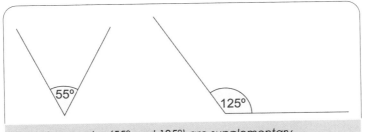

These two angles (55° and 125°) are supplementary.

Estimate and then Measure Angles Accurately

Angles are usually measured in degrees.

As before, when we write an actual measurement, we use the symbols | | to show this.

$|\angle ABC| = 50°$.

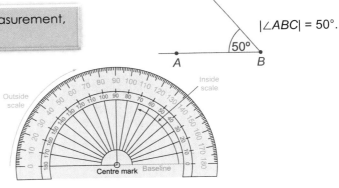

We use a **protractor** to measure an angle accurately. However, it is good practice to make an estimate of the angle before we use a protractor.

A protractor has two scales, a centre point and a baseline.

 ## Worked Example 11.1

Measure the angle *ABC*.

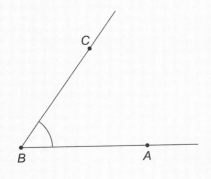

Solution

Step 1   Place the centre point of the protractor on the vertex of the angle. Make sure that one arm of the angle is lined up with the baseline.

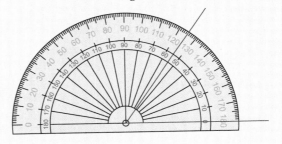

Step 2 Read the angle between the two arms of the angle. Here we need to use the inside scale.

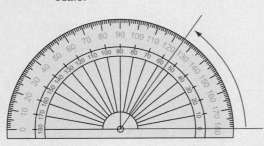

Step 3 Write in the measurement in the angle. $|\angle ABC| = 55°$.

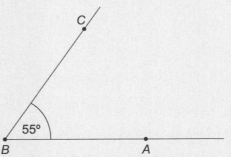

Note: When measuring angles with the protractor, we must be careful to use the right scale. We use the **inner scale** of the protractor if the arm of the angle that is lined up with the baseline of the protractor passes through the zero of the inner scale.

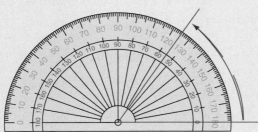

We use the **outer scale** of the protractor if the arm of the angle that is lined up with the baseline of the protractor passes through the zero of the outer scale.

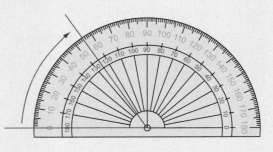

🔷 **ACTIVITIES** 11.4, 11.5, 11.6, 11.7, 11.8, 11.9

11.4 PERPENDICULAR, PARALLEL, VERTICAL AND HORIZONTAL LINES

There are many different ways to describe how lines are related to each other.

Perpendicular lines are lines that are at right angles or 90° to each other.

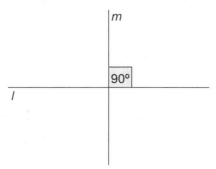

> **Perpendicular lines** are at right angles to each other.

The line *l* is perpendicular to the line *m*. This can be written as $l \perp m$ (*l* perpendicular to *m*).

> $l \perp m$ (*l* perpendicular to *m*)

Parallel lines are lines that never meet. This means that they are always the same distance from each other.

p ⟶

q ⟶

> Parallel lines are an equal distance apart and therefore never meet.

The line *p* is parallel to the line *q*. This can be written as *p* ∥ *q* (*p* parallel to *q*).

Lines that are parallel to each other have arrows on them to show that they are parallel.

> *p* ∥ *q* (*p* parallel to *q*)

A line that is parallel to level ground is called a **horizontal line**.

A **vertical line** is a line that is perpendicular to the horizontal.

ACTIVITIES 11.10, 11.11

11.5 AXIOMS

An **axiom** is a statement that we accept **without any proof**. We use axioms as the basic building blocks to understand geometry better.

Axiom 1 (Two Points Axiom)

There is exactly one line through any two given points.

We can draw only one line between the points *A* and *B*.

Axiom 2 (Ruler Axiom)

The properties of the distance between points.

The distance between two points has the following properties:

1. The distance between two points is never negative.

   We would never say that $|AB| = -3$ cm.

2. $|AB| = |BA|$.

   If $|AB| = 5$ mm, then $|BA| = 5$ mm also. This makes sense, as [AB] and [BA] are the same line segment.

3. If point C lies on AB, between A and B, then |AB| = |AC| + |CB|.

If |AB| = 10 cm, and |AC| = 4 cm, then |CB| = 6 cm. If we divide a line segment into two or more parts, then the sum of the lengths of each of these parts will equal the length of the original line segment.

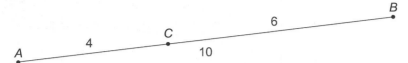

4. Given any ray from the point A and a distance d ⩾ 0, there is exactly one point B on the ray whose distance from A is d.

This property means that we can mark off a distance of 5 cm on a ray from a point A and call this point B. There is no other point on the ray that is 5 cm from A. The length of the line segment [AB] will also be 5 cm.

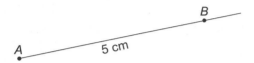

Axiom 3 (Protractor Axiom)

The properties of the degree measure of an angle.

The number of degrees in an angle is always a number between 0° and 360°. This axiom has the following properties.

1. A straight angle has 180°.

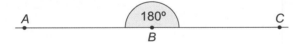

This means that all the angles at a point add up to 360°, as they make up two straight angles.

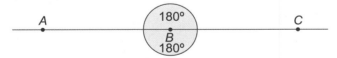

2. Given a ray [AB and a number between 0 and 180, there is exactly one ray from A, on each side of the ray [AB, that makes an (ordinary) angle having d degrees with the ray [AB.

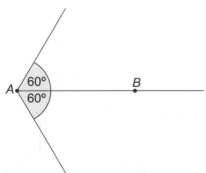

This property of the protractor axiom means that, for example, there is only one 60° angle on each side of the ray [AB.

3. If an angle is divided into two smaller angles, then these two angles add up to the original angle.

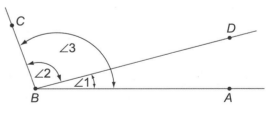

|∠1| + |∠2| = |∠3|

or

|∠ABD| + |∠DBC| = |∠ABC|

Worked Example 11.2

Without using a protractor, find the measure of the angle *ABC*.

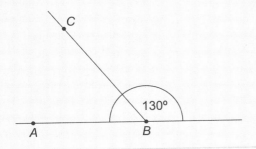

Solution

> Remember to show as much work as possible.

A straight angle = 180°.

$$|\angle ABC| = 180° - 130°$$
$$|\angle ABC| = 50°$$

 ## Worked Example 11.3

Without measuring, find the measure of ∠1.

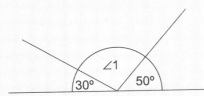

Solution

A straight angle = 180°.

$$|\angle 1| = 180° - 30° - 50°$$
$$|\angle 1| = 100°$$

Worked Example 11.4

Using your knowledge of the geometry axioms, find the measure of ∠β.

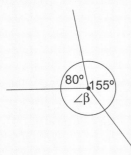

Solution

Angle at a point = 360°.

$$|\angle \beta| = 360° - 80° - 155°$$
$$|\angle \beta| = 125°$$

Axiom 5 (Axiom of Parallels)

Given any line *l* and a point *P*, there is exactly one line through *P* that is parallel to *l*.

It is clear that we can draw only one line through the point *P* that would be parallel to the line *l*.

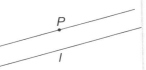

 ACTIVITIES 11.12, 11.13, 11.14, 11.15, 11.16, 11.17

1. Draw a line segment [AB], such that |AB| = 10 cm.

   (i) What other name could we give to this line segment?

   (ii) Draw a point C anywhere on the line segment [AB].

   (iii) Measure the length of the line segment [AC] and [CB].

   (iv) Is |AC| + |CB| = |AB|?

2. On a plane, label the points D and E.

   (i) Draw a line through the points D and E.

   (ii) What name could you give to this line?

   (iii) Can you draw any other line through these two points?

3. Examine the diagram shown below and fill in the missing word(s):

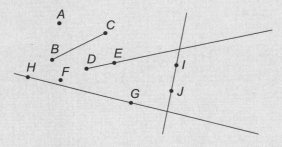

   (i) A is a _____.

   (ii) [BC] is a _____.

   (iii) [DE is a _____.

   (iv) HG is a _____.

   (v) IJ is a _____.

   (vi) F is a _____.

   (vii) Is it true to say that H, F and G are collinear?

4. (i) What do we mean when we say three points are collinear?

   (ii) Draw four points that are collinear.

   (iii) Draw another point on the same plane that is not collinear.

5. (i) Draw a ray [AB on a plane.

   (ii) Draw a ray [BA on the same plane.

   (iii) Are the rays [AB and [BA the same? Give a reason for your answer.

6. Draw two different examples of the following angles. In each case, measure the angle:

   (i) Acute   (iv) Straight
   (ii) Right-angled   (v) Reflex
   (iii) Obtuse   (vi) Ordinary

7. Use a protractor to measure the following angles. In each case, name and identify the type of angle:

   (i)
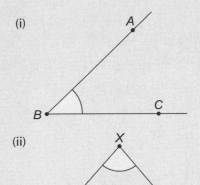

   (ii)
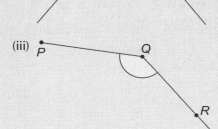

   (iii)
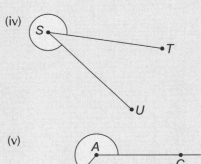

   (iv)

   (v)
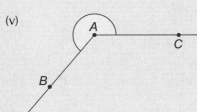

8. Use a protractor to draw the following angles:

   (i) 45°   (iv) 200°
   (ii) 70°   (v) 270°
   (iii) 335°

9. Consider the two angles below:

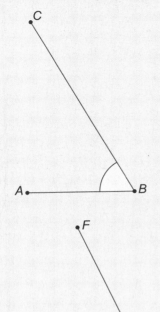

(i) Estimate which angle is the biggest.

(ii) Check your answer using a protractor.

(iii) Does the length of the arm of the angle affect the measure of the angle? Give a reason for your answer.

10. In the diagram below, name all the lines that are:

(i) Parallel to each other

(ii) Perpendicular to each other

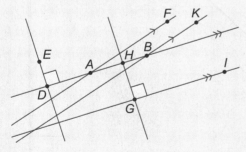

11. Find the measure of each of the unknown angles without measuring them:

(i)

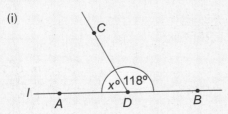

(ii)

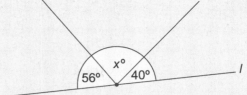

(iii)

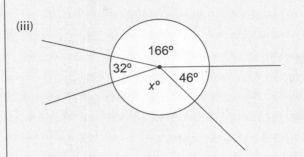

(iv)

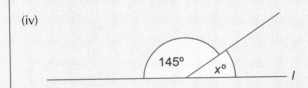

(v)

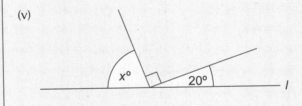

(vi)

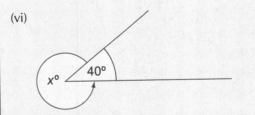

(vii)

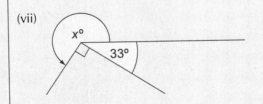

12. (a) Look at the information in each diagram and write an equation in x.

(b) Solve each equation to find the value of x.

Note: *l* is a straight line.

(i)
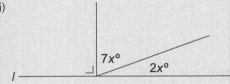

(iii)
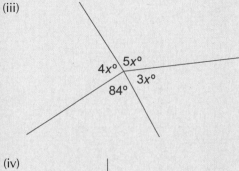

(ii)
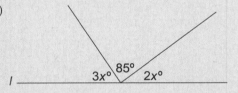

(iv)
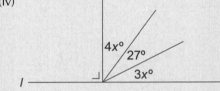

13. Find x and y in each case.
Note: *l* is a straight line.

(i)
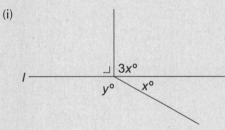

(ii)
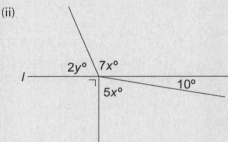

14. Find the value of A in each case:
Note: *l* is a straight line.

(i)
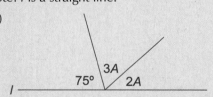

(iii)

(ii)
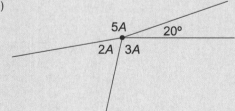

(iv)
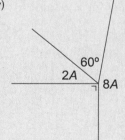

chapter 12

Constructions I

Learning Outcomes

In this chapter you will learn how to do the following constructions:

- A bisector of any given angle, using only a compass and a straight edge
- A perpendicular bisector of a line segment, using only a compass and a straight edge
- A line perpendicular to a given line *l*, passing through a given point on *l*
- A line parallel to a given line, passing through a given point
- Division of a line segment into two or three equal segments, without measuring it
- A line segment of a given length on a given ray
- An angle of a given number of degrees with a given ray as one arm

12.1 GEOMETRY CONSTRUCTIONS

When we look at the Egyptian pyramids, the megaliths at Stonehenge or the passage tomb at Newgrange, we wonder how they were constructed thousands of years ago. However, without an understanding of geometry, these wonders of the world could not have been built.

Everywhere around us we can see geometry constructions:

- A wall must be built perpendicular to the ground or else it will fall down.
- Would a TV be better to watch if it were in the shape of a square instead of a rectangle?
- Would the wheels of a car roll if they were not in the shape of a circle?

By studying these geometry constructions, you are continuing a tradition begun over 2,000 years ago by Euclid when he published his book *The Elements*.

These words were written above the door of Plato's Academy, a famous school in Athens run by the philosopher Plato (429–347 BC). Plato considered geometry to be one of the most important branches of knowledge.

'Let no man ignorant of geometry enter here.'

12.2 CONSTRUCTION EQUIPMENT

Compass

The compass is a very important tool for constructions.

It is used to draw arcs...

By adjusting the compass width, we can change the size of the arcs or circles that we draw.

...and circles.

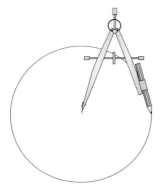

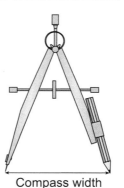

Compass width

Protractor

The protractor is used to construct angles. It can also be used to check the accuracy of some constructions.

Straight Edge

A straight edge is a tool that is used to draw a straight line. It has no markings, so it can not be used for measuring lines. In reality, we just use the ruler found in the construction set.

Ruler

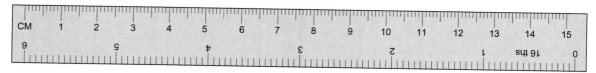

A ruler is used to construct line segments of certain lengths.

> A **cubit** was one of the earliest recorded units of length. It originated in Egypt around 3,000 BC. One cubit is equal to the distance from the tip of the middle finger to the elbow.

Set Square

Set squares are rulers in the shape of triangles. We can use set squares to draw lines and certain angles. They are used especially for constructing right angles. Two set squares are used: the 45° set square, which has angles of 45°, 45° and 90°, and the 30° or 60° set square, which has angles of 30°, 60° and 90°.

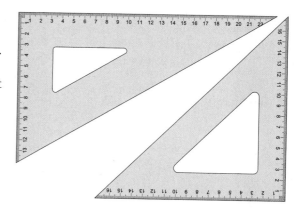

Pencil

Make sure that your pencil has a sharp point. Remember NEVER to rub out any lines, arcs, etc. that you have used in your constructions. These construction lines are very important, as they show that you have followed the correct method.

ACTIVITIES 12.1, 12.2

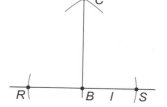

12.3 CONSTRUCTION 1

A Bisector of Any Given Angle, Using Only a Compass and a Straight Edge

Worked Example 12.1

Construct the **bisector** of ∠*ABC*.

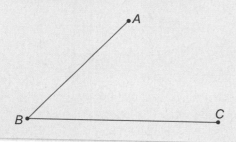

> To **bisect** is to cut into two equal parts. The **bisector** is the line that cuts an angle into two equal parts.

Solution

1 Place the compass point on the angle's **vertex** B.

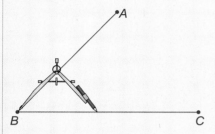

> The vertex of an angle is the point where the two rays of an angle meet.

2 Draw an arc of the same width across each ray of the angle. Label X, Y.

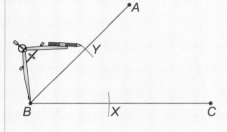

3 Place the compass on the point X and draw an arc.

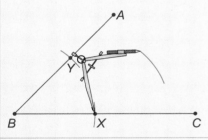

4 Without changing the compass width, place the compass on the point Y and draw an overlapping arc.

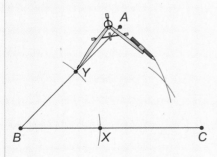

5 Mark the point where the two arcs intersect.

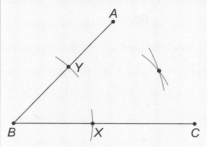

6 Using a straight edge, draw a line from this point to the vertex B.

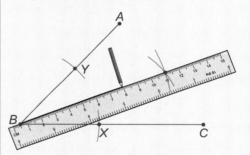

7 This line is the bisector of the angle ABC.

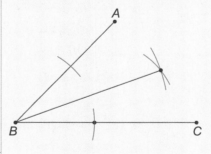

ACTIVITIES 12.3, 12.4

Exercise 12.1

1. Copy the following angles into your copybook. Bisect the indicated angles using only a compass and a straight edge. Remember, you can check your construction with a protractor.

(i)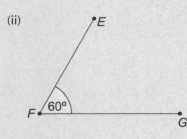

(ii)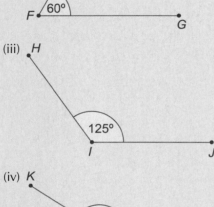

(iii)

(iv)

(v)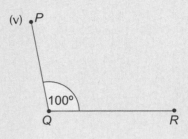

(vi)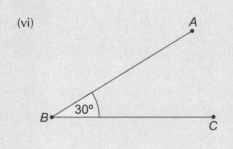

(vii)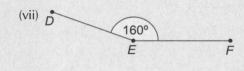

(viii)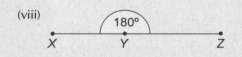

2. Construct the following angles using a protractor:

(i) 40°

(ii) 150°

(iii) 90°

(iv) 230°

(v) 315°

Bisect each of the constructed angles using only a compass and a straight edge.

12.4 CONSTRUCTION 2

A Perpendicular Bisector of a Line Segment, Using Only a Compass and a Straight Edge

A **perpendicular bisector** of a line segment cuts the line segment into two equal parts and also creates a line at right angles to the original line segment.

Construct the perpendicular bisector of the line segment [CD].

Solution

1 Place the compass point on *C*, an endpoint of the line segment.	**4** Mark the two points where the arcs intersect.
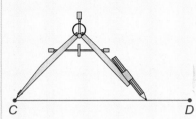	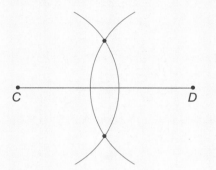
2 Set the compass width to **more than half** the length of [*CD*] and draw an arc.	**5** Using a straight edge, draw a line through these two points.
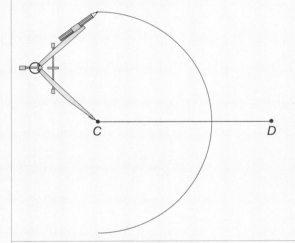	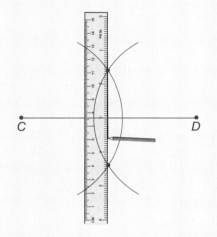
3 Without changing the compass width, place the compass point on *D* and draw an arc.	**6** This line is the perpendicular bisector of the line segment [*CD*].
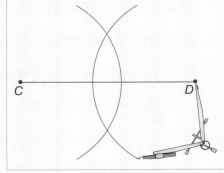	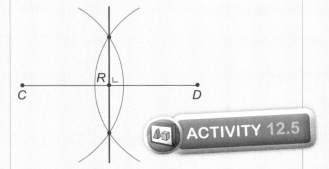

ACTIVITY 12.5

Constructing the perpendicular bisector of a line segment also finds the **midpoint** of the line segment. In the example above, *R* is the midpoint of [*CD*].

Exercise 12.2

1. Copy the following line segments into your copybook. Construct the perpendicular bisector of each line segment using only a compass and a straight edge.
   Remember, you can check your construction with a protractor and ruler.

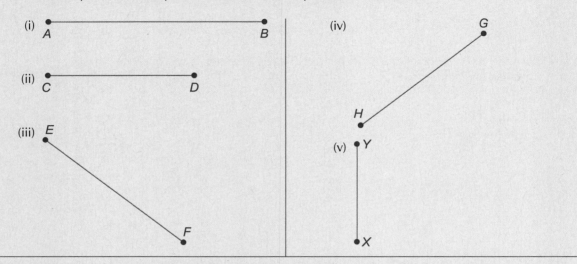

(i) A ————————— B

(ii) C ————— D

(iii) E ... F

(iv) G ... H

(v) Y ... X

2. Draw a line segment [AB] of length 10 cm. Construct the perpendicular bisector of [AB].

3. Draw a line segment [CD] of length 5.5 cm. Construct the perpendicular bisector of [CD].

4. Draw a line segment [EF] of length 85 mm. Construct the perpendicular bisector of [EF].

5. Draw a line segment [GH] of length 7 cm. Construct the perpendicular bisector of [GH].

6. Copy the following line segments into your copybook. Construct the perpendicular bisector of each line segment.

   (i) Draw a line segment from A to C. What is the shape ABC called?

   (ii) Mark the point of intersection of the perpendicular bisectors.

   (iii) Using this point as the centre of a circle, draw a circle which passes through the points A, B and C.

12.5 CONSTRUCTION 4

Note: Constructions 3 and 7 are not included in the Ordinary Level course.

A Line Perpendicular to a Given Line *l*, Passing Through a Given Point on *l*

Two methods are shown, both of which must be known.

Worked Example 12.3

Construct a line perpendicular to the line *l*, passing through the point *B* on the line *l*.

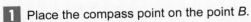

Solution Using a Compass and a Straight Edge

1 Place the compass point on the point *B*.

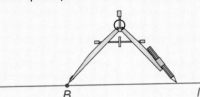

4 Without changing the compass width, place the compass point on *S* and draw an overlapping arc.

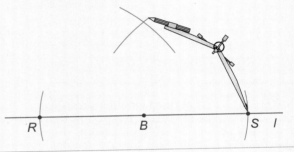

2 Using a small compass width, draw an arc that intersects the line *l* at two points. Label *R, S*.

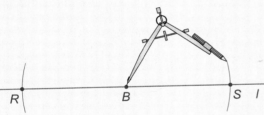

5 Mark the point where the arcs intersect.

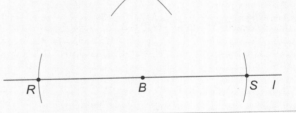

3 Increase the compass width, place the compass point on *R*, and draw an arc.

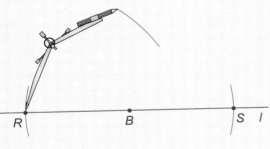

6 Using a straight edge draw a line through this point and the point *B*.

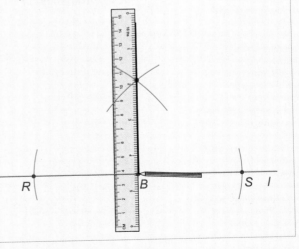

7 This line is perpendicular to the line *l* and passes through the point *B*.

R ⌐ B S *l*

Solution Using a Set Square or Protractor

1 Line up one side of the right angle of the set square at point *B* and the other side on the line *l*.

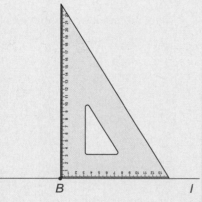

B *l*

3 This line is perpendicular to the line *l* and passes through the point *B*.

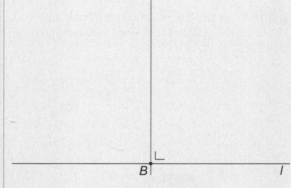

B *l*

2 Draw a line from the line *l* through the point *B*.

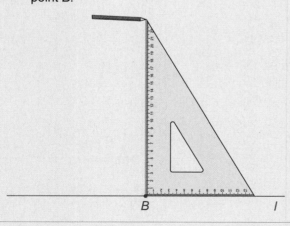

B *l*

ACTIVITIES 12.6, 12.7

Exercise 12.3

1. Copy the following lines into your copybook. Construct a line perpendicular to the given line passing through the given point, **using only a compass and a straight edge**.

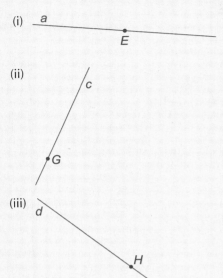

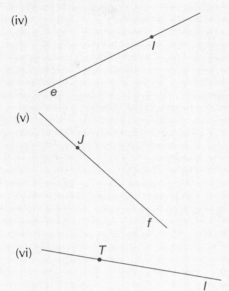

2. Copy the following lines into your copybook. Construct a line perpendicular to the given line passing through the given point, **using a set square or protractor**.

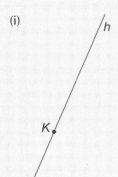

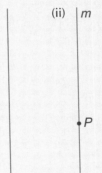

3. Copy the following figure into your copybook. Using only a compass and straight edge:

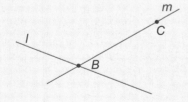

(i) Construct a line perpendicular to the line *l* passing through the point *B*.

(ii) Construct a line perpendicular to the line *m* passing through the point *C*.

12.6 CONSTRUCTION 5

A Line Parallel to a Given Line, Passing Through a Given Point

Two methods are shown, both of which must be known.

Worked Example 12.4

Construct a line parallel to the line *m*, passing through the point *C*.

C

_____ *m*

Solution Using a Compass and a Straight Edge

1 Draw a line through the point *C* to the line *m*. Label the intersection of these two lines *D*.

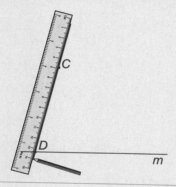

2 Place the compass point on *D*, and draw an arc across both lines. Ensure that the arc does not go above the point *C*.

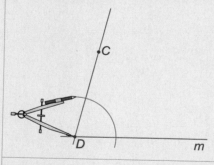

3 Label the points of intersection *X* and *Y*.

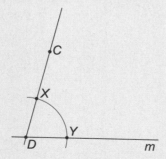

4 Without changing the compass width, place the compass point on *C* and draw an arc.

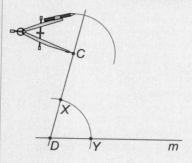

5 Use the compass to measure the distance between *X* and *Y*.

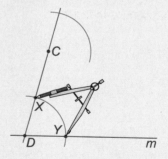

6 Using this compass width, place the compass point where the upper arc and line meet. Draw a new arc across the upper arc.

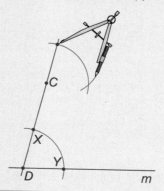

7 Mark the point where the arcs intersect.

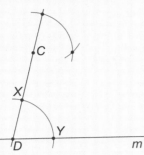

9 This line is parallel to the line *m* and passes through the point *C*.

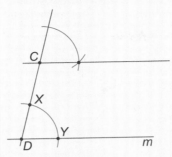

8 Using a straight edge, draw a line from this point through the point *C*.

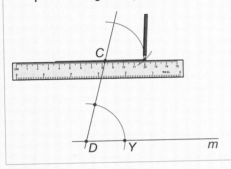

Solution Using a Set Square

1 Using a set square, draw a perpendicular line through the point *C* to the line *m*.

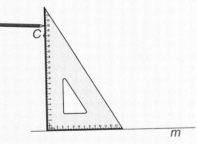

3 Draw a line through the point *C*.

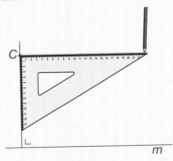

2 Line up one side of the right angle of the set square at point *C* and the other side on the perpendicular line.

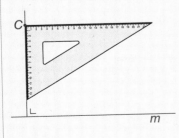

4 This line is parallel to the line *m* and passes through the point *C*.

ACTIVITIES 12.8, 12.9

Exercise 12.4

1. Copy the following figures into your copybook. In each case construct a line parallel to the given line and passing through the given point, **using only a compass and a straight edge**.

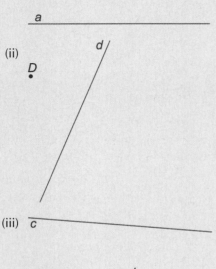

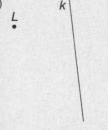

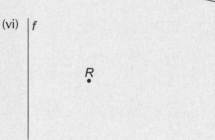

2. Copy the following figures into your copybook. In each case construct a line parallel to the given line and passing through the given point, **using a set square**.

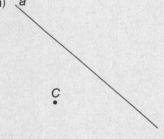

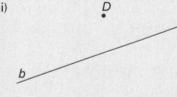

3. Draw a line *p,* and then mark a point *E* 3 cm above this line, and a point *D* 7 cm below this line. Using only a compass and a straight edge:

   (i) Construct a line parallel to the line *p* passing through the point *E*.

   (ii) Construct a line parallel to the line *p* passing through the point *D*.

12.7 CONSTRUCTION 6

Division of a Line Segment into Two or Three Equal Segments, Without Measuring It

Worked Example 12.5

Divide the line segment [AB] into **three** equal parts.

A •————————————————• B

Solution

CONSTRUCTIONS I

1 From point A (or B), draw a ray at an acute angle to the given line segment.

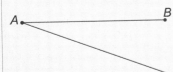

2 Place the compass point on A.

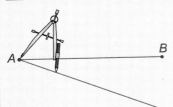

3 Using the same compass width, mark off **three** equal arcs along the ray. (Use a small compass width.)

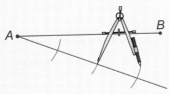

4 Label the points of intersection R, S and T.

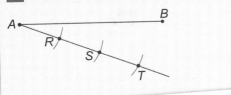

5 Join the last point T to the point B on the line segment.

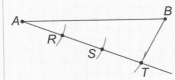

6 Using a set square and straight edge, line the set square up with the line segment [TB].

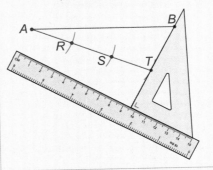

7 Slide the set square along, using the straight edge as a base. Using the set square, draw a line segment from S and R to the line segment [AB].

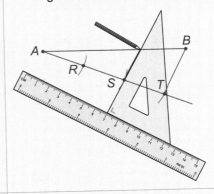

8 Label the points of intersection with the line segment [AB] as points C and D.

The line segment [AB] has now been divided into three equal segments.

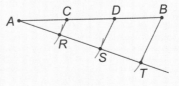

ACTIVITIES 12.10, 12.11

Exercise 12.5

1. Draw a line segment [*AB*] of length 11 cm.
   Divide this line segment into three equal parts without measuring it.

2. Draw a line segment [*CD*] of length 6 cm. Divide this line segment into three equal segments, using only a compass, a straight edge and a set square.

3. Draw a line segment [*EF*] of length 13 cm.
   Divide this line segment into three equal segments without measuring it.

4. Draw a line segment [*GH*] of length 7.5 cm.
   Divide this line segment into three equal parts without measuring it.

5. Copy the following figures into your copybook.
   Divide each line segment into three equal parts without measuring it.

   (i)   *B*   (ii) *C*   (iii) *E*   (iv) *H*

   A   *D*   *F*   *G*

6. Draw a line segment [*IJ*] of length 10 cm. Divide this line segment into two equal parts without measuring.

7. Draw a line segment [*XY*] of length 9 cm. Divide this line segment into two equal parts without measuring it.

12.8 CONSTRUCTION 8

A Line Segment of a Given Length on a Given Ray

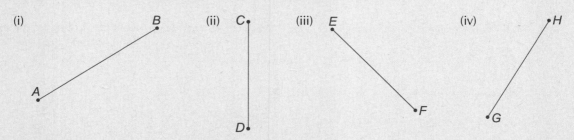

Worked Example 12.6

Construct a line segment 5 cm in length on the given ray.

X ———————————————— *Y*

Solution

1 Using a ruler, draw a line segment [*EF*] of length 5 cm.	**2** Place the compass on the point *E*. Adjust the compass width until it is at point *F*, i.e. 5 cm.
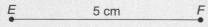 *E* 5 cm *F*	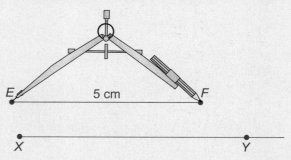 *X* *Y*

3 Using this compass width, place the compass point on the point *X*.

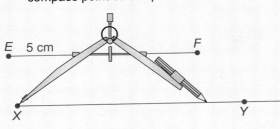

5 Connect *X* to *Z* with a straight edge.

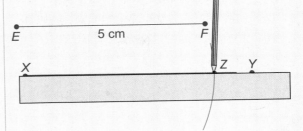

4 Without adjusting the compass width, draw an arc that crosses the ray.
Label this point of intersection as *Z*.

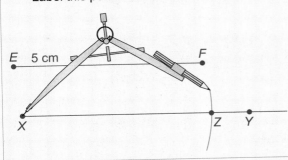

6 The line segment of a given length has been constructed on the given ray.

|XZ| = 5 cm

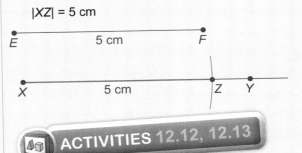

ACTIVITIES 12.12, 12.13

 Exercise 12.6

1. Copy the following figures into your copybook.
In each case construct the given line segment on the given ray.

(i)

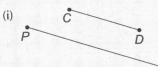

(ii)

(iii) W

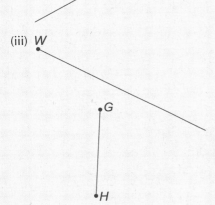

(iv)

(v)

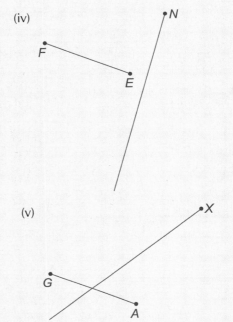

2. Draw a line segment [AB] of length 6 cm.

   (i) Draw a ray above the line segment [AB].

   (ii) Draw a ray below the line segment [AB].

   (iii) Construct a line segment on each ray where the length of each segment equals |AB|.

12.9 CONSTRUCTION 9

An Angle of a Given Number of Degrees With a Given Ray as One Arm

Worked Example 12.7

Construct an angle of 50° on the ray [AB.

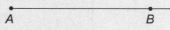

Solution

1 Place the centre of the protractor on the point A.

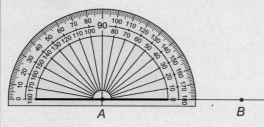

2 At the required angle, mark a point C using the protractor.

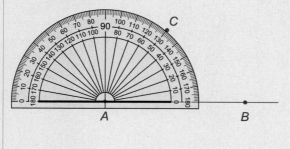

3 Draw a ray from A through C with a straight edge.

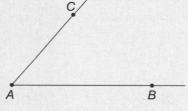

4 Write in the required angle value, i.e. 50°.

An angle of the given length has been constructed on the given ray.

|∠BAC| = 50°.

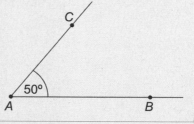

ACTIVITY 12.14

Exercise 12.7

1. Copy the following rays into your copybook.
   Using a protractor, construct the following angles on the given rays.

   (i) $|\angle ABC| = 40°$ on the ray [BA.

   (ii) $|\angle DEF| = 100°$ on the ray [EF.

   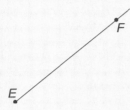

   (iii) $|\angle GHI| = 170°$ on the ray [HG.

   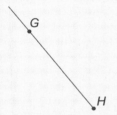

   (iv) $|\angle JKL| = 235°$ on the ray [KL.

   (v) $|\angle MNO| = 300°$ on the ray [NM.

2. Construct the following angles using a protractor.

   (i) $|\angle PQR| = 190°$ on the ray PQ].   (iv) $|\angle ABC| = 108°$ on the ray [BA.

   (ii) $|\angle STV| = 280°$ on the ray [TV.   (v) $|\angle LMN| = 270°$ on the ray [MN.

   (iii) $|\angle XYZ| = 340°$ on the ray [YZ.   (vi) $|\angle UVW| = 333°$ on the ray [VW.

Revision Exercises

Unless otherwise stated, constructions should be attempted using a compass and a straight edge only.

1. Draw two lines that intersect at a point, as in the figure below.

   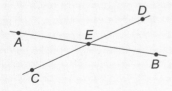

   (i) Measure all four angles at the point E. Are any angles equal?

   (ii) Using a compass and straight edge, bisect ∠DEB.

2. Draw a line segment [XY] such that $|XY| = 100$ mm.

   (i) Using only a compass, find the midpoint of the line segment [XY].

   (ii) Construct a circle of diameter 100 mm, using the midpoint of [XY] as its centre.

3. Draw a line segment [AB] such that $|AB| = 15$ cm.
   Construct the perpendicular bisector of this line segment.

4. Draw a line segment [PQ] where |PQ| = 10 cm.

   (i) Construct the perpendicular bisector of [PQ].

   (ii) Label as point R the point of intersection of the bisector and line segment.

   (iii) Construct a circle of radius 5 cm, using R as its centre.

   (iv) How does this show that R is the midpoint of the line segment [PQ]?

5. (i) Draw a line segment [AB] where |AB| = 12 cm.

   (ii) Divide [AB] into three equal parts without measuring it.

6. Construct the following line segments and angle into your copybook.

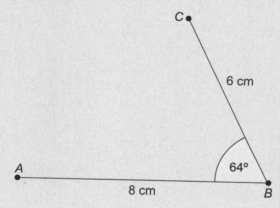

   (i) Construct the perpendicular bisector of each line segment.

   (ii) Draw a line segment from A to C. What is the shape ABC called?

   (iii) Mark the point of intersection of the perpendicular bisectors.

   (iv) Using this point as the centre of a circle, draw a circle that passes through the points A, B and C.

7. Copy the figure below into your copybook.

Construct a line perpendicular to the line PQ through the point R.

8. Draw line segment [AB] where |AB| = 8 cm.

   (i) Mark a point C on [AB], such that |AC| = 2 cm.

   (ii) Using a compass, construct a line perpendicular to [AB] through the point C.

   (iii) Mark a point D on the line segment [AB], such that |BD| = 3 cm.

   (iv) Using a protractor, construct a line perpendicular to the line segment [AB] through the point D.

9. Draw a line l and then mark a point E at least 5 cm above this line. Construct a line parallel to l through the point E.

10. Draw a line segment [GH] where |GH| = 7 cm. Construct the perpendicular bisector of [GH].

11. Draw the line segment [EF] where |EF| = 10 cm.

   (i) Divide this line segment into three equal parts without measuring it.

   (ii) Label the points as shown below.

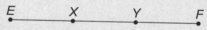

   (iii) Construct the line segment [FG] where |FG| = 6 cm as shown in the diagram below.

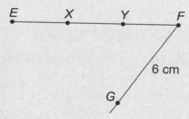

   (iv) Divide this line segment into three equal parts without measuring it.

   (v) Label the points as shown below.

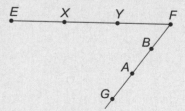

   (vi) Construct the line segments [EG], [XA] and [YB]. What do you notice about these line segments?

12. Construct the following figure:
$|AB| = 7$ cm and $|\angle ABC| = 110°$.
Place the point X above the line segment $[AB]$.

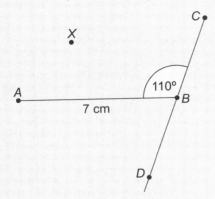

(i) Construct a line through X parallel to $[AB]$. Label as P the point of intersection of this line and $[DC]$.

(ii) Construct a line through X parallel to $[DC]$. Label as Q the point of intersection of this line and $[AB]$.

(iii) What is the four-sided figure $XPBQ$ called?

(iv) Confirm this by listing the measurements of angles and line segments in $XPBQ$.

13. Copy the figure below into your copybook.

(i) Without measuring, construct a line segment $[XY]$ that is three times the length of $[CD]$.

(ii) On a separate ray, without measuring, construct a line segment $[PQ]$ that is half the length of $[CD]$.

14. Using only a protractor and a straight edge, construct angles that satisfy the following:

(i) $|\angle ABC| = 90°$ on the ray $[BC$

(ii) $|\angle DEF| = 45°$ on the ray $FE]$

(iii) $|\angle PQR| = 60°$ on the ray $[QP$

(iv) $|\angle XYZ| = 30°$ on the ray $[YZ$

15. Two fences enclosing a park meet at an angle of 110° as shown.

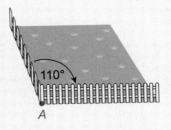

A path is to be built through the park from the point A.

This path must always be the same distance from the two fences.

Show on a diagram where this new path is to be built.

16. A clock designer is given a design for a new clock.

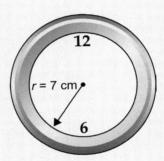

The design gives the position of the 12 o'clock and 6 o'clock positions only. Reproduce this design and mark on your design where the rest of the numbers should be placed.

17. Two schools are 8.25 km apart as shown.

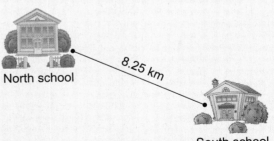

A new secondary school is to be built 5 km from the North school and 7 km from the South school.

Show on a diagram the two locations at which this secondary school could be built.
(Use a scale of 1 cm = 1 km.)

18. A section of a field is shown below.

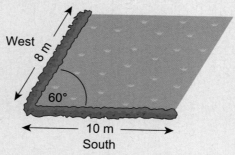

West
8 m
60°
10 m
South

Two drainage ditches are to be dug in this field. One ditch is to be dug beside the western side of the field, and another is to be dug beside the southern side of the field.

Each ditch must be exactly 2 m away from its side of the field.

Show on a diagram where these ditches should be placed.

Explain your work, showing all construction marks clearly.

19. For a game, Emily stands at X, 8 m away from point A, and Joan stands at Y, 6 m away from point A.

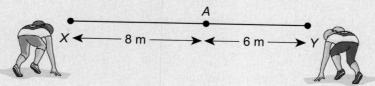

A
X ← 8 m → ← 6 m → Y

(i) Using a scale of 1 cm = 1 m, draw this diagram in your copy.

In the game, they must run in a straight line to a certain point B that will always be directly opposite point A.
The first one to reach this point wins.

(ii) Using a compass and a straight edge only, construct the line that this point B lies on.

Emily runs a distance of 10 m to reach point B.

(iii) Mark this point on your diagram.

(iv) Using your diagram, find out how far away point B is from Joan (to the nearest metre).

20. Three groups decide to camp in a field as shown.
They decide to dig the latrine (toilet) at an equal distance from each campsite.

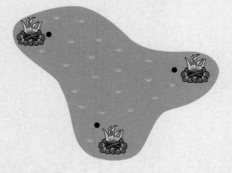

Show on a diagram where this latrine should be dug. Show all construction marks.

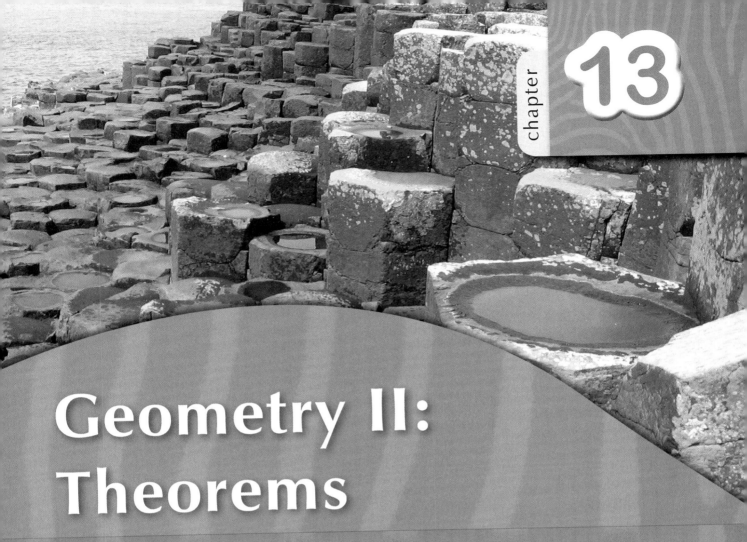

chapter

13

Geometry II: Theorems

Learning Outcomes

In this chapter, you will learn the following theorems:

- Theorem 1. Vertically opposite angles are equal in measure.

- Theorem 2. In an isosceles triangle, the angles opposite the equal sides are equal. Conversely, if two angles are equal, then the triangle is isosceles.

- Theorem 3. If a transversal makes equal alternate angles on two lines, then the lines are parallel (and converse).

- Theorem 4. The angles in any triangle add up to 180°.

- Theorem 5. Two lines are parallel if, and only if, for any transversal, the corresponding angles are equal.

- Theorem 6. Each exterior angle of a triangle is equal to the sum of the interior opposite angles.

- Theorem 9. In a parallelogram, opposite sides are equal and opposite angles are equal.

- Theorem 10. The diagonals of a parallelogram bisect each other.

13.1 THEOREMS

A **theorem** is a rule that you can prove by following a certain number of logical steps or by using a previous theorem or axiom that you already know.

You may even know some geometry theorems already without realising it!

Hint: What do you know about this shape?

In most cases, you only need to understand what each theorem means and how to use them in different situations.

KEY WORDS

- **Theorem**
- **Vertically opposite**
- **Alternate**
- **Corresponding**
- **Right-angled triangle**
- **Isosceles triangle**
- **Exterior angle**
- **Interior angle**
- **Quadrilateral**
- **Square**
- **Rhombus**
- **Rectangle**
- **Parallelogram**
- **Transversal**

Thales of Miletus (*c.* 624–546 BC) was a Greek scientist and mathematician. He is believed to have developed some of the first geometry theorems. We will encounter the Theorem of Thales in a later chapter. Thales showed how geometry could have practical uses – he lived in Egypt and impressed the Egyptians by using geometry to estimate the height of the pyramids!

Thales of Miletus

13.2 VERTICALLY OPPOSITE ANGLES

In the previous chapter, we looked at many different types of angles. There are also different types of relationships between angles. **Vertically opposite angles** are an important example of this.

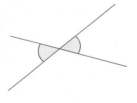 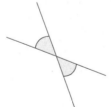

Vertically opposite angles are angles that have the same vertex and are directly opposite each other.

ACTIVITIES 13.1, 13.2, 13.3

All of these angles are vertically opposite each other.
Vertically opposite angles use the same rays to form the angle.

A way to spot vertically opposite angles is to look for the **X shape**.

Vertically opposite angles have a special property. You can see this for yourself by doing Activities 13.2 and 13.3. From these activities, it is clear that:

Theorem 1

Vertically opposite angles are equal in measure.

Worked Example 13.1

Find the measure of the angle *A* and the angle *B*.

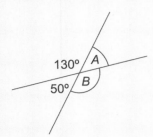

Solution

Angle *A* = 50° (angle vertically opposite is 50°).

Angle *B* = 130° (angle vertically opposite is 130°).

> Remember, it is always a good idea to show as much work as possible or to write down the reason for your answer.

 ## Worked Example 13.2

Find $|\angle B|$ and $|\angle C|$.

Solution

$|\angle B| = 110°$ (vertically opposite angle).

Once we know $|\angle B|$, we can then use another axiom or theorem to find $|\angle C|$.

$\angle B$ and $\angle C$ make a straight angle, so we know that these angles add up to 180°.

$|\angle C| = 180° - 110°$

$|\angle C| = 70°$

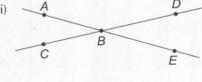

 ## Exercise 13.1

1. Identify the pairs of vertically opposite angles in each of the following diagrams:

(i)

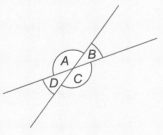

(ii)

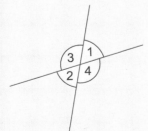

(iii)

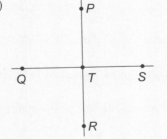

(iv)

(diagram: lines intersecting at T with points P, Q, T, S, R)

2. Find the value of angle *A* in each of the following diagrams. Make sure to show all your work and give a reason for your answer.

(i)

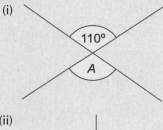

(ii)

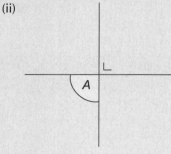

(iii)

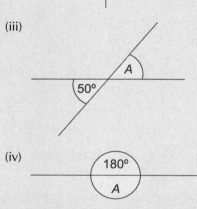

(iv)

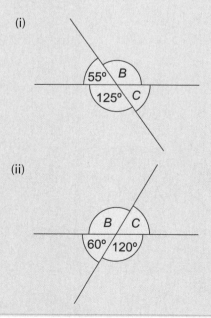

3. Find the measure of |∠*B*| and |∠*C*| in each of the following diagrams. Make sure to show all your work and give a reason for your answer.

(i)

(ii)

(iii)

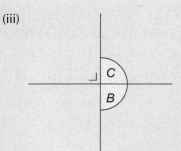

(iv)

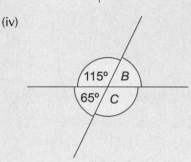

4. Find the size of each of the angles marked with letters in each of the following diagrams. Make sure to show all your work and give a reason for your answer.

(i)

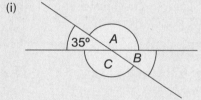

(ii)

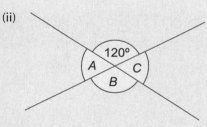

(iii)

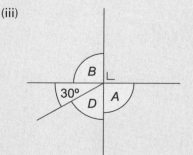

(iv)

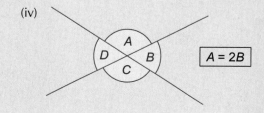

A = 2*B*

5. Find the size of each of the angles in the following diagrams. Make sure to show all your work and give a reason for your answer.

(i)

|∠ABC| =
|∠DBE| =
|∠ABE| =

(ii)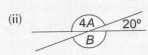

|∠ A| =
|∠ B| =

13.3 ALTERNATE AND CORRESPONDING ANGLES IN PARALLEL LINES

When a **transversal** intersects (cuts across) two or more other lines, certain angles are formed.

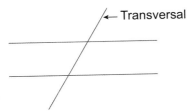

Transversal

> A transversal is a line that intersects two or more lines.

Two types of angles are formed when a transversal intersects two lines:

(i) **Alternate** angles   (ii) **Corresponding** angles

When a transversal cuts two parallel lines, the alternate and corresponding angles formed by this line will have certain properties.

Remember, we can spot parallel lines from the arrows drawn on them to show they are parallel to each other.

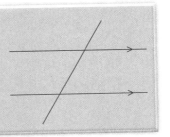

Alternate Angles

The angles shown in the diagrams below are **alternate angles**.

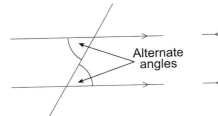 Alternate angles

 Alternate angles

> Alternate angles are on **opposite sides** of the transversal that cuts two parallel lines but are **between** the two parallel lines.

ACTIVITY 13.4

It is very important to be able to identify which angles are alternate.

An easy way to remember which angles are **alternate** is to look for the **Z shape**.

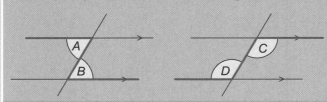

Once we can identify which angles are alternate, we can then explore the properties of alternate angles.

ACTIVITIES 13.5, 13.6

From Activities 13.5 and 13.6, we can conclude that:

> If we have two parallel lines, then the alternate angles formed by a transversal are equal.

If $l \parallel m \Rightarrow |\angle 1| = |\angle 2|$

The converse (reverse) of this statement also applies:

> If the alternate angles are equal, the transversal has cut two parallel lines.

If $|\angle 1| = |\angle 2| \Rightarrow l$ is parallel to m

From these two statements, we can show that:

> ### Theorem 3
> If a transversal makes equal alternate angles on two lines, then the lines are parallel (and converse).

ACTIVITY 13.7

Corresponding Angles

The angles shown in the diagrams below are **corresponding angles**.

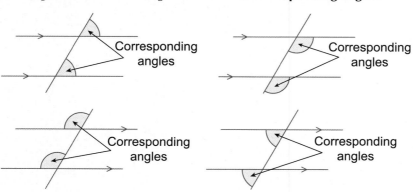

Corresponding angles

Corresponding angles

Corresponding angles

Corresponding angles

ACTIVITY 13.8

> **Corresponding angles** are on the **same side** of the transversal that cuts two parallel lines and are **either above or below** the two parallel lines.

An easy way to remember which angles are **corresponding** is to look for the **F shape**.

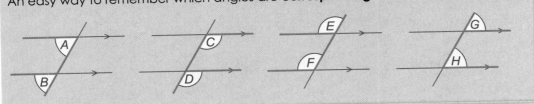

Once we can identify which angles are corresponding, we can then explore the properties of corresponding angles.

From Activities 13.9 and 13.10, we can show that:

ACTIVITIES 13.9, 13.10

> If we have two parallel lines, then the corresponding angles formed by a transversal are equal.

If $p \parallel q \Rightarrow |\angle 1| = |\angle 2|$

The converse (reverse) of this statement also applies:

> If the corresponding angles are equal, the transversal has cut two parallel lines.

If $|\angle 1| = |\angle 2| \Rightarrow p \parallel q$

From these two statements, we can conclude that:

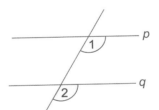

Theorem 5

Two lines are parallel if, and only if, for any transversal, the corresponding angles are equal.

ACTIVITY 13.11

 Worked Example 13.3

Without measuring, find the value of $|\angle 1|$, $|\angle 2|$ $|\angle 3|$ and $|\angle 4|$.

Solution

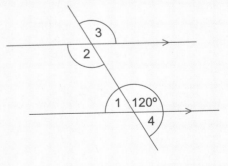

$|\angle 1| = 180° - 120°$ (straight angle)

$|\angle 1| = 60°$

$|\angle 2| = 120°$ (alternate angle)

$|\angle 3| = 120°$ (corresponding angle or vertically opposite angle)

$|\angle 4| = 60°$ (straight angle or vertically opposite angle)

> Remember, in most questions there are many different ways to find the measure of an angle.
> Also, the interior angles between two parallel lines add up to 180°. That is, $|\angle 1| + |\angle 2| = 180°$.

Worked Example 13.4

Without measuring, find the value of $|\angle A|$.

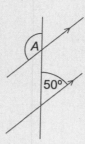

This question is more difficult, as we must determine ourselves which angles to use.

Solution

Fill in angle B.

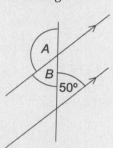   **or**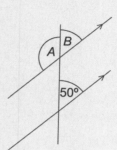

$|\angle B| = 50°$ (alternate angle)

$|\angle A| = 180° - 50°$ (straight angle)

$|\angle A| = 130°$

$|\angle B| = 50°$ (corresponding angle)

$|\angle A| = 180° - 50°$ (straight angle)

$|\angle A| = 130°$

Exercise 13.2

1. For each of the diagrams below, state which angle is **alternate** to angle A and which angle is **corresponding** to angle A.

(i)

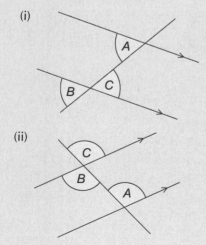

(ii)

(iii)

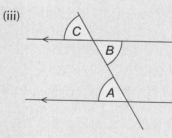

(iv)

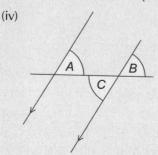

2. Find the measure of $|\angle 1|$ and $|\angle 2|$ in each of the following diagrams. Make sure to give a reason for your answer.

(i)

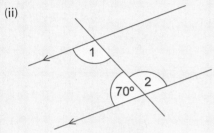

(ii)

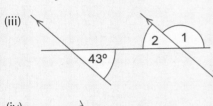

(iii)

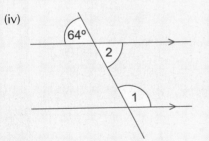

(iv)

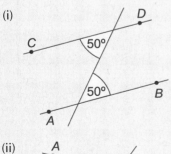

3. Investigate by using **alternate angles** if the line *AB* is parallel to the line *CD* in each of the following diagrams:

(i)

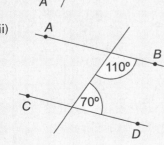

(ii)

4. Investigate by using **corresponding angles** if *l* ∥ *m* in each of the following diagrams:

(i)

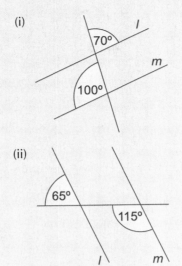

(ii)

5. Find the size of each of the angles marked with letters in each of the following diagrams. Make sure to show all your work and give a reason for your answer.

(i)

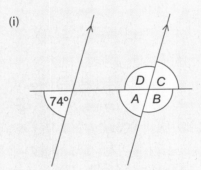

(ii)

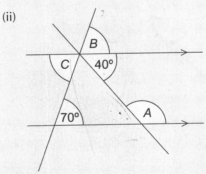

(iii)

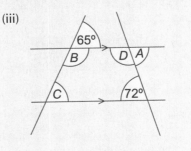

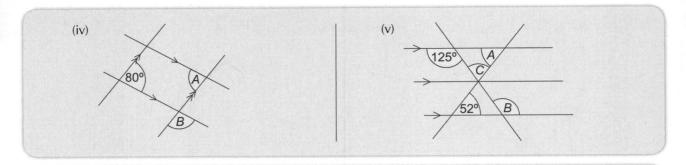

13.4 TRIANGLES

Triangles come in many different shapes and sizes.

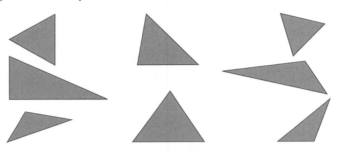

Triangles are often seen in construction, as the triangle is a very stable shape.

When we name a triangle, we usually call it after its three vertices. The triangle shown on the right could be called the triangle *ABC* or △*ABC*.

Types of Triangles

Triangles are usually divided into three types. This is done by looking at their side lengths and angle sizes.

From Activities 13.12, 13.13 and 13.14, we can identify the following triangles and their properties:

ACTIVITIES 13.12, 13.13, 13.14

Equilateral	Isosceles	Scalene
All sides the same length	Two sides the same length	No side the same length
All angles the same size (60°)	Two angles the same size	No angles the same size

Usually, if a triangle's three sides are the same length, a mark is drawn through each side. This is called an equilateral triangle.

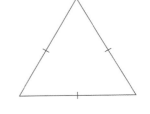

If a triangle has two sides of the same length, the same two marks are drawn through the two equal sides.
This is called an isosceles triangle.

If any angles in the triangle are equal, they are also marked.

In the triangle shown here, two angles are equal.

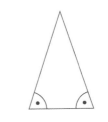

Another type of triangle is a **right-angled triangle**.
A right-angled triangle can be either a scalene or an isosceles triangle.

We can now look at the various properties of triangles.

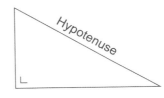

A triangle is a right-angled triangle if one of its angles is a right angle (90° angle). The side opposite the right angle is called the hypotenuse.

The word **hypotenuse** is thought to derive from the Greek *hypo* ('under') and *teinein* ('to stretch').

Isosceles Triangles

From the previous activities, we have already determined that:

A triangle that has two equal sides is an isosceles triangle.

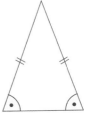

We can also investigate the relationship between the angles and the sides of an isosceles triangle.

ACTIVITIES 13.15, 13.16

From Activities 13.15 and 13.16, it is clear that:

In an isosceles triangle, the angles opposite the equal sides are equal as well.

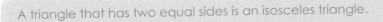

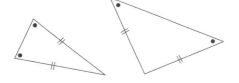

The word **isosceles** derives from the Greek *iso* ('same') and *skelos* ('leg') because an isosceles triangle looks like a human's two legs on the ground.

Combining the two statements above, we get the following theorem:

> ### Theorem 2
> In an isosceles triangle, the angles opposite the equal sides are equal. Conversely, if two angles are equal, then the triangle is isosceles.

Angles in a Triangle

We have already discovered that the angles in a triangle add up to 180°. This can also be illustrated in another way.

From our investigations, we can now say that:

> ### Theorem 4
> The angles in any triangle add up to 180°.

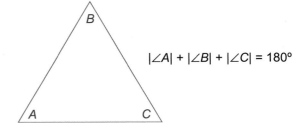

$|\angle A| + |\angle B| + |\angle C| = 180°$

Exterior Angles of a Triangle

The **exterior angle** (external or outside angle) of a triangle also has some interesting properties.

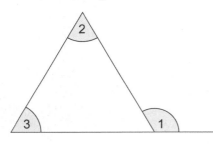

> An **exterior angle** of a triangle is the angle formed when one side of a triangle is extended.

The exterior angle is ∠1. The angles ∠2 and ∠3 are said to be **interior opposite angles**. They are also know as **interior remote angles**.

We can now look at the relationship between these two types of angles.

From our explorations of these angles, it is clear that:

> ### Theorem 6
> Each exterior angle of a triangle is equal to the sum of the interior opposite angles.

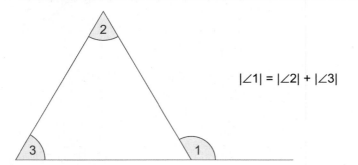

$|\angle 1| = |\angle 2| + |\angle 3|$

Worked Example 13.5

Without measuring, find the value of $|\angle A|$.

Solution

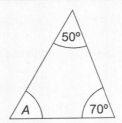

$|\angle A| + 50° + 70° = 180°$ (angles in a triangle)

$\therefore |\angle A| = 180° - 50° - 70°$

$|\angle A| = 60°$

Worked Example 13.6

Find the measure of $|\angle ABC|$.

Solution

It is usually much easier if we use the notation $\angle A$ instead of $\angle BAC$, $\angle C$ instead of $\angle ACB$ and $\angle B$ instead of $\angle ABC$.

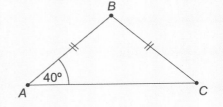

$|\angle A| = 40°$

$\therefore |\angle C| = 40°$ (isosceles triangles)

$|\angle B| + 40° + 40° = 180°$ (angles in a triangle)

$\therefore |\angle B| = 180° - 40° - 40°$

$|\angle B| = 100°$

$|\angle ABC| = 100°$

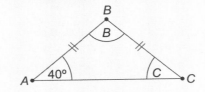

Worked Example 13.7

Find the measure of $|\angle C|$ without measuring the angle.

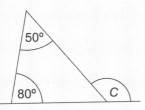

Solution

$|\angle C| = 80° + 50°$ (exterior angle)

$\therefore |\angle C| = 130°$

Worked Example 13.8

Find $|\angle 1|$. The diagram is not drawn to scale.

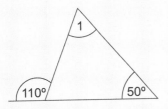

Solution

$|\angle 1| + 50° = 110°$ (exterior angle)

$\therefore |\angle 1| = 110° - 50°$

$|\angle 1| = 60°$

Exercise 13.3

1. Find the value of the angle *A* in each of the
   following triangles. Remember to show as
   much work as possible.

   (i)
   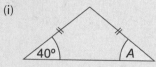

   (ii)
   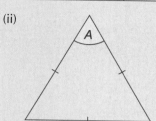

   (iii)
   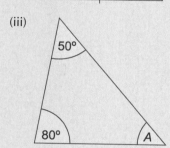

   (iv)
   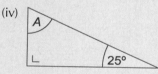

   (v)
   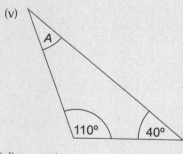

   (vi)
   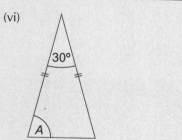

2. Find the measure of angle *A* in each case:

   (i)
   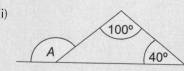

   (ii)
   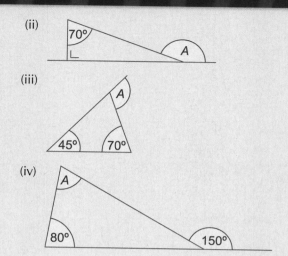

   (iii)

   (iv)

3. Find the value of the angle *B* in each of the
   following triangles. Remember to show as
   much work as possible.

   (i)

   (ii)

   (iii)

   (iv)
   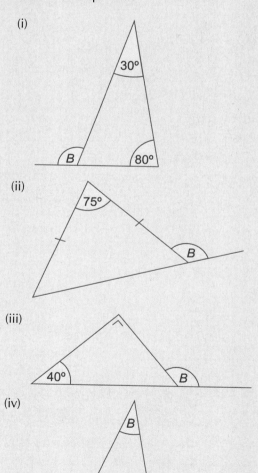

GEOMETRY II: THEOREMS

4. Find the size of each of the angles marked with letters in each of the following triangles. Make sure to show all your work and give a reason for your answer.

(i)

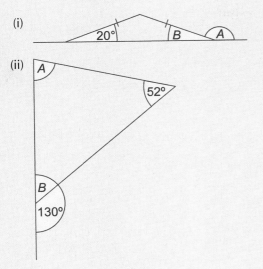

(ii)

(iii)

(iv)

(v)

The following questions may require you to use the knowledge that you gained in the previous sections of this chapter.

5. Find the size of each of the angles marked with letters in each of the following diagrams. Make sure to show all your work and give a reason for your answer.

(i)

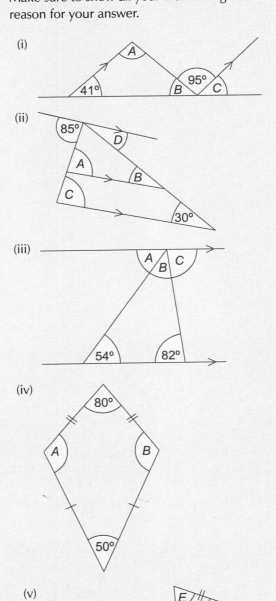

(ii)

(iii)

(iv)

(v)

13.5 QUADRILATERALS

Many two-dimensional shapes are **polygons**.

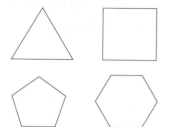

> A **polygon** is a flat, two-dimensional shape whose sides only meet at their endpoints. A polygon has at least three sides.

When we name a polygon, we name it after its vertices, following a circular path around the polygon.

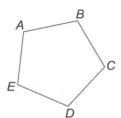

This is the polygon *ABCDE* or *EDCBA*.

You will often encounter a type of polygon called a **quadrilateral**.

> A **quadrilateral** is a four-sided figure with four corners or vertices.

Remember, a **quad** bike has **four** wheels.

Quadrilaterals come in many shapes and sizes. However, there are special types of quadrilaterals that appear most often in everyday life.

Special Quadrilaterals

We can now investigate the most common types of quadrilaterals and their properties.

 ACTIVITIES 13.20, 13.21, 13.22, 13.23

From Activities 13.20–13.23, we can identify the different quadrilaterals and list their properties:

Type of quadrilateral	Sides	Parallel sides	Angles	Diagonals
Square	Four equal sides	Opposite sides are parallel	All angles the same size (90°)	Bisect each other – angle of 90° formed
Rectangle	Opposite sides are equal	Opposite sides are parallel	All angles the same size (90°)	Bisect each other
Parallelogram	Opposite sides are equal	Opposite sides are parallel	Opposite angles are equal	Bisect each other
Rhombus	Four equal sides	Opposite sides are parallel	Opposite angles are equal	Bisect each other – angle of 90° formed

Parallelograms

A square, a rectangle and a rhombus could all be described as **parallelograms**.

 ACTIVITY 13.24

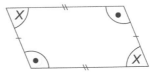

A **parallelogram** is a quadrilateral whose opposite sides and angles are equal.

From Activity 13.24 we can now state:

Theorem 9

In a parallelogram, opposite sides are equal and opposite angles are equal.

We also know through our investigations that:

Theorem 10

The diagonals of a parallelogram bisect each other.

The converse of Theorem 9 also applies:

For a quadrilateral, if opposite sides and opposite angles are equal, the quadrilateral is a parallelogram.

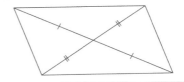

Worked Example 13.9

In the following parallelogram, find $|AB|$ and $|\angle DCB|$.

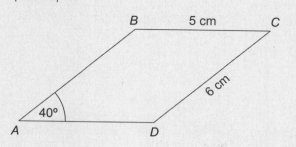

Solution

$|AB| = 6$ cm (opposite side)

$|\angle DCB| = 40°$ (opposite angle)

Worked Example 13.10

In the following parallelogram, find $|\angle A|$.

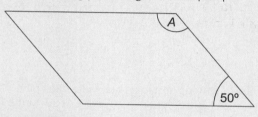

Solution

> A parallelogram is made up of two triangles. This means that the angles in a parallelogram add up to 360°.

We know that angles opposite each other are equal in a parallelogram.

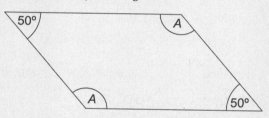

$\therefore |\angle A| + |\angle A| + 50° + 50° = 360°$

$2|\angle A| + 100° = 360°$

$2|\angle A| = 360° - 100°$

$2|\angle A| = 260°$

$|\angle A| = 130°$

Worked Example 13.11

In the following parallelogram, find $|\angle 1|$, $|\angle 2|$ and $|\angle 3|$.

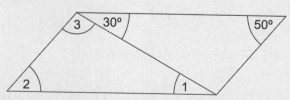

> When answering any question on parallelograms, remember that they also have **alternate** and **corresponding angles**.

Solution

$|\angle 1| = 30°$ (alternate angle)

$|\angle 2| = 50°$ (opposite angle)

$|\angle 1| + |\angle 2| + |\angle 3| = 180°$ (angles in a triangle)

$30° + 50° + |\angle 3| = 180°$

$\therefore |\angle 3| = 180° - 50° - 30°$

$|\angle 3| = 100°$

Worked Example 13.12

In the rhombus $ABCD$, $|AX| = 3$ cm, $|\angle ACB| = 35°$ and $|\angle ABD| = 55°$.

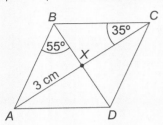

Find:

   (i) $|XC|$

   (ii) $|\angle BXC|$

   (iii) $|\angle CBX|$

Solution

   (i) $|XC| = 3$ cm (diagonals bisect)

   (ii) $|\angle BXC| = 90°$ (rhombus diagonals)

   (iii) $|\angle CBX|$

This question is more difficult, as it involves a couple of steps.

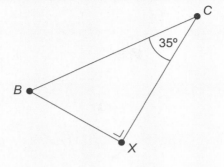

Consider $\triangle BXC$.

$35° + 90° + |\angle CBX| = 180°$ (angles in a triangle)

$|\angle CBX| = 180° - 90° - 35°$

$|\angle CBX| = 55°$

Note from this that a diagonal bisects the angle in a rhombus, i.e. $|\angle 1| = |\angle 2|$.

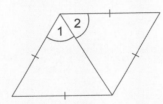

Exercise 13.4

1. Find $|\angle BAD|$ and $|AB|$ in each of the following parallelograms. Remember to show as much work as possible.

(i)

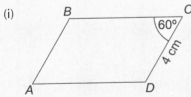

(ii)

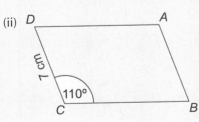

(iii)

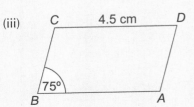

(iv)

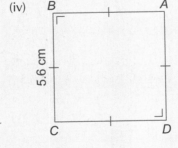

(v)

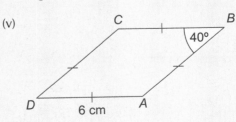

2. Find the value of the angle A and the angle B in each of the following parallelograms. Remember to show as much work as possible.

(i)
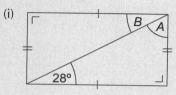

(ii)
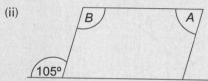

(iii)
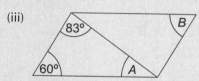

(iv)
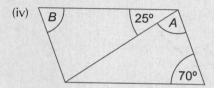

(v)
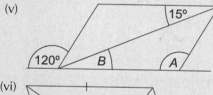

(vi)
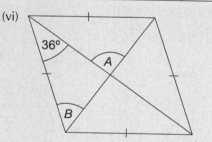

3. In the parallelograms below, identify all the angles that are equal in measure and all the sides that are equal in length.

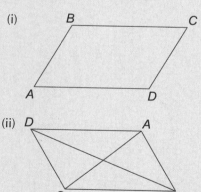

4. Find $|AC|$ in each of the following parallelograms. Make sure to show all your work and give a reason for your answer.

(i)
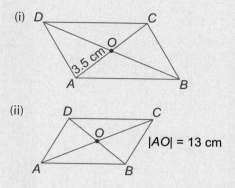

(ii)
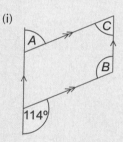

$|AO|$ = 13 cm

5. Find the size of each of the angles marked with a letter in the following diagrams. Make sure to show all your work and give a reason for your answer.

(i)
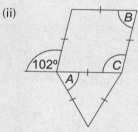

(ii)
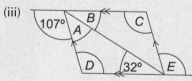

(iii)
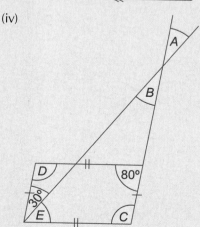

(iv)

Revision Exercises

1. (a) Find the missing angles. Give reasons for your answers.

(i)

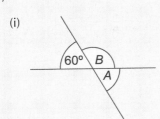

(ii)

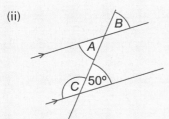

(iii)

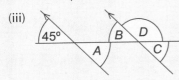

(iv)

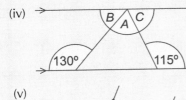

(v)

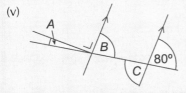

(b) Classify each of the following pairs of angles using the diagram below. The first pair have been done for you.

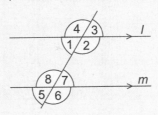

(i) ∠1 and ∠3: *Vertically opposite*

(ii) ∠3 and ∠7:

(iii) ∠8 and ∠7:

(iv) ∠2 and ∠8:

(v) ∠5 and ∠1:

(c) In your own words, explain what each of the following terms means. Use diagrams where necessary to help explain your answers:

(i) Transversal

(ii) Theorem

(iii) Axiom

(iv) Quadrilateral

(v) Parallelogram

2. (a) Find the missing angles, which are lettered in the diagrams below. Show as much work as possible.

(i)

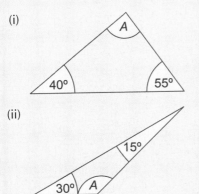

(ii)

(iii)

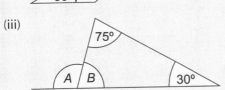

(iv)

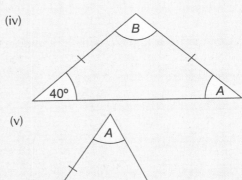

(v)

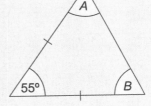

(b) The three main types of triangles are isosceles, equilateral and scalene. Construct each type of triangle.

Using your constructions, fill in the following table, which shows the properties of each type of triangle:

	Equilateral	Isosceles	Scalene
How many sides are equal?			
How many angles are equal?			
Sum of all the angles			

(c) Find the value of x in each of the following diagrams:

(i)

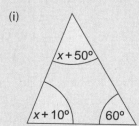

(ii)

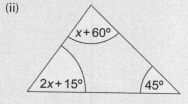

(iii)

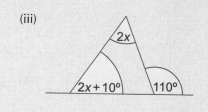

3. (a) Find the missing angles in the following diagrams. Show as much work as possible.

(i)

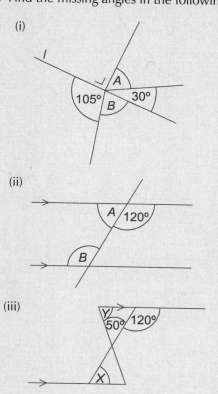

(ii)

(iii)

(iv)

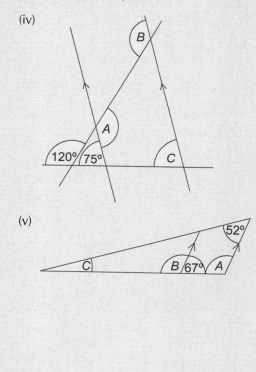

(v)

(b) Draw any two parallel lines p and q. Draw a transversal through these two lines.

(i) Measure any two pairs of alternate angles. What do you notice?

(ii) Measure any two pairs of corresponding angles. What do you notice?

(iii) How does this show that the two lines p and q are parallel?

(c) Find the size of each angle marked with a letter in the following diagrams.

(i)

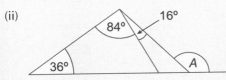

(iv)

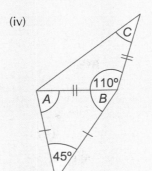

(ii)

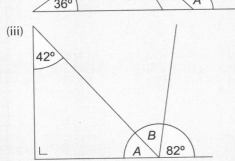

(v)

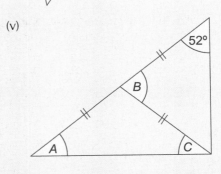

(iii)

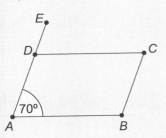

4. (a) *ABCD* is a parallelogram. Find the measure of the following angles (show as much of your work as possible):

(i) $|\angle BCD|$

(ii) $|\angle ADC|$

(iii) $|\angle EDC|$

(iv) $|\angle ABC|$

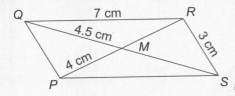

(b) *PQRS* is a parallelogram. Find the measure of the following line segments (show as much of your work as possible):

(i) $|QP|$

(ii) $|PS|$

(iii) $|MR|$

(iv) $|MS|$

(c) *DEFG* is a square. The triangle *DHG* is an isosceles triangle. Find the measure of the following angles (show as much of your work as possible):

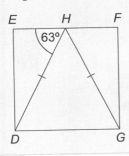

(i) $|\angle HDG|$

(ii) $|\angle DHG|$

(iii) $|\angle FHG|$

(iv) $|\angle EDH|$

5. (a) Using the diagram of a parallelogram *ABCD*, find the measure of the following angles. Show all your work.

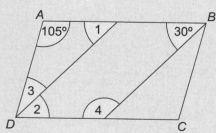

(i) $|\angle 1|$

(ii) $|\angle 2|$

(iii) $|\angle 3|$

(iv) $|\angle 4|$

(b) The following shape shows a type of parallelogram. Find the size of each of the following angles, remembering to show as much of your work as possible.

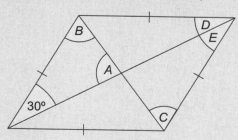

(i) $|\angle A|$

(ii) $|\angle B|$

(iii) $|\angle C|$

(iv) $|\angle D|$

(v) $|\angle E|$

(c) Consider the following two triangles.

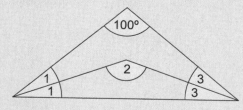

(i) Using the angles in the diagram, write an equation to show that the angles in the smaller triangle add up to 180°.

(ii) Now write an equation to show what the angles in the larger triangle add up to.

Find, using your two equations:

(iii) $|\angle 1| + |\angle 3| =$

(iv) $|\angle 2| =$

chapter 14

Statistics

Learning Outcomes

In this chapter you will learn about statistics in today's world, including:

- ⮑ How to find, collect and organise data

- ⮑ How to deal with different types of data

- ⮑ How to present data in a frequency table

- ⮑ How to represent data on a line plot, a bar chart, a pie chart, a stem-and-leaf diagram and a histogram

- ⮑ Measures of central tendency: mean, median and mode

- ⮑ Recognise how sampling variabilty influences the use of sample information to make statements about the population

- ⮑ How to use a spreadsheet to generate charts and provide summary statistics

- ⮑ How to recognise misuses and understand the limitations of statistics

Have you ever put a list of names in alphabetical order, or taken a set of scores and ordered them from the smallest to the largest? If you have taken any unordered list and ordered it in some way, then you have been doing some **statistics**.

> The word **statistics** comes from the Latin word *status*, which means 'state'.

'Number-crunching' is a slang term used by computer scientists to describe a program performing millions of arithmetic operations (addition, subtraction, multiplication and division) every second. Nowadays, some people describe doing statistics as 'number-crunching'. When statisticians 'number-crunch', they collect lots of data and try to make sense of this data.

14.1 STATISTICS IN TODAY'S WORLD

Statistics play a very important part in understanding the world we live in. When we turn on our TVs, browse the Internet or open a newspaper, we encounter numbers, charts, tables, graphs and other statistical results. Statistics are used:

- in weather reports
- in stock market reports
- in compiling football league tables
- in compiling music charts
- in compiling summaries of road traffic deaths
- in making predictions about the outcome of an election

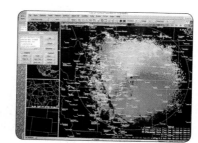

This list is not exhaustive. Can you think of any other areas in which statistics are used?

ACTIVITY 14.1

14.2 STATISTICAL INVESTIGATIONS

Scientists, economists, engineers and several other professionals rely on statistical investigations to solve many of their problems. A large part of any statistical investigation is the production of **data**.

> Any unordered list is called data. When this list is ordered in some way, it becomes information.

KEY WORDS

- **Primary data**
- **Secondary data**
- **Categorical data**
- **Numerical data**
- **Survey**
- **Questionnaire**
- **Population**
- **Census**
- **Sample**
- **Line plot**
- **Pie chart**
- **Bar chart**
- **Stem-and-leaf**
- **Histogram**
- **Mean**
- **Median**
- **Mode**
- **Range**

STATISTICS

Types of Data

All data is either **categorical** data or **numerical** data.

Categorical Data

Questions that cannot be answered with numbers provide categorical data. The following are examples of such questions:

- What colour is your hair?
- What TV programmes do you watch?
- What is your favourite band?

- What colour is your car?
- What grade did you get in your maths exam?

All categorical data is either **nominal** or **ordered**. Ordered data can be arranged in some order. Nominal categorical data cannot be ordered. Exam grades are an example of ordered categorical data.

Numerical Data

Questions that can be answered with numbers provide numerical data:

- How many Irish people holidayed abroad in 2009?
- What is the present rate of unemployment?
- How many golf Majors has Tiger Woods won?
- How many houses were built in Ireland in 2009?
- What is the average height of First Year students in your school?

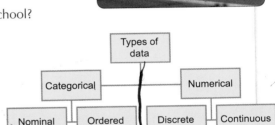

All numerical data is either **discrete** or **continuous**.
As a young person you are always growing. The rate at which you grow is so slow that we do not have any instrument to measure how much you have grown in a single day. However, your height is changing all the time and, for your age, could have any value within a certain range. We call such measurements **continuous numerical data**.
Numbers or measurements that can have only certain values, for example shoe size, are called **discrete numerical data**.

Primary and Secondary Data

Primary data is collected by or for the person who is going to use it. Secondary data is **not** collected by or for the person who is going to use it.

- Sources for primary data are **experiments** and **surveys**.
- Sources for secondary data include *The Guinness Book of Records*, the Census of Population or Internet-based sources such as CensusAtSchools.

Steps in a Statistical Investigation

All statistical investigations begin with a question. Here are the steps in a statistical investigation:

- Pose a question.
- Collect data.
- Present the data.
- Analyse the data.
- Interpret the data.

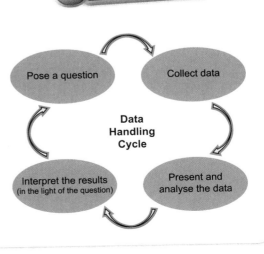

STATISTICS

14.3 COLLECTING DATA

Statisticians may collect data from everybody of interest to their investigation. We call such a collection of data a **census**.
If it is not possible to collect data from everybody, then data is collected from a smaller group.

Populations and Samples

Suppose that you wish to do a study on the TV viewing habits of students in your school, and now realise that it is impractical to interview everybody. You decide to interview 80 out of the 800 students in the school. In this case, the group of all 800 students is called the **population.**

> The population is the entire group that is being studied.

The group of 80 students is called a **sample**.

It is very important that a sample is representative of the population. For example, the sample of 80 students mentioned above would not be representative of the whole school if they were all First Year students. Unrepresentative samples give biased results. **Bias** is a distortion of the results.

> A sample is a group that is selected from the population.

Reliability of Data

When choosing a sample, you should always ensure that:

- The sample is large enough.
- A random sample is picked from the whole population.
- Everybody has an equal chance of being selected.

A simple method of selecting a random sample is to assign a number to every member of the population and then use your calculator to generate a set of random numbers. A member becomes part of the sample if their number corresponds to one of the numbers in the generated set. 'Picking names from a hat' is another method of random sampling.

Choosing a Random Sample with Excel

When choosing a sample, it is useful to be able to choose a random set of whole numbers between two given numbers. For example, to choose a sample of size 40 from a population of 800, you need to generate 40 random numbers between 1 and 800. Most spreadsheet applications will do this for you.

Worked Example 14.1

Generate 80 random numbers between 1 and 1,000 using Excel.

Solution

Excel 2007

(i) Move the cursor to cell A1.

(ii) Type the formula =RANDBETWEEN (1,1000) and press RETURN. ↵

(iii) Highlight cells A1 to A80.

(iv) Now use Excel's FILL DOWN command.

or

Excel 2003

(i) Move the cursor to cell A1.

(ii) Type the formula =RAND() and press RETURN. ↵

(iii) Highlight cells A1 to A80.

(iv) Now use Excel's FILL DOWN command.

(v) Move the cursor to cell B1.

(vi) Type the formula =INT(A1*1000)+1 and press RETURN.

(vii) Highlight cells B1 to B80.

(viii) Now use Excel's FILL DOWN command.

(ix) You should now see 80 numbers randomly selected from the numbers 1–1,000.

Microsoft Excel - Book2

File Edit View Insert Format Tools Data Window Help Adobe PDF

A1 =RAND()

	A	B	C	D	E	F	G
1	0.60023	600					
2	0.69713	697					
3	0.70354	703					
4	0.26089	260					
5	0.95556	955					
6	0.6224	622					
7	0.3761	376					
8	0.6456	645					
9	0.34983	349					
10	0.16506	165					
11	0.5339	533					
12	0.32716	327					
13	0.9099	909					
14	0.0782	78					
15	0.15234	152					
16	0.78169	781					
17	0.77952	779					
18	0.27432	274					
19	0.79897	798					
20	0.85012	850					
21	0.34045	340					
22	0.18671	186					
23	0.3798	379					
24	0.3146	314					
25	0.11969	119					
26	0.70209	702					
27	0.93735	937					
28	0.58333	583					
29	0.07516	75					
30	0.81083	810					
31	0.77456	774					
32	0.01765	17					
33	0.6964	696					
34	0.09878	98					

Sheet1 / Sheet2 / Sheet3 /

Ready

If you wanted to generate 10 random numbers between 1 and 30, you would highlight and fill down 10 cells at steps (iii) and (iv), and you would type =INT(A1*30)+1 at step (vi).

- RAND() generates a number between 0 and 1.

- Multiplying this by 1,000 yields a number between 0 and 1,000.

- The INT function removes the decimal parts of the number, leaving only the integer part, e.g. INT(314.867) = 314. So this produces a whole number between 0 and 999.

- Adding 1 to this creates a random whole number between 1 and 1,000, as desired.

ACTIVITY 14.5

Surveys

The most common way of collecting data is by survey. Most surveys use a questionnaire. The survey can be carried out by:

- Face-to-face interview
- Telephone interview
- Sending the questionnaire out by post
- Making the questionnaire available online

Surveys can also be carried out by observation. Suppose you wish to record the gender of all the people using a gym on a particular night. This is done by observing every person who enters the gym on that night and recording your results on an observation sheet.

Here are some of the advantages and disadvantages of each type of survey:

Survey	Advantages	Disadvantages
Face-to-face interview	Questions can be explained to the interviewee.	Not random Expensive to carry out.
Telephone	It is possible to select the sample from almost the entire adult population. Questions can be explained to the interviewee.	Expensive in comparison to postal and online surveys.
Postal	Inexpensive	People do not always reply to postal surveys, and those who do reply may not be representative of the whole population.
Online	Very low cost The anonymity of respondants ensures more honest answers to sensitive questions.	Not representative of the whole population – only those who go online and do online surveys are represented.

Designing a Questionnaire

A **questionnaire** is an important method for collecting data.
In the next activity you will get a chance to design a questionnaire. Here are some important points to note when designing questionnaires.

Questionnaires should:

- be useful and relevant to the survey you are undertaking
- use clear and simple language
- be as brief as possible
- begin with simple questions to encourage people to complete the questionnaire
- accommodate all possible answers
- be clear where answers should be recorded
- have no leading questions that give a clue as to how you would like the person to respond. For example, 'Manchester United are losing a lot of games this season. Do you think their manager should resign?'
- not ask for a response to more than one topic. For example, 'Do you think the government spends too much money on sport and should be voted out of office in the next election?'

> A **questionnaire** is a set of questions designed to obtain data from a population.

 **ACTIVITIES** 14.6, 14.7

STATISTICS

14

Designed Experiments

In a designed experiment, we apply some treatment to a group of subjects and then observe the effects of the treatment on the subjects. Pharmaceutical companies carry out many designed experiments when they are testing new drugs.

Exercise 14.1

1. Tanya has carried out a survey on the colour of cars in the school car park and will present the results of her findings to the class. Explain why the data collected by Tanya is primary data.

2. List three methods of collecting primary data.

3. Conor would like to predict the winning time for the men's 100 m final in the next Olympic Games. He gathers data from past editions of *The Guinness Book of Records*. Explain why the data collected by Conor is secondary data.

4. List two sources of secondary data.

5. List two advantages of telephone surveys.

6. What are the disadvantages of face-to-face interviews as a method of collecting data?

7. Explain the terms 'population' and 'sample'.

8. What do we call a survey of the whole population?

9. Assign a two-digit number to each student in your class (the first student is 01, the second 02, and so on.) Using the random integer generator on your calculator, select a random sample of size five from your class.

10. Make a list of 30 famous people. Using the random integer generator on your calculator, select a random sample of size six from the list.

11. Make a list of the 32 counties of Ireland. Using the random integer generator on your calculator, select a random sample of six counties from the list.

12. List six qualities of a good questionnaire.

13. Jane has designed a questionnaire that includes the following question:

    How old are you?

    Young ☐   Middle-aged ☐   Old ☐

    (i) What is wrong with the question?

    (ii) Improve the question.

14. John is doing a survey on football. In his questionnaire, he has asked this question:

    How often do you watch a football game?

    Never ☐   Once a week ☐   When I can ☐

    (i) What is wrong with the question?

    (ii) Improve the question.

STATISTICS

231

ACTIVE MATHS 1

15. Andrew receives a questionnaire about a new TV station. Here are some of the questions asked. Give one criticism of each question.

(i) How many hours have you spent watching TV in the past year?

(ii) What is your annual income?

<20,000 ☐   20,000–40,000 ☐   >50,000 ☐

16. Sinéad is doing a survey and has included the following question in a questionnaire:

Where did you grow up?

Country ☐   Farm ☐   City ☐

What is wrong with this question?

17. What is wrong with the following question:

Would you be in favour of amending Article 4 of the Irish Constitution?

Yes ☐   No ☐   Undecided ☐

18. Aisling is doing a survey on people's TV habits. She wants to know how much time people spend watching TV. Write down three questions Aisling should ask in her survey.

14.4 FREQUENCY TABLES

When data is collected, it is often convenient to put it together in a **frequency table**. Frequency tables show you how frequently each piece of data occurs. It is good practice to include a **tally** row in your frequency table. Tallies are simply marks to help you keep track of counts. The marks are bunched together in groups of five.

Worked Example 14.2

A class sits a mathematics test. Their marks out of 10 are as follows:

7	8	9	7	9	10
8	8	6	9	7	5
9	6	4	8	6	9
7	8	9	7	9	10
9	7	5	9	8	8

(i) Sort the data into a frequency table. Include a tally column in your table.

(ii) How many students sat the test?

(iii) What percentage of students scored 8 or better?

 **ACTIVITIES 14.8, 14.9**

Solution

(i)

Mark	4	5	6	7	8	9	10
Tally	I	II	III	₩	₩ II	₩ IIII	II
Frequency	1	2	3	6	7	9	2

Note that ₩ represents 5. Four vertical lines and one diagonal line gives a total of five lines.

(ii) 1 + 2 + 3 + 6 + 7 + 9 + 2 = 30 students

(iii) Number of students who scored 8 or better

= 7 + 9 + 2

= 18 students

∴ Percentage = $\frac{18}{30} \times 100 = 60\%$

Exercise 14.2

1. Listed below are the ages of students who attended a school disco.

15	12	14	12	14	15
14	14	13	13	14	12
13	13	12	12	14	15
14	14	13	12	14	12
12	13	14	12	13	14

   (i) Sort the data into a frequency table. Include a tally row in your table.

   (ii) How many students attended the disco?

2. Aoife tosses a die 50 times. Her scores are listed below.

5	3	3	3	5	1	2	5	1	5
1	3	3	6	4	6	1	2	1	1
1	6	5	6	3	4	2	2	5	2
4	6	5	1	2	6	1	1	6	2
2	6	2	5	2	3	4	4	6	6

   (i) Sort the data in a frequency table that includes a tally row.

   (ii) How many times did Aoife throw a six?

   (iii) How many times did Aoife throw a one?

   (iv) What percentage of the throws were fours?

3. Below is some data selected at random from the CensusAtSchools database. The data gives the different modes of transport a group of students uses to go to school.

Walk	Bus	Walk	Walk	Walk
Bus	Walk	Car	Car	Bus
Walk	Bus	Car	Walk	Walk
Car	Rail	Bus	Walk	Rail

   (i) Sort the data into a frequency table.

   (ii) What is the most popular means of travel?

   (iii) What is the least popular means of travel?

4. A teacher has given all her classes a spelling test that consists of 10 spellings. She is tabulating the results. However, she has not completed the frequency table.
   Copy the table and fill in the frequency row.

Mark	4	5	6	7	8	9	10
Tally	II	I	IIII	ℕℕ	ℕℕ	ℕℕ IIII	IIII
Frequency							

   (i) How many students took the test?

   (ii) What fraction of the students got all spellings correct?

5. A group of students is asked how many children there are in their family. The findings were as follows:

1	2	4	3	2	3
2	3	6	2	1	3
1	4	2	3	5	3
2	3	1	4	5	6
2	2	3	4	1	1

   (i) Sort the data into a frequency table.

   (ii) How many children come from families that have four or more children?

   (iii) What percentage of the children come from families with three or fewer children?

6. A survey is made of the number of goals scored in a series of soccer matches. The findings are as follows:

2	0	1	2	2	1	3
1	1	4	0	1	3	4
0	2	0	4	2	0	4
3	1	2	4	2	2	0
1	1	2	1	2	2	0

   (i) Sort the data into a frequency table.

   (ii) How many soccer matches were played?

   (iii) How many scoreless draws were there?

   (iv) What is the maximum number of games that could have been drawn?

   (v) What is the minimum number of games that could have been drawn?

7. Cathal takes three coins from his pocket and tosses the three coins together. He repeats this experiment 25 times and records his results as follows:

TTT	TTH	HTT	THT	HHH
HTH	THH	HHT	HHH	HTT
TTH	HHT	TTT	THH	HHH
THT	HTH	HTH	HTH	THH
THT	TTH	HHT	HTH	HTT

Result	3 Heads	2 Heads	1 Head	0 Head
Tally				
Frequency				

(i) Copy and complete the frequency table.

(ii) What percentage of the throws revealed one head only?

 ACTIVITY 14.10

14.5 GRAPHING DATA

In this section we look at important methods of graphing sets of data. Data that is graphed is always easier to analyse and interpret.

Line Plots

A line plot is a simple and effective way of representing data. A line plot uses symbols – usually x's – to represent the frequency of a piece of data.

Worked Example 14.3

Tom, a car salesman, sells second-hand cars that have been manufactured by four different manufacturing companies. The line plot below shows the number of cars he sold during January.

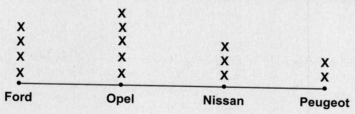

(i) How many cars did Tom sell in January?

(ii) What percentage of the total were Nissan (give your answer to the nearest percentage)?

(iii) What type of car sold the best?

(iv) What was the least popular type?

Solution

(i) $4 + 5 + 3 + 2 = 14$ cars

(ii) $\frac{3}{14} \times 100 = 21\%$

(iii) Opel

(iv) Peugeot

Exercise 14.3

1. The table below shows the number of DVDs rented by John in different shops during his mid-term break.

Shop	Planet DVD	Cinema Station	Movie Corner
Number	2	3	5

Draw a line plot comparing the numbers of DVDs rented in the three shops.

2. The table below shows the number of houses built in a particular townland over the past three years.

Year	2007	2008	2009
Number	4	7	2

Draw a line plot comparing the number of houses built during the past three years.

3. The table below shows the number of cars sold by a dealer over a four-month period.

Month	Jan	Feb	Mar	Apr
Number	7	2	3	1

Represent the data using a line plot.

4. Anne has decided to use a line plot to show the number of days that she and three of her friends have been absent from school.

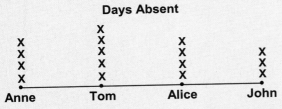

(i) Who has been absent the most number of days?

(ii) Who has been absent the least number of days?

(iii) How many days in total have the four friends missed between them?

(iv) Express the number of days Anne has missed as a percentage of this total.

Bar Charts

Bar charts are a simple graphical way of representing data. The bars on the chart may be horizontal or vertical. The height or length of the bars is proportional to the numbers in each category. All bars in a bar chart are the same width.

Worked Example 14.4

The following table gives the different modes of transport that a First Year class uses to travel to school.

Mode	Car	Walk	Bicycle	Bus	Train
Number	6	3	5	8	2

(i) Draw a bar chart to illustrate the data.

(ii) How many students are in the class?

(iii) What fraction of the students travels to school by bus?

Solution

(i)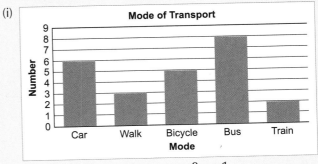

(ii) $6 + 3 + 5 + 8 + 2$
= 24 students

(iii) $\dfrac{8}{24} = \dfrac{1}{3}$

The following table gives marks for five students in two different maths tests:

Name	Seán	Máire	Eoin	Caitlin	Aoife
Test 1	69	64	78	56	92
Test 2	60	68	43	52	84

(i) Draw a bar chart to compare the results in both tests.

(ii) Using your bar chart, say whether the results from Test 1 are better than those from Test 2.

Solution

(i)

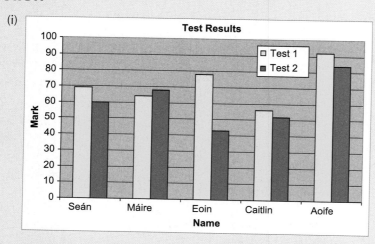

(ii) The chart indicates that all students with the exception of Máire scored better in Test 1.

STATISTICS

The bar chart below shows the monthly rainfall in an area over a six-month period.

(i) Which was the wettest month?

(ii) Which was the driest month?

(iii) What was the total rainfall for the six-month period?

(iv) What fraction of the rain for the period fell during May?

Solution

(i) April

(ii) July

(iii) $9 + 6 + 5 + 3 + 4 + 6 = 33$ cm

(iv) $\dfrac{6}{33} = \dfrac{2}{11}$

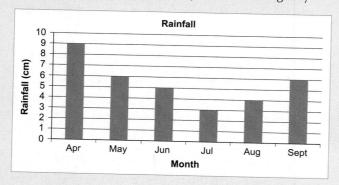

ACTIVITIES 14.11, 14.12

Exercise 14.4

1. A survey was carried out in a Second Year mathematics class. Students were asked to select their favourite colour from a list of colours. The results are shown in the table below:

Colour	Blue	Red	Green	Yellow	Black	Orange
Frequency	7	8	4	4	3	2

   (i) Represent the data with a bar chart.

   (ii) What is the most popular colour?

   (iii) What is the least popular colour?

   (iv) How many students are in the class?

   (v) What percentage of students have blue as their favourite colour?

2. The bar chart below shows the number of goals scored by five students in a penalty competition.

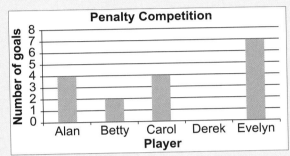

   (i) Who was the top scorer?

   (ii) Who scored no goals?

   (iii) How many goals were scored altogether?

   (iv) Which two players scored the same number of goals?

   (v) Did Betty and Evelyn score more or fewer than half the goals?

3. A class has to elect two representatives to the student council. An election is held and the results are as follows:

Student	Paula	Seán	James	Tanya	Rosie
Vote	8	4	3	7	5

   (i) Draw a bar chart to illustrate the data.

   (ii) Which students were elected?

   (iii) What fraction of the vote did James get?

4. The table below gives the ages of 30 pupils in a homework club.

Age	7	8	9	10	11
Number	2	5	6	11	6

   (i) Represent the data on a bar chart.

   (ii) What is the most common age in the club?

   (iii) Write the most common age as a fraction of all the children in the club.

   (iv) What is the percentage of students aged 7? Give your answer to two decimal places.

5. Below is a bar chart that shows the number of newspapers sold in a newsagent's shop over one week.

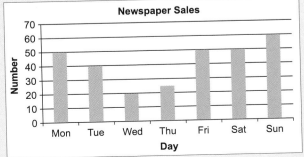

   (i) How many newspapers were sold on Tuesday?

   (ii) How many newspapers were sold during the week?

   (iii) What is the percentage of newspapers sold on Sunday?

   (iv) Why, do you think, were more newspapers sold on Sunday than on any other day?

6. Here are the areas (in 10,000 km²) of five European countries.

Country	Belgium	Denmark	Ireland	Holland	Austria
Area	3	4	7	4	8

(i) Represent the data on a bar chart.

(ii) What is the area of Denmark (in km²)?

(iii) Which two countries combine to have the same area as Austria?

(iv) Express the area of Belgium as a percentage of Ireland. Give your answer to the nearest whole number.

7. Anne decided to survey her class to find out each student's favourite sport. Below is a frequency table containing her results.

Sport	Soccer	Rugby	Football	Hurling	Basketball	Tennis
Number	6	3	2	5	8	6

(i) Represent the data on a bar chart.

(ii) How many students are in Anne's class?

(iii) What is the most popular sport in the class?

(iv) What percentage of the class likes soccer?

(v) What fraction of the class has rugby as their favourite sport?

8. John carried out a survey of his Third Year maths class. He wanted to find out the shoe sizes of the students in the class. John represented the data in the following bar chart.

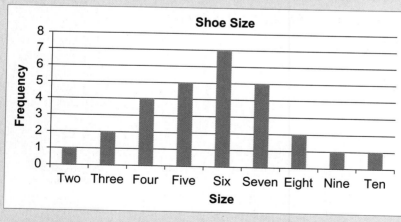

(i) How many students are in John's class?

(ii) What is the most popular shoe size?

(iii) How many students in the class wear a size 8 or bigger?

(iv) What percentage of the class wears the most popular shoe size?

9. The following bar chart compares money spent by a group of students on two different days of the week.

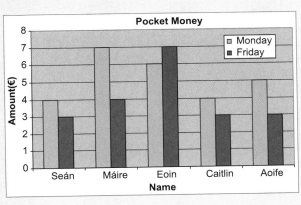

(i) Who spent the most on Monday?

(ii) Who spent the most on Friday?

(iii) What was the total amount spent on Monday?

(iv) What was the total amount spent on Friday?

(v) Write out the differences between the amount spent on Monday and the amount spent on Friday, for each student.

Pie Charts

If you want to show how data is shared or divided, then a pie chart is a good way of displaying this information. A pie chart is a circle divided into sectors, and the areas of the sectors are proportional to the size of each share.

Worked Example 14.7

The students in a class are asked to name their favourite indoor sport.
Here are their findings:

Sport	Basketball	Badminton	Squash	Table tennis
Frequency	12	6	5	1

Represent this information on a pie chart.

Solution

Step 1 Find the total number of students.
Total = 12 + 6 + 5 + 1 = **24**.

Step 2 Find the angle in each sector.

Basketball $= \dfrac{12}{24} \times 360° = \dfrac{1}{2} \times 360° = 180°$

Badminton $= \dfrac{6}{24} \times 360° = \dfrac{1}{4} \times 360° = 90°$

Squash $= \dfrac{5}{24} \times 360° = 75°$

Table tennis $= \dfrac{1}{24} \times 360° = 15°$

Step 3 Draw a circle (usually a circle with radius 5–8 cm looks best), and mark its centre.
Using your protractor, construct and label the sectors.

STATISTICS

Worked Example 14.8

A group of students were surveyed and asked to select their favourite colour from a list of colours. The results are displayed in the following pie chart.

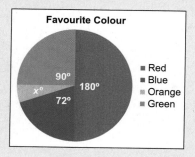

Favourite Colour

■ Red
■ Blue
■ Orange
■ Green

(i) What is the value of x?

(ii) If eight people chose blue as their favourite colour, how many students were surveyed?

(iii) Copy and complete the following table:

Colour	Red	Blue	Orange	Green
Number				

Solution

(i) $360° - (180° + 90° + 72°) = 18°$

(ii) $\dfrac{72}{360} = \dfrac{1}{5}$

$\dfrac{1}{5}$ of the pie is 8 students

$\dfrac{5}{5}$ of the pie is $8 \times 5 = 40$ students

(iii) Red: $\dfrac{180}{360} \times 40 = 20$

Orange: $\dfrac{18}{360} \times 40 = 2$

Green: $40 - (20 + 8 + 2) = 10$

Colour	Red	Blue	Orange	Green
Number	20	8	2	10

Exercise 14.5

1. The pie chart shows how 24 students in a class travelled home from school.

   (i) What is the value of x, the angle in the sector representing those students who walked home from school?

   (ii) Copy and complete the frequency table.

Mode	Bus	Car	Train	Walk	Bicycle
Frequency					

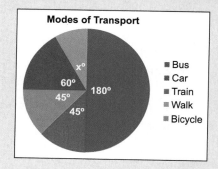

Modes of Transport

■ Bus
■ Car
■ Train
■ Walk
■ Bicycle

2. Twenty students took part in a survey. They were asked to identify their favourite sport. The results are given in the pie chart below.

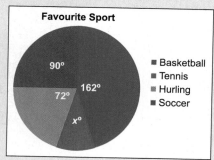

Favourite Sport

■ Basketball
■ Tennis
■ Hurling
■ Soccer

   (i) What is the value of x?

   (ii) Copy and complete the frequency table.

Sport	Basketball	Tennis	Hurling	Soccer
Number				

   (iii) What percentage of the students chose soccer?

3. A total of 120 First Year students were asked to choose one of three subjects: technology, music or art.

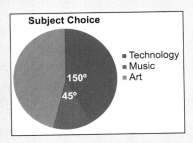

Subject Choice
- Technology
- Music
- Art

150°
45°

(i) What is the size of the angle representing Art?

(ii) Copy and complete the frequency table.

Subject	Technology	Music	Art
Frequency			

4. A farmer has a mixed farm. The pie chart shows how the farmer has divided his farm.

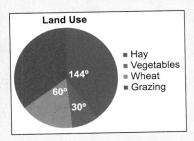

Land Use
- Hay
- Vegetables
- Wheat
- Grazing

144°
60°
30°

(i) What is the size of the angle representing grazing?

(ii) If the farmer has 15 acres of vegetables, then what is the size of his farm?

(iii) How many acres of wheat has he planted?

5. The pie chart below gives the breakdown of grades achieved by a group of students in a maths exam. Forty students achieved an A grade in the exam.

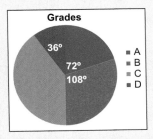

Grades
36°
72°
108°
- A
- B
- C
- D

(i) How many students sat the test?

(ii) What is the size of the angle representing Grade C?

(iii) Copy and complete the following table.

Grade	A	B	C	D
Number	40			
Percentage	20%			

6. In a class of 20 students, 5 are girls and 15 are boys. Draw a pie chart to represent this data.

7. Thirty Second Year students are asked to choose one of the following languages: French, German or Spanish. Fifteen choose French, 10 choose Spanish and the rest study German.

(i) Represent this information on a pie chart.

(ii) What is the percentage of students who choose to study German?

8. The following table gives the composition of the air we breathe.

Draw a pie chart to represent this information.

Gas	Nitrogen	Oxygen	Other Gases
Percentage in air	78%	21%	1%

9. The table below gives the composition of the 31st Dáil.

Party	Fine Gael	Labour	Fianna Fáil	Sinn Féin	ULA	Independents
Number	76	37	20	14	5	14

(i) How many seats are there in the 31st Dáil?

(ii) Draw a pie chart to represent the composition of the 31st Dáil.

(iii) What percentage of seats did Fine Gael win?

10. In a survey, 100 students were asked to name their favourite soap. The results are given in the table.

Soap	Fair City	EastEnders	Coronation Street	Home and Away	Other
Number	15	10	10	60	5

Represent the information on a pie chart.

Stem-and-Leaf Diagrams

Stem-and-leaf diagrams represent data in a similar way to bar charts.

A stem-and-leaf diagram represents data by separating each value into two parts: the stem and the leaf (the final digit). This allows you to show the distribution in the same way as a bar chart.

 Worked Example 14.9

Here are the marks obtained by 30 boys in a maths test:

87, 57, 29, 79, 84, 7, 55, 53, 65, 69, 62, 44, 52, 39, 43, 9, 13, 91, 61, 57, 75, 44, 73, 74, 68, 58, 52, 37, 35, 14

Represent the data on a stem-and-leaf diagram.

Solution

Step 1: Decide on the size of numbers in the stem. The marks range from 7 to 91. This range would suggest a stem in 10's.

Step 2: Construct an unordered stem-and-leaf diagram.

Stem	Leaf
0	7, 9
1	3, 4
2	9
3	9, 7, 5
4	4, 3, 4
5	7, 5, 3, 2, 7, 8, 2
6	5, 9, 2, 1, 8
7	9, 5, 3, 4
8	7, 4
9	1

Step 3: Order the leaves from the smallest to the largest.

Step 4: Give the diagram a key.

Stem	Leaf
0	7, 9
1	3, 4
2	9
3	5, 7, 9
4	3, 4, 4
5	2, 2, 3, 5, 7, 7, 8
6	1, 2, 5, 8, 9
7	3, 4, 5, 9
8	4, 7
9	1 Key: 3|5 = 35

 Worked Example 14.10

Twenty people go on a historic bus tour of Galway. Their ages are as follows:

15	14	25	23	33
45	13	51	60	48
19	57	47	56	44
11	38	46	21	16

(i) Represent the data on a stem-and-leaf diagram.

(ii) How many people aged between 50 and 65 were on the bus?

Solution

(i)

Stem	Leaf
1	1, 3, 4, 5, 6, 9
2	1, 3, 5
3	3, 8
4	4, 5, 6, 7, 8
5	1, 6, 7
6	0 Key: 1|4 = 14 years

(ii) Reading from our stem-and-leaf diagram, we see that four people were aged between 50 and 65.

 **ACTIVITIES** 14.14, 14.15

Exercise 14.6

1. Here are the marks obtained by 20 students in a maths test:

70	86	100	52	71
57	72	86	32	40
46	61	72	76	89
77	98	86	46	48

(i) Using the data from the table above, complete the stem-and-leaf diagram.

(ii) What percentage of students achieved a mark greater than 50?

Stem	Leaf
3	
4	
5	
6	
7	0, 1
8	
9	
10	Key: 8|6 = 86

2. A group of students were asked to choose a number between 50 and 100. Here are the results:

72	77	60	72	51	62
75	60	63	77	67	72
79	63	82	93	89	97
60	73	83	99	69	70
67	83	76	51	55	90

Represent the data on the stem-and-leaf diagram below.

Stem	Leaf
5	1, 1
6	
7	
8	
9	Key: 5|1 = 51

3. Siobhán measures the heights (in centimetres) of all students in her class. Here are her results:

149	156	165	154	148
158	177	175	166	153
154	168	138	149	155
157	157	165	156	181
165	143	139	183	178

(i) Copy and complete the stem-and-leaf diagram.

Stem	Leaf
13	8, 9
14	
15	
16	
17	
18	Key: 13|8 = 138 cm

(ii) Siobhán's height is 158 cm. What fraction of the class is taller than her?

4. The stem-and-leaf diagram shows the time in minutes spent by customers in a cafeteria on a particular morning.

0	4, 5, 5, 6, 7, 8, 8, 9
1	3, 3, 4, 5, 5, 5, 6, 6, 8, 8
2	1, 1, 2, 2, 3, 3, 7, 8, 9
3	2, 2, 2, 3, 4, 4, 4
4	1, 2, 2
5	2
6	3, 3 Key: 3|2 = 32 mins

(i) How many customers visited the cafeteria that morning?

(ii) How many customers spent at least 40 minutes in the cafeteria?

(iii) What fraction of the customers spent less than 20 minutes in the cafeteria?

5. Here are the times in seconds for 20 athletes who ran a 100 m race:

10.6	13.1	12.3	11.8	11.0
11.6	12.3	11.2	12.5	12.5
10.5	12.0	12.7	11.2	10.8
11.1	13.1	11.5	10.7	12.2

(i) Draw a stem-and-leaf diagram for this data.

(ii) How many athletes had times under 11 seconds?

(iii) What is the difference between the fastest time and the slowest time?

6. John records the ages of the first 20 people who line up at a bus stop in the morning. Here are his results:

20	32	28	13	15	46	32	48	31	19
19	21	32	42	13	27	45	34	13	24

(i) Draw a stem-and-leaf diagram for this data.

(ii) If **only** the teenagers in the group were on their way to school, what percentage of the group was **not** going to school that morning?

7. The stem-and-leaf diagram below shows the time (in seconds) it took contestants to answer a general knowledge question. All contestants answered in less than 7 seconds.

2	1, 2, 2
3	2, 4, 8, 9
4	1, 3, 4, 6, 7
5	1, 5
6	8

Key: 5|1 = 5.1 s

(i) How many contestants answered the question?

(ii) What percentage of contestants took longer than 5 seconds to answer?

8. The stem-and-leaf diagram shows the number of emails that each of 15 students received last week:

1	1, 2, 2, 3, 7, 9
2	2, 4, 9, 9
3	1, 3, 9
4	1, 6

Key: 2|2 = 22

(i) What was the highest number of emails received by a student?

(ii) How many emails in total were received by the group?

(iii) If $\frac{2}{3}$ of all emails received by the group were junk mail, then how many of the group's emails were junk?

Histograms

If you wish to graph height, foot length or arm span, then you could use a histogram.
Histograms are used to represent continuous data.

Histograms are similar to bar charts. In a bar chart, the height of the bar represents the frequency. In a histogram, the area of the bar represents the frequency. However, in our course we will deal only with histograms in which the bars have a width of 1. Therefore, the **area** of the bar will have the same value as the **height** of the bar.

Worked Example 14.11

The following frequency table shows the times, in minutes, spent by a group of people in a museum.

Time	0–10	10–20	20–30	30–40	40–50
Number	1	4	8	7	9

Note: 10–20 means 10 or more but less than 20, and so on.

Represent the data on a histogram.

Solution

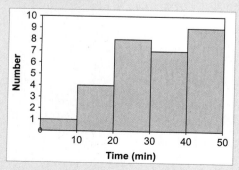

ACTIVITY 14.16

Exercise 14.7

1. The histogram shows the distances, in kilometres, that some students have to travel to school.

   Complete the following table:

Distance	0–2	2–4	4–6	6–8	8–10
Number					

   Note: 0–2 means 0 or more but less than 2, etc.

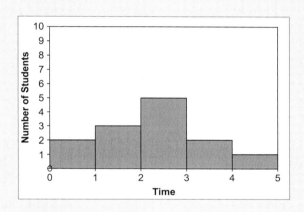

2. The ages in years of a group at a party were recorded. The results are shown in the table below.

Age (in years)	15–20	20–25	25–30	30–35	35–40
Frequency	4	8	16	12	4

   Note: 15–20 means 15 or more but less than 20, etc.

   Draw a histogram that will represent the data.

3. The time, in minutes, taken by each member of a group of students to solve a problem is represented in the histogram.

   Copy and complete the following table:

Time (min)	0–1	1–2	2–3	3–4	4–5
Number					

   Note: 1–2 means 1 or more but less than 2, etc.

   (i) How many students solved the problem in less than 3 minutes?

   (ii) What percentage of students solved it in less than a minute?

4. The number of hours' sleep taken by 50 people on a certain night was tabled as follows:

Time (hours)	0–3	3–6	6–9	9–12
Number	4	11	20	15

   Note: 0–3 means 0 is included but 3 is not, etc.

   (i) Draw a histogram that will represent the data.

   (ii) What is the greatest possible number of people who had over 8 hours' sleep?

   (iii) What is the least possible number who had over 8 hours' sleep?

5. Twenty students are asked how many minutes they spent watching television on a particular day. The following frequency distribution summarises their replies.

Time	0–20	20–40	40–60	60–80	80–100
Frequency	2	6	5	3	4

   Note: 0–20 means 0 is included but 20 is not, etc.

   (i) Draw a histogram to represent the data.

   (ii) What percentage spent less than 20 minutes watching television?

6. The stem-and-leaf diagram below shows the time (in seconds) it took contestants to answer a general knowledge question. All contestants answered in less than 7 seconds.

2	1, 2, 2
3	2, 4, 8, 9
4	1, 3, 4, 6, 7
5	1, 5
6	8 Key: 5|1 = 5.1 s

(i) Copy and complete the table.

Time (s)	2–3	3–4	4–5	5–6	6–7
Number		4			

Note: 2–3 means 2 is included but 3 is not, etc.

(ii) Draw a histogram to represent the data.

7. In a restaurant, the times taken (in minutes) for customers' meals to arrive are recorded. The results are given in the table below:

Time (min)	0–5	5–10	10–15	15–20	20–25	25–30
Number	1	6	7	8	6	2

Note: 0–5 means 0 is included but 5 is not, etc.

(i) Draw a histogram for this data.

In a popular TV programme, a well-known food critic stated that people should not have to wait longer than 17 minutes for their meals.

(ii) What is the highest possible number of people that could have waited for longer than 17 minutes?

(iii) What is the lowest possible number of people that could have waited for longer than 17 minutes?

14.6 MEASURES OF CENTRAL TENDENCY: MEAN, MEDIAN AND MODE

Statisticians are often interested in finding one number that represents a data set. This number is known as an **average**. There are different ways of working out the average.
We will look at three averages: the **mean**, the **mode** and the **median**.

The Mean

For example, the mean of the set {1, 2, 3, 4, 6, 8} is:

Mean $= \dfrac{1 + 2 + 3 + 4 + 6 + 8}{6} = \dfrac{24}{6} = 4$

> The mean of a set of values is found by adding the values and dividing the total by the number of values.

The Mode

The **mode** of the set {1, 2, 2, 2, 3, 3, 4, 5, 6} is 2, as 2 occurs more often than any other value.

> The mode of a set of values is the value that occurs most often.

Not all sets of data will have a mode, e.g. {1, 3, 5, 7}, and some data sets may have more than one mode, e.g. {1, 2, 2, 3, 5, 7, 7}.

The Median

To learn how to find the **median** of a data set, we need to know how to rank data. Ranking data means putting the data in order, either from the lowest value to the highest, or the highest value to the lowest.

Ranking the set {4, 7, 11, 9, 12, 10, 8, 11, 14, 2, 6}

gives   {2, 4, 6, 7, 8, 9, 10, 11, 11, 12, 14}

The number in the middle of the ranked set is called the **median**.

To find the median, cross out the smallest and largest, then the second smallest and second largest, and so on until you are left with the middle number.

$\{\cancel{2}, \cancel{4}, \cancel{6}, \cancel{7}, \cancel{8}, 9, \cancel{10}, \cancel{11}, \cancel{11}, \cancel{12}, \cancel{14}\}$.

The median equals 9.

What happens if the set contains an even number of values? For example, consider the set $\{4, 1, 3, 2\}$.

Rank the set: $\{1, 2, 3, 4\}$.

But this set contains an even number of values. In this case, we sum the two middle numbers (2 and 3) and divide our result by 2: $\{\cancel{1}, 2, 3, \cancel{4}\}$

Median $= \dfrac{2+3}{2} = \dfrac{5}{2} = 2.5$

> The median of a data set is the middle number after the data has been ranked. If there is an even number of values in the set, then the median is the mean of the middle two numbers.

Sampling Variability

If we select a number of samples from a population and find the average (mean, median or mode) of each sample, then we will find that these averages vary from sample to sample. This is known as **sampling variability**.

Worked Example 14.12

There are 20 members in a badminton club. Their ages are shown in the frequency table below:

Age	11	12	13	14	15
Frequency	4	3	4	7	2

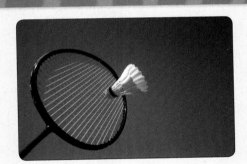

Find:

  (i) The mean of the data

  (ii) The mode of the data

  (iii) The percentage of members who have ages greater than the mean

Solution

  (i) Mean $= \dfrac{\text{Total of all the ages}}{\text{Total number of people}}$

$= \dfrac{(4 \times 11) + (3 \times 12) + (4 \times 13) + (7 \times 14) + (2 \times 15)}{4 + 3 + 4 + 7 + 2}$

$= \dfrac{44 + 36 + 52 + 98 + 30}{6}$

$= \dfrac{260}{20}$

∴ Mean $= 13$

  (ii) Mode $=$ most common age $= 14$ years (14 has the highest frequency).

  (iii) Those whose ages are greater than the mean are the 14-year-olds and 15-year-olds, of whom there are nine (since $7 + 2 = 9$).
  Percentage $= \dfrac{9}{20} \times 100 = 45\%$

14

 Worked Example 14.13

The percentages for a maths test are represented on the stem-and-leaf diagram below.

Stem	Leaf
3	6, 7, 8, 9
4	0, 1, 3, 5, 7, 9
5	1, 2, 3, 4, 8, 8, 9
6	4, 6, 7
7	3, 8
8	0 Key: 5|8 = 58

(i) Find the median percentage.

(ii) Write down the mode.

Solution

(i) To find the median, cross out the smallest and the largest number (in this case 36 and 80), then the second smallest and second largest, and so on until you are left with the number in the middle.

Stem	Leaf
3	6, 7, 8, 9
4	0, 1, 3, 5, 7, 9
5	1, ②, 3, 4, 8, 8, 9
6	4, 6, 7
7	3, 8
8	0 Key: 5|8 = 58

Median = 52%   Median

(ii) Mode = 58%   (the most common result)

 Exercise 14.8

1. Find the mean of these sets of numbers:

(i) {2, 5, 7, 3, 3}   (iii) {8.2, 7.9, 8.1, 7.8}   (v) {6, 9, 2, 7, 4, 2}

(ii) {5, 8, 6, 4, 5, 3, 4}   (iv) {1, 2, 3, 8, 7}   (vi) {6, 7, 8, 6, 7, 8, 6, 7, 8, 7}

2. Find the median and mode of these sets of numbers:

(i) {5, 8, 6, 4, 5, 3, 5}   (iii) {6, 2, 2, 2, 6}   (v) {0, 0, 0}

(ii) {2, 5, 7, 3, 3}   (iv) {6, 7, 8, 6, 7, 8, 6, 7, 8, 7}

3. The ages of a group of people entering a shopping centre are summarised in the following stem-and-leaf plot:

2	1, 2, 4, 5, 5, 5, 5, 6, 7, 7, 8
3	0, 0, 1, 1, 1, 2, 2, 3, 3, 6, 7, 8, 8
4	1, 1, 1, 2, 2, 3, 3, 4, 8, 9
5	0, 1, 1, 2, 7, 7
6	1, 2, 2, 6, 6 Key: 4|1 = 41 years

(i) Find the mode of the data.

(ii) Find the median of the data.

4. A teacher marks a test for 20 students and summarises the results in a stem-and-leaf diagram.

0	6
1	3
2	1
3	6, 7
4	3, 3, 3, 5, 5
5	3, 8, 9
6	3, 7
7	7, 8
8	2, 5
9	9 Key: 6|3 = 63

(i) Find the mode of the data.

(ii) Find the median of the data.

5. There are 16 students taking part in a school play. Here is a list of their ages:

12, 15, 16, 15, 16, 14, 16, 12, 14, 15, 12, 15, 12, 13, 12, 14

   (i) Find the mode of the data.   (iii) Find the median.

   (ii) Rank the data.   (iv) Find the mean. (Round your answer to two decimal places.)

6. The foot lengths (to the nearest centimetre) of a group of students are given below.

20, 22, 23, 25, 26, 25, 22, 25

24, 25, 25, 24, 22, 24, 23, 25

   (i) Find the mode of the data.   (iii) Find the median.

   (ii) Rank the data.   (iv) Find the mean.

7. The following are the number of goals scored by 20 teams in a soccer league:

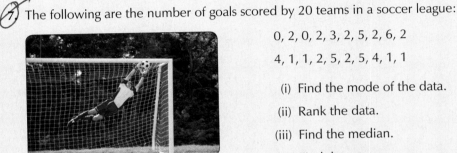

0, 2, 0, 2, 3, 2, 5, 2, 6, 2

4, 1, 1, 2, 5, 2, 5, 4, 1, 1

   (i) Find the mode of the data.

   (ii) Rank the data.

   (iii) Find the median.

   (iv) Find the mean.

8. The stem-and-leaf diagram below displays the weights, in kilograms, of 10-week-old babies:

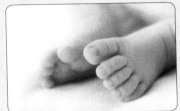

3	7, 9
4	2, 4, 7, 8, 8, 8
5	0, 1, 3, 6, 7, 7, 9
6	0, 1, 2, 3, 5
7	1, 2 Key: 4|2 = 4.2 kg

   (i) What is the weight of the lightest baby?   (iii) Find the median.

   (ii) Find the mode of the data.   (iv) Find the mean, to two decimal places.

9. *I Gotta Feeling*, *She Wolf* and *Hotel Room Service* were the top three singles downloaded from iTunes during October 2009. During that month, Max downloaded all three singles and calculated that the average price of a top three single at that time was €1.19.

   (i) How might Max have calculated this average?

   (ii) If Max has used the mean as the average, then how much did he pay in total for the three singles?

   (iii) If Max has used the median as the average, then write down two different sets of prices that Max *could* have paid.

10. For each of the following data sets, find the value of x. The mean of each data set is given.

   (i) {6, x, 7, 2, 3, 5} Mean = 5   (iv) {x, 3, 8, 11, 9} Mean = 8

   (ii) {5, 13, x, 6, 2, 8, 3} Mean = 7   (v) {22, x, 42, 52, 62} Mean = 40

   (iii) {5, 2, 6, x} Mean = 4

11. The frequency table below shows the grades achieved by a First Year maths class in an end-of-term test.

Grade	A	B	C	D	E
Number	3	8	7	2	1

(i) What is the mode and median of this distribution?

(ii) Explain why you cannot write down the mean of this distribution.

12. Four girls and six boys received text messages. The mean number of messages received by the four girls was 42, and the mean number of messages received by the six boys was 40.

(i) How many messages in total were received by the girls?

(ii) How many messages in total were received by the boys?

(iii) Is it possible to say that a girl must have received the most messages? Explain.

13. Alice removes all the Aces and picture cards from a deck of playing cards. She then deals out six cards. She reveals four of the cards to her audience. The four cards are the Three of Clubs, the Three of Hearts, the Three of Spades and the Three of Diamonds.

(a) Is it possible for Alice's audience to give:

(i) The median of the six numbers on the cards

(ii) The mode of the six numbers

(iii) The mean of the six numbers

Explain your reasoning.

(b) Alice then reveals that the number on one of the hidden cards is less than three and the number on the other hidden card is greater than three. If the mean of the six numbers is 4, find the numbers on the hidden cards.

14. A list contains seven odd numbers. The largest number is 23. The smallest number is 12 less than the largest. The mode is 13 and the median is 15. Two of the numbers add up to 38. What are the seven numbers?

Deciding Which Average to Use

The mean, median and mode of a set of data are all averages, but each one has a different meaning. The average, or measure of central tendency, that we choose depends on the characteristics of the data set we are studying. The following table will help you decide when to use the mean, median or mode.

Average	When to use	Advantages/Disadvantages
Mode	■ If data is **categorical**, then the mode is the only sensible measure of centre to use. Therefore, for data on hair colour, eye colour, gender, etc. use only the mode. ■ The mode can also be used with **numerical** data.	*Advantages* ■ It can be used with any type of data. ■ It is easy to find. ■ It is not affected by extreme values. *Disadvantage* ■ There is not always a mode.
Median	■ Used **only** with **numerical** data. ■ If there are **extreme values** in the data set, then use the median.	*Advantages* ■ It is easy to calculate. ■ It is not affected by extreme values.
Mean	■ Used **only** with **numerical** data. ■ If there are **not extreme values** in the data set, use the mean.	*Advantage* ■ It uses all the data. *Disadvantage* ■ It is affected by extreme values.

Worked Example 14.14

The value of seven houses in a rural area are as follows:

€150,000   €160,000   €180,000   €180,000
€180,000   €190,000   €2,500,000

(i) Find the mean house price for the area.

(ii) Find the median house price for the area.

(iii) Which of the above averages is the most typical of house prices in the area?

Solution

(i) Mean

$$= \frac{150{,}000 + 160{,}000 + 180{,}000 + 180{,}000 + 180{,}000 + 190{,}000 + 2{,}500{,}000}{7}$$

= €505,714 (to the nearest euro)

(ii) {150,000, 160,000, 180,000, 180,000, 180,000, 190,000, 2,500,000}
Median = €180,000

(iii) The median is the better average. The extreme value of €2,500,000 affects the mean, and this is the value of just one house in the area.

Exercise 14.9

1. Decide which average you would use for each of the following. Give a reason for your answer.

   (i) The average height of students in your class

   (ii) The average eye colour of all teachers in the school

   (iii) The average mark in a maths exam

   (iv) The average colour of all cars in the school car park

   (v) The average wage of 100 workers in a company, given that 90 of the workers earn between €30,000 and €40,000 per year, five workers earn between €60,000 and €80,000 per year, and the remaining five workers earn over €600,000 per year

2. Write down the type of average in each case:

   (i) This average uses all values of the data.

   (ii) This average is used with categorical data.

   (iii) This average is useful with data that contains extreme values.

3. Below is some data selected at random from the CensusAtSchools database. The data gives the different modes of transport a group of students uses to go to school.

Walk	Bus	Walk	Walk	Walk
Bus	Walk	Car	Car	Bus
Walk	Bus	Car	Walk	Walk
Car	Rail	Bus	Walk	Rail

   (i) What type of data is contained in this sample?

   (ii) What average are you using when you refer to the most popular type of transport used by these students?

STATISTICS

4. Rex has just been given the result of his last maths test. He does not know the results his classmates received, but would like to know how his result compares with those of his classmates. The teacher has given the class the modal mark, the mean mark and the median mark for the test.

   (i) Which average tells Rex whether he is in the top half or the bottom half of the class?

   (ii) Is the modal mark useful to Rex? Explain.

   (iii) Which average tells Rex how well he has done in comparison to everyone else?

5. (i) Find the mean, the mode and the median of the following set of numbers: 1, 2, 12, 12, 18, 19, 20, 24, 188.

   (ii) Which average would you use to describe these numbers? Give a reason for your answer.

6. Generate some primary data from within your class. Find the average of the data using a suitable measure, e.g. the number of pets they have.

14.7 MEASURE OF SPREAD

Range

The mean, median and mode supply us with one number to describe a set of data. However, such numbers give no indication of data spread.

Consider the sets A = {8, 8, 9, 11, 14} and B = {1, 3, 8, 17, 21}:

$$\text{The mean of set A} = \frac{8 + 8 + 9 + 11 + 14}{5} = \frac{50}{5} = 10$$

$$\text{The mean of set B} = \frac{1 + 3 + 8 + 17 + 21}{5} = \frac{50}{5} = 10$$

Both sets have the same mean, but the members of set A are more tightly bunched around the mean than the members of set B. To measure the spread of values, we could use the **range**.

> The **range** of a set of data is the <u>difference between</u> the <u>maximum value</u> and the <u>minimum value</u> in a set.
> Range = Maximum value – Minimum value.

$\underline{\text{Range}}_A = 14 - 8 = 6$ $\text{Range}_B = 21 - 1 = 20$

This indicates that the elements of set B may have a greater spread of values.

The range is affected by extreme values called **outliers**.

> An <u>outlier</u> is an individual <u>value</u> that <u>falls outside</u> the overall pattern.

1, 2, 3, 4, 7, 1, 88

ACTIVITY 14.18

14.8 SPREADSHEETS

Spreadsheets are a very useful tool for generating charts and providing summary statistics. We can generate bar charts, pie charts and histograms, as well as finding measures of central tendency and variation using a spreadsheet such as Excel.

STATISTICS

Worked Example 14.15

All the cars in a car park were surveyed to find their country of origin. The results were tabulated in a spreadsheet.

	A	B	C	D	E	F	G
1	**Country**	Ireland	Poland	UK	Lithuania	France	Total
2	**Number**	24	6	2	5	1	
3							

Sheet1 / Sheet2 / Sheet3 /

Ready — NUM

(i) Copy this table into a spreadsheet of your own.

(ii) Use the spreadsheet to generate a bar chart.

(iii) Use the spreadsheet's SUM function to find the total number of cars in the car park.

Solution

(i)

	A	B	C	D	E	F	G
1	**Country**	Ireland	Poland	UK	Lithuania	France	
2	**Number**	24	6	2	5	1	
3							

Sheet1 / Sheet2 / Sheet3 /

Ready — NUM

(ii) (a) Highlight cells A1:F2.

(b) Using the mouse, click on the following:
INSERT ⟶ CHART ⟶ COLUMN ⟶ NEXT ⟶ NEXT

(c) Enter 'Cars in the Car Park' in chart title box.
Enter 'Country' in x-axis box.
Enter 'Number of cars' in y-axis box.

(d) Click on FINISH.

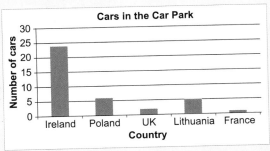

(iii) Here we need to sum the numbers in the cells B2 to F2, and we would like to put our answer in cell G2. So we type = SUM(B2:F2) into cell G2. Here is the result:

	A	B	C	D	E	F	G
1	**Country**	Ireland	Poland	UK	Lithuania	France	Total
2	**Number**	24	6	2	5	1	38
3							

Sheet1 / Sheet2 / Sheet3 /

Ready — NUM

Worked Example 14.16

A committee holds an election for a leader. The votes for the four candidates are counted and tabulated in a spreadsheet.

	A	B	C	D	E	F	G
1	**Candidate**	Allison	Brian	Cathy	Dermot	Total	
2	**No. of votes**	4	3	5	6		
3							

(i) Copy the data into your own spreadsheet.

(ii) Use the spreadsheet to generate a pie chart.

(iii) Use the SUM command to find the total number of votes cast.

Solution

(i)

	A	B	C	D	E	F	G
1	**Candidate**	Allison	Brian	Cathy	Dermot	Total	
2	**No. of votes**	4	3	5	6		
3							

(ii) (a) Highlight cells B1:E2.

(b) Using the mouse, click on the following:
INSERT ⟶ CHART ⟶ PIE ⟶ NEXT ⟶ NEXT

(c) Enter 'Election Result' in the chart title box.

(d) Click on FINISH.

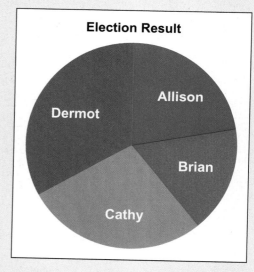

(iii) Here we need to sum the numbers in the cells B2 to E2, and we would like to put our answer in cell F2. So we type =SUM(B2:E2) into cell F2. Here is the result:

	A	B	C	D	E	F	G
1	**Candidate**	Allison	Brian	Cathy	Dermot	Total	
2	**No. of votes**	4	3	5	6	18	
3							

Worked Example 14.17

The following spreadsheet shows students' results in four tests:

	A	B	C	D	E
1	**Student**	**Test 1**	**Test 2**	**Test 3**	**Test 4**
2					
3	K Murphy	51	55	68	60
4	A Browne	74	82	79	80
5	C Guerin	40	70	48	55
6	D Keane	90	94	89	100
7	E O'Shea	56	60	82	85
8	F Langford	12	41	58	60
9	G Moran	51	82	46	85

Sheet1 / Sheet2 / Sheet3

Ready   NUM

(i) Copy the data into your own spreadsheet.

(ii) Using the spreadsheet's MAX and MIN commands, find the maximum and minimum result for each test. Hence, find the range for each test.

(iii) Find the mean mark for each test.

(iv) Find the median mark for each test.

Solution

	A	B	C	D	E
1	**Student**	**Test 1**	**Test 2**	**Test 3**	**Test 4**
2					
3	K Murphy	51	55	68	60
4	A Browne	74	82	79	80
5	C Guerin	40	70	48	55
6	D Keane ← my results	90	94	89	100
7	E O'Shea	56	60	82	85
8	F Long	12	41	58	60
9	G Moran	51	82	46	85
10	Max	=MAX(B3:B9)	=MAX(C3:C9)	=MAX(D3:D9)	=MAX(E3:E9)
11	Min	=MIN(B3:B9)	=MIN(C3:C9)	=MIN(D3:D9)	=MIN(E3:E9)
12	Range	=B10–BII	=C10–C11	=D10–D11	=E10–E11
13	Mean	=AVERAGE (B3:B9)	=AVERAGE (C3:C9)	=AVERAGE (D3:D9)	=AVERAGE (E3:E9)
14	Median	=MEDIAN (B3:B9)	=MEDIAN (C3:C9)	=MEDIAN (D3:D9)	=MEDIAN (E3:E9)

Sheet1 / Sheet2 / Sheet3

Ready   NUM

1. The spreadsheet below gives the marks out of 10 scored by a class in a maths test.

	A	B	C	D	E	F	G	H	I	J	K	L
1	**Mark**	0	1	2	3	4	5	6	7	8	9	10
2	**Freq.**	0	1	1	2	4	6	8	4	2	1	1

Sheet1 / Sheet2 / Sheet3 /
Ready   NUM

   (i) Copy the data into your own spreadsheet.

   (ii) Use the spreadsheet to generate a bar chart.

   (iii) Using the SUM command, find out the number of students in the class and place your answer in cell B3.

2. Alan, a Junior Certificate student, has logged in a spreadsheet the number of hours he has spent studying over the past week. Below is a copy of a section of the spreadsheet Alan used:

	A	B	C	D	E	F	G
1	**Day**	Mon	Tue	Wed	Thu	Fri	
2	**Hours**	3	2	4	1	0	
3							

Sheet1 / Sheet2 / Sheet3 /
Ready

   (i) Copy the data into your own spreadsheet.

   (ii) Use the spreadsheet to generate a bar chart.

   (iii) Using the SUM command, find how many hours' study Alan did over the past week.

3. John works out how he spends a typical 24-hour day and tabulates his findings in a spreadsheet:

	A	B	C	D	E	F	G
1	**Activity**	School	Study	Play	TV	Sleep	
2	**No. of hours**	7	3	x	2	10	
3							

Sheet1 / Sheet2 / Sheet3 /
Ready   NUM

   (i) Copy this information into your own spreadsheet, and find the value of x.

   (ii) Use your spreadsheet to generate a pie chart.

4. There are 72 people on a campsite: 27 are Irish, 34 are from mainland Europe and the rest are British.

   (i) What percentage (to the nearest whole number) of the campsite population is British?

   (ii) Put the information in a spreadsheet and generate a pie chart.

5. Collect the following data from your class: (a) wrist circumference and (b) eye colour.

   (i) Enter the data in a spreadsheet.

   (ii) Generate appropriate charts to represent the data.

   (iii) Find the mean and median wrist measurements for the class.

   (iv) Find the maximum and minimum wrist measurements.

   (v) Find the range for wrist measurements.

   (vi) Print your spreadsheet.

STATISTICS

6. The table shows the results that a sample of five students, from two different classes, received in a maths test.

Class A	70	42	58	68	49
Class B	69	43	50	100	59

(i) Enter the data as a spreadsheet.

(ii) Use two bar charts to display the data.

(iii) Comment on the shape of the charts.

(iv) Find the mean and median measurements for each class.

(v) Is there an outlier in any of the data sets?

(vi) Find the range for each class.

(vii) Comment on the spread of the results for each class.

14.9 MISUSES OF STATISTICS

Statistics presented in newspapers, on TV, on websites and in other media can sometimes be misleading. It is important that we, as consumers, are able to spot errors and exaggerations in such statistics. The following is a list of possible errors and exaggerations that may mislead the consumer.

1. *Arithmetic errors or omissions.* Always check that everything adds up. Do all percentages add up to 100? Does the number in each group add up to the total number surveyed?

2. *Sample size.* Many advertisements or newspaper articles contain statements such as 'Four out of five owners said their cats preferred KAT food.' How many cat owners were surveyed? If only 10 cat owners were surveyed and eight said that their cats preferred KAT, we cannot say that this number is representative of all cat owners, as the number surveyed is too small.

3. *Misleading comparisons.* Newspaper articles and TV reports sometimes make misleading comparisons. For example:

   The unemployment situation in the country at present is twice as bad as it was in the 1980s. There are twice as many unemployed now than at any time in the 1980s.

   However, there is a larger workforce now than in the 1980s. Unemployment figures should always be given as a percentage of the workforce. This is an example of a misleading comparison.

4. *Sources.* Always check the source of the information. Surveys are sometimes sponsored by companies with vested interests to promote. Very often, the sponsor can gain financially from the results of the survey.

5. *Misleading graphs.* The chart below summarises the results of 500 throws of a die. Do you think the die is biased?

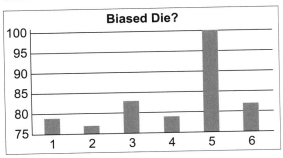

What makes the chart exaggerate the difference between the number of times a 5 was thrown and the number of times a 3 was thrown?

Now look at a different chart that summarises the same results:

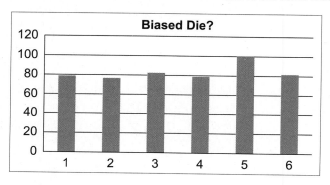

This graph is more correct, as it starts with zero at the bottom of each bar.

6. *Non-representative samples.* A sample should always be representative of the population it is taken from, otherwise the results will be misleading. For example, suppose you want to find the average height of 16-year-olds in your school, and you wish to do it by taking a sample. You decide to randomly choose thirty 16-year-olds. However, you limit your sample to girls only. This is not a representative sample, as boys have been deliberately omitted from the sample. This will lead to misleading results.

7. *Response bias.* This will occur when people have a choice of whether or not to take part in a survey. For example, a television show might ask people to phone in and vote on some issue. First, the people who watch that particular show may not be representative of the overall population; second, people who do phone in might be more or less likely to vote 'Yes' than people who don't want to phone in.

ACTIVITY 14.19

Revision Exercises

1. The following data was downloaded from the CensusAtSchools database.

Right-handed	Right-handed	Right-handed	Right-handed	Right-handed
Ambidextrous	Right-handed	Left-handed	Right-handed	Right-handed

(i) Show the data on a frequency table
(ii) Represent the information on a pie chart.
(iii) You would like to collect this data from your class. What question should you pose?
(iv) Using your question from (iii), collect the data from your class.
(v) Represent the information on a line plot.
(vi) Find the percentage of students that are right-handed in the CensusAtSchools sample.
(vii) Find the percentage of students in your class that are right-handed.

2. The marks, out of 5, in a maths quiz for a class of 20 pupils are as follows:

4	2	3	5	4
1	1	2	3	5
4	3	1	5	3
3	1	3	5	3

(i) Show the data on a frequency table.
(ii) Represent the data on a bar chart.
(iii) If 2 is the mark needed to pass the test, then how many students failed the test?
(iv) What percentage of students passed the test?
(v) Represent the data on a pie chart.

3. A company has been asked to design and market a magazine for teenagers.

Explain what primary data sources and secondary data sources the company might use in its research.

4. A sample of young people were asked how many magazines they buy during the week. Here are the results:

0	1	2	2	1
0	0	1	1	1
4	2	1	3	0
0	0	1	4	2

  (i) Sort the data into a frequency table. Include a tally row in your table.

  (ii) How many people were surveyed?

  (iii) Represent the data on a pie chart.

  (iv) What percentage of those surveyed bought just one magazine?

  (v) Suppose you are asked to carry out a similar survey in your school. Explain how you would select a sample from your school.

5. The table below gives the number of pairs of football boots sold by a sports shop during a particular week.

Day	Mon	Tue	Wed	Thu	Fri	Sat
No. sold	5	10	10	20	15	50

  (i) Represent the data using a bar chart.

  (ii) What is the total number of shoes sold during the week?

  (iii) Write the number sold on Saturday as a fraction of the total sold during the whole week.

  (iv) What was the mean number sold per day for this particular week?

  (v) Why, in your opinion, are the sales figures for Saturday much greater than those for any other day?

6. A group of students carried out a survey one morning to find the modes of transport used by students to travel to school. The results were as follows:

Mode	Walk	Bus	Cycle	Car	Train
Number	5	20	6	2	1

  (i) Represent the data on a bar chart.

  (ii) How many students were surveyed?

  (iii) What is the most popular mode of transport? Can you suggest a reason why?

  (iv) Two members of the class were late and were not included in the original survey. They had both walked to school. With this extra data, make out an updated frequency table.

  (v) Represent the new information on a pie chart.

7. John asked a group of friends to write down a number greater than 0 and less than 7. Here are his results:

4	5	5	6	6
2	4	2	3	6
4	6	6	6	3
6	3	3	1	2

  (i) Sort the data into a frequency table. Include a tally row in your table.

  (ii) How many friends did John survey?

  (iii) Use a bar chart to represent the data.

  (iv) What is the most popular number?

  (v) What is the least popular number?

8. The number of students in each of the 20 classes in a school is given in the table below.

23	10	20	18	24
29	18	20	25	15
16	20	30	18	26
32	17	24	32	28

  (i) Represent the data on a stem-and-leaf diagram.

  (ii) What is the total number of students attending this school?

  (iii) What percentage of classes contain more than 30 students?

  (iv) What percentage of students in the school belong to classes with more than 30 students? Give your answer to the nearest percentage point.

9. The table below shows the weight in grams of 50 apples:

Weight	20–30	30–40	40–50	50–60	60–70
Frequency	3	14	11	18	4

Note: 20–30 means 20 is included but 30 is not, etc.

(i) Draw a histogram to represent this data.

(ii) What percentage of the apples weighed 60 grams or more?

10. The answers to survey questions can be classified as:

(i) Categorical data where the categories are not ordered

(ii) Ordered categorical data

(iii) Discrete numerical data

(iv) Continuous numerical data

In each row in the table below, write a short question that you could include in a survey and that will give the type of data stated.

Question	Type of data
Q. 1	Categorical data where the categories are not ordered
Q. 2	Ordered categorical data
Q. 3	Discrete numerical data
Q. 4	Continuous numerical data

SEC Sample Paper, Junior Cert Ordinary Level, 2010

11. Here are the marks scored by 20 students in a science test.

51	74	50	33	35	47	55	44	28	87
72	55	44	76	84	93	56	67	92	50

(i) Construct a stem-and-leaf diagram to show these results.

(ii) What percentage of students scored over 90?

12. The frequency table below shows the ages of people living in a rural area.

Age	0–10	10–20	20–30	30–40	40–50	50–60	70–80	80–90
Frequency	5	5	7	10	18	12	6	2

Note: 0–10 means 0 or more but less than 10, etc.

(i) Construct a histogram to represent this data.

(ii) What percentage of the population is aged 50 or more?

13. A survey of shoe sizes of all students in Third Year in a particular school gave the following results:

Shoe size	3	4	5	6	7	8	9
Number	5	12	20	25	15	5	2

Find:

(i) The mean of the data in the frequency table, correct to two decimal places

(ii) The median of the data in the frequency table

(iii) The mode of the data in the frequency table

14. A class of 30 pupils received the following grades in a maths test:

A	B	B	C	A	D
C	B	A	B	B	B
B	C	B	D	B	C
A	B	C	B	B	A
B	A	D	C	C	B

(i) Is this data categorical data or numerical data? Explain.

(ii) Copy and complete the frequency table below:

Grade	A	B	C	D
Number				

(iii) What is the mode of the data?

(iv) Choose a suitable graph or chart to represent the data. Explain why you have chosen this graph or chart.

15. The heights of 20 tomato plants in a glasshouse are measured (in centimetres):

37	28	42	38	44
36	37	49	42	37
47	37	42	39	42
36	37	41	39	43

(i) Show the results in a stem-and-leaf diagram.

(ii) What is the modal height?

(iii) What is the median height?

(iv) What is the mean height?

(v) Which average best describes the data? Explain your answer.

(vi) What is the range of the data?

(vii) The plants measured were located in a shaded section of the glasshouse. How could this sample be biased as a result?

16. The frequency table below shows the time spent by a group of students on a difficult maths problem:

Time (min)	0–4	4–8	8–12	12–16
Number	8	12	10	7

Note: 0–4 means 0 is included but 4 is not, etc.

(i) Construct a histogram for the data.

(ii) What is the modal time interval for this data?

(iii) How many students worked on the problem?

17. Twenty people attend a meeting on healthy diets. Their ages are summarised in the following stem-and-leaf diagram:

Stem	Leaf
1	1, 1, 1, 4, 5,
2	1, 3, 5
3	3, 8
4	4, 5, 6, 7, 8
5	9, 9
6	8, 9, 9 Key: 1|4 = 14 years

Using the stem-and-leaf diagram, calculate:

(i) The median age $\frac{38+44}{2} = 82 ; 41$ (ii) The range   (iii) The mean age   (iv) The modal age

18. There are 15 boys and 13 girls in a maths class. The mean time spent on homework each week for the boys is 5.5 hours. The mean time spent on homework for the girls is 7.2 hours. Find the mean time spent on homework for all students in the class. Round your answer to two decimal places.

19. The table shows the monthly salaries (in euro) of 20 families living in a particular neighbourhood.

2,451	2,580	2,595	2,635
2,635	2,530	2,550	2,680
2,654	2,520	2,560	2,575
2,462	2,540	2,890	2,740
2,635	2,635	2,673	2,480

(i) Copy and complete the grouped frequency distribution:

Salary (€)	2,450–2,500	2,500–2,550	2,550–2,600	2,600–2,650	2,650–2,700	2,700–2,750
Number						

Note: 2,450–2,500 includes 2,450 but excludes 2,500, etc.

(ii) Draw a histogram to represent the distribution.

(iii) Comment on the shape of the histogram.

(iv) Using the original table, calculate the mean and the median salary.

Another family has moved into the neighbourhood. One member of the family is a very successful writer and earns €10,000 a month.

(v) Comment on how this will affect the mean salary for the neighbourhood.

(vi) Which average will now be more representative of salaries for the neighbourhood? Explain.

20. The following table shows the diameter (in centimetres) of a sample of 20 ball bearings:

1.738	1.740	1.735	1.737
1.736	1.724	1.736	1.745
1.740	1.725	1.732	1.739
1.739	1.730	1.732	1.739
1.739	1.732	1.746	1.729

(i) Copy and complete the grouped frequency distribution below:

Length	1.720–1.725	1.725–1.730	1.730–1.735	1.735–1.740	1.740–1.745	1.745–1.750
Freq.						

Note: 1.720–1.725 includes 1.720 but excludes 1.725, etc.

(ii) Draw a histogram to represent the distribution.

(iii) Comment on the shape of the histogram.

(iv) Using the original table, calculate the mean and median diameter.

21. For each of the following scenarios, explain how the statistics could mislead.

(a) ABC Polls recently said that seven out of every 10 teenagers are habitual smokers. The statement was based on the result of a survey. Twenty teenagers were surveyed. → *not enough of the teenage population*

(b) A radio show host asked her listeners for their opinion on the proposed construction of a new airport in Dublin. Of those who phoned the show, 75% were not in favour of the proposal. ← *unfair selection*

(c) Éamonn carried out a survey of all Leaving Certificate students in his school. One of the questions was as follows: 'Would you be in favour of a new uniform for the school?' ← *making the questioner get the person to answer yes.*

Of those surveyed, 80% answered no. Éamonn then announced that 80% of the respondents in his survey said no to a new school uniform, and that it was therefore the opinion of the majority of students in the school that the uniform should not change. ↑ *only leaving certificate students were asked not a sample of the population*

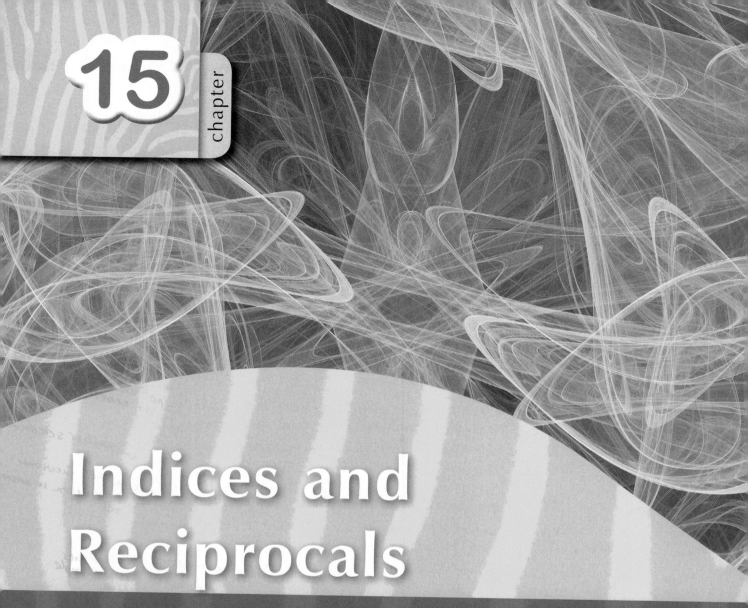

15 chapter

Indices and Reciprocals

Learning Outcomes

In this chapter you will learn:

- ➲ To work with indices and square roots
- ➲ The laws of indices and how to apply them
- ➲ How to work with numbers in scientific notation
- ➲ How to compare numbers using orders of magnitude
- ➲ How to compute reciprocals

15.1 INDICES AND SQUARE ROOTS

Bacteria are very small organisms that are found almost everywhere on earth (even in the human body!). Bacteria can reproduce very quickly, sometimes doubling in number every 10 minutes.

Alice is a scientist who studies bacteria. She has managed to isolate one bacterium in her laboratory. She knows that this type of bacterium will reproduce every 10 minutes by dividing in two. Therefore, after 10 minutes there will be two bacteria, after 20 minutes four bacteria, and so on. Can you help Alice by completing the following table?

Minutes elapsed	10	20	30	40	50	60	70	80
Number of bacteria	2	4				64		

The table above can also be laid out as follows:

Minutes elapsed	Number of bacteria
10	2
20	2 × 2
30	2 × 2 × 2
40	2 × 2 × 2 × 2
50	2 × 2 × 2 × 2 × 2
60	2 × 2 × 2 × 2 × 2 × 2
70	2 × 2 × 2 × 2 × 2 × 2 × 2
80	2 × 2 × 2 × 2 × 2 × 2 × 2 × 2

The work in the second column of this table can be written in a simpler form if we use **index notation**.

If six 2s are multiplied together, i.e. $2 \times 2 \times 2 \times 2 \times 2 \times 2$, it is written as 2^6 (pronounced '2 to the power of 6').

We call 2 the **base** and 6 the **index** or **power**.

Worked Example 15.1

Evaluate the following, without using a calculator:

(i) 3^4

(ii) 7^3

Solution

(i) $3^4 = 3 \times 3 \times 3 \times 3 = 81$

(ii) $7^3 = 7 \times 7 \times 7 = 343$

Worked Example 15.2

Using a calculator, evaluate the following:

(i) 20^4　　(ii) 5^8

Solution

(i) To begin, locate the $\boxed{x^y}$ button on your calculator. This allows us to input the required power.

Type the following:

20　$\boxed{x^y}$　4　$\boxed{=}$

Note: Individual calculators may differ.

The answer 160,000 will display on your screen.

(ii) Type the following:

5　$\boxed{x^y}$　8　$\boxed{=}$

The answer 390,625 will display on your screen.

Square Roots

What non-negative number, when multiplied by itself, gives an answer of 9?

The answer is 3.

We use the symbol $\sqrt{}$ to denote square root. We find the non-negative root.

$$3 \times 3 = 9$$

We say that the **square root** of 9 is 3. This is written $\sqrt{9} = 3$.
Similarly, $\sqrt{4} = 2$ and $\sqrt{16} = 4$. Remember that $x^2 = 9 \Rightarrow x = \pm\sqrt{9} = \pm 3$; but $\sqrt{9} = 3$ (not -3).

Worked Example 15.3

Evaluate the following, without using a calculator:

(i) $\sqrt{49}$

(ii) $\sqrt{10,000}$

Solution

(i) We are looking for a non-negative number that, when multiplied by itself, gives an answer of 49:

$7 \times 7 = 49$, therefore $\sqrt{49} = 7$.

(ii) We are looking for a non-negative number that, when multiplied by itself, gives 10,000:

$100 \times 100 = 10,000$, therefore $\sqrt{10,000} = 100$.

 Worked Example 15.4

Use a calculator to evaluate the following. Give answers correct to two decimal places.

 (i) $\sqrt{78}$ (ii) $\sqrt{12.4}$

Solution

(i)

   The answer 8.831760866 is displayed.

   Answer = 8.83

(ii)

   The answer 3.521363372 is displayed.

   Answer = 3.52

Exercise 15.1

1. Without using a calculator, evaluate the following (show all your work):

 (i) 2^3 (iv) 6^2

 (ii) 3^3 (v) 1^{10}

 (iii) 5^2 (vi) 4^3

2. Without using a calculator, evaluate the following (show all your work):

 (i) 2^1 (iv) 4^1

 (ii) 2^2 (v) 4^2

 (iii) 3^2 (vi) 3^4

3. Without using a calculator, evaluate the following:

 (i) $\sqrt{4}$ (iv) $\sqrt{36}$

 (ii) $\sqrt{9}$ (v) $\sqrt{144}$

 (iii) $\sqrt{49}$ (vi) $\sqrt{169}$

4. Without using a calculator, evaluate the following:

 (i) $\sqrt{25} \times \sqrt{36}$ (v) $\sqrt{16} \div \sqrt{4}$

 (ii) $\sqrt{16} \times \sqrt{49}$ (vi) $\sqrt{100} \div \sqrt{25}$

 (iii) $\sqrt{81} \times \sqrt{9}$ (vii) $\sqrt{16} + \sqrt{9}$

 (iv) $\sqrt{25} \times \sqrt{4}$ (viii) $\sqrt{64} - \sqrt{36}$

5. Complete the following number wheels:

(i)

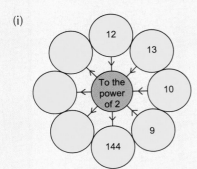

(ii)

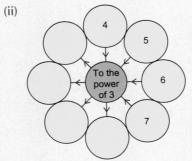

(iii)

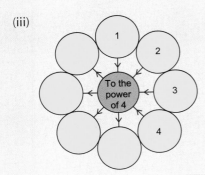

(iv)

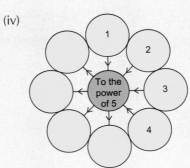

6. Match the numbers in column A with the numbers in column B.

A	B
2^3	27
4^2	64
1^6	16
$\sqrt{49}$	25
3^3	8
4^3	7
5^2	81
$\sqrt{25}$	5
9^2	1
5^3	125

7. Using your calculator, evaluate:

  (i) 20^3 (iii) 25^2 (v) 7^6

  (ii) 15^4 (iv) 9^5 (vi) 4^7

8. Using your calculator, evaluate the following (give your answer correct to two decimal places):

  (i) $\sqrt{12}$ (iii) $\sqrt{97}$ (v) $\sqrt{500}$

  (ii) $\sqrt{28}$ (iv) $\sqrt{122}$ (vi) $\sqrt{1460}$

9. Using your calculator, evaluate:

  (i) 12^3 (iii) 21^3 (v) 17^2

  (ii) 15^5 (iv) 19^4 (vi) 26^4

10. Using your calculator, evaluate the following (give your answer correct to two decimal places):

  (i) $\sqrt{15}$ (iii) $\sqrt{69}$ (v) $\sqrt{950}$

  (ii) $\sqrt{29}$ (iv) $\sqrt{135}$ (vi) $\sqrt{1371}$

11. If $a^n = b$, find the values of a, b and n in each of the following cases:

  (i) a is the only even prime number and n is the number of days in a week.

  (ii) b is 9^2 and a is the first odd prime number.

  (iii) n is the HCF of 6 and 9. b is the sum of 5^2 and 10^2.

12. Complete the following tables:

(i)

2^1	2^2	2^3	2^4	2^5	2^6	2^7	2^8
			16				

(ii)

3^1	3^2	3^3	3^4	3^5	3^6	3^7
				243		

(iii)

4^1	4^2	4^3	4^4	4^5	4^6
				1,024	

ACTIVITY 15.1

15.2 FIRST AND SECOND LAWS OF INDICES

In Activity 15.1, we derived the First Law of Indices:

Multiplying: add powers

FORMULA

Law 1: $a^p \times a^q = a^{p+q}$

This formula is on page 21 of *Formulae and Tables*.

 **Worked Example 15.5**

Simplify the following products, giving your answer in index notation:

  (i) $3 \times 3 \times 3 \times 3 \times 3$

  (ii) $4 \times 5 \times 4 \times 5 \times 5 \times 4$

  (iii) $r \times s \times t \times r \times s \times s \times r$

Solution

(i) $3 \times 3 \times 3 \times 3 \times 3 = 3^5$

(ii) $4 \times 5 \times 4 \times 5 \times 5 \times 4 = (4 \times 4 \times 4) \times (5 \times 5 \times 5) = 4^3 \times 5^3$

(iii) $r \times s \times t \times r \times s \times s \times r = (r \times r \times r) \times (s \times s \times s) \times t = r^3 \times s^3 \times t$

a^{pq} Worked Example 15.6

Simplify the following, giving your answer in index notation:

(i) $(-5)^4$ (iii) $(-6)^2$

(ii) $(-3)^3$ (iv) $(-2)^5$

Solution

(i) $(-5)^4 = -5 \times -5 \times -5 \times -5$

$= (-5 \times -5) \times (-5 \times -5)$

$= 25 \times 25$

$= 5^2 \times 5^2$

$= 5^4$

(ii) $(-3)^3 = -3 \times -3 \times -3$

$= (-3 \times -3) \times -3$

$= 9 \times -3$

$= -27$

$= -3^3$

(iii) $(-6)^2 = -6 \times -6$

$= 36$

$= 6^2$

(iv) $(-2)^5 = -2 \times -2 \times -2 \times -2 \times -2$

$= (-2 \times -2) \times (-2 \times -2) \times -2$

$= 4 \times 4 \times -2$

$= 16 \times -2$

$= -32$

$= -2^5$

In general:

■ A negative number raised to an even power gives a positive answer.

■ A negative number raised to an odd power gives a negative answer.

a^{pq} Worked Example 15.7

Simplify the following, giving your answer in index notation:

(i) $5^3 \times -5^2$

(ii) $-6^3 \times -6^2$

Solution

(i) $5^3 \times -5^2 = -5^5$ ($(+)(-) = (-)$ and $a^p \times a^q = a^{p+q}$)

(ii) $-6^3 \times -6^2 = 6^5$ ($(-)(-) = (+)$ and $a^p \times a^q = a^{p+q}$)

 Worked Example 15.8

Simplify the following, using the First Law of Indices:

(i) $7^4 \times 7^5$

(ii) $15^{12} \times 15^7$

 ACTIVITY 15.2

Solution

(i) Law 1: $a^p \times a^q = a^{p+q}$

$\therefore 7^4 \times 7^5 = 7^{4+5} = 7^9$

(ii) Law 1: $a^p \times a^q = a^{p+q}$

$\therefore 15^{12} \times 15^7 = 15^{12+7} = 15^{19}$

In Activity 15.2, we derived the Second Law of Indices:

Division: Subtract powers

FORMULA

Law 2: $\dfrac{a^p}{a^q} = a^{p-q}$

This formula is on page 21 of *Formulae and Tables*.

 Worked Example 15.9

Simplify the following, using the Second Law of Indices:

(i) $8^6 \div 8^2$

(ii) $\dfrac{4^{12}}{4^3}$

Solution

(i) Law 2: $\dfrac{a^p}{a^q} = a^{p-q}$

$\therefore 8^6 \div 8^2 = 8^{6-2} = 8^4$

(ii) Law 2: $\dfrac{a^p}{a^q} = a^{p-q}$

$\therefore \dfrac{4^{12}}{4^3} = 4^{12-3} = 4^9$

 Exercise 15.2

1. Simplify the following, using powers:

(i) $2 \times 2 \times 2 \times 2 \times 2$

(ii) $5 \times 5 \times 5 \times 5 \times 5 \times 5$

(iii) $2 \times 2 \times 2 \times 5 \times 5$

(iv) $2 \times 2 \times 2 \times 2 \times 2 \times 3 \times 3 \times 3 \times 3 \times 3 \times 3$

(v) $2 \times 5 \times 2 \times 2 \times 5 \times 2 \times 2 \times 5 \times 5 \times 2 \times 5$

(vi) $2 \times 3 \times 2 \times 5 \times 2 \times 3 \times 3 \times 5 \times 2 \times 3 \times 3$

2. Simplify the following, using powers:

(i) $4 \times 4 \times 4 \times 4 \times 4$

(ii) $5 \times 2 \times 5 \times 2 \times 5 \times 2$

(iii) $2 \times 2 \times 3 \times 3 \times 5 \times 5$

(iv) $2 \times 2 \times 2 \times 2 \times 5 \times 3 \times 3 \times 5 \times 3 \times 3 \times 5$

(v) $2 \times 3 \times 4 \times 2 \times 3 \times 4 \times 2 \times 3 \times 4 \times 2 \times 3 \times 4$

(vi) $2 \times 3 \times 4 \times 5 \times 2 \times 3 \times 4 \times 5 \times 2 \times 3 \times 4$

3. Simplify the following, using powers (Note: x, y and z represent numbers):

(i) $x \times x \times x \times x \times x \times x$

(ii) $y \times y \times y \times y \times y \times y$

(iii) $x \times y \times z \times x \times x \times y \times z$

(iv) $z \times z \times z \times z \times z \times x \times x \times x \times x \times x \times x \times x \times x$

(v) $x \times x \times x \times x \times x \times y \times y \times y \times x \times x \times y \times x \times x \times y$

(vi) $x \times y \times x \times x \times z \times x \times x \times y \times y \times z \times x \times x \times y \times y$

4. Simplify the following, using powers:

(i) $y \times y \times y \times y \times y$

(ii) $x \times y \times y \times x \times y \times x$

(iii) $x \times y \times y \times z \times z$

(iii) $x \times x \times y \times x \times z \times x \times x \times z \times x \times x \times y \times z$

(iv) $x \times y \times z \times x \times x \times y \times z \times x \times x \times y \times z \times x \times x \times y \times z$

(v) $x \times y \times z \times z \times y \times x \times x \times x \times z \times y \times x \times x \times z$

5. Rewrite the following as products, without using powers, e.g. $2^4 = 2 \times 2 \times 2 \times 2$.

(i) 2^3 (iv) 6^5 (vii) 2^6 (x) 8^6 (xiii) z^5

(ii) 3^4 (v) 7^6 (viii) 5^5 (xi) x^6 (xiv) a^2

(iii) 5^2 (vi) 3^5 (ix) 7^2 (xii) y^3 (xv) b^4

6. Use the law $a^p \times a^q = a^{p+q}$ to fill in the numbers in the boxes:

(i) $6^2 \times 6^3 = 6^\square$ (iv) $5^3 \times 5^4 = 5^\square$

(ii) $8^3 \times 8^5 = 8^\square$ (v) $7^2 \times 7^3 = 7^\square$

(iii) $2^8 \times 2^{10} = 2^\square$

7. Use the law $a^p \times a^q = a^{p+q}$ to simplify the following. Give your answer in index form.

(i) $3^5 \times 3^4$ (iv) $5^{16} \times 5^2$

(ii) $4^6 \times 4^5$ (v) $10^4 \times 10^5$

(iii) $5^9 \times 5^4$

8. Use the law $a^p \div a^q = a^{p-q}$ to fill in the numbers in the boxes.

(i) $5^8 \div 5^3 = 5^\square$ (iv) $2^9 \div 2^3 = 2^\square$

(ii) $7^{12} \div 7^5 = 7^\square$ (v) $3^8 \div 3^6 = 3^\square$

(iii) $10^5 \div 10^2 = 10^\square$

9. Use the law $a^p \div a^q = a^{p-q}$ to simplify the following. Give your answer in index form.

(i) $\dfrac{4^6}{4^2}$ (iv) $\dfrac{2^7}{2^3}$

(ii) $\dfrac{6^{13}}{6^{10}}$ (v) $\dfrac{10^8}{10^3}$

(iii) $\dfrac{8^{22}}{8^{18}}$

10. Use the law $a^p \times a^q = a^{p+q}$ to simplify the following. Give your answer in index notation.

(i) -3×3^3 (vi) $2^5 \times -2^3$

(ii) $5^2 \times -5^3$ (vii) $-6^3 \times -6^2$

(iii) $-7^3 \times -7^4$ (viii) $8^2 \times 8^5$

(iv) $4^3 \times 4^2$ (ix) $-9^6 \times -9^4$

(v) $-9^3 \times -9^2$ (x) $-10^3 \times 10^2$

11. Use the law $a^p \div a^q = a^{p-q}$ to simplify the following. Give your answer in index notation.

(i) $2^4 \div -2^2$ (vi) $8^{10} \div -8^3$

(ii) $-4^3 \div -4$ (vii) $-7^{13} \div 7^6$

(iii) $-6^8 \div 6^3$ (viii) $-10^{10} \div -10^2$

(iv) $6^9 \div -6^2$ (ix) $3^9 \div -3^6$

(v) $-5^8 \div -5^3$ (x) $-1^9 \div -1^7$

12. Simplify the following, giving your answer in index notation:

(i) $(-4)^3$ (vi) $(-3)^3 \times (-3)^2$

(ii) $(-2)^6$ (vii) $(-4)^2 \times -4$

(iii) $\dfrac{-2^3 \times 2^5}{2^4}$ (viii) $\dfrac{5^3 \times -5^5}{-5^2 \times 5^4}$

(iv) $\dfrac{-3^2 \times -3^3}{3^2}$ (ix) $\dfrac{6^3 \times (-6)^2}{6 \times -6}$

(v) $(-2)^2 \times 2^3$ (x) $\dfrac{6^2 \times 6^3 \div 6}{-6 \times -6^2 \times (-6)^2}$

ACTIVITY 15.3

15.3 THIRD LAW OF INDICES

In Activity 15.3, we derived the Third Law of Indices:

FORMULA

Law 3: $(a^p)^q = a^{pq}$

This formula is on page 21 of *Formulae and Tables*.

Worked Example 15.10

Use the Third Law of Indices to simplify the following. Give your answer in index notation.

(i) $(3^6)^4$ (ii) $(2^4)^8$ (iii) $(-5^3)^7$ (iv) $(-5^2)^9$

Solution

(i) $(a^p)^q = a^{pq}$

   $(3^6)^4 = 3^{6 \times 4} = 3^{24}$

(ii) $(2^4)^8 = 2^{4 \times 8}$

   $= 2^{32}$

(iii) $(-5^3)^7 = -(5^3)^7$

   $= -5^{21}$

(iv) $(-5^2)^9 = -(5^2)^9$

   $= -5^{18}$

Exercise 15.3

1. (i) Explain why $(2^3)^5 = 2^3 \times 2^3 \times 2^3 \times 2^3 \times 2^3$.
   (ii) Hence, show that $(2^3)^5 = 2^{15}$.

2. (i) Explain why $(3^6)^3 = 3^6 \times 3^6 \times 3^6$.
   (ii) Hence, show that $(3^6)^3 = 3^{18}$.

3. (i) Explain why $(5^5)^4 = 5^5 \times 5^5 \times 5^5 \times 5^5$.
   (ii) Hence, show that $(5^5)^4 = 5^{20}$.

4. Use the law $(a^p)^q = a^{pq}$ to fill in the numbers in the boxes.

   (i) $(2^3)^4 = 2^{\square}$ (vii) $(4^5)^6 = 4^{\square}$

   (ii) $(3^3)^5 = 3^{\square}$ (viii) $(2^2)^2 = 2^{\square}$

   (iii) $(5^2)^4 = 5^{\square}$ (ix) $(7^6)^7 = 7^{\square}$

   (iv) $(6^4)^5 = 6^{\square}$ (x) $(10^{11})^9 = 10^{\square}$

   (v) $(10^5)^5 = 10^{\square}$ (xi) $(8^5)^3 = 8^{\square}$

   (vi) $(6^2)^7 = 6^{\square}$ (xii) $(16^2)^3 = 16^{\square}$

5. Use the law $(a^p)^q = a^{pq}$ to simplify the following (leave your answers in index form):

   (i) $(8^3)^4$ (iv) $(5^6)^9$

   (ii) $(7^9)^5$ (v) $(18^5)^8$

   (iii) $(10^4)^5$ (vi) $(12^5)^7$

6. Use the laws of indices to simplify the following (leave your answers in index notation):

   (i) $3^5 \times 3^7$ (vii) $19^8 \div 19^3$

   (ii) $(5^2)^3$ (viii) $-10^7 \div -10^3$

   (iii) $12^7 \div 12^4$ (ix) $3^8 \times -3^7$

   (iv) $(8^4)^{10}$ (x) $-5^9 \times 5^4$

   (v) $16^2 \times 16^4$ (xi) $(6^3)^4$

   (vi) $\dfrac{18^9}{18^5}$ (xii) $\dfrac{12^9}{12^2}$

7. $16 = 2^4$

   or $= 2^2 \times 2^2$

   or $= (2^2)^2$

   or $= 2^9 \div 2^5$

   Represent the following numbers in four different ways, using indices each time.

   (i) 32

   (ii) 81

   (iii) 64

   (iv) 625

8. Use the law $(a^p)^q = a^{pq}$ to simplify the following. Leave your answer in index notation.

   (i) $(-3^2)^3$ (iii) $(-2^8)^5$ (v) $(-6^3)^3$ (vii) $(-8^3)^9$ (ix) $(-10^3)^7$ (xi) $(-20^3)^4$

   (ii) $(-4^3)^4$ (iv) $(-5^2)^6$ (vi) $(-4^5)^7$ (viii) $(-11^2)^5$ (x) $(-12^5)^9$ (xii) $(-3^7)^9$

15.4 SCIENTIFIC NOTATION

ACTIVITY 15.4

When doing calculations, scientists often use very large numbers.
For example, the speed of light is about 300,000,000 metres per second.

Very large numbers can be awkward to write down. So scientists use scientific notation to write down these numbers.

In Activity 15.4, you learned how to write very large numbers in **scientific notation**.

A number is written in **scientific notation** if it is of the form $a \times 10^n$, where $1 \leqslant a < 10$ and $n = 0$ or $n \in N$.

Another name for scientific notation is **standard form**.

Worked Example 15.11

Write the following numbers in scientific notation:

(i) 673

(ii) 980,000

(iii) 725,000,000,000

Solution

(i) $673 = 6.73 \times 10^2$

(ii) $980,000 = 9.8 \times 10^5$

(iii) $725,000,000,000 = 7.25 \times 10^{11}$

Orders of Magnitude

A number rounded to the nearest power of 10 is called an **order of magnitude**.

Orders of magnitude are generally used to make very approximate comparisons. If two numbers differ by one order of magnitude, one is about 10 times larger than the other.

Worked Example 15.12

By how many orders of magnitude does 345,632 differ from 567,123,423?

Solution

Write both numbers in scientific notation:

$345,632 = 3.45632 \times 10^5$ Rounded to the nearest power of 10 $= 10^0 \times 10^5 = 10^5$.

$567,123,423 = 5.67123423 \times 10^8$ Rounded to the nearest power of 10 $= 10^1 \times 10^8 = 10^9$.

$\dfrac{10^9}{10^5} = 10^{9-5} = 10^4$

Note: $10^0 = 1$.

Therefore, both numbers differ by four orders of magnitude.

1. Write the following numbers in scientific notation.

   (i) 15

   (ii) 150

   (iii) 1,500

   (iv) 15,000

   (v) 150,000

   (vi) 150,000,000

2. Write the following in the form $a \times 10^n$, where $1 \leqslant a < 10$, and $n = 0$ or $n \in N$.

   (i) 350

   (ii) 5,600

   (iii) 3,450,000

   (iv) 630,000,000

   (v) 78,900

   (vi) 47,823

3. Write the following numbers in the form $a \times 10^n$, where $1 \leqslant a < 10$, and $n = 0$ or $n \in N$.

   (i) 680

   (ii) 3,280

   (iii) 65,780

   (iv) 3,000,000

   (v) 456,800

   (vi) 6

4. Write the following numbers in scientific notation.

   (i) 165

   (ii) 17,850

   (iii) 1,500,000

   (iv) 195,000,000

   (v) 1,750,000,000

   (vi) 787,000

5. The following numbers are written in scientific notation. Rewrite the numbers in ordinary form.

   (i) 3×10^5

   (ii) 9×10^6

   (iii) 2.4×10^2

   (iv) 6.4×10^4

   (v) 6.12×10^3

   (vi) 7.38×10^5

6. The following numbers are written in scientific notation. Rewrite the numbers in ordinary form.

   (i) 2×10^6

   (ii) 1.69×10^4

   (iii) 2.48×10^3

   (iv) 6.47×10^5

   (v) 6.12×10^1

   (vi) 8.67×10^3

7. Write the following in the form $a \times 10^n$, where $1 \leqslant a < 10$, and $n = 0$ or $n \in N$.

   (i) 36

   (ii) 5,613

   (iii) 345

   (iv) 6,349

   (v) 7,890,000

   (vi) 68,000

   (vii) 3,280,000

   (viii) 65,780,000

   (ix) 9,000,000,000

   (x) 56,000,000

8. The following numbers are written in scientific notation. Rewrite the numbers in ordinary form.

   (i) 1.5×10^3

   (ii) 2.54×10^4

   (iii) 3.5×10^5

   (iv) 6.67×10^6

   (v) 8.15×10^2

   (vi) 9.182×10^7

9. By how many orders of magnitude do the following numbers differ?

   (i) 1,239,868 and 345

   (ii) 345,789,213 and 4,538

   (iii) 767,894,567,000 and 23,000,000

   (iv) 23 and 234,678

   (v) 1.8 and 234

15.5 RECIPROCALS

Study the table below:

$2 \times \dfrac{1}{2} =$	1
$3 \times \dfrac{1}{3} =$	1
$\dfrac{3}{5} \times \dfrac{5}{3} =$	1
$-\dfrac{6}{7} \times -\dfrac{7}{6} =$	1
$-\dfrac{4}{3} \times -\dfrac{3}{4} =$	1

If the product of two numbers is 1, then both numbers are **reciprocals** of each other.

From the table, we see that the reciprocal of 2 is $\frac{1}{2}$ and the reciprocal of $\frac{1}{2}$ is 2. Similarly the reciprocal of $\frac{3}{5}$ is $\frac{5}{3}$.

Worked Example 15.13

Write out the reciprocals of the following numbers:

(i) 4   (ii) $\dfrac{9}{10}$ (iii) $-\dfrac{1}{5}$

Solution

(i) The reciprocal of 4 is $\dfrac{1}{4}$.

$$4 \times \dfrac{1}{4} = 1$$

(ii) The reciprocal of $\dfrac{9}{10}$ is $\dfrac{10}{9}$.

$$\dfrac{9}{10} \times \dfrac{10}{9} = 1$$

(iii) The reciprocal of $-\dfrac{1}{5}$ is -5.

$$-5 \times -\dfrac{1}{5} = 1$$

Exercise 15.5

1. Write as a fraction the reciprocal of each element of the following sets of numbers:

   (i) $\{2, 4, 6, 8, 10\}$

   (ii) $\{1, 3, 5, 7, 9\}$

   (iii) $\{2, 3, 5, 7, 11, 13\}$

   (iv) $\{5, 10, 15, 20, 25, 30\}$

2. Write as whole numbers the reciprocals of each element of the following sets:

   (i) $\left\{\dfrac{1}{2}, \dfrac{1}{4}, \dfrac{1}{6}, \dfrac{1}{8}, \dfrac{1}{10}\right\}$

   (ii) $\left\{\dfrac{1}{3}, \dfrac{1}{5}, \dfrac{1}{7}, \dfrac{1}{9}, \dfrac{1}{11}, \dfrac{1}{13}\right\}$

   (iii) $\left\{\dfrac{1}{5}, \dfrac{1}{10}, \dfrac{1}{15}, \dfrac{1}{20}, \dfrac{1}{25}, \dfrac{1}{30}\right\}$

   (iv) $\left\{\dfrac{1}{23}, \dfrac{1}{29}, \dfrac{1}{31}, \dfrac{1}{37}, \dfrac{1}{41}\right\}$

   (v) $\left\{\dfrac{1}{4}, \dfrac{1}{9}, \dfrac{1}{16}, \dfrac{1}{25}, \dfrac{1}{36}, \dfrac{1}{49}\right\}$

3. Write as fractions the reciprocals of each element of the following sets:

   (i) $\left\{\dfrac{2}{3}, \dfrac{3}{4}, \dfrac{4}{5}, \dfrac{5}{6}, \dfrac{6}{7}, \dfrac{7}{8}\right\}$

   (ii) $\left\{\dfrac{3}{5}, \dfrac{5}{7}, \dfrac{7}{9}, \dfrac{9}{11}, \dfrac{11}{13}\right\}$

   (iii) $\left\{\dfrac{2}{5}, \dfrac{4}{7}, \dfrac{2}{3}, \dfrac{8}{11}, \dfrac{10}{13}\right\}$

4. Find the reciprocals of each of the following mixed numbers:

   (i) $2\dfrac{1}{2}$ (iii) $4\dfrac{1}{4}$ (v) $6\dfrac{1}{6}$

   (ii) $3\dfrac{1}{3}$ (iv) $5\dfrac{1}{5}$ (vi) $7\dfrac{1}{7}$

5. (a) By rounding each of the following denominators to the nearest whole number, estimate the answer.

   (b) Use the reciprocal button $\boxed{x^{-1}}$ or $\boxed{\tfrac{1}{x}}$ on your calculator to find the true value of the expression. Give your answer correct to three decimal places.

   (i) $\dfrac{1}{5.246}$ (iii) $\dfrac{1}{4.245}$ (v) $\dfrac{1}{3.981}$

   (ii) $\dfrac{1}{9.876}$ (iv) $\dfrac{1}{19.742}$ (vi) $\dfrac{1}{2.459}$

6. Find the reciprocal of each of the following numbers:

   (i) $-\dfrac{1}{2}$ (vi) $-\dfrac{1}{8}$

   (ii) -4 (vii) $-\dfrac{12}{7}$

   (iii) $-2\dfrac{1}{5}$ (viii) $-1\dfrac{1}{5}$

   (iv) $-\dfrac{3}{10}$ (ix) $-\dfrac{3}{4}$

   (v) $-11\dfrac{2}{5}$ (x) $-\dfrac{15}{8}$

Revision Exercises

1. (a) Without using a calculator, evaluate the following:

    (i) 3^4
    (ii) 5^3
    (iii) 2^6
    (iv) $(-3)^4$
    (v) $(-5)^3$
    (vi) $(-2)^6$

    (b) Without using a calculator, evaluate the following:

    (i) $\sqrt{64}$
    (ii) $\sqrt{64} + \sqrt{16}$
    (iii) $\sqrt{64} + \sqrt{16} \times 2$

2. Copy and complete the following sentences:

    (i)   The square root of 25 is ___.
    (ii) The square of 4 is ___.
    (iii) The square root of 81 is ___.
    (iv) 10 is the square root of ___.
    (v)   1 is the square root of ___.

3. (a) Using your calculator, evaluate the following to two decimal places:

    (i) 2.5^6 (ii) $\dfrac{3.1^4}{2.8^3}$ (iii) $(5.2^3)^2$

    (b) The approximate distances in kilometres between some of the planets and the sun are given in the table below:

Planet	Distance from the sun
Earth	1.5×10^{11} m
Mercury	6.0×10^{10} m
Mars	2.5×10^{11} m
Venus	1.1×10^{11} m

    (i)   Which planet is furthest from the sun?
    (ii) Which planet is nearest the sun?
    (iii) What is the difference between Earth's distance from the sun and Mercury's distance from the sun?

4. (a) Evaluate the following sums and give your answer in scientific notation:

    (i) $70,000 + 800,000$
    (ii) $340,000 + 56,000$
    (iii) $7,600 + 4,300,000$

    (b) (i) By rounding to the nearest whole number, estimate the value of:
    $$\sqrt{16.35} \times \frac{10.34}{1.87} - (1.98)^2$$
    (ii) Now use your calculator to find the answer correct to two decimal places.

5. (a) Write 3.14×10^4 as a natural number.

    (b) If $x = 65$ and $y = 63$, evaluate $\sqrt{x^2 - y^2}$.

    (c) The mass of the earth is 6×10^{25} kilograms. The mass of Jupiter is 300 times this mass. Write the mass of Jupiter in scientific notation.

6. Use the laws of indices to simplify the following. Give your answers in index notation.

    (i) $2^3 \times 2^8$
    (ii) $-3^4 \times -3^8$
    (iii) $\dfrac{5^8}{5^3}$
    (iv) $(-5^2)^{15}$
    (v) $\dfrac{-7^9}{7^4}$
    (vi) $(4^3)^7$
    (vii) $-5^2 \times 5^8$
    (viii) $\dfrac{7^3 \times 7^5}{7 \times -7^2}$

7. Using your calculator or otherwise, evaluate the following to two decimal places:

    (i)   The reciprocal of $\dfrac{3}{8}$
    (ii) The reciprocal of 13
    (iii) $\dfrac{1}{\sqrt{3}} + \dfrac{1}{4.9}$
    (iv) $\dfrac{3}{4.5} + \dfrac{5}{4.5^2} - \dfrac{1}{\sqrt{4.5}}$

8. (a) Estimate the following by rounding appropriately.

    (b) Using your calculator, evaluate each one correct to two decimal places.

    (i) $(5.9)^2 - \sqrt{26}$
    (ii) $\dfrac{5.3 - \sqrt{10}}{(1.2)^2 + 1}$
    (iii) $\sqrt{17} \times \dfrac{15.02}{3.19} - (2.3)^2$

9. By completing the table below, find the smallest value of n for which $5^n > 8^5$.

n	5^n
6	
7	
8	

10. The mass of Saturn is 5.69×10^{29} kilograms. The mass of the earth is 6.04×10^{24} kilograms. By how many orders of magnitude does the mass of Saturn differ from the mass of the earth?

11. (a) Use your calculator to divide 112,200 by 0.0011. Write your answer in the form $a \times 10^n$, where $1 \leqslant a < 10$ and $n = 0$ or $n \in N$.

  (b) (i) Use the rules of indices to simplify:
  $$\frac{c^4 \times c^3}{c \times c^5}$$

  (ii) Using your answer to part (i), evaluate:
  $$\frac{28^4 \times 28^3}{28 \times 28^5}$$

12. A man puts two grains of rice on the first square of a chessboard, four on the second square, eight on the third square, and so on.

  (i) Write, in powers of two, the number of grains of rice he puts on the second, third and fourth squares.

  (ii) How many grains of rice does he put on the last square, i.e. the 64th square? Give your answer in index form.

  (iii) On which square are there 128 grains?

16

chapter

Applied Arithmetic

Learning Outcomes

In this chapter, you will learn to solve problems that involve finding:

- ⮑ Income tax (standard rate only)
- ⮑ Net pay (including other deductions of specified amounts)
- ⮑ VAT
- ⮑ Profit or loss
- ⮑ Percentage profit or loss on the cost price
- ⮑ Discount
- ⮑ Percentage discount
- ⮑ Selling price
- ⮑ Compound interest for not more than three years

16.1 INCOME TAX

Income and Deductions

Employees expect to earn money for the work they carry out.

- If you are paid according to the number of hours worked or goods produced, this is called a **wage**.

- If you are paid the same amount regardless of the number of hours worked or goods produced, this is called a **salary**.

Most people cannot keep all the money they earn. Employees have several **deductions** made to their earnings before they receive their money.

> **YOU SHOULD REMEMBER...**
> - How to calculate percentages
> - How to work with decimals

> **Gross pay** or **gross income** is money earned before deductions are made.

> **Net pay** or **net income** is money received after all deductions have been made.

> **KEY WORDS**
> - Gross income
> - Net/take-home income
> - Statutory deductions
> - Non-statutory deductions
> - Income tax (PAYE)
> - Standard rate of tax
> - Standard rate cut-off point
> - Tax credit
> - Gross tax
> - Tax payable
> - VAT
> - Interest payable
> - Investment interest

- Deductions
- Net Pay

Statutory and Non-Statutory Deductions

Deductions can be **statutory** or **non-statutory**.

> **Statutory deductions** are payments that must be made to the government. They are taken from gross pay by the employer.

Statutory deduction	What is it used for?
Income tax (PAYE – Pay As You Earn)	Payment of public services, e.g. Gardaí, health care, education, etc.
Pay-Related Social Insurance (PRSI)	Old-age pensions, jobseeker's benefit, jobseeker's allowance, child benefit, etc.

> **Non-statutory deductions** are voluntary deductions. They are taken from gross pay by the employer at the request of the employee.

Examples of voluntary deductions include healthcare payments, union fees, pension payments, etc.

Income Tax Rates

There are two rates of income tax in Ireland.

- The lower rate is called the **standard rate** of tax.

- The higher rate is called the **higher rate** of tax.

> Note that tax rates can vary from year to year and from country to country.

For example, the first €32,800 that a single person earns is taxed at 20%, and any income above this amount is taxed at 41% (figures accurate for 2011).

For a married couple where both people are working, the first €65,600 is taxed at 20% and any additional income is taxed at 41%.

Every employee receives a **tax credit** certificate. This shows the employee's tax credit. This amount can change for individual employees.

The amount up to which an employee is taxed at the standard rate is called the **standard rate cut-off point.**

Gross tax is the amount of tax owed to the state before tax credits are deducted.

Standard rate cut-off point → } Taxed at 41%

} Taxed at 20%

Tax payable is gross tax less tax credit.

Tax credit is a sum deducted from the total amount (gross tax) a taxpayer owes to the state.

Calculating Income Tax and Net Income

 Worked Example 16.1

Miriam earns €35,000. She pays tax at a rate of 20%. Her tax credit is €1,830.

Calculate her tax payable.

Solution

Step 1

Gross tax = €35,000 × 20%

= €35,000 × 0.20

∴ Gross tax = €7,000

Step 2

Tax payable = Gross tax – Tax credit

= €7,000 – €1,830

∴ Tax payable = €5,170

 **ACTIVITIES 16.1, 16.2**

Worked Example 16.2

Will's gross annual pay is €36,000. His standard rate cut-off point is €36,400. The standard rate of tax is 21% and he has a tax credit of €2,400. Calculate:

(i) The tax payable   (ii) Will's net pay

Solution

Note that, in this example, Will earns an amount less than the standard rate cut-off point, so tax is calculated only on the €36,000.

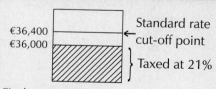

€36,400
€36,000

Standard rate cut-off point

} Taxed at 21%

(i) **Step 1** Find gross tax

Gross tax = €36,000 × 21%

= €36,000 × 0.21

= €7,560

Step 2 Find tax payable

Tax payable = Gross tax – Tax credit

= €7,560 – €2,400

= €5,160

∴ Tax payable = €5,160

(ii) Find net pay

Net pay = Gross pay – Tax payable

= €36,000 – €5,160

∴ Net pay = €30,840

Worked Example 16.3

Michael earns €27,000. He pays tax at a rate of 20%. He has a tax credit of €1,950. He has instructed his employer to pay his annual health insurance premium of €550 directly from his salary. Find Michael's:

   (i) Tax payable   (ii) Total deductions   (iii) Net pay

Solution

(i)   Gross tax = €27,000 × 20%

                 = €27,000 × 0.20

      ∴ Gross tax = €5,400

      Tax payable = Gross tax − Tax credit

                 = €5,400 − €1,950

      ∴ Tax payable = €3,450

(ii)   Total deductions = Tax payable + Health insurance

                 = €3,450 + €550

      ∴ Total deductions = €4,000

(iii)   Net pay = Gross pay − Total deductions

                 = €27,000 − €4,000

      ∴ Net pay = €23,000

 ACTIVITY 16.3

Exercise 16.1

1. A man earns €26,000 annually. He pays tax at a rate of 20%.

   What is his gross tax bill for the year?

2. A woman earns €32,000 per year. She pays tax at a rate of 18%.

   What is her gross tax bill for the year?

3. James earns €35,000 per annum. He pays tax at a rate of 20%. He has a tax credit of €2,140. Calculate:

   (i) Gross tax

   (ii) Net pay

4. Niamh and Declan are married and have a joint income of €73,000. They have a tax credit of €4,300 and pay tax at a rate of 21%. Calculate:

   (i) Gross tax

   (ii) Net pay

5. Jack earns €36,000 in a year. His tax credit is €1,830. He pays tax at the standard rate of 20%. Calculate:

   (i) Gross tax

   (ii) Tax due

   (iii) Net pay

6. Laura earns €34,000 per annum. The standard rate cut-off point is €36,400. The standard rate of tax is 20%. Her tax credit is €2,600. Calculate:

   (i) Gross tax

   (ii) Tax due

   (iii) Net pay

7. Seán has a gross annual income of €36,300. The standard rate cut-off point is €37,000. He pays tax at a rate of 22%. His tax credit is €2,016. What is Seán's net income?

8. Orla has a gross annual income of €29,400. She pays tax at a rate of 20%. Her tax credit is €1,890. Her employer deducts her union fee of €300 per year from her salary. What is:

   (i) Her tax payable

   (ii) Her net pay after all deductions

9. Ian earns €37,000 in a year. The standard rate cut-off point is €37,400. The standard rate of tax is 21%. His tax credit is €2,100. His union fees are €450 and his annual health insurance is €350. Calculate:

   (i) Ian's tax payable

   (ii) His take-home pay after all deductions

10. Tadhg earns €33,500 per annum. The standard rate cut-off point is €36,000. The standard rate of tax is 20%. His tax credit is €2,200. His health insurance is €400, and he pays €600 into his savings in the year. Calculate:

   (i) Tadhg's tax payable

   (ii) His take-home pay after all deductions

11. Abdul earns €33,000. His tax bill for the year is €6,930. What percentage of his income is paid in tax?

12. Neasa's net tax bill for last year was €6,300. Her tax credit was €1,300. Her gross income for the year was €38,000. She paid tax at the standard rate only.

   (i) How much was her gross tax?

   (ii) What rate did she pay tax at?

13. A married couple earn €74,000 per annum. They have a tax credit of €4,600. Last year they paid tax of €10,940. They pay tax at the standard rate.
   What is the standard rate in this case?

16.2 VAT: VALUE ADDED TAX

VAT is a tax charged by the government on consumer spending.

For example, if you buy a computer game, you pay **VAT** on the game.

VAT is collected by the Revenue Commissioner. It is collected in stages, starting with the manufacturing stage and ending with the sale of the finished product to the consumer. VAT is collected at the following stages from the following people:

- Manufacturer
- Wholesaler
- Distributor
- Retailer
- Consumer

A tax is placed on the value added to the product or service at each stage, and this is where the name 'value-added tax' comes from.

VAT Rates

There are several different rates of VAT (figures accurate for 2010):

Standard rate	Applies to most goods and services	21%
Reduced rate	Applies to labour-intensive services, e.g. hairdressing	13.5%
Zero rate	Applies to many foods and medicines and to children's clothes	0%
Special rate	Applies to the sale of livestock	4.8%

Remember that these rates can change from year to year and country to country.

You can find which rate of VAT applies to different goods and services by checking the list available on the Revenue website at www.revenue.ie.

Rates of VAT vary depending on the product or service being purchased. For example, chocolate spread has a zero rate but chocolate biscuits have a 21% rate.

Worked Example 16.4

Michelle sees a camera in a shop window. The sign says '€250 + VAT @ 21%'.
How much will she pay for the camera?

Solution

Step 1   Find 21% of €250

VAT = 250 × 0.21

∴ VAT = €52.50

Step 2   Find the total price

Total price = €250 + VAT

= €250 + 52.50

∴ Price paid = €302.50

Worked Example 16.5

Carol gets her hair done and the bill comes to €56.75. VAT is charged at the reduced rate of 13.5%.

What was the original bill before VAT was added?

Solution

Original bill = 100%

Original bill + VAT = 113.5%

113.5% = €56.75

∴ 1% = $\frac{€56.75}{113.5}$

1% = €0.50

100% = €0.50 × 100

= €50

∴ Original bill = €50

Worked Example 16.6

Stefan loves to go to the cinema. On his last trip, the tickets for two people cost him €22.50. He later found his receipt and he noticed the amount of VAT charged was €2.50. What rate of VAT was charged?

Solution

Step 1   Find the cost before VAT

Cost before VAT = Final cost – VAT

= €22.50 – €2.50

∴ Cost before VAT = €20

∴ VAT = €2.50 (€22.50 – €20)

Step 2   Express the VAT as a percentage of the initial cost

Rate of VAT = $\frac{\text{VAT}}{\text{Cost before VAT}} \times \frac{100}{1}$

= $\frac{2.50}{20} \times \frac{100}{1}$

∴ Rate of VAT = 12.5%

> Note that VAT is charged on the **original** cost figure.

 **ACTIVITIES** 16.4, 16.5

Exercise 16.2

1. If VAT charged on hairdressing is 13.5%, find the VAT to be charged on each of the following haircuts if the cost before VAT is:

   (i) €10   (iii) €18

   (ii) €14   (iv) €20

2. The VAT charged on TVs is 21%. Find the **total price** of the following TVs if the price before VAT is:

   (i) €150   (iii) €800

   (ii) €500   (iv) €1,999

3. Find the total price of ordering a movie on Sky Box Office if the price of the movie is €5 + VAT @ 21%.

4. While shopping, Karen buys the following items:

   ■ Milk: €1.20 + VAT @ 0%

   ■ Chocolate biscuits: €3.00 + VAT @ 21%

   ■ Tea: €2.00 + VAT @ 13.5%

   How much does her shopping bill amount to?

5. A shopkeeper bought 300 light bulbs from a wholesaler at €0.50 each + VAT @ 21%.

   Find the total cost of the light bulbs.

6. Dinner in a restaurant for four people costs €140 excluding VAT. Find the total bill when VAT is charged at 13.5%.

7. Brian is on holidays with his family. He buys two DVDs for his friend on his way home. The DVDs cost €8 and €12 excluding VAT. VAT is charged at 20%.

   What is the total cost of the DVDs?

8. Craig brought his girlfriend out for dinner. When the bill arrived, he was shocked to see the total was €170.25.

   If VAT is charged at 13.5%, what was the cost of the bill before the VAT was added?

9. The government of a country has decided to charge one standard rate of VAT @ 25%.

   If the price of a car including VAT is €9,000, how much of this price is VAT?

10. A refrigerator can be purchased for €968, including VAT @ 21%. How much would this refrigerator cost without VAT?

11.

    A laptop costs €1,452 and this includes VAT at 21%. How much of the selling price should be given to the Revenue Commissioner?

12. An auctioneer charges VAT at a rate of 21%. If the auctioneer is successful in selling a house, she gets a fee of 1.25% of the selling price.

    If she sells a house for €270,000, how much will her fee to the client be:

    (i) Before VAT

    (ii) After VAT

16.3 HOUSEHOLD BILLS

Households have bills for many things, from groceries to TV licences and utilities such as electricity and gas. Two regular bills in households are electricity and gas bills.

The amount of electricity or gas used by a household is recorded by a meter. The meter is usually read every two months. Bills show the present and previous meter readings.

Worked Example 16.7

Calculate the values of A, B, C, D, E and F on the following electricity bill.

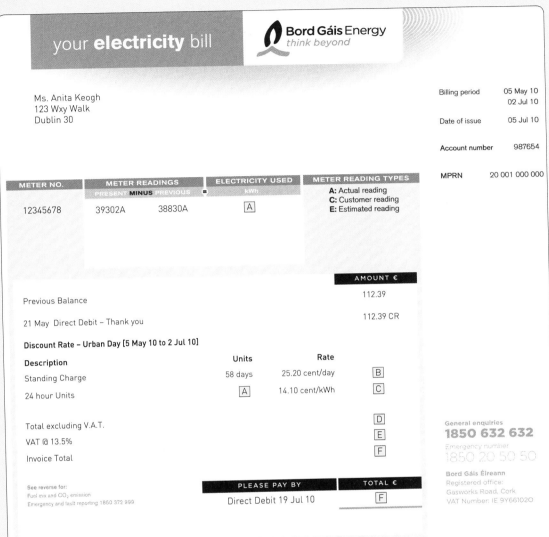

Solution

Step 1 Find the number of units used:

Present meter reading – Previous meter reading

39,302 – 38,830 = 472 units $\boxed{A}$

> On an electricity bill, units are measured in kilowatt hours (kWh).

Step 2 Calculate charges based on units used:

Standing charge = 25.20 cent for 58 days = €14.62 $\boxed{B}$

Unit rate = 14.10 cent for 472 kWh = €66.55 $\boxed{C}$

Total excluding VAT = €14.62 + €66.55 = €81.17 $\boxed{D}$

VAT @ 13.5% (€81.17 × 0.135) = €10.96 $\boxed{E}$

Total including VAT = €81.17 + €10.96 = €92.13 $\boxed{F}$

> The standing charge is a charge that you must pay regardless of the amount of electricity used. It is based on the number of days you have the service.

Worked Example 16.8

Calculate the values of A, B, C, D, E, F, G and H on the following gas bill.

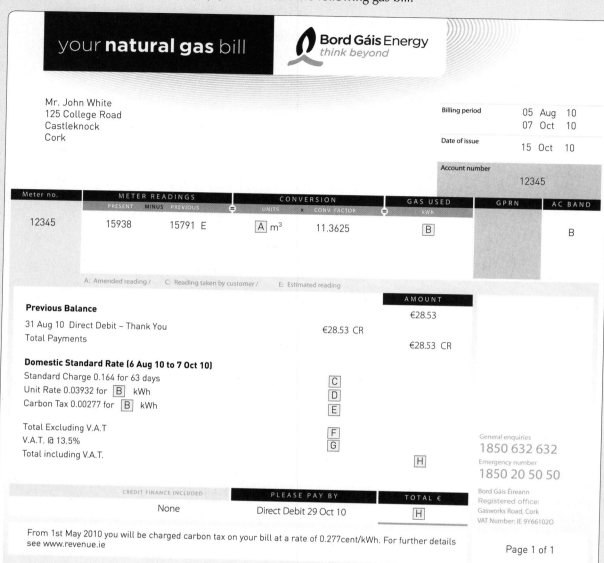

Solution

> The amount of gas that is used is measured by volume and recorded in units.

Step 1 Find the number of units used:

Present meter reading – Previous meter reading

15,938 –15,791 = 147 units $\boxed{A}$

Step 2 Convert the units to kilowatt hours:

Units × conversion factor = kWh

147 × 11.3625 = 1,670 (rounded to nearest kWh) $\boxed{B}$

Step 3 Calculate charges based on units used:

> The standing charge is a charge you must pay regardless of the amount of gas used. It is based on the number of days you have the service.

Standing charge = 0.164 for 63 days	= €10.33	C
Unit rate = 0.03932 for 1,670 kWh		
0.03932 × 1670 ≈ 65.66	= €65.66	D
Carbon tax = 0.00277 for 1,670 kWh	= €4.63	E
Total excluding VAT = €10.33 + €65.66 + €4.63	= €80.62	F
VAT @ 13.5% (€80.62 × 0.135)	= €10.88	G
Total including VAT = €80.62 + €10.88	= €91.50	H

When calculating bills for various services, it is important to remember the following:

- Measure the amount of the service or product used (in units).
- Calculate the cost of the total units used.
- Include any standing charges for the service or product.
- Calculate the VAT using the correct rate.
- Amounts are normally rounded to the nearest cent.
- kWh are rounded to the nearest whole number.

Worked Example 16.9

Paul has his telephone service with Digicell. His monthly standing charge is €50. This includes 300 minutes of calls and 200 text messages. If he exceeds the number of minutes allowed, he is charged 15c per minute. Every additional text message costs 12c.

In the month of December, Paul sends 210 text messages and the duration of all his calls is 320 mins. VAT is charged at 21%. What is the total cost of his bill this month?

Solution

Standing charge		= €50.00
Text messages (210) = 200 × 0	= € 0.00	
	10 × €0.12	= € 1.20
Calls (320 minutes) = 300 × 0	= € 0.00	
	20 × €0.15	= € 3.00
Total (excluding VAT)		= €54.20
VAT @ 21%		= €11.38
Total (including VAT)		= €65.58

 ACTIVITY 16.6

Exercise 16.3

1. Calculate the values of A, B, C, D, E and F on the following electricity bill.

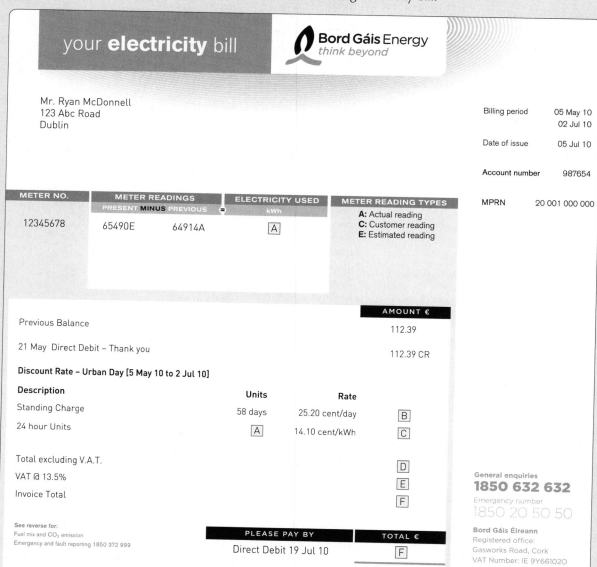

your **electricity** bill

Bord Gáis Energy
think beyond

Mr. Ryan McDonnell
123 Abc Road
Dublin

Billing period	05 May 10
	02 Jul 10
Date of issue	05 Jul 10
Account number	987654
MPRN	20 001 000 000

METER NO.	METER READINGS		ELECTRICITY USED	METER READING TYPES
	PRESENT MINUS PREVIOUS =		kWh	A: Actual reading
12345678	65490E	64914A	A	C: Customer reading
				E: Estimated reading

	AMOUNT €
Previous Balance	112.39
21 May Direct Debit – Thank you	112.39 CR

Discount Rate – Urban Day [5 May 10 to 2 Jul 10]

Description	Units	Rate	
Standing Charge	58 days	25.20 cent/day	B
24 hour Units	A	14.10 cent/kWh	C
Total excluding V.A.T.			D
VAT @ 13.5%			E
Invoice Total			F

See reverse for:
Fuel mix and CO$_2$ emission
Emergency and fault reporting 1850 372 999

PLEASE PAY BY	TOTAL €
Direct Debit 19 Jul 10	F

General enquiries
1850 632 632
Emergency number
1850 20 50 50

Bord Gáis Éireann
Registered office:
Gasworks Road, Cork
VAT Number: IE 9Y661020

2. Calculate the values of A, B, C, D, E, F, G and H on the following gas bill.

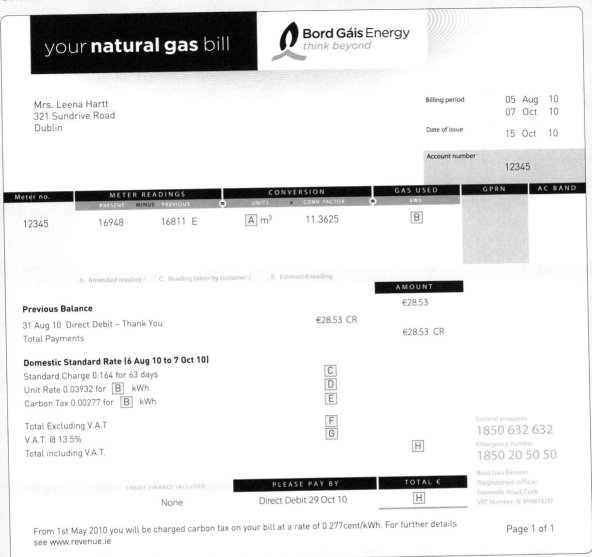

3. Study the following meter readings taken from electricity bills and calculate for **each** bill:

  (i) The number of units used

  (ii) The cost if each unit costs 12 cent

	Present	Previous
Bill 1	9,556	9,487
Bill 2	10,004	8,754
Bill 3	5,492	4,879
Bill 4	12,345	11,687

  (iii) If the standing charge is €12 and VAT is charged at 13.5%, calculate the total cost of each bill in part (ii).

4. Calculate the cost of gas used for each of the following households if gas costs €0.04 for every kilowatt hour used (exclusive of VAT).

	kWh used
Bill 1	1,680
Bill 2	1,984
Bill 3	1,782
Bill 4	1,002

5. Frances has the following bill pay option on her phone:

For €65 per month, she has unlimited calls to numbers within Ireland and 300 free text messages.

All calls to destinations outside Ireland are charged at 45c per minute.

Last month, Frances made an overseas call lasting 20 minutes. She did not exceed her quota for text messages.

(i) How much did her overseas call cost?

(ii) How much was her bill before VAT is added?

(iii) If VAT is charged at 21%, what was the total of her bill?

6. The following gas bill arrived in the Makim household.
Calculate the total cost of the bill for the last two months (61 days).

Meter no.	Meter readings (Present – Previous)	Conversion factor	Standing charge
77,775	14,986 – 13,789	11.305	0.155 for 61 days
VAT charged @ 13.5%		Unit rate 0.04132	

7. A local call from a landline costs 6c per minute. If Alan has to pay line rental of €24 per month and in a particular month he makes calls lasting 94 minutes, calculate:

(i) The cost of his bill before VAT

(ii) The cost of the bill if VAT is charged at 20%

8. If a text message costs €0.07 and Milo has €3.78 credit on his phone, how many text messages can he send before he runs out of credit?

9. Marie pays a standing charge of €12 per month for her phone. Her calls cost €0.19 per minute. If Marie does not want to spend more than €50 on her next phone bill, what is the maximum number of minutes she can use this month? (Ignore VAT.)

10. Aaron and Robbie are thinking of changing mobile phone networks. Each researches the different networks and they come up with the following: Robbie says network A will cost the least and Aaron says network B is the best option.

If both make calls for 120 minutes and send 150 text messages each month, which is the better network to choose?

	Network A	Network B
Standing charge	€20	€15
Free text messages	100	85
Free minutes	100	100
Additional texts	10c per text	12c per text
Cost per minute for calls	15c	25c

11. The following is a gas meter reading for Deirdre's apartment.

Present = 12,348 units	Previous = 11,938 units
Conversion factor = 11.3625	Unit rate = €0.03 per kWh used

Calculate:

(i) The number of units used

(ii) The number of kilowatt hours used (to the nearest whole number)

(iii) The cost of the gas used before VAT

(iv) The total cost of the bill if VAT is charged at 13.5%

16.4 PERCENTAGE PROFIT AND LOSS AND SELLING PRICE

> If a product or service is sold for more than it cost to buy or produce, then the seller has made a profit.

> If a product or service is sold for less than it cost to buy or produce, then the seller has made a loss.

> The percentage profit mark-up is the profit expressed as a percentage of the cost price: $\dfrac{\text{Profit}}{\text{Cost price}} \times 100$.

> The selling price is the cost price plus profit/loss.

 ## Worked Example 16.10

Tony buys an iPod for €75 on eBay. He then sells it for €100.

What is:

(i) The cost price

(ii) The selling price

(iii) The profit or loss made

(iv) The percentage mark-up

Solution

(i) Cost price = €75 (price Tony paid)

(ii) Selling price = €100 (price Tony sells for)

(iii) Profit = Selling price – Cost price

$\quad\quad$ = €100 – €75

∴ Profit = €25

(iv) Percentage mark-up = $\dfrac{\text{Profit}}{\text{Cost price}} \times \dfrac{100}{1}$

$\quad\quad = \dfrac{25}{75} \times \dfrac{100}{1}$

$\quad\quad = 33\dfrac{1}{3}\%$

 ## Worked Example 16.11

A company manufactures a computer game for €10 and sells it to games stores, making a profit of 30%. What is the selling price?

Solution

Profit = 10 × 0.30

∴ Profit = €3

Selling price = Cost price + Profit

$\quad\quad$ = €10 + €3

$\quad\quad$ = €13

The selling price is €13.

Worked Example 16.12

Rory has a business selling medical supplies. The company's policy is to sell all goods at cost plus 20% mark-up.

If he sells first-aid boxes for €15, what is the cost price of a first-aid box?

Solution

Selling price = Cost price + Profit

$$= 100\% + 20\%$$

$$\therefore \text{Selling price} = 120\%$$

This means that the selling price is 120% of the cost price. We now need to find the cost price (100%).

$$\therefore 120\% = €15$$

$$\therefore 1\% = \frac{15}{120}$$

$$= €0.125$$

$$\therefore 100\% = 0.125 \times 100$$

$$= €12.5$$

The cost price is €12.50.

Worked Example 16.13

Lisa owns a clothes shop. She decides to sell off last season's stock at a loss of 10%. She sells a hoody for €18. How much did it cost her originally?

Solution

Selling price = Cost price – Loss

$$= 100\% - 10\%$$

$$\therefore \text{Selling price} = 90\%$$

This means that the selling price is 90% of the cost price. We now need to find the cost price (100%).

$$\therefore 90\% = €18$$

$$\therefore 1\% = \frac{18}{90}$$

$$= €0.20$$

$$\therefore 100\% = 0.20 \times 100$$

$$= €20$$

The cost price is €20.

ACTIVITY 16.7

 Exercise 16.4

1. Fill in the missing figures below:

	Cost price	Selling price	Profit/loss	% Profit/loss
1	€25.00	€30.00	€5.00	
2	€31.00	€36.00		
3	€25.00	€20.00		
4	€14.00		€14.00	
5	€12.00	€18.00	€6.00	
6	€18.00	€18.90		
7		€3.00	−€3.00	
8		€2.80	−€0.70	
9	€10.00		€2.00	
10	€11.00		€4.50	
11		€20.00	€4.00	
12	€16.00	€18.00		
13	€70.00	€90.00		
14	€1,100.00	€990.00		
15	€1,904.00		€660.00	
16		€2,475.00	−€275.00	
17	€8,375.00	€10,050.00		
18	€1,238.00		€16.00	
19	€91.20		€28.80	
20	€512.00		−€64.00	

2. Find the selling price of each of the following:

	Cost price	% Mark-up
(i)	€50.00	5.00%
(ii)	€120.00	6.00%
(iii)	€240.00	12.50%
(iv)	€650.00	21.50%
(v)	€2,250.00	16.00%

3. Find the selling price of each of the following:

	Cost price	% Loss
(i)	€50	5.00%
(ii)	€1,250	15.00%
(iii)	€34,000	25.00%
(iv)	€12,800	37.50%
(v)	€14,400	12.00%

4. A product costs €13,250 to produce.

Find the percentage mark-up if a company sells the product for €15,900.

5. Jack imports jerseys for €10. He sells the jerseys at cost plus 12.5%.

What is the selling price?

6. A retailer buys goods from a cash and carry for €120. The recommended selling price is cost plus 15%.

How much should she sell the goods for?

7. As part of a mini company project, Robbie sells personalised hoodies. He sells them for €15 and this includes a mark-up of 25%.

How much did he pay for them?

8. By selling a TV for €1,116, a retailer makes a profit of 24%. During a sale, the price is reduced to €1,035.

(i) How much did the store pay for the TV?

(ii) What percentage profit is made on the TV during the sale?

9. A Second Year student wants to buy a new app for her iPhone. She decides to sell her maths book for €10 at a loss of 60%.

How much did she originally pay for the book?

16.5 DISCOUNTS (ALLOWED AND RECEIVED)

Discounts are offered for several reasons, e.g. to encourage customers to buy a product or to encourage a customer to pay for goods quickly or with cash.

> A **discount** is a reduction in the price of a bill or charge.

Some manufacturers offer trade discounts. This is done to encourage wholesalers and retailers to sell their product. For example, the selling price of a product is €100, and the manufacturer offers a trade discount of 10%. The wholesaler now has to pay €100 – 10% of €100 = €90.

10% discount

The wholesaler can now sell the goods for €100, making a profit of €10.

Discounts are also offered to encourage customers to buy the goods or pay for goods bought on credit quickly. On an invoice (the bill sent by a seller to the customer for goods purchased), you may often see the word 'Terms'. This describes the discount that is offered for prompt payment.

€ Worked Example 16.14

Murphy Table Tennis Supplies sends an invoice to TT Youth Club. The terms tell us that if this is paid within one month, a discount of 5% is applied.

Murphy Table Tennis Supplies Ltd, Dublin Rd, Wicklow
Invoice No. 14

To: TT Youth Club
     Dublin 15

Order No: 5
Terms: 5%, 1 month otherwise net

Quantity	Description	Unit price (€)		Total ex. VAT (€)
500	Balls	€0.60		€300.00
15	Bats	€4.00		€60.00
				€360.00
			VAT 21%	€75.60
			Total due	€435.60

Calculate:

  (i) The amount of discount

  (ii) The price after discount

Solution

  (i) From the invoice, we can see that TT Youth Club owes Murphy Table Tennis Supplies €435.60.

  The discount is 5% (if paid within one month).

  ∴ We need to find 5% of €435.60.

  €435.60 @ 5% = 435.60 × 0.05

  $\qquad\qquad\quad$ = 21.78

  The 5% discount is €21.78.

  (ii) €435.60 – €21.78 = €413.82

  ∴ The price to be paid after discount is €413.82.

1. In each of the following, calculate:

(i) The discount

(ii) The price after the discount

	Selling price	% Discount
(a)	€1,200	5%
(b)	€200	15%
(c)	€1,600	15%
(d)	€4,400	2%
(e)	€1,400	25%
(f)	€1,500	12%
(g)	€1,460	37.50%
(h)	€28,400	12%

2. In each of the following, calculate the % discount:

	Selling price	Discount
(i)	€50.00	€2.50
(ii)	€144.00	€8.64
(ii)	€270.00	€40.50
(iv)	€789.75	€126.36
(v)	€2,610.00	€313.20

3. For the invoice below, calculate:

(i) The discount received if paid within one month

(ii) The price to be paid after discount

Invoice no. 234			
Terms: Discount 6% if paid within 1 month			
Quantity	**Description**	**Unit price**	**Total ex. VAT**
200	Apples	€0.20	€40.00
120	Nectarines	€0.25	€30.00
			€70.00
		VAT 0%	€0.00
		Total due	€70.00

4. For the invoice below, calculate:

(i) The discount received if paid within one month

(ii) The price to be paid after discount

Invoice no. 3546			
Terms: Discount 12% if paid within 1 month			
Quantity	**Description**	**Unit price**	**Total ex. VAT**
200	Bandages	€1.00	€200.00
120	Ice packs	€1.25	€150.00
			€350.00
		VAT 21%	€73.50
		Total due	€423.50

5. Rick owns a camera shop. He purchases 10 cameras at €120 each. The wholesaler offers him a trade discount of 20%. How much does Rick pay in total for the cameras?

6. Fiona has an apartment in the city centre. She charges €450 rent per month. She tells her tenants that she will offer them a 7% discount if they pay the rent in cash before the last day of every month.

How much rent will she receive if they pay before the end of the month?

7. Ciara and Barbara are shopping in Mahon Point. Ciara sees a sign on a shop window:

   (i) Ciara bought a cardigan for €12. What was the original price?
   (ii) Barbara bought a jacket for €25. What was the original price?

20% off

8. (i) Complete the invoice below, which was sent to a phone shop.

Invoice no. 3567

Terms: Discount 5% if paid within 1 month

Quantity	Description	Unit price	Total ex. VAT
50	iPod (8GB)	€60.00	€3,000.00
10	iPhone (16GB)	€320.00	€3,200.00
10	iTouch (16GB)	€120.00	€1,200.00
			€7,400.00
		Trade discount 20%	
		Price (ex. VAT)	
		VAT 21%	
		Total due	

(ii) The phone shop must pay for these goods within one month. Calculate the price they must pay after all discounts have been applied.

16.6 CURRENCY EXCHANGE

In the eurozone, the unit of currency is the euro. If you travel to any country within the eurozone, there is no need to change your money. However, if you travel to any country outside the eurozone, you will need to change your money. For example, if you travel to Japan, you will need to convert your money from euro into Japanese yen.

Worked Example 16.15

On a certain day, €1 = £0.87. Chris is travelling to London tomorrow and wants to change €200 into sterling (£). How much sterling will he get?

Solution

$$€1 = £0.87$$
$$€1 × 200 = £0.87 × 200$$
$$€200 = £174$$

Chris will get £174.

Worked Example 16.16

The Ethiopian currency is called the birr. On a particular day, the euro–birr exchange rate was €1 = 22 birr.

Alicia was returning home from Ethiopia and converted her money in the airport.

How much did she receive in euro (to the nearest cent) for 1,000 birr?

Solution

$$22 \text{ birr} = €1$$
$$1 \text{ birr} = \frac{€1}{22}$$
$$1 \times 1,000 \text{ birr} = \frac{€1}{22} \times 1,000$$
$$1,000 \text{ birr} = €45.4545$$
$$1,000 \text{ birr} \approx €45.45 \text{ (rounded to the nearest cent)}$$

> Always arrange the exchange rate to have the currency you are looking for on the right-hand side.

Foreign currency can be bought and sold at a **bureau de change**. Many banks, building societies and department stores offer this service. However, they do not all offer the same exchange rates.

At a bureau de change, you will see the following signs:

- If you are going on holiday and want to buy foreign currency, the bank is selling it to you. So use the 'SELL at' exchange rate.
- If you have returned from holiday and want to sell back the currency you have left over, it is the 'BUY at' rate that you must use.

These two different rates are used so that the operators of the bureau de change can make a profit. Another cost that you should consider is the **commission** the bureau de change will charge you. This is an extra charge for the service they have provided.

Worked Example 16.17

Cian is going on holidays to America and wants to change €250 into dollars. He goes to his local bank. At the bureau de change counter, he sees a sign that says:

	We buy	We sell
US dollars	1.34	1.30

(i) How much will he get in dollars for €250?

(ii) If commission is charged at 1.5% of the euro value, how much will Cian pay in total?

Solution

(i) First, ask the question: Is Cian buying or selling US dollars?

Cian is buying dollars – therefore, the bank is selling.

So, the exchange rate is €1 = $1.30 (the rate the bank sells at).

$$€1 = \$1.30$$
$$€1 \times 250 = \$1.30 \times 250$$
$$€250 = \$325$$

Cian will get $325.

(ii) Commission = €250 × 0.015
$$= €3.75$$
∴ Total cost = €250 + €3.75
$$= €253.75$$

Exercise 16.6

1. On a day when €1 = £0.68, find:

   (i) The value in pounds of €60

   (ii) The value in euro of £816

2. On a day when €1 = $1.34, find:

   (i) The value in dollars of €350

   (ii) The value in euro of $871

3. A pair of trainers costs £21 online. If £1 = €0.84, how much will the trainers cost in euro?

4. A ticket to a New York Knicks game costs $104. How much will it cost in euro if €1 = $1.30?

5. If €1 = $1.42 (Australian dollar), €1 = ¥111.87 (Japanese yen) and €1 = £0.87:

   (i) How many Australian dollars would you get for €60?

   (ii) How many Japanese yen would you get for €150?

   (iii) How many pounds would you get for €50?

   (iv) How many euro would you get for ¥67,122?

   (v) How many euro would you get for $106.50?

   (vi) Are you better off if you have (a) ¥44,748 or (b) £347?

6. A bank quotes the following exchange rates for euro:

	We buy	We sell
Sterling £	0.87	0.82
US dollar $	1.38	1.34
Yen ¥	111	108

   (i) Mark has €900 and wants sterling. How much will he get?

   (ii) Ali has ¥5,994. How much will he get in euro?

   (iii) Mia has £104.40 and wants to change this to euro. How much will she get?

   (iv) Jake has $1,100. How much will he get in euro?

   (v) Ava has €1500. How many yen will she get?

7. Ursula is importing wine for her restaurant. She is charged $3.66 (New Zealand dollars) for each bottle of wine. There are 12 bottles in each case.

   If she imports 10 cases, how much will she pay in euro if €1 = $1.83?

8. Aoidhbhin is going on holiday to Bali. She changes €800 in the airport. The exchange rate she is offered is €1 = IDR12,450.50 (Indonesian rupiah). When she arrives in Bali, she notices that the exchange rate is €1 = IDR12,449.

   How much did she gain in rupiah by changing her money in the airport?

9. Karl is travelling to New York and wishes to convert €500 into dollars. At the local bank he sees the following sign:

	We buy	We sell
US $	1.34	1.30

   *Commission 2.5% applied to all transactions.

   (i) How much will Karl get in dollars for €500?

   (ii) How much commission will he have to pay in euro?

10. Chloe came home from the bureau de change with £90.20 (sterling). The exchange rate was €1 = £0.82.

    (i) How much did she exchange in euro?

    (ii) If commission was 3%, how much did she pay in total?

16.7 COMPOUND INTEREST

Individuals and businesses don't always have enough cash to buy what they want or pay their bills. It is sometimes necessary for them to borrow money. At the same time, there are individuals and businesses that have great amounts of cash, and so they decide to invest it.

If you borrow money from a bank or any financial institution, they will expect you to pay back the money you borrowed, but they will also charge you for the use of the money they loaned you. This is called **interest payable**.

When you invest money in an investment account or a financial institution, you are giving the people who run the account or institution the use of your money. So they have to pay you a charge for the use of this money. This is called **investment interest**.

When a loan or an investment is paid back in full, the total amount is the sum borrowed plus the interest that was paid.

When dealing with interest, we use the following symbols:

FORMULA

$F = P(1 + i)^t$
This formula appears on page 30 of *Formulae and Tables*.

- F = Final value (amount borrowed or invested + interest)
- P = Principal (amount borrowed or invested)
- i = Rate of interest per annum (year) (always use decimal form)
- t = Time (length of time you had the loan or investment)

 Worked Example 16.18

Sam borrows €300 for one year at 2% per annum. How much interest will he pay for the year?

Solution

Interest = Principal × i

= 300 × 2%

= 300 × 0.02

= 6

Sam will pay interest of €6.

Worked Example 16.19

Aoife invests €200,000 for two years at 3% per annum.

How much will her investment be worth at the end of the two years?

Solution

$P = €200,000$ $t = 2$ years $i = 3\%$

$F = P(1 + i)^t$

$\therefore F = 200,000(1 + 0.03)^2$

     $= 200,000(1.03)^2$

     $= 200,000(1.0609)$

$\therefore F = 212,180$

 **ACTIVITY 16.8**

The investment will be worth €212,180.

Worked Example 16.20

€10,000 is invested at 3% per annum. At the beginning of the second year, €1,450 is withdrawn from this amount. The interest rate for the second year rises to 3.5%.

Calculate:

(i) The value of the investment at the end of Year 1

(ii) The value of the investment at the end of Year 2

Solution

(i) Value of investment at end of Year 1

$P_1 = €10,000 \qquad t = 1 \text{ year} \qquad i = 3\%$

$F = P(1 + i)^t$

$\therefore F = 10,000(1 + 0.03)^1$

$\qquad = 10,000(1.03)^1$

$\qquad = 10,000(1.03)$

$\therefore F = 10,300$

Value at the end of Year 1 = €10,300.

(ii) Value of investment at end of Year 2

At the beginning of Year 2, €1,450 is withdrawn:

$P_2 = €10,300 - €1,450 = €8,850$

$t = 1 \text{ year}$

$i = 3.5\%$

$F = P(1 + i)^t$

$F = 8,850(1+0.035)^1$

$\qquad = 8,850(1.035)^1$

$\qquad = 8,850(1.035)$

$\therefore F = 9,159.75$

Value at the end of Year 2 = €9,159.75.

 Exercise 16.7

1. Calculate the amount of interest earned/paid for each of the following:

	Principal	i
(i)	€1,000	5%
(ii)	€2,500	10%
(iii)	€300	12%
(iv)	€1,450	15%
(v)	€600	6%
(vi)	€24,500	3%
(vii)	€17,000	4%
(viii)	€800	25%
(ix)	€950	30%
(x)	€14,400	0.5%

2. Calculate the final value of each of the following after one year:

	Principal	i
(i)	€300	5%
(ii)	€1,400	10%
(iii)	€1,200	12%
(iv)	€1,250	15%
(v)	€96	6%
(vi)	€750	3%
(vii)	€110	4%
(viii)	€13	25%
(ix)	€5,400	30%
(x)	€98,010	0.5%

3. €2,500 is invested at 5% for two years. Calculate the final value.

4. €600 is invested at 3% for one year. Calculate the interest payable.

5. €1,200 is invested at 4% for two years. Calculate the final value.

6. €10,000 is borrowed at 8% for three years. Calculate the final value.

7. €15,000 is borrowed at 6% for three years. Calculate the interest payable.

8. €25,400 is borrowed at 3% for one year. Calculate the interest payable.

9. €2,500 is invested at 4% for two years. Calculate the interest payable.

10. €1,500 is borrowed at 5% for two years. Calculate the final value of the debt.

11. €10,000,000 is invested at 10.5% for three years. Calculate the final value of the debt.

12. €9,600 is borrowed at 2% for one year. Calculate the interest payable.

13. Kyle borrows €60,000 at 3%. At the end of Year 1 he repays €16,000. The rate of interest is then lowered to 2%.

   How much will he owe at the end of the second year?

14. A football club borrowed €12,000,000 to revamp their stadium. The rate of interest for the first year was 8% and the rate for the second year was 10%. At the end of Year 1 €500,000 is repaid. Calculate the amount owing at the end of the second year.

15. A business secures a three-year loan for €30,000 with the following conditions attached:

   ■ The loan must be repaid in full by the end of the third year.

   ■ The rate of interest is 3% for the first two years. Then it decreases by 0.5%.

   Calculate the total interest that will be paid on this loan (to the nearest euro).

Revision Exercises

1. Calculate the tax due for each of the following employees:

   Tadhg – Gross income €340, rate of tax 20%, tax credit €36

   Helen – Gross income €380, rate of tax 21%, tax credit €35

   Eoin – Gross income €260, rate of tax 20%, tax credit €28

   Jenny – Gross income €580, rate of tax 21%, tax credit €44

2. Andy earns €26,000. His tax credit is €1,830. He pays tax at the standard rate of 20%.

   Calculate his net pay.

3. Paula has a take-home pay of €30,000. She pays tax of €5,000 at the standard rate. She has no tax credit.

   What rate of tax does she pay (to two decimal places)?

4. Rob has a gross income of €36,000 and a standard rate cut-off point of €36,700.

   He pays tax at a rate of 20% and he has a tax credit of €2,300.

   How much does the Revenue Commissioner receive in tax from Rob?

5. Niall is paid weekly. He earns €26,000 per annum. He pays tax at 21% and he has an annual tax credit of €1,820. How much does Niall:

   (i) Pay in tax per year

   (ii) Take home every year

   (iii) Take home per week (allow 52 weeks exactly for one year)

6. VAT of €65 is added to a bill of €255. Calculate:

   (i) The total bill

   (ii) The rate at which VAT is charged (to two decimal places)

7. Find the price, including VAT, of each of the following:

   (i) A camera priced at €300 + VAT @ 21%

   (ii) A DVD priced at €18 + VAT @ 21%

   (iii) A bottle of Coca Cola priced at €2 + VAT @ 13.5%

   (iv) A meal priced at €120 + VAT @ 13.5%

8. The price of a laptop, including VAT @ 10%, is €715. If the VAT rate is increased to 13%, calculate:

   (i) The price before VAT

   (ii) The price with the new VAT

9. An accountant charges a client €290.40 for work carried out. If this includes VAT at 21%, how much is the VAT on this bill?

10. Paul's weekly wage is €690. He pays income tax at the rate of 20%. His weekly tax credit is €65. What is Paul's take-home pay?

Gross pay	€690
Tax @ 20%	
Tax credit	
Tax due	
Take-home pay	

11. (a) Study the following meter readings taken from electricity bills and calculate for each bill:

   (i) The number of units used

   (ii) The cost of the electricity used if each unit costs 12 cent

	Present	Previous
Bill 1	8,445	8,387
Bill 2	10,004	9,754
Bill 3	3,182	2,013
Bill 4	2,691	1,208

   (b) If the standing charge is €12 and VAT is charged at 13.5%, calculate the total cost of each bill in part (a).

12. The following gas bill arrived in the Gorman household.

Meter no.	Meter readings (Present – Previous)	Conversion factor	Standing charge
77,885	14,896 – 13,879	11.305	0.145 for 61 days
VAT charged @ 13.5%		Unit rate 0.045	

   Calculate the total cost of the bill for the last two months (61 days).

13. Nicola pays a standing charge of €15 per month for her phone. Her calls cost €0.19 per minute. If Nicola does not want to spend more than €60 on her next phone bill, what is the maximum number of minutes she can use this month? (Ignore VAT.)

14. Fill in the missing figures below:

	Cost price	Selling price	Profit	% Mark-up
1	€200.00	€300.00		
2	€24.00	€32.00		
3	€25.00		€5.00	
4		€28.00	€14.00	
5	€12.00		€6.00	

15. Luke has his own business selling copies to other boys in his class. He sells a copy for €0.50 and it costs him €0.20 to buy one. What is his percentage mark-up?

16. Paul sells his old PlayStation for €70. This is at a loss of 65%. How much did he originally pay for it?

17. (i) Complete the following invoice.

Invoice no. 24564			
Terms: Discount 5% if paid within 1 month			
Quantity	**Description**	**Unit price**	**Total ex. VAT**
50	TVs	€70.00	€3,500.00
10	Laptops	€500.00	€5,000.00
10	Blu-ray players	€120.00	€1,200.00
			€9,700.00
		Trade Discount 20%	
		Price (ex. VAT)	
		VAT @ 21%	
		Total due	

(ii) Calculate the price the shop will pay after all discounts have been deducted, given that the shop pays within one month.

18. A bank quotes the following exchange rates for euro:

(i) Niall has €850 and wants sterling. How much will he get in sterling?

(ii) Albert has ¥4,248. How much will he get in euro?

(iii) Chloe has £51.09 and wants to change this to euro. How much will she get in euro?

(iv) Ben has $8,970. How much will he get in euro?

(v) Lucy has €500. How many yen will she get?

	We buy	**We sell**
Sterling £	0.78	0.74
US dollar $	1.38	1.34
Yen ¥	118	115

19. €16,000 was invested at 5% for two years at compound interest. Calculate the final value.

20. €2,450 was invested at 3% for one year at compound interest. Calculate the interest.

21. €44,000 was invested at 4% for two years at compound interest. Calculate the final value.

22. €33,330 was borrowed at 10% for three years at compound interest. Calculate the final value.

23. €7,800,000 was borrowed at 2% for three years at compound interest. Calculate the interest.

24. Celia invests €15,000 at 2% per annum at compound interest. At the end of the first year, she withdraws €2,500. In Year 2, the rate of interest is changed to 2.5%.

What is the final value of Celia's investment at the end of Year 2?

Distance, Speed and Time

Learning Outcomes

In this chapter you will learn to:

- Calculate, interpret and apply units of measure and time
- Solve problems that involve calculating average speed, distance and time

17.1 TIME

From setting our alarm clock, to checking a bus timetable, to remembering when our favourite television program starts, time plays an important role in our lives.

'Time is money.'

Benjamin Franklin (1706–1790)

YOU SHOULD REMEMBER...

■ How to read the 24-hour clock

■ How to read the 12-hour clock

KEY WORDS

■

■ **Distance**

■ **Speed**

■ **Time**

For simplicity and to avoid confusion, we use the 24-hour (hr) clock when dealing with timetables and questions related to time.

For example, in the 24-hour clock system, 4.40 a.m. would be 04:30 (hours) and 5.15 p.m. would be 17:15 (hours).

 ## Worked Example 17.1

A car starts its journey at 12:20 and takes $5\frac{3}{4}$ hours to reach its destination.

At what time does the car arrive at its destination?

Solution

$5\frac{3}{4}$ hours needs to be changed into minutes.

> Remember that there are 60 minutes in 1 hour.

$\frac{3}{4} \times 60 = 45$ minutes

$\therefore 5\frac{3}{4}$ hours = 5 hours 45 minutes

We can write this as 5:45.

$$
\begin{array}{r}
12:20 \\
+\ 05:45 \\
\hline
17:65 \\
\end{array}
$$

Of course, there is no such time as 17:65, so we 'carry' the hour:

Add 1 to the hour and subtract 60 from the minutes.

The car arrives at 18:05.

> As the question used the 24-hr clock, we give our answer in that format.

Worked Example 17.2

A train leaves a station at 14:35 and reaches the next station at 16:07. How long does the journey take?

Solution

```
  16:07
− 14:35
```

As the number of minutes above is less than the number of minutes below, we change 16:07 into 15:67 so that we can subtract more easily:

```
  15:67
− 14:35
  1:32
```

 ACTIVITY 17.1

∴ The journey takes 1 hour 32 minutes.

 Exercise 17.1

1. Convert each of the following into 24-hr clock time:

   (i) 12.25 a.m.   (iv) 2.26 p.m.

   (ii) 3.56 p.m.   (v) 7.28 a.m.

   (iii) 11.55 p.m.   (vi) 12.00 p.m.

2. Convert each of the following into 12-hr clock time.

   (i) 14:12   (iv) 11:46

   (ii) 22:10   (v) 18:36

   (iii) 0:15   (vi) 20:31

3. Convert the following into hours **and minutes**:

   (i) $2\frac{1}{2}$ hours   (iv) $10\frac{5}{6}$ hours

   (ii) $4\frac{1}{3}$ hours   (v) $\frac{1}{12}$ hour

   (iii) $1\frac{1}{5}$ hours   (vi) $2\frac{4}{15}$ hours

4. How many seconds are there in:

   (i) 2 minutes

   (ii) $10\frac{2}{3}$ minutes

   (iii) 2 hours

   (iv) $3\frac{7}{8}$ hours

   (v) $1\frac{1}{2}$ days

5. Calculate the arrival time for each of the following journeys:

	A	B	C	D	E
Start time	12:05	13:05	08:14	18:35	22:20
Duration of journey	52 mins	1 hr 15 mins	2 hrs 47 mins	4 hrs 37 mins	3 hrs 4 mins

Note: h or hr(s) can be used as a shortcut for writing the word hour(s).

	F	G	H	I	J
Start time	15:02	23:41	00:10	23:05	14:23
Duration of journey	$1\frac{1}{4}$ hrs	25 hrs 28 mins	130 mins	$2\frac{3}{5}$ hrs	$1\frac{3}{4}$ days

DISTANCE, SPEED AND TIME

6. Calculate the departure (start) time for each of the following journeys:

	A	B	C	D	E
End time	11:56	07:40	13:14	20:12	04:08
Duration of journey	36 mins	2 hr 24 mins	1 hr 23 mins	5 hrs 19 mins	3 hrs 38 mins

	F	G	H	I	J
End time	09:47	02:41	00:10	23:05	19:42
Duration of journey	3.75 hrs	3 hrs 29 mins	$10\frac{3}{20}$ hrs	420 mins	$\frac{3}{8}$ day

7. Calculate the time taken for each of the following journeys:

	A	B	C	D	E
End time	11:53	09:14	22:18	15:06	00:45
Start time	10:47	08:03	21:21	12:48	22:56

	F	G	H	I	J
End time	08:41	20:12	23:31	22:07	03:51
Start time	04:55	18:11	12:44	19:46	23:57

8. Classes start in a school at 09:00 and finish at 15:45. There is a 15-minute small break and 45 minutes off for lunch. Find:

   (i) The length of the school day

   (ii) The time a student spends in classes

9. A engine for a car can be manufactured in a factory every 35 minutes. The factory starts production at 8:45 and stops at 16:55.

   (i) Find the number of engines that can be produced in a single working day.

   After a refit of the factory, an engine can be produced 4 minutes more quickly than before.

   (ii) Find the number of completed engines that can now be produced in a single working day.

10. A school starts at 8:55 with nine classes, each 35 minutes in length. There are two breaks per day, one for 10 minutes and a 30-minute lunch break. Find the time at which the school finishes.

11. A train passes a station every 45 minutes. The first train is at 06:30 and the last train is at 22:15. Calculate:

   (i) The length of time between the first and last train

   (ii) The number of trains that pass the station in a day

   (iii) The number of trains that pass the station before 12:15

17.2 TIMETABLES

We read timetables in some form nearly every day, from checking when the next bus is due to checking what class we have next.

	Mon.	Tue.	Wed.	Thur.	Fri.
9.00–9.45	English	Irish	Science	P.E.	Maths
9.45–10.30	Maths	History	Maths	History	CSPE
10.30–11.15	Geography	P.E.	English	Irish	English
11.15–11.30	*Break*	*Break*	*Break*	*Break*	*Break*
11.30–12.15	Science	German	Irish	Geography	Art

A timetable is used to show a lot of information regarding time in a compact and easily read way.

 Worked Example 17.3

A section of a Bus Éireann timetable is shown.

MONDAY TO FRIDAY			
SERVICE NUMBER	233	233	233
		D	**D**
Cork (Parnell Place) dep.	0650	0735	0845
Model Farm Road			
Mount Desert		0745	0857
Carrigrohane	0700		
Leemount Cross		0750	0900
Cloghroe Church			
Cannon Cross			
Ballincollig	0710		0910
Ballincollig West			
Inniscarra		0755	0912
Coachford		0820	0935
Ovens			
Killumney			
Srelane			
Farran			
Farnanes	0730		
Cloughduv		....	
Crookstown		....	
Kilmurry		....	
Lissarda		....	
Macroom arr.		 0855	1010

(i) Which bus is the first to stop at Macroom?

(ii) Which bus reaches Macroom in the shortest time?

(iii) Which buses stop at Coachford?

(iv) Which bus takes the shortest time to reach Ballincollig from Cork?

(v) After Ballincollig, what is the next stop for the 06:50 bus?

Solution

(i) The first bus to stop at Macroom is the 07:35 bus.

> We usually identify buses by their start time.

(ii)

End time	08:55	10:10
Start time	07:35	08:45
Time taken	1:20	1:25
	1 hr 20 mins	1 hr 25 mins

The 08:55 bus reaches Macroom in the shortest time.

(iii) The 07:35 and 08:45 buses stop at Coachford.

(iv)

End time	07:10	09:10
Start time	06:50	08:45
Time taken	0:20	0:25
	20 mins	25 mins

The 06:50 bus takes the shortest time to reach Ballincollig from Cork.

(v) Farnanes is the next stop.

 **ACTIVITY 17.2**

Exercise 17.2

1. A bus timetable for Galway to Clifden is shown.

Galway to Clifden...	Timetable valid from 1st December 2010				
Operates...	Daily	Daily	Daily	Daily	Tuesday & Friday only
GALWAY Tourist Office	**0900**	**1200**	**1600**	**1730**	**1730**
Moycullen	0925	1225	1625	1755	1755
Rosscahill	0930	1230	1630	1800	1800
Oughterard	0940	1240	1640	1810	1810
Maam Cross	0950	1250	1650	1820	1820
Recess	1010	1310	1710	1840	1840
Canal Bridge	1015	1315	1715	1845	1845
CLIFDEN, CONNEMARA	**1030**	**1330**	**1730**	**1900**	**1900**
Cleggan	1045	1345	1745	-	1915
Letterfrack	1055	-	1755	1915	1925

(i) What bus does not service Letterfrack?

(ii) How long does it take for the bus to reach Clifden from Galway?

(iii) How long does it take for the bus to reach Cleggan from Moycullen?

(iv) If you arrive at the bus stop at Maam Cross at 14:25, at what time will you arrive in Clifden?

2. An airline's timetable for flights between the City of Derry airport and Dublin airport is shown.

CITY OF DERRY

City of Derry to Dublin

FLIGHT	DEPART	ARRIVE	M T W T F S S
RE 282	08.10	09.00	• • • • • – –
RE 282	09.40	10.30	– – – – – • –
RE 282	12.15	13.05	– – – – – – •
RE 288	16.55	17.45	– – – – – • –
RE 288	19.45	20.35	• • • • • – •

Dublin to City of Derry

FLIGHT	DEPART	ARRIVE	M T W T F S S
RE 281	07.00	07.50	• • • • • – –
RE 281	08.30	09.20	– – – – – • –
RE 281	11.00	11.50	– – – – – – •
RE 287	15.35	16.25	– – – – – – •
RE 287	18.30	19.20	• • • • • – •

(i) If Henry travels on Saturday, what is the earliest flight he can get from Dublin to Derry?

(ii) How long does it take to fly from the city of Derry to Dublin airport?

Priscilla must check into Dublin airport 45 minutes before her flight. If it takes her $1\frac{1}{4}$ hours to reach the airport, what is the latest time she can leave at to get flight RE 281 if she travels on:

(iii) A Sunday

(iv) A weekday

3. The Dublin to Belfast rail timetable is shown.

		MON TO SAT	MON TO SAT	MON TO SAT	MON TO SAT	FRI ONLY	MON TO FRI	SAT ONLY	MON TO SAT	MON TO SAT	MON TO SAT	SUN	SUN
DUBLIN Connolly	Dep	07.35	09.35	11.00	13.20	14.45	15.20	15.20	16.50	19.00	20.50	10.00	13.00
Drogheda MacBride	Dep	08.07	10.06	11.36	13.50	15.27	15.50	15.53	..	19.32	21.20	10.32	13.32
Dundalk Clarke	Dep	08.30	10.30	11.58	14.15	15.52	16.12	16.15	17.43	19.55	21.42	10.54	13.54
Newry	Dep	08.48	10.48	12.16	14.33	..	16.30	16.33	18.01	20.13	22.00	11.12	14.12
Portadown	Dep	09.09	11.09	12.37	14.56	....	16.51	16.57	18.22	20.34	22.21	11.34	14.34
Lurgan	Dep	..	..	..	..	..	..	..	..	..	20.58	....	11.44	..
Lisburn	Dep	....	11.33	....	15.20	....	....	....	....	20.58	....	12.03	....
BELFAST Central	Arr	09.45	11.50	13.15	15.35	..	17.27	17.35	18.57	21.15	22.57	12.16	15.07

Baile Átha Cliath – Béal Feirste – Luan go Domhnach (gan Saoire Phoiblí san áireamh)
Dublin – Belfast – Monday – Sunday (excluding public holidays)

(i) Name the train that stops at Lurgan.

(ii) Which train is the last to leave for Belfast on a weekday?

(iii) What is the fastest time the train takes to get from Dublin to Belfast?

(iv) Which Dublin to Belfast train is the slowest?

4. Here is part of the southbound DART timetable.

(i) How long does it take the DART to travel from Blackrock to Salthill?

(ii) Which two consecutive stations are 4 minutes apart?

(iii) A passenger travels from Blackrock to Bray. How long will the journey take?

(iv) Joe goes to Glenageary station to catch a southbound DART. He arrives at 1830 hours. How long will he have to wait before the train arrives?

(v) At what time will the 1852 train from Blackrock arrive in Bray?

Blackrock	1817	1827	1852
Seapoint	1818	1828	1853
Salthill	1820	1830	1855
Dún Laoghaire	1822	1832	1857
Sandycove	1824	1834	1859
Glenageary	1826	1836	1901
Dalkey	1828	1838	1903
Killiney	1832	1842	1907
Shankill	1834	1844	1909
Bray	1840	1850	1915

(vi) Which two consecutive stations are the furthest apart? (You may assume that the DART travels at the same average speed between stations.)

5. Part of the Dublin to Cork rail timetable is shown.

Baile Átha Cliath –Corcaigh – Seirbhísí Díreacha – Luan go Satharn (gan Saoire Phoiblí san áireamh) Dublin – Cork – Direct Services – Monday – Sunday (excluding public holidays)		MON TO SAT	MON TO SAT	MON TO SAT	MON TO SAT	MON TO SAT	MON TO SAT	MON TO SAT	MON TO SAT
DUBLIN Heuston	Dep	07.00	08.00	09.00	10.00	11.00	11.00	13.00	14.00
Newbridge	Dep	..	..	..	..	..	..	..	..
Kildare	Dep	....	....	....	....	11.30	....	13.30	....
Monasterevin	Dep	..	..	..	..	..	..	..	..
Portarlington	Dep	....	....	....	....	11.44	....	13.44	....
Portlaoise	Dep	07.52	..	09.54	10.52	11.56	..	13.56	..
Ballybrophy	Dep	....	....	....	10.07	....	....	14.09	....
Templemore	Dep	..	09.14	10.18	..	12.18	..	14.20	..
Thurles	Dep	08.21	09.22	10.26	11.21	12.26	13.18	14.28	15.18
Limerick Junction	Dep	08.46	09.47	10.50	11.47	12.50	13.43	14.52	15.43
Charleville	Dep	....	....	11.07	....	13.09	15.11	....	....
Mallow	Arr	09.18	10.17	11.22	12.19	13.24	14.15	15.26	16.15
Mallow	Dep	09.18	10.17	11.22	12.19	13.24	14.15	15.26	16.15
CORK	Arr	09.53	10.52	11.50	12.53	13.55	14.50	15.55	16.50

(i) Identify the trains that stop at Ballybrophy.

(ii) Which trains are the fastest from Dublin to Cork?

(iii) Which train is the slowest from Dublin to Cork?

(iv) Which train takes the longest time to go from Charleville to Cork?

(v) If you arrive at Portlaoise station at 9:58, how long will you have to wait for the next train to Templemore?

6. Here is part of the timetable for the northbound Arklow–Bray train service.

(i) How long does the train take to go from Arklow to Greystones?

(ii) Write down the missing times XXXX and YYYY. (Assume same journey times.)

Arklow	0657	0919
Rathdrum	0715	0937
Wicklow	0730	0952
Greystones	0750	XXXX
Bray	0806	YYYY

(iii) Which two consecutive stations are the greatest time apart? (Assume the same average speed between stations.)

(iv) David Toland wants to go from Rathdrum to Wicklow by train. He walks to Rathdrum station, arriving there at 0655 hours. How long will he have to wait for the next train?

(v) How many minutes does it take to travel from Arklow to Bray?

DISTANCE, SPEED AND TIME

17.3 DISTANCE, SPEED AND TIME

The world record for the 100 m sprint as of 2010 stands at 9.58 seconds by Usain Bolt. Can you calculate the average speed for that run?

An aeroplane travels between two airports at an average speed of 250 kilometres per hour for 1,000 km. How long did the flight take?

Light travels at around 300,000,000 metres per second. How far will light travel in 1 minute?

All of these question can be answered with the aid of the following diagram, called the Distance–Speed–Time triangle or DST triangle.

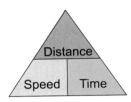

We can remember the DST triangle by the mnemonic 'Dad's Silly Triangle'.

To calculate average **speed**, we just cover up Speed on the triangle:

FORMULA

$$S = \frac{D}{T} = \frac{\text{Distance}}{\text{Time}}$$

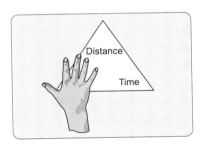

We must also be familiar with the units of speed. These are usually given in kilometres per hour (km/h) or metres per second (m/s).

To calculate **distance**, we just cover up Distance on the triangle:

FORMULA

$$D = S \times T = \text{Speed} \times \text{Time}$$

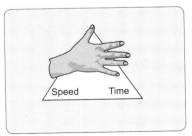

To calculate **time**, we just cover up Time on the triangle:

FORMULA

$$T = \frac{D}{S} = \frac{\text{Distance}}{\text{Speed}}$$

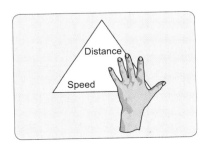

Worked Example 17.4

A train travels 100 km in 1 hr 15 minutes. What is the average speed of the train?

Solution

As the speed will be in kilometres/hour, we must first express 1 hr 15 minutes as hours only.

1 hr 15 minutes can be expressed as $1\frac{15}{60}$ hours.

Using a calculator, we can change this into 1.25 or $1\frac{1}{4}$ hours.

$$\text{Speed} = \frac{\text{Distance}}{\text{Time}} = \frac{100}{1.25} = 80 \text{ km/h}$$

 ## Worked Example 17.5

A rocket travels at 150 m/s. How long will it take to reach a height of 75 km?

Solution

We must make sure that the units are correct.

As the speed is in metres/second, we will change kilometres into metres:
75 km = 75,000 m

$$\text{Time} = \frac{\text{Distance}}{\text{Speed}} = \frac{75,000}{150} = 500 \text{ seconds}$$

 ## Worked Example 17.6

A hiker travels at an average speed of 6 km/h for 40 minutes. How far did she walk?

Solution

As the speed is in kilometres/hour, we must change the time given into hours as well:

$$40 \text{ minutes} = \frac{40}{60} = \frac{2}{3} \text{ hour}$$

$$\text{Distance} = \text{Speed} \times \text{Time} = 6 \times \frac{2}{3} = 4 \text{ km}$$

We may encounter questions which involve two or more parts and may also be asked to find the overall average speed.

 ## Worked Example 17.7

Alexander travels by car for $1\frac{1}{2}$ hours to his nearest railway station, which is 90 km away. He then takes a train at an average speed of 150 km/h for 3 hours.

(i) What was the average speed of the car?

(ii) What distance did the train travel?

(iii) What was the total distance travelled?

(iv) What was the overall time taken for the journey?

(v) What was the overall average speed of his journey?

Solution

(i) Speed = $\dfrac{\text{Distance}}{\text{Time}} = \dfrac{90}{1.5} = 60$ km/h

(ii) Distance = Speed × Time
$= 150 \times 3 = 450$ km

(iii) Total distance:

90 km + 450 km = 540 km

(iv) Overall time:

1.5 hrs + 3 hrs = 4.5 hours

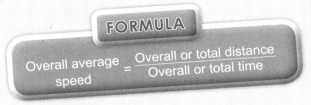

FORMULA

Overall average speed $= \dfrac{\text{Overall or total distance}}{\text{Overall or total time}}$

(v) Overall average speed $= \dfrac{540}{4.5} = 120$ km/h

Exercise 17.3

1. Calculate the average speed in km/h of each of the following:

	A	B	C	D	E	F	G	H
Distance	100 km	250 km	450 km	900 km	12 km	100 km	3,000 m	1,100 m
Time	5 hrs	4 hrs	8 hrs	6 hrs	30 mins	$\frac{1}{3}$ hr	900 secs	$1\frac{1}{4}$ mins

2. Calculate the time taken in hours for each of the following:

	A	B	C	D	E	F	G	H
Distance	100 km	150 km	3,000 km	9 km	8,800 km	6,000 m	1,500 km	180,000 m
Speed	100 km/h	75 km/h	60 km/h	0.5 km/h	100 km/h	12 km/h	80 km/h	$33\frac{1}{3}$ km/h

3. Calculate the distance travelled in kilometres for each of the following:

	A	B	C	D	E
Time	$2\frac{1}{4}$ hrs	$7\frac{1}{3}$ hrs	$3\frac{1}{6}$ hrs	2 hrs 30 mins	21 mins
Speed	50 km/h	120 km/h	24 km/h	95 km/h	85 km/hr

4. An runner runs at an average speed of 5 m/s. How long will it take her to run a 200 m race?

5. A car travels at an average speed of 60 km/h.

   (i) How far will the car travel in $1\frac{1}{2}$ hours?

   (ii) How long would the car take to travel 150 km?

6. A boat travels 750 metres in $2\frac{1}{2}$ minutes. What is the boat's average speed in m/s?

7. A hillwalking group sets out at 09:30. At 12:00, they have walked 10 km.
   What is the group's average speed in km/h?

8. A train travels at an average speed of 90 km/h.

   (i) How long would this train take to travel 210 km?

   (ii) How far would this train travel between 13:50 and 15:40?

9. An airplane travels from Shannon to New York, a distance of 4,950 km, between 08:50 and 13:20.

    (i)   What is the average speed of the plane?

    (ii) It leaves New York on the return flight at 17:15 and travels at an average speed of 990 km/h. At what time will it arrive?

10. A runner runs a 40 km race. He runs the first half of the race at an average speed of 10 km/h and the rest at 8 km/h. How long will he take to run the entire race?

11. Convert 18 km/h to m/s.

12. Convert 7.5 m/s to km/h.

13. Convert 150 metres per minute to kilometres per hour.

14. The speed of light is 300,000,000 m/s. The Sun is 150 million kilometres away from the Earth. If a solar flare takes place on the Sun, how many seconds will elapse before it is seen on the Earth?

15. A ferry travels 200 km in 4 hours to the nearest port. It then travels 45 km in 1 hour 15 minutes.

    (i)   What was the average speed of the ferry for the first part of its voyage?

    (ii) What was the average speed of the ferry for the second part of its voyage?

    (iii) What was the overall distance sailed?

    (iv) What was the total time for the voyage?

    (v)   What was the ferry's overall average speed?

16. A car travels at 50 km/h for 4 hours 12 minutes. On the next stage of its journey, the car travels 300 km at an average speed of 60 km/h.

    (i)   What was the distance travelled by the car for the first part of its journey?

    (ii) How long did it take the car to complete the second part of its journey?

    (iii) What was the overall distance travelled by the car?

    (iv) What was the total time for the journey?

    (v)   What was the car's overall average speed to the nearest kilometre/hour?

17. In a competition, an athlete cycles 50 km in $1\frac{1}{3}$ hours and then runs 10 km in at an average speed of 15 km/h.

    (i)   What was the average speed of the athlete cycling?

    (ii) How long did it take him to run 10 km?

    (iii) What was the total distance travelled?

    (iv) What was the athlete's overall time?

    (v)   What was the athlete's overall average speed to the nearest kilometre/hour?

Revision Exercises

1. (a) A school opens each day at 09:10 and closes at 16:40. For how long is the school open each day?

    (b) An interviewer interviews candidates for a job. Each interview takes 9 minutes. How many candidates will be interviewed in 3 hours if no breaks are taken?

    (c) A student spends 35 minutes at his maths homework and 20 minutes each on Irish, English, History and Science. How long (in hours and minutes) will it take him to complete this homework?

2. (a) A train leaves Dublin at 11.25 a.m. and arrives in Tralee at 5.50 p.m. Convert these times to the 24-hour clock and hence find the time which the journey takes.

(b) Copy and complete this table:

12-hr clock	7.00 p.m.		10.20 p.m.
24-hr clock		16:00	

12-hr clock		11.40 a.m.	11.40 p.m.
24-hr clock	06:30		

(c) Here are the times for the songs on U2's *Zooropa* album. The times are given in minutes and seconds (e.g. *Numb* takes 4 minutes and 18 seconds).

Side 1		Side 2	
Zooropa	6.30	Daddy's gonna pay	5.19
Babyface	4.30	Some days	4.15
Numb	4.18	The first time	3.45
Lemon	6.56	Dirty day	5.24
Stay	4.58	The wanderer	4.44

(i) How long is side 1?

(ii) How long is side 2?

(iii) How long is the entire album?

3. (a) A garda is trying to find out facts about a burglary. He gets the following statements:

(i) 'I saw a man entering the house at half-past eleven in the morning.'

(ii) 'I saw a man leaving the house with a DVD player 20 minutes after midday.'

(iii) 'I arrested the man three-quarters of an hour after he left the house.'

Fill in this table:

Event	Man enters house	Man leaves house	Man is arrested
12-hr clock			
24-hr clock			

(b) A boat put out to sea at 9.30 p.m. on Monday. $2\frac{1}{4}$ hours later, it developed engine failure. Forty minutes later, it sent out an SOS signal. The crew was rescued 55 minutes later. Complete this log, using the 24-hour clock.

Event	Put to sea	Engine failure	SOS sent	Rescued
Day	Mon			
Time	21:30			

(c) Here is part of a timetable for the northbound DART.

Connolly	1222	1237	1250	DDDD
Killester	1226	1241	1254	CCCC
Harmonstown	1228	1243	1256	1313
Raheny	1230	1245	1258	1315
Kilbarrack	1233	1248	BBBB	1318
Howth Junction	AAAA	1250	1303	1320

(i) How long does it take to go from Connolly to Howth Junction?

(ii) Write down the missing times *AAAA, BBBB, CCCC, DDDD* (assuming same journey times).

(iii) James wants to travel by DART from Connolly station to a lunch-time meeting in Raheny. When he gets to Raheny station, he will have a 5-minute walk to the meeting, which starts at 1300 hours. What is the latest time at which he should arrive at Connolly station to catch his train?

4. (a) A woman works at a car-assembly factory. She has to put wing mirrors on each car. She can fit one mirror every $2\frac{1}{2}$ minutes. How many will she fit in an hour?

(b) Here are the evening viewing times for October 26 on RTÉ:

RTÉ 1	RTÉ 2
1800 *Angelus*	1755 *Hullaballoo*
1801 *Six-One News*	1825 *Home and Away*
1900 *Fair City*	1855 *Nuacht*
1930 *Head to Toe*	1903 *Cúrsaí*
2000 *Bob*	2002 *Poirot*
2030 *Check Up*	2100 *The Bill*
2100 *News*	2132 *Cheers*
2130 *Tuesday File*	2200 *Fanning Profiles*
2210 *Radio Days*	2230 *Network News*
2335 *Late News*	2250 *Pole to Pole*
2345 Close	2345 Close

(i) How Long did *Head to Toe* last?

(ii) How long did *Cheers* last?

(iii) *Radio Days* was the only film on RTÉ that evening. How many minutes did it last?

(iv) Sheila watches all the above programmes on RTÉ 2. For how many hours and minutes was she watching TV?

(v) Two programmes on RTÉ 2 were in the Irish language. What was the total length of Irish broadcasting that evening?

(vi) Was more or less than $\frac{1}{10}$ of the total viewing time on RTÉ 2 that evening in Irish?

(vii) A student wrote to RTÉ 1 to complain that too much time was given over to news programmes. She wrote, 'There were over 2 hours of news programmes (including *Nuacht*) on RTÉ (between RTÉ 1 and RTÉ 2) on October 26th.' Was this true or false?

(c) Here are the departing times for the No. 1 bus route from City Hospital to Central Station, a journey which lasts 25 minutes.

0726	0800	0840	0920	1120	1215
1305	1345	1430	1550	1630	1717
1752	1830	2030	2120		

(i) What time does the 1550 bus arrive at Central Station?

(ii) Which bus arrives at Central Station at 1817?

(iii) A doctor at City Hospital wants to catch a train at Central Station at 1400. Which is the latest bus that she should catch?

5. (a) A student cycles to school, a distance of 6 km. She travels this distance in 20 minutes. What is her average speed in km/h?

(b) A train leaves Limerick at 09:55 and arrives at Wexford at 12:25.

(i) How long did the journey take?

(ii) If the distance travelled is 180 km, find the average speed of the train in km/h.

(c) This table shows the driving distances (in km) between some major Irish towns. For example, the highlighted reading shows that the distance from Belfast to Ennis is 330 km.

Athlone					
220	Belfast				
218	420	Cork			
180	190	390	Donegal		
110	330	140	260	Ennis	
90	310	200	200	260	Galway

(i) Which two towns are the same distance from Galway?

(ii) Which is further from Athlone – Belfast or Cork?

(iii) If you drive from Athlone to Donegal at an average speed of 60 km/h, how long will the journey take?

(iv) A cyclist travels from Ennis to Cork in 6 hours. What is the average speed of the cyclist?

(v) A car leaves Belfast at 1050 hours, to go to Donegal. It travels at an average speed of 57 km/h.
At what time will it reach Donegal?

(vi) A family wants to travel from Donegal to Cork. They travel for 4 hours at an average speed of 65 km/h. They complete the journey in a further 2 hours. What is their average speed for the last two hours?

6. (a) Here is a part of a DART timetable for a certain day:

Howth	1450	1510	1530	1550
Sutton	1453	1513	1533	1553
Bayside	1455	1515	1535	1555
Howth Junction	1457	1517	*BBBB*	1557
Kilbarrack	1459	1519	1539	1559
Raheny	*AAAA*	1521	1541	1601

(i) How long does it take the DART to go from Howth to Raheny?

(ii) How often did DART trains run on the day?

(iii) Write down the missing times *AAAA* and *BBBB*.

(iv) Which two stations are the furthest time apart?

(v) If Sutton and Bayside are 1.5 km apart, what is the average speed of the train between these two stations?

(b) A student kept a record of the times spent on five consecutive activities. Fill in the missing parts.

Event	Time	Duration
Getting ready	07:10–08:05	
Going to school	08:05–09:15	
School day	09:15–	6 hrs 35 mins
Sport		$1\frac{1}{4}$ hrs
Going home after school	–18:00	

7. (a) If I travel at 1 m/s, how many kilometres will I travel in an hour?

(b) A car travels at an average speed of 48 km/h.

(i) How many hours and minutes would it take to go a distance of 160 kilometres?

(ii) How far would it travel between 10:45 and 15:25?

(c) A man runs a 30 kilometre race in 5 hours. For the first two hours, his average speed is 7.2 km/h. Find his average speed for the remaining 3 hours.

8. (a) A car travels 63 km in $2\frac{1}{4}$ hours. What is its average speed?

(b) Here are the evening departure times for buses from a university campus to the general train station, a journey which takes 35 minutes

1800	1815	1836	1847	1905
1912	1933	1952	2011	2024
2041	2100	2116	2133	2154
2209	2224	2241		

(i) Karen wants to go from the campus to the station to catch a train at 2227 hours. What is the latest bus which she could catch?

(ii) If you arrive at the campus bus stop at 1925 hours, at what time will you reach the train station?

(iii) If the journey is 14 kilometres in length, what is the average speed of the bus in km/h?

(c) Edward decides to visit his friend in Donegal. He leaves his home at 06:15 and travels for $2\frac{1}{3}$ hours at an average speed of 55 km/hr.

He then stops for something to eat at a café and restarts his journey 45 minutes later.

After travelling 100 km for 80 minutes, he reaches his friend's house.

Calculate:

(i) How far he travelled for the first part of his journey

(ii) The time at which he reached his first stop

(iii) The time at which he restarted his journey

(iv) The average speed for the second part of his journey

(v) The time that he arrived at his friend's house

(vi) The overall average speed for the total journey (to the nearest km/hr)

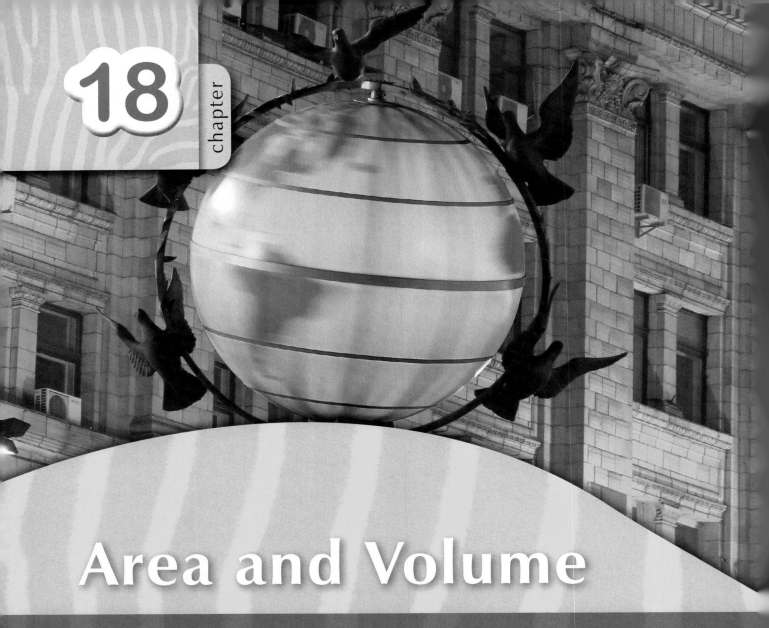

Area and Volume

Learning Outcomes

In this chapter you will learn to:

- ➲ Find the area and perimeter of two-dimensional (2D) shapes
- ➲ Find the area and circumference of a circle
- ➲ Solve problems involving area
- ➲ Investigate the nets of rectangular solids
- ➲ Find the surface area of rectangular solids
- ➲ Find the volume of rectangular solids and cylinders
- ➲ Solve problems involving surface area and volume
- ➲ Draw and interpret scaled diagrams

18.1 AREA AND PERIMETER OF 2D SHAPES

From designing a garden to designing a tower block, **area** and **perimeter** are important concepts to understand and be able to use.

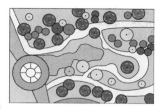

Area is the amount of flat space that a shape occupies.

ACTIVITY 18.1

Perimeter is the sum of the length of all the sides of a shape.

YOU SHOULD REMEMBER...

- How to find the perimeter and area of basic two-dimensional (2D) shapes

KEY WORDS

- Length
- Width
- Area
- Perimeter
- Circumference
- π (pi)
- Net
- Surface area
- Volume
- Scale

AREA AND VOLUME

From Activity 18.1, we can state the following:

Rectangle	**Square**
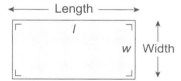 Area = (length × width) = $l \times w$ Perimeter = $2l + 2w$ or $2(l + w)$	Area = (length)^2 = l^2 Perimeter = $4l$
Triangle	**Parallelogram**
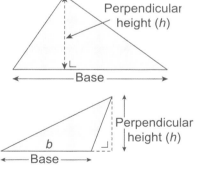 Area = $\frac{1}{2}$ × base × perpendicular height = $\frac{1}{2} bh$	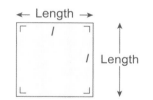 Area = base × perpendicular height = bh

The units of area will always be units^2, for example: mm^2, cm^2, m^2, km^2, etc. When finding the area of a shape, make sure that you use the **same** units: mm × mm, cm × cm, etc.

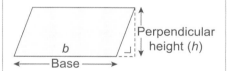

Worked Example 18.1

Find the area of each of the following shapes:

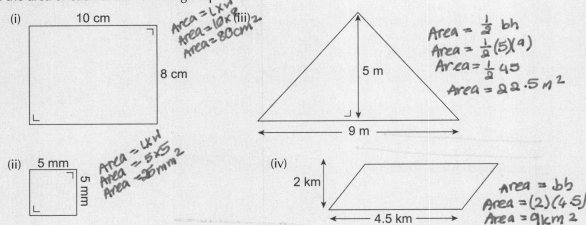

(i) 10 cm, 8 cm

Area = L x w
Area = 10 x 8
Area = 80 cm²

(ii) 5 mm, 5 mm

Area = L x w
Area = 5 x 5
Area = 25 mm²

(iii) 5 m, 9 m

Area = ½ bh
Area = ½ (5)(9)
Area = ½ 45
Area = 22.5 m²

(iv) 2 km, 4.5 km

Area = bh
Area = (2)(4.5)
Area = 9 km²

Solution

(i) Rectangle ∴ area = $l \times w = 10 \times 8 = 80$ cm².

(ii) Square ∴ area = $l^2 = 5 \times 5 = 25$ mm².

(iii) Triangle ∴ area = $\frac{1}{2} bh = \frac{1}{2} \times 9 \times 5 = 22.5$ m².

(iv) Parallelogram ∴ area = $bh = 4.5 \times 2 = 9$ km².

> When finding the area of triangles and parallelograms, it is very important to pick the correct base and perpendicular height.

We may also meet 2D shapes made up of a number of different shapes. These are referred to as **compound shapes**.

Worked Example 18.2

Find the area of this shape.

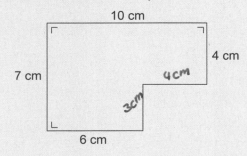

10 cm, 7 cm, 4 cm, 4 cm, 3 cm, 6 cm

Solution

It may help to fill in any side length or width that is missing:

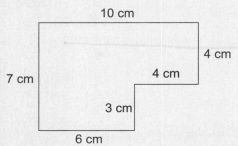

10 cm, 7 cm, 4 cm, 4 cm, 3 cm, 6 cm

Method 1

We divide the shape into different parts and then work out the area of each part.

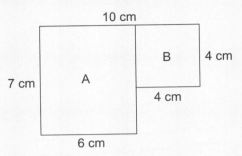

Part A   **Part B**

Area: $7 \times 6 = 42$ cm²   Area: $4 \times 4 = 16$ cm²

The total area of the shape is now found by adding these two areas:

Area of shape $= 42$ cm² $+ 16$ cm² $= 58$ cm²

Method 2

We redraw the shape as a rectangle and then subtract the area of the part that has been added to form this rectangle.

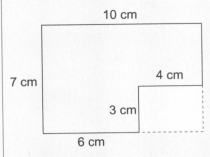

Total area   **Area of added part**

$7 \times 10 = 70$ cm² $3 \times 4 = 12$ cm²

The area of the shape is now found by subtracting the smaller area from the larger area:

Area of shape $= 70$ cm² $- 12$ cm² $= 58$ cm²

Exercise 18.1

1. Find the area and perimeter of each of the following rectangles and squares.

(i) 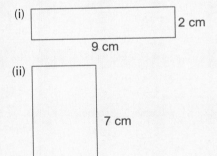 2 cm, 9 cm

(ii) 7 cm, 4 cm

(iii) 7.5 mm, 7.5 mm

(iv) 0.15 m, 0.75 m

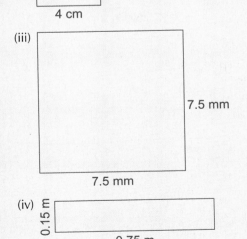

(v) 500 m, 500 m

(vi) 1.25 km, 2200 m

(vii) 5.8 cm, 55 mm

(viii) 9 km, 400 m

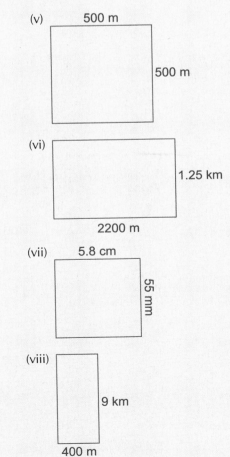

2. Find the area of each of the following triangles and parallelograms.

(i)
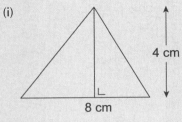
4 cm
8 cm

(ii)
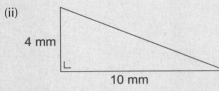
4 mm
10 mm

(iii)
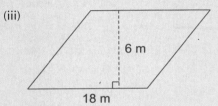
6 m
18 m

(iv)
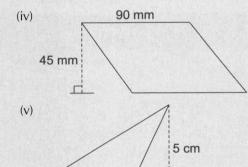
90 mm
45 mm

(v)
5 cm
92 mm

(vi)
12 cm
5 cm

(vii)
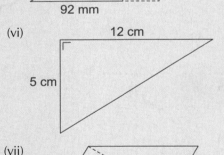
7 m
9 m
8 m

(viii)
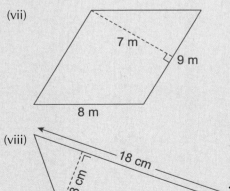
18 cm
8 cm
21 cm

3. Find the area of the coloured regions of each shape.

(i)
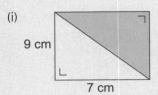
9 cm
7 cm

(ii)
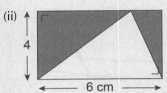
4
6 cm

(iii)
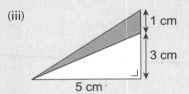
1 cm
3 cm
5 cm

(iv)
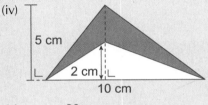
5 cm
2 cm
10 cm

(v)
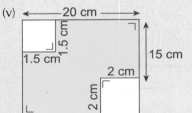
20 cm
1.5 cm
1.5 cm
2 cm
2 cm
15 cm

(vi)
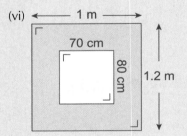
1 m
70 cm
80 cm
1.2 m

(vii)
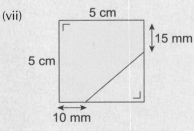
5 cm
15 mm
5 cm
10 mm

(viii)
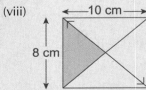
10 cm
8 cm

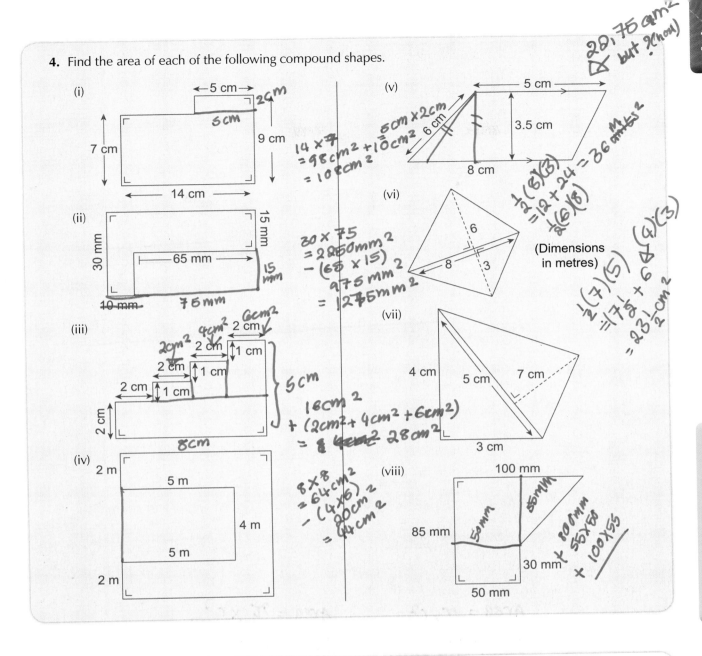

4. Find the area of each of the following compound shapes.

(i)

(handwritten)
14×7
$= 98\,cm^2 + 5cm \times 2cm = 10cm^2$
$= 108\,cm^2$

(ii)

(handwritten)
30×75
$= 2250\,mm^2$
$- (65 \times 15)$
$\quad 975\,mm^2$
$= 1275\,mm^2$

(iii)

(handwritten)
$16\,cm^2$
$+ (2cm^2 + 4cm^2 + 6cm^2)$
$= 28\,cm^2$

(iv)

(handwritten)
8×8
$= 64\,cm^2$
$- (4 \times 6)$
$\quad 20\,cm^2$
$= 44\,cm^2$

(v)

(handwritten top)
28.75 cm² but I don't

(handwritten)
$\frac{1}{2}(6)(8)$
$= \frac{1}{2}(8)(3)$
$= 12 + 24 = 36\,M\,ts\,2$

(vi)

(Dimensions in metres)

(handwritten)
$\frac{1}{2}(7)(5) \quad \frac{1}{2}(4)(3)$
$= (7\frac{1}{2} + 6$
$= 23\frac{1}{2}\,cm^2$

(vii)

(viii)

(handwritten)
$+ 800mm$
$+ 55 \times 50$
$+ 100 \times 55$

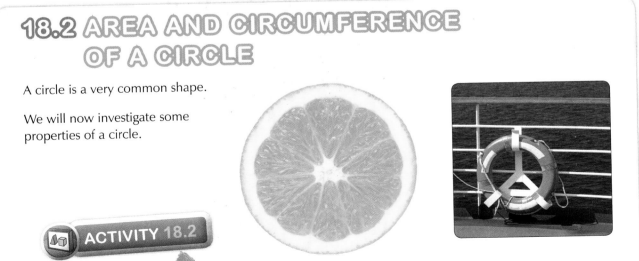

18.2 AREA AND CIRCUMFERENCE OF A CIRCLE

A circle is a very common shape.

We will now investigate some properties of a circle.

ACTIVITY 18.2

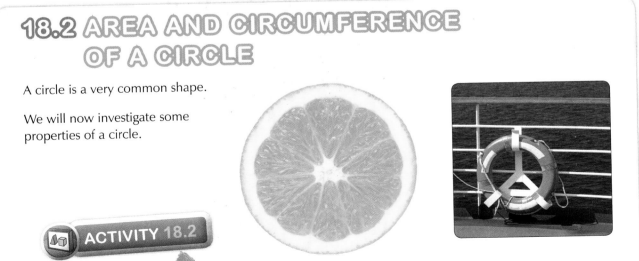

From Activity 18.2, we can see that the length of the circumference of any circle divided by the length of its diameter is always the same. This number is π (pronounced 'pi').

We use π to help calculate the area and circumference (perimeter) of a circle.

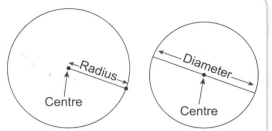

Area

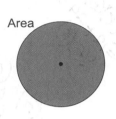

Circumference

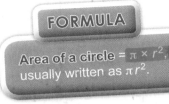

FORMULA

Area of a circle = π × r², usually written as πr².

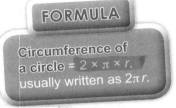

FORMULA

Circumference of a circle = 2 × π × r, usually written as 2πr.

These formulae appear on page 8 of *Formulae and Tables*.

π = 3.141592… is an infinite decimal which never ends and never repeats.
Therefore, in calculating the area or circumference of a circle, we may be told to use one of the following values for π:

- π = 3.14
- π = $\frac{22}{7}$
- The value of π from the calculator

Sometimes we don't give π a value but just leave it as π. This is referred to as 'leaving our answer in terms of π'.

Worked Example 18.3

Find the area and circumference of a circle of radius length 21 cm, taking:

(i) π = 3.14   Area = π × r² (ii) π = $\frac{22}{7}$ Area = π × r²
Solution Area = 3.14 × (21)²   Area = $\frac{22}{7}$ × (21)²
(i) π = 3.14   Area = 3.14 × 441   Area = $\frac{22}{7}$ × 441
                Area ≈ 1,384.74 cm² ✓   Area = 1,386 cm² ✓

(i) π = 3.14

Area of a circle = π × r²   Circumference of a circle = 2 × π × r

= 3.14 × (21)²   circumference = 2 × π × r   = 2 × 3.14 × 21
                                  circ = 2 × 3.14 × 21
= 3.14 × 441   circ. = 6.28 × 21   = 6.28 × 21

= 1,384.74 cm²   circ. = 131.88 cm   = 131.88 cm

(ii) π = $\frac{22}{7}$

Area of a circle = π × r²   Circumference of a circle = 2 × π × r

= $\frac{22}{7}$ × (21)²   circ. = 2 × π × r   = 2 × $\frac{22}{7}$ × 21
                                  circ = 2 × $\frac{22}{7}$ × 21
= $\frac{22}{7}$ × 441   circ. = $\frac{44}{7}$ × 21   = $\frac{44}{7}$ × 21

= 1,386 cm²   circ. = 132 cm   = 132 cm

Changing the value of π will affect the answer slightly.

Worked Example 18.4

Find, in terms of π, the area and circumference of a circle of diameter length 5 cm.

Solution

If the diameter length is 5 cm, then the radius length is 2.5 cm.

Area of a circle $= \pi \times r^2$

$\quad = \pi \times (2.5)^2$

$\quad = \pi \times 6.25$

$\quad = 6.25\pi$ cm^2

Circumference of a circle $= 2 \times \pi \times r$

$\quad = 2 \times \pi \times 2.5$

$\quad = 5 \times \pi$

$\quad = 5\pi$ cm

> When we are asked to leave our answer in terms of π, the answer must contain the π symbol.

(handwritten) Area $= \pi \times r^2$
Area $= \pi \times (2.5)^2$
Area $= \pi \times 6.25$
Area $= 6.25\pi$ cm^2

(handwritten) circ. $= 2 \times \pi \times r$
circ. $= 2 \times \pi \times 2.5$
circ. $= 5 \times \pi$
circ. $= 5\pi$ cm

Worked Example 18.5

A wire is bent into the following semicircular shape. Taking $\pi = 3.14$, find:

  (i) The area of the shape

  (ii) The length of wire needed to make the shape

— 9 cm —

Solution

(i) Area of a circle $= \pi \times r^2$

    Area of a half a circle $= \dfrac{\pi \times r^2}{2}$

$\quad = \dfrac{3.14 \times (9)^2}{2}$

$\quad = \dfrac{254.34}{2}$

$\quad = 127.17$ cm^2

(ii) Length of wire needed to make the shape
    = Circumference of half the circle
      + length of wire used as the diameter

Circumference of a circle $= 2 \times \pi \times r$

Circumference of a half a circle $= \dfrac{2 \times \pi \times r}{2}$ (or πr)

$\quad = \dfrac{2 \times 3.14 \times 9}{2}$

$\quad = \dfrac{56.52}{2}$

$\quad = 28.26$ cm

Length of wire used as the diameter $= 9 \times 2 = 18$ cm

Length of wire needed to make the shape
$= 28.26 + 18 = 46.26$ cm

Exercise 18.2

1. Taking $\pi = 3.14$, find the area and circumference of each of the following circles:

  (i) Radius length = 6 cm

  (ii) Radius length = 14 cm

  (iii) Radius length = 10.4 mm

  (iv) Diameter length = 30 m

  (v) Radius length = 8.25 cm

  (vi) Radius length = 6.28 cm

  (vii) Diameter length = 100 m

  (viii) Radius length = 0.001 m

(handwritten) (i) Area $= \pi \times r^2$
Area $= 3.14 \times 6^2$
Area $= 3.14 \times 36$
Area $= 3.14 \times 36$
Area $= 113.04$ cm^2 ✓

(handwritten) (vii) circumference $= \pi \times r \times 2$
circ. $= 3.14 \times 50 \times 2$
circ. $= 6.28 \times 50$
circ. $= 314$ m ✓

2. Taking $\pi = \frac{22}{7}$, find the area and circumference of each of the following circles:

  (i) Radius length = 7 cm

  (ii) Diameter length = 70 cm

  (iii) Radius length = 10.5 cm

  (iv) Radius length = 14 cm

  (v) Radius length = 3.5 cm

  (vi) Radius length = 0.49 m

  (vii) Diameter length = 84 mm

  (viii) Radius length = $\frac{7}{11}$ m

3. Find the area and circumference of each of the following circles, in terms of π:

   (i) Radius length = 10 cm   (iii) Diameter length = 12 m   (v) Diameter length = 50 cm

   (ii) Radius length = 4 mm   (iv) Radius length = 0.5 cm   (vi) Radius length = 1 m

4. Measure the radius length of each of the following circles and, hence, find the area and length of each circle. Take the value of π from your calculator and give your answers to two decimal places.

(i)

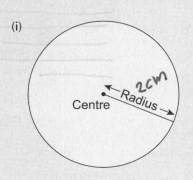

(ii)

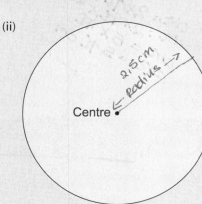

(handwritten annotations)
Area = $\pi \times r^2$
Area = 4π cm^2
Area = 12.57 cm^2
circumference = $2 \times \pi \times r$
circ = $2 \times \pi \times 2$
circ = 4π cm
circ. = 12.57 cm

5. Find the area and perimeter of each of the following figures (answers correct to two decimal places).

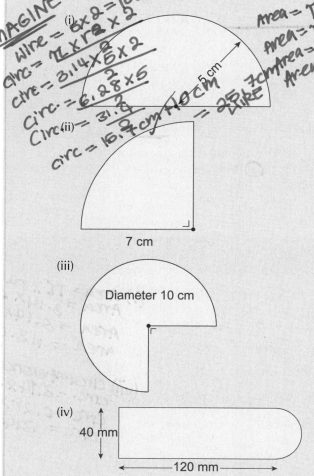

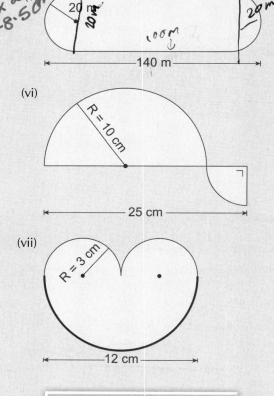

Note: The highlighted curve is a semicircle.

6. Find the area of the shaded regions of each of the following shapes (correct to three decimal places):

(i)

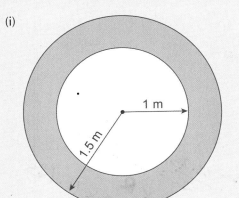

1 m

1.5 m

(iii)

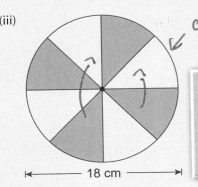

← cemicircle

18 cm

Note: Angles at the centre for each sector are equal.

(iv)

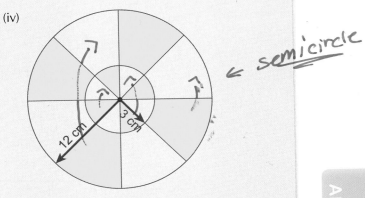

← semicircle

12 cm

3 cm

Note: Angles at the centre for each sector are equal.

(ii)

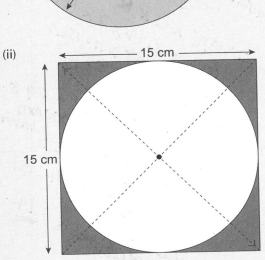

15 cm

15 cm

18.3 PROBLEMS INVOLVING AREA AND PERIMETER

Using what we have learned in the previous sections of this chapter, we can now try to solve real-life problems involving area and perimeter.

Worked Example 18.6

A lawn is 10 m long and 4 m wide. It is surrounded by a path of 1 m width as shown.

(i) Find the area of the path.

(ii) Find the cost of the path if paving costs €4 per m².

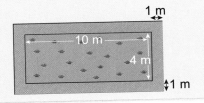

1 m

10 m

4 m

1 m

Solution

(i) Lawn area $= 10 \times 4 = 40$ m²

Lawn area including path $= 12 \times 6$
$= 72$ m²

∴ Area of path $= 72 - 40 = 32$ m²

(ii) Paving costs €4 per m²

∴ Cost $= 32 \times 4 = €128$

Worked Example 18.7

The diameter of a 20c coin is 22.25 mm.

Taking $\pi = 3.14$:

    (i) Calculate the circumference of the coin.

If the coin is rolled along the ground, find:

    (ii) The distance travelled if the coin makes 10 complete revolutions

    (iii) The number of complete revolutions the coin makes if it rolls 1 m

Solution

We must first find the radius of the 20c coin:

$$\text{Radius} = \frac{22.25}{2} = 11.125 \text{ mm}$$

  (i) Circumference of a circle $= 2 \times \pi \times r$

$$= 2 \times 3.14 \times 11.125$$

$$= 6.28 \times 11.125$$

$$= 69.865 \text{ mm}$$

It may be more appropriate to use centimetres in our answer:

69.865 mm = 6.9865 cm (10 mm = 1 cm)

  (ii) The distance travelled if the coin makes 10 complete revolutions:
      6.9865 cm × 10 = 69.865 cm

> One complete revolution = one circumference.

  (iii) 1 m = 100 cm

$$\text{Number of revolutions} = \frac{\text{Total distance travelled}}{\text{Distance travelled in one revolution}}$$

$$= \frac{100}{6.9865} = 14.31\ldots$$

Number of complete revolutions = 14

Handwritten annotations:

(i) Radius = $\frac{22.25}{2}$ = 11.125mm

arc. = $\pi \times 2 \times R$
circ. = 3.14 × 2 × 11.125
circ. = 6.28 × 11.125
circ. = 69.865

(ii) 69.865 × 10 = 698.65 cm

(iii) 1m = 100cm = 1000mm
No Revolutions $\frac{\text{Total distance}}{\text{one}}$
$\frac{1000}{69.865}$ = 14.31
COMPLETE Revolutions = 14

Exercise 18.3

1. Here is the plan of a floor (in metres).

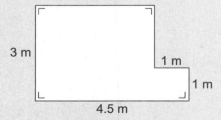

3 m   1 m   1 m   4.5 m

The floor is to be covered in square tiles with sides of length 25 cm. How many tiles are needed to cover the floor?

2. A wall is to be built according to the following plan:

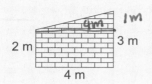

Handwritten work:
$\frac{1}{2}4(1) = 2m^2$
$2 \times 4 = 8m^2 + 2m^2 = 10m^2$ ✓
$12m^2$

(i) Find the area of the wall.

It is then decided to build a window into the wall. Two designs are shown.

Handwritten: design 2 $40 \times 3 = 1200 \text{cm}^2 = 12m^2$

Design 1	Design 2

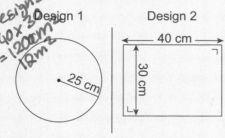

(ii) Which window design uses the least area?

Handwritten: Design 2

(iii) Using the window of least area, what is the remaining area of the wall?

Handwritten: $2m^2$

3. A circular patio surrounds a flower bed as shown.

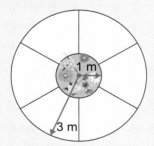

Taking $\pi = \frac{22}{7}$, find:

(i) The area covered by the patio (correct to one decimal place)

(ii) The cost of paving the patio, if paving costs €19.50 per m²

4. A design for a helipad of a hospital is shown.

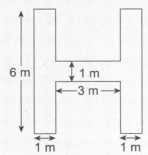

(i) Find the area covered by this design.

(ii) If 1 litre of paint covers 5 m², calculate how many litres of paint are needed to paint this design.

(iii) Find the total cost of painting this design if 1 litre of paint costs €10 and two coats of paint are required.

5. A window of a church is shown. It consists of a semicircle on top of a rectangle as shown.

Handwritten:
Design 1)
area = $\pi \times r^2$
area = $\pi \times 25^2$
area = $\pi \times 625$
area = $685\pi \text{ cm}^2$
area = $1963.32 \text{cm}^2 \div 100$
$19.6356 m^2$

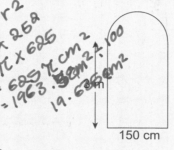

Handwritten: Design 2 $98,880 \text{cm}^2$

(i) Find the area covered by this design (in metres squared correct to two decimal places).

(ii) A lead strip is to surround this window. If this strip cost €5 per 50 cm, find the cost of installing the lead strip.

6. A bicycle wheel has a diameter of 49 cm. Taking $\pi = \frac{22}{7}$, find:

(i) The distance travelled in 20 complete turns of the wheel.

(ii) The number of complete turns the wheel makes in travelling 1 km.

7. *pqrs* is a rectangular field. *A*, *B* and *C* are rectangular areas of forest inside this field. Each area of forest is completely surrounded by a 'fire-break': a grassy area, 20 m wide.

(a) Write down the missing lengths *w*, *x*, *y* and *z*.

(b) Find, in hectares, the area of:

  (i) The field *pqrs*

  (ii) The entire forest

  (iii) The grassy part

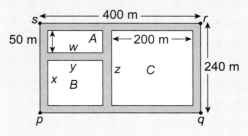

(Remember: 10,000 m² = 1 hectare.)

8. A plan for a courtyard is shown.

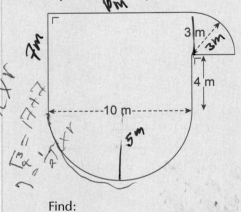

Find:

  (i) The area covered by this courtyard.

  (ii) The cost to tarmac the courtyard, if it costs €45 per m².

  (iii) The cost to build a wall around the courtyard, at a cost of €12.50 per metre.

9.

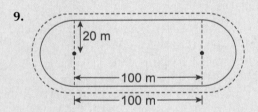

Two runners run around this track. One runs around the inside track, the other around the outer track, which is 1 m further out. How much extra track does the second runner cover in one full lap? (Take $\pi = 3.14$.)

10. A computer graphic is designed for a game as shown.

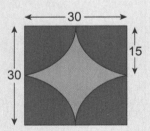

  (i) Find the area covered by this graphic (units for area are in pixels).

  (ii) Find the area covered by the blue shaded region of the graphic ($\pi = 3.14$).

  (iii) A HDTV screen has a resolution of 1,280 × 720 pixels. How many of these graphics will fit on the screen?

  (iv) What percentage, to the nearest whole number, of the screen will be red?

11. A bridge is to be rebuilt over a river. A diagram is produced for the project engineer. Each arc is a semicircle.

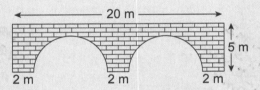

  (i) Find the width of the bridge arcs.

  (ii) It is decided to restore the side of the bridge shown to its original colour. This will cost €5 per m². Calculate the total cost.

12. A car manufacturer has a choice of two designs, A and B, for a windscreen wiper of its car. The shaded region indicates the area that is wiped by each design.

Type A

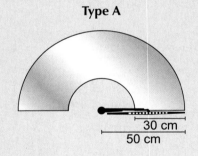

Type B

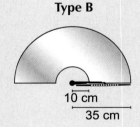

Which blade wipes the largest area of windscreen?

Show clearly how you got your answer.

AREA AND VOLUME

18.4 RECTANGULAR SOLIDS

In this section, we will deal with three-dimensional (3D) objects and their characteristics.

Volume

In everyday life, we measure many things by **volume**.
Ten litres of petrol or 500 ml of a soft drink are examples
of volume.

  **ACTIVITY 18.3**

From Activity 18.3, we can get a clear understanding of what volume is.

> **Volume (capacity)** is the amount of space an object occupies.

> When measuring volume, the units of measurement will always be units^3, for example: mm^3, cm^3, m^3, km^3, etc.

To find the volume of a rectangular solid (cuboid), we multiply out the three dimensions given.

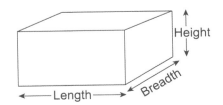

FORMULA

Volume of a cuboid = Length × breadth × height

∴ Volume = lbh

If all sides of the rectangular solid are equal,
then it can be referred to as a **cube**.

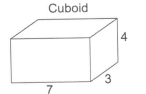
Cuboid

Cube

FORMULA

Volume of a cube = Length × length × length

∴ Volume = l^3

Surface Area and Nets

A cube or cuboid has six flat sides or faces.

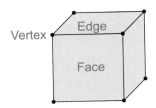
Vertex
Edge
Face

> The line where two faces meet is called an **edge**.
>
> The corner where two edges meet is called a **vertex**.

If we cut along the edges of a rectangular solid, we can create a **net** of that solid.

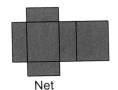
Net

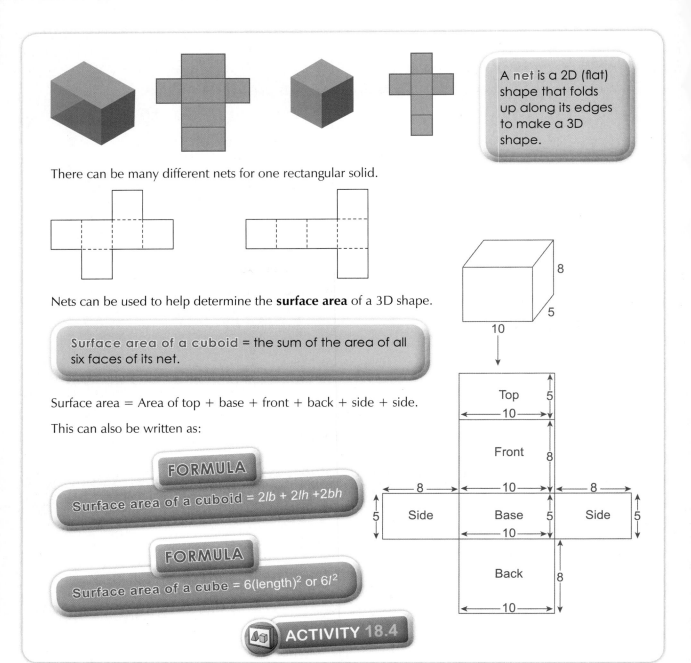

A net is a 2D (flat) shape that folds up along its edges to make a 3D shape.

There can be many different nets for one rectangular solid.

Nets can be used to help determine the **surface area** of a 3D shape.

Surface area of a cuboid = the sum of the area of all six faces of its net.

Surface area = Area of top + base + front + back + side + side.

This can also be written as:

FORMULA

Surface area of a cuboid = $2lb + 2lh + 2bh$

FORMULA

Surface area of a cube = $6(\text{length})^2$ or $6l^2$

ACTIVITY 18.4

Worked Example 18.8

Find the volume and surface area of the following cuboid.

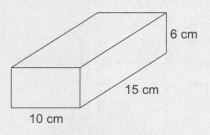

Solution

Volume = lbh = length × breadth × height

$= 10 \times 15 \times 6 = 900 \text{ cm}^3$

Surface area = $2lb + 2lh + 2bh$

$= 2(10)(15) + 2(10)(6) + 2(15)(6)$

$= 300 + 120 + 180 = 600 \text{ cm}^2$

Remember: When working out the volume or surface area, make sure that the units are all the same.

Worked Example 18.9

A sheet of metal is folded along the dotted lines into an open box as shown.

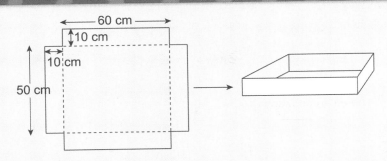

(i) Find the capacity of the box in litres.

(ii) Find the surface area of the exterior of the box.

Solution

(i) Capacity = volume = lbh
$$= 60 \times 50 \times 10$$
$$= 30{,}000 \text{ cm}^3$$

Remember that 1 litre = 1,000 ml = 1,000 cm³

$$\therefore 30{,}000 \text{ cm}^3 = \frac{30{,}000}{1{,}000} \text{ litres}$$

Capacity = 30 litres

(ii) Surface area of the exterior of the box.

Using the net of the shape:

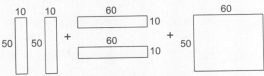

$(50 \times 10) + (50 \times 10) + (60 \times 10) + (60 \times 10) + (60 \times 50)$

$500 + 500 + 600 + 600 + 3{,}000$

$1{,}000 + 1{,}200 + 3{,}000 = 5{,}200 \text{ cm}^2$

Exercise 18.4

1. By counting the 1 cm³ blocks, find the volume and surface area of each of the following rectangular solids:

 = 1 cm³

(i)

(iv)

(ii)

(v)
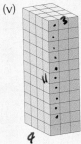

(iii)

2. Which of the following nets can be used to form cubes?

(i)
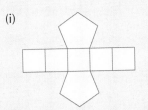

(ii)
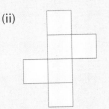

(iii)
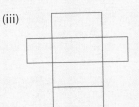

(iv)
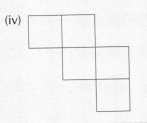

3. Use the following nets of each rectangular solid to find their volume and surface area:

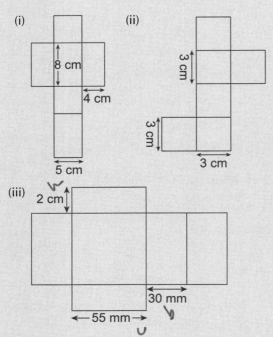

(i) 8 cm, 4 cm, 5 cm

(ii) 3 cm, 3 cm, 3 cm

(iii) 2 cm, 30 mm, 55 mm

4. Find the volume and surface area of each of the following rectangular solids:

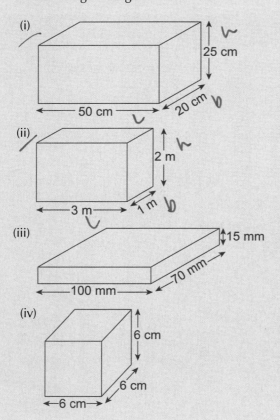

(i) 25 cm, 50 cm, 20 cm

(ii) 2 m, 3 m, 1 m

(iii) 15 mm, 70 mm, 100 mm

(iv) 6 cm, 6 cm, 6 cm

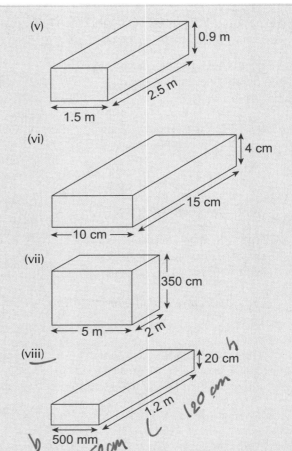

(v) 0.9 m, 2.5 m, 1.5 m

(vi) 4 cm, 15 cm, 10 cm

(vii) 350 cm, 5 m, 2 m

(viii) 20 cm, 1.2 m, 500 mm

5. A rectangular solid is 5 mm long, 3 mm wide and 10 mm high. Find:

(i) The volume in mm³

(ii) The surface area in cm²

6. A wooden box with no lid is shown. What is the area of the wood (in cm²) needed to make this box?

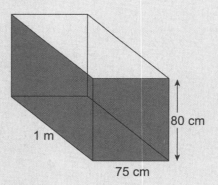

1 m, 80 cm, 75 cm

7. Rectangular boxes are to be packed inside a freight container as shown.

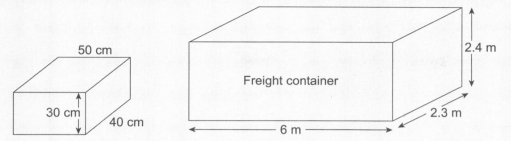

How many complete boxes can fit inside the freight container?

8. An empty rectangular water tank has length 1.5 m, width 1.4 m and height 0.9 m. A rectangular bucket has length 21 cm, width 10 cm and height 8 cm.

(a) Find (in cubic centimetres) the capacity of:

  (i) The tank

  (ii) The bucket

(b) The bucket is repeatedly filled with water and the water is then poured into the tank. How many bucketfuls does the tank hold?

18.5 VOLUME OF CYLINDERS

A cylinder is a very common 3D shape that can be used for a variety of different purposes.

From Activity 18.5, we have shown that the volume of a cylinder is:

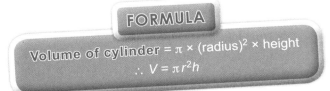

FORMULA

Volume of cylinder = π × (radius)² × height

∴ $V = \pi r^2 h$

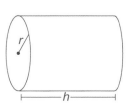

Worked Example 18.10

Find the volume of the following metal cylinder, taking $\pi = 3.14$.

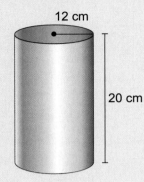

12 cm

20 cm

Solution

Volume of cylinder $= \pi r^2 h$

$= 3.14 \times (12)^2 \times 20$

$= 3.14 \times 144 \times 20$

$\therefore$ Volume $= 9{,}043.2 \text{ cm}^3$

Worked Example 18.11

Rainwater is collected from a garden and poured into a water storage cylinder.
If the radius of the cylinder is 25 cm and the height of the water in the cylinder is 77 cm, how much water has been collected? Give your answer in litres. $\left(\text{Take } \pi = \frac{22}{7}.\right)$

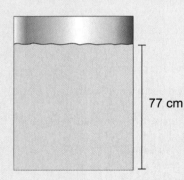

77 cm

Solution

We need to find the volume of a cylinder that is 77 cm high with a radius of 25 cm.

Volume $= \pi r^2 h = \frac{22}{7} \times (25)^2 \times 77$

$= \frac{22}{7} \times 625 \times 77$

$= 151{,}250 \text{ cm}^3$

Now convert to litres (1 litre $= 1{,}000 \text{cm}^3$):

$151{,}250 \text{ cm}^3 = \frac{151{,}250}{1{,}000} \text{ litres} = 151.25 \text{ litres}$

Exercise 18.5

1. Taking $\pi = 3.14$, find the volume of each of the following cylinders:

   (i) Radius length 6 cm, height 5 cm

   (ii) Radius length 2 m, height 12 m

   (iii) Radius length 11 mm, height 18 mm

2. Taking $\pi = \frac{22}{7}$, find the volume of each of the following cylinders (correct to two decimal places):

   (i) Radius length 3 mm, height 2 mm

   (ii) Radius length 1 m, height 30 cm

   (iii) Diameter length 30 cm, height 15 cm

3. Find the volume in cubic centimetres of each of the following cylinders, in terms of π.

(i)

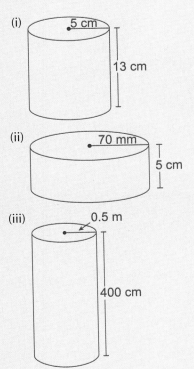

5 cm

13 cm

(ii)

70 mm

5 cm

(iii)

0.5 m

400 cm

4. A jeweller has a choice of two silver cylindrical rods to buy. Which cylinder has the most silver?

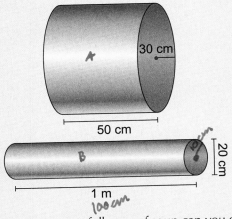

A

30 cm

50 cm

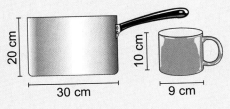

B

20 cm

1 m
100 cm

5. (i) How many full cups of soup can you get from the saucepan full of soup as shown?

20 cm

30 cm

10 cm

9 cm

(ii) On closer inspection, it is found that the level of the soup in the saucepan is only 15 cm high. How many full cups of soup can you get from the saucepan now?

6. A hollow plastic water pipe is shown. Find the volume of plastic that was used to make this pipe. $\left(\pi = \frac{22}{7}\right)$

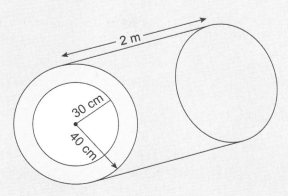

2 m

30 cm

40 cm

7. Two cylinders are to be cut out of a rectangular block as shown.

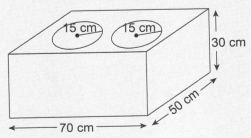

15 cm   15 cm

30 cm

50 cm

70 cm

Taking $\pi = 3.14$, find:

(i) The total volume of the two cylinders

(ii) The remaining volume of the metal block

8. A half-cylindrical trough is filled with water from a tap. $\left(\pi = \frac{22}{7}\right)$

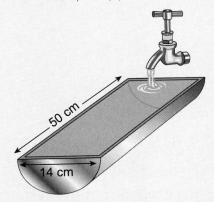

50 cm

14 cm

(i) Find the volume of water in the trough.

(ii) If water leaks from the trough at a rate of 550 ml every 15 minutes, how long will it take for the trough to empty?

18.6 SCALE DIAGRAMS

Drawing to scale can be a very useful tool in aiding our understanding of a shape or object.

In a scale of 1 : 10, every one unit on the diagram represents 10 units in real life.

ACTIVITY 18.6

Worked Example 18.12

The map shows the distance between two cities, Dublin and Cork.
The map uses a scale of 1 : 5,000,000.

(i) Using the map, find the distance between Dublin and Cork to the nearest kilometre.

(ii) If Donegal is 400 km away from Cork, how far would this be on the map?

Solution

We must first change the scale into one that is more useful to us.

1 cm : 5,000,000 cm

1 cm : 50,000 m (divide by 100 to change centimetres into metres)

1 cm : 50 km (divide by 1,000 to change metres into kilometres)

1 cm on the map represents 50 km.

(i) Using a ruler, we find that the distance between the cities on the map is 5.1 cm.

∴ Actual distance = 5.1 × 50 = 255 km

(ii) If Donegal is 400 km away from Cork, how far would this be on the map?

400 ÷ 50 = 8 cm

Dublin

5.1 cm

Cork

Exercise 18.6

1. A diagram has a scale of 1 : 200. Calculate the actual lengths of lines represented as:

    (i) 5 cm   (iii) 120 mm

    (ii) 2.5 cm   (iv) 0.09 m

2. A map has a scale of 1 : 1,000,000. Calculate the scaled lengths that need to be drawn on the map to represent:

    (i) 10 km   (iii) 24 km

    (ii) 5.5 km   (iv) 800 m

3. Draw on graph paper each of the following lines and shapes. In each case, write down the scale you used.

(i)

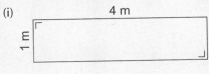

(ii)

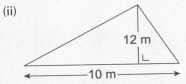

(iii)

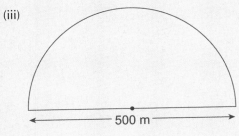

(iv)

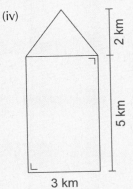

4. A map of three local towns is shown. The scale of the map is 1 : 50,000.

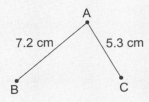

(i) Calculate the distance between Town A and Town B to the nearest kilometre.

(ii) Calculate the distance between Town A and Town C to the nearest kilometre.

(iii) If Town D is 25 km away from Town A, how far is this on the map?

5. Joan walks in a straight line for 150 m. She then turns 90° and walks another 80 m.

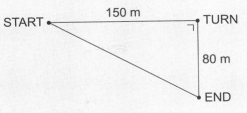

(i) Draw a scaled diagram of her journey, using a scale of 1 : 1,000.

(ii) Using this drawing, calculate the distance between her starting and end points.

6. A model car is made using a scale of 1 : 75.

(i) If the model car is 5 cm long, how long is the real car?

(ii) If the model car is 2 cm wide, how wide is the real car?

(iii) If the car is 1.5 m high, how high is the model car?

7. The following is a sketch of the ground floor of a house that has not been drawn to scale. Draw on graph paper a scaled diagram of this ground floor, using a scale of 1 : 50.

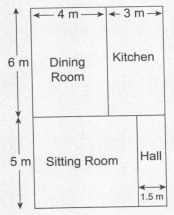

8. A diagram of a human being 1.5 m tall is shown. Find the heights of all the other objects shown. (Use a ruler to help you.)

1. (a) Find the area of each of these rectangles (all dimensions are in centimetres):

(i)
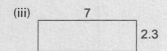
5
3

(iii)
7
2.3

(v)
$6\frac{1}{2}$
$4\frac{1}{2}$
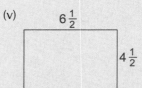

(ii)
4
3.2

(iv)
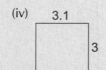
3.1
3

(b) Find the area of each of these triangles (all dimensions are in centimetres):

(i)
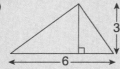
3
6

(iii)

4
4

(v)
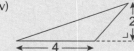
2
4

(ii)
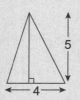
5
4

(iv)
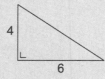
4
6

(c) Find the area of the shaded regions in square centimetres (all dimensions are in centimetres):

(i)
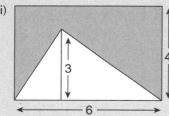
4
3
6

(iii)
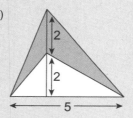
2
2
5

(v)
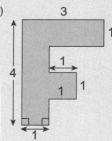
3
1
4
1
1
1
1

(ii)
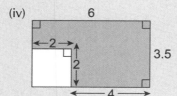
3
5

(iv)
6
2
2
3.5
4

2. (a) Find the area of the shaded regions (all dimensions are in millimetres):

(i)
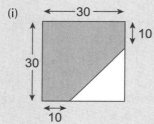
30
10
30
10

(ii)
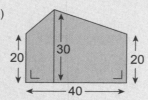
20
30
20
40

(iii)
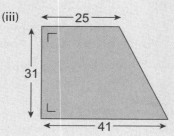
25
31
41

AREA AND VOLUME

(iv)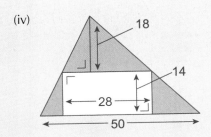

(v)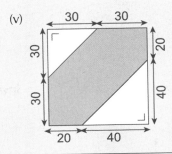

(b) A rectangular swimming pool 25 m long and 8 m wide is shown. It is surrounded by a path that is 1 m wide.

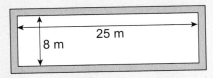

(i) Find the area of the path.

(ii) Find the cost of paving the path if paving costs €7.50 per m².

(c) Angela Reilly builds a rectangular patio, 6 m wide and 9 m long, as shown. She surrounds it with a flower bed, which is 2 m wide along the length and 3 m wide along the width. Find the area of the flower bed.

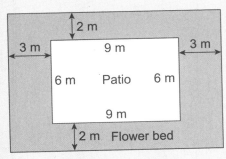

3. (a) (i) How many mm² are in 1 cm²?

(ii) How many cm² are in 1 m²?

(iii) How many mm² are in 1 m²?

(b) Find the area of these quadrilaterals:

(i)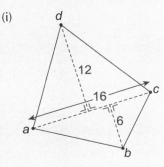

(ii)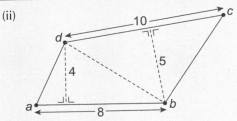

(iii)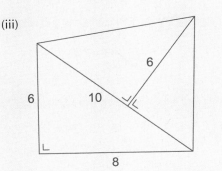

(c) Here is the plan of the floor of a room.

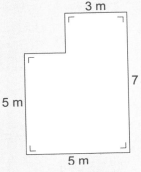

(i) Calculate the area of the floor.

(ii) Find the cost of carpeting the floor if carpet costs €14 per square metre.

(iii) Calculate the perimeter of the room.

(iv) The entire room is surrounded by a wall that is 3 m high. Find the area of the surface of this wall. (You may ignore windows and doors.)

(v) Find the cost of wallpapering this wall if wallpaper costs €1.50 per m².

Area = πr^2 circumference = $2\pi r$

18

4. (a) (i) The radius of a circle is 5 cm in length. Using $\pi = 3.14$, find the length of the circumference.

   (ii) The length of the radius of a circle is 7 cm. Find the length of the circumference, taking $\frac{22}{7}$ as an approximation for π.

   (iii) The radius of a circle is 4 cm long. Taking $\pi = 3.14$, find the length of:

      (a) The diameter

      (b) The circumference

   (iv) The diameter of a circle is 21 cm in length. Taking $\pi = \frac{22}{7}$:

      (a) Find the length of the radius.

      (b) Find the length of the circumference.

 (b) For each diagram write down:

   (i) The fraction of a full circle shown

   (ii) The length of the arc $\left(\pi = \frac{22}{7}\right)$

   (iii) The area of the shape $\left(\pi = \frac{22}{7}\right)$

   (iv) The perimeter of the shape

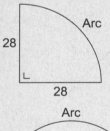

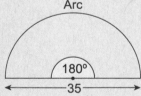

 (c) Find the length of the perimeter of these two racing tracks with semicircular ends:

   (i) $\left(\pi = \frac{22}{7}\right)$

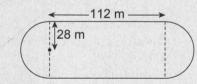

   (ii) $(\pi = 3.14)$

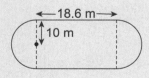

5. (a) Find the area of each of these figures. All dimensions are in centimetres.

   (i) $\left(\pi = \frac{22}{7}\right)$

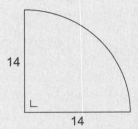

   (ii) $\left(\pi = \frac{22}{7}\right)$

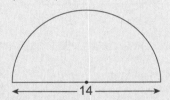

   (iii) $(\pi = 3.14)$

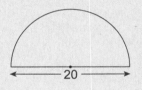

   (iv) $(\pi = 3.14)$

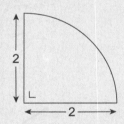

   (v) $(\pi = 3.14)$

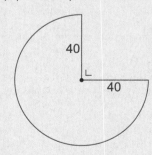

 (b) (i) Find the length of a wheel of radius 20 cm, taking $\pi = 3.14$.

   (ii) How far (in metres) will the wheel travel if it turns 1,000 times?

   (iii) How many times does the wheel turn if it travels a distance of 3,140 m?

AREA AND VOLUME

(c) The radii of two circles are 12 cm and 4 cm, respectively. Find the ratio:

  (i) Length circle 1 : Length circle 2

  (ii) Area circle 1 : Area circle 2

6. (a) Find the area of the shaded region in each diagram (take $\pi = \frac{22}{7}$):

  (i)
  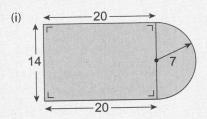

  (ii)
  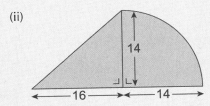

  (iii)
  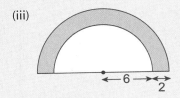

  (iv)
  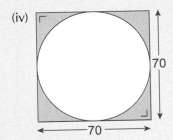

(b) The diameter of each wheel of a bicycle is 70 cm. Take $\pi = \frac{22}{7}$.

  (i) How far (in metres) will the bicycle travel if each wheel turns 150 times?

  (ii) How many times does each wheel complete a full turn if the bicycle travels a distance of 5,280 m?

(c) This is a semicircle of radius 6 cm inside a rectangle. Find:

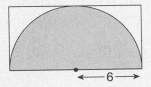

  (i) The area of the rectangle

  (ii) The ratio
  Area semi-circle: Area rectangle, taking $\pi = 3$

7. (a) A circular swimming pool has radius 10 m. It is surrounded by a path of width 1 m.

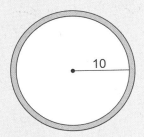

  (i) Using $\pi = \frac{22}{7}$, find the area of the path.

  (ii) Find the cost of paving the path if paving costs €5.50 per square metre.

(b) Find the area of the shaded region, using $\pi = \frac{22}{7}$ where necessary:

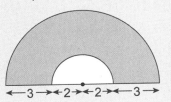

(c)
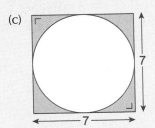

Find the area of the shaded region, using $\pi = \frac{22}{7}$.

8. (a) A rectangular room has length 6 m, width 5 m and height 2 m. Find the volume of the room.

(b) A cereal box has the following dimensions:

Length = 25 cm
Breadth = 10 cm
Height = 30 cm

Find the volume of the box.

(c) A rectangular wine box has length 10 cm, breadth 15 cm and height 20 cm.

(i) How many litres of wine does the box hold?

(ii) If the average wine glass has a capacity of 150 cm³, how many glassfuls does the box contain?

9. (a) A rectangular warehouse is 50 m long, 20 m wide and 6 m high.

(i) Find the volume of the warehouse.

(ii) Cubic boxes of side 2 m are stored in the warehouse. How many boxes will fit in the warehouse?

(b) A cubic container is made of cardboard and contains fruit juice. Each side is of length 15 cm.

(i) Find the volume of juice in litres.

(ii) Find the area of cardboard needed for the box.

(c) A square sheet of paper has sides 1 m in length. Square pieces of side 20 cm are cut from the four corners. The flaps are then folded up and an open rectangular box is formed.

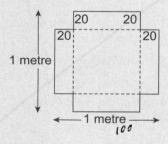

(i) Find the capacity of the box in litres.

(ii) Find the surface area of the box in cm².

10. (a) A solid cylinder has radius 10 cm and height 10 cm. Using $\pi = 3.14$, find its volume.

(b) A cylindrical tin of paint has radius 7 cm and height 20 cm. Using $\frac{22}{7}$ as an approximation for π, find the volume of paint in the tin (when full).

(c) A rectangular ingot of gold is 20 cm in length, 8 cm in breadth and 6 cm in height.

(i) Find the volume of the ingot.

(ii) Find (in kilograms) the mass of the ingot if 1 cm³ has mass 18 grams.

(iii) The gold is to be melted down and made into charm bracelets, each of which requires 25cm³ of gold. How many bracelets will be made, and what volume of gold will be left over?

11. (a) Two cylinders have height 10 cm, but their radii have length 8 cm and 4 cm, respectively.

(i) Find their volumes in terms of π.

(ii) Find the ratio of their volumes.

(b) (i) Find the volume of a cylindrical cup of radius 2 cm and height 7 cm, taking $\pi = \frac{22}{7}$.

(ii) A rectangular water tank has length 20 cm, breadth 22 cm and height 40 cm. Find its capacity in cm³.

(iii) The tank is empty. The cup is repeatedly filled with water and the water is poured into the tank. How many times must this be done before the tank is full?

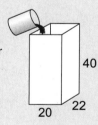

(c) (i) A metal rod is in the shape of a cylinder of radius 0.2 cm and height 4.2 cm. Find its volume, taking $\pi = \frac{22}{7}$.

(ii) Four such rods are enclosed in a rectangular packet, as in the diagram. Find the capacity of the packet.

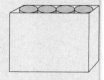

(iii) Find the difference between the capacity of the packet and the volume of the four rods.

AREA AND VOLUME

chapter 19

Algebra: Solving Simultaneous Equations

Learning Outcomes

In this chapter you will learn to:

⮑ Solve first-degree equations in two variables

19.1 SIMULTANEOUS EQUATIONS

- How to add/subtract terms
- How to multiply terms
- How to solve equations

Gottfried Leibniz (1646–1716), a German mathematician, is credited with the idea of solving simultaneous equations.

The financial world uses simultaneous equations to model the balance between the supply and demand for a product or service.

$x + y = 5$

$x + 2y = 8$

These two equations are referred to as **simultaneous equations**.

From this information, we can solve that $x = 2$ and $y = 3$:

$x + y = 5 \quad \rightarrow \quad 2 + 3 = 5$

$x + 2y = 8 \quad \rightarrow \quad 2 + 2(3) = 8$

Simultaneous equations are also used to find the intersection point of two lines:

Gottfried Leibniz

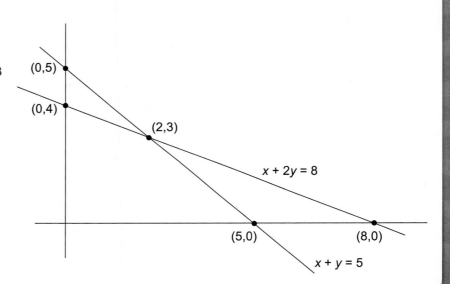

x^2 Worked Example 19.1

Is $x = 3$ and $y = 2$ the correct solution for the simultaneous equations:

$x + 6y = 15$

$3x + 4y = 10$

Solution

We let $x = 3$ and $y = 2$ for both equations.

$x + 6y = 15$

$(3) + 6(2) = 3 + 12 = 15 \qquad 15 = 15 \qquad$ Yes

$3x + 4y = 10$

$3(3) + 4(2) = 9 + 8 = 17 \qquad 17 \neq 10 \qquad$ No

$x = 3$ and $y = 2$ is not the correct solution.

(The solution must satisfy **both** equations.)

x^2 Worked Example 19.2

Is $x = -3$ and $y = 1$ the correct solution for the simultaneous equations:

$-2x + 7y = 13$

$3x + y = -8$

Solution

$-2x + 7y = 13$

$-2(-3) + 7(1) = 6 + 7 = 13$ $\qquad$ $13 = 13$ $\qquad$ Yes

$3x + y = -8$

$3(-3) + 1 = -9 + 1 = -8$ $\qquad$ $-8 = -8$ $\qquad$ Yes

$x = -3$ and $y = 1$ is correct.

 ACTIVITY 19.1

Exercise 19.1

Check if the given solution in each case is correct for the simultaneous equations:

1. $x + 6y = 38$

$x - y = 3$

Solution: $x = 8, y = 5$

2. $x + 6y = 19$

$x + 3y = 10$

Solution: $x = 7, y = 2$

3. $x + y = 8$

$4x - 3y = 11$

Solution: $x = 2, y = -1$

4. $5x + 4y = 34$

$x - 2y = 4$

Solution: $x = 4, y = 1$

5. $x - 5y = -5$

$3x - 2y = -2$

Solution: $x = 0, y = 1$

6. $-3x + 10y = 5$

$2x + 3y = -13$

Solution: $x = -5, y = -2$

7. $a + 9b = 14$

$-2a + b = 10$

Solution: $a = -4, b = 2$

8. $4p - 3p = 14$

$p - 4q = 10$

Solution: $p = 1, q = -2$

9. $-2m = 3 - n$

$1 = 4m - 3n$

Solution: $m = -5, n = -7$

19.2 SOLVING SIMULTANEOUS EQUATIONS

To solve two simultaneous equations, we must follow a certain method.

In this method, when we add or subtract the two equations, we must be left with an equation which has only one unknown.

x^2 Worked Example 19.3

Solve for x and y:

$x + y = 7$

$3x - 2y = 6$

> A **coefficient** is a number or symbol multiplied with a variable, e.g. 8 in the term 8x.

Solution

First, we make either the x or y term in each equation have the same **coefficient**.

> Often, it is easier to make the x's have the same value.

We do this by multiplying each equation:

$x + y = 7$ $(\times 3)$ $\rightarrow$ $3x + 3y = 21$

$3x - 2y = 6$ $(\times 1)$ $\rightarrow$ $\underline{3x - 2y = 6}$

> When we solve simultaneous equations, they should always be in the form shown in this example: Two variables on one side and a constant on the other side of the equal sign.

We now must decide if we will subtract or add the bottom line.

As the x's are the same sign, we will subtract. We put the bottom line in brackets with the subtract sign:

$$3x + 3y = 21$$
$$\underline{-(3x - 2y\ \ = 6)}$$

We will now subtract. This will affect the signs of all the terms on the bottom line:

$$3x + 3y = 21$$
$$\underline{-3x + 2y = -6}$$
$$5y = 15$$
$$\frac{5y}{5} = \frac{15}{5}$$
$$\therefore y = 3$$

$3x - 3x = 0$
$3y + 2y = 5y$
$21 - 6 = 15$

Now we put this value of y into **one** of the equations to find the value of x:

$$x + y = 7$$
$$x + 3 = 7$$
$$x = 7 - 3$$
$$x = 4$$

So our answer is $x = 4$, $y = 3$.

x^2 Worked Example 19.4

Solve for x and y:

$3x - 2y = 6$

$2x + 3y = 4$

Solution

We will make the y's have the same value:

$3x - 2y = 6$ $(\times 3)$ $\rightarrow$ $9x - 6y = 18$

$2x + 3y = 4$ $(\times 2)$ $\rightarrow$ $4x + 6y = 8$

As the y's are different signs, we will add:

$$9x - 6y = 18$$
$$\underline{+(4x + 6y = 8)}$$
$$13x = 26$$
$$\frac{13x}{13} = \frac{26}{13}$$
$$\therefore x = 2$$

If $x = 2$, we will now find the value of y:

$$3x - 2y = 6$$
$$3(2) - 2y = 6$$
$$6 - 2y = 6$$
$$-2y = 0$$
$$y = 0$$

So our answer is $x = 2$, $y = 0$.

ACTIVITY 19.2

x^2 Worked Example 19.5

Solve for x and y:

$3x = -2 + 5y$

$2x + y = -10$

Solution

First, change the top equation so that it is in the correct form:

$3x - 5y = -2$

$2x + y = -10$

We will make the x's have the same value:

$3x - 5y = -2$ $(\times 2)$ $\rightarrow$ $6x - 10y = -4$

$2x + y = -10$ $(\times 3)$ $\rightarrow$ $6x + 3y = -30$

The x's are the same sign, so we will subtract:

$$6x - 10y = -4 \quad \rightarrow \quad 6x - 10y = -4$$
$$-(6x + 3y = -30) \quad \rightarrow \quad \underline{-6x - 3y = +30}$$
$$-13y = 26$$
$$\frac{-13y}{-13} = \frac{26}{-13}$$
$$y = -2$$

As $y = -2$, we will now find the value of x:

$$3x - 5y = -2$$
$$3x - 5(-2) = -2$$
$$3x + 10 = -2$$
$$3x = -2 - 10$$
$$3x = -12$$
$$x = -4$$

So our answer is $x = -4$, $y = -2$.

Note: It may have been easier to eliminate y at the beginning. Check.

Exercise 19.2

Solve for x and y in each of the following questions:

1. $x + y = 5$
$x - y = 1$

2. $x + y = 14$
$x - y = 2$

3. $x + y = 15$
$x - y = 7$

4. $x + y = 21$
$x - y = 7$

5. $2x + y = 12$
$x - y = 3$

6. $3x + y = 13$
$2x - y = 7$

7. $x + 2y = 11$
$3x - 2y = 9$

8. $2x + y = 7$
$x - y = 2$

9. $5x + 2y = 16$
$2x - y = 1$

10. $2x + y = 11$
$x - 2y = 3$

11. $3x + 2y = 13$
$x - y = 1$

12. $x + 2y = 10$
$x - y = 1$

13. $x + 3y = 10$
$5x - y = 18$

14. $x + y = 3$
$6x - 5y = 7$

15. $x - y = 5$
$2x + 3y = 15$

16. $x + 3y = 4$
$2x - y = 8$

17. $3x + y = 4$
$5x - 4y = 1$

18. $2x - y = 5$
$x + 7y = 10$

19. $x + y = 9$
$6x - 5y = 10$

20. $x + y = 5$
$11x - 2y = 3$

21. $2x + 3y = 12$
$7x - 2y = 17$

22. $7x - 3y = 14$
$5x - 2y = 10$

23. $x - y = 1$
$x = 2y - 2$

24. $x - 4y = 0$
$x = y + 6$

25. $x = y + 4$
$x + 2y - 1 = 0$

26. $x - y + 3 = 0$
$2x = -y$

27. $x = y$
$3x + 5y = 32$

28. $x = -2y$
$y = x - 9$

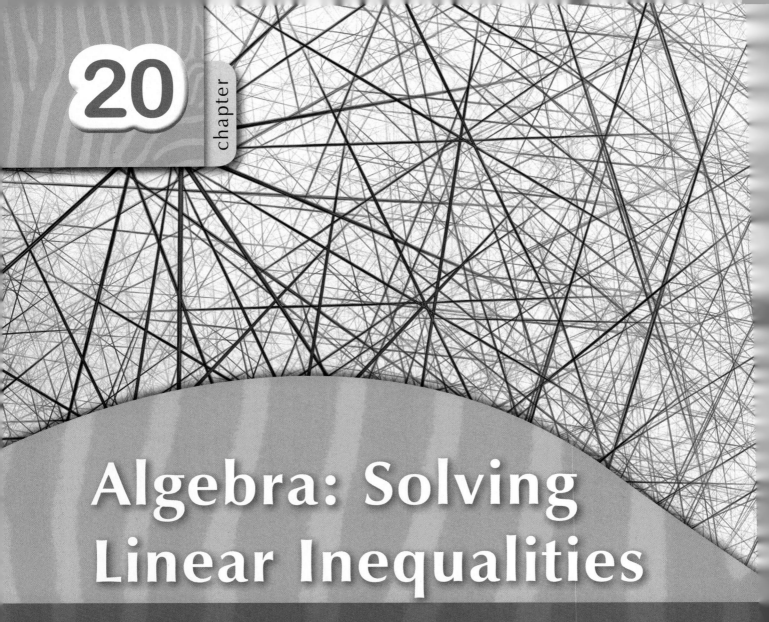

20 chapter

Algebra: Solving Linear Inequalities

Learning Outcomes

In this chapter you will learn to:

- Understand the concept of equality
- Solve linear inequalities in one variable

20.1 INEQUALITIES

When one expression is different to another, it can be referred to as an **inequality**.

In maths, one side of an equation = the other side of the equation.

In an inequality, one side of the inequality is:

- greater than,
- greater than or equal to,
- less than, or
- less than or equal to the other side.

When trying to solve an inequality, we must be able to distinguish between different inequality signs.

Inequality Signs

> Greater than	$x > 4$	The value of x is greater than 4.
≥ Greater than or equal to	$x \geq 4$	The value of x is greater than or equal to 4.
< Less than	$x < 2$	The value of x is less than 2.
≤ Less than or equal to	$x \leq 2$	The value of x is less than or equal to 2.

x^2 Worked Example 20.1

State if the following inequalities are true or false.

    (i) $5 > 3$ (ii) $10 < 5$ (iii) $-5 > -6$ (iv) $-10 < -11$

Solution

    (i) $5 > 3$ (ii) $10 < 5$ (iii) $-5 > -6$ (iv) $-10 < -11$

    True   False   True   False

ACTIVITY 20.1

Exercise 20.1

1. State whether each of the following inequalities is true or false.

    (i) $5 > 2$ (vi) $-4 < -5$

    (ii) $3 < 4$ (vii) $1 > -2$

    (iii) $1 > 6$ (viii) $-9 > -8$

    (iv) $-3 < 7$ (ix) $-2 < -3$

    (v) $-2 < 0$ (x) $-10 > -12$

2. Write the correct inequality sign between the following pairs of numbers.

    (i) 10   4   (vi) −7   −9

    (ii) 3   5   (vii) −4   0

    (iii) −2   4   (viii) −2   2

    (iv) −3 −10   (ix) −5   −4

    (v) 0   −3   (x) −20 −19

20.2 GRAPHING INEQUALITIES

When dealing with inequalities, we can be asked to show our answer (solution set) on a numberline. To do this, we must first understand the three different types of numbers we may meet when solving inequalities.

Natural Numbers – N

A **natural number** is any positive whole number greater than 0.

$N = \{1, 2, 3, 4, ...\}$

These numbers are denoted by the letter N.

> We are usually told when we are dealing with natural numbers – the question will say $x \in N$. This means that x is an element of N, i.e. from the set of natural numbers.

As natural numbers are whole numbers, in order to graph them on the numberline we use dots.

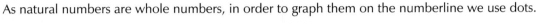

Integers – Z

An **integer** is any whole number.

$Z = \{ ..., -3, -2, -1, 0, 1, 2, 3, ...\}$

These numbers are denoted by the letter Z.   > This is written as $x \in Z$.

As integers are also whole numbers, in order to graph them on the numberline we use dots.

Real Numbers – R

Real numbers are all the numbers on the numberline. They can be positive, negative or neutral (zero) whole numbers, decimals or fractions. They also include irrational numbers, e.g. $\sqrt{2}$.

These numbers are denoted by the letter R.   > This is written as $x \in R$.

As real numbers can be any number, in order to show them on the numberline we use a solid line.

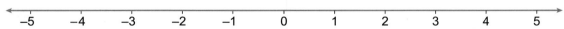

x^2 Worked Example 20.2

Draw separate numberlines to show the following inequalities:

    (i) $x > 3, x \in N$ (ii) $x \leqslant 2, x \in N$

Solution

    (i) $x > 3, x \in N$

        As $x \in N$, we use dots on the numberline.

$x > 3$ means that x represents all the natural numbers that are greater than 3.

The next natural number greater than 3 is 4. We continue the dots and then draw an arrow to the right to show that the inequality continues in this direction.

> The dots/line go in the direction the inequality sign is pointing.
> Think of > as pointing to the right and < as pointing to the left.

(ii) $x \leqslant 2, x \in N$ means that x represents all the natural numbers that are less than or equal to 2.

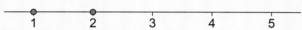

The first natural number less than or equal to 2 is 2 itself. We draw a dot on 2 and then on 1. As the smallest natural number is 1, there are no further values. Therefore, we don't put an arrow on the number line.

---

x^2 Worked Example 20.3

Draw a numberline to show the following inequality:

$x < 1, x \in Z$

Solution

$x < 1, x \in Z$ means that x represents all the integers that are less than 1.

As integers include 0 and negative whole numbers, we draw an arrow to show that the inequality continues.

---

x^2 Worked Example 20.4

Draw separate numberlines to show the following inequalities:

   (i) $x < 4, x \in R$ (ii) $x \geqslant 1, x \in R$

Solution

   (i) $x < 4, x \in R$ means that x represents **all** numbers less than 4.

   As 4 is not included but $3.\dot{9}$ could be, we use an **empty circle** to show this on the numberline.

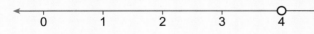

   (ii) $x \geqslant 1, x \in R$ means that x represents **all** numbers greater than or equal to 1.

   To show that 1 is included, we use a **full circle** to show this on the numberline.

> We only use empty-circle and full-circle symbols when graphing real-number inequalities ($X \in R$). We use dots (full circles) when graphing elements of N and Z.

ACTIVITY 20.2

Exercise 20.2

1. Write down the first three values of the following inequalities:

   (i) $x > 4, x \in N$ (v) $x < -5, x \in Z$

   (ii) $x \leqslant 12, x \in N$ (vi) $x > 0, x \in Z$

   (iii) $x \geqslant -1, x \in Z$ (vii) $x < 3, x \in N$

   (iv) $x < 2, x \in Z$ (viii) $x \geqslant 1, x \in N$

2. Draw separate numberlines to show the following inequalities ($x \in N$):

   (i) $x > 1$ (iv) $x < 4$ (vii) $x \geqslant 2$

   (ii) $x > 5$ (v) $x < 2$ (viii) $x \leqslant 1$

   (iii) $x \geqslant 10$ (vi) $x \geqslant 5$

3. Draw separate numberlines to show the following inequalities ($x \in Z$):

   (i) $x > 0$ (v) $x < 7$

   (ii) $x < -3$ (vi) $x \geqslant -6$

   (iii) $x \leqslant 3$ (vii) $x \leqslant 6$

   (iv) $x > -1$ (viii) $x \geqslant 0$

4. Draw separate numberlines to show the following inequalities ($x \in R$):

   (i) $x > 3$ (iv) $x \leqslant -3$ (vii) $x \leqslant 0$

   (ii) $x \geqslant -5$ (v) $x < 8$ (viii) $x \geqslant 4$

   (iii) $x < 2$ (vi) $x > -1$

5. Draw separate numberlines to show the following inequalities:

   (i) $x \leqslant 3, x \in N$ (iii) $x \geqslant -1, x \in R$ (v) $x < 5, x \in R$

   (ii) $x \geqslant -5, x \in Z$ (iv) $x < -4, x \in Z$ (vi) $x < 2, x \in N$

20.3 SOLVING INEQUALITIES

Solving an inequality is very similar to solving an equation.

$2x - 8 > -4$

$\quad 2x > -4 + 8$

$\quad 2x > 4$

$\quad \dfrac{2x}{2} > \dfrac{4}{2}$

$\quad x > 2$

When solving an inequality, we usually end up with a range of values for the unknown. This range or set of values is called the **solution set**.

In this case, $x > 2$ is the solution set.

x^2  ## Worked Example 20.5

Solve the following inequality and show the solution on a numberline.

$2x - 1 < 9, x \in N$

Solution

$2x - 1 < 9$

We treat the $<$ like an equal sign and solve:

$2x - 1 + 1 < 9 + 1$

$\quad 2x < 10$

$\quad \dfrac{2x}{2} < \dfrac{10}{2}$

$\quad x < 5, x \in N$

We then draw this set on a numberline. Remember that $x \in N$.

```
 ———•————•————•————•————————————
    1    2    3    4    5    6
```

Occasionally, we may also be asked to list the elements of the set or all the possible values of the set.

In this case, $x < 5, x \in N$. So the answer is all the natural numbers less than 5, i.e. {1, 2, 3, 4}.

x^2 Worked Example 20.6

Solve $3x - 4 > 5$, $x \in R$ and show the solution on a numberline:

Solution

$3x - 4 > 5$

$\quad 3x > 5 + 4$

$\quad 3x > 9$

$\quad\quad x > 3$, $x \in R$

As we are dealing with real numbers, we draw an empty circle at 3 and shade to the right.

x^2 Worked Example 20.7

Solve the following inequality and show the solution on a numberline:

$6(x + 3) \leqslant 5(x + 3)$, $x \in R$

Solution

$6(x + 3) \leqslant 5(x + 3)$

$6x + 18 \leqslant 5x + 15$

$6x - 5x \leqslant 15 - 18$

$\quad\quad x \leqslant -3$, $x \in R$

As we are dealing with real numbers, we draw a full circle at -3.

An Important Case

On our course we are not required to solve $-x$'s. When solving an inequality, however, we may end up faced with $-x$'s.

Consider the inequality $-3x > 9$.

To correct this, we **flip** the sign of the inequality.

If $-3x > 9$, then $3x < -9$.

> When we multiply or divide both sides of an inequality by a negative number, we flip or reverse the inequality sign.
> E.g. $5 > 4$ but $-5 \ngtr -4$, whereas $-5 < -4$.

ACTIVITY 20.3

Exercise 20.3

Solve each of the following inequalities and show the solution on a numberline.

1. $2x > 6$, $x \in N$
2. $x + 3 > 4$, $x \in N$
3. $3x - 9 \leqslant 12$, $x \in N$
4. $4x + 3 > -9$, $x \in Z$

5. $5x + 5 \leqslant 5$, $x \in Z$
6. $5x > 2x + 18$, $x \in N$
7. $2x + 11 > 9$, $x \in R$
8. $3x + 3 < -3$, $x \in R$

9. $4x - 5 \geqslant 23$, $x \in R$
10. $6x + 10 \leqslant -2$, $x \in R$
11. $7x - 5 > 23$, $x \in R$
12. $4x \leqslant 3x - 10$, $x \in R$

13. $3x + 6 > 2x - 5, x \in Z$

14. $9x + 4 \leqslant 5x + 12, x \in N$

15. $7x - 3 \geqslant 6x + 4, x \in R$

16. $18 + 8x < 12 + 5x, x \in R$

17. $5x - 3 \leqslant 2x + 3, x \in R$

18. $4(x - 2) \geqslant 5(x - 1), x \in Z$

19. $6(x - 1) \leqslant 3(2 + x), x \in N$

20. $3x + 5(2x - 4) \geqslant 2(x + 3) + 7, x \in N$

21. $4(x + 3) < 2(x + 4), x \in Z$

22. $5(x - 1) - 2(x - 3) \leqslant 4, x \in R$

23. $2(x + 1) - 4(x - 4) > 5 - (4x - 3), x \in R$

24. $3(x - 5) + 5x > 6(x - 3) + 1, x \in R$

Revision Exercises

1. (a) Solve each of the following inequalities and show the solution on a numberline.

   (i) $x + 1 \leqslant 5, x \in N$ (iii) $3x + 1 < 10, x \in N$ (v) $2x + 3 < 11, x \in R$

   (ii) $x - 1 < 6, x \in N$ (iv) $2x - 1 \geqslant 7, x \in N$

   (b) Write down the inequality shown in each of the following diagrams.

   (i) $x \in N$

   (ii) $x \in Z$

   (iii) $x \in R$

   (iv) $x \in R$

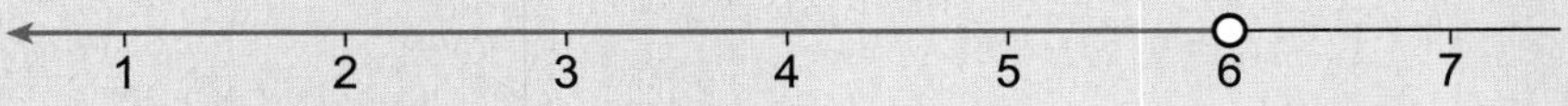

   (v) $x \in N$

2. (a) Solve each of the following inequalities and show the solution on a numberline.

   (i) $2x + 1 \leqslant 7, x \in Z$ (iii) $5x + 2 < 32, x \in Z$ (v) $2x - 5 > 1, x \in R$

   (ii) $4x + 3 \geqslant 31, x \in R$ (iv) $x - 5 \leqslant 3, x \in N$

   (b) Solve each of the following inequalities and show the solution on a numberline.

   (i) $3x + 5 > 8, x \in N$ (iv) $11(x - 2) - 4 > 2(x - 4), x \in R$

   (ii) $-2(x - 3) + 5(x - 3) \leqslant 3, x \in R$ (v) $5(2x - 3) - (4 - x) - 3(x + 3) - 4 \geqslant 0, x \in R$

   (iii) $2(x - 5) + 3(x - 3) > 4(x - 4), x \in Z$

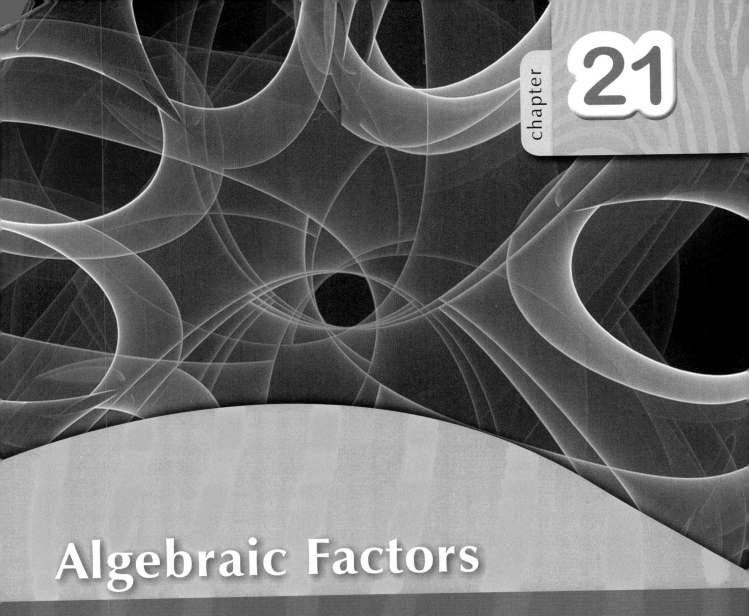

chapter 21

Algebraic Factors

Learning Outcomes

In this chapter you will learn to:

- Understand the concept of factors in algebra
- Factorise an expression by:
    - Taking out the highest common factor
    - Grouping
- Factorise quadratic trinomials where the coefficient of x^2 is 1
- Factorise using the difference of two squares

21.1 ALGEBRAIC FACTORS

4 is a factor of 20.

$\frac{20}{4} = 5$ with no remainder.

So a factor is a number that divides evenly into another number.

In algebra, we need to be able to find the factors of terms and expressions.

This process is called **factorising**.

$x(x + 5) = x^2 + 5x \rightarrow$ Expanding

$x^2 + 5x = x(x + 5) \rightarrow$ Factorising

Factorising is the reverse of expanding. We turn the given expression into a **product**.

YOU SHOULD REMEMBER...

- What factors are
- How to simplify algebraic expressions
- How to work with indices

KEY WORDS

- **Factor pair**
- **Factors**
- **Highest common factor**
- **Grouping**
- **Quadratic trinomials**
- **Difference of two squares**

Worked Example 21.1

If 5 is a factor of the terms below, find the other factor in the pair.

(i) 10

(ii) $15x$

(iii) $20x^2$

Solution

(i) $\frac{10}{5} = 2$

(ii) $\frac{15x}{5} = 3x$

(iii) $\frac{20x^2}{5} = 4x^2$

Worked Example 21.2

If $4x$ is a factor of these terms, find the other factor in the pair.

(i) $8x$ (ii) $12x^2$ (iii) $16x^3$

Solution

(i) $8x$

$4x \times \textcircled{2}$

We can check to see if we have the correct answer: $4x \times 2 = 8x$

(ii) $12x^2$

$4x \times \textcircled{3x} = 12x^2$

(iii) $16x^3$

$4x \times \textcircled{4x^2} = 16x^3$

Exercise 21.1

1. If 2 is a factor of these terms, write down the other factor in the factor pair.

   (i) 8   (iv) $2x^2$

   (ii) 2   (v) $20x^2$

   (iii) 2x   (vi) $8x^3$

2. If 3 is a factor of these terms, write down the other factor in the factor pair.

   (i) 9   (iv) $9x^2$

   (ii) 27   (v) $18x^3$

   (iii) 81x   (vi) $6y^2$

3. If 5 is a factor of these terms, write down the other factor in the factor pair.

   (i) 5   (iv) 50xy

   (ii) 200   (v) $30x^3$

   (iii) 20x   (vi) $25y^2$

4. If x is a factor of these terms, write down the other factor in the factor pair.

   (i) 5x   (iv) −2xy

   (ii) x^2 (v) $-2x^3$

   (iii) x   (vi) $6x^2y$

5. If a is a factor of these terms, write down the other factor in the factor pair.

   (i) 3a   (iv) $-2ba^2$

   (ii) $6a^2$ (v) $-8a^3$

   (iii) 10a   (vi) $12ab^2$

6. If x^2 is a factor of these terms, write down the other factor in the factor pair.

   (i) $4x^2$ (iv) x^4

   (ii) $36x^2y^2$ (v) $3x^3$

   (iii) $-x^2$ (vi) $4x^3y^2$

7. If −4x is a factor of these terms, write down the other factor in the factor pair.

   (i) −8x   (iv) −4xy

   (ii) $16x^2$ (v) $-20x^4$

   (iii) 4x   (vi) $-16x^2y^2$

8. If $2y^2$ is a factor of these terms, write down the other factor in the factor pair.

   (i) $2y^2$ (iv) $-2x^2y^3$

   (ii) $8y^2$ (v) $8y^6$

   (iii) $4xy^2$ (vi) $8x^2y^3$

21.2 HIGHEST COMMON FACTOR

We have already seen that factorising is the reverse of expanding.

    $4x(x + 3) = 4x^2 + 12x$ → Expanding

When we factorise, we are given the expanded answer and have to work backwards.

We have to pick the term that will go on the outside of the bracket. We always pick the **highest common factor** (HCF) of the two terms.

    $4x^2 = 4(x)(x)$

    $12x = 4(3)(x)$

So the highest common factor is $4(x) = 4x$.

We can then work out what goes inside the brackets. These are the remaining factors.

    $4x(x) + 4x(3)$

Working in reverse:

    $4x(x + 3)$

It is advisable always to check your answer by multiplying it back out.

x^2 **Worked Example 21.3**

Factorise fully the following:

    (i) $2x + 6$ (ii) $3x^2 - 15x$ (iii) $18y + 6y^2$ (iv) $y^2 - 3y^3$

Solution

    (i) $2x + 6$

        $2x = 2(x)$

        $6 = 2(3)$

        The highest common factor of $2x$ and 6 is 2.

        $\therefore 2x + 6 = 2(x) + 2(3)$

                   $= 2(x + 3)$

> We can always check our answer by multiplying it back out:
>
> $2(x + 3) = 2x + 6$

    (ii) $3x^2 - 15x$

        $3x^2 = 3(x)(x)$

        $15x = 3(5)(x)$

        So $3x$ is the outside term of our bracket.

        $\therefore 3x^2 - 15x = 3x(x) - 3x(5)$

                       $= 3x(x - 5)$

    (iii) $18y + 6y^2$

        The highest common factor of 18 and 6 is 6.

        The highest common factor of y and y^2 is y.

        So $6y$ is the outside term of our bracket.

        $\therefore 18y + 6y^2 = 6y(3 + y)$

    (iv) $y^2 - 3y^3 = 1y^2 - 3y^3$

        The highest common factor of 1 and 3 is 1.

        The highest common factor of y^2 and y^3 is y^2.

        So y^2 is the outside term of our bracket.

        $\therefore y^2 - 3y^3 = y^2(1 - 3y)$

> It is important to put 1 as the first term inside the bracket.

 **ACTIVITY 21.1**

📖 **Exercise 21.2**

Factorise fully the following:

  1. $6x + 10y = 2(\quad)$ **11.** $6x + 9y$ **21.** $6p^2 - 12pq$

  2. $9a + 6b = 3(\quad)$ **12.** $4a + 10b$ **22.** $22x^2 - 33xy$

  3. $25a + 35b = 5(\quad)$ **13.** $14p + 21q$ **23.** $24xy - 16xz$

  4. $21p + 28q = 7(\quad)$ **14.** $15a + 25b$ **24.** $35b^2 - 25ab$

  5. $12x - 15y = 3(\quad)$ **15.** $12k - 15m$ **25.** $a^2 - a$

  6. $40m + 60n = 20(\quad)$ **16.** $22c - 33d$ **26.** $25ab - 75ac$

  7. $2x + xy = x(\quad)$ **17.** $15x^2 - 25x$ **27.** $xy - xz$

  8. $a^2 + ab = a(\quad)$ **18.** $4x - 6$ **28.** $2x^2 - 6x$

  9. $12p^2 - 3p = 3p(\quad)$ **19.** $14y - 7$ **29.** $6p - 9pq$

 10. $9ab - 15ac = 3a(\quad)$ **20.** $5d - 35e$ **30.** $x^3 - x^2$

31. $6x^2 + 8xy$

32. $16xy - 24y^2$

33. $40a^2 - 5a$

34. $18t + 27t^2$

35. $75xy + 100xy^2$

36. $44a^2 - 66a$

37. $24x - 28y + 44z$

38. $35a - 45b - 15c$

39. $12a^3b + 15ab^2$

40. $16a^2x^2 - 24ax^3 - 32a^3x$

41. $x^4 - x^3$

42. $2x^2 - x^3$

21.3 GROUPING FACTORS I

If we are asked to multiply or expand two expressions, we follow the usual rules.

$(2a + b)(x + 3y) = 2a(x + 3y) + b(x + 3y)$

$\qquad\qquad\qquad = 2ax + 6ay + bx + 3by$

When we wish to factorise an expression that has four terms, we:

(1) Remove the common factor from two pairs of terms.

(2) Remove the common factor from the new expression.

x^2 Worked Example 21.4

Factorise:

(i) $ax + ay + bx + by$

(ii) $3ap - 6bp + 6aq - 12bq$

Solution

(i) $ax + ay + bx + by$

$\quad = a(x + y) + b(x + y)$ **Step 1**

$\quad = (x + y)(a + b)$ **Step 2**

(ii) $3ap - 6bp + 6aq - 12bq$

$\quad = 3p(a - 2b) + 6q(a - 2b)$ **Step 1**

$\quad = (a - 2b)(3p + 6q)$ **Step 2**

 ACTIVITY 21.2

Exercise 21.3

Factorise the following:

1. $px + py + qx + qy$

2. $ma + mb + na + nb$

3. $3a + 3b + ka + kb$

4. $wx + wy + 5x + 5y$

5. $ac + 3c + ab + 3b$

6. $px + py + 6x + 6y$

7. $ax + ay + 7x + 7y$

8. $ac + bc + 3a + 3b$

9. $ak + bk + 4a + 4b$

10. $x + xy + 5 + 5y$

11. $px - py + qx - qy$

12. $ab - ax + by - xy$

13. $mr - ms + nr - ns$

14. $ax - 2ay + bx - 2by$

15. $2ac - 2ad + bc - bd$

16. $6xy - 3ay + 10bx - 5ab$

17. $15ax - 6bx + 5ay - 2by$

18. $6mx - 3my + 2nx - ny$

19. $pq - 3py + 2qx - 6xy$

20. $50bx - 10xy + 30ab - 6ay$

21. $a^2 + 3a + ab + 3b$

22. $x^2 - wx + 9x - 9w$

23. $5 + 5b + a + ab$

24. $xy - y + 8x - 8$

25. $2x - 3xy + 2ax - 3ay$

26. $10a - 8b + 5a^2 - 4ab$

27. $20p^2 - 16pq + 15p - 12q$

28. $9x^2 - 6xy + 21xz - 14yz$

29. $7a - 21b + a^2 - 3ab$

30. $x^2 - x + 4kx - 4k$

21.4 GROUPING FACTORS II

When dealing with grouping, we may encounter examples that have a negative common factor or that need to be rearranged in order to factorise them.

Worked Example 21.5

Factorise $2ax - 2bx - ay + by$.

Solution

$2ax - 2bx - ay + by$

| We must be careful with the signs. |

$= 2x(a - b) - y(a - b)$

$= (a - b)(2x - y)$

| Remember that $-y(a - b) = -ay + by$. A negative multiplied by a negative is a positive. |

Worked Example 21.6

Factorise $15as - 2bt - 3at + 10bs$.

Solution

Method 1

$15as - 2bt - 3at + 10bs$

$= 15as + 10bs - 3at - 2bt$ (rearranging)

$= 5s(3a + 2b) - t(3a + 2b)$

$= (3a + 2b)(5s - t)$

Method 2

$15as - 2bt - 3at + 10bs$

$= 15as - 3at + 10bs - 2bt$ (rearranging)

$= 3a(5s - t) + 2b(5s - t)$

$= (5s - t)(3a + 2b)$

Exercise 21.4

Copy these and fill in the brackets, but watch the signs carefully!

1. $-5a + 10b = -5(\quad)$

2. $-6x - 8y = -2(\quad)$

3. $-15t + 21s = -3(\quad)$

4. $-24a - 28b = -4(\quad)$

5. $-2x - x^2 = -x(\quad)$

6. $-6x + 14z = -2(\quad)$

7. $-2x + 3y = -1(\quad)$

8. $-15p + 9r - 12s = -3(\quad)$

9. $-xy - xz = -x(\quad)$

10. $-x^2 + x = -x(\quad)$

Factorise fully:

11. $ax - ay - cx + cy$

12. $3x + 3y - ax - ay$

13. $7x - 7y - kx + ky$

14. $ak + at - 5k - 5t$

15. $x^2 - 4x - ax + 4a$

16. $pq + ps - 9q - 9s$

17. $ab - ac - b^2 - bc$

18. $ak - bk + at - bt$

19. $3ax - 6ay - x^2 + 2xy$

20. $15xy - 20y^2 - 9x + 12y$

Rearrange these and then factorise:

21. $ak + bt + at + bk$

22. $2ac + bd + 2ad + bc$

23. $3ax - by + 3bx - ay$

24. $5ac - 2b - 10a + bc$

25. $10ac + b - 5bc - 2a$

26. $ab + 3 + 3a + b$

27. $15ac + 2bd + 10bc + 3ad$

28. $3xy - 7 - x + 21y$

29. $35ab + 6 - 21b - 10a$

30. $22wx + yz - 2wy - 11xz$

Factorise this collection of expressions:

31. $10ax - 2ay - 5bx + by$

32. $ab + mn + bm + an$

33. $ab - b - a + 1$

34. $7x^2 + xy - 7x - y$

35. $a^2 - 3ab + 7(a - 3b)$

36. $y^2(a + 6) - 2(a + 6)$

37. $t(x - 5) - x + 5$

38. $k(a + b) + a + b$

39. $c - a + p(a - c)$

40. $(a - b) - k(b - a)$

21.5 QUADRATIC TRINOMIALS I

When we multiply or expand the two expressions $(x + 5)(x + 2)$, we end up with a special type of expression.

$$(x + 5)(x + 2) = x(x + 2) + 5(x + 2)$$
$$= x^2 + 2x + 5x + 10$$
$$= x^2 + 7x + 10$$

This expression is called a **quadratic trinomial**.

When asked to factorise this quadratic trinomial, we need to notice that:

A quadratic trinomial in x has an x^2 term, an x term and a constant.

$$5 \times 2 = 10$$

This is the constant, i.e. the number by itself.

5 and 2 are factors of 10.

$5 + 2 = 7$. This is the number in front of the x term.

So if we are asked to factorise $x^2 + 7x + 10$, we know we are looking for the factors of 10 (the factors of the constant) that add up to 7 (the coefficient of x).

x^2 Worked Example 21.7

Factorise $x^2 + 8x + 15$.

Solution

We are looking for the factors of 15 that add up to 8.

The factors of 15 are:

$$1 \times 15$$
$$3 \times 5$$
$$1 + 15 = 16$$
$$\mathbf{3 + 5 = 8} \checkmark$$

So our factors are $(x + 3)(x + 5)$.

We must always check our answer:

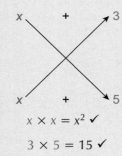

$$x \times x = x^2 \checkmark$$
$$3 \times 5 = 15 \checkmark$$

We now use the arrows:

$$x \times 5 = 5x$$
$$x \times 3 = \underline{3x +}$$
$$8x \checkmark$$

So $(x + 3)(x + 5)$ is correct.

> $(x + 3)(x + 5)$ could also be written as $(x + 5)(x + 3)$ (multiplication is commutative).

x^2 Worked Example 21.8

Factorise $x^2 + 10x + 24$.

Solution

We are looking for the factors of 24 that add up to 10.

The factors of 24 are:

$$1 \times 24$$
$$2 \times 12$$
$$3 \times 8$$
$$4 \times 6$$
$$1 + 24 = 25$$
$$2 + 12 = 14$$
$$3 + 8 = 11$$
$$\mathbf{4 + 6 = 10} \checkmark$$

So the factors are $(x + 4)(x + 6)$:

Now we check our answer:

$$x \times x = x^2 \checkmark$$
$$6 \times 4 = 24 \checkmark$$

We now use the arrows:

$$x \times 4 = 4x$$
$$x \times 6 = 6x +$$
$$\underline{}$$
$$10x \checkmark$$

So $(x + 4)(x + 6)$ is correct.

 ACTIVITY 21.3

Exercise 21.5

Factorise the following:

1. $x^2 + 3x + 2$

2. $x^2 + 4x + 4$

3. $x^2 + 7x + 10$

4. $x^2 + 6x + 5$

5. $x^2 + 7x + 12$

6. $x^2 + 5x + 4$

7. $x^2 + 12x + 11$

8. $x^2 + 2x + 1$

9. $x^2 + 16x + 15$

10. $a^2 + 6a + 8$

11. $x^2 + 12x + 20$

12. $x^2 + 9x + 14$

13. $x^2 + 9x + 20$

14. $x^2 + 11x + 10$

15. $x^2 + 8x + 16$

16. $x^2 + 6x + 9$

17. $p^2 + 8p + 7$

18. $x^2 + 9x + 18$

19. $x^2 + 11x + 18$

20. $x^2 + 10x + 25$

21. $x^2 + 12x + 27$

22. $x^2 + 11x + 28$

23. $x^2 + 13x + 36$

24. $x^2 + 14x + 33$

25. $x^2 + 8x + 12$

26. $x^2 + 11x + 30$

27. $x^2 + 13x + 30$

28. $x^2 + 17x + 30$

29. $x^2 + 31x + 30$

30. $x^2 + 12x + 36$

31. $x^2 + 13x + 42$

32. $x^2 + 14x + 49$

33. $x^2 + 12x + 32$

34. $x^2 + 11x + 24$

35. $x^2 + 13x + 40$

36. $x^2 + 18x + 81$

37. $x^2 + 29x + 100$

38. $x^2 + 14x + 48$

39. $x^2 + 27x + 50$

40. $x^2 + 20x + 51$

21.6 QUADRATIC TRINOMIALS II

Quadratic trinomials can also have one or two negative factors. We must be very careful when dealing with these types of expressions.

x^2 Worked Example 21.9

Factorise $x^2 - 6x + 8$.

Solution

We are looking for the factors of $+8$ that add to give us -6.

The only way two factors of a positive number would give a negative number when added together is if both factors are negative.

Negative × negative = positive.

The factors of 8 (both factors being negative) are:

$$-1 \times -8$$
$$-2 \times -4$$
$$(-1) + (-8) = -9$$
$$\mathbf{(-2) + (-4) = -6} \checkmark$$

So the factors are $(x - 2)(x - 4)$.

Now we check our answer:

$$x \times x = x^2 \checkmark$$
$$-2 \times -4 = +8 \checkmark$$

We now use the arrows:

$$x \times -4 = -4x$$
$$x \times -2 = \underline{-2x +}$$
$$-6x \checkmark$$

So $(x - 2)(x - 4)$ is correct.

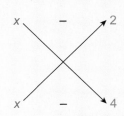

x^2 Worked Example 21.10

Factorise $y^2 + 3y - 18$.

Solution

We are looking for the factors of -18 that add to give us $+3$.

Negative × positive = negative.

3×-6

-3×6

$3 + (-6) = -3$

$\mathbf{-3 + 6 = +3}$ ✓

So the factors are $(y - 3)(y + 6)$.

Now we check our answer:

$y \times y = y^2$ ✓

$-3 \times +6 = -18$ ✓

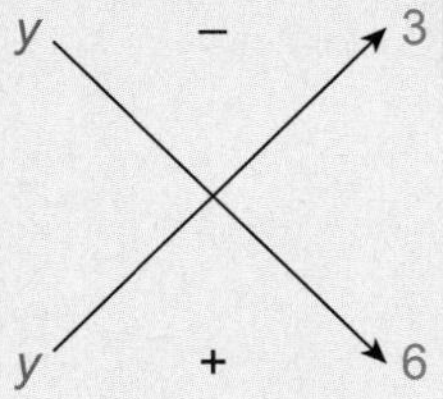

We now use the arrows:

$y \times +6 = +6y$

$y \times -3 = \underline{-3y +}$

$+3y$ ✓

So $(y - 3)(y + 6)$ is correct.

If the constant is positive, then the factors are either both positive or both negative.

If the constant is negative, then one factor is positive and the other is negative.

Exercise 21.6

Factorise the following:

1. $x^2 - 3x + 2$

2. $x^2 - 5x + 6$

3. $x^2 - 4x + 3$

4. $x^2 - 7x + 10$

5. $x^2 - 8x + 12$

6. $x^2 - 9x + 20$

7. $x^2 - 15x + 26$

8. $x^2 - 10x + 21$

9. $x^2 - 8x + 15$

10. $x^2 - 5x + 4$

11. $x^2 - 2x - 8$

12. $x^2 - 8x - 20$

13. $x^2 - 5x - 24$

14. $x^2 - 2x - 15$

15. $x^2 - 14x - 15$

16. $x^2 - 2x - 3$

17. $x^2 + 2x - 15$

18. $x^2 - x - 12$

19. $x^2 + x - 6$

20. $x^2 - x - 6$

21. $x^2 + 2x - 3$

22. $x^2 + 6x - 7$

23. $x^2 + 3x - 10$

24. $x^2 + 6x - 16$

25. $x^2 + 4x - 32$

26. $x^2 + 5x - 14$

27. $x^2 - 11x + 30$

28. $x^2 + 11x + 30$

29. $x^2 - 4x - 5$

30. $x^2 - x - 30$

31. $x^2 + 9x - 22$

32. $x^2 - 4x + 4$

33. $x^2 - 6x + 9$

34. $x^2 + 5x - 24$

35. $x^2 - x - 90$

36. $x^2 + 2x - 63$

37. $x^2 - 15x + 56$

38. $x^2 + x - 42$

39. $x^2 + 3x - 70$

40. $x^2 - 10x + 24$

21.7 THE DIFFERENCE OF TWO SQUARES

Another type of quadratic equation that we may come across occurs when we multiply two expressions that differ only by their sign.

$$(x - 5)(x + 5)$$

$$= x(x + 5) - 5(x + 5)$$

$$= x^2 + 5x - 5x - 25$$

$$= x^2 - 25$$

$$= x^2 - 5^2$$

Which is the difference of two square terms.

Working backwards, we can factorise:

$$x^2 - 25$$

First we write each term as a square:

$$(x)^2 - (5)^2$$

We know that the the two terms of the expression differ only by their sign.

$$(x - 5)(x + 5) \text{ or } (x + 5)(x - 5)$$

This factorising method is called **the difference of two squares**.

There must always be a minus sign between the two terms in order to use this method.

x^2 Worked Example 21.11

Factorise the following:

(i) $y^2 - 81$

(ii) $x^2 - 225$

Solution

(i) $y^2 - 81$

$(y)^2 - (9)^2$ (writing as two square terms)

$(y - 9)(y + 9)$

The difference of two squares will always have a minus sign in one bracket and a plus sign in the other bracket.

(ii) $x^2 - 225$

$(x)^2 - (15)^2$

$(x - 15)(x + 15)$

 ACTIVITY 21.4

Exercise 21.7

Factorise the following:

1. $x^2 - 9$

2. $x^2 - 4$

3. $y^2 - 36$

4. $x^2 - 16$

5. $x^2 - 25$

6. $x^2 - 100$

7. $x^2 - 64$

8. $p^2 - 121$

9. $196 - a^2$

10. $x^2 - 81$

11. $y^2 - 144$

12. $x^2 - 1$

Factorise and evaluate the following:

13. $8^2 - 6^2$

14. $100^2 - 99^2$

15. $51^2 - 49^2$

16. $21^2 - 20^2$

17. $7.6^2 - 2.4^2$

1. Factorise:

   (i) $x^2 - 36$

   (ii) $x^2 - x - 72$

   (iii) $x^2 - xy + 7x - 7y$

   (iv) $px - 2qx - 11p + 22q$

   (v) $y^2 - 49$

2. Factorise:

   (i) $ax + 6a + px + 6p$

   (ii) $x^2 + 3x - 54$

   (iii) $y^2 - 9$

   (iv) $5y^2 - 45$

   (v) $pr + qs + qr + ps$

3. Factorise:

   (i) $x^2 - 11x + 30$

   (ii) $2x^2 - 3xy - 2x + 3y$

   (iii) $3a^2b + 30ab^2$

   (iv) $3a^2b + 30ab^2 - a - 10b$

   (v) $x^2 - x - 42$

4. (a) The factors of $x^2 + ax + b$ are $(x - 1)$ and $(x + 8)$.

   Find the values of a and b.

   (b) The factors of $x^2 + px + q$ are $(x - 7)$ and $(x - 9)$.

   Find the values of p and q.

   (c) The factors of $x^2 - kx - t$ are $(x - 2)$ and $(x + 1)$.

   Find the values of k and t.

5. (a) Factorise $a^2 - 64$.

   (b) One factor of $x^2 + 8x - 65$ is $(x - 5)$. What is the other?

   (c) (i) Copy and fill in the bracket:
   $-2a^3b + 4a^2b^2 = -2a^2b(\qquad)$

   (ii) Factorise $13a - 26b - 2a^3b + 4a^2b^2$.

6. (a) (i) Factorise $x^2 + 4x - 32$.

   (ii) Evaluate the expression $x^2 + 4x - 32$ when $x = -8$.

   (b) Factorise:

   (i) $ab - bc - a + c$

   (ii) $x^2 + 2x - 63$

   (c) Factorise and hence evaluate $30.3^2 - 29.7^2$.

7. (a) Factorise:

   (i) $x^2 - 4$

   (ii) $x^2 - 4x$

   (iii) $x^2 - 4x + 4$

   (b) The factors of $x^2 + ax + b$ are $(x - 17)$ and $(x + 3)$. Find the values of a and b.

   (c) Factorise fully:

   (i) $7x^2 - 28$

   (ii) $x^2 - 169$

   (iii) $x^2 - 49x$

chapter 22

Algebra: Solving Quadratic Equations

Learning Outcomes

In this chapter you will learn to:

➲ Understand the concept of solving quadratic equations in algebra

➲ Solve quadratic equations by factorising

22.1 SOLVING QUADRATIC EQUATIONS

A **quadratic expression** is one of the form $ax^2 + bx + c$, $a \neq 0$.

A **quadratic equation** is of the form $ax^2 + bx + c = 0$, $a \neq 0$.

When we solve a quadratic equation, the solutions are the x-values of the points at which the graph cuts the x-axis.

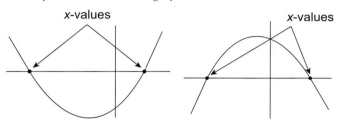

In general, quadratic equations have two different solutions.

We have learned in Chapter 21 how to factorise quadratic expressions. This turns the expression into a **product**.

When dealing with factors, remember this important point:

If two factors or numbers, when multiplied, give us zero, then one of the following is true:

- The first factor is equal to zero.

OR

- The second factor is equal to zero.

OR

- Both factors are equal to zero.

This fact is used to solve quadratic equations that factorise.

YOU SHOULD REMEMBER...

- How to solve linear equations
- How to find the factors of quadratic expressions

KEY WORDS

- **Solve**
- **Solution**
- **Roots**
- **Factors**
- **Highest common factor**
- **Difference of two squares**
- **Quadratic trinomials**

x^2 Worked Example 22.1

Solve the following equations:

    (i) $(x - 3)(x + 5) = 0$ (ii) $(x - 2)(x + 2) = 0$ (iii) $(x)(x + 8) = 0$

Solution

  (i) $(x - 3)(x + 5) = 0$ (ii) $(x - 2)(x + 2) = 0$ (iii) $(x)(x + 8) = 0$

      $x - 3 = 0$ **OR** $x + 5 = 0$ $x - 2 = 0$ **OR** $x + 2 = 0$ $x = 0$ **OR** $x + 8 = 0$

        $x = 3$ **OR** $x = -5$ $x = 2$ **OR** $x = -2$ $x = 0$ **OR** $x = -8$

This answer could also be written as $x = \pm 2$.

The equation $(x)(x + 8) = 0$ could also be written as $x(x + 8)$.

Exercise 22.1

Solve the following equations:

1. $(x - 4)(x - 3) = 0$
2. $(x + 6)(x + 2) = 0$
3. $(x - 2)(x + 2) = 0$
4. $(x)(x - 10) = 0$
5. $(x + 3)(x + 1) = 0$
6. $(x + 1)(x - 7) = 0$
7. $(x)(x + 4) = 0$
8. $(x - 12)(x - 11) = 0$
9. $(x + 2)(x + 2) = 0$
10. $x(x - 9) = 0$
11. $(x - 4)(x) = 0$
12. $0 = (x + 3)(x - 7)$

22.2 HIGHEST COMMON FACTOR

One type of quadratic equation is where we have an x^2 term and an x term only.

For example: $x^2 - 5x = 0$ or $x^2 + 10x = 0$.

To solve equations of this type, we find the highest common factor (HCF).

x^2 Worked Example 22.2

Solve for x: (i) $x^2 + 9x = 0$ (ii) $x^2 = 12x$

Solution

(i) $x^2 + 9x = 0$

$x(x + 9) = 0$

$x = 0$ **OR** $x + 9 = 0$

$x = 0$ **OR** $x = -9$

(ii) $x^2 = 12x$

Bring all terms to one side.

$x^2 - 12x = 0$

$x(x - 12) = 0$

$x = 0$ **OR** $x - 12 = 0$

$x = 0$ **OR** $x = 12$

Exercise 22.2

Solve the following:

1. $x^2 - 5x = 0$
2. $x^2 - 2x = 0$
3. $x^2 - 3x = 0$
4. $x^2 + 7x = 0$
5. $x^2 + 4x = 0$
6. $x^2 - 11x = 0$
7. $x^2 - x = 0$
8. $x^2 - 7x = 5x$
9. $x^2 - 5x = -4x$
10. $x^2 + x = 0$
11. $x^2 = -12x$
12. $x^2 = 9x$
13. $x^2 - 4x - 3 = -3$
14. $3x = -x^2$
15. $4 = x^2 + 3x + 4$
16. $0 = x^2 - 7x$

22.3 DIFFERENCE OF TWO SQUARES

Another quadratic equation that we may be asked to solve is one that has an x^2 term minus a number.

For example: $x^2 - 100 = 0$ or $x^2 - 64 = 0$.

To solve equations of this type, we factorise using the **difference of two squares** method.

It is easy to confuse **taking out the highest common factor** and the **difference of two squares**:

HCF	Difference of two squares
$x^2 - 4x = 0$	$x^2 - 4 = 0$
x^2 and x term	x^2 and a constant term

ACTIVITY 22.3

x^2 Worked Example 22.3

Solve for x:

   (i) $x^2 - 49 = 0$ (ii) $x^2 - 144 = 0$

Solution

(i) $x^2 - 49 = 0$

Method 1	Method 2
$x^2 - 49 = 0$ $(x)^2 - (7)^2 = 0$ $(x - 7)(x + 7) = 0$	$x^2 - 49 = 0$ $x^2 = 49$
$x - 7 = 0$ OR $x + 7 = 0$	$x = \pm \sqrt{49}$
$x = 7$ OR $x = -7$	$x = \pm 7$

(ii) $x^2 - 144 = 0$

Method 1	Method 2
$x^2 - 144 = 0$ $(x)^2 - (12)^2 = 0$ $(x - 12)(x + 12) = 0$	$x^2 - 144 = 0$ $x^2 = 144$
$x - 12 = 0$ OR $x + 12 = 0$	$x = \pm \sqrt{144}$
$x = 12$ OR $x = -12$	$x = \pm 12$

Note: $\sqrt{}$ is defined as 'the positive root of'.
For example, $\sqrt{25} = 5$, but $x^2 = 25$ has solutions $x = \pm\sqrt{25} = \pm 5$.

Exercise 22.3

Solve the following:

1. $x^2 - 4 = 0$

2. $x^2 - 121 = 0$

3. $y^2 - 16 = 0$

4. $x^2 - 100 = 0$

5. $x^2 - 1 = 0$

6. $x^2 - 25 = 0$

7. $a^2 - 196 = 0$

8. $x^2 - 64 = 0$

9. $x^2 - 81 = 0$

10. $a^2 - 225 = 0$

11. $x^2 - 140 = 4$

12. $x^2 = 400$

13. $x^2 + 5 = 630$

14. $-x^2 + 1 = 0$

22.4 QUADRATIC TRINOMIALS

The final type of quadratic that we may have to solve is that of a **quadratic trinomial**.

For example: $x^2 + 2x - 15 = 0$.

 ACTIVITY 22.4

'Trinomial' means that there are three terms in the expression.

A quadratic trinomial has an x^2 term, an x term and a number (constant).

x^2 Worked Example 22.4

Solve: (i) $x^2 + 10x + 16 = 0$ (ii) $x^2 - 4x - 21 = 0$

Solution

(i) $x^2 + 10x + 16 = 0$

$(x + 8)(x + 2) = 0$

$x + 8 = 0$ **OR** $x + 2 = 0$

$x = -8$ **OR** $x = -2$

(ii) $x^2 - 4x - 21 = 0$

$(x - 7)(x + 3) = 0$

$x - 7 = 0$ **OR** $x + 3 = 0$

$x = 7$ **OR** $x = -3$

x^2 Worked Example 22.5

Solve: $x^2 + 8x + 15 = 0$ and verify both solutions.

Solution

$x^2 + 8x + 15 = 0$

$(x + 5)(x + 3) = 0$

$x + 5 = 0$ **OR** $x + 3 = 0$

$x = -5$ **OR** $x = -3$

Verify:

$x = -5 \Rightarrow (-5)^2 + 8(-5) + 15 = 0$

$25 - 40 + 15 = 0$

$-15 + 15 = 0$

$0 = 0$ $\therefore x = -5$ is a solution.

$x = -3 \Rightarrow (-3)^2 + 8(-3) + 15 = 0$

$9 - 24 + 15 = 0$

$-15 + 15 = 0$

$0 = 0$ $\therefore x = -3$ is a solution.

Exercise 22.4

Solve the following quadratic trinomials:

1. $x^2 + 4x + 3 = 0$

2. $x^2 + 12x + 35 = 0$

3. $x^2 + 7x + 12 = 0$

4. $x^2 + 6x + 5 = 0$

5. $x^2 + 11x + 28 = 0$

6. $x^2 + 12x + 11 = 0$

7. $x^2 + 3x + 2 = 0$

8. $x^2 + 14x + 13 = 0$

9. $x^2 - 8x + 15 = 0$

10. $x^2 + 4x + 4 = 0$

11. $x^2 - 4x + 4 = 0$

12. $x^2 - 9x + 8 = 0$

13. $x^2 - 6x - 27 = 0$

14. $x^2 - 10x + 21 = 0$

15. $x^2 + 14x + 49 = 0$

16. $x^2 + 15x + 54 = 0$

17. $x^2 + 3x - 40 = 0$

18. $x^2 + 5x - 24 = 0$

19. $x^2 + 4x - 21 = 0$

20. $x^2 + 3x - 10 = 0$

21. $x^2 - 14x + 45 = 0$

22. $x^2 + 12x + 36 = 0$

23. $x^2 - 4x - 12 = 0$

24. $x^2 - 6x + 5 = 0$

25. $x^2 - 16x + 63 = 0$

26. $x^2 - 2x - 35 = 0$

27. $x^2 + 9x + 14 = 0$

28. $x^2 - 18x + 72 = 0$

29. $x^2 + 13x + 42 = 0$

30. $x^2 - x - 6 = 0$

31. $x^2 - 13x + 42 = 0$

32. $x^2 - 3x = 10$

33. $x^2 - 18x = -45$

34. $x^2 - 7x = 8$

35. $x^2 - 21 = -4x$

36. $x^2 + 2 = 3x$

37. $x^2 = 5x + 24$

38. $12 - 4x = x^2$

39. $(x + 2)^2 = 16$

 ## Revision Exercises

Solve the following quadratic equations:

1. $x^2 - 2x - 8 = 0$

2. $a^2 + 3a - 10 = 0$

3. $b^2 - 7b + 12 = 0$

4. $x^2 - x - 12 = 0$

5. $x^2 + x - 20 = 0$

6. $x^2 - 9x = 0$

7. $x^2 - 16 = 0$

8. $x^2 - 3x - 40 = 0$

9. $x^2 + 8x = 0$

10. $x^2 - 11x + 28 = 0$

11. $x^2 - 3x + 2 = 0$

12. $x^2 - 4 = 0$

13. $x^2 - 4x = 0$

14. $q^2 + 4q - 21 = 0$

15. $x^2 - 49 = 0$

16. $x^2 + x - 6 = 0$

17. $x^2 - 5x - 14 = 0$

18. $p^2 - 225 = 0$

19. $x^2 - 13x + 30 = 0$

20. $x^2 + 7x + 10 = 0$

21. $x^2 - 6x - 16 = 0$

22. $x^2 + 3x = 0$

23. $x^2 - x = 0$

24. $x^2 + x - 42 = 0$

25. $x^2 + 3x - 54 = 0$

26. $x^2 - 2x = 0$

27. $x^2 - 4x - 12 = 0$

28. $x^2 + 13x = 0$

29. $x^2 - 169 = 0$

30. $x^2 - 20x + 100 = 0$

31. $x^2 + 7x - 18 = 0$

32. $x^2 + 3x + 2 = 0$

33. $x^2 - 13x + 22 = 0$

34. Solve $x^2 - 10x + 16 = 0$ and verify both solutions.

35. Solve $x^2 - 2x - 63 = 0$ and verify both solutions.

36. Solve $x^2 + 10x + 9 = 0$ and verify both solutions.

37. Solve $x^2 - 6x + 9 = 0$ and verify both solutions.

38. Solve $x^2 - 5x - 14 = 0$ and verify both solutions.

Write Q.39–Q.50 in the form $x^2 + bx + c = 0$ before solving:

39. $x^2 = 2x + 24$

40. $x^2 + x = 30$

41. $x^2 = x + 90$

42. $x^2 + x = 4(x + 7)$

43. $x^2 = 2(x + 24)$

44. $x(x + 1) = 3x - 1$

45. $x(x + 1) = 10(3x - 10)$

46. $x^2 = 4$

47. $x^2 = 4x$

48. $13(x + 1) = x(x + 1)$

49. $(x - 2)(x + 3) = 24$

50. Solve $(x - 1)(x + 1) = 8x - 17$ and verify the only solution.

chapter 23

Algebraic Fractions

Learning Outcomes

In this chapter you will learn to:

- Simplify algebraic fractions
- Solve equations that contain fractions
- Divide algebraic terms

23.1 FRACTIONS

We may sometimes encounter algebraic terms that involve fractions. In order to simplify these type of terms, we must first understand how to deal with fractions with numbers only.

 ACTIVITY 23.1

x^2 Worked Example 23.1

If $p = 4$ and $q = 5$, find the value of:

(i) $\dfrac{1}{p} + \dfrac{1}{q}$ (ii) $\dfrac{p}{3} - \dfrac{q}{2}$

Solution

(i) $p = 4$ and $q = 5$

$\therefore \dfrac{1}{p} + \dfrac{1}{q} = \dfrac{1}{4} + \dfrac{1}{5}$

The lowest common multiple or LCD of 4 and 5 is 20.

$\dfrac{5(1) + 4(1)}{20} = \dfrac{5 + 4}{20} = \dfrac{9}{20}$

(ii) $\dfrac{p}{3} - \dfrac{q}{2}$

$= \dfrac{4}{3} - \dfrac{5}{2}$

LCD = 6

$\dfrac{2(4) - 3(5)}{6} = \dfrac{8 - 15}{6} = \dfrac{-7}{6}$

Exercise 23.1

ALGEBRAIC FRACTIONS

1. If $x = 2$ and $y = 3$, find the value of:

   (i) $\dfrac{1}{x} + \dfrac{1}{y}$ (iii) $\dfrac{3}{x} + \dfrac{5}{y}$

   (ii) $\dfrac{1}{x} - \dfrac{1}{y}$ (iv) $\dfrac{1}{2x} + \dfrac{1}{y}$

2. If $a = 3$, $b = 4$ and $c = 5$, find the value of:

   (i) $\dfrac{1}{a} + \dfrac{1}{b} + \dfrac{1}{c}$ (iii) $\dfrac{a}{c} - \dfrac{4b}{a} - c$

   (ii) $\dfrac{2}{a} + \dfrac{5}{b} - \dfrac{3}{c}$ (iv) $\dfrac{a - b}{c} + \dfrac{3c}{2}$

3. If $x = 3$, $y = 5$ and $z = 2$, find the value of:

   (i) $\dfrac{1}{x} - \dfrac{1}{y} + \dfrac{1}{z}$ (iii) $\dfrac{x + y}{3} + \dfrac{z - y}{8}$

   (ii) $\dfrac{x - 2y}{5} - \dfrac{3z}{4}$ (iv) $\dfrac{y + x}{5} - \dfrac{z - y}{2}$

4. If $p = 1$, $q = \dfrac{1}{2}$ and $r = \dfrac{1}{3}$, find the value of:

   (i) $p + q + r$ (iii) $2(q + r) - p$

   (ii) $2p + 3q - 5r$ (iv) $\dfrac{p + q}{r - q}$

23.2 ALGEBRAIC FRACTIONS

We can identify an algebraic fraction, as it will have a variable, for example an x:

$$\frac{x}{5} + \frac{x}{6}$$

When we are asked to add or subtract two algebraic fractions, we use the same method that we would normally use for numerical fractions.

Worked Example 23.2

Simplify $\frac{x}{3} + \frac{5x}{2}$.

Solution

The LCD of 2 and 3 is 6:

- 3 into 6 goes 2 times.
- 2 into 6 goes 3 times.

$$\frac{x}{3} + \frac{5x}{2}$$

$$= \frac{2(x) + 3(5x)}{6}$$

$$= \frac{2x + 15x}{6}$$

$$= \frac{17x}{6}$$

---

x^2 **Worked Example 23.3**

Write as a single fraction:

$$\frac{x + 2}{3} - \frac{2x - 1}{4}$$

Solution

The LCD of 3 and 4 is 12:

- 3 into 12 goes 4 times.
- 4 into 12 goes 3 times.

$$\frac{x + 2}{3} - \frac{2x - 1}{4}$$

$$= \frac{4(x + 2) - 3(2x - 1)}{12}$$

$$= \frac{4x + 8 - 6x + 3}{12}$$

$$= \frac{-2x + 11}{12}$$

> Remember that
> $-3 \times -1 = +3$.

 ACTIVITY 23.2

📖 **Exercise 23.2**

Simplify each of the following:

1. $\frac{x}{3} + \frac{x}{4}$

2. $\frac{x}{5} + \frac{x}{3}$

3. $\frac{y}{7} + \frac{y}{2}$

4. $\frac{y}{5} + 3$

5. $\frac{2x}{3} + \frac{x}{4}$

6. $\frac{3x}{8} - \frac{2x}{5}$

7. $\frac{4x}{5} + \frac{x}{2}$

8. $\frac{x}{4} + \frac{x}{3} + \frac{x}{2}$

9. $\frac{x}{2} + \frac{x}{6} + \frac{x}{8}$

10. $\frac{2x}{3} + \frac{3x}{7} - \frac{x}{6}$

11. $\frac{4x}{5} - \frac{2x}{3} + \frac{3}{1}$

12. $\frac{7x}{9} - \frac{5x}{3} + 2$

13. $\frac{4}{3} - \frac{5x}{6} + \frac{3}{5}$

14. $\frac{4x}{5} - \frac{2x}{3} + \frac{8x}{9}$

15. $\frac{11x}{3} - \frac{3}{8} - \frac{x}{2}$

16. $\frac{x + 1}{2} + \frac{x + 3}{3}$

17. $\frac{x + 4}{2} + \frac{x + 1}{5}$

18. $\frac{x + 7}{3} + \frac{x + 5}{4}$

19. $\frac{x - 1}{5} + \frac{x - 2}{4}$

20. $\frac{2x + 1}{4} + \frac{3x - 2}{8}$

21. $\frac{5x - 2}{4} + \frac{2x - 6}{3}$

22. $\frac{x + 2}{4} + \frac{3x - 5}{6}$

23. $x + 7 + \frac{3x + 4}{5}$

24. $\frac{4x - 1}{5} - \frac{2x + 1}{2}$

25. $\frac{2x + 1}{3} - \frac{4x + 3}{5}$

26. $\frac{3x + 2}{2} - \frac{5x - 3}{3}$

27. $\frac{8x - 5}{4} - \frac{2x - 7}{3}$

28. $\frac{x - 10}{4} - \frac{3x + 12}{5}$

29. $\frac{4x - 16}{5} - 2x - 1$

30. $\frac{5x - 1}{3} - 3x$

31. $\frac{x + 3}{2} + \frac{4x + 1}{4} + \frac{1}{3}$

32. $\frac{x - 2}{4} + \frac{2x + 1}{8} - \frac{2}{3}$

33. $\frac{3x + 3}{7} + \frac{3}{14} - \frac{5x + 1}{4}$

34. $\frac{2x - 2}{5} - \frac{3x + 1}{3} + \frac{2}{15}$

35. $\frac{6x + 2}{9} - \frac{2x + 1}{18} - \frac{2x - 4}{6}$

36. $\frac{4x - 3}{2} - \frac{7x + 12}{3} - \frac{x - 4}{6}$

23.3 SOLVING EQUATIONS WITH FRACTIONS

When trying to solve equations that have fractions, it can be easier to multiply every term by the LCD. By doing this, we end up with terms that consist of whole numbers.

x^2 Worked Example 23.4

Solve: $\dfrac{2x}{3} - \dfrac{3x}{5} = \dfrac{2}{15}$

Solution

The LCD of 3, 5 and 15 is 15.

We will multiply every term in the equation by 15:

$$\dfrac{15(2x)}{3} - \dfrac{15(3x)}{5} = \dfrac{15(2)}{15}$$

$$\dfrac{\overset{5}{\cancel{15}}(2x)}{\cancel{3}_1} - \dfrac{\overset{3}{\cancel{15}}(3x)}{\cancel{5}_1} = \dfrac{\overset{1}{\cancel{15}}(2)}{\cancel{15}_1}$$

$$5(2x) - 3(3x) = 1(2)$$

$$10x - 9x = 2$$

$$x = 2$$

> No term should still have a fraction part.

x^2 Worked Example 23.5

Solve: $\dfrac{2x-1}{3} - \dfrac{x+1}{9} = 4$

> Note that 4 can be written as $\dfrac{4}{1}$.

Solution

The LCD of 3, 9 and 1 is 9.

We will multiply every term in the equation by 9.

$$\dfrac{9(2x-1)}{3} - \dfrac{9(x+1)}{9} = \dfrac{9(4)}{1}$$

$$\dfrac{\overset{3}{\cancel{9}}(2x-1)}{\cancel{3}_1} - \dfrac{\overset{1}{\cancel{9}}(x+1)}{\cancel{9}_1} = \dfrac{\overset{9}{\cancel{9}}(4)}{\cancel{1}_1}$$

$$3(2x-1) - 1(x+1) = 9(4)$$

$$6x - 3 - 1x - 1 = 36$$

$$5x - 4 = 36$$

$$5x = 40$$

$$x = 8$$

> No term should still have a fraction part.

ACTIVITY 23.3

Exercise 23.3

Solve the following equations:

1. $\dfrac{x+2}{2} = 5$

2. $\dfrac{x+5}{3} = 2$

3. $\dfrac{x-3}{4} = 3$

4. $\dfrac{3x+1}{5} = 5$

5. $\dfrac{9x-4}{2} = 7$

6. $\dfrac{x}{4} + \dfrac{x}{2} = 3$

7. $\dfrac{x}{5} + \dfrac{x}{3} = 8$

8. $\dfrac{x}{3} - \dfrac{x}{6} = 1$

9. $\dfrac{x}{4} + \dfrac{x}{5} = \dfrac{9}{10}$

10. $\dfrac{x}{2} - \dfrac{x}{5} = \dfrac{3}{2}$

11. $\dfrac{x}{4} + \dfrac{2x}{5} = \dfrac{13}{20}$

12. $\dfrac{2x}{3} - \dfrac{4x}{9} = \dfrac{10}{3}$

13. $\dfrac{3x}{8} - \dfrac{x}{4} = \dfrac{5}{2}$

14. $\dfrac{4x}{7} - \dfrac{3x}{14} = 5$

15. $\dfrac{8x}{9} - \dfrac{5x}{6} = \dfrac{5}{18}$

16. $\dfrac{x+1}{3} + \dfrac{x-1}{7} = 4$

17. $\dfrac{4x+2}{3} + \dfrac{2x+2}{4} = 3$

18. $\dfrac{3x+1}{2} - \dfrac{2x+1}{5} = 8$

19. $\dfrac{8x-3}{3} - \dfrac{4x-2}{5} = 5$

20. $\dfrac{3x+1}{15} + \dfrac{x+1}{5} = \dfrac{2}{3}$

21. $\dfrac{3x-5}{7} + \dfrac{2x-1}{14} = \dfrac{3}{2}$

22. $\dfrac{4x+3}{5} - \dfrac{2x-1}{2} = \dfrac{1}{10}$

23. $\dfrac{3x-1}{2} - \dfrac{4x-1}{4} = \dfrac{5}{4}$

24. $\dfrac{2x+1}{6} - \dfrac{x+2}{12} = \dfrac{5}{4}$

25. $\dfrac{3x+1}{4} - \dfrac{2x+1}{5} = \dfrac{5}{2}$

26. $\dfrac{x+3}{3} + \dfrac{2x+6}{4} = 5$

27. $\dfrac{2x-5}{4} - \dfrac{4x+3}{5} = -\dfrac{19}{20}$

28. $\dfrac{14-x}{2} - \dfrac{x+3}{5} = 5$

29. $\dfrac{x-3}{2} = \dfrac{x+4}{4}$

30. $\dfrac{1}{2}(x+1) - \dfrac{1}{3}(2x-1) = 0$

23.4 SIMPLIFYING ALGEBRAIC FRACTIONS

When asked to simplify a fraction, we are being asked to change it into a simpler form, for example $\frac{4}{16} = \frac{1}{4}$. This is also the same as $4 \div 16 = \frac{1}{4}$.

When we simplify an algebraic fraction $\left(\text{e.g. simplify } \dfrac{12x^2}{3x}\right)$ we are also being asked to **divide**.

$$\frac{12x^2}{3x} = 12x^2 \div 3x$$

$$\therefore \frac{12x^2}{3x} = \frac{^4\cancel{12} \times x \times \cancel{x}}{\cancel{3}_1 \times \cancel{x}} = 4x$$

Simplifying algebraic fractions is similar to simplifying normal fractions.

ACTIVITY 23.4

x^2 Worked Example 23.6

Simplify the following:

(i) $\dfrac{50xy}{2x}$

(ii) $\dfrac{20a^2b}{5a}$

(iii) $\dfrac{12y^2}{4y^3}$

Solution

(i) $\dfrac{50xy}{2x}$

$= \dfrac{\overset{25}{\cancel{(50)}}\overset{1}{\cancel{(x)}}(y)}{\underset{1}{\cancel{(2)}}\underset{1}{\cancel{(x)}}}$

$= 25y$

(ii) $\dfrac{20a^2b}{5a}$

$= \dfrac{\overset{4}{\cancel{(20)}}\overset{1}{\cancel{(a)}}(a)(b)}{\underset{1}{\cancel{(5)}}\underset{1}{\cancel{(a)}}}$

$= 4ab$

(iii) $\dfrac{12y^2}{4y^3}$

$= \dfrac{\overset{3}{\cancel{(12)}}\overset{1}{\cancel{(y)}}\overset{1}{\cancel{(y)}}}{\underset{1}{\cancel{(4)}}\underset{1}{\cancel{(y)}}\underset{1}{\cancel{(y)}}(y)}$

$= \dfrac{3}{y}$

ALGEBRAIC FRACTIONS

x^2 **Worked Example 23.7**

Simplify the following:

(i) $\dfrac{4x + 8}{x + 2}$ (ii) $\dfrac{a^2 + 2a - 8}{a + 4}$ (iii) $\dfrac{x^2 - 1}{x^2 + x}$

Solution

(i) $\dfrac{4x + 8}{x + 2}$

We factorise the **top** part of the fraction:

$$\dfrac{4 \times (x + 2)}{(x + 2)} = \dfrac{4\cancel{(x + 2)}}{\cancel{(x + 2)}} = 4$$

Remember that $\frac{5}{5} = 1$ so $\frac{x+2}{x+2} = 1$ also.

(ii) $\dfrac{a^2 + 2a - 8}{a + 4}$

$$= \dfrac{(a - 2) \times (a + 4)}{(a + 4)} = \dfrac{(a - 2) \times \cancel{(a + 4)}^1}{\cancel{(a + 4)}_1}$$

$$= a - 2$$

(iii) $\dfrac{x^2 - 1}{x^2 + x}$

We factorise both the numerator and the denominator:

$$= \dfrac{(x - 1) \times (x + 1)}{x(x + 1)} = \dfrac{(x - 1) \times \cancel{(x + 1)}}{x \cancel{(x + 1)}}$$

$$= \dfrac{x - 1}{x}$$

When factorising, there should be at least **one** factor that is common to both the top and the bottom of the fraction.

 Exercise 23.4

Simplify each of the following algebraic fractions:

1. $\dfrac{10x^2}{5}$

2. $\dfrac{27y^3}{3}$

3. $\dfrac{18x^2}{9}$

4. $\dfrac{45a^2}{3a}$

5. $\dfrac{20x^3}{4x}$

6. $\dfrac{15y^3}{5y}$

7. $\dfrac{20x}{20x}$

8. $\dfrac{2x^2}{x^3}$

9. $\dfrac{4y^2}{y^3}$

10. $\dfrac{7y}{14y^3}$

11. $\dfrac{10x^2y}{5y}$

12. $\dfrac{100y^3}{40y^2}$

13. $\dfrac{25x^3y^2}{20xy}$

14. $\dfrac{3x^3y^2z^2}{9xyz}$

15. $\dfrac{14a^2b^2c}{7ab^2c}$

16. $\dfrac{3x + 12}{x + 4}$

17. $\dfrac{5x + 10}{x + 2}$

18. $\dfrac{3x - 9}{x - 3}$

19. $\dfrac{4x - 2}{2x - 1}$

20. $\dfrac{15x - 20}{3x - 4}$

21. $\dfrac{x^2 - 4x}{x - 4}$

22. $\dfrac{2x^2 - 2x}{2x - 2}$

23. $\dfrac{6x^2 - 21x}{3x}$

24. $\dfrac{12x^2 - 4x}{3x - 1}$

25. $\dfrac{14x^2 - 35x}{2x - 5}$

26. $\dfrac{x^2 + 3x + 2}{x + 2}$

27. $\dfrac{x^2 + 7x + 12}{x + 4}$

28. $\dfrac{x^2 + 7x + 10}{x + 2}$

29. $\dfrac{x^2 - 5x + 6}{x - 3}$

30. $\dfrac{x^2 + 5x - 14}{x + 7}$

31. $\dfrac{x^2 - 2x + 1}{x - 1}$

32. $\dfrac{x^2 - 25}{x + 5}$

33. $\dfrac{x^2 + 3x - 18}{x + 6}$

34. $\dfrac{8x - 4x^2}{2 - x}$

35. $\dfrac{x^2 - 100}{x - 10}$

36. $\dfrac{x^2 + 2x - 24}{(x - 4)(x + 6)}$

Revision Exercises

Express each of the following as single fractions in their simplest form:

1. $\dfrac{x}{5} + \dfrac{x}{2}$

2. $\dfrac{x}{2} + \dfrac{x}{4}$

3. $\dfrac{x}{2} - \dfrac{x}{7}$

4. $\dfrac{k}{4} - \dfrac{k}{8}$

5. $\dfrac{x}{4} + \dfrac{x}{3} + \dfrac{x}{12}$

6. $\dfrac{b}{7} + \dfrac{b}{2} - \dfrac{b}{14}$

7. $\dfrac{x+1}{2} + \dfrac{x+2}{3}$

8. $\dfrac{x+3}{5} + \dfrac{x+4}{2}$

9. $\dfrac{3x+2}{4} + \dfrac{2x+1}{3}$

10. $\dfrac{2x+4}{5} + \dfrac{4x+1}{2}$

11. $\dfrac{x+2}{3} + \dfrac{x+3}{2}$

12. $\dfrac{5x+3}{3} - \dfrac{3x+2}{6}$

13. $\dfrac{3y-1}{5} - \dfrac{2y+3}{4}$

14. $\dfrac{3y-1}{7} - \dfrac{y+2}{14}$

15. $\dfrac{5x+1}{2} - \dfrac{3x-1}{3}$

16. $\dfrac{x-1}{2} + \dfrac{x-1}{3} - \dfrac{x-2}{6}$

17. $\dfrac{x+10}{5} - \dfrac{x+4}{2} + \dfrac{x+7}{10}$

18. $\dfrac{x+11}{3} - \dfrac{x-1}{8} + \dfrac{x-4}{6}$

19. $\dfrac{3x-1}{5} + \dfrac{x+4}{2}$

20. $\dfrac{11x-2}{3} - \dfrac{x+1}{2}$

Solve each of the following equations:

21. $\dfrac{x+10}{11} = 2$

22. $\dfrac{3x-2}{5} = 5$

23. $\dfrac{8x+1}{3} = 11$

24. $\dfrac{x}{3} + \dfrac{x}{4} = 7$

25. $\dfrac{x}{2} + \dfrac{x}{3} = 15$

26. $\dfrac{x}{2} - \dfrac{x}{5} = 9$

27. $\dfrac{2x}{3} - \dfrac{x}{4} = 5$

28. $\dfrac{x+3}{7} + \dfrac{x+5}{4} = 6$

29. $\dfrac{4x+2}{3} - \dfrac{x-2}{2} = 5$

30. $\dfrac{1-x}{2} - \dfrac{x-6}{3} = 0$

31. $\dfrac{x}{3} + \dfrac{x}{4} = 21$

32. $\dfrac{3x+2}{5} - \dfrac{x}{2} = 1$

33. $\dfrac{4x-4}{9} + \dfrac{2x+3}{18} = \dfrac{5}{6}$

34. $\dfrac{3x+1}{5} - \dfrac{x+1}{3} = \dfrac{6}{15}$

35. $\dfrac{6x-1}{12} + \dfrac{4x-2}{6} = \dfrac{3}{4}$

36. $\dfrac{x+12}{20} - \dfrac{5x+10}{4} = \dfrac{-7}{10}$

37. $\dfrac{3}{8}(5x+1) + \dfrac{1}{4}(x-1) = \dfrac{13}{2}$

38. $\dfrac{5}{8}(3x+5) - \dfrac{3}{4}(x+11) = 5$

39. (i) Write the following as a single fraction:
$$\dfrac{3x-4}{5} - \dfrac{x+7}{2}$$

(ii) Hence or otherwise, solve the equation:
$$\dfrac{3x-4}{5} - \dfrac{x+7}{2} = -4$$

Simplify each of the following algebraic fractions:

40. $\dfrac{3x^2+9x}{x+3}$

41. $\dfrac{2x-3x^2}{3x-2}$

42. $\dfrac{4x^2+16x}{x+4}$

43. $\dfrac{x^2+12x+27}{x+9}$

44. $\dfrac{x^2-21x+110}{x-10}$

45. $\dfrac{x^2-8x}{x-8}$

46. $\dfrac{x^2-2x-35}{x^2+5x}$

47. $\dfrac{x^2-400}{x+20}$

48. $\dfrac{x-3}{x^2-6x+9}$

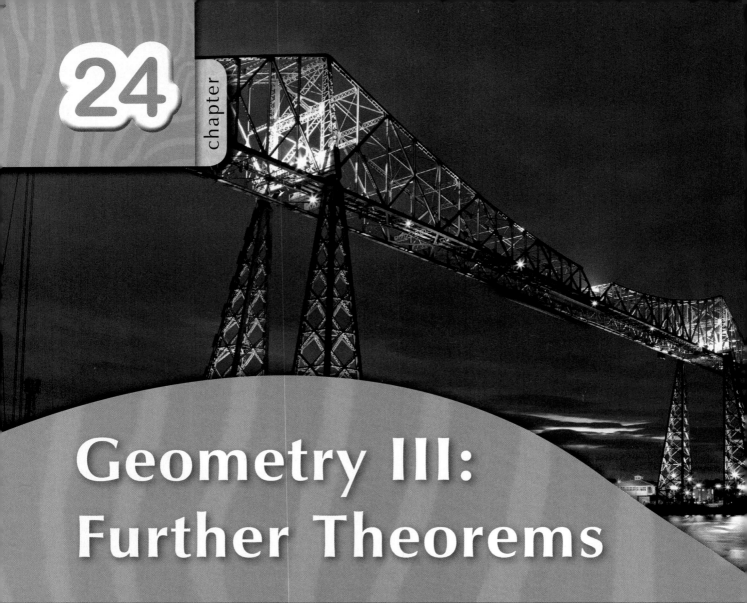

24 chapter

Geometry III: Further Theorems

Learning Outcomes

In this chapter you will learn the following theorems, corollaries and axioms:

- Theorem 13. If two triangles are similar, then their sides are proportional, in order.

- Axiom 4. Congruent triangles (SAS, ASA, SSS and RHS).

- Theorem 14. The theorem of Pythagoras: In a right-angled triangle, the square of the hypotenuse is the sum of the squares of the other two sides.

- Theorem 15. If the square of one side of a triangle is the sum of the squares of the other two sides, then the angle opposite the first side is a right angle.

- Corollary 3. Each angle in a semicircle is a right angle.

- Corollary 4 . If the angle standing on a chord [BC] at some point of the circle is a right angle, then [BC] is a diameter.

24.1 SIMILAR TRIANGLES

We use many different terms to describe triangles: for example, triangles can be scalene, isosceles or equilateral. There are also terms to describe the **relationship** between two or more triangles. In the following section, we will look at the relationship between **similar triangles**.

We can see from this example that two shapes can be similar to each other even though they are not the same size. 'Similar' means they have the same shape.

If we examine these two triangles, we may notice something about the angles in each one.

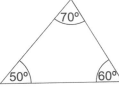

KEY WORDS

- Similar
- Congruent
  - SSS
  - SAS
  - ASA
  - RHS
- Pythagoras
- Right angle
- Diameter

Triangles whose angles are the same are said to be **similar**.

If two pairs of angles in each triangle are the same, then the triangles are similar. The third angle in each triangle must have the same measurement, as the total measure is 180°.

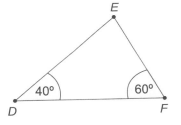

In similar or equiangular triangles, all three pairs of angles are equal.

$|\angle ACB| = 180° - 40° - 60°$

$|\angle ACB| = 80°$

$|\angle DEF| = 180° - 40° - 60°$

$|\angle DEF| = 80°$

ACTIVITY 24.1

It is important to remember that while the angles are equal, the sides are not. However, the **corresponding sides** of two similar triangles do have a special property.

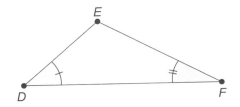

The corresponding sides of similar triangles are in the same ratio.

Corresponding sides are the sides that match each other in the two triangles. For example, in the triangles above, [AB] and [DE] are corresponding sides.

ACTIVITY 24.2

GEOMETRY III: FURTHER THEOREMS

Theorem 13

If two triangles are similar, then their sides are proportional, in order.

In the similar triangles shown, this relationship can be written as:

$$\frac{|AB|}{|DE|} = \frac{|AC|}{|DF|} = \frac{|BC|}{|EF|}$$

In practice, we only need to use two of the ratios to determine the missing side.

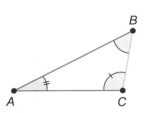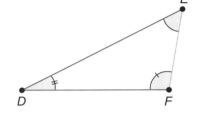

The converse of Theorem 13 also applies:

If the sides of two triangles are proportional (in order), the two triangles are similar.

Worked Example 24.1

Find the length of the side marked x in the following pair of similar triangles.

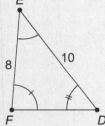

Solution

Identify which sides correspond to each other.

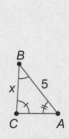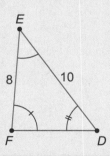

It is a good idea to put the triangle with the unknown side first.

We know that $\frac{|BC|}{|EF|} = \frac{|AB|}{|DE|}$.

Start with the unknown side and put it over the corresponding side in the other triangle:

$$\frac{x}{8}$$

We let this be equal to another known triangle side over its corresponding side:

$$\frac{x}{8} = \frac{5}{10}$$

Remember that the order in which we put one side over the other must not be changed once we start to find the unknown side.

Cross-multiply to eliminate fractions:

$$10x = 5(8)$$

$$10x = 40$$

$$x = 4$$

Worked Example 24.2

Find the length of the side marked *y* in the following pair of similar triangles.

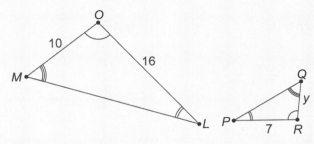

Solution

Identify which sides correspond to each other. It is helpful to redraw the triangles so that the corresponding sides match.

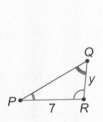 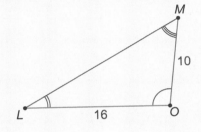

Start with the side we are looking for: $\dfrac{y}{10} = \dfrac{7}{16}$

Cross-multiply: $16y = 70$

$$y = 4.375$$

Exercise 24.1

1. Identify the pairs of corresponding sides in each of the following similar triangles:

(i)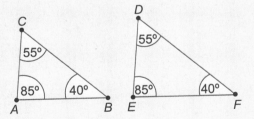

(ii)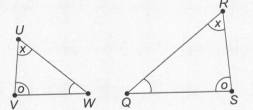

(iii)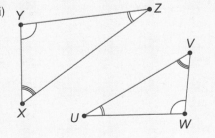

(iv)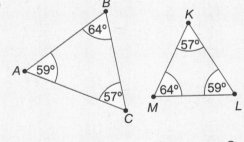

(v)

2. Find the value of x in each of the following pairs of similar triangles.

(i)
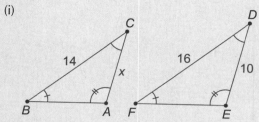

(ii)
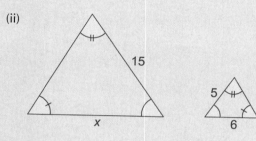

(iii)
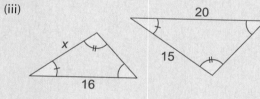

(iv)
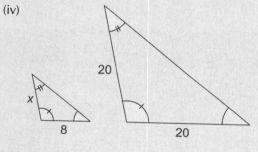

(v)
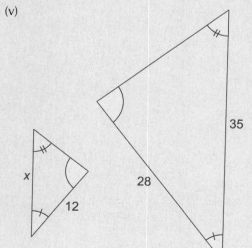

3. Find the value of y in each of the following pairs of similar triangles.

(i)
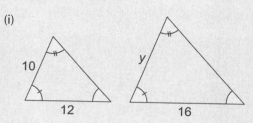

(ii)
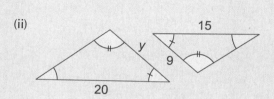

(iii)
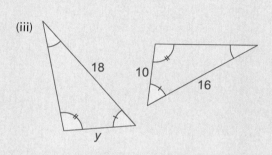

(iv)
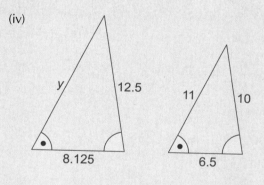

(v)
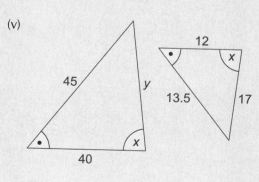

4. Find the value of *x* and *y* in the following pairs of similar triangles.

(i)

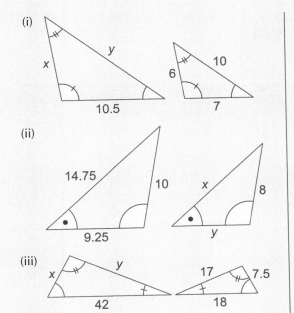

(ii)

(iii)

(iv)

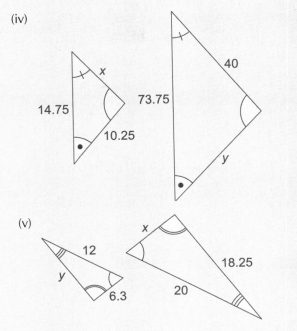

(v)

24.2 CONGRUENT TRIANGLES

If we look at the two triangles shown,
we can see that they are exactly the same.
They are identical to each other.

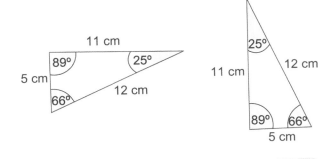

Congruent triangles
are triangles in which all
the corresponding sides
and angles are equal.

ACTIVITY 24.3

These two triangles can be described as **congruent triangles**.

Corresponding angles are the angles that match each other in the two triangles.

There are different ways to show that two triangles are congruent. These methods are listed in Axiom 4:

Axiom 4

Congruent triangles (SAS, ASA, SSS and RHS)

Congruent Triangles: Side, Side, Side (SSS)

SSS is a shorthand way to write 'Side, Side, Side'.

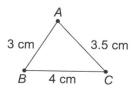 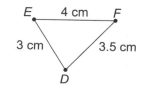

ΔABC is congruent to ΔDEF.

The side lengths in ΔABC are the same as the side lengths in ΔDEF.

Congruent Triangles: Side, Angle, Side (SAS)

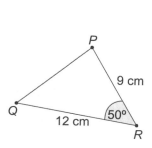 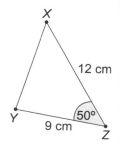

ΔPQR is congruent to ΔXYZ.

Two sides and the angle between them are equal.

The **in-between** angle can also be called the **included angle**.

Congruent Triangles: Angle, Side, Angle (ASA)

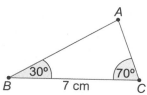 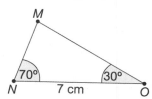

ΔABC is congruent to ΔMNO.

Two angles and the included side are equal.

The included side is the side between the vertices of the two angles.

Congruent Triangles: Right Angle, Hypotenuse, One Other Side (RHS)

Both of these triangles are right-angled, their hypotenuse is the same length and they have one other side that is equal.

The **hypotenuse** is the side opposite the right angle. It is also the longest side in the triangle.

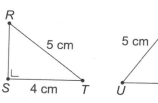 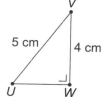

The areas of congruent triangles are equal as well.

ACTIVITY 24.4

ΔRST is congruent to ΔUVW.

Worked Example 24.3

State whether the following triangles are congruent or not, and give a reason for your answer.

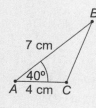 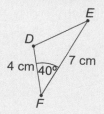

GEOMETRY III: FURTHER THEOREMS

Solution

$|AB| = |EF|$ (7 cm)

$|AC| = |DF|$ (4 cm)

$|\angle BAC| = |\angle DFE|$ (40°)

The triangle ABC is congruent to the triangle DEF.

We must now give our reason: the triangles are congruent because the two corresponding sides and the included angle are equal.

This statement can be written as follows:

$\triangle ABC \equiv \triangle DEF$ (SAS)

> The symbol ≡ is a shorthand way of describing two triangles as congruent.

 ## Worked Example 24.4

Is the triangle $\triangle XYZ \equiv \triangle PQR$?

Solution

We must first find $|\angle P|$, as this is one of the corresponding angles.

$|\angle P| = 180° - 80° - 60°$

$\Rightarrow |\angle P| = 40°$

$|XY| = |PR|$ (9 cm)

$|\angle X| = |\angle P|$ (40°)

$|\angle Y| = |\angle R|$ (60°)

$\therefore \triangle XYZ \equiv \triangle PQR$ (ASA)

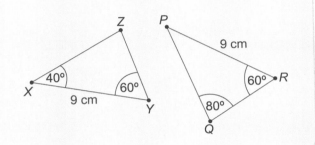

 ## Exercise 24.2

1. State whether the following triangles are congruent or not.
   Give a reason for your answer (SSS, SAS, ASA, RHS).

(i)

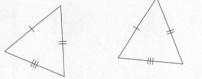

(ii)

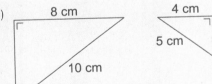

(iii)

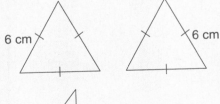

(iv)

(v)

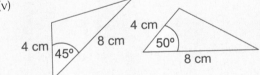

(vi)

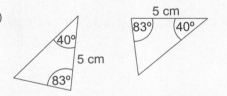

(vii)

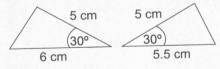

(viii)

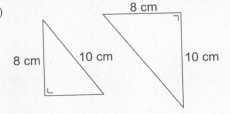

2. State whether the following pairs of triangles are congruent or not. Explain your answer fully.

(i)

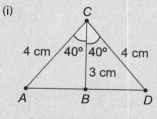

Is ΔABC ≡ ΔBCD?

(ii)

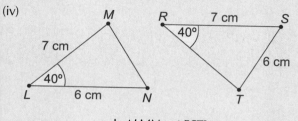

Is ΔDEF ≡ ΔXYZ?

(iii)

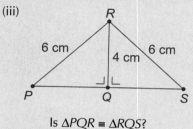

Is ΔPQR ≡ ΔRQS?

(iv)

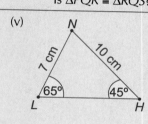

Is ΔLMN ≡ ΔRST?

(v)

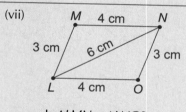

Is ΔLNH ≡ ΔABC?

(vi)

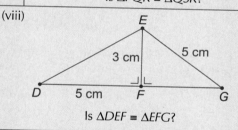

Is ΔPQR ≡ ΔQSR?

(vii)

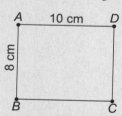

Is ΔLMN ≡ ΔLNO?

(viii)

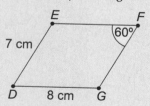

Is ΔDEF ≡ ΔEFG?

3. ABCD is a rectangle.

(i) Write down |CD| and |BC|.

(ii) Join B to D.

What name do we give to [BD]?

(iii) Say why the triangle ABD is congruent to the triangle BDC.

4. DEFG is a parallelogram.

(i) Write down |EF| and |FG|.

(ii) What is |∠EDG|?

(iii) Join E to G.

(iv) Show that ΔEDG ≡ ΔEFG.

5. In the following diagram, AB ∥ CD.

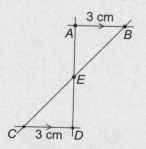

Show that triangle ABE is congruent to the triangle CDE.

24.3 THE THEOREM OF PYTHAGORAS

Pythagoras of Samos was a Greek philosopher and mathematician who lived in the sixth century BC. He is famous for the theorem that bears his name, although we cannot be sure that he himself discovered it. Pythagoras and his followers believed that numbers were the ultimate reality – for example, they believed that the number 10 was sacred. They also observed many strange rules based on Pythagoras' beliefs, including a rule that forbade them to eat beans!

This image shows Pythagoras using a stick to draw a proof of his theorem in the sand.

The theorem of Pythagoras is based on the properties of a right-angled triangle.

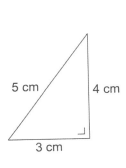

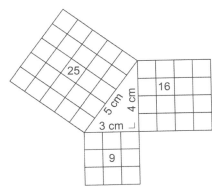

In the right-angled triangle shown on the left, we can see that $5^2 = 25$ and that $3^2 + 4^2$ is also equal to 25.

ACTIVITY 24.5

We can show that:

Theorem 14: The theorem of Pythagoras

In a right-angled triangle, the square of the hypotenuse is the sum of the squares of the other two sides.

This leads to the famous equation:

FORMULA

$$c^2 = a^2 + b^2$$

This formula appears on page 16 of *Formulae and Tables*.

In this equation, c is the hypotenuse (the longest side and also the side opposite the right angle); a and b are the other two sides of the triangle (it does not matter which side we call a and which side we call b).

If we know that in a certain triangle the square of one side is equal to the sum of the squares of the other two sides, we can show that the triangle is a right-angled triangle.

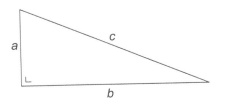

$$13^2 = 5^2 + 12^2$$

We can also show that the angle opposite the longest side is a right angle.

ACTIVITY 24.6

This then leads us to the next theorem, which is the converse of Pythagoras' theorem:

Theorem 15

If the square of one side of a triangle is the sum of the squares of the other two sides, then the angle opposite the first side is a right angle.

 Worked Example 24.5

Find the value of $|AB|$.

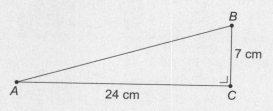

Solution

It is important to identify which side we are trying to find, i.e. the hypotenuse or another side.

Write Pythagoras' theorem.	$c^2 = a^2 + b^2$
Write down the given values.	$a = 7, b = 24$
Put these values into the equation and solve.	$c^2 = 7^2 + 24^2$
	$c^2 = 49 + 576$
	$c^2 = 625$
Find the square root.	$c = \sqrt{625}$
	$c = 25$
$\therefore |AB| = 25$ cm	

We ignore –25, as we are dealing with length.

 Worked Example 24.6

Find the value of $|XY|$.

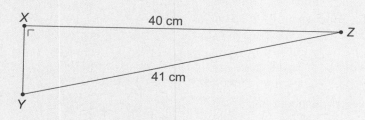

Solution

In this case, we are trying to find the length of one of the other sides (not the hypotenuse).

Write Pythagoras' theorem.	$c^2 = a^2 + b^2$
Write down the given values.	$c = 41, b = 40$
Put these values into the equation.	$41^2 = a^2 + 40^2$
	$1{,}681 = a^2 + 1{,}600$
We now put the unknown value on one side and everything else on the other side.	$1{,}681 - 1{,}600 = a^2$
	$81 = a^2$
Find the square root.	$a = \sqrt{81}$
	$a = 9$
$\therefore |XY| = 9$ cm.	

When given the hypotenuse and another side, we will always subtract the square of one from the square of the other.

Worked Example 24.7

Which of the following triangles are right-angled triangles? (Triangles are not drawn to scale.)

Triangle 1

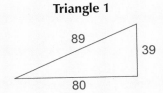

Triangle 2

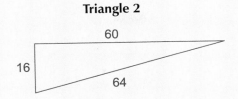

Solution

If a triangle is right-angled, then $c^2 = a^2 + b^2$.

We must first identify which side we will use as the hypotenuse. The hypotenuse is always the longest side.

Once we have identified one side as the hypotenuse, we call the two other sides a and b.

Triangle 1	Triangle 2
$c = 89$ (longest side)	$c = 64$ (longest side)
$\therefore c^2 = (89)^2 = 7{,}921$	$\therefore c^2 = (64)^2 = 4{,}096$
If the triangle is right-angled, then $a^2 + b^2$ will also be equal to 7,921: $a = 80 \rightarrow a^2 = (80)^2 = 6{,}400$ $b = 39 \rightarrow b^2 = (39)^2 = 1{,}521$	$a^2 + b^2$ should be equal to 4,096 if the triangle has a right angle: $a = 60 \rightarrow a^2 = (60)^2 = 3{,}600$ $b = 16 \rightarrow b^2 = (16)^2 = 256$
$6{,}400 + 1521 = 7{,}921$	$3{,}600 + 256 = 3{,}856$ $3{,}856 \neq 4{,}096$
$\therefore$ Triangle 1 is a right-angled triangle.	$\therefore$ Triangle 2 is **NOT** a right-angled triangle.

Exercise 24.3

1. Find the length of the hypotenuse in each of the following triangles.

(i)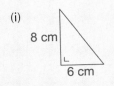

(ii)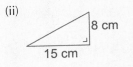

(iii)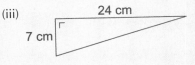

(iv)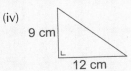

(v)

(vi)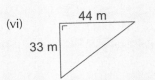

(vii)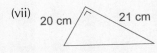

(viii)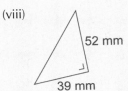

(ix)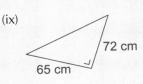

(x)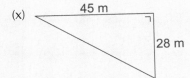

GEOMETRY III: FURTHER THEOREMS

24

2. Find the length of the unknown side in each of the following triangles.

(i)

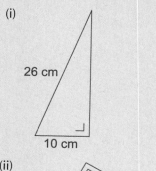

26 cm

10 cm

(ii)

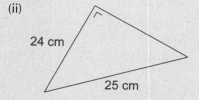

24 cm

25 cm

(iii)

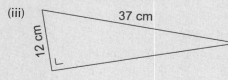

37 cm

12 cm

(iv)

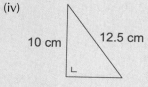

10 cm

12.5 cm

(v)

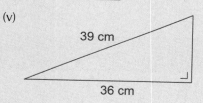

39 cm

36 cm

(vi)

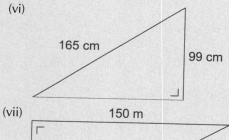

165 cm

99 cm

(vii)

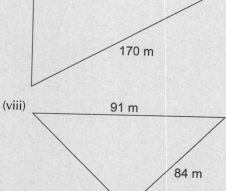

150 m

170 m

(viii)

91 m

84 m

(ix)

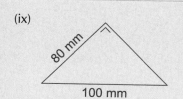

80 mm

100 mm

(x)

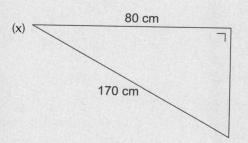

80 cm

170 cm

3. Five triangles are shown (not to scale). Which triangles are right-angled triangles?

(i)

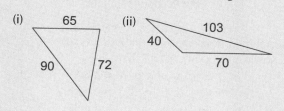

65

90   72

(ii)

103

40

70

(iii)

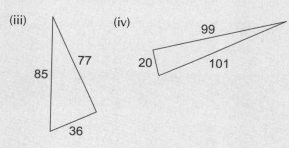

85   77

36

(iv)

99

20   101

(v)

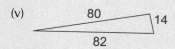

80

14

82

4. Find the length of the unknown side correct to two decimal places.

(i)

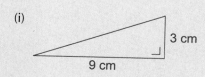

3 cm

9 cm

(ii)

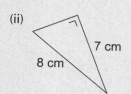

7 cm

8 cm

(iii)

2 cm   2 cm

(iv)

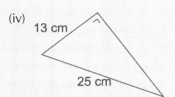

13 cm

25 cm

(v)

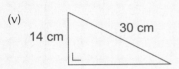

14 cm   30 cm

(vi)

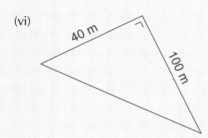

40 m

100 m

(vii)

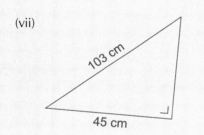

103 cm

45 cm

(viii)

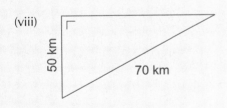

50 km   70 km

(ix)

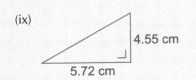

4.55 cm

5.72 cm

(x)

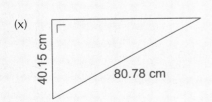

40.15 cm

80.78 cm

5. The side lengths of triangles are shown. Which lengths will form right-angled triangles?

  (i) 11, 60, 61

 (ii) 20, 24, 30

(iii) 36, 77, 80

(iv) 145, 408, 433

 (v) 115, 252, 277

6. Find unknown side lengths in each of the following triangles. Correct to two decimal places where necessary.

(i)

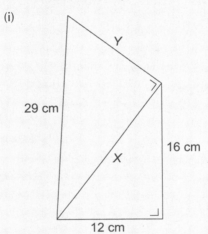

29 cm

Y

16 cm

X

12 cm

(ii)

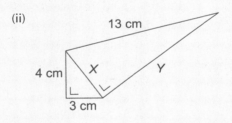

13 cm

4 cm

X   Y

3 cm

(iii)

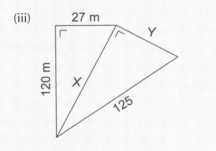

27 m

Y

120 m

X

125

(iv)

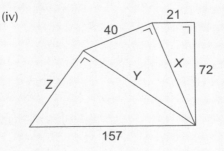

21

40

Z   Y   X   72

157

24.4 CIRCLES

A **circle** is a very common shape found in all aspects of everyday life. Can you name items in your house that are circular?

A circle is a set of points at a given radius from a fixed point, its centre.

Every single point on the circle is the same distance from the centre. This distance is called the radius length.

To understand some of the properties of circles, we must first be familiar with some terms that are commonly used:

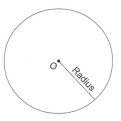

The radius is the line segment from the centre of the circle to any point on the circle. The centre of a circle is usually marked with a dot and sometimes the letter O.

The plural of radius is **radii**.

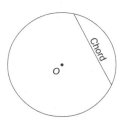

A chord is a line from one point on the circle to any other point on the circle. A chord does not have to go through the centre.

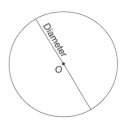

The diameter is a chord through the centre of a circle. The diameter is twice the radius.

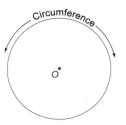

The circumference is the perimeter, or length, of the circle.

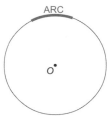

An arc is any part of the circumference, or curve, of the circle.

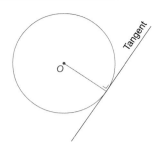

A **tangent** is a line which touches the circle at one point only.

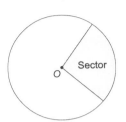

A **sector** is the area of the circle enclosed by an arc and two radii.

Properties of Circles

We can now try to discover some properties of circles. From this, we can show some corollaries based on our findings.

A **corollary** is a statement that follows readily from a previous theorem.

It is clear from our explorations of circles in Activity 24.7 that the angle opposite the diameter in a circle is a right angle, or 90°. From this, we get the following corollary:

Corollary 3

Each angle in a **semicircle** is a right angle.

A **semicircle** is half a circle whose base is its diameter.

From this corollary, we can also show another property of a circle:

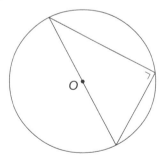

It is clear from Activity 24.8 that:

Corollary 4

If the angle standing on a chord [BC] at some point of the circle is a right angle, then [BC] is a diameter.

Corollary 3 is sometimes referred to as Thales' theorem, as it is claimed that it was discovered by the mathematician Thales of Miletus.

This corollary could be considered the converse (opposite) of Corollary 3.

Worked Example 24.8

Find |∠A| and |∠B| in the following diagram.

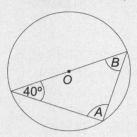

Solution

|∠A| = 90° (angle in a semicircle)

|∠B| = 180° − 90° − 40° (angles in a triangle)

∴ |∠B| = 50°

Worked Example 24.9

Without measuring, find |∠B| and |∠C|.

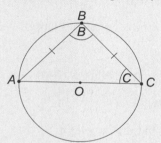

Solution

|∠B| = 90° (angle in a semicircle)

ΔABC is an isosceles triangle.

∴ |∠C| = (180° − 90°) ÷ 2

|∠C| = 45°

Worked Example 24.10

A, B and C are three points on a circle, centre O.

Find (i) |∠AOB| and (ii) |∠BCO| in the diagram shown.

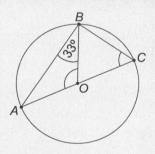

Solution

(i) |∠AOB|

Triangle AOB is an isosceles triangle as [AO] and [BO] are radii.

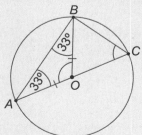

|∠OAB| and |∠OBA| are equal

⇒ |∠OAB| = 33°

∴ |∠AOB| = 180° − 33° − 33°

|∠AOB| = 114°

ACTIVE MATHS 1

(ii) $|\angle BCO|$

Triangle *BOC* is also an isosceles triangle. [*CO*] and [*BO*] are radii.

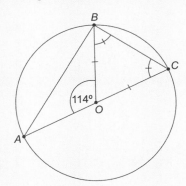

Method 1	Method 2
$|\angle BOC| = 180° - 114°$ (straight angle)	$|\angle AOB| = 114°$
$|\angle BOC| = 66°$	$|\angle OBC| + |\angle BCO| = 114°$ (exterior angle)
$|\angle BCO| = (180° - 66°) \div 2$ (isosceles triangle)	$|\angle OBC| = |\angle BCO|$ (isosceles triangle)
$|\angle BCO| = 57°$	$|\angle BCO| = 114° \div 2$
	$|\angle BCO| = 57°$

Exercise 24.4

1. In each of the following diagrams, identify and name the 90° angle. Also name the diameter of each of the circles. *O* is the centre in each case.

(i)
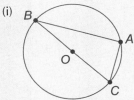

(ii)

(iii)
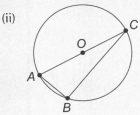

(iv)
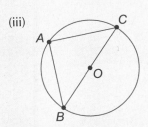

2. Find the value of $|\angle A|$ and $|\angle B|$ in each of the following diagrams. Remember to show as much work as possible. *O* is the centre in each case.

(i)
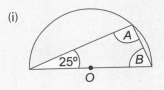

(ii)
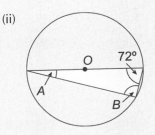

(iii)
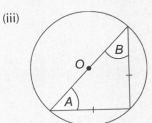

(iv)
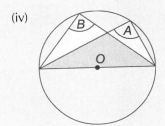

3. Find the value of $|\angle C|$ and $|\angle D|$ in each of the following diagrams. Remember to show as much work as possible. *O* is the centre in each case.

(i)
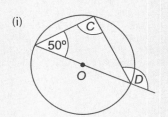

(ii)
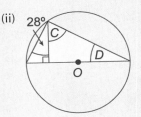

(iii)
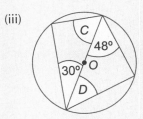

(iv)
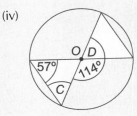

4. Find the value of $|\angle 1|$ and $|\angle 2|$ in each of the following diagrams. Remember to show as much work as possible. *O* is the centre in each case.

(i)

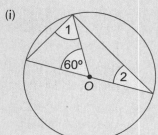

(iii)

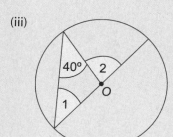

(ii)

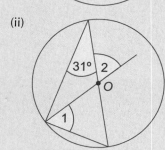

(iv)

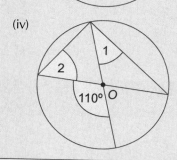

5. Consider the following circle, in which *O* is the centre of the circle.

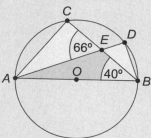

Find:

(i) $|\angle CAE|$

(ii) $|\angle DBE|$

(iii) $|\angle EAB|$

(iv) $|\angle AEB|$

Are the triangles *ACE* and *BDE* similar? Explain your answer fully.

6. Consider the following diagram, in which *O* is the centre of the circle.

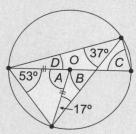

Find:

(i) $|\angle A|$

(ii) $|\angle B|$

(iii) $|\angle C|$

(iv) $|\angle D|$

7. Find the length of the diameter of the given circle in each of the following diagrams. *O* is the centre in each case.

(i)

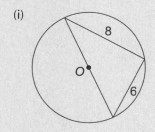

(ii)

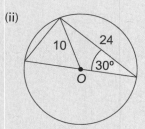

(iii)

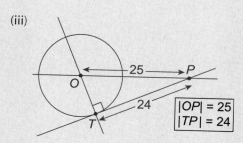

$|OP| = 25$
$|TP| = 24$

Revision Exercises

1. (a) State whether each of the following pairs of triangles are congruent or not. Explain how you reached your decision.

(i)
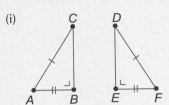

(ii)
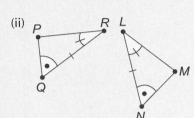

(iii)
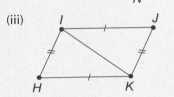

(iv)
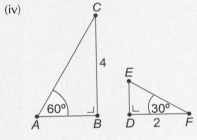

(v)
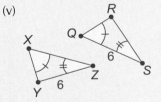

(vi)
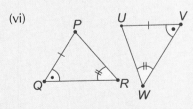

(b) Draw a line segment [AB] of length 8 cm. Using a compass, find the midpoint of the line segment [AB]. Mark this point as D.

Mark a point C that is 4 cm directly above the midpoint D, as shown on the diagram.

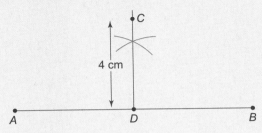

(i) Draw line segments [AC] and [BC].

(ii) Are the triangles CAD and BCD congruent? Justify your answer.

(c) The parallelogram ABCD is shown below:

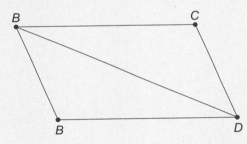

(i) Show that the two triangles formed by drawing a diagonal are congruent.

(ii) If the two triangles formed are congruent, what can we say about the area of each of the triangles?

(iii) What does this tell us that a diagonal does to the area of a parallelogram?

2. (a) Find the value of x and y in the following pairs of similar triangles.

(i)
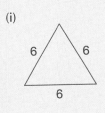
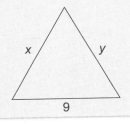

(ii)
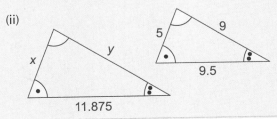

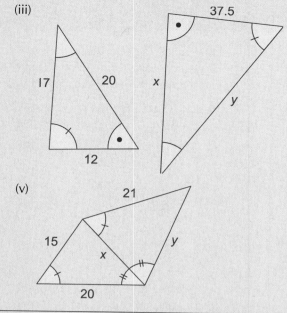 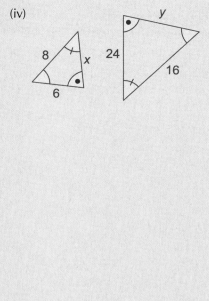

(iii) (iv)

(v)

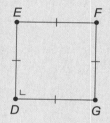

(b) Copy the following quadrilateral *DEFG* into your copybook:

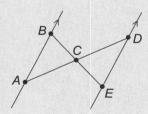

(i) What type of quadrilateral is *DEFG*?

(ii) Draw the diagonal [*EG*].

(iii) State why $\triangle EDG \equiv \triangle EFG$.

(iv) Draw the diagonal [*DF*]. Let *M* be the point of intersection of [*EG*] and [*DF*].

(v) Name three triangles congruent to $\triangle EFM$.

(c) The lines *AB* and *DE* are parallel to each other.

(i) Is $\triangle ABC$ similar to $\triangle CDE$? Explain your answer.

(ii) Is $\triangle ABC$ congruent to $\triangle CDE$? Explain your answer.

3. (a) Find the length of the unknown side in each of the following triangles:

(i)

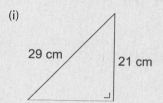

(ii)

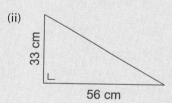

(iii)

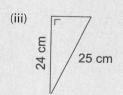

(iv)

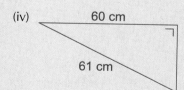

(v)

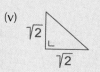

(b) An architect is given three designs for a roof. Unfortunately, some measurements are missing from the blueprints. Find the missing measurements p and q in each of the following designs.

(i) Design 1

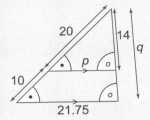

To help her calculate the missing measurements, the architect redraws the roof, dividing it into two similar triangles as shown.

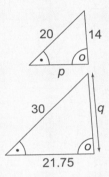

(ii) Design 2

Split into two pairs of similar triangles, and calculate p and q.

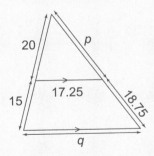

(iii) Design 3

Split into two pairs of similar triangles, and calculate p and q.

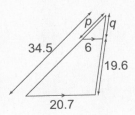

(c) A ramp is designed as follows:

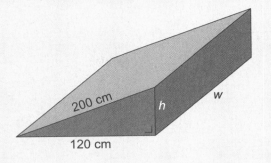

The vertical height (h) of the ramp is one-third of the width (w) of the ramp.

(i) Find the vertical height and the width of the ramp.

(ii) If 10 of these ramps are stored one on top of the other, what is the height of the smallest container in which these 10 ramps could be stored?

(iii) What is the minimum volume of this smallest container?

4. (a) Which of these triangles are right-angled triangles? Show clearly how you arrived at your answer.

(i)
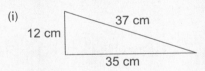

(ii)
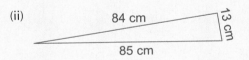

(iii)
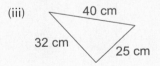

(iv)
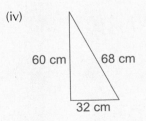

(v)
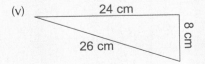

(b) In each of the following, find the lengths X and Y.

(i)
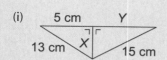

(ii)
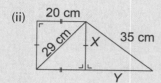

(iii)
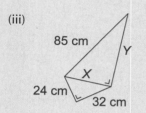

(c) A rectangular manufacturing frame made of metal bars is shown below:

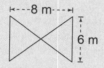

Find the total length of the metal bars required to make this shape.

5. (a) Find the value of |∠A| and |∠B| in each of the following diagrams. Show as much work as possible. O is the centre of the circle in each case.

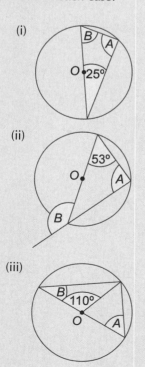

(iv)
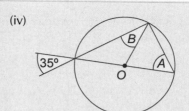

(v)
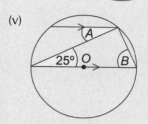

(b) Consider the following diagram, in which O is the centre of the circle.

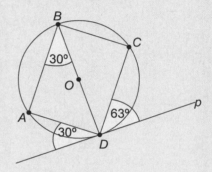

(i) Find |∠ADB| and |∠ADC|.

(ii) The line p touches the circle at the point D. What name is given to the line p?

(iii) Is the quadrilateral ABCD a parallelogram? Explain your answer.

(c) [AB] is the diameter of a circle with centre O. DO ∥ BC.

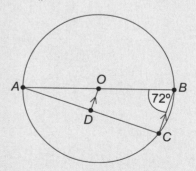

Find:

(i) |∠ACB|

(ii) |∠ADO|

(iii) |∠BOD|

(iv) |∠DAO|

6. (a) A ladder is 2 m long, as shown in the diagram.

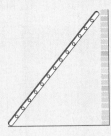

    (i) If it is set 1.6 m from the bottom of the wall, how far up the wall will it reach?

    (ii) If the ladder is moved to 1 m from the bottom of the wall, how far up will the ladder now reach? (Give your answer correct to two decimal places.)

(b) Rachel and Sarah live on roads which are at right angles to each other as shown.

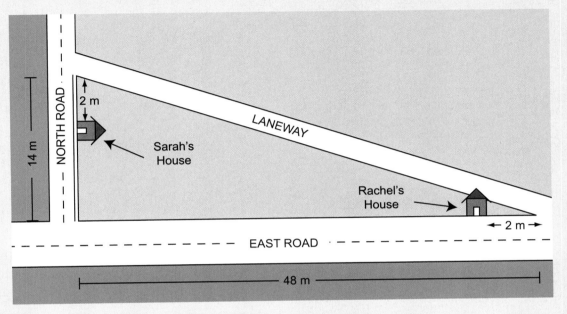

Rachel wants to walk to Sarah's house using the shortest distance.
Should she go by road or use the laneway?

(c) A design is given for a flower-bed (shaded region) in a circular lawn. C is the centre of the lawn.

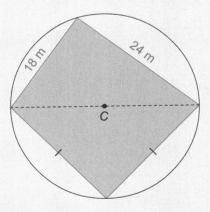

    (i) Calculate the radius of the lawn.

    (ii) It costs €9.50 per metre to build a fence around this flower-bed. Find the cost of building this fence to the nearest euro.

7. (a) The perpendicular distance between two airports and a town is shown.

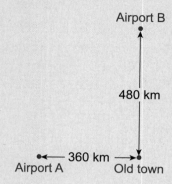

(i) What is the flight distance between the two airports?

(ii) A plane takes off at one airport at 14:15 and lands at the other airport at 16:50. Find the speed of this plane to the nearest km/hr.

(b) A square piece of land is shown.

The diagonal distance between two opposite corners of this land is 100 m.

Find the perimeter of this piece of land to the nearest metre.

(c) A design for a roof is shown.

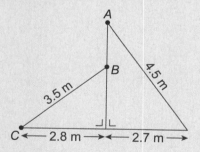

It is decided that a solar panel will be fitted between the points A and B.

(i) What is the height of the solar panel?

(ii) A cable linking the solar panel to the house will run from A to C. What is the shortest length (to the nearest centimetre) this cable can be?

8. (a) The dimensions of a television are given as the length of the diagonal of the screen.

The length and width for two television screens are given.

Calculate the dimension of each television.

(b) Three diagrams for a new sculpture are given to an engineer to construct.

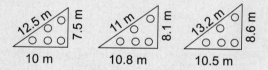

It is decided that the sculpture must **not** have a right angle. Which of the above designs meet this condition?

(c) The penalty box for a soccer pitch is shown. The penalty spot is 11 m directly from the goal line.

A penalty kick is awarded and the ball is placed on the penalty spot. The referee stands at position A and the linesman stands at position B.

How far away (to the nearest metre) is each of the officials from the ball?

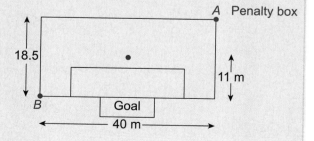

chapter 25

Constructions II

Learning Outcomes

In this chapter you will learn to construct:

- A triangle, given the lengths of three sides (SSS)
- A triangle, given SAS data
- A triangle, given ASA data
- A right-angled triangle, given the length of the hypotenuse and one other side
- A right-angled triangle, given one side and one of the acute angles (several cases)
- A rectangle, given side lengths

25.1 CONSTRUCTING TRIANGLES AND RECTANGLES

In this chapter we deal with constructing triangles and rectangles. These constructions use the methods we learned in Chapter 12. It is important that you are confident in these methods before you attempt the constructions in this chapter.

When dealing with more complicated constructions, it is always better to follow a certain approach before you begin the actual construction.

■ Draw a rough sketch of the shape.

■ Label the corners, or vertices.

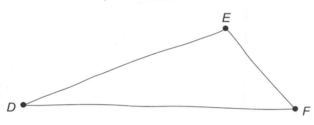

■ We put the length of the side of the triangle given in the question on the bottom of the sketch. If two sides are given, we usually put the longest side on the bottom of the sketch.

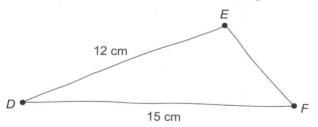

■ Fill in any other information given about the triangle.

Don't forget, when you have finished your construction, to label all the angles and side lengths that were given in the question. It is always a good idea to check that your construction has the same dimensions as given in the question.

25.2 CONSTRUCTION 10

Construct a Triangle, Given Lengths of Three Sides (SSS)

SSS means **Side, Side, Side**.

Worked Example 25.1

Construct a triangle *ABC* where |*AB*| = 6 cm, |*BC*| = 8 cm and |*AC*| = 4 cm.

Solution

1 Draw a rough sketch of the construction.

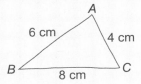

2 Using a ruler, draw the line segment [*BC*]. This will be the base of the triangle, as it is the longest side.

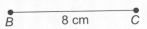

3 Next, use |*AB*| = 6 cm. Set the compass width to 6 cm.

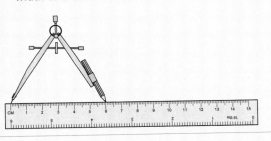

4 Using this width, place the compass point on *B* and draw an arc.

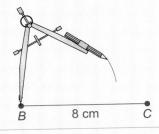

5 Now use |*AC*| = 4 cm. Set the compass width to 4 cm.

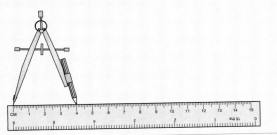

6 Using this width, place the compass point on *C* and draw an overlapping arc.

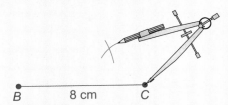

7 Label the intersection of the two arcs as point *A*.

8 Join *A* to *B* and *A* to *C*.

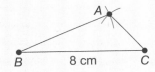

9 Fill in the remaining lengths.

The triangle is now constructed as required.

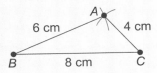

ACTIVITY 25.1

CONSTRUCTIONS II

ACTIVE MATHS 1 **409**

Exercise 25.1

Construct the following triangles. Don't forget to check to see if your construction has the correct dimensions. Diagrams are not to scale.

1. Triangle ABC where $|AB| = 8$ cm, $|BC| = 7$ cm and $|AC| = 6$ cm.

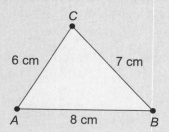

2. Triangle DEF where $|DE| = 11$ cm, $|EF| = 7$ cm and $|DF| = 10$ cm.

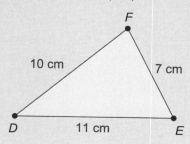

3. Triangle PQR, using the measurements as shown in the diagram.

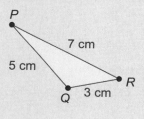

4. Triangle STU, using the measurements as shown in the diagram.

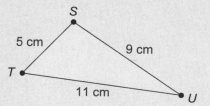

5. Triangle WVZ, using the measurements as shown in the diagram.

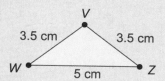

6. Triangle GHI where $|GI| = 5.5$ cm, $|GH| = 12$ cm and $|HI| = 8$ cm.

7. Triangle JKL where $|JK| = 4$ cm, $|KL| = 7$ cm and $|JL| = 8$ cm.

8. Triangle MNO where $|MN| = 7.5$ cm, $|NO| = 7.5$ cm and $|MO| = 5$ cm.

9. Triangle ABC where $|AB| = 8$ cm, $|BC| = 8$ cm and $|AC| = 8$ cm.

10. Triangle XYZ where $|XY| = 6$ cm, $|XZ| = 2|XY|$ and $|YZ| = \frac{4}{3}|XY|$.

25.3 CONSTRUCTION 11

Construct a Triangle, Given Two Sides and the Angle Between the Two Sides (SAS)

SAS means **Side, Angle, Side**.

Worked Example 25.2

Construct a triangle *EDF* having |*ED*| = 10 cm, |∠*DEF*| = 40° and |*EF*| = 7 cm.

Solution

1 Draw a rough sketch of the construction, putting the longest side as the base.

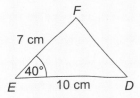

2 Using a ruler draw the line segment [*ED*] where |*ED*| = 10 cm.

3 Using a protractor, construct an angle of 40° at the point *E*.

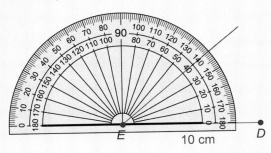

4 Set the compass width to 7 cm.

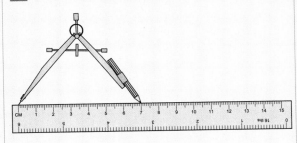

5 Using this width, place the compass point on *E* and draw an arc on the arm of the angle.

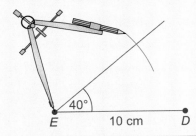

6 Mark and label this intersection as the point *F*.

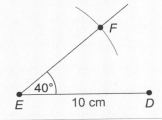

7 Join *F* to *D*.

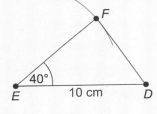

8 Fill in the remaining lengths and the angle.

The triangle is now constructed as required.

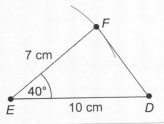

 **ACTIVITY** 25.2

Exercise 25.2

Construct the following triangles. Don't forget to check to see if your construction has the correct dimensions. Diagrams are not to scale.

1. Triangle *RST* where |*RS*| = 8 cm, |*RT*| = 6 cm and |∠*TRS*| = 30°.

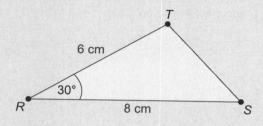

2. Triangle *XYZ* where |*XZ*| = 10 cm, |*YZ*| = 6 cm and |∠*XZY*| = 60°.

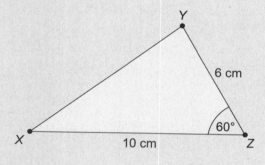

3. Triangle *ABC* where |*AB*| = 5 cm, |*AC*| = 8 cm and |∠*BAC*| = 120°.

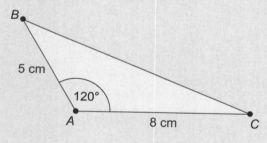

4. Triangle *DEF*, using the measurements as shown in the diagram.

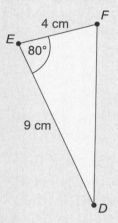

5. Triangle *GHI*, using the measurements as shown in the diagram.

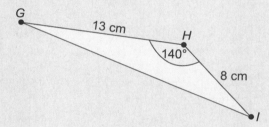

6. Triangle *JKL* where |∠*JKL*| = 35°, |*KL*| = 7 cm and |*JK*| = 9 cm.

7. Triangle *MNO* where |∠*MON*| = 105°, |*NO*| = 9 cm and |*MO*| = 7 cm.

8. Triangle *PQR* where |*QP*| = 10 cm, |*PR*| = 8 cm and |∠*QPR*| = 160°.

9. Triangle *TUV* where |*TV*| = 4.5 cm, |*UV*| = 6 cm and |∠*TVU*| = 68°.

25.4 CONSTRUCTION 12

Construct a Triangle, Given Two Angles and the Side Between the Two Angles (ASA)

ASA means **Angle, Side, Angle**.

Worked Example 25.3

Construct a triangle *ABC* where |*AB*| = 7 cm, |∠*ABC*| = 80° and |∠*BAC*| = 50°.

Solution

1 Draw a rough sketch of the construction.

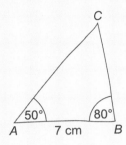

2 Using a ruler construct a horizontal line segment |*AB*| = 7 cm.

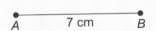

3 Using a protractor, construct an angle of 50° at the point *A*.

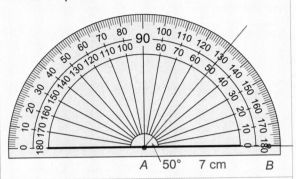

4 Using a protractor, construct an angle of 80° at the point *B*.

Mark and label the intersection of these angles' arms as the point *C*.

The triangle is now constructed as required.

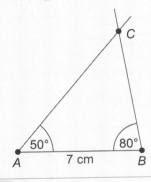

 **ACTIVITY 25.3**

 Exercise 25.3

Construct the following triangles. Diagrams are not to scale.

1. Triangle *ABC* where |∠*BAC*| = 45°, |*AC*| = 9 cm and |∠*BCA*| = 40°.

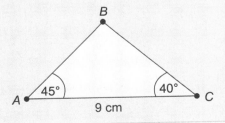

2. Triangle *GHI*, using the measurements as shown in the diagram.

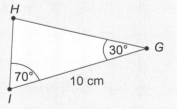

3. Triangle *DEF* where |∠*EFD*| = 40°, |∠*FDE*| = 115° and |*FD*| = 5 cm.

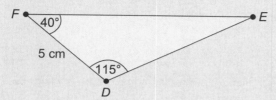

4. Triangle *JKL* where |∠*J*| = 135°, |∠*L*| = 30° and |*JL*| = 3 cm.

5. Triangle *MNO* where |∠*NMO*| = 35°, |∠*ONM*| = 85° and |*MN*| = 8 cm.

6. Triangle *PQR* where |∠*QPR*| = 120°, |*PQ*| = 5 cm and |∠*PQR*| = 40°.

7. Triangle *TUV* where |*TV*| = 5 cm, |∠*VTU*| = 40° and |∠*UVT*| = 70°.

What type of triangle is the triangle *TUV*? Give a reason for your answer.

25.5 CONSTRUCTION 13

Construct a Right-Angled Triangle, Given the Length of the Hypotenuse and One Other Side

Remember that the hypotenuse is the side opposite the right angle.

Worked Example 25.4

Construct a triangle *EDF* where |*ED*| = 8 cm, |∠*EDF*| = 90° and |*EF*| = 10 cm.

Solution

1 Make a rough sketch of the triangle. It is important to identify where the right angle is and not use the hypotenuse as the horizontal line.

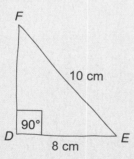

2 Using a ruler construct the horizontal line segment |*ED*| = 8 cm.

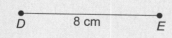

3 Using your protractor or set square, draw an angle of 90° at *D*.

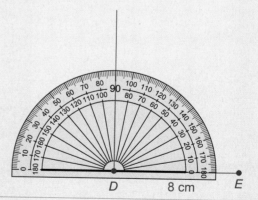

4 Set the compass width to the length of the hypotenuse: |*EF*| = 10 cm.

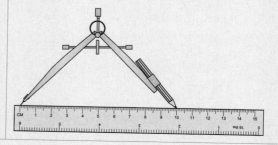

5 Using this width, place the compass point on E and draw an arc.

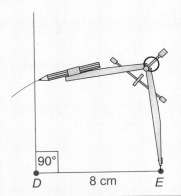

7 Using a ruler, draw a line from F to E.

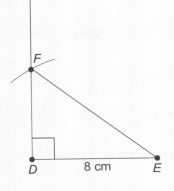

6 Mark and label where the arc meets the vertical line as point F.

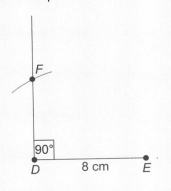

8 The triangle is now drawn as required. Label all given measurements.

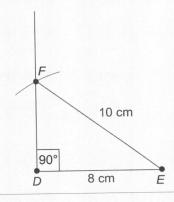

ACTIVITY 25.4

Exercise 25.4

Construct the following triangles. Diagrams are not to scale.

1. Triangle ABC where $|\angle ABC| = 90°$, $|AC| = 9$ cm and $|AB| = 7$ cm.

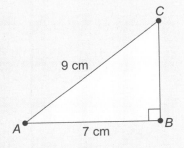

2. The triangle DEF where $|\angle DEF| = 90°$, $|FD| = 14$ cm and $|EF| = 11$ cm.

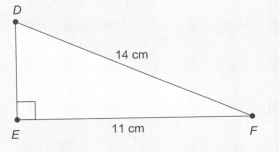

CONSTRUCTIONS II

3. The triangle *GHI*, using the measurements as shown in the diagram.

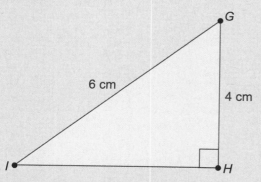

4. Triangle *JKL*, using the measurements as shown in the diagram.

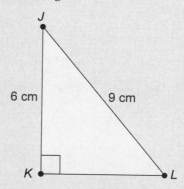

Construct the following triangles, and use Pythagoras' theorem to find the length of the side not given. (Give your answer correct to one decimal place.)

5. Triangle *MNO* where $|MN| = 6$ cm, $|\angle NOM| = 90°$ and $|NO| = 3$ cm.

6. Triangle *PQR* where $|\angle QPR| = 90°$, $|RQ| = 5$ cm and $|PR| = 2$ cm.

7. Triangle *TUV* where $|TU| = 7$ cm, $|UV| = 3$ cm and $|\angle UVT| = 90°$.

8. Triangle *ABC* where $|AC| = 10$ cm, $|BC| = 9$ cm and $AB \perp BC$.

9. Triangle *XYZ* where $|XY| = 4$ cm, $|XZ| = 2|XY|$ and $XY \perp YZ$.

25.6 CONSTRUCTION 14

Construct a Right-Angled Triangle, Given One Side and One of the Acute Angles (Several Cases)

 Worked Example 25.5

Construct a triangle *ABC* where $|AB| = 8$ cm, $|\angle ABC| = 90°$ and $|\angle ACB| = 50°$.

Solution

1 Make a rough sketch of the triangle. Identify where the right angle is. Fill in all the angles.

As $|\angle ACB| = 50°$, then $|\angle BAC| = 40°$ (angles in a triangle).

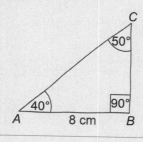

2 Using a ruler, construct the line segment $|AB| = 8$ cm.

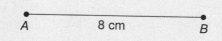

3 Using your protractor or set square, draw an angle of 90° at the point *B*.

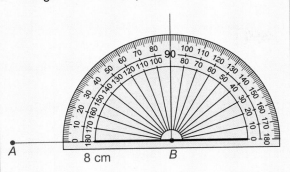

4 Using a protractor, construct an angle of 40° at the point *A*.

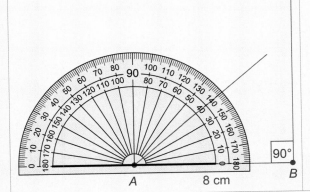

5 Mark and label where this angle's arm meets the right angle's arm as the point *C*.

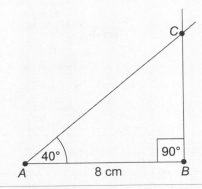

6 Fill in |∠*ACB*| = 50°.

The triangle is now constructed as required.

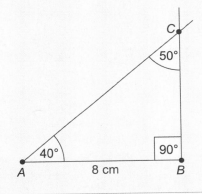

Worked Example 25.6

Construct a triangle *EDF* where |*ED*| = 6.5 cm, |∠*EFD*| = 90° and |∠*FDE*| = 70°.

This triangle is more difficult, as the only side length we are given is the hypotenuse. It is simpler to use the hypotenuse as the base of our triangle.

Solution

1 Make a rough sketch of the triangle. Identify where the right angle is. Fill in all the angles.

|∠*FED*| = 20°

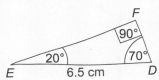

2 Using a ruler, construct the horizontal line segment. |*ED*| = 6.5 cm (hypotenuse)

CONSTRUCTIONS II

3 Using a protractor, construct an angle of 70° at the point *D*.

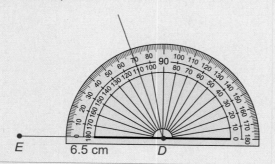

5 Mark and label where the arms of these two angles meet as point *F*.

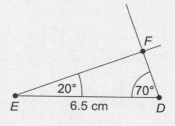

4 Using a protractor, construct an angle of 20° at the point *E*.

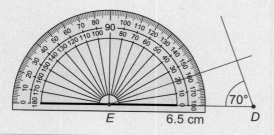

6 Fill in the remaining lengths and angles.

The triangle is now constructed as required.

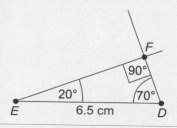

ACTIVITIES 25.5, 25.6

Exercise 25.5

Construct the following triangles. Diagrams are not to scale.

1. Triangle *ABC* where |∠*ABC*| = 90°, |*AC*| = 5 cm and |∠*BAC*| = 30°.

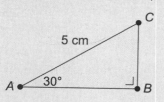

2. Triangle *DEF* where |∠*DEF*| = 55°, |∠*EFD*| = 90° and |*EF*| = 6 cm.

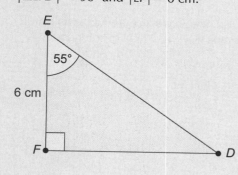

3. Triangle *GHI*, using the measurements as shown in the diagram.

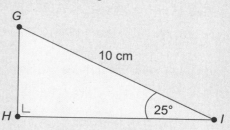

4. Triangle *JKL*, using the measurements as shown in the diagram.

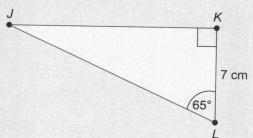

5. Triangle *MNO* where $|\angle MNO| = 90°$, $|\angle MON| = 15°$ and $|MN| = 3$ cm.

6. Triangle *PQR* where $|\angle RQP| = 45°$, $|QR| = 10$ cm and $|\angle PRQ| = 90°$.

7. Triangle *STU* where $|ST| = 7$ cm, $|\angle STU| = 80°$ and $|\angle SUT| = 90°$.

8. Triangle *XYZ* where $|XY| = 12$ cm, $|\angle XZY| = 90°$ and $|\angle ZXY| = 35°$.

9. Triangle *ABC* where $|\angle CAB| = 10°$, $|AB| = 6$ cm and $|\angle ABC| = 90°$.

25.7 CONSTRUCTION 15

Construct a Rectangle, Given Side Lengths

If you are asked to construct a rectangle, you use a protractor and a ruler.

Worked Example 25.7

Construct a rectangle *ABCD*, where $|AB| = 9$ cm and $|BC| = 4$ cm.

Solution

1 Make a rough sketch of the rectangle.

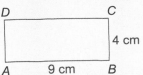

2 Draw a line *l*.

_____ *l*

3 Construct the line segment [*AB*] where $|AB| = 9$ cm.

4 Place the centre of the protractor on the point *A* and draw a 90° angle.

You could also use a set square here.

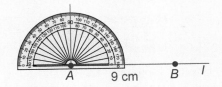

5 Using your compass, mark a point on this line at the given distance from *A* (4 cm). Label this point *D*.

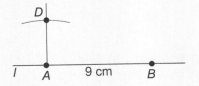

6 Place the centre of the protractor on the point *B* and draw a 90° angle.

You could also use a set square here.

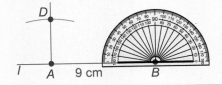

7 Using your compass, mark a point on this line at the given distance from *B* (4 cm). Label this point *C*.

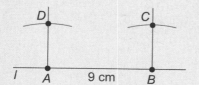

8 Join *C* to *D*. Label all given measurements.

The rectangle *ABCD* is now drawn.

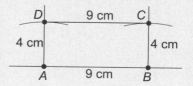

ACTIVITIES 25.7, 25.8

Exercise 25.6

Construct the following quadrilaterals:

1. Rectangle *ABCD* where $|AB| = 7$ cm and $|BC| = 4$ cm.

2. Rectangle *EFGH* where $|EF| = 8$ cm and $|FG| = 5$ cm.

3. Square *IJKL* where $|IJ| = 6$ cm.

4. Rectangle *MNOP* where $|MN| = 7$ cm and $|NO| = 10$ cm.

5. Rectangle *QRST* where $|QR| = 65$ mm and $|RS| = 35$ mm.

6. Rectangle *UVWX* where $|UV| = 8$ cm and the area of the rectangle *UVWX* is 40 cm².

7. Rectangle *ABCD* where $|AB| = 15$ cm and $|BC| = \frac{1}{3}|AB|$.

8. Square *EFGH* whose area is 100 cm².

Revision Exercises

1. (i) Construct a triangle *ABC* where $|AB| = 7$ cm, $|\angle ABC| = 40°$ and $|\angle BAC| = 40°$.

   (ii) Verify by measuring that $|AC| = |BC|$.

2. (i) Construct a triangle *PQR* where $|PQ| = 6$ cm, $|PR| = 4$ cm and $|QR| = 3$ cm.

   (ii) Measure the interior angle at each vertex of the triangle and find the sum of these angles.

3. (i) Construct an equilateral triangle *MNO* of side 5 cm.

   (ii) Measure the interior angle at each vertex of the triangle.

4. (i) Construct a triangle *RST* where $|RT| = 12$ cm, $|\angle RST| = 90°$ and $|\angle STR| = 35°$.

   (ii) Find the length of the sides [RS] and [ST].

   (iii) Using your measurements, check the accuracy of your construction by using the theorem of Pythagoras. Comment on the accuracy of this method.

5. (i) Construct the triangle *XYZ* where $|XY| = 60$ mm, $|ZY| = 45$ mm and $|\angle ZYX| = 20°$.

   (ii) Measure $|XZ|$.

   (iii) Calculate the perimeter of $\triangle XYZ$.

6. (i) Construct a triangle *DEF* where $|DE| = 8$ cm, $|DF| = 6$ cm and $|\angle EDF| = 30°$.

   (ii) Construct a line perpendicular to [DE] through the point *F*.

   (iii) Explain how this line can be used to help find the area of the triangle *DEF*.

   (iv) Find the area of the triangle *DEF*.

7. (i) Construct the triangle *GHI* where |*GH*| = 8 cm, |∠*IGH*| = 40° and |∠*IHG*| = 55°.

(ii) By measuring, find the longest side and the biggest angle.

(iii) Construct the triangle *JKL* where |*KL*| = 8 cm, |*JK*| = 6 cm and |∠*JKL*| = 90°.

(iv) By measuring, find the longest side and the biggest angle.

(v) What do you notice about the longest side and the biggest angle in these two triangles?

8. (i) Construct the rectangle *ABCD* where |*AB*| = 7 cm and |*BC*| = 4 cm.

(ii) Construct the line segments [*AC*] and [*DB*].

(iii) What name can be given to the line segments [*AC*] and [*DB*]?

(iv) Using a ruler, measure [*AC*] and [*DB*]. What do you notice?

9. (i) Construct the square *PQRS* where |*PQ*| = 5 cm.

(ii) Bisect the angles ∠*SPQ* and ∠*PQR*.

(iii) Label the point of intersection of these two lines as the point *X*.

(iv) Measure all four angles at the point *X*. What do you notice about all the angles?

(v) Measure [*SX*]. What other line segments have the same length as [*SX*]?

10. (i) With the aid of the diagram below, construct the quadrilateral *ABCD*.

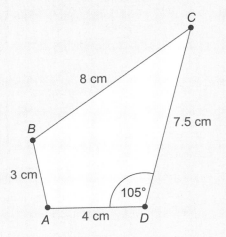

(ii) Measure all four interior angles. What do they add up to? ~~18·~~ 360°

11. (i) Draw the line segment [*DE*] where |*DE*| = 7 cm.

(ii) Using only a protractor and ruler, construct the square *DEFG*.

12. (i) Construct the triangle *ABC* where |*AC*| = 10 cm, |*AB*| = 6 cm and |∠*ABC*| = 90°.

(ii) Measure the side [*BC*].

(iii) What type of triangle is *ABC*?

(iv) Show that |*AB*|² + |*BC*|² = |*AC*|².

13. (i) Construct the triangle *MNO* where |*MN*| = 5 cm, |*MO*| = 4 cm and |*NO*| = 4 cm.

(ii) What type of triangle is the triangle *MNO*?

(iii) Find all three angles in the triangle *MNO*.

(iv) Construct the triangle *RST* where |*RS*| = 10 cm, |*RT*| = 8 cm and |*ST*| = 8 cm.

(v) Find all three angles in the triangle *RST*.

(vi) What do you notice about the angles in the triangles *MNO* and *RST*?

14. A blueprint for the roof of a house is shown below.

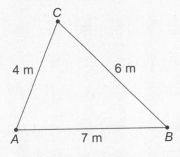

(i) Construct a drawing of △*ABC*, using 1 cm for every metre.

(ii) Use your construction to find the height of the roof in metres (to one decimal place).

15. (i) Construct the triangle *XYZ* where |*XY*| = 8.5 cm, |*YZ*| = 7.5 cm and |∠*XYZ*| = 90°.

(ii) Construct the perpendicular bisector of [*XZ*]. Use this line to mark the midpoint of [*XZ*] as *A*.

(iii) Draw a circle using point *A* as the centre of the circle, with a radius of |*AX*|.

(iv) What name could we now give [*XZ*]?

16. (i) Construct the triangle *DEF* where |*DE*| = 6.5 cm, |*DF*| = 4.5 cm and |∠*FDE*| = 55°.

(ii) Construct the perpendicular bisector of [*DE*].

(iii) Construct the perpendicular bisector of [*DF*].

(iv) Label the point of intersection of the bisectors as *X*.

(v) Draw a circle, with centre *X* and with radius length equal to |*DX*|.

17. A construction company is asked to build a bridge. This bridge consists of nine triangles, the design of one of which is shown.

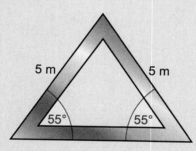

(i) Using a scale of 1 cm : 1 m, construct the triangle shown.

(ii) Using your drawing, calculate the length of this bridge to the nearest metre.

18. A bracket for a hanging basket is shown. By constructing the triangle shown, calculate how far the chain is from the wall to the nearest millimetre.

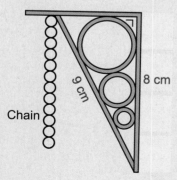

19. A garden is being designed as shown. The garden consists of a smaller square inside a bigger square. The four triangular corners of the garden will be raised flower beds.

The midpoints of the larger sides of the square, *A*, *B*, *C* and *D*, are to be used to draw the smaller square.

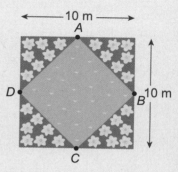

(i) Using a scale of 1 cm : 1 m, reproduce this design.

Using your construction:

(ii) Find the sides of the smaller square, to the nearest centimetre.

(iii) Calculate the area of the smaller square, to the nearest m².

(iv) Calculate the area of one of the triangular flower beds.

20. A map showing the road distances between three towns is shown.

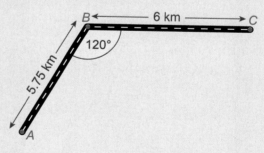

A new road is planned to bypass Town *B* and connect Town *A* directly to Town *C*.

(i) Using an appropriate scale, construct a scale drawing of this map.

(ii) From your construction, calculate to the nearest kilometre how much distance will be saved by using the bypass to go from Town *A* to Town *C*.

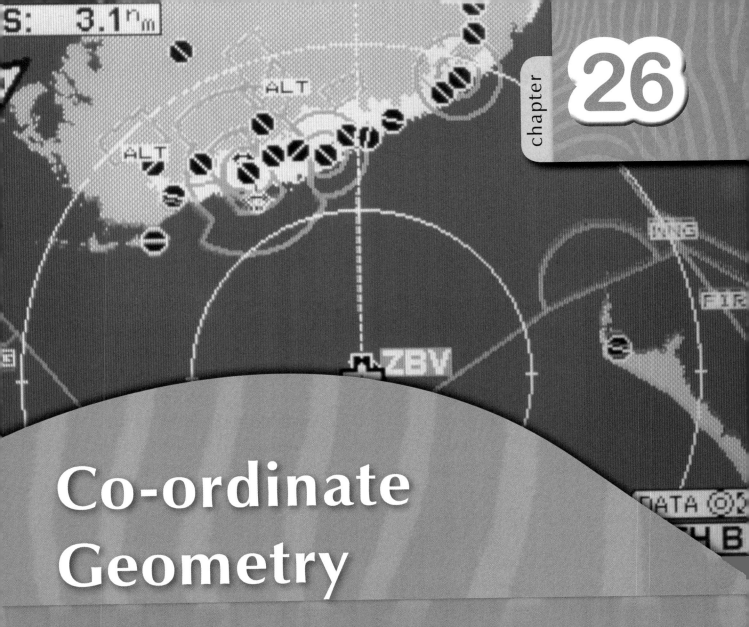

chapter 26

Co-ordinate Geometry

Learning Outcomes

In this chapter you will learn how to:

- ➲ Co-ordinate the plane
- ➲ Find the distance between two points
- ➲ Find the midpoint of two points
- ➲ Find the slope of a line
- ➲ Find the equation of a line
- ➲ Find the x-intercept and the y-intercept of a line

Co-ordinate geometry was invented by the French mathematician René Descartes (1596–1650). His work on co-ordinate geometry first appeared in 1631 in a book entitled *Discourse on Method.* Co-ordinate geometry is sometimes called Cartesian geometry in honour of Descartes.

René Descartes

The co-ordinate system invented by Descartes has many applications in everyday life, including air traffic control, global positioning systems (GPS), architecture, engineering and cartography (map-making).

For example, when you look up the location of a place on a map, it is usually given as a set of co-ordinates. The location of a ship at sea is determined by longitude and latitude, which is an application of the co-ordinate system to the curved surface of the earth. Computer graphic artists use digital co-ordinates on the screen to create computer animations.

YOU SHOULD REMEMBER...

- The theorem of Pythagoras
- How to find the area of a rectangle
- How to find the area of a triangle
- A circle is the set of all points that are a fixed distance from a given point.

KEY WORDS

- **Distance**
- **Midpoint**
- **Slope of a line**
- **Equation of a line**
- **Intercept**

26.1 CO-ORDINATING THE PLANE

In co-ordinate geometry, we refer to the two-dimensional plane on which we work as the x–y plane, or the Cartesian plane. Every point on the plane is represented by a pair of numbers. To begin, we draw a scaled horizontal line called the x-axis and a scaled vertical line called the y-axis. The x-axis and y-axis intersect at the **origin**.

The **origin** is the point where the x-axis and the y-axis intersect.

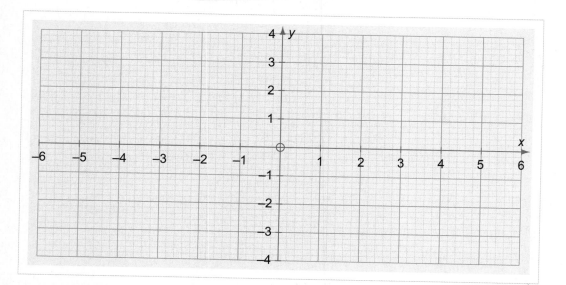

The *x*-axis and *y*-axis divide the plane into four sections called **quadrants**.

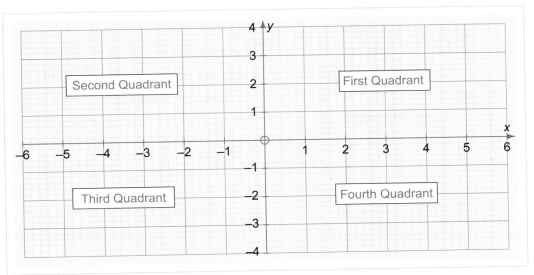

Every point on the plane is represented by a set of co-ordinates (x,y). The *x* co-ordinate is the point's position as read from the *x*-axis, and the *y* co-ordinate is the point's position as read from the *y*-axis. The co-ordinates of the origin are $(0,0)$.

Worked Example 26.1

Using graph paper, construct an *x*-axis and a *y*-axis, with *x* from −5 to 5 and *y* from −5 to 3. Now plot the following points:

$A(-1,2)$, $B(3,2)$, $C(3,-5)$, $D(-4,-1)$, $E(4,-2)$ $F(-1,-2)$, $G(0,1)$, $H(2,0)$, $I(0,-4)$, $J(-3,0)$

Solution

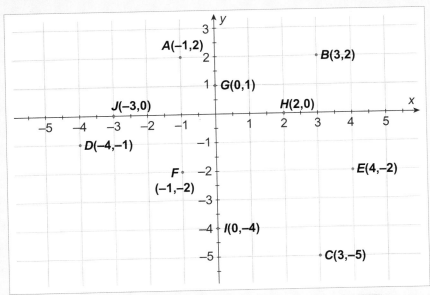

Exercise 26.1

1. Write down the co-ordinates of the points A to U shown below:

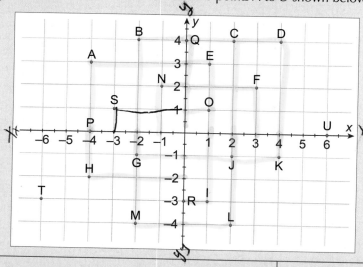

2. Using graph paper, construct an x-axis and a y-axis, with x from −5 to 5 and y from −5 to 5. Now plot the following points:

   A(1,2), B(3,4), C(5,5), D(2,−2), E(4,3)

   F(−1,2), G(−2,1), H(−4,0), I(0,−3), J(3,0)

3. Using graph paper, construct an x-axis and a y-axis, with x from −4 to 4 and y from −5 to 5. Now plot the following points:

   A(−1,3), B(−3,−4), C(2,−5), D(−3,−2), E(4,−2)

   F(−1,−2), G(0,4), H(3,0), I(0,−2), J(−1,0)

4. On which axis do the following points lie?

Point	Axis
A(0,3)	y-axis
B(−3,0)	
C(2,0)	
D(0,−2)	
E(4,0)	

5. Plot the following points and say to which quadrant each point belongs:

Point	Quadrant
V(−1,4)	Second
W(−3,−2)	
X(2,−5)	
Y(3,2)	
Z(−5,−2)	

6. Using graph paper, construct an x-axis and a y-axis, with x from −5 to 5 and y from −4 to 4. Now plot any two points in each of the following:

   (i)   First quadrant

   (ii) Second quadrant

   (iii) Third quadrant

   (iv) Fourth quadrant

7. Plot the following points:

   V(−1,3), W(4,3), X(4,−2), Y(−1,−2)

   (i)   Are these points the vertices of a square? Explain.

   (ii) Write down an angle that measures 90°.

8. Plot these four vertices of a rectangle:

   R(0,−3), S(4,−3), T(4,2), U(0,2)

   (i)   Write down the length of each side of the rectangle.

   (ii) What is the area of the rectangle?

9. Using graph paper, plot these points:

   V(−2,−3), W(−1,−1), X(0,1), Y(1,3), Z(2,5)

   What do you notice about these points?

10. Plot the triangle whose vertices are M(−4,−1), N(2,−1) and O(0,5). Hence, find the area of the triangle MNO.

26.2 DISTANCE BETWEEN TWO POINTS

A very useful measurement in co-ordinate geometry is the distance between two points, or length of a line segment. In Exercise 26.1, we used a graph to find the lengths of vertical and horizontal line segments.

> Graphs can only be used to measure distance if the two points can be joined by either a vertical or horizontal line segment.

Consider the points $A(1,1)$, $B(4,4)$ and $C(4,1)$.

Can you suggest different ways of finding $|AB|$, the distance between A and B?

 **ACTIVITY 26.2**

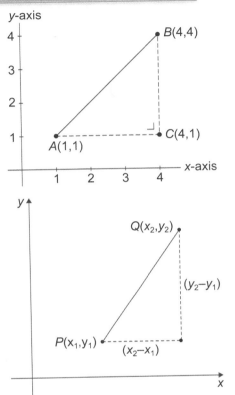

If P has co-ordinates (x_1,y_1) and Q has co-ordinates (x_2,y_2), then by the theorem of Pythagoras:

FORMULA

$$|PQ| = \sqrt{(x_2 - x_1)^2 + (y_2 - y_1)^2}$$

This formula appears on page 18 of *Formulae and Tables*.

Worked Example 26.2

Find the distance between $A(2,1)$ and $B(3,5)$.

Solution

FORMULA

$$D = \sqrt{(x_2 - x_1)^2 + (y_2 - y_1)^2}$$

$x_1 = 2$
$x_2 = 3$
$y_1 = 1$
$y_2 = 5$

$$D = \sqrt{(3 - 2)^2 + (5 - 1)^2}$$
$$= \sqrt{(1)^2 + (4)^2}$$
$$= \sqrt{1 + 16}$$
$$= \sqrt{17}$$
$$\therefore |AB| = \sqrt{17}$$

Worked Example 26.3

Find the distance between $A(-1,1)$ and $B(2,5)$.

Solution

FORMULA

$$D = \sqrt{(x_2 - x_1)^2 + (y_2 - y_1)^2}$$

$x_1 = -1$
$x_2 = 2$
$y_1 = 1$
$y_2 = 5$

$$D = \sqrt{(2 + 1)^2 + (5 - 1)^2}$$
$$= \sqrt{(3)^2 + (4)^2}$$
$$= \sqrt{9 + 16}$$
$$= \sqrt{25}$$
$$\therefore |AB| = 5$$

Exercise 26.2

1. Find the distance between the following pairs of points:

   (i)   (1,2) and (5,5)

   (ii) (1,5) and (13,10)

   (iii) (3,7) and (5,7)

   (iv) (2,2) and (2,6)

2. Find the distance between the following pairs of points:

   (i)   (−1,5) and (4,6)

   (ii) (5,−1) and (0,1)

   (iii) (6,−4) and (0,0)

   (iv) (−5,−2) and (3,−6)

3. Find |AB| in each of the following:

   (i)   A(1,2) and B(3,-4)

   (ii) A(−1,−2) and B(3,−2)

   (iii) A(5,3) and B(2,1)

   (iv) A(6,7) and B(−1,−4)

4. A(−1,2), B(−1,5), C(2,5) and D(2,2) are the vertices of the square ABCD.

   (i)   Plot the points A, B, C, and D.

   (ii) Find the length of the side [AB].

   (iii) Find the length of the diagonal [AC].

5. A(−3,−1), B(1,1), C(2,−1) and D(−2,−3) are the vertices of a parallelogram ABCD.

   (i)   Plot the points A, B, C, and D.

   (ii) Find the length of the side [AB].

   (iii) Find the length of the diagonal [AC].

   (iv) Find the length of the diagonal [BD].

6. A(0,−2), B(3,2) and C(6,6) are the co-ordinates of three points.

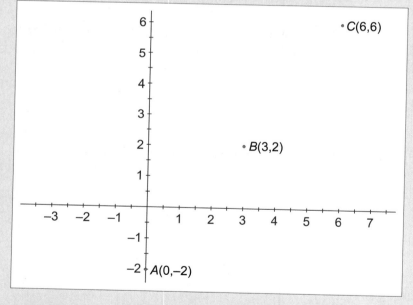

A, B and C will lie on a straight line if |AB| + |BC| = |AC|.
Show that the points A, B and C lie on a straight line.

7. A(5,0), B(−4,3) and C(4,4) are the co-ordinates of three points.

   (i)   Which of these points is furthest from the origin, (0,0)?

   (ii) On graph paper, plot the points A, B and C.

   (iii) Explain why the points A(5,0) and B(−4,3) lie on the circle of radius length 5 and with its centre at the origin, (0,0).

8. Show that the triangle with vertices $A(1,3)$, $B(2,5)$ and $C(3,2)$ is an isosceles triangle.

9. If a circle is drawn with centre $(0,0)$ and radius length 6, would the point $(5,3)$ be inside or outside the circle? Explain your answer.

10. A circle has centre $C(3,4)$, and the point $A(-1,2)$ is on its circumference.
    Calculate $|CA|$, its radius length.

11. A cow is tethered to the point $A(5,2)$ by a rope of length 6 m.

$A(5,2)$

The base of the barn door is at the point $B(0,5)$. Is it possible for the cow to reach the barn door? Explain your answer.

12. $A(4,-1)$, $B(1,3)$ and $C(0,1)$ are the vertices of a triangle ABC.

   (i)   Plot the triangle.

   (ii) Find the lengths of the three sides.

   (iii) Use the theorem of Pythagoras to prove that the triangle is a right-angled triangle.

26.3 MIDPOINT OF A LINE SEGMENT

The point that bisects a line segment is called the midpoint of the line segment.

Consider the points $A(1,1)$ and $B(5,4)$.

Discuss possible methods for finding the midpoint of $[AB]$.

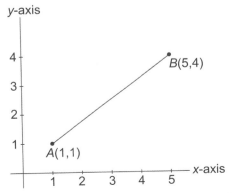

If A has co-ordinates (x_1, y_1) and B has co-ordinates (x_2, y_2), then the midpoint of the line segment $[AB]$ is

FORMULA

$$\left(\frac{x_1 + x_2}{2}, \frac{y_1 + y_2}{2}\right)$$

This formula appears on page 18 of *Formulae and Tables*.

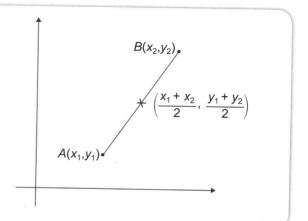

Worked Example 26.4

$A(1,-2)$ and $B(-3,4)$ are two points. Find the midpoint of $[AB]$.

Solution

$x_1 = 1$

$x_2 = -3$

$y_1 = -2$

$y_2 = 4$

FORMULA

$$\text{Midpoint} = \left(\frac{x_1 + x_2}{2}, \frac{y_1 + y_2}{2}\right)$$

Midpoint of $[AB] = \left(\dfrac{1 + (-3)}{2}, \dfrac{-2 + 4}{2}\right)$

$\qquad\qquad\qquad = \left(\dfrac{-2}{2}, \dfrac{2}{2}\right)$

$\therefore$ Midpoint $= (-1, 1)$

Worked Example 26.5

$A(1,3)$ and $C(2,5)$ are two points. Find the co-ordinates of the point B, if C is the midpoint of $[AB]$.

Solution

Let the co-ordinates of B be (x_2, y_2).

Then $\left(\dfrac{1 + x_2}{2}, \dfrac{3 + y_2}{2}\right) = (2,5)$.

A(1,3)   C(2,5)   B(x₂,y₂)

Therefore, $\qquad \dfrac{1 + x_2}{2} = 2 \qquad$ and $\qquad \dfrac{3 + y_2}{2} = 5$.

Now, cross-multiply:

$\qquad 1 + x_2 = 4 \qquad$ and $\qquad 3 + y_2 = 10$

$\qquad\qquad x_2 = 4 - 1 \qquad$ and $\qquad\qquad y_2 = 10 - 3$

$\qquad\qquad x_2 = 3 \qquad$ and $\qquad\qquad y_2 = 7$

So, the co-ordinates of B are $(3,7)$.

Exercise 26.3

1. Find the midpoints of the line segments joining the following pairs of points:

(i) (3,2) and (5,4) (iii) (3,7) and (5,9)

(ii) (1,5) and (7,3) (iv) (2,2) and (4,6)

2. Find the midpoints of the line segments joining the following pairs of points:

(i) (−1,4) and (5,6) (iii) (4,−4) and (0,0)

(ii) (4,−1) and (0,1) (iv) (−5,−2) and (3,−6)

3. Find the midpoint of [AB] in each of the following:

(i) A(1,2) and B(3,−4)

(ii) A(−1,−2) and B(3,−2)

(iii) A(5,3) and B(2,1)

(iv) A(6,7) and B(−1,−4)

4. The line k bisects the line segment [AB].

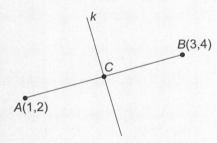

Find the co-ordinates of the point C.

5. A computer game has a buried treasure located halfway between the base of a palm tree and the corner of a large boulder.

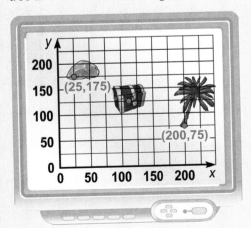

Find the co-ordinates of the buried treasure.

6. [AB] is a diameter of the circle shown below.

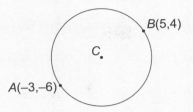

Find the co-ordinates of the centre of the circle.

7. ABCD is a parallelogram. The diagonals AC and BD bisect each other at the point E.

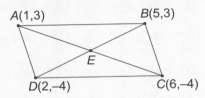

(i) Find E by getting the midpoint of [AC].

(ii) Show that E is also the midpoint of [BD].

8. A(1,3) and B(5,−7) are the co-ordinates of two points.

(i) Find M, the midpoint of [AB].

(ii) Verify that |AM| = |MB|.

9. FHKI is a rectangle.

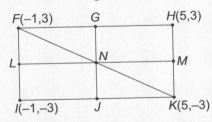

(i) Find N, the midpoint of [FK].

(ii) Find G and J, the midpoints of the midpoints [FH] and [IK], respectively.

(iii) Find L and M, the midpoints of [FI] and [HK], respectively.

(iv) Verify that N is also the midpoint of [GJ] and [LM].

10. For each of the following, find the co-ordinates of B, if C is the midpoint of [AB].

(i) A(2,2), C(3,−5) (iii) A(6,3), C(2,2)

(ii) A(−1,−2), C(4,−2) (iv) A(6,7), C(−1,−4)

11. [AB] and [DE] are diameters of the circle shown below.

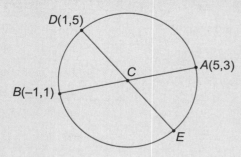

(i) Find the co-ordinates of C, the centre of the circle.

(ii) Find the co-ordinates of E, the end point of diameter [DE].

(iii) Find the length of the radius of the circle.

(iv) Find the length of the diameter of the circle.

(v) Hence, show that $\dfrac{\sqrt{40}}{\sqrt{10}} = 2$.

26.4 SLOPE OF A LINE

The slope of a line is a measure of the 'steepness' of the line. We measure the slope of a line by finding how much the line rises or falls as we move from left to right along it.

Consider the line *l* which contains the points A(1,1) and B(4,3).

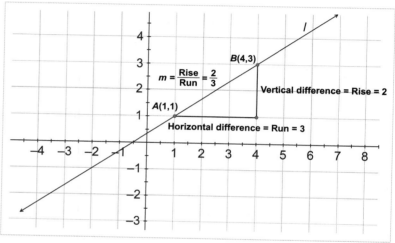

The horizontal difference between A and B is 3. We sometimes call this number the *run*. The vertical difference between A and B is 2. This number is called the *rise*.

The slope of *l* is $\dfrac{rise}{run} = \dfrac{2}{3}$. We use the letter *m* to denote slope; therefore $m = \dfrac{2}{3}$ for the line *l*.

Consider the line *k*, which contains the points C(–2,3) and D(2,1).

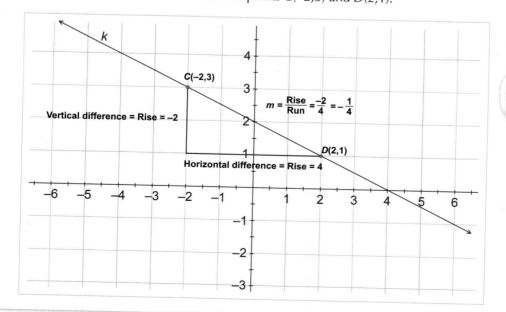

Slope = $\dfrac{\text{Rise}}{\text{Run}}$

The horizontal difference (the *run*) between C and D is 4.
The vertical difference (the *rise*) between C and D is –2.
The *rise* is negative here, as we are dropping down from C to D.

The slope of k is $m = \dfrac{rise}{run} = \dfrac{-2}{4} = -\dfrac{1}{2}$.

If A has co-ordinates (x_1, y_1) and B has co-ordinates (x_2, y_2), then the slope of the line AB is given by:

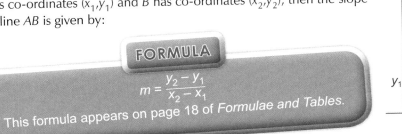

FORMULA

$$m = \frac{y_2 - y_1}{x_2 - x_1}$$

This formula appears on page 18 of *Formulae and Tables*.

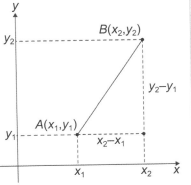

ACTIVITY 26.4

Worked Example 26.6

Find the slope of the line containing the points E(–2,4) and F(3,1).

Solution

$x_1 = -2$

$x_2 = 3$

$y_1 = 4$

$y_2 = 1$

$m = \dfrac{1 - 4}{3 + 2} = -\dfrac{3}{5}$

FORMULA

$$m = \frac{y_2 - y_1}{x_2 - x_1}$$

Exercise 26.4

1. Find the slope of the line which passes through these pairs of points:

   (i) (2,2) and (3,5)

   (ii) (1,5) and (3,1)

   (iii) (4,7) and (5,7)

   (iv) (2,2) and (3,6)

   (v) (–1,5) and (4,6)

   (vi) (5,–1) and (2,1)

2. Find the slope of the line which passes through these pairs of points:

   (i) (3,–4) and (0,0)

   (ii) (–5,–2) and (4,–6)

   (iii) A(1,2) and B(3,–4)

   (iv) A(–1,–2) and B(3,–2)

   (v) A(5,3) and B(2,–1)

   (vi) A(6,7) and B(–2,–4)

3. Find the slope of each of these lines:

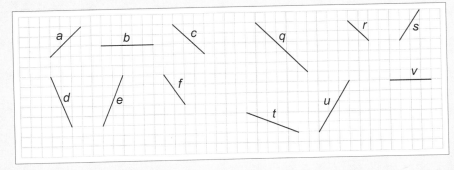

4. Using graph paper, draw lines with slopes of:

   (i) $\dfrac{2}{3}$ (ii) $\dfrac{-3}{5}$ (iii) $-\dfrac{4}{3}$ (iv) $\dfrac{1}{2}$ (v) $\dfrac{3}{4}$ (vi) -2

5. Using the same axes and scales, draw two lines with slope $\dfrac{1}{2}$. What do you notice about the two lines?

6. Using the same axes and scales, draw two lines with slope $-\dfrac{3}{2}$. What do you notice about the two lines?

7. $P(-1,3)$, $Q(6,2)$, $R(5,-1)$ and $S(-2,0)$ are four points.

   (i) Plot the quadrilateral $PQRS$ on the x–y plane.

   (ii) Prove that $PQRS$ is a parallelogram by showing that opposite sides have the same slope.

8. You are given the following points $A(1,3)$, $B(2,1)$, $C(7,2)$ and $D(6,4)$.

   (i) Plot the points.

   (ii) Verify that the slope of AB is equal to the slope of CD.

   (iii) Verify that the slope of AD is equal to the slope of BC.

   (iv) Show that $|AB| = |CD|$ and $|AD| = |BC|$.

   (v) Find M, the midpoint of $[AC]$.

   (vi) Verify that M is also the midpoint of $[BD]$.

26.5 EQUATION OF A LINE

The equation of a line gives us information on how the x co-ordinate and the y co-ordinate of every point on the line are related to each other.

For example, consider the equation $x + y = 6$. This equation tells us that, for every point on this line, the x co-ordinate added to the y co-ordinate equals 6. Therefore, points on this line would include $(0,6)$, $(6,0)$, $(1,5)$, $(5,1)$, $(2,4)$, $(4,2)$, $(7,-1)$, $(-1,7)$, and so on.

Worked Example 26.7

l is the line $3x - y = 7$.

   (i) Find three points on l.

   (ii) Sketch the line.

   (iii) Find the slope of l.

   (iv) Investigate if $(100,293)$ is on l.

Solution

   (i) To find three points on l, we randomly select values for x and y. Substitute into the given equation to find the corresponding ordinate.

$l: 3x - y = 7$

Let $x = 5$.	Let $y = 5$.	Let $x = 3$.
$3(5) - y = 7$	$3x - (5) = 7$	$3(3) - y = 7$
$15 - y = 7$	$3x - 5 = 7$	$9 - y = 7$
$-y = 7 - 15$	$3x = 7 + 5$	$-y = 7 - 9$
$-y = -8$	$3x = 12$	$-y = -2$
$y = 8$	$x = 4$	$y = 2$
$\therefore$ Point $(5,8)$	$\therefore$ Point $(4,5)$	$\therefore$ Point $(3,2)$

(ii)

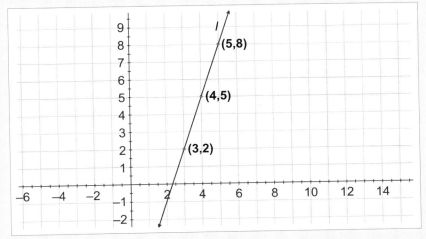

(iii) We can now use any two points on *l* to find the slope. Let us use (4,5) and (5,8).

$x_1 = 4$

$x_2 = 5$

$y_1 = 5$

$y_2 = 8$

FORMULA

$m = \dfrac{y_2 - y_1}{x_2 - x_1}$

$m = \dfrac{8 - 5}{5 - 4} = \dfrac{3}{1} = 3$

(iv) Is (100, 293) on *l*?

Substitute for *x* and *y* into *l*:

l: $3x - y = 7$

$3(100) - 293 = 7$

$300 - 293 = 7$

$7 = 7$

$\therefore$ (100,293) is on *l*.

Exercise 26.5

1. Which of these lines passes through (1,2)? Show clearly how you got your answer.

Line	Tick ✓ or ✗
$2x + y = 4$	✓
$x + y = 3$	✓
$2x + y = 5$	✗
$x - y + 1 = 0$	✓
$3x + y = 6$	✗

2. Which of these lines passes through the point (−1,3)? Show clearly how you got your answer.

Line	Tick ✓ or ✗
$x + y = 2$	✓
$3x + y = 0$	✓
$2x + y = 4$	✗
$3000x + 1000y = 0$	✓
$x - y = 4$	

3. In each case below, find four points on the line and then sketch the line.

   (i) $x + y = 5$ (ii) $x + y = 7$

 (iii) $x - y = 2$ (iv) $2x + y = 7$

  (v) $3x + y = 10$ (vi) $x + 2y = 6$

 (vii) $x + 3y = 9$ (viii) $x - y = 7$

4. The line $5x - 7y - 11 = 0$ contains only one of the following points: (−5,−2), (2,0), (5,2) and (8,4). Which one of the points is on the line? Justify your answer.

5. The line $4x - 5y = 7$ contains only three of the following points: (3,1), (−7,−7), (−1,−2) and (8,5). Which of the points is **not** on the line? Justify your answer.

6. *l* is the line $2x - y = 8$.

  (i) Find three points on *l*.

 (ii) Sketch the line.

(iii) Find the slope of *l*.

(iv) Investigate if (50,92) is on *l*.

7. k is the line $x + 3y = 6$.

   (i) Find three points on k.

   (ii) Sketch the line.

   (iii) Find the slope of k.

   (iv) Investigate if $(-54, 20)$ is on k.

8. j is the line $x - y = 8$.

   (i) Find three points on j.

   (ii) Sketch the line.

   (iii) Find the slope of j.

   (iv) Investigate if $(50, 43)$ is on j.

9. $(4, -1)$ is on the line $4x + 3y = k$. Find the value of k.

10. $(-2, 5)$ is on the line $2x - y + k = 0$. Find the value of k.

11. $(2, -1)$ is on the line $5x + 3y = c$. Find the value of c.

12. The point $(k, 3)$ is on the line $3x + y = 15$. Find the value of k.

13. The point $(c, -4)$ is on the line $2x + y = 10$. Find the value of c.

26.6 EQUATIONS OF THE FORM $y = mx + c$

Many equations that model or represent real-life situations are of the form $y = mx + c$.

For example, the equation that converts degrees Fahrenheit to degrees Celsius is:

$$y = \frac{5}{9}x - \frac{160}{9}$$

Here, x represents degrees Fahrenheit and y represents degrees Celsius.

 **ACTIVITY 26.5**

If an equation is in the form $y = mx + c$, then m is the slope of the line and c is the y-intercept (the point where the line intersects the y-axis).

FORMULA

Equation of a line:
$$y = mx + c$$
Where m = slope and
c = y-intercept

This formula appears on page 18 of *Formulae and Tables*.

 Worked Example 26.8

l is the line $y = \frac{3}{4}x + 3$.

   (i) Write down the slope of l. $\frac{3}{4}$

   (ii) Write down the co-ordinates of the **y-intercept** of l.

   (iii) Graph the line l.

   (iv) Find the **x-intercept** of l.

The x-intercept is the point where a line crosses the x-axis; the y-intercept is where a line crosses the y-axis.

Solution

(i) $m = \dfrac{3}{4}$

(ii) $(0,3)$

(iii) $(0,3)$ is a point on l.

$m = \dfrac{3}{4} = \dfrac{\text{Rise}}{\text{Run}}$

Start at $(0,3)$, rise 3 and run 4. This gives us a second point on l, $(4,6)$.

(iv) The y co-ordinate of any point on the x-axis is 0.
Let $y = 0$ in the equation of l, and solve the equation to find x.

$0 = \dfrac{3}{4}x + 3$ (multiply all terms by 4)

$0 = 3x + 12$

$-12 = 3x$

$-4 = x$

$\therefore (-4,0)$ is the x-intercept.

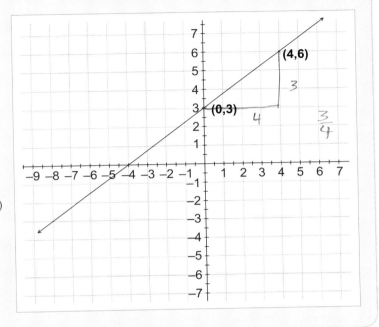

Worked Example 26.9

k is the line $3x - 4y = 12$.

(i) Find the co-ordinates of the point where k cuts the x-axis.

(ii) Find the co-ordinates of the point where k cuts the y-axis.

(iii) Hence, sketch the line k.

Solution

(i) The y co-ordinate of any point on the x-axis is 0.
Let $y = 0$ in the equation of k, and solve the equation to find x.

$3x - 4(0) = 12$

$3x = 12$

$x = \dfrac{12}{3}$

$x = 4$

$(4,0)$ are the co-ordinates of the point where k cuts the x-axis.

> x-intercept:
> Let y = 0.

(ii) The x co-ordinate of any point on the y-axis is 0.
Let $x = 0$ in the equation of k, and solve the equation to find y.

$3(0) - 4y = 12$

$-4y = 12$

$y = -\dfrac{12}{4}$

$y = -3$

$(0,-3)$ are the co-ordinates of the point where k cuts the y-axis.

> y-intercept:
> Let x = 0.

(iii)

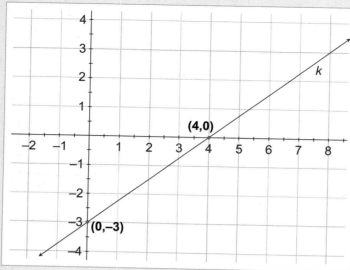

Exercise 26.6

1. Write down the slopes of the following lines:

    (i) $y = 3x + 6$

    (ii) $y = x + 2$

    (iii) $y = 4x + 5$

    (iv) $y = \frac{1}{2}x + 5$

2. Write down the slopes of the following lines:

    (i) $y = 3x - 8$

    (ii) $y = \frac{2}{3}x + 4$

    (iii) $y = -5x + 12$

    (iv) $y = -\frac{6}{5}x - 15$

3. Find the co-ordinates of the y-intercept of the following lines (i.e. the point where the lines cross the y-axis):

    (i) $y = \frac{4}{5}x + 2$

    (ii) $y = 3x - 2$

    (iii) $y = \frac{1}{2}x + 5$

    (iv) $y = -2x - \frac{1}{3}$

4. Find the co-ordinates of the y-intercept of the following lines (i.e. the point where the lines cross the y-axis).

    (i) $y = \frac{2}{3}x - 8$

    (ii) $y = 3x - 2$

    (iii) $y = \frac{5}{2}x - 9$

    (iv) $y = -3x - \frac{2}{5}$

5. Using graph paper, graph the following lines:

    (i) $y = \frac{4}{5}x + 4$

    (ii) $y = 3x - 4$

    (iii) $y = \frac{1}{2}x + 2$

    (iv) $y = -3x - \frac{1}{3}$

    (v) $y = \frac{2}{3}x - 8$

    (vi) $y = 3x - 2$

    (vii) $y = \frac{3}{2}x - 10$

    (viii) $y = 3x - \frac{2}{5}$

6. Using graph paper, graph the following lines:

    (i) $y = 3x + 1$

    (ii) $y = 2x + 3$

    Using your graph, find the co-ordinates of the point where the two lines meet.

7. Using graph paper, graph the following lines:

    (i) $y = \frac{1}{3}x + 3$

    (ii) $y = \frac{1}{4}x + 2$

    Using your graph, find the co-ordinates of the point where the two lines meet.

8. Using graph paper, graph the following lines:

    (i) $y = x + 3$

    (ii) $y = 2x$

    Using your graph, find the co-ordinates of the point where the two lines meet.

9. Find the co-ordinates of the x-intercept of the following lines:

    (i) $y = 3x + 6$

    (ii) $y = x - 2$

    (iii) $y = 4x + 8$

    (iv) $y = 5x - 15$

10. Find the co-ordinates of the y-intercept of the following lines:

    (i) $y = 2x + 6$

    (ii) $y = 2x - 2$

    (iii) $y = 4x - 8$

    (iv) $y = 3x - 15$

11. Find the co-ordinates of the x-intercept and the y-intercept for each of the following lines, and hence draw the lines:

    (i) $x + y = 6$ (iv) $3x - y = 12$

    (ii) $x + 2y = 5$ (v) $5x + 3y = 15$

    (iii) $2x + y = 4$

12. Find the co-ordinates of the x-intercept and the y-intercept for each of the following lines, and hence draw the lines:

    (i) $x + y = 4$ (iv) $3x - 4y = 12$

    (ii) $x + 5y = 5$ (v) $5x + 10y = 50$

    (iii) $2x - 4y = 4$

26.7 FINDING THE EQUATION OF A LINE

l is a line containing the point (x_1, y_1), and (x, y) is any other point on l.

Then, $m = \dfrac{y - y_1}{x - x_1}$ where m is the slope of the line l.

Now cross-multiply:

FORMULA

$$y - y_1 = m(x - x_1)$$

This formula appears on page 18 of *Formulae and Tables*.

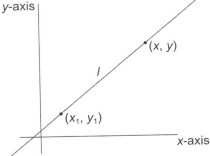

This is the equation of the line. Therefore, to find the equation of a line we need the slope of the line, m, and a point on the line, (x_1, y_1).

Worked Example 26.10

Find the equation of the line which passes throught the points $(-2,3)$ and $(3,6)$.

Solution

$x_1 = -2$

$x_2 = 3$

$y_1 = 3$

$y_2 = 6$

$m = \dfrac{y_2 - y_1}{x_2 - x_1}$

$m = \dfrac{6 - 3}{3 - (-2)}$

$m = \dfrac{3}{3 + 2}$

$m = \dfrac{3}{5}$

$m = \dfrac{3}{5}$ Point $= (-2,3)$

$y - y_1 = m(x - x_1)$

$y - 3 = \dfrac{3}{5}(x + 2)$ (Multiply across by 5)

$\therefore 5(y - 3) = 3(x + 2)$

$5y - 15 = 3x + 6$

$\therefore 3x - 5y + 21 = 0$

Exercise 26.7

1. Find the equation of the line containing the point A and with slope m:

    (i) $A(2,2);\ m = 1$ (iv) $A(4,-3);\ m = \dfrac{1}{2}$

    (ii) $A(-2,3);\ m = -1$ (v) $A(1,-7);\ m = -\dfrac{1}{3}$

    (iii) $A(5,2);\ m = -4$ (vi) $A(2,-8);\ m = -\dfrac{1}{4}$

2. Find the equations of the following lines containing the point B and with slope m:

    (i) $B(-2,2);\ m = \dfrac{1}{2}$ (iv) $B(2,3);\ m = -\dfrac{1}{2}$

    (ii) $B(-4,3);\ m = -\dfrac{4}{3}$ (v) $B(6,-7);\ m = -\dfrac{2}{5}$

    (iii) $B(-5,2);\ m = \dfrac{2}{3}$ (vi) $B(-2,6);\ m = \dfrac{2}{7}$

3. Find the equation of the line through the points A and B:

   (i) $A(1,1); B(2,2)$ (iv) $A(-1,4); B(3,-2)$

   (ii) $A(-1,3); B(2,4)$ (v) $A(1,3); B(-2,-5)$

   (iii) $A(-5,-6); B(3,4)$ (vi) $A(-3,6); B(5,-2)$

4. Find the equation of the line through the points A and B:

   (i) $A(-1,2); B(-2,3)$ (iv) $A(1,5); B(-3,-1)$

   (ii) $A(1,4); B(-2,5)$ (v) $A(-1,4); B(2,-4)$

   (iii) $A(5,-5); B(-3,5)$ (vi) $A(1,1); B(-2,-2)$

5. Find the equation of each line on this graph:

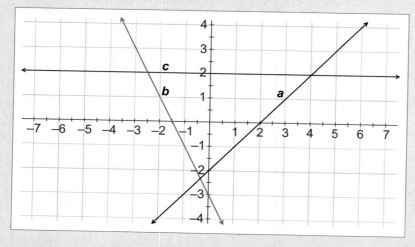

6. Find the equation of each line on this graph:

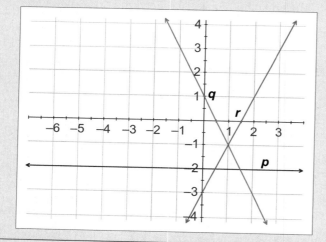

7. Plot the points A and B, and hence, write down the equation of the line containing A and B:

   (i) $A(1,1); B(1,2)$ (iv) $A(-1,4); B(3,4)$

   (ii) $A(-1,3); B(-1,4)$ (v) $A(1,3); B(-2,3)$

   (iii) $A(-5,-6); B(-5,4)$ (vi) $A(2,-2); B(-3,-2)$

8. Plot the points A and B, and hence, write down the equation of the line containing A and B:

   (i) $A(5,1); B(5,2)$ (iv) $A(1,5); B(3,5)$

   (ii) $A(-1,4); B(1,4)$ (v) $A(1,-2); B(-2,-2)$

   (iii) $A(-5,6); B(-5,3)$ (vi) $A(0,-1); B(6,-1)$

9. Find the equation of the line through the points $A(3,1)$ and $B(-5,2)$.
Show that the line contains $C(-13,3)$.

10. Find the equation of the line through the points $A(2,1)$ and $B(-1,-1)$.
Show that the line contains $C(8,5)$.

11. Find the equation of the line through $C(3,1)$ that contains the midpoint of $A(1,4)$ and $B(-5,2)$.

1. (a) Plot the points (–1,3), (5,3), (–1,–1) and (5,–1) on the co-ordinate plane below.

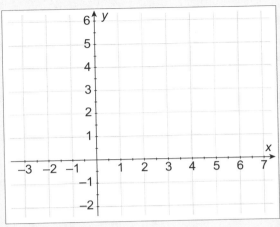

(b) Join the four points to form a shape.

(c) Name the shape.

(d) Write down two properties of that shape.

(e) On your diagram above, draw two axes of symmetry of the shape.

SEC Sample Paper, Junior Certificate, 2010

2. (a) Write down the co-ordinates of the point A and the point B on the diagram.

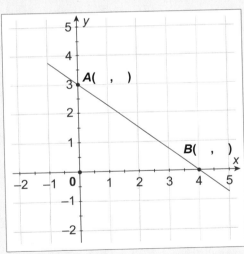

(b) Use the distance formula to find $|AB|$.

(c) Write down the distance from O to A and the distance from O to B.

(d) Use the theorem of Pythagoras to find the length of the hypotenuse of the triangle OAB.

SEC Sample Paper, Junior Certificate, 2010

3. A(1,1) and B(–3,5) are two points.

(i) Plot the two points.

(ii) Find M, the midpoint of [AB].

(iii) Verify that $|AM| = |MB|$.

(iv) Find the equation of AB.

(v) Find the co-ordinates of the point where AB cuts the x-axis.

4. $P(2,-1)$, $Q(3,6)$ and $R(-1,6)$ are three points.

    (i) Plot the three points.

    (ii) Find M, the midpoint of $[PQ]$.

    (iii) Find the slope of RM.

    (iv) Find the equation of RM.

    (v) Find the co-ordinates of the point where RM cuts the y-axis.

    (vi) Working from your graph, find the area of the triangle PQR.

5. $M(-5,1)$ and $N(2,6)$ are two points.

    (i) Plot the two points.

    (ii) Find the slope of MN.

    (iii) Find the equation of MN.

    (iv) Find the co-ordinates of the point where MN cuts the y-axis.

    (v) Hence, write the equation of MN in the form $y = mx + c$.

6. The graph below is a conversion graph between ounces and grams.

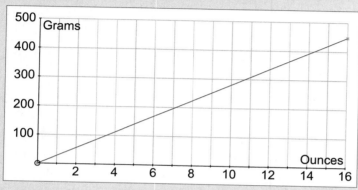

    (i) Using the graph, convert 16 ounces to grams.

    (ii) Using the graph, convert 200 grams to ounces.

    (iii) Find the slope of the line.

    (iv) Hence, write down the equation of the line in the form $y = mx$.

    (v) Use your equation to convert 50 ounces to grams. Round your answer to two decimal places.

7. l is the line $3x + y = 6$.

    (i) Verify that $(2,0)$ lies on l.

    (ii) If $(0,k)$ is a point on l, then find the value of k.

    (iii) Plot the line l.

    (iv) Find the slope of l using the slope formula.

    (v) Find the slope of l by writing the equation in the form $y = mx + c$.

8. Find the equation of the line l.

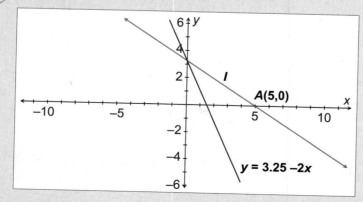

9. $P(1,3)$, $Q(2,0)$ and $R(4,4)$ are the vertices of the triangle PQR.

   (i) Plot the points P, Q and R.

   (ii) Show that $|PR| = |PQ|$.

   (iii) Find $|RQ|^2$.

   (iv) Verify that $|RQ|^2 = |PR|^2 + |PQ|^2$.

   (v) What can you say about triangle PQR?

10.

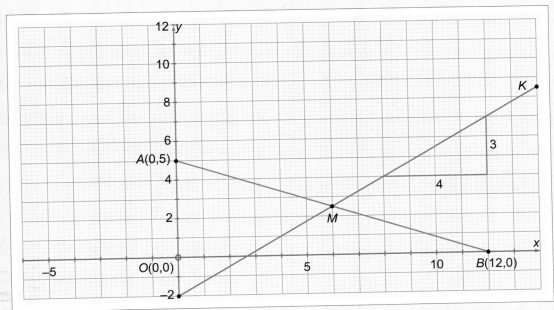

   (i) Write down $|OA|$ and $|OB|$.

   (ii) Using the theorem of Pythagoras, find $|AB|$.

   (iii) Find M, the midpoint of $[AB]$.

   (iv) Hence, find the equation of the line k.

11. A computer game shows the location of some flowers on a grid. The object of the game is to collect all the nectar from the flowers in the shortest time.

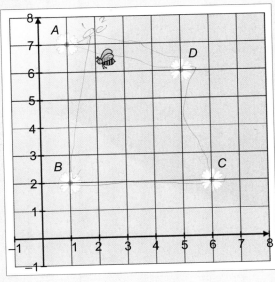

(a) A bee found a hidden flower half-way between flower B and flower D.
    Find the co-ordinates of this hidden flower.

(b) Another flower E can be located by completing the square $ABCE$.

    $E =$ _____

(c) Bee 1 and Bee 2 are on flower A. Bee 1 flies directly from flower A to B and then on to C. Bee 2 flies from flower A directly to D and then on to C.
    Write down which bee has travelled the shorter distance, giving a reason for your answer.

SEC Project Maths Paper 2 sample paper, Junior Certificate, 2011

12. Orcas Island is located in Washington State, USA. A co-ordinate grid covers the map. Each square measures 1 km². A pilot takes a group of tourists on a trip along the path marked on the map.

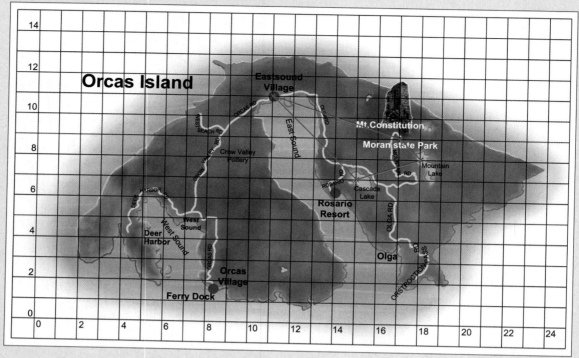

(a) Calculate the following distances (leaving your answers in surd form):

   (i) Eastsound village to Cascade Lake

   (ii) Cascade Lake to Mountain Lake

   (iii) Mountain Lake to Mount Constitution

   (iv) Mount Constitution to Eastsound Village

(b) What was the total distance, to the nearest kilometre, covered by the group?

(c) One of the group observed that the plane flew over a road midway between Cascade Lake and Mountain Lake. Use the midpoint formula to find out if this is correct.

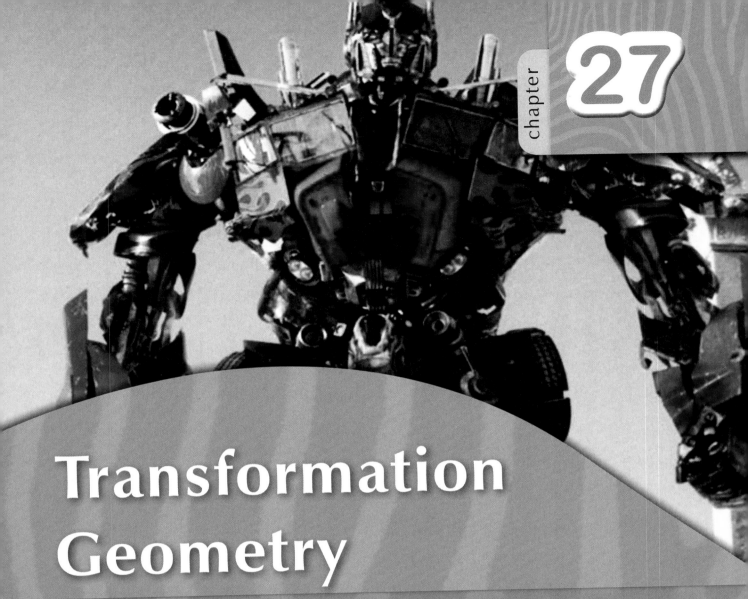

chapter 27

Transformation Geometry

Learning Outcomes

In this chapter you will learn to:

⮑ Locate the axis of symmetry

⮑ Recognise images of points and objects under different transformations

  ⮑ Translation

  ⮑ Central symmetry

  ⮑ Axial symmetry

⮑ Locate the centre of symmetry

27.1 AXIS OF SYMMETRY

What do we mean when we say that something is **symmetrical** or shows symmetry? We see examples of symmetry every day, especially in nature.

Symmetrical shapes are pleasing to the eye and are used widely in construction and engineering.

KEY WORDS

- **Symmetrical**
- **Axis of symmetry**
- **Translation**
- **Object**
- **Image**
- **Central symmetry**
- **Axial symmetry**

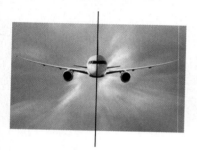

If an imaginary line can be drawn through a shape which divides the shape into two halves that are reflections or mirror images of each other, then the shape is symmetrical.

This line is called an axis of symmetry.

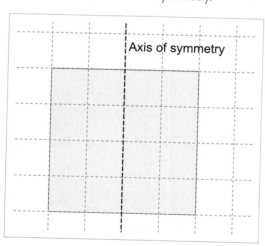

Axis of symmetry

Shapes can have more than one line of symmetry or axis of symmetry.

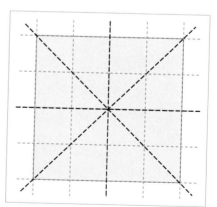

ACTIVITIES 27.1, 27.2

TRANSFORMATION GEOMETRY

Worked Example 27.1

How many axes of symmetry do the following shapes have?
Draw the axis (or axes) of symmetry of each shape.

(i)

(ii)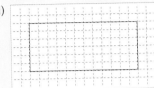

Solution

(i)

This shape has one
axis of symmetry.

(ii)

This shape has two axes of symmetry.

If a shape has only **one line of symmetry**, this is called an **axis**; if it has **two or more lines of symmetry**, these are called **axes**.

 Exercise 27.1

1. Copy these shapes into your copybook and draw in all the lines of symmetry. (Note that some shapes may not have any axis of symmetry.)

(i)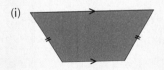

(ii)

(iii)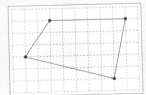

(iv)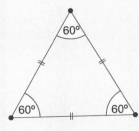

(v)

(vi)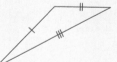

(vii)

(viii)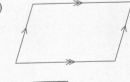

(ix)

(x)

(xi)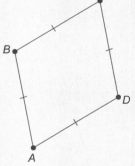

(xii)

2. Copy these shapes into your graph copy, and complete them using the line of symmetry given.

(i)
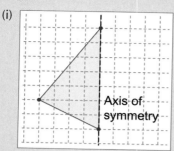

(ii)
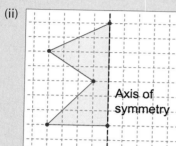

(iii)
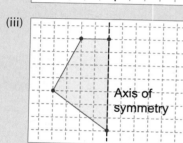

(iv)
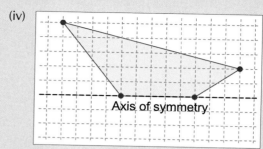

(v)
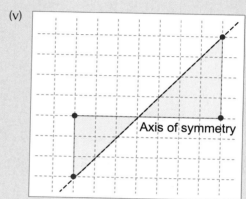

3. Copy these letters into your copybook and show every axis of symmetry. (Note that some letters may not have any axis of symmetry.)

B H D U F

27.2 TRANSFORMATIONS

In geometry, a transformation is when a shape's size or position is changed or **transformed**.

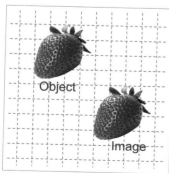

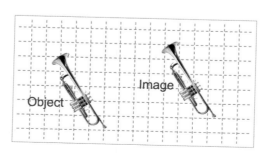

The point or shape we start with is called the **object**. The transformed shape is called the **image**.

Translation

One type of transformation is a **translation**.

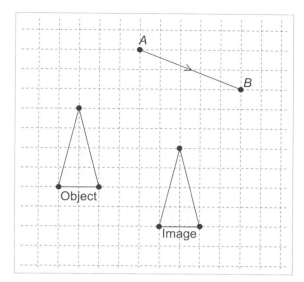

Each point in the object shape has been moved the same distance as $|AB|$, parallel to AB and in the direction of A to B.

> A **translation** is when we move a point or shape in a straight line. A translation moves every point the same distance and in the same direction.

In a translation, the image and the object are identical and face the same way.

We can move the square $ABCD$ under the translation which moves the point X to the point Y.

This can also be written as the translation $\overrightarrow{XY}$.

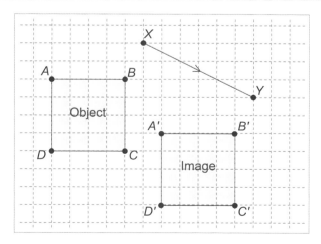

Every point on the square $ABCD$ has been moved the same distance and in the same direction as moving the point X to the point Y. The image of A is called A'.

Notice that if we moved the square *ABCD* under the translation which maps the point *Y* onto the point *X* (translation $\overrightarrow{YX}$), it would move in the opposite direction.

> The word **map** is sometimes used instead of the word **move**.

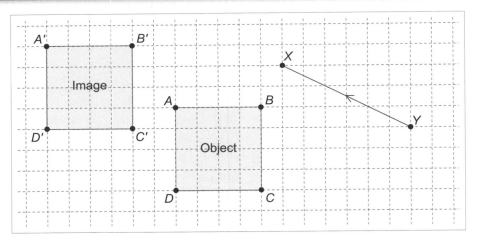

A translation may also be given by using one letter.

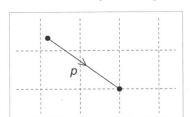

This would be the translation $\vec{p}$.

Central Symmetry

Another type of transformation is a **central symmetry** (in a point).

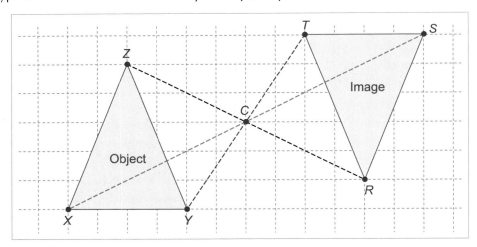

Each point is mapped through the point *C* and reflected out the other side.

Note: $|XC| = |CS|$, $|YC| = |CT|$ and $|ZC| = |CR|$.

> A central symmetry is a reflection in a point.

The point used for the central symmetry may also be part of the shape. In the diagram below, we are finding the image of *P* under a central symmetry through the point C.

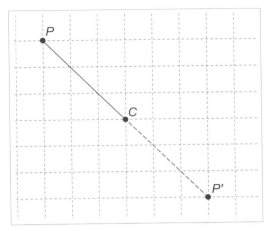

If *P* is the object to be transformed by a central symmetry, then the image can be labelled as *P'*.

In a central symmetry, the image will be upside down and facing the object.

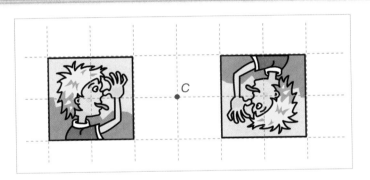

Centre of Symmetry

Certain shapes can be mapped onto themselves under a central symmetry in a point.

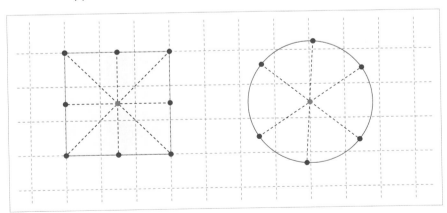

If a shape can be mapped onto itself under a central symmetry in a point, this point is called a **centre of symmetry.**

Under a central symmetry in the point C, the image of H is in the same position as the object shape H.

C is the centre of symmetry.

However, not all shapes have a centre of symmetry. For example, the triangle does not have a centre of symmetry.

Can you see why not?

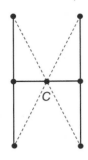

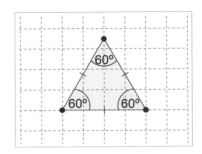

Axial Symmetry

Another type of transformation is an axial symmetry (in the x-axis or y-axis).

Axial symmetry in the y-axis

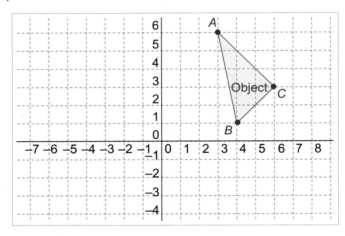

Each point is mapped through the y-axis and reflected out the same distance on the other side.

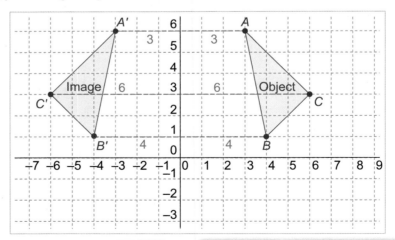

An **axial symmetry** is a reflection in a line or axis. The line acts as a mirror.

In an axial symmetry, the image and object are the same distance from the axis used and one is a mirror image of the other.

Worked Example 27.2

The following images are produced by a translation, an axial symmetry in the x-axis and a central symmetry in the point E. Match each image with the correct transformation.

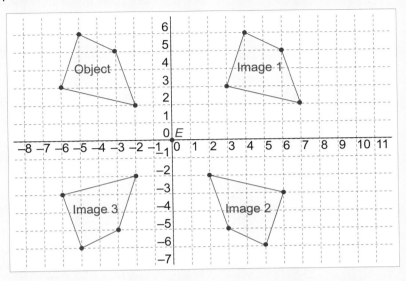

Solution

Image 1: Translation (the image is facing the same way as the object, all points are moved in a straight line, for the same distance).

Image 2: Central symmetry (the image is facing the object, each point is mapped through the point E).

Image 3: Axial symmetry in the x-axis (the image is a mirror image of the object).

Exercise 27.2

1. Identify in each diagram the image of the object under the translation $\overrightarrow{AB}$.

(i)

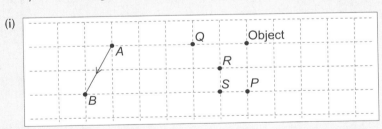

(ii)

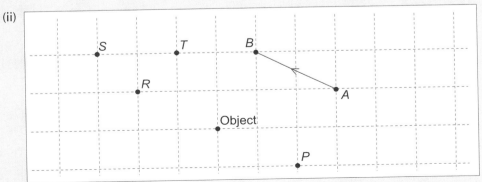

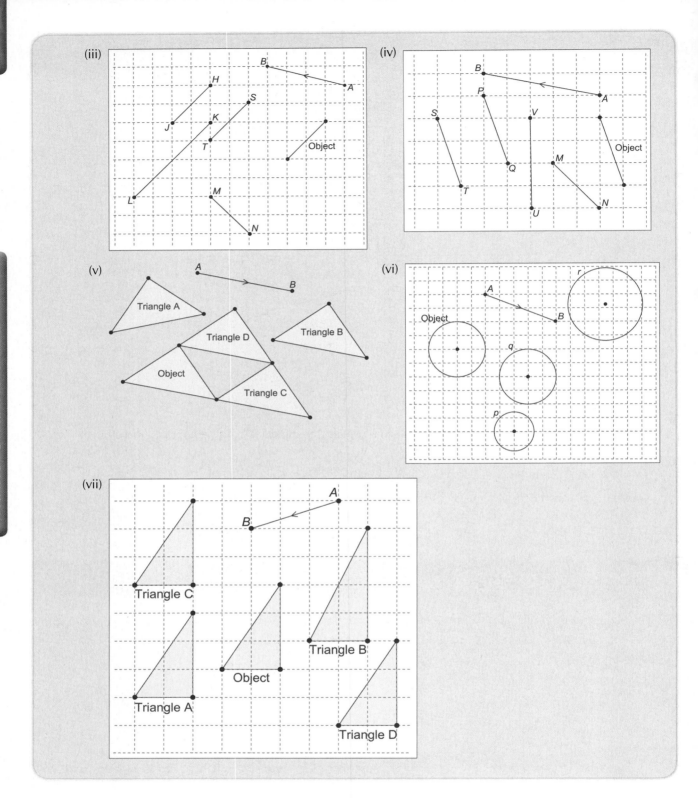

(viii)

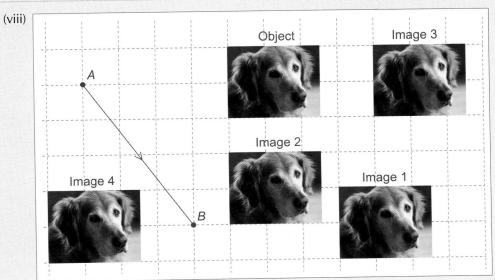

(ix)

2. Identify in each diagram the image of the object under a central symmetry in the point C.

(i)

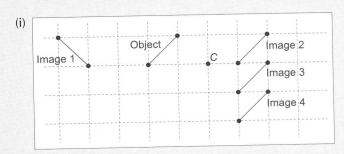

(ii)

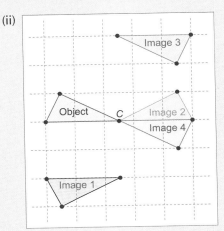

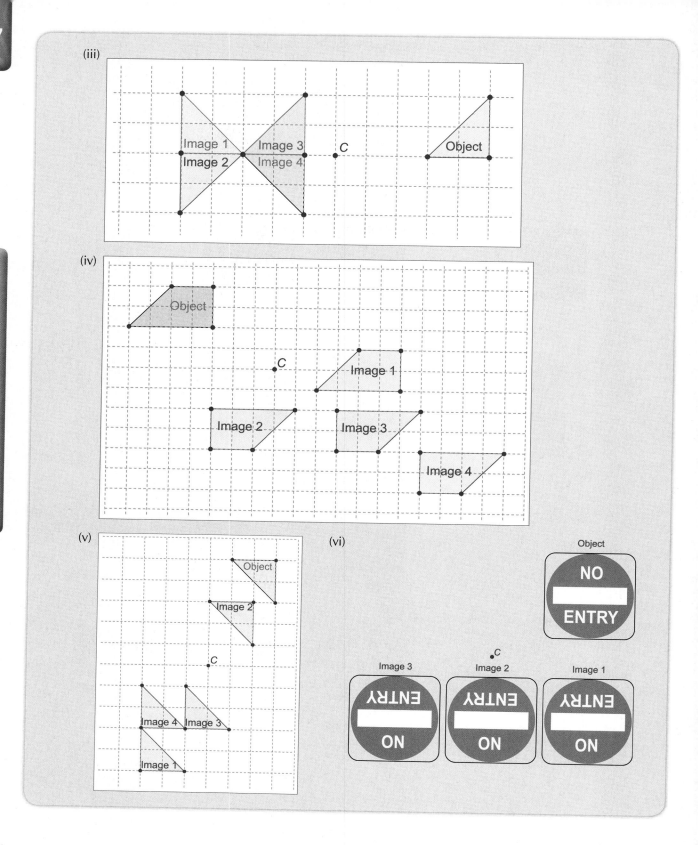

(vii)

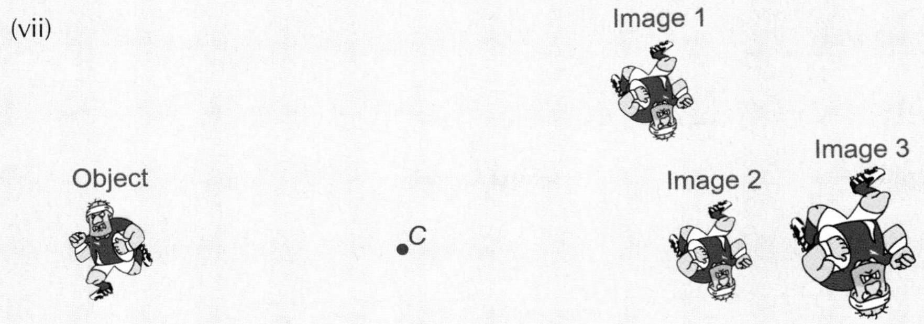

Image 1

Object

Image 2

Image 3

.C

3. In each case, show the centre of symmetry of each of these shapes, and label with the letter C. (Note that some shapes may not have a centre of symmetry.)

(i)

(ii)

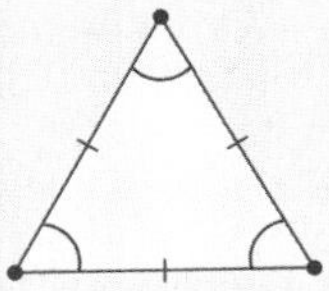

(iii) **S**

(iv) **D**

(v) **I**

(vi)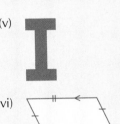

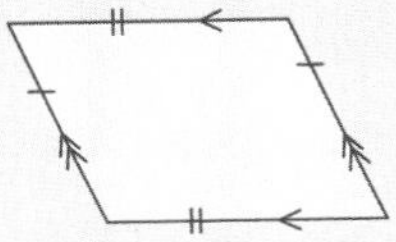

(vii)

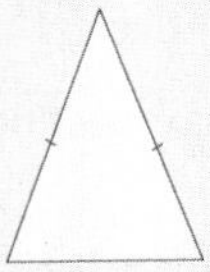

(viii) **X**

4. Fill in each box with the correct number.

(i) **A** has ☐ axes of symmetry and ☐ centres of symmetry.

(ii) **N** has ☐ axes of symmetry and ☐ centres of symmetry.

(iii)  △ has ☐ axes of symmetry and ☐ centres of symmetry.

5. Identify in each diagram the image of the object under an axial symmetry in the named axis.

(i) Axial symmetry in the *y*-axis

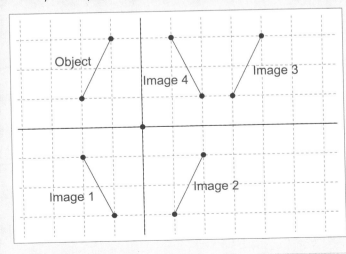

(ii) Axial symmetry in the x-axis

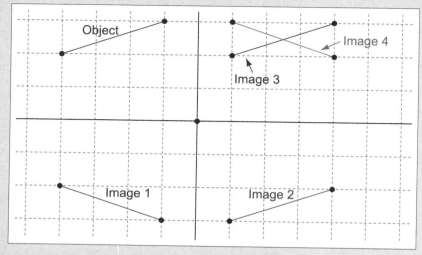

(iii) Axial symmetry in the y-axis

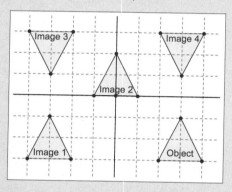

(iv) Axial symmetry in the x-axis

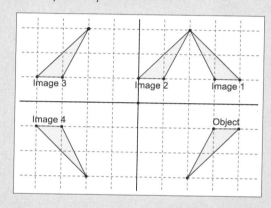

(v) Axial symmetry in the y-axis

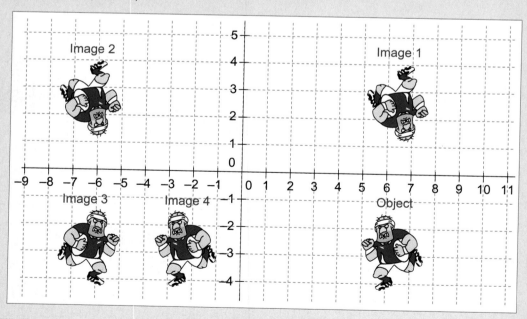

6. In each case, identify the transformation that maps:

   (i) Image A onto Image B

   (ii) Image D onto Image C

   (iii) Image A onto Image D

   (iv) Image B onto Image D

Can any of the above answers be a translation? Give a reason for your answer.

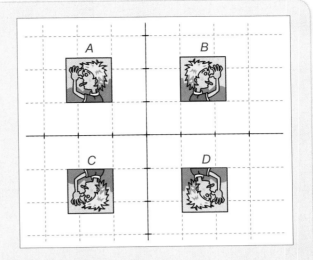

7. In each question below, three images labelled A, B and C are the images of the object under a transformation. The transformations could be a translation, an axial symmetry or a central symmetry.

For each image, state which transformation is used.

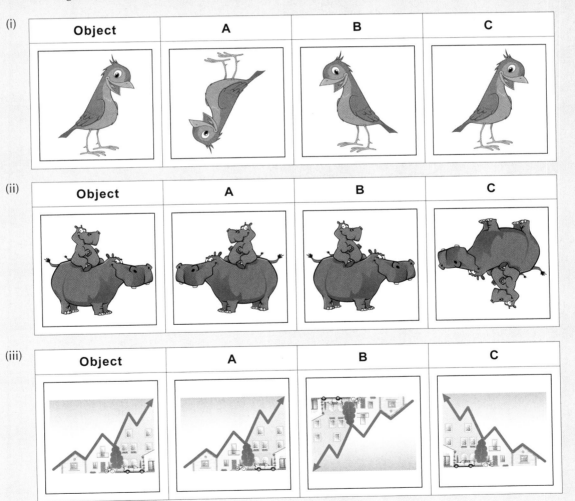

28
chapter

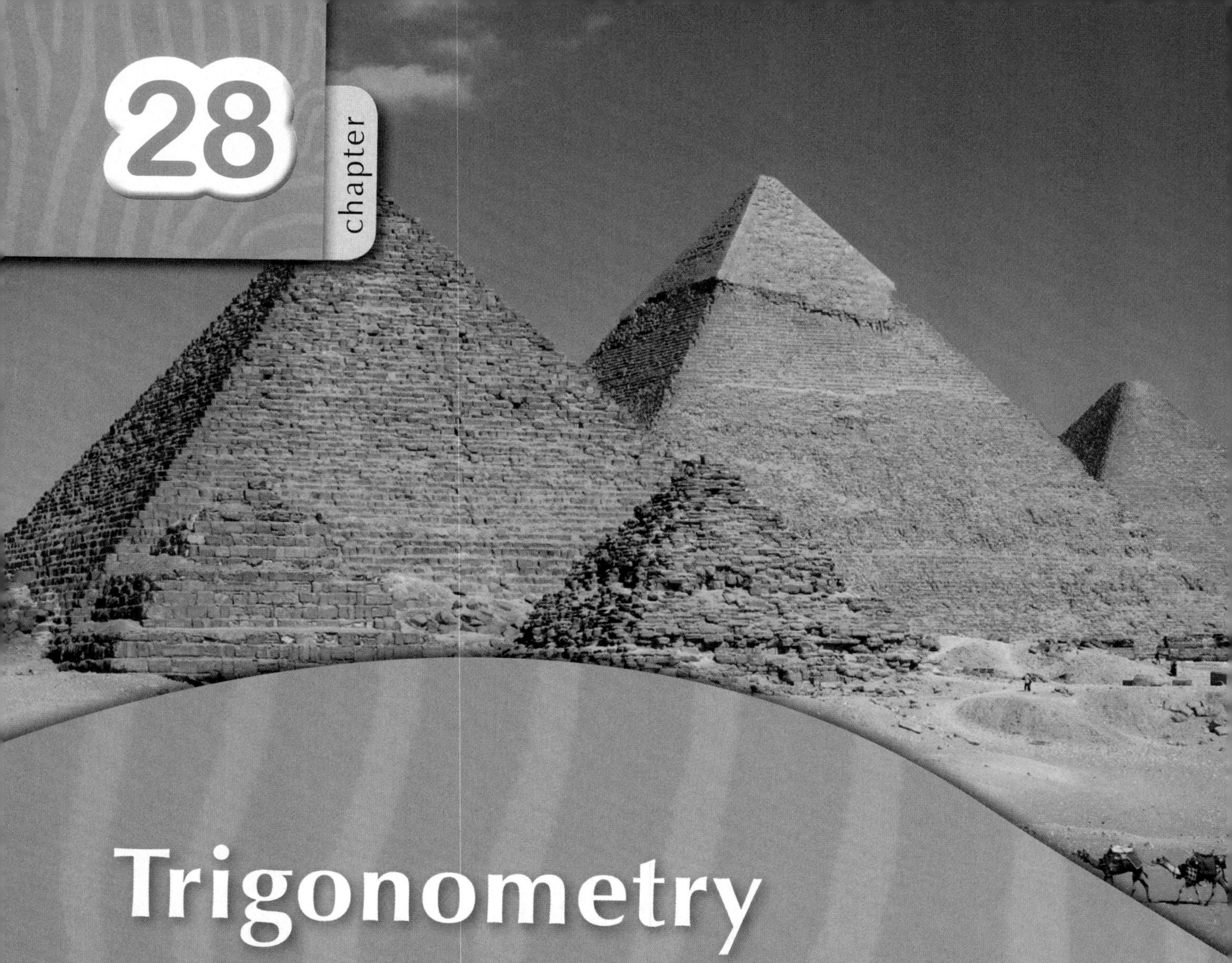

Trigonometry

Learning Outcomes

In this chapter you will learn about:

- Right-angled triangles
- The theorem of Pythagoras
- The trigonometric ratios: sin, cos and tan
- Using the trigonometric ratios to solve problems

Trigonometry is the study of triangles, their angles, areas and lengths. It has been studied since ancient times. As early as 300 BC, the Babylonians, who lived in the Middle East, had discovered how to measure angles and used this knowledge to study astronomy.

Today, trigonometry is still used by astronomers, but it is also important in many other fields: building, land surveying, economics, acoustics (the study of sound waves), seismology (the study of earth tremors) and even music theory!

TRIGONOMETRY

28.1 RIGHT-ANGLED TRIANGLES AND THE THEOREM OF PYTHAGORAS

In our course we will deal only with right-angled triangles.

The longest side in a right-angled triangle is always opposite the right angle. We call this side the **hypotenuse**. Pythagoras, an ancient Greek mathematician, studied right-angled triangles and discovered a very famous result. Today, this result is known as the **theorem of Pythagoras.**

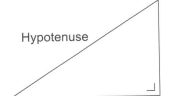

Hypotenuse

The Theorem of Pythogoras

In a right-angled triangle, the area of the square on the hypotenuse is equal to the sum of the areas of the squares on the other two sides.

When to use Pythagoras' theorem:

■ You are given two side lengths of a right-angled triangle and want to calculate the length of the third side.

■ You are given three side lengths and want to investigate if the triangle is right-angled.

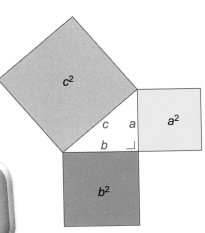

ACTIVITY 28.1

FORMULA

$c^2 = a^2 + b^2$
This formula is on page 16 of *Formulae and Tables.*

Worked Example 28.1

Use the theorem of Pythagoras to find the value of x.

Solution

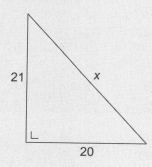

$x^2 = 21^2 + 20^2$ (Theorem of Pythagoras)

$x^2 = 441 + 400$

$x^2 = 841$

$x = \sqrt{841}$

$x = 29$

 Worked Example 28.2

A ladder is 5 m long. It is leaning against a vertical wall. The foot of the ladder is 3 m from the foot of the wall. How far up the wall does the ladder reach?

Solution

Let x be the distance from the top of the ladder to base of the wall:

$3^2 + x^2 = 5^2$ (Theorem of Pythagoras)

$9 + x^2 = 25$

$x^2 = 25 - 9$

$x^2 = 16$

$x = \sqrt{16}$

$x = 4$

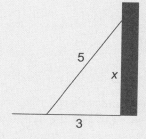

Therefore, the ladder reaches 4 m up the wall.

 Exercise 28.1

1. Find the value of x in each case.

(i)

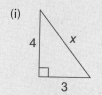

(ii)

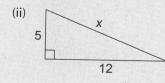

(iii)

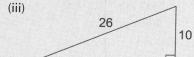

(iv)

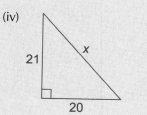

(v)

(vi)

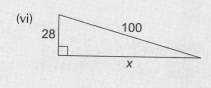

TRIGONOMETRY

2. Find the value of x in each case (leave your answers in surd form).

(i)

(ii)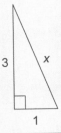

(iii)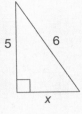

(iv)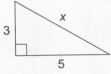

3. A ladder is 10 m long and rests against a vertical wall. The top of the ladder reaches a point on the wall which is 8 m above the ground. Find the distance from the wall to the foot of the ladder.

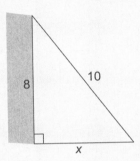

4. Use the theorem of Pythagoras to find the value of x.

(i)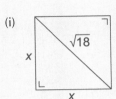

(ii)

5. Find the value of x and y in each case.

(i)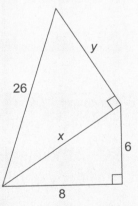

(iii)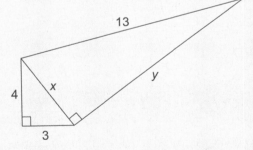

(ii)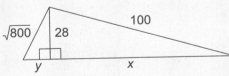

(iv)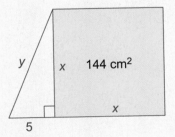

6. How long is the diagonal of a square with a side of length 4 m? Correct your answer to two decimal places.

7. A rectangle has length 80 cm. Its perimeter has length 280 cm. Find the length of a diagonal of the rectangle.

8. The sides of a triangle are of lengths 85, 77 and 36.
   By applying the theorem of Pythagoras, investigate if the triangle is right-angled.

9. The sides of a triangle are of lengths 3530, 3526 and 168.
   By applying the theorem of Pythagoras, investigate if the triangle is right-angled.

10. Health and Safety regulations state that a 5 m ladder should be placed 1.3 m from the foot of the wall. How far up the wall does the ladder reach? Give your answer to three significant figures.

28.2 RIGHT-ANGLED TRIANGLES AND THE TRIGONOMETRIC RATIOS

In a right-angled triangle we have the following special ratios:

SOH
$$\sin A = \frac{\text{opposite}}{\text{hypotenuse}}$$

CAH
$$\cos A = \frac{\text{adjacent}}{\text{hypotenuse}}$$

TOA
$$\tan A = \frac{\text{opposite}}{\text{adjacent}}$$

These ratios appear on page 16 of *Formulae and Tables*.

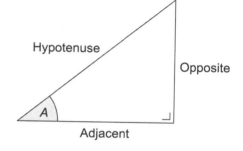

Worked Example 28.3

In the following right-angled triangle, write down the value of each of the following ratios:
sin A, cos A and tan A; also sin B, cos B and tan B.

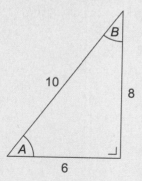

Solution

$$\sin A = \frac{8}{10} = \frac{4}{5} \qquad \sin B = \frac{6}{10} = \frac{3}{5}$$

$$\cos A = \frac{6}{10} = \frac{3}{5} \qquad \cos B = \frac{8}{10} = \frac{4}{5}$$

$$\tan A = \frac{8}{6} = \frac{4}{3} \qquad \tan B = \frac{6}{8} = \frac{3}{4}$$

Note that the hypotenuse does not change, but the opposite and adjacent do change, depending on the angle used.

Worked Example 28.4

Use your calculator to find the value of each of the following, correct to four decimal places:

(a) sin 52°   (b) cos 45°   (c) tan 22°

Solution

Make sure your calculator is in degree mode.

(a) To find sin 52°, key the following into your calculator:

= 0.788010753

= 0.7880 correct to four decimal places

> Your calculator may do these steps in a different order.

(b) To find cos 45°, key the following into your calculator:

= 0.707106781

= 0.7071 correct to four decimal places

(c) To find tan 22°, key the following into your calculator:

ACTIVITY 28.2

= 0.404026225

= 0.4040 correct to four decimal places

Exercise 28.2

1. For each of the following triangles, write down the values of sin A, cos A, and tan A:

(i)

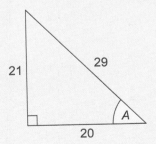

(ii)

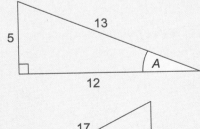

(iii)

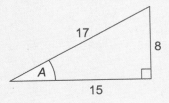

2. For each of the following triangles, write down the values of sin A, cos A, tan A, sin B, cos B and tan B:

(i)

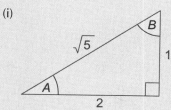

(ii)

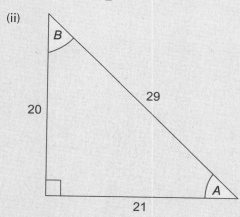

(iii)

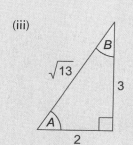

3. Use your calculator to find the value of these, correct to four decimal places:

(i) cos 15°   (vii) tan 12°

(ii) cos 30°   (viii) tan 30°

(iii) cos 75°   (ix) tan 80°

(iv) sin 14°   (x) sin 20°

(v) sin 42°   (xi) cos 66°

(vi) sin 85°   (xii) tan 44°

4. Using your calculator, find:

(i) sin 10° and cos 80°

(ii) cos 20° and sin 70°

(iii) sin 50° and cos 40°

(iv) sin 60° and cos 30°

(v) cos 75° and sin 15°

Can you spot a rule here?

5. Copy and complete these sentences:

(i) sin 25° is the same as cos…

(ii) cos 42° is the same as sin…

(iii) sin 55° is the same as cos…

(iv) cos 82° is the same as sin…

(v) cos x° is the same as sin…

28.3 FINDING THE LENGTH OF A SIDE IN A RIGHT-ANGLED TRIANGLE

In a right-angled triangle, if we know the length of just **one** side and the measure of just **one** angle (other than the right angle), then we can find the lengths of the remaining two sides.

Worked Example 28.5

Consider the triangle ABC shown below.
If $|AB| = 8$ cm and $|\angle BAC| = 35°$, then find $|BC|$ to one decimal place.

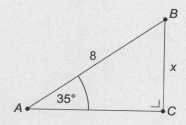

Solution

Let $|BC| = x$

$\sin 35° = \dfrac{x}{8}$

$x = 8 \sin 35°$ (cross-multiplying)

$x = 4.5886$ (calculator)

$\therefore x = 4.6$ cm (one decimal place)

Worked Example 28.6

Find (i) $|BC|$ and (ii) $|BD|$. Give your answers to two decimal places.

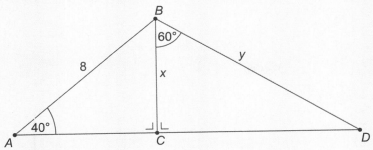

Solution

(i) Let $|BC| = x$

$\sin 40° = \dfrac{x}{8}$

$x = 8 \sin 40°$ (cross-multiplying)

$x = 5.1423$ (calculator)

$\therefore x = 5.14$ (two decimal places)

(ii) Let $|BD| = y$

$\cos 60° = \dfrac{5.14}{y}$

$y \cos 60° = 5.14$ (cross-multiplying)

$y = \dfrac{5.14}{\cos 60°}$

$\therefore y = 10.28$ (calculator)

Exercise 28.3

1. Find the value of x in the following triangles (where necessary, round to two decimal places):

(i)
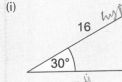

(ii)
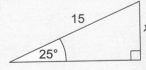

(iii)
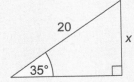

SOH
CAH
TOA

(iv)
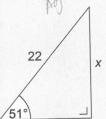

(v)
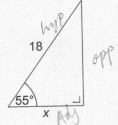

(vi)
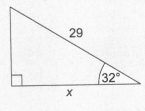

(vii)

(viii)
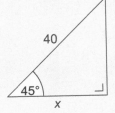

(ix)
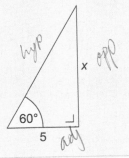

2. (a) Find the value of *y* in the following triangles.

(b) Hence, find the measures of the third side in each triangle.

Give your answers correct to two decimal places where necessary.

(i)
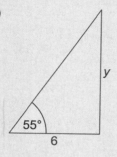

(ii)
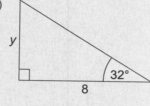

(iii)
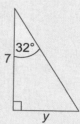

(iv)
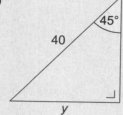

(v)
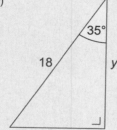

(vi)
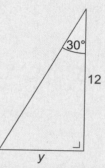

(vii)
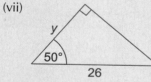

(viii)
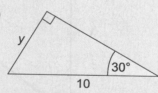

(ix)
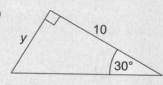

3. Solve for *x* and *y* to two decimal places.

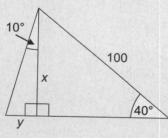

4. Solve for *x*, *y* and *z* to two significant figures.

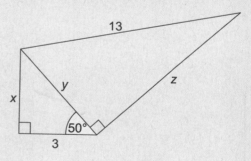

28.4 FINDING ANGLES

How can we find the measure of the angle *A*?

From the triangle we can see that $\sin A = \frac{3}{7} = 0.42857$.

We can now use the calculator to find *A*.

Key in the following:

This gives the answer 25.37684293, which is 25° to the nearest degree.

This is written as $A = \sin^{-1}\left(\frac{3}{7}\right) \approx 25°$.

Worked Example 28.7

If tan A = 0.7096, use your calculator to find the measure of the angle A to the nearest degree.

Solution

Key in the following:

(2nd F) (tan) (0.7096) (=)

This gives an answer 35.35951174, which is 35°
to the nearest degree.
This is written as $A = \tan^{-1}(0.7096) \approx 35°$.

Exercise 28.4

1. Use your calculator to find the measure of the angle X. Give your answer to the nearest degree.

   (i)   sin X = 0.3452   (v)   cos X = 0.6593   (ix)   tan X = 0.9128
   (ii) cos X = 0.7659   (vi)   tan X = 0.4678   (x)   sin X = 0.1538
   (iii) tan X = 0.5467   (vii) sin X = 0.7654   (xi)   cos X = 0.3472
   (iv) sin X = 0.4521   (viii) cos X = 0.8345   (xii) tan X = 0.4523

2. Use your calculator to find the measure of the angle X. Give your answer to the nearest degree.

   (i)   sin X = 0.2543   (v)   cos X = 0.3956   (ix)   tan X = 0.5275
   (ii) cos X = 0.9567   (vi)   tan X = 0.8764   (x)   sin X = 0.6431
   (iii) tan X = 0.7645   (vii) sin X = 0.1236
   (iv) sin X = 0.1254   (viii) cos X = 0.4376

sin x = 0.2543
x = sin⁻¹ (0.2543)

3. (a) Calculate to the nearest degree the value of the angle A.

   (b) Calculate the length of the missing side.

   (i)    (ii) 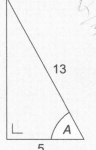   (iii)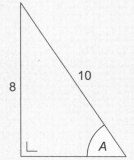

4. Calculate to the nearest degree the value of the angles A and B.

   (i) 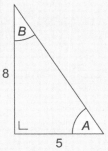   (ii) 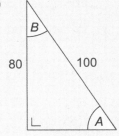   (iii)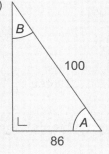

5. (a) Calculate to the nearest degree the value of the angle *A*.

(b) Calculate the length of the third side in each triangle (correct to two decimal places where necessary).

(i)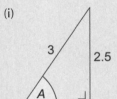

(ii)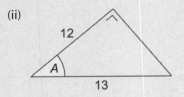

(iii)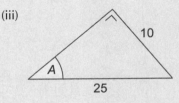

6. In the following parallelograms, calculate to the nearest degree the value of the angle *B*:

(i)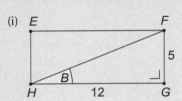

(ii)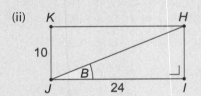

(iii)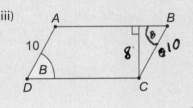

28.5 USING TRIGONOMETRY TO SOLVE PRACTICAL PROBLEMS

Angles of Elevation and Depression

If you look up at a tall building, the angle that your line of vision makes with the horizontal is called the **angle of elevation**.

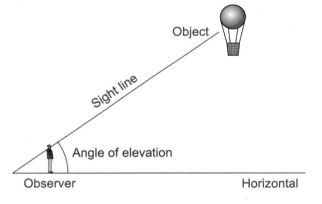

The **angle of elevation** is the angle above the horizontal.

If you stand on top of a cliff and observe a swimmer out at sea, the angle that your line of vision makes with the horizontal is called the **angle of depression**.

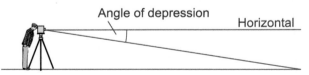

The **angle of depression** is the angle below the horizontal.

Worked Example 28.8

The Petronas Towers in Kuala Lumpur, Malaysia, are among the world's tallest buildings. Using the information given in the diagram below, calculate the height, to the nearest metre, of the towers.

Solution

Let x = height of the towers

$\tan 78° = \dfrac{x}{100}$

$x = 100 \tan 78°$

$x = 470.463$

$x = 470$ m

78°
←100 m→

Worked Example 28.9

From a point C on a cliff top a surveyor, using a clinometer, measures the angle of depression of a point B on the beach below, to be 63°. A is a point vertically below the point C. $|AB| = 7$ m. Calculate to two decimal places the height, h.

A 7 m B

Solution

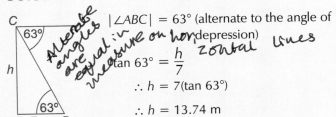

$|\angle ABC| = 63°$ (alternate to the angle of depression)

Alternate angles are equal in measure on horizontal lines

$\tan 63° = \dfrac{h}{7}$

$\therefore h = 7(\tan 63°)$

$\therefore h = 13.74$ m

C
63°
h
63°
A 7 m B

ACTIVITY 28.3

Exercise 28.5

1. A girl stands on level ground when the sun's elevation is 30°. The girl casts a shadow of length 2.94 m. Find the girl's height to the nearest centimetre.

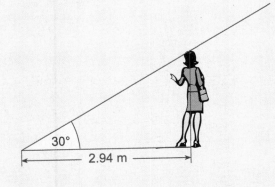

30°
← 2.94 m →

2. The Statue of Liberty pictured below is one of New York's tallest structures. Using the information given, calculate the height of the structure.

77°
10.62 m

3. A ladder rests against a vertical wall. The ladder makes an <u>angle of 60°</u> with the horizontal and reaches a point on the wall <u>4 m</u> above the ground. Find to the nearest centimetre the distance from the foot of the ladder to the wall.

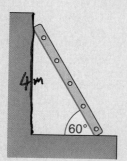

4. *P* and *Q* are two islands 32 km apart in an east–west direction. *H* is a small island between *P* and *Q*, 11 km from *P* and 21 km from *Q*.

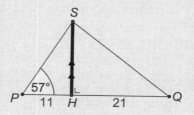

A ship sails north from *H* for two hours until it reaches a point *S*, as shown. Find (correct to one decimal place):

 (i) The distance travelled by the ship

 (ii) The speed of the ship

 (iii) The distance |SQ|

5. A plane takes off from a level runway at an angle of 10° (see diagram). Calculate the value of *x* when the nose of the plane is 20 m above the runway.

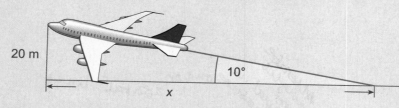

6. John is standing on a cliff top and observes a boat drifting towards the base of the cliff. He decides to call the emergency services and give them the position of the boat. He measures the angle of depression of the boat from the cliff top to be 30°, and he knows the cliff top is 200 m above sea level. How far is the boat from the base of the cliff?

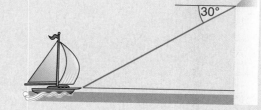

7. A vertical pole is tied to the horizontal ground by means of two wires. The longer wire is 22 m long and makes an angle of 47° with the ground. The shorter wire makes an angle of 63° with the ground. Find to the nearest metre:

 (i) The height of the pole

 (ii) The length of the shorter wire

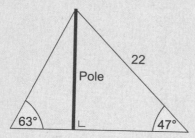

8. The Sears Tower in Chicago is one of the world's tallest structures. A tourist wishing to calculate the height of the tower makes the measurements shown in the diagram. Using these measurements, calculate the height of the tower. Using the Internet or some other source, find out the height of the tower.

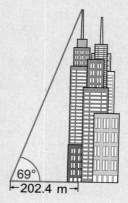

9. Alan wants to know the height of a tree in his back garden. Standing 5 m from the foot of the tree, and using a clinometer, he measures the angle of elevation of the top of the tree to be 33°. If Alan is 170 cm in height, find the height of the tree.

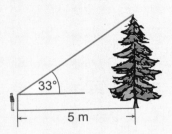

10. A flagpole *AB*, with *A* at the top, is held upright by two ropes, *AC* and *AD*, fixed on horizontal ground at *C* and *D*. |*AC*| = 10. If |∠*ACB*| = 25° and |∠*ADB*| = 36°, find |*BD*| correct to one decimal place.

11. A football pitch *ABCD* is shown. During a training session, a coach asks each player to run from *A* to *C* and back to *A*. The pitch is 120 m long and 90 m wide. Calculate the distance covered by each player during this exercise.

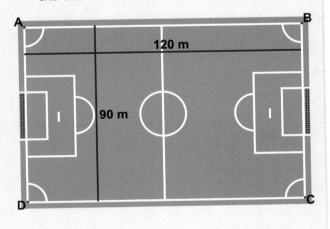

Revision Exercises

1. Use the theorem of Pythagoras to evaluate *x* in each of the following:

(i)

(ii)
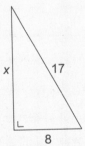

(iii)

(iv)
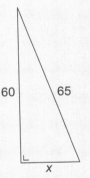

2. Use your calculator to find the value of these correct to four decimal places:

  (i) sin 54°   (ii) cos 68°   (iii) tan 15°   (iv) sin 60°   (v) cos 20°

(vi) tan 85°   (vii) tan 45°   (viii) sin 45°   (ix) cos 45°   (x) sin 70°

3. For each of the following triangles, write down the values of sin *A*, cos *A* and tan *A*; also sin *B*, cos *B* and tan *B*:

(i)
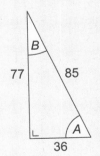

(ii)
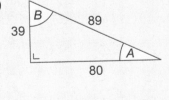

(iii)
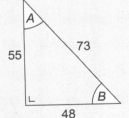

(iv)
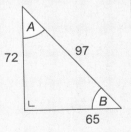

---

4. Use your calculator to find, correct to the nearest decimal, the measure of the angle B.

   (i) $\cos B = 0.4823$ (vi) $\sin B = 0.3142$

  (ii) $\sin B = 0.1684$ (vii) $\sin B = 0.2689$

 (iii) $\tan B = 0.4219$ (viii) $\tan B = 1.4628$

 (iv) $\sin B = 0.6834$ (ix) $\tan B = 2.7918$

  (v) $\cos B = 0.5128$ (x) $\cos B = 0.5214$

5. The measure of the angle A is 22°. The angle B is twice the measure of the angle A.

   (i) Write down the measure of the angle B.

  (ii) Using your calculator, find $\sin A$ and $\sin B$.

 (iii) Is $2\sin(A) = \sin(2A)$? Explain.

 (iv) Using your calculator, show that $\sin(2A) = 2\sin A \cos A$.

6. (i) Find the measure of the angle A.

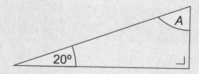

  (ii) Use the theorem of Pythagoras to find the value of x.

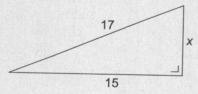

 (iii) If $\sin A = \dfrac{3}{5}$, find the value of x.

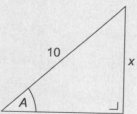

7. (i) Use your calculator to find (a) $\sin 51°$ and (b) $\sin 28°$.

  (ii) Find the value of x and y, correct to three significant figures.

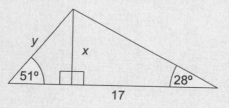

8. (i) If $\sin A = \dfrac{3}{5}$, find $\cos A$.

  (ii) The angle of elevation of the top of a TV mast, from a point 20 m from the base of the mast, is 55°. Find the height of the mast, to two decimal places.

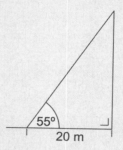

9. (i) Find x and, hence, the value of sin θ, in the form $\dfrac{a}{b}$.

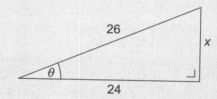

  (ii) Calculate $|CB|$ to one decimal place.

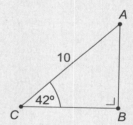

10. Johnny is flying a kite. The string makes an angle of 30° with the horizontal. If the height of the kite is 10 m, find the length of string that Johnny has used. Note that Johnny holds the string in his hand 1 m above the ground.

11. Two ships *A* and *B* leave a port *O* at the same time. Both ships sail for 2 hours. Ship *A* sails in the direction shown, at a speed of 12 km/h. Ship *B* sails in the direction shown, at a speed of 16 km/h. Find the distance between the ships after two hours' sailing.

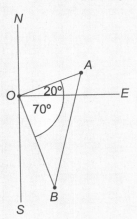

12. Max and Mo are standing on the same side of a tall building. Max observes the angle of elevation of the top of the building to be 45°, and Mo observes the angle of elevation to be 60°. The building is 100 m high.

Ignoring their heights, find the distance between Max and Mo.

13. (i) Find the measure of *A*, *B* and *x*, giving angle measurements correct to the nearest degree.

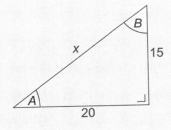

(ii) A rectangular tile contains two right-angled triangles. Dimensions are shown in the diagram. Find the area of the tile.

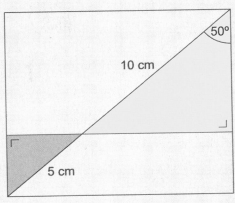

14. When the angle of elevation of the sun is 30°, a vertical tree casts a shadow 5 m long on horizontal ground.

(i) Find the height of the tree.

(ii) Find, correct to one decimal place, the length of the shadow when the angle of elevation is 20°.

15. *ABCD* is a parallelogram. Find the area of *ABCD*.

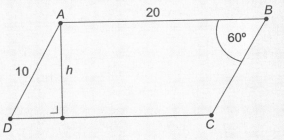

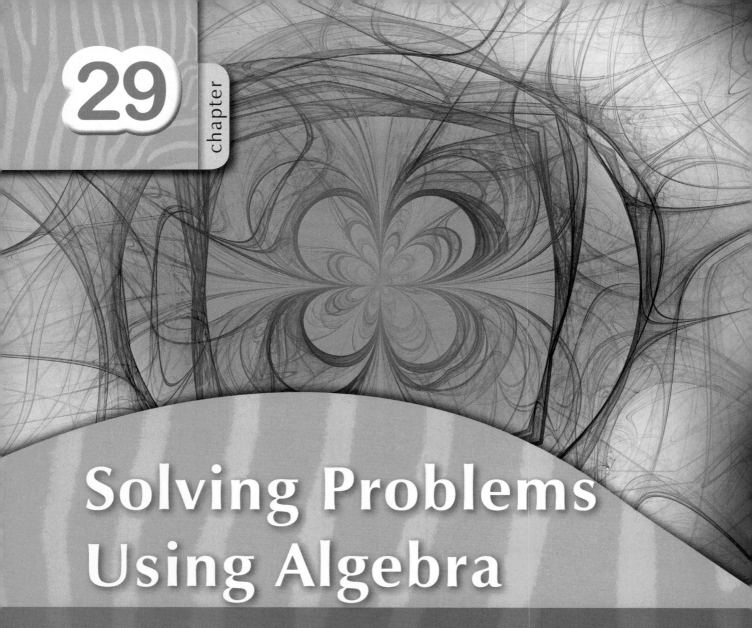

29

Solving Problems Using Algebra

Learning Outcomes

In this chapter you will learn to:

➲ Write problems as algebraic expressions

➲ Solve problems using:

   ➲ Linear equations

   ➲ Simultaneous equations

   ➲ Quadratic equations

29.1 WRITING EXPRESSIONS

Some mathematical problems may be written in words instead of using numbers and letters.

If five times a number plus four is equal to 39, what is the number?

By letting x be equal to the unknown number in the problem, we can begin the process of trying to find out what that unknown number is.

To begin with, we must first practise changing words into algebraic expressions.

For example, five times a number can be written as $5x$.

 ACTIVITY 29.1

x^2 Worked Example 29.1

Mia is x years old. Ben is five years younger than Mia. Alex is one year older than Ben. Emma is three times the age of Alex. Write expressions for:

   (i) Ben's age   (ii) Alex's age   (iii) Emma's age

Solution

Our starting point is that Mia is x years old.

   (i) Ben is five years younger.

      Ben's age = Mia's age – 5 years

$$= x - 5$$

   (ii) Alex is one year older than Ben

      Alex's age = Ben's age + 1 year

$$= x - 5 + 1$$
$$= x - 4$$

   (iii) Emma is three times the age of Alex

      Emma's age = 3 × Alex's age

$$= 3(x - 4)$$
$$= 3x - 12$$

x^2 Worked Example 29.2

n is equal to an even number. Write expressions for the next four even numbers.

Solution

2, 4, 6, 8 and 10 are even numbers. The difference or gap between each number is 2.

2	4	6	8	10
n	$n + 2$	$n + 4$	$n + 6$	$n + 8$

The next four even numbers would be $n + 2$, $n + 4$, $n + 6$ and $n + 8$.

SOLVING PROBLEMS USING ALGEBRA

1. John is x years old. Michelle is two years older than John. Write down an expression for Michelle's age.

2. Anne is x years old. Bob is three years younger. Write down an expression for Bob's age.

3. Paul has x dollars. His wife, who has twice as much money, gives $5 to her husband. How much does each of them have now (in terms of x)?

4. (i) 12 is a natural number.

   Write down the next two consecutive natural numbers.

   (ii) n is a natural number.

   Write down the next two consecutive natural numbers.

5. Aidan has 15 computer games – all for either the PS3 or Xbox. If y of them are for the PS3, write an expression for the number of Xbox games he has.

6. Juan has 14 shirts. If x are short-sleeved, how many are long-sleeved?

7. A woman had to get from Bray to Dublin, a distance of 25 kilometres. She cycled the first x kilometres and then took the bus for the next x kilometres. She then walked the rest of the journey. Write an expression for how far she walked.

8. A swimming pool has a length of $5x$ metres and a width of $(2x - 3)$ metres.

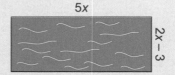

   Write an expression for:

   (i) The perimeter of the swimming pool

   (ii) The area of the swimming pool

9. A wall is made up 30 rectangular bricks. Each brick is 20 cm by x cm.

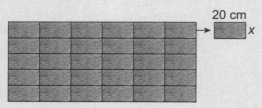

   (i) Write down an expression for the area of the wall.

   (ii) Five bricks are removed from the wall. Write an expression for the area of the remaining wall.

10. (i) 20 is an even number.

    Write down the next two consecutive even numbers.

    (ii) m is also an even number.

    Write down the next two consecutive even numbers.

11. Write an expression for the area and perimeter of the following shapes.

(i)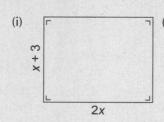

(ii)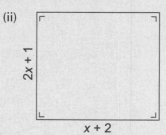

(iii)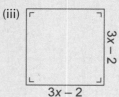

(iv)

12. Find an expression for the total area of each of the following rectangles:

(i)
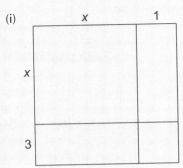

(ii)
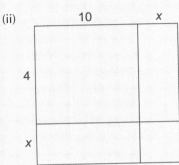

(iii)
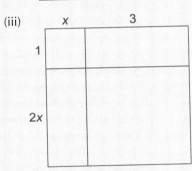

(iv)
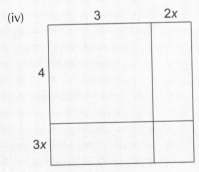

13. A Chewy bar costs three cents more than a Stikky bar. Caitríona has 90 cents. She buys two Chewy bars and a Stikky bar. If a Stikky bar costs x cents, write down expressions for:

(i) The cost of a Chewy bar

(ii) The amount of money that Caitríona spends

(iii) The amount of money that she has left

14. How many hours are there in:

(i) Two days (ii) Ten days (iii) x days

15. Patrick has 80 cents. He buys x bars at five cents each.
How much money does he have left?

16. How many months are there in:

(i) One year (ii) Two years (iii) y years

17. A Gaelic football team scored x goals and $(x + 5)$ points. If a goal is worth three points, what is their total score in points?

18. The San Francisco 49ers scored x touchdowns and three fewer field goals. They converted all of the touchdowns except one. The scoring system is:

(i) Converted touchdown = 7 points

(ii) Unconverted touchdown = 6 points

(iii) Field goal = 3 points

Write an expression for their total score.

19. Veronica is x years old. Walter is four times as old as Veronica. How old (in terms of x) will Walter be in 10 years' time?

20. The area of each of three rectangles is shown. By factorising each expression, write an expression for the perimeter of each rectangle.

(i)
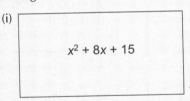
$x^2 + 8x + 15$

(ii)
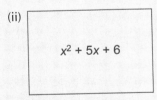
$x^2 + 5x + 6$

(iii)
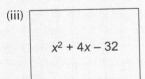
$x^2 + 4x - 32$

29.2 SOLVING PROBLEMS USING LINEAR EQUATIONS

In the previous section we learned how to write expressions when given the information in words.

 ACTIVITY 29.2

From this, we can now solve for x and so find the actual value of the unknown.

x^2 Worked Example 29.3

Bob is six years older than Heather. The sum of their ages is 42. Find their ages.

Solution

Bob is six years older than Heather.

Let Heather's age = x.

> It is usually better to use the smallest number as the starting variable.

∴ Bob's age = x + 6.

> When trying to solve a problem using algebra, we always follow these steps:
> - Identify the unknown and represent it using a letter.
> - Let the unknown be the smaller value, if you have a choice.
> - Change the word equation into a maths equation.
> - Solve for x.
> - **Then** answer the question asked.

Word equation: The sum of their ages is 42. Bob's age added to Heather's age equals 42.

Maths equation:

$$x + x + 6 = 42$$
$$2x + 6 = 42$$
$$2x = 42 - 6$$
$$2x = 36$$
$$x = 18$$

We now must write down Heather's and Bob's ages:

- Heather's age = x = 18 years.
- Bob's age = x + 6 = 18 + 6 = 24 years.

We can now check our answer:

$$18 + 24 = 42$$

x^2 Worked Example 29.4

There are 21 animals on a farm. All of them are either chickens or cows. Altogether, the animals have 52 legs. How many chickens are on the farm, and how many cows are on the farm?

Solution

Let the number of chickens on the farm = x.

Let the number of cows on the farm = 21 − x.

> If there were 10 chickens on the farm, to find the number of cows we would subtract 10 from 21 (21 − 10).

Chickens have two legs
⇒ Number of chickens' legs = 2x.

Cows have four legs
⇒ Number of cows' legs = 4(21 − x).

Word equation: Altogether, the animals have 52 legs.

The number of chickens' legs plus the number of cows' legs equals 52.

Maths equation:

$$2x + 4(21 - x) = 52$$
$$2x + 84 - 4x = 52$$
$$-2x + 84 = 52$$
$$-2x = 52 - 84$$
$$-2x = -32$$
$$\frac{-2x}{-2} = \frac{-32}{-2}$$
$$x = 16$$

Number of chickens on the farm = x = 16.

Number of cows on the farm = 21 − x
$$= 21 - 16 = 5.$$

Exercise 29.2

1. If you double a number and add seven, the result is 29. Find the number.

2. When you double a number and add one, you get 23. Find the number.

3. When you multiply a number by five and add seven, you get 22. Find the number.

4. When you treble a number and take away five, the result is 22. Find the number.

5. When a number is multiplied by three and four is added, the answer is ten.
   What is the number?

6. When you double a number and take away 13, the answer is 47. Find the number.

7. The diagram shows two equilateral triangles. Find the value of a and b.

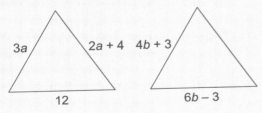

8. Fred is two years older than Harry. The sum of their ages is 26. Find their ages.
   (Hint: Let x = Harry's age.
   ∴ x + 2 = Fred's age.)

9. Yousef is one year older than Paul. The sum of their ages is 73. Find their ages.

10. Find two consecutive numbers that add up to 21.
    (Hint: Let x = the first number.
    ∴ x + 1 = the next consecutive number.)

11. Find two consecutive numbers that add up to 43.

12. Nishi is three years older than Emer. The sum of their ages is 31. Find their ages.

13. Find two consecutive numbers that add up to 39.

14. Find three consecutive numbers that add up to 33.

15. Barry has x cents. Colm has twice as much as Barry. Dave has three cents less than Colm. They have 57 cents altogether. How much does each of them have?

16. Henry says 'I am thinking of a number. When 13 is added to four times the number, the result is the same as when 20 is subtracted from seven times the number.'
    What number is Henry thinking of?

17. Find the value of x and y in each of the following parallelograms:

(i)

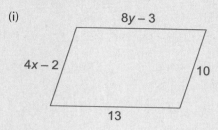

8y – 3

4x – 2

10

13

(ii)

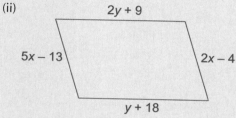

2y + 9

5x – 13

2x – 4

y + 18

18. Four expressions are shown:

A: 4x + 18

B: 5x + 7

C: 2(x – 3)

D: 12(1 – x)

(i) Find the value of A + B.

(ii) Find the value of D + C.

(iii) If A + B = D + C, find the value of x.

19. The sum of half of a number and one-third of the number is 25. Find the number.

20. Joanne is 18 and her mother is 43. In how many years will her mother be twice as old as Joanne? (Hint: Let x = the number of years, ∴ 18 + x = Joanne's age in x years' time and 43 + x = her mother's age in x years' time.)

21. Find four consecutive even numbers so that the sum of all four is the same as three times the biggest number.
(Hint: Let x = the smallest.
∴ x + 2 = the next, x + 4 = the next and x + 6 = the biggest.)

22. Find three consecutive numbers, where one-seventh of the sum of the first two is equal to one-quarter of the last number.

23. Peter is five times as old as Kristin. In two years' time, Peter will be three times as old as Kristin. How old are they now?

24. A pet shop has rabbits and gerbils for sale. They have 20 animals altogether. They sell two rabbits. Then one of the gerbils has twins. The shop now has three times as many gerbils as rabbits. How many of each did they start with?

25. A Gaelic football team scored 18 times, a mixture of points and goals. A goal is worth three points. If their total score was 28 points, how many goals did they get?

26. One hundred and ninety students go on a tour. They go in minibuses that carry 14 passengers each and in buses that carry 40 passengers each. There were eight vehicles used, all full. How many of each type of vehicle were used?

27. A packet of eggs contains six eggs. Abraham buys x packets. He uses two eggs for his breakfast.

(i) Write an expression for the number of eggs that he has left.

(ii) If he has 28 eggs left, how many packets did he buy?

28. Jane ate x mince pies. Her father ate five times as many. Her mother ate one more than Jane and her father combined. They ate 37 mince pies altogether. How many did each of them eat?

29. Pete is 14 years old and his mother is 39. In how many years will Pete's mother be exactly twice as old as Pete?

30. Emer and Beth pick a number x.

■ Emer multiplies the number by six and adds four.

■ Beth adds five to the number and multiplies by four.

They both get the same answer having done this.

(i) Write an equation to show this information.

(ii) Solve the equation in order to find the number.

29.3 SOLVING PROBLEMS USING SIMULTANEOUS EQUATIONS

We may also encounter equations where there are two unrelated unknowns, usually referred to as x and y, which may be solved using simultaneous equations.

x^2 Worked Example 29.5

Three apples and two oranges cost 91 cents.
Two apples and five oranges cost €1.45. Find the cost of each fruit.

Solution

Let the cost of an apple $= x$, and let the cost of an orange $= y$.

Word equation 1: Three apples and two oranges cost 91 cents.

Maths equation 1: $3x + 2y = 91$

Word equation 2: Two apples and five oranges cost €1.45.

Maths equation 2: $2x + 5y = 145$

> Both equations **must** be equal to the same units, in this case cents.

We now solve for x and y:

$3x + 2y = 91 \quad (\times 2) \rightarrow 6x + 4y = 182$

$2x + 5y = 145 \ (\times 3) \rightarrow 6x + 15y = 435$

First we find the value of y:

$$6x + 4y = 182$$
$$-(6x + 15y = 435)$$
$$-11y = -253$$
$$\frac{-11y}{-11} = \frac{-253}{-11}$$
$$y = 23$$

If $y = 23$, we can now find the value of x:

$$3x + 2y = 91$$
$$3x + 2(23) = 91$$
$$3x + 46 = 91$$
$$3x = 91 - 46$$
$$3x = 45$$
$$x = 15$$

Cost of an apple $= x = 15$ cents.

Cost of an orange $= y = 23$ cents.

> Remember to answer the question asked.

x^2 Worked Example 29.6

Thirty adults and children visited a cinema. Tickets cost €5 for an adult and €3 for a child. The total cost of the visit was €114.

Find the number of adults who visited the cinema and the number of children who visited the cinema.

Solution

Let the number of adults = x, and let the number of children = y.

Word equation 1

€5 by the number of adults plus €3 by the number of children equals a total cost of €114.

Maths equation 1: $5x + 3y = 114$

We now solve for x and y:

$5x + 3y = 114$ $(\times 1)$ → $5x + 3y = 114$

$x + y = 30$ $(\times 5)$ → $5x + 5y = 150$

First we find the value of y:

$5x + 3y = 114$

$-(5x + 5y = 150)$

$-2y = -36$

$\dfrac{-2y}{-2} = \dfrac{-36}{-2}$

$y = 18$

Word equation 2

30 adults and children visited a cinema.

Maths equation 2: $x + y = 30$

If $y = 18$, we can now find the value of x:

$x + y = 30$

$x + 18 = 30$

$x = 30 - 18$

$x = 12$

Number of adults = 12.

Number of children = 18.

Exercise 29.3

1. A pen and a marker cost 30 cents. Two pens and three markers cost 80 cents. Let x = the cost of a pen and y = the cost of a pencil. Write down two equations and, hence, find the cost of each.

2. An apple and two oranges cost 39 cents. Two apples and an orange cost 42 cents. Let x = the cost of an apple and y = the cost of an orange. Write down the two equations and, hence, find the cost of each fruit.

3. A new points system is introduced into a league, so that you get x points for a win and y for a draw. Team A wins three matches and draws one. They get 17 points. Team B wins one match and draws two. They get nine points. Write down two equations in x and y and, hence, find the values of x and y.

4. Entrance to a fun-park costs €2 for adults and €1 for children. A Scout leader brings a troop (12 people in all) to the fun-park. It costs her €17. Let x = the number of adults and y = the number of children. Write down two equations in x and y and, hence, find their values.

5. Old Chris is a farmer. He has 15 animals on his farm. All of them are chickens or pigs. When he counts the legs of all the animals he gets a total of 38.
Let x = the number of chickens and y = the number of pigs. Write down two equations in x and y and, hence, find their values.

6. Find the value of x and y in the following parallelogram.

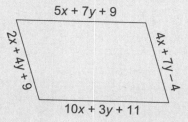

7. In Gaelic football, you get three points for a goal and one point for a 'point'. A team scores 14 times in all during a match, equating to 20 points. Let x = the number of goals and y = the number of points. Write down two equations in x and y and, hence, find their values.

8. Two adults and three children pay €19 to get into a cinema. One adult and four children pay €17. Let x = the cost for an adult and y = the cost for a child.
Write down two equations in x and y and, hence, find the price of each ticket.

9. A bus company has a fleet of coaches and minibuses for hire. Three minibuses and four coaches cost €1,000 to hire and two minibuses and one coach cost €500 to hire. Find the cost of hiring a coach and a minibus separately.

10. A clothes shop buys a total of 100 shirts. Theses shirts are either short- or long-sleeved. A long-sleeved shirt costs €5 and a short-sleeved shirt €3. If the shop spent €350 buying these shirts, find how many of each type the shop bought.

11. There are 14 caravans on a site: x of them are large, and y of them are small. Large caravans sleep five people; small caravans sleep three people. When all caravans are full, 62 people can sleep on the site.
Write down two equations in x and y and, hence, find their values.

12. One thousand tickets were sold for a concert. Tickets were priced at €30 or €40. Ticket sales amounted to €33,500. Let x be the number of €30 tickets sold and y be the number of €40 tickets sold. Write down two equations in x and y and, hence, find the number of each type of ticket sold.

13. A farmer has 100 hectares of land for wheat or vegetables. Each hectare of wheat yields €400 and each hectare of vegetables yields €500. He makes €42,000. How many hectares of each crop did he sow?

14. A manufacturer produces both steel forks and knives. It takes 31 minutes to manufacture five forks and seven knives, while it takes an hour and a half to produce 15 forks and 20 knives. Calculate the time needed to produce 100 forks and 100 knives.

29.4 SOLVING PROBLEMS USING QUADRATIC EQUATIONS

When a problem involves squaring or multiplying so that the unknown is squared, we are dealing with quadratic equations.

x^2 Worked Example 29.7

The length of a rectangular room is 3 m longer than its width. The area of the rectangle is 54 m^2. Find the length and width of the room.

Solution

It can help to draw a diagram.

Width of room = x.

Length of room = $x + 3$.

Word equation:

Area of rectangle = length × width

= 54 m^2

Maths equation: $(x + 3)x = 54$

$x^2 + 3x = 54$

As this is a quadratic equation, we must first bring all the terms over to one side before we solve.

$x^2 + 3x - 54 = 0$

The factors of −54 that would give us a 3 are:

-9×6 \qquad 9×-6

$-9 + 6 = -3$ (incorrect) \quad **9 − 6 = +3** (✓)

Factors: $(x + 9)(x - 6)$

$\therefore (x + 9)(x - 6) = 0$

$x + 9 = 0$ **or** $x - 6 = 0$

$x = -9$ \qquad **or** \qquad $x = 6$

x cannot be equal to −9, as this would mean that the width would be negative, which is not possible.

Width of room = x = 6 m

Length of room = $x + 3$

$= 6 + 3$

$= 9$ m

x^2 Worked Example 29.8

Find three **consecutive** numbers so that the first number squared is equal to the second and third added together.

Solution

First number = x.

Second number = $x + 1$.

Third number = $x + 2$.

Consecutive means one number after the other in order, for example 11, 12 and 13.

Word equation: The first number squared is equal to the second and third added together.

Maths equation:

$x^2 = (x + 1) + (x + 2)$

$x^2 = x + 1 + x + 2$

$x^2 = 2x + 3$

$x^2 - 2x - 3 = 0$

Factors: $(x + 1)(x - 3)$

$\therefore (x + 1)(x - 3) = 0$

$x + 1 = 0$ **or** $x - 3 = 0$

$x = -1$ \qquad **or** \qquad $x = 3$

As we have not been told if the first number is negative or positive, we must check both answers:

First number = x = −1	First number = x = 3
Second number = $x + 1 = -1 + 1 = 0$	Second number = $x + 1 = 3 + 1 = 4$
Third number = $x + 2 = -1 + 2 = 1$	Third number = $x + 2 = 3 + 2 = 5$
−1, 0, 1	**3, 4, 5**

As both answers show three consecutive numbers, we must use both answers.

Answer: −1, 0 and 1 **or** 3, 4 and 5.

Exercise 29.4

1. Let x be equal to a number.

   This number is squared and two times the number is then added to give a total of 15.

   Find two possible values for the number.

2. Let y be equal to a number.

   The sum of this number squared and four times the number is 12.

   Find two possible values for the number.

3. A positive number is squared and twice the number is then added. The result is 35.

   Find the number.

4. A number is squared. This is equal to multiplying the number by 6 and subtracting 8. Find two possible values for the number.

5. Find two consecutive natural numbers whose product is 20.

6. The length of a room is 3 m more than the breadth. The area of the room is 28 m². Find the dimensions of the room.

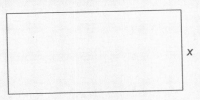

7. Let x be equal to a number. Another number is 5 less than x. When the two numbers are multiplied, the answer is 36.
   Find two possible values for the number.

8. One natural number is 4 bigger than another. Their product is 12. Find the numbers.

9. When 10 is added to the square of a number, the result is equal to seven times the number. Find two possible values for the number.

10. The area of this rectangle is 21 units squared. Find the value of x.

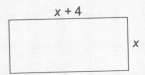

11. Two numbers differ by 4. The product of the two numbers is 96. List all the possible correct answers for the two numbers.

12. When the square of a number and six times the number are added, the total is 40. Find two possible values for the number.

13. n and $(n + 2)$ are two consecutive odd natural numbers. Their product is 15. Write down an equation in n and, hence, find its value.

14. Find two consecutive even natural numbers whose product is 80.

15. Two natural numbers add up to 12. Their product is 32.

   (i) If $x =$ the first number, write the second number in terms of x

   (ii) Write an equation in x.

   (iii) Find the two numbers.

16. The sum of the areas of these two rectangles is 47. Find the value of x.

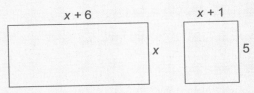

17. The sum of two numbers is 14. Their product is 33. Find the numbers.

18. Find three consecutive natural numbers so that the product of the first two numbers is 2 more than twice the last number.

19. The perimeter of a rectangle is 20 m.

   (i) If $x =$ the length, write down (in terms of x) an expression for the width.

   (ii) If the area of this rectangle is 21 m², find its dimensions.

20. Find three consecutive odd natural numbers so that the product of the first number and the last number is 11 greater than two times the middle number. (Hint: Let x, $x + 2$ and $x + 4$ be the three numbers.)

21. A garden in the shape of a rectangle is shown.

The shaded region in the diagram represents the area of the garden that is to be covered in wooden decking.

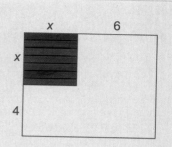

(i) Write an expression for the area of the garden in terms of x.

If the area of the garden is 48 m², find:

(ii) The dimensions of the garden

(iii) The area of the garden that will not be decked

Revision Exercises

1. Alfie is x years old. Linda is four times as old as Alfie. Write down an expression for Linda's age.

2. Kilian has eight pets – all cats and dogs. If x of them are cats, how many are dogs?

3. Sandra puts 20 songs on her iPod playlist. x of these songs are from one band. How many of the songs on the playlist are not from this band?

4. (i) 15 is a natural number. Write down the next two natural numbers.

(ii) a is a natural number. Write down the next two natural numbers.

(iii) 15 is also an odd number. Write down the next two odd numbers.

(iv) a is also an odd number. Write down the next two odd numbers.

5. Jessica has a call card for 20 phone calls. She rings her mother x times and her boyfriend twice as many times as she rings her mother.

She then has only two calls left on her card. Solve for x.

6. Liam, Michael and Noreen pick strawberries. Liam and Michael put their pickings together. They have 5 kilograms between the two of them. Noreen picked twice as much as Michael. If Liam picked x kilograms, write an expression for the amount Noreen picked.

7. How many minutes are there in:

(i) 3 hours

(ii) 4 hours and 25 minutes

(iii) x hours

(iv) x hours and y minutes

8. Dave is x years old. His sister Paula is five years older. His father is five times as old as Dave. Copy this chart and fill in their ages:

	Age now	Age in 7 years	Age 2 years ago
Dave	x		
Paula			
Father			

9. When you multiply a number by 10 and take away 3, the result is 37. Find the number.

10. When you treble a number and take away 6, the answer is 30. Find the number.

11. Simon is one year older than John. The sum of their ages is 31. Find their ages.
(Hint: Let x = John's age.)

12. Patricia is four years older than Roberta. The sum of their ages is 28. Find their ages.

13. Find two consecutive numbers which add up to 45.

14. Find two consecutive numbers which add up to 121.

SOLVING PROBLEMS USING ALGEBRA

15. Alan has x cents. Bertie has three times as much as Alan. Carol has 2 cents more than Bertie. They have 51 cents altogether. How much does each of them have?

16. Find three consecutive numbers which add up to 54.

17. Henrietta says, 'If you add 11 to my age and multiply the result by 3, the answer is one more than 7 times my age.' How old is Henrietta?

18. Find two consecutive numbers such that five times the smaller one added to seven times the bigger one gives 91.

19. Find three consecutive numbers such that 13 times the smallest number is the same as five times the sum of the other two numbers.

20. James is x years old. His sister Karen is four times as old as James. In 6 years' time, Karen will be twice as old as James. How old is James?

21. A mother gives 40 cents to be divided between her two sons, Peter and Quentin. If Peter's share were doubled, he would have 11 cents more than Quentin's initial share. How much did each get? (Hint: Let x = Peter's share, so (40 − x) = Quentin's share.)

22. Divide 17 into two parts so that three times the first part is 2 more than four times the other part.

23. Barry has x CDs in his collection. His sister Ann has three times as many. She gives five CDs to Barry. Now she has twice as many as her brother. How many CDs do they have altogether?

24. Thirty people work in a fast-food shop. The people who work in the kitchen get €5 per hour. The people who serve the customers get €4 per hour. The total labour cost is €129 per hour. How many people work in the kitchen?

25. A pen and a pencil cost 32 cents. Two pens and three pencils cost 76 cents. Let x = the cost of a pen and y = the cost of a pencil. Write down two equations and, hence, find the cost of each.

26. A cone and an ice-pop cost 60 cents. Three cones and two ice-pops cost €1.65. Write down two equations and, hence, find the cost of each item.

27. There are 24 students in a class. Three times the number of boys is 2 more than twice the number of girls. Let x = the number of girls and y = the number of boys. Write down two equations in x and y and, hence, find their values.

28. In a second-hand book stall, there are 120 books for sale. Paperbacks are 10 cents each and hardbacks are 20 cents each. They are all sold, bringing in a total of €15.50. How many paperbacks and how many hardbacks were there?

29. A tour operator hires x taxis which carry three people each and y minibuses which carry 12 people each. She hires an equal number of taxis and minibuses. She transports 75 people. Write down two equations and, hence, find the values of x and y.

30. A woman is told by her nutritionist that she must take 30 mg of vitamin C and 18 mg of vitamin E each day. She can take orange and/or blue tablets. Each orange tablet contains 3 mg of vitamin C and 3 mg of vitamin E. Each blue tablet contains 5 mg of vitamin C and 1 mg of vitamin E. How many of each should she take each day?

31. The sum of two numbers is 11. The sum of their squares is 65. Find the numbers.

32. A small rectangular swimming pool in a fitness centre measures 4 metres by 10 metres. It is surrounded by a path of width x metres. The area of the path is 32 m². Find x.

```
┌─────────────────┐
│  ┌───────────┐  │
│  │    10     │  │
│  │         4 │  │
│  └───────────┘  │
└─────────────────┘
```

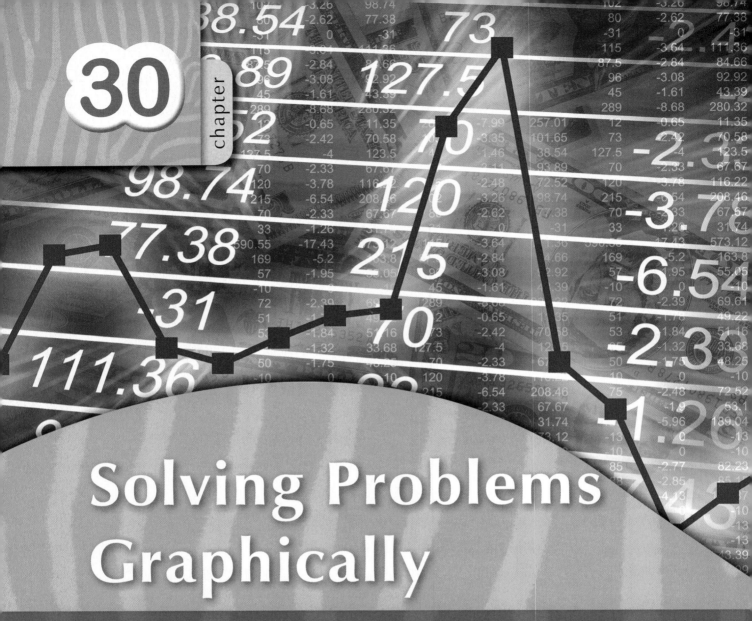

30

chapter

Solving Problems Graphically

Learning Outcomes

In this chapter you will learn to:

- ➲ Use graphs as a tool for representing and analysing linear, quadratic and exponential patterns and equations

- ➲ Graph linear functions and find if they have a point of intersection from the graph

- ➲ Understand rate of change and the y-intercept with regard to linear graphs

- ➲ Recognise proportional relationships

- ➲ Use graphs to represent phenomena quantitatively

YOU SHOULD REMEMBER...

- Co-ordinate geometry of the line
- How to graph functions
- Patterns
- Ratio and proportion

Sometimes we have to deal with a lot of data that is hard to understand and communicate. To show this data more clearly, we can present it in graphical form. There are many types of graphs.

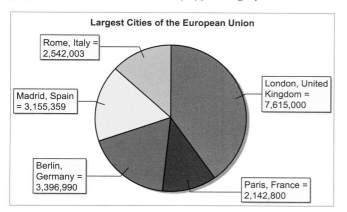

Largest Cities of the European Union

Rome, Italy = 2,542,003

Madrid, Spain = 3,155,359

Berlin, Germany = 3,396,990

London, United Kingdom = 7,615,000

Paris, France = 2,142,800

KEY WORDS

- **x-axis and y-axis**
- **Slope**
- **Rate of change**
- **y-intercept**
- **Start term**
- **Difference**
- **Linear**
- **Quadratic**
- **Exponential**

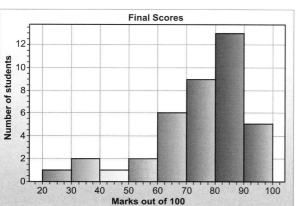

Final Scores

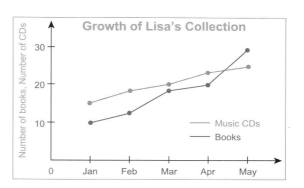

Growth of Lisa's Collection

Music CDs
Books

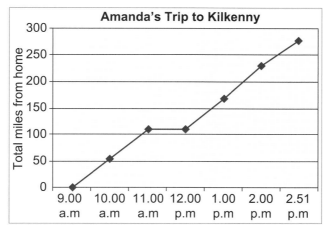

Amanda's Trip to Kilkenny

Graphs are useful tools, as they show information in a way that makes it easier to grasp.

One of the most familiar types of graph is a **linear graph**, or **line graph**.

To draw a line, we must have either two points on the line or the equation of the line.

Drawing a Line, Given Two Points on the Line

If we are given any two points of a line, we should be able to plot the points and then draw the line.

Worked Example 30.1

Plot the points (3,1) and (−4,3) and draw a line between these two points.

Solution

We first construct an *x*-axis and a *y*-axis on graphed paper. We plot these two points and draw a line through them.

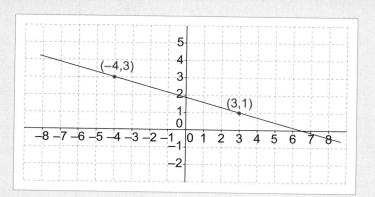

Drawing a Line, Given the Equation of the Line

Usually, however, we are given the equation of a line and then asked to plot the line. These equations can be in two forms:

$ax + by + c = 0$ **OR** $y = mx + c$

Worked Example 30.2

Using graph paper, graph the line $4x + 5y = 20$.

Solution

$4x + 5y = 20$	
Let $x = 0$	Let $y = 0$
$4(0) + 5y = 20$	$4x + 5(0) = 20$
$5y = 20$	$4x = 20$
$y = 4$	$x = 5$
If $x = 0$, then $y = 4$.	If $y = 0$, then $x = 5$.
Point (0,4)	Point (5,0)
y-intercept	*x*-intercept

We now use these points to graph the line:

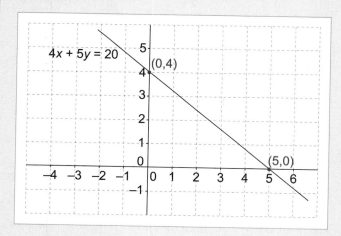

Another approach is to use a table.

Worked Example 30.3

Using graph paper, graph the line $y = 3x$.

Solution

If we let $x = 0$, then y is also $= 0$.

Construct a table and pick three x-values to use:

x	$y = 3x$	y	Point
-2	$3(-2)$	-6	$(-2,-6)$
0	0	0	$(0,0)$
2	$3(2)$	6	$(2,6)$

Note: Picking three x-values is good practice to help eliminate errors that may not be spotted if you take only two x-values.

Using these three points, we draw the line:

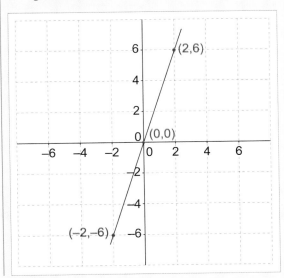

Any line in the form $y = mx$ will go through the origin $(0,0)$.

ACTIVITY 30.1

Using the methods described, we can now find the **point of intersection** of two lines by graphing both lines on the same axes.

The **point of intersection** of two lines is where the two lines meet or cross.

Worked Example 30.4

m is the line $2x + 3y = 12$, and n is the line $x - 3y = -3$.

(i) Graph both these lines using the same axes and scales.

(ii) Reading from your graph, find where these two lines intersect.

Solution

(i)

$2x + 3y = 12$		$x - 3y = -3$	
Let $x = 0$	Let $y = 0$	Let $x = 0$	Let $y = 0$
$2(0) + 3y = 12$	$2x + 3(0) = 12$	$(0) - 3y = -3$	$x - 3(0) = -3$
$3y = 12$	$2x = 12$	$-3y = -3$	$x = -3$
$y = 4$	$x = 6$	$y = 1$	
If $x = 0$, then $y = 4$.	If $y = 0$, then $x = 6$.	If $x = 0$, then $y = 1$.	If $y = 0$, then $x = -3$.
Point $(0,4)$	Point $(6,0)$	Point $(0,1)$	Point $(-3,0)$

We graph these two lines and mark the point of intersection.

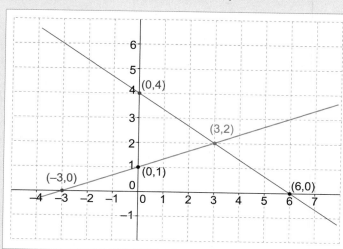

(ii) From our graph, the point of intersection is (3,2).

Exercise 30.1

1. Graph the following lines on a co-ordinate plane.

   (i) $2x + 3y = 6$ (iii) $7x - 3y = 21$ (v) $3x - y = 0$

   (ii) $5x + 3y = 15$ (iv) $2x - 5y = 30$ (vi) $4x + 3y = 12$

2. Graph the following lines on a co-ordinate plane.

   (i) $y = 2x + 6$ (iii) $y = \frac{1}{2}x + 3$ (v) $y = -\frac{3}{4}x - 6$

   (ii) $y = -x + 2$ (iv) $y = -\frac{1}{3}x + 3$ (vi) $y = 5x$

3. In each of the following graphs, name the point of intersection of the two lines.

(i)
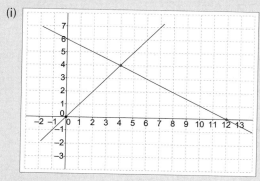

(ii)
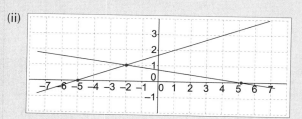

(iii)
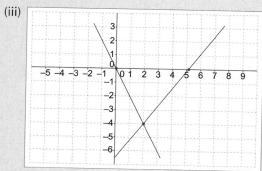

(iv)
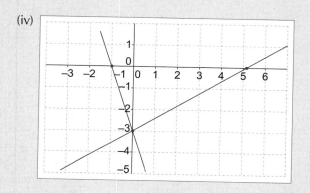

4. Find the point of intersection of each of the following pairs of lines.

(i) $x + 3y = 12$
$x - 2y = 2$

(iii) $x - 3y = -12$
$2x + 3y = 30$

(v) $x + 2y = 8$
$x - 2y = 0$

(vii) $y = x + 1$
$y = -3x + 5$

(ix) $y = 2x - 4$
$y = \frac{2}{3}x$

(ii) $x + y = 6$
$2x + y = 8$

(iv) $5x - 2y = -10$
$x - y = 1$

(vi) $y = 2x + 4$
$y = 3x - 3$

(viii) $y = -x + 1$
$y = -\frac{1}{2}x + 2$

(x) $3x - 4y = 0$
$y = -\frac{1}{4}x + 4$

5. Do the following pairs of lines intersect? In each case, explain your reason by drawing a graph.

(i) $5x - 2y = -10$
$5x - 2y = 20$

(ii) $3x - y = 6$
$2x - y = 4$

(iii) $y = 4x - 2$
$y = 2x - 5$

(iv) $y = 2x - 4$
$y = 2x + 8$

30.2 INTERPRETING GRAPHS OF LINEAR EQUATIONS

Linear graphs have some important features that we must understand if we wish to interpret the graphs correctly.

The following graph shows the fare for a taxi journey.

The equation that represents this graph is $y = 2x + 5$.

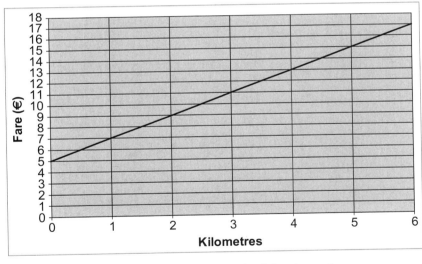

From this graph and equation, we notice the following points.

(a) Slope

$y = 2x + 5$

> The slope of a line is how much the y-value changes when the x-value changes by one unit.

The **slope** of the line is 2.

This corresponds to the rate of change of the fare (y-value) per kilometre (x-value).

The fare changes €2 per kilometre. From our graph, we can see that:

- 1 km costs €7.
- 2 km costs €9.
- 3 km costs €11.

(b) *y*-intercept

$y = 2x + 5$

The *y*-intercept of this line is 5.

The *y*-intercept (where the line intercepts or hits the *y*-axis) gives us the start value of the fare. This is the standard fare to hire a taxi, i.e. €5.

Worked Example 30.5

The graph of the cost of a meal for a wedding is shown.

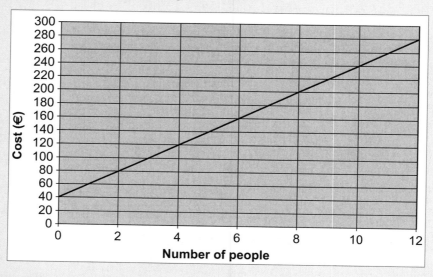

Using your graph, answer the following:

  (i)   Find the cost of the meal for 10 people.

 (ii)   How many people could eat for €180?

(iii)   Find the slope of the line.

(iv)   Find the equation used to calculate the cost of the meal per person.

 (v)   What could the *y*-intercept value represent in this graph?

Solution

For parts (i) and (ii), if we start with a value on one axis, we draw a line so that we can read off a value from the other axis.

  (i)   Using the graph, we can draw a vertical line from 10 people (on the *x*-axis) up to the graph line. We then draw a horizontal line across to the *y*-axis to read off 240.

        The cost for 10 people would be €240.

 (ii)   Using a graph, we can draw a horizontal line from €180 (on the *y*-axis) across to the graph line. We then draw a vertical line down to the *x*-axis to read off 7.

        Seven people could eat for €180.

(iii)   Find the slope of the line.

        This can be done by two methods.

Method 1

We pick two points on the line: (0,40) and (2,80).

Using the formula $m = \dfrac{y_2 - y_1}{x_2 - x_1}$:

$$m = \frac{80 - 40}{2 - 0} = \frac{40}{2}$$

$$\therefore m = 20$$

Method 2

The slope is the rate of change of the y-value in relation to the x-value.

The y-value changes by 40 every two people
$\Rightarrow$ changes by 20 for one person.

$\therefore m = 20$

y-value	x-value
40	0
80	2
120	4

(iv) When asked for a linear equation, it is usually better to use the form $y = mx + c$.

m = slope = 20 c = y-intercept = 40

Equation of line $\Rightarrow y = 20x + 40$

(v) The y-intercept value of €40 could represent the booking fee.

Directly Proportional Graphs

We may also encounter graphs that are directly proportional.

Worked Example 30.6

A graph for converting euros into dollars is shown.

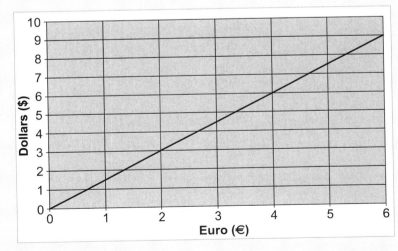

Using your graph:

(i) Convert \$6 into euros.

(ii) Calculate how much €5 would be worth in dollars.

(iii) Find the equation used to change euros into dollars.

(iv) Find out if the two currencies are directly proportional to each other.

Solution

(i) From the graph, \$6 is worth €4.

(ii) From the graph, €5 is worth \$7.50.

(iii) Use the formula $y = mx + c$.

Use the points $(0,0)$ and $(2,3)$.

$m = \dfrac{3-0}{2-0} = \dfrac{3}{2}$

$c = y\text{-intercept} = 0$

$y = mx + c = \dfrac{3}{2}x + 0$

$\therefore y = \dfrac{3}{2}x$

(iv) Consider the following table:

Euro	Dollar
2	3
4	6
6	9

- If we double the euro amount, the dollar amount doubles as well.
- If we multiply the euro amount by 3, the dollar amount also trebles as well.

Either one of these facts shows that these two quantities are **directly proportional**.

> **Directly proportional quantities** can be represented as a line in the form $y = mx$. The line will go through the origin $(0,0)$.

 ## Worked Example 30.7

A customer has a choice of two electricity companies, A and B. The cost of electricity is shown on the graph.

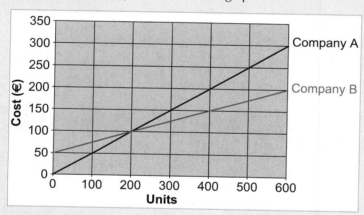

Using this graph:

(i) Identify which company's cost per unit is directly proportional.

(ii) Explain what the point of intersection represents in this graph.

(iii) Which company represents the better value for money?

Solution

(i) Company A, as the line for this company goes through the origin.
The equation for this line would be in the form $y = mx$.

(ii) At the point of intersection, both companies charge the same price for the same amount of electricity.
200 units cost €100.

(iii) For those customers who use less than 200 units, it would be better to go with Company A.
For those customers who use more than 200 units, it would be better to go with Company B.

 ACTIVITY 30.3

Exercise 30.2

1. A car rental company charges a basic fee of €20 for hiring one of its Economy cars and a fee of 20 cents per kilometre for every kilometre driven. The graph shows the cost of renting the car for journeys of less than 1,000 km.

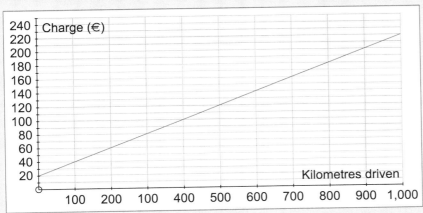

Use the graph to answer the following questions.

(i) John rents one of the Economy cars. He drives the car a total distance of 800 km, before returning it to the car rental company. How much does the company charge John?

(ii) Anne rents an Economy car to drive to Dublin. She returns the car to a garage in Dublin. Her journey was 200 km. How much does Anne have to pay?

(iii) Rex rented an Economy car. The car rental company charged him €130. What distance did Rex travel in the car?

(iv) Find the equation of the straight line in the graph above.

(v) If y represents the cost of renting a car and x represents distance travelled, use your equation to find the cost of renting an Economy car for a journey of 1,220 km.

2. A taxi driver charges a fixed minimum price of €3. The graph shows the cost of hiring the taxi for journeys of between 0 and 6 km.

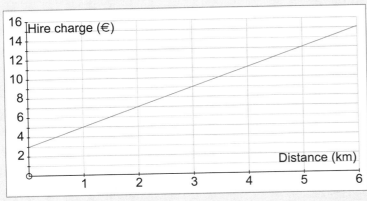

Use the graph to answer the following questions.

(i) John hires the taxi to take him from his home to the airport, a distance of 4 km. How much does the taxi driver charge John?

(ii) Alice hires the taxi to take her from her home to the cinema, a distance of 3 km. How much does the taxi driver charge Alice?

(iii) Anne has hired the taxi to take her from school to the shop. The taxi driver has charged Anne €12. What is the distance from Anne's school to the shop?

(iv) Find the equation of the straight line in the graph above.

(v) If y represents hire charge and x represents distance travelled, use your equation to find the cost of hiring the taxi for a journey of 10 km.

3. Electricity bills are issued every two months. At present, electricity bills have a fixed charge of €22.12. The graph below shows the charges for electricity for customers who use between 0 and 1,000 units of electricity every two months. Use the graph to answer the following questions.

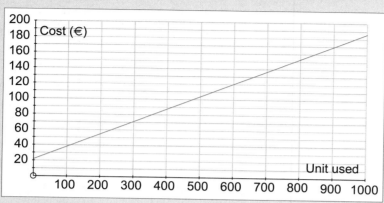

(i) Estimate the bill for a customer who has used 700 units of electricity.

(ii) Estimate the bill for a customer who has used 920 units of electricity.

(iii) John has received an electricity bill for €170 for this period. How many units of electricity has John used in this period?

(iv) The equation of the straight line in the graph is y = 0.164x + 22.12.

If y represents cost of electricity and x represents number of units used, use the equation to find the cost of 1,500 units of electricity.

4. The graph below shows charges for gas.

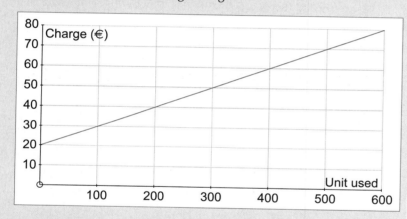

(i) What is the bill for a customer who has used 200 units of gas?

(ii) What is the bill for a customer who has used 350 units of gas?

(iii) Sharon has received a gas bill for €60. How many units of gas has Sharon used?

(iv) Find the equation of the line in this graph.

(v) Use the equation to find the cost of 800 units of gas.

5. The following equation converts degrees Celsius to degrees Fahrenheit:

$$y = \frac{9}{5}x + 32$$

Here, x represents degrees Celsius and y represents degrees Fahrenheit.

(i) Using graph paper, sketch the equation for x between 0 and 100.

(ii) Use your graph to convert 0°C to °F.

(iii) Use your graph to convert 41°F to °C.

(iv) Use the equation to convert 100°C to °F.

6. The graph below shows that the cost of hiring a conference centre depends on the number of people attending the conference:

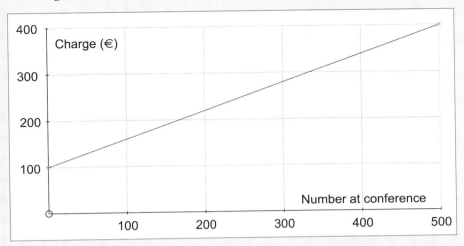

(i) What is the basic fee for hiring the conference centre?

(ii) If 200 people attend a conference, then from the graph estimate the cost of hiring the centre for this group.

(iii) The organiser of a conference has just received a bill of €280 for hiring the centre. From the graph, estimate the number of people that attended the conference.

(iv) Find the equation of the line in the form $y = mx + c$.

(v) Use your equation to find the cost of hiring the centre for a group of 350 people.

7. This graph shows the relationship between the value of a car and its age. The car has had only one owner.

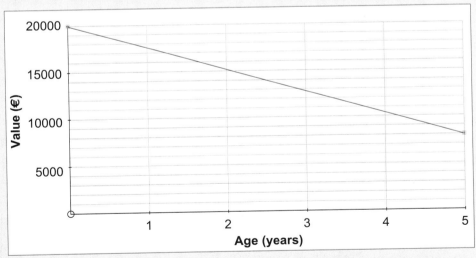

(i) How much did the owner pay for the car?

(ii) If the owner has owned the car for three years, what is the present value of the car?

(iii) If she intends selling the car in two years' time, how much should she expect to get for the car?

(iv) Find the equation of the line in the form $y = mx + c$.

(v) Use your equation to find the value of the car after six years.

8. Jamie, a professional footballer, has just bought a new apartment for €50,000 and a new car for €100,000. The graph below predicts the value of the car and the value of the apartment over the next five years.

(i) From the graph, estimate the value of the car after two years.

(ii) From the graph, estimate the value of the apartment after five years.

(iii) If Jamie bought the car and the apartment in 2010, then in what year will the car have the same value as the apartment?

(iv) Jamie has decided to sell both the car and the apartment in five years' time. He hopes to raise enough money from the sales to buy a yacht. The yacht will cost €150,000. Will Jamie have enough money from the sales to buy the yacht? Explain your answer.

30.3 GRAPHS OF LINEAR PATTERNS

Linear patterns can be represented using line graphs. We can use what we have learned about line graphs in the previous sections of this chapter and apply this to linear patterns.

 Worked Example 30.8

The table below shows how a plant grows over a period of 35 days. (Heights are in centimetres).

Start height	8
Day 5	12
Day 10	16
Day 15	20
Day 20	24
Day 25	28
Day 30	32
Day 35	36

(i) Draw a graph to show this table.

(ii) What does the slope represent in this pattern? Give a value for the slope.

(iii) What does the y-intercept represent in this pattern?

(iv) Find the equation of this line.

(v) What will be the height of the plant after 62 days?

Solution

(i) We normally put the first column of a table as the x-axis and the second as the y-axis.

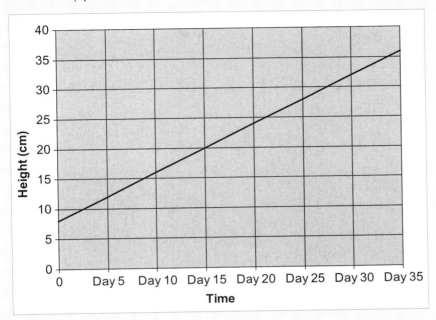

(ii) The slope represents the rate of change of the pattern.

The plant grows 4 cm every five days.

The slope is the rate of change of the y-value in relation to the x-value.

$\therefore$ Slope $= \frac{4}{5}$

(iii) The line starts at a value of $y = 8$.

$\therefore$ The y-intercept represents the start value of the pattern.

The plant's start height is 8 cm.

(iv) $y = mx + c$

$m =$ slope $= \frac{4}{5}$ $c =$ y-intercept $= 8$

Equation of line $\Rightarrow y = \frac{4}{5}x + 8$

(v) We can use the formula for the equation of the line to help with this pattern: 62 days would be on the x-axis, and the y-axis represents the height of the plant.

$\therefore x = 62$

$y = \frac{4}{5}x + 8$

$\Rightarrow y = \frac{4}{5}(62) + 8$

$\Rightarrow y = 49.6 + 8$

$\therefore y = 57.6$ cm

The plant will be 57.6 cm high after 62 days.

Orla's parents give her a choice on how she receives her pocket money, as shown by the linear graph. Orla will save all her pocket money for seven weeks.

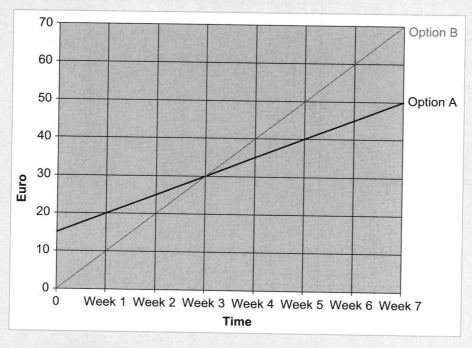

(i) Using the graph, fill in the following table:

	Option A	Option B
Start amount		
Week 1		
Week 2		
Week 3		
Week 4		
Week 5		
Week 6		
Week 7		

(ii) Describe in words both linear patterns.

(iii) In what week will Orla have saved the same amount with either option?

(iv) What option would you advise Orla to take?

Solution

(i)

	Option A	Option B
Start amount	15	0
Week 1	20	10
Week 2	25	20
Week 3	30	30
Week 4	35	40
Week 5	40	50
Week 6	45	60
Week 7	50	70

(ii) Option A: Orla is given €15 to start with and gets €5 per week.

Option B: She is given no money to start with and gets €10 per week.

(iii) The point of intersection of both lines is at Week 3.
∴ In Week 3, Orla will have saved the same amount with either option.

(iv) Option B will give her the most money after seven weeks.

Exercise 30.3

1. Christine saves €50 per week in her savings account. She already had €300 in her account.

   (i) Show how much she will have saved in five weeks, using a table and graph.

   Let the x-axis on your graph represent weeks and the y-axis euros saved.

   (ii) Use your graph to estimate how much money she will have in her account in 10 days' time.

   (iii) How much money will she have in her account in 25 days' time?

2. Fran is hiring a plumber. The plumber charges a call-out fee of €50 and €30 an hour for labour.

   (i) Copy and complete the following table:

	Cost (€)
Call-out charge	
1 hour	80
2 hours	
3 hours	
4 hours	

   (ii) Draw a graph of this table.

   (iii) Does this graph represent a directly proportional relationship between the two values? Explain your answer.

   (iv) Use your graph to estimate how much money the plumber would charge for five hours' work.

   (v) How much would it cost Fran if the plumber worked for eight hours?

3. A comic collector graphs how many comics he had in January and how many comics he has now.

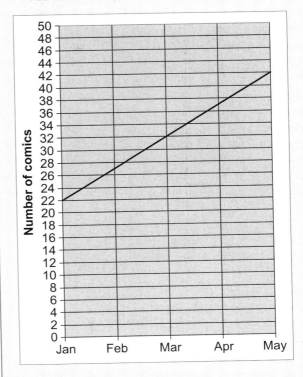

   (i) Draw a table to show this graph.

   (ii) Describe this pattern in your own words.

   (iii) If he continues to collect comics at the same rate, how many will he have collected by December?

4. A plant was planted on a given day. After it was planted, its height was measured every week. A graph of its height versus its weekly growth is shown.

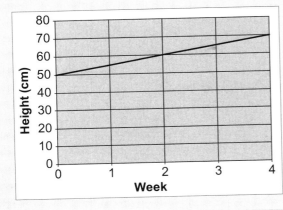

   (i) Draw a table to show this graph.

   (ii) How tall was the plant when it was planted?

   (iii) Describe this pattern in your own words.

   (iv) Assuming that the plant continues to grow in the same pattern, how tall will the plant be in nine weeks?

   (v) The plant grows to a maximum height of 1 m. How many weeks will this take?

5. Kieran is training for a marathon. He records the number of kilometres he runs per week for the first three weeks of his training.

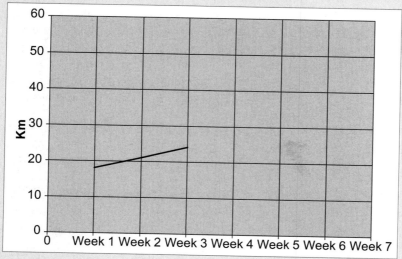

(i) Complete the following table:

	Kilometres run
Week 1	
Week 2	
Week 3	

(ii) Kieran continues to increase the number of kilometres run per week at the same rate. Describe this pattern in your own words.

(iii) Continue the graph on to show how many kilometres Kieran will run in seven weeks.

(iv) Explain why this value may not be correct.

6. To purchase and install a new central heating system costs €1,000. Each radiator installed costs an extra €125.

  (i) Show as a table how much it would cost to install up to seven radiators.

  (ii) Draw a graph of this table.

  (iii) How much would it cost in total to install 10 radiators?

  (iv) A homeowner has €3,000 to spend on installing the system. How many radiators could be purchased with this amount?

7. An advertising agency produces an ad campaign for a new toy. The start-up costs for the ad campaign are €50,000. Each day that the ad campaign runs costs an additional €20,000.

  (i) Show as a table how much it costs to run the campaign for eight days.

  (ii) Draw a graph of this table.

  (iii) From your graph, determine when €120,000 has been spent on the campaign.

  (iv) It is decided to run the campaign for another six days.
What is the total cost of this advertising campaign?

  (v) After 14 days, sales of the toy advertised amount to €500,000. The cost of manufacturing the toy is €100,000.

If we include the cost of the advertising campaign, how much profit does the company make on this toy?

8. Seán knows how to correctly spell 10 words from a page in his spelling book. He decides to learn to spell five new words from this page every day.

Ciara does not know how to correctly spell any words from this page of the spelling book. She decides to learn to spell seven new words from this page every day.

  (i) Show as a table how many words both Seán and Ciara will know how to spell in 10 days.

  (ii) Draw a graph of this table.

3. The number of bacteria on a kitchen surface is estimated. A graph shows the estimated number of bacteria present on the kitchen surface each hour.

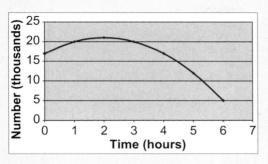

(i) How many bacteria were present on the kitchen surface initially?

(ii) Give a name to this type of pattern.

(iii) How many bacteria were present after five hours?

(iv) A disinfectant was applied to the surface at a certain time. If the bacteria were first counted at 8 a.m., at what time do you think the disinfectant was applied? Give a reason for your answer.

4. The area covered by weed in a lake is shown in a graph.

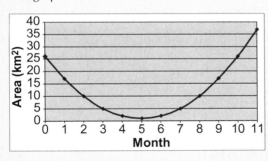

(i) Explain what type of pattern this graph represents.

(ii) In which number month was the area covered by the weed at its biggest?

(iii) In which number month was the area covered by the weed at its smallest?

(iv) If in Month 9 the weed covered 30% of the lake's surface, estimate the area of the lake.

(v) Which month numbers do you think represent the summer months? Give a reason for your answer.

5. The table below shows how high a plant grows over five days.

Start height (cm)	6
Day 1	15
Day 2	22
Day 3	27
Day 4	30
Day 5	31

(i) Draw a graph to show this table. (Let the x-axis on your graph represent time and the y-axis height.)

(ii) How tall was the plant when it was planted?

(iii) Between which two consecutive days was the plant growing most slowly?

(iv) Between which two consecutive days was the plant growing fastest?

(v) After Day 5 the plant begins to wilt and die. Assuming that the plant's height still follows the same pattern as before, how tall will the plant be on Day 7?

30.5 GRAPHS WITHOUT FORMULAE

There are many types of graphs that may be used to represent various situations and problems. When numbers are used in the graph, it is referred to as a **quantitative** graph.

This section deals with graphs where we do not know the formulae used to produce them.

One of the most common examples of this type of graph is the **distance–time graph**.

Worked Example 30.11

A student cycles to school on a particular day. She leaves her house at 8 a.m. and arrives in school at 9 a.m. The graph below shows her journey.

> Is is important to realise that in distance–time graphs the speed can be represented by the slope (gradient) between two points.

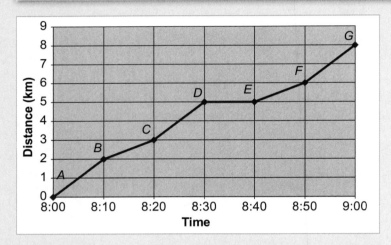

- (i) How far is the school from her house?
- (ii) Give one explanation for the graph between 8:30 and 8:40.
- (iii) What is the student's average speed in km/hr between the points *B* and *D*?
- (iv) What is her average speed for the whole journey?

Solution

- (i) Reading from the graph, we see that the school is 8 km from her house.

- (ii) At this time the student stays the same distance from her house.

  - She must have stopped at this time, perhaps for a rest.

- (iii) At point *B*, she is 2 km from her house.

  At point *D*, she is 5 km from her house.

  In 20 minutes (8:10–8:30), she travelled 3 km.

  3 km per 20 minutes = 9 km/hr (3 × 3)

- (iv) In 1 hour she travelled 8 km.

  ∴ Overall average speed = 8 km/hr.

> It is important to realise the role of **slope** or rate of change in graphs.
>
> - Remember that Slope = $\frac{\text{Rise}}{\text{Run}}$, i.e the rate of change of the *y*'s with respect to the *x*'s.
>
> - It is also important to note what the *x*-axis and *y*-axis represent.
>
> - In distance–time graphs, the steeper the slope, the faster the average speed.

Describe the speed of each of the following graphs.

Figure A

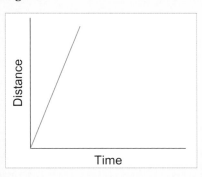

Figure B

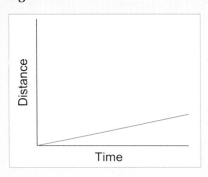

Figure C

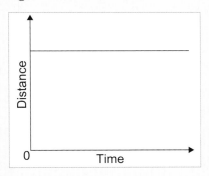

Figure D

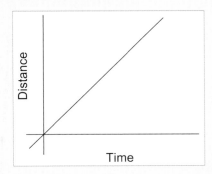

Figure E

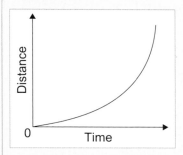

Solution

Faster-moving objects travel a greater distance over a given time.

Figure A: The slope of this graph is positive (going up from left to right) and quite steep.

The y-value (distance) is increasing quickly with respect to time.

∴ The graph represents an object moving at a fast speed.

Figure B: The slope of this graph is positive and shallow.

The y-value (distance) is increasing slowly with respect to time.

∴ The graph represents an object moving at a slow speed.

Figure C: The slope of this graph is flat, i.e = 0.

The y-value (distance) does not change with respect to time.

∴ The graph represents an object that is not moving.

Figure D: The slope of this graph is roughly 1.

It increases one unit of distance for every one unit of time.

∴ The graph represents an object moving at a steady, moderate speed.

Figure E: As this is a non-linear graph, the rate of change varies. At the start, the gradient appears to be shallow, but further on it becomes steeper.

∴ The graph represents an object that moves slowly at the start but then speeds up.

Speed–Time Graphs

It is also important to note what the x-axis and especially the y-axis represent.

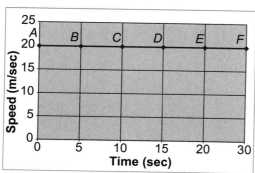

In this graph, we can see that the speed does not change with respect to time.

This graph shows a speed–time graph of a car travelling at the same (or a **constant**) speed of 20 m/sec.

Exercise 30.5

1. A family travels from A to their destination D in a car. The distance from their home to their destination versus the time is shown.

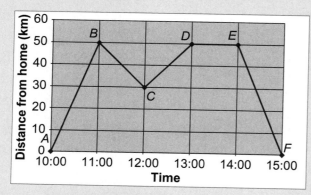

(i) How far did they travel?

(ii) At what time did they reach their destination?

(iii) They stopped for a meal during the journey. Where is this represented in the graph?

2. Claire decides to visit her friends, who live 5 km away.
   She travels as follows:

   (A) She leaves her house at 7.30 p.m. and walks to the bus stop, which is 1 km away. This takes her 10 minutes.

   (B) She waits five minutes for the bus.

   (C) The bus drops her off at a stop 1 km away from her friend's house. The bus takes 15 minutes to get to this stop.

   (D) She meets one of her friends and arrives at their house at 8.15 p.m.

   Draw a distance–time graph that represents Claire's journey.
   Let the distance from her home be on the y-axis and the time taken be on the x-axis.

3. The graph shown presents a journey taken over a five-hour period. Make up a story to describe the journey between each point. Make sure to include a reference to the time taken.

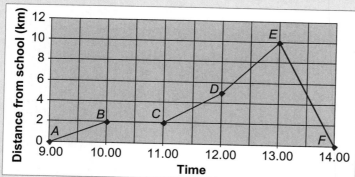

4. The following graphs show different representation of a bath filling with water. Match each statement with the correct graph.

Statement	Graph
Statement 1: A bath that is empty and is being filled up with water from a tap.	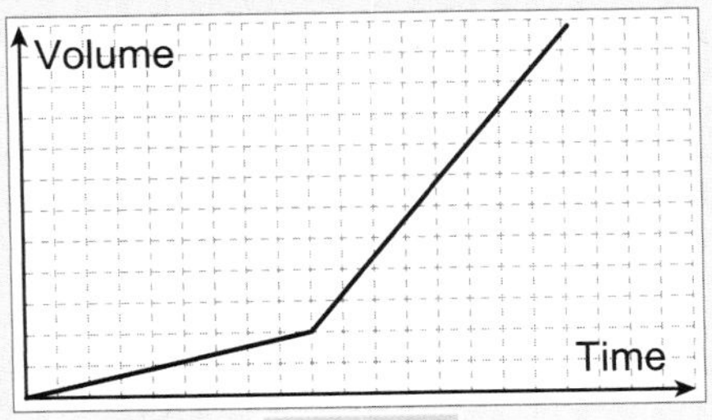 *Figure A*
Statement 2: A bath that is $\frac{1}{3}$ full and is being filled up with water from a tap.	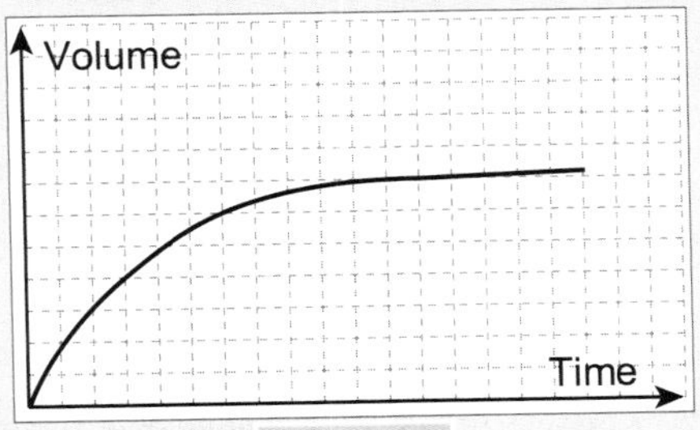 *Figure B*
Statement 3: A bath that is empty and is being filled up with water from a tap that is suddenly tuned off.	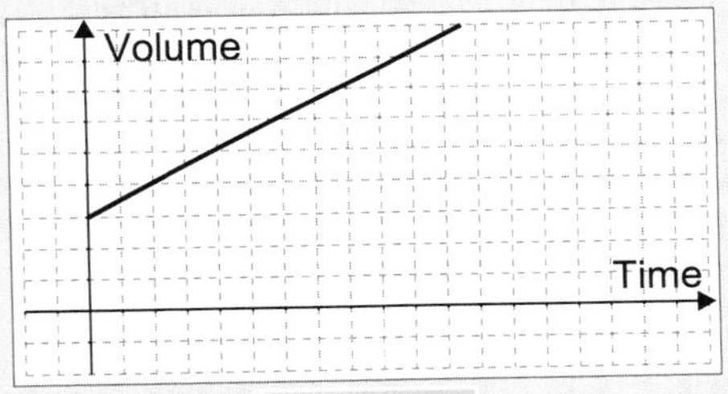 *Figure C*
Statement 4: A bath that is empty and is being filled up with water from a tap that is slowly losing water pressure.	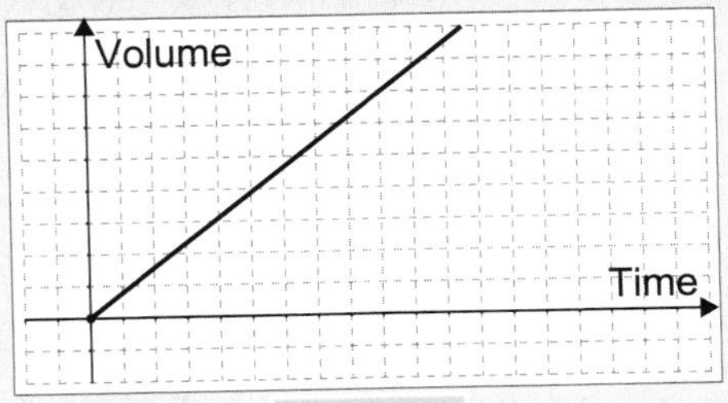 *Figure D*
Statement 5: A bath that is empty and is being filled up with water from a tap whose water pressure suddenly increases.	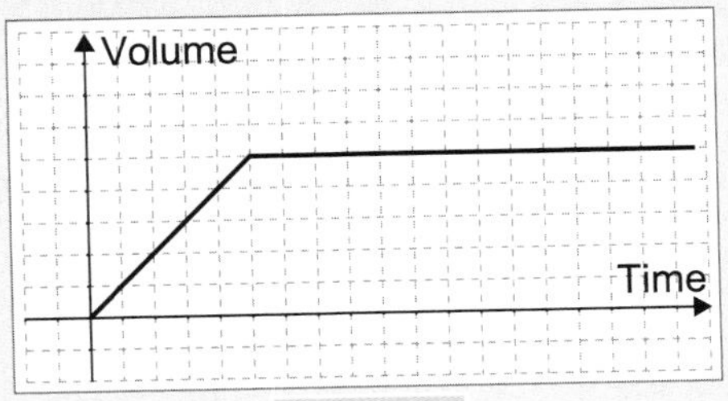 *Figure E*

5. The graph of the speed of a car in the first six seconds of a race is shown.

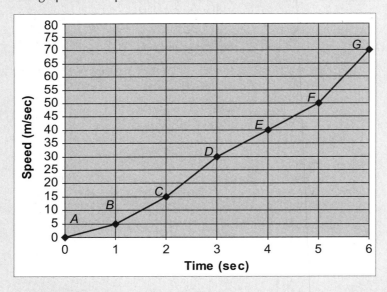

(i) Copy this graph into your graph copy.

(ii) Estimate how long it took for the car to reach 25 m/sec.

(iii) What was the speed of the car at 4.5 seconds?

A second car starts the race at the same time and the speed at which it travels is shown in the table.

(iv) Using the same axes and scales, represent this table using a suitable graph.

Time (sec)	Speed (m/sec)
0	0
1	2
2	10
3	20
4	40
5	45
6	80

Revision Exercises

1. Find the point of intersection of the following pairs of lines:

(i) $2x - y = -8$
$2x - 7y = -8$

(ii) $x - 2y = -5$
$4x - y = -6$

(iii) $4x + 3y = 18$
$y = \frac{1}{3}x + 1$

(iv) $y = x$
$y = \frac{1}{3}x + 8$

2. The graph show how much money an employee earns per hour.

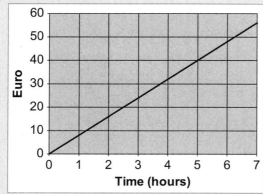

(i) Find the slope of the line.

(ii) What does the slope tell us about what the employee earns per hour?

(iii) Estimate, from your graph, how much the employee earns in four hours.

(iv) Using an alternative method, calculate how much the employee earns in eight hours.

(v) Explain which method is more accurate and why.

3. The cost in euros to produce a magazine is given by the equation $y = 2x + 5$.

   (i) Draw a graph of this equation. (Let the x-axis on your graph represent the number of magazines produced and let the y-axis be the cost in euros.)

   (ii) What could the y-intercept value represent in this graph?

   (iii) Using your graph, estimate the cost of producing seven magazines.

   (iv) What would be the cost of producing 35 magazines?

4. Henry borrows €500 from a friend. He agrees to pay his friend back €75 per month.

   (i) Copy and complete the following table:

Time	Money owed (€)
0	500
1st month	425
2nd month	
3rd month	

   (ii) Draw a graph to show this table.

   (iii) From your graph, determine how long it takes Henry to pay off his loan.

5. The cost of hiring an electrician is shown on the graph.

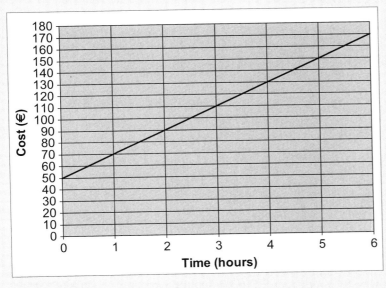

   (i) Copy and complete the following table:

Time (hours)	Cost (€)
0	
1	
2	
3	
4	
5	
6	

   (ii) Find the equation of the line shown.

   (iii) What does the y-intercept value represent?

   (iv) What does the slope of this line represent?

   (v) What is the cost if the electrician works for 8.5 hours?

6. This graph shows a bus tour journey from Ballyshannon to Letterkenny.

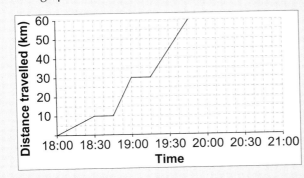

   (i) At what time did the bus first stop?

   (ii) At what time was the bus travelling the fastest?

   (iii) What was the average speed for the whole journey (correct to two decimal places)?

7. Without the aid of a diagram, explain which of the following pairs of lines will intersect each other and which will not.

(i) $y = 2x - 3$
$ y = 3x - 2$

(ii) $y = \frac{1}{3}x - 4$
$ 4x - 3y = 11$

(iii) $4x + 3y = 9$
$ y = \frac{1}{3}x + 5$

(iv) $4x + 5y = 8$
$ 8x + 10y = 20$

8. This graph shows a train journey after the train passes a certain point.

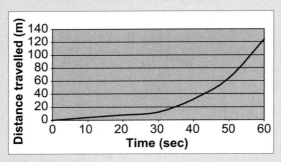

(i) How far does the train travel in the first 20 seconds?

(ii) Describe the train's journey, according to this graph, in terms of speed.

(iii) This graph shows either a train leaving or approaching a station stop. State which case it is and give a reason for your answer.

9. The following graphs show different rates of change with respect to time. Make up a story that represents each graph.

(a)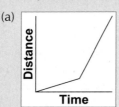

(b)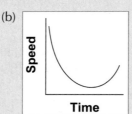

(c)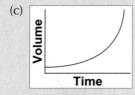

(d)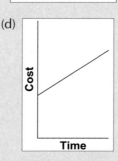

(e)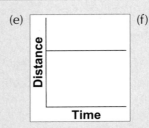

(f)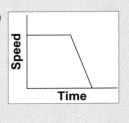

10. The graph below is a conversion graph between ounces and grams.

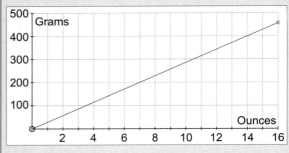

(i) Using the graph, convert 16 ounces to grams.

(ii) Using the graph, convert 200 grams to ounces.

(iii) Find the slope of the line.

(iv) Hence, write down the equation of the line in the form $y = mx$.

(v) Use your equation to convert 50 ounces to grams. Round your answer to one decimal place.

11. The number of birds in a bird sanctuary is recorded for five days in the table below.

Day 1	6
Day 2	10
Day 3	18
Day 4	30
Day 5	46

(i) Draw a graph to show this table.

(ii) What type of pattern does this graph represent?

(iii) Between which two consecutive days did the number of birds increase the most?

(iv) According to this pattern, how many birds will be in the bird sanctuary on Day 6 and on Day 7?

12. The table below shows how a plant grows over a 35-day period.

Time	Height (cm)
Start	8
Day 5	12
Day 10	16
Day 15	20
Day 20	24
Day 25	28
Day 30	32
Day 35	36

(i) Draw a graph to show this table.

(ii) What do you notice about the rate of increase of the plant height?

(iii) Estimate the plant's height on Day 23.

(iv) After 17 days, how much will the plant have grown?

13. The graph shows the cost of renting a van from two different companies, Vans R Us and Cheaper Vans.

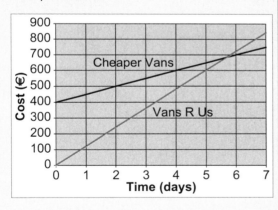

(i) How much does Vans R Us charge per day?

(ii) What is Cheaper Vans' fixed fee?

(iii) Describe in your own words the cost of hiring a van from both companies.

(iv) Which firm charges less to hire a van for 10 days?

(v) How much would it cost to hire a van for 15 days from either company?

14. Alex knows four words of Chinese. He sets himself a target of doubling the number of Chinese words he knows every day.

(i) What type of pattern does this information represent?

(ii) Draw a table and graph to represent the number of Chinese words he plans to know in seven days.

(iii) How many Chinese words does he plan to know in 12 days? Is this answer realistic?

15. A carrier pigeon is released from the top of a building. The height of the pigeon is measured every second. A table is produced to show these heights.

Seconds	Height (m)
0	16
1	9
2	4
3	1
4	0
5	1

(i) Draw a graph to represent this table.

(ii) What type of pattern is shown?

(iii) What is the height of the pigeon after 1.5 seconds?

(iv) At what time is the pigeon 4 m from the ground?

(v) Explain what might be happening to the pigeon after 4 seconds.

16. For a promotion, a supermarket decides to stack a certain brand of beans as a tower on the shop floor. The number of cans required for the first three levels of this tower pattern are shown.

Level	No. of cans
1	49
2	42
3	35

(i) Draw a graph to represent the number of cans in these three levels.

(ii) Find how many cans are needed to finish this pattern.

(iii) If each can is 12 cm high, how high will this tower be?

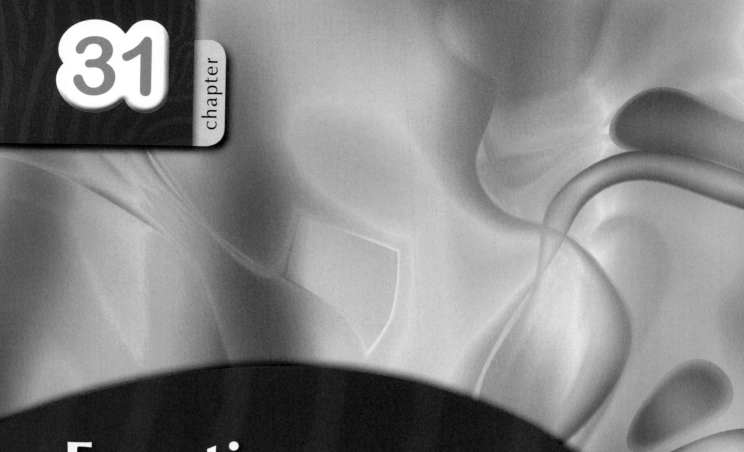

31
chapter

Functions
and Graphs

Learning Outcomes

In this chapter you will learn to:

⊃ Understand the concept of a function

⊃ Recognise couples, domain, codomain and range

⊃ Write functions using different notations

⊃ Draw graphs of linear functions

⊃ Draw graphs of quadratic functions

⊃ Use graphs to solve problems

31.1 IDEA OF A FUNCTION

A function is like a machine. If you put in a number, the machine changes the number and sends out a new number. *input*

For example, let us take set $A = \{4, 10, 11.5\}$. Let f be a function which doubles the input. If you put in 4, then 8 will come out. We write $f(4) = 8$. If the input is 10, the output will be 20. This can be written $f(10) = 20$. If you send in 11.5, 23 will emerge. In other words $f(11.5) = 23$.

The **domain** of this function is $\{4, 10, 11.5\}$, the set of inputs.

The **range** of this function is $\{8, 20, 23\}$, the set of outputs.

A function which doubles numbers could be represented in many other ways:

$f(x) = 2x \qquad y = 2x \qquad f : x \rightarrow 2x$

It is important to note that the variable x is usually used to represent the input.

y or $f(x)$ are used to represent the corresponding output.

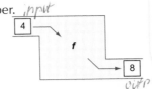
inputs — *input*

4 → f → 8
output

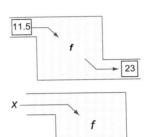
10 → f → 20

11.5 → f → 23

x → f → y or $f(x)$

A function can also be written as a set of **couples**. The input is written as the first component, and the output is written as the second component. For example, the function f could be written:

$f = \{(4,8), (10,20), (11.5,23)\}$

When a function is written as a set of couples, all the first components will be different.

31.2 DOMAIN AND RANGE

> When a function is written as a set of couples, then the set of first components is called the domain, and the set of second components is called the range.

Worked Example 31.1

$f : x \rightarrow 3x - 1$ is a function defined on the domain $\{1, 2, 3, 4\}$. Find the range.

Solution

'$f : x \rightarrow 3x - 1$' means 'If you put in a number, you will get out three-times-the-number-minus-one'. See what happens to the members of the domain 1, 2, 3 and 4:

$f(1) = 3(1) - 1 = 3 - 1 = 2 \qquad$ (If you put in 1, you get out 2.)

$f(2) = 3(2) - 1 = 6 - 1 = 5 \qquad$ (If you put in 2, you get out 5.)

$f(3) = 3(3) - 1 = 9 - 1 = 8 \qquad$ (If you put in 3, you get out 8.)

$f(4) = 3(4) - 1 = 12 - 1 = 11 \quad$ (If you put in 4, you get out 11.)

$\therefore f = \{(1,2), (2,5), (3,8), (4,11)\}$

$\therefore$ The range of this function is $\{2, 5, 8, 11\}$ (the set of outputs).

Worked Example 31.2

g is the function $g : x \rightarrow 5x + 4$. Find the values of v, w and x, as in the diagram.

Solution

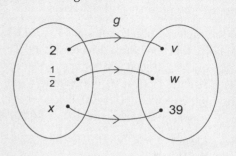

$g(2) = 5(2) + 4 = 10 + 4 = 14 \quad \therefore v = 14$

$g\left(\frac{1}{2}\right) = 5\left(\frac{1}{2}\right) + 4 = 2\frac{1}{2} + 4 = 6\frac{1}{2} \quad \therefore w = 6\frac{1}{2}$

$g(x) = 5x + 4 = 39$

$\therefore 5x = 35 \quad$ (taking 4 from both sides)

$\therefore x = 7 \quad$ (dividing both sides by 5)

Codomain

Let $A = \{-1, 0, 1\}$

Let $B = \{0, 1, 2\}$

Let $f : A \rightarrow B : x \rightarrow x^2 + 1$

This means that f is a function which transforms elements of the set A into elements of the set B, and the output is the input squared plus one.

A is the **domain**. B is the **codomain**, the set of allowable outputs.

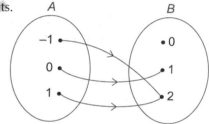

$f(-1) = (-1)^2 + 1 = 1 + 1 = 2$

$f(0) = (0)^2 + 1 = 0 + 1 = 1$

$f(1) = (1)^2 + 1 = 1 + 1 = 2$

$\therefore f = \{(-1,2), (0,1), (1,2)\}$

$A = \{-1, 0, 1\} = $ the **domain**.

$B = \{0, 1, 2\} = $ the **codomain** = the set of **allowable** outputs.

$\{1, 2\} = $ the **range** = the set of **actual** outputs.

Life is full of functions. For example, here is a function which shows the average seasonal temperatures (in degrees Fahrenheit) in Alaska:

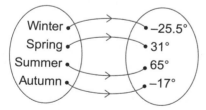

Here is another function which shows the prices of various items in a local grocery store:

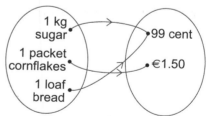

Here is a function which tells you the code to dial if you want to telephone someone in a particular place:

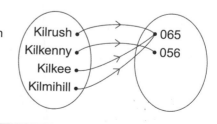

Finally, $f : x \rightarrow 20 + 45x$ is a function in which the input is the mass of a roast beef (in kilograms) and the output is the time (in minutes) which the roast should spend in the oven.

Exercise 31.1

1. $f : x \rightarrow 5x + 2$ is a function. Find $f(3)$.

2. $g : x \rightarrow 7x - 1$ is a function. Evaluate $g(2)$.

3. $f : x \rightarrow 10x + 3$. Find $f(7)$.

4. $g : x \rightarrow 6x - 10$. Find $g(5)$.

5. $f : x \rightarrow 2x + 1$ is a function.

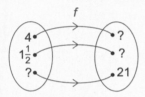

Copy and complete the diagram, replacing the question marks with the appropriate values.

6. $g : x \rightarrow 4x - 3$ is a function.

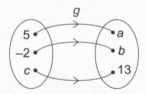

Write down the values of a, b and c, as in the diagram.

7. $f : x \rightarrow 9 - x$ is a function, as shown in the diagram.

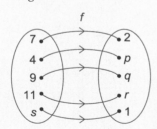

Write down the values of p, q, r and s.

8. $f : x \rightarrow 5x - 2$ is a function. The domain of f is {1, 2, 3}. Find the range of f.

9. f is a function such that $f(x) = 10 - x$.

   (i) Find $f(6)$.

   (ii) If the domain of f is {6, 7, 8, 9, 10, 11}, find the range.

10. $f : x \rightarrow x^2 + 1$ is a function defined on the domain {−2, −1, 0, 1, 2}. Find the range.

11. $f : x \rightarrow 3x + 11$ is a function.
    The domain is {1, 2, 3}. Find the range.

12. $f : x \rightarrow 7x - 10$ is a function.
    The domain is {0, 1, 2, 3}. Find the range.

13. $g : x \rightarrow x^2 + 4$ is a function.
    The domain is {−5, 0, 5}. Find the range.

14. $f : x \rightarrow 2x^2$ is a function. Evaluate:

    (i) $f(3)$ (ii) $f(5)$ (iii) $f(10)$

15. $f : x \rightarrow 3x^2 - 5$ is a function.
    If the domain is {2, 3, 4, 5}, find the range.

16. $f : x \rightarrow 10x^2 - 3$ is a function. Evaluate:

    (i) $f(1)$ (ii) $f(2)$ (iii) $f(3)$

17. $f : x \rightarrow 5x - 8$ is a function. Find:

    (i) $f(7)$

    (ii) $f(-7)$

    (iii) The value of p if $f(p) = 17$

    (iv) The range of q if $f(q) = q$

18. $g : x \rightarrow 2x + 3$ is a function defined on the domain N (the set of natural numbers).

    (i) Find the values of $g(1)$, $g(2)$ and $g(3)$.

    (ii) Investigate if $g(3) = g(1) + g(2)$.

    (iii) Find the value of x if $g(x) = 53$.

19. f is a function such that $f : x \rightarrow 3x^3 - 5$.
Fill in the missing numbers in the diagram.

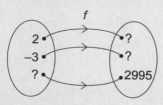

20. $f : x \rightarrow 5x^2 + 1$ is a function.
Fill in the missing numbers in the diagram.

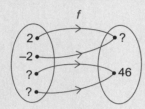

21. $A = \{0, 1, 2\}$ and $B = \{0, 1, 2, 3, 4, 5\}$
are two sets. $f : A \rightarrow B : x \rightarrow 2x + 1$
List the elements of these sets:

   (i) The range of f (ii) The codomain of f

22. $A = \{-1, 0, 1\}$, $B = \{0, 1, 2, 3\}$.
$f : A \rightarrow B : x \rightarrow x^2 + 2$
List the elements of these sets:

   (i) The range of f (ii) The codomain of f

23. $f : x \rightarrow x^2 + 2x + 3$ is a function. Evaluate $f(5)$.

24. $f : x \rightarrow 100 - 2x^2$ is a function. Evaluate:

   (i) $f(5)$ (ii) $f(7)$ (iii) $f(2)$

25. $f : x \rightarrow x^2 - x - 6$. Evaluate $f(3)$ and $f(-2)$.

26. $f : x \rightarrow (2x - 1)(x - 3)$. Evaluate:

   (i) $f(5)$ (ii) $f(3)$ (ii) $f\left(\frac{1}{2}\right)$

27. $f : x \rightarrow (6 - x)(x + 1)$. Evaluate:

   (i) $f(4)$ (ii) $f(6)$ (iii) $f(-1)$

28. The number of hours homework which
a student should do per day is estimated to
be $\frac{x+1}{2}$, where $x =$ the number of the year
in secondary school. How many hours' study
should be done by a student:

   (i) In Third Year?   (ii) In Second Year?

29. $f : x \rightarrow 2x + k$. If $f(6) = 22$, find k.

30. $f : x \rightarrow ax + 7$.

   (i) If $f(5) = 22$, find the value of a.

   (ii) Show on the numberline the solution
of $f(x) \leqslant 16$.

31.3 GRAPHS

In the 1700s one of Europe's experts on the study of graphs
was an Italian woman called Maria Agnesi. Because she was
a woman, many academic institutions refused to give her a
post. The French Academy, the leading academy of its day,
would not allow her a research post in Paris. The graph she
invented was called (in Italian) 'la versiera d'Agnesi' – the rope
of Agnesi, but was mistranslated as 'l'avversiera d'Agnesi' – the
witch of Agnesi. It is known as 'the witch of Agnesi' to this day.

La Versiera d'Agnesi

$$y = \frac{8a^3}{x^2 + 4a^2}$$

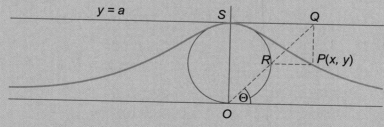

Graph of a Linear Function

Worked Example 31.3

$f : x \rightarrow 2x - 1$ is a function.

    (i) Draw the graph of f in the domain $-1 \leqslant x \leqslant 4$.

    (ii) Estimate from the graph the value of $f(2.2)$. *input is x*

    (iii) If $f(x) = 1.8$, find the value of x. *output y*

Solution

This function can be written in various other ways:
$y = 2x - 1$; $f(x) = 2x - 1$; $x \rightarrow 2x - 1$

All of these mean: 'If you want to find the output, you must double-the-input-and-subtract-one.'

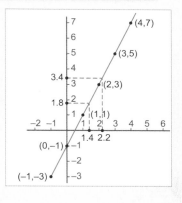

    (i) The domain (the set of inputs) of this function is $\{-1, 0, 1, 2, 3, 4\}$.

       The couples of f will be $\{(-1,-3), (0,-1), (1,1), (2,3), (3,5), (4,7)\}$.

       If we plot these points, we see that they form a straight line. By joining these points we form the graph of this function.

    (ii) This means: 'If the input is 2.2, find the output.' Draw a dotted line from 2.2 on the x-axis to the graph and then to the y-axis.

       Answer: 3.4

    (iii) This means: 'If the output is 1.8, find the input.' Draw a dotted line from 1.8 on the y-axis to the graph and then to the x-axis.

       Answer: 1.4

Worked Example 31.4

Solve **graphically** the simultaneous equations $y = 4 - x$ and $y = 2x - 5$, by graphing both functions in the domain $0 \leqslant x \leqslant 5$.

Solution

Here are the couples of the first function:
$\{(0,4), (1,3), (2,2), (3,1), (4,0), (5,-1)\}$

Here are the couples of the second function:
$\{(0,-5), (1,-3), (2,-1), (3,1), (4,3), (5,5)\}$

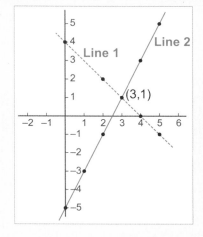

On the right we see the graphs of the two functions simultaneously. The point of intersection is (3,1), which is the only point which satisfies both equations simultaneously

Answer: $x = 3$, $y = 1$

Exercise 31.2

1. Draw the graph of the function:
   $f : x \rightarrow 2x + 1$ in the domain $-1 \leqslant x \leqslant 4$.

2. Draw the graph of the function:
   $y = 3x + 1$ in the domain $-1 \leqslant x \leqslant 5$.

3. (i) Draw the graph of the function:
   $f : x \rightarrow 3x - 3$ in the domain $0 \leqslant x \leqslant 5$.

   (ii) From your graph, estimate the value of $f(3.3)$.

4. (a) Draw the graph of the function:
   $f : x \rightarrow 2x + 3$ in the domain $-2 \leqslant x \leqslant 4$.

   (b) Estimate (from your graph):

   (i) The value of $f(1.5)$

   (ii) The value of x for which $f(x) = 8$

5. (a) Draw the graph of the function:
   $y = 5 - x$ in the domain $-1 \leqslant x \leqslant 4$.

   (b) Estimate from your graph:

   (i) The value of y if $x = 3.3$

   (ii) The value of x if $y = 5.4$

6. (a) Draw the graph of the function:
   $y = 6 - 2x$ in the domain $-2 \leqslant x \leqslant 4$.

   (b) Estimate from your graph:

   (i) The value of y if $x = 1.3$

   (ii) The value of x if $y = 1.4$

7. (a) Draw the graph of the function:
   $f : x \rightarrow 4x - 5$ in the domain $-2 \leqslant x \leqslant 3$.

(b) Estimate from your graph:

   (i) The value of $f(0.2)$

   (ii) The value of x if $f(x) = 6$

8. (i) Using the same scales and axes, draw the graphs of the two functions $y = 3 - x$ and $y = x - 1$ in the domain $0 \leqslant x \leqslant 4$.

   (ii) Use your graphs to solve the simultaneous equations $y = 3 - x$ and $y = x - 1$.

9. (i) Using the same scales and axes, draw the graphs of the two functions $y = -2x$ and $y = 3x - 5$ in the domain $-1 \leqslant x \leqslant 3$.

   (ii) Use your graphs to solve the simultaneous equations $y = -2x$ and $y = 3x - 5$.

10. (i) Using the same scales and axes, draw (in the domain $-3 \leqslant x \leqslant 1$) the graphs of the two functions $y = -x$ and $y = 2x + 3$.

    (ii) Use your graphs to solve the simultaneous equations $y = -x$ and $y = 2x + 3$.

11. (i) Using the same scales and axes, draw the graphs of these two functions in the domain $0 \leqslant x \leqslant 5$:
    $f : x \rightarrow \frac{1}{2}x - 3$ and $g : x \rightarrow 3 - x$

    (ii) Use your graphs to solve the simultaneous equations $y = \frac{1}{2}x - 3$ and $y = 3 - x$.

12. (a) Solve the simultaneous equations $y = 2 - x$ and $y = 3x - 10$ using an **algebraic** method.

    (ii) Solve these equations by **graphing** the functions $y = 2 - x$ and $y = 3x - 10$ in the domain $0 \leqslant x \leqslant 5$.

Quadratic Graphs

Worked Example 31.5

(a) Draw the graph of the function $f : x \rightarrow x^2 + x - 6$ in the domain $-4 \leqslant x \leqslant 3$.

(b) Estimate, from your graph:

   (i) The value of $f(2.2)$

   (ii) The values of x for which $f(x) = 0$

   (iii) The values of x for which $x^2 + x - 6 = 4$

Solution

(a) This grid will help us to evaluate $f(x)$ for the domain:

x	−4	−3	−2	−1	0	1	2	3
x^2	16	9	4	1	0	1	4	9
x	−4	−3	−2	−1	0	1	4	9
−6	−6	−6	−6	−6	−6	−6	−6	−6
y	6	0	−4	−6	−6	−4	0	6

The points are (−4,6), (−3,0), (−2,−4), (−1,−6), (0,−6), (1,−4), (2,0), (3,6)

Here is the graph:

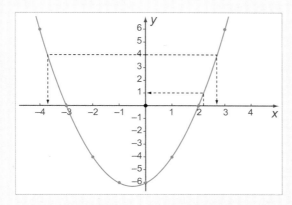

(b) (i) This means: 'If $x = 2.2$, what is the value *of y?*' The dotted line from 2.2 to the graph and then to the y-axis gives us the estimate:
$f(2.2) = 1$

(ii) This means: 'If $y = 0$, find x.' The graph cuts the x-axis at (−3,0) and (2,0).
Hence the values of x for which $f(x) = 0$ are −3 and 2.

(iii) This means: 'If $y = 4$, find x.' Draw lines both East and West from 4 on the y-axis.
These give us the estimates:
$x = −3.7$ and 2.7

 Worked Example 31.6

(a) Draw the graph of $y = 5 + 4x − x^2$ in the domain $−1 \leqslant x \leqslant 5$.

(b) Zero on the x-axis represents midday, while 1, 2, 3, etc. represent 1 p.m., 2 p.m., 3 p.m., etc. The readings on the y-axis represent the depth of water (in metres) in a harbour. Find:

(i) The depth at 3.30 p.m. (ii) The greatest depth and the time at which it occurs

Solution

(a)

x	−1	0	1	2	3	4	5
5	5	5	5	5	5	5	5
$+4x$	−4	0	4	8	12	16	20
$−x^2$	−1	0	−1	−4	−9	−16	−25
y	0	5	8	9	8	5	0

The points are (−1,0), (0,5), (1,8), (2,9), (3,8), (4,5), (5,0)

Here is the graph: It is shaped like an upside-down wine glass.

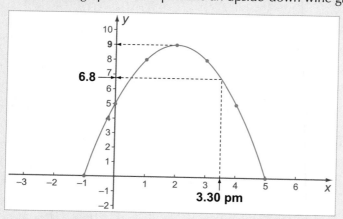

3.30 pm

(b) (i) To find the depth at 3.30 p.m., we start at 3.5 on the x-axis (not at 3.3 of course!). The corresponding reading on the y-axis is 6.8.

Answer: The depth at 3.30 p.m. is about 6.8 m.

(ii) **Answer:** The greatest depth is 9 m at 2 p.m.

Exercise 31.3

1. Draw the graph of the function $y = x^2 - 4x + 5$ in the domain $0 \leqslant x \leqslant 4$.

   Use your graph to find:

   (i) The value of y when $x = 3.5$

   (ii) The values of x if $y = 2$

2. Draw the graph of the function $y = x^2 - 6x + 7$ in the domain $0 \leqslant x \leqslant 6$.

   Use your graph to find:

   (i) The value of y when $x = 0.5$

   (ii) The values of x if $y = 0$

3. Draw the graph of the function $f : x \rightarrow x^2 - 3x - 4$ in the domain $-2 \leqslant x \leqslant 5, x \in R$.

   Find from your graph:

   (i) The value of $f(4.5)$

   (ii) The solution to $x^2 - 3x - 4 = 0$

   (iii) The approximate solutions to $x^2 - 3x - 4 = -2$

4. Draw the graph of the function $y = x^2 + x - 12$ in the domain $-4 \leqslant x \leqslant 3, x \in R$.

   Use your graph to find:

   (i) The value of y when $x = 1.5$

   (ii) The values of x if $y = 0$

   (iii) The approximate values of x for which $y = -4$

5. Draw the graph of the function $y = x^2 - x - 5$ in the domain $-3 \leqslant x \leqslant 4, x \in R$.

   (i) The value of y when $x = 1.8$

   (ii) The values of x if $y = 0$

   (iii) The values of x for which $y = 4$

6. Draw the graph of the function $x \rightarrow x^2 - 2x - 1$ in the domain $-2 \leqslant x \leqslant 4, x \in R$.

   Use your graph to find:

   (i) The value of $x^2 - 2x - 1$ when $x = -1\frac{1}{2}$

   (ii) The values of x if $x^2 - 2x - 1 = 0$

   (iii) The least value of $x^2 - 2x - 1$

7. Draw the graph of the function $y = x^2 - 3x + 1$ in the domain $-1 \leqslant x \leqslant 4$.

   Use your graph to find:

   (i) The value of y when $x = 1.5$

   (ii) The values of x if $y = 5$

   (iii) The values of x for which $y = 0$

8. Draw the graph of the function $x \rightarrow x^2 + 2x - 4$ in the domain $-4 \leqslant x \leqslant 2, x \in R$.

   Use your graph to find:

   (i) The value of $x^2 + 2x - 4$ when $x = 0.5$

   (ii) The values of x if $x^2 + 2x - 4 = 0$

   (iii) The least value of $x^2 + 2x - 4$ and the value of x at which it occurs

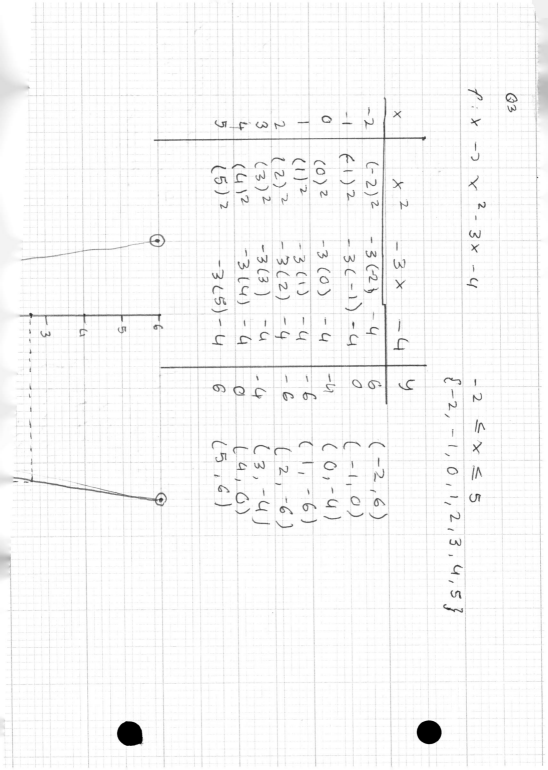

Q3

$f: x \rightarrow x^2 - 3x - 4$ $-2 \leq x \leq 5$ $\{-2, -1, 0, 1, 2, 3, 4, 5\}$

x	x^2	$-3x$	-4	y	
-2	$(-2)^2$	$-3(-2)$	-4	6	$(-2, 6)$
-1	$(-1)^2$	$-3(-1)$	-4	0	$(-1, 0)$
0	$(0)^2$	$-3(0)$	-4	-4	$(0, -4)$
1	$(1)^2$	$-3(1)$	-4	-6	$(1, -6)$
2	$(2)^2$	$-3(2)$	-4	-6	$(2, -6)$
3	$(3)^2$	$-3(3)$	-4	-4	$(3, -4)$
4	$(4)^2$	$-3(4)$	-4	0	$(4, 0)$
5	$(5)^2$	$-3(5)-4$		6	$(5, 6)$

P2

Area & Volume

Statistics
mean - -
stem-leaf

Probability
theorems
constructs
co-ord geometry
trigonometry
graphs

patterns
sequence
slopes
time
algebra
probability

Paper 1.

Rational Number

Natural "

Venn Diagrams

Surds

VAT

DIRT

%'s

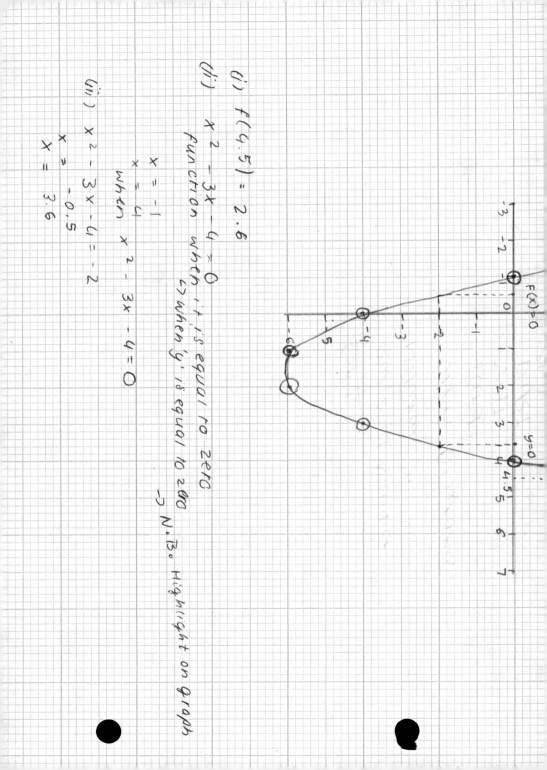

(i) $f(4.5) = 2.6$

(ii) $x^2 - 3x - 4 = 0$
function when it is equal to zero
↳ when 'y' is equal to zero
→ N.B. Highlight on graph

$x = -1$
$x = 4$
when $x^2 - 3x - 4 = 0$

(iii) $x^2 - 3x - 4 = -2$
$x = -0.5$
$x = 3.6$

9. Draw the graph of the function $y = x^2 + 4x$ in the domain $-5 \leqslant x \leqslant 1, x \in R$.

Use your graph to find:

(i) The value of y when $x = 0.3$

(ii) The values of x if $y = 0$

(iii) The values of x for which $y = -2$

(iv) The least value of y and the value of x at which it occurs

10. Draw the graph of the function $y = x^2 - 6$ in the domain $-4 \leqslant x \leqslant 4, x \in R$.

Use your graph to find:

(i) The value of y when $x = 1.4$

(ii) The values of x if $y = 0$

(iii) The values of x for which $y = 5$

11. Draw the graph of the function $y = x^2 - 6x + 5$ in the domain $0 \leqslant x \leqslant 6, x \in R$.

Take zero on the x-axis to be midnight and 1, 2, 3, etc. to represent 1 a.m., 2 a.m., 3 a.m., etc. The readings on the y-axis represent temperature (in degrees Celsius).

Find, from your graph:

(i) The temperature at half past five in the morning.

(ii) The lowest temperature reached and the time at which it occurred

(iii) The times at which the temperature was zero

12. Draw the graph of $f : x \rightarrow 2x^2 - 3x - 7$ in the domain $-2 \leqslant x \leqslant 3, x \in R$.

Find, from your graph:

(i) The value of $f(1.7)$

(ii) The values of x for which $f(x) = 0$

13. Draw the graph of the function $y = 3x^2 - 3x - 4$ in the domain $-2 \leqslant x \leqslant 3, x \in R$.

Use your graph to estimate:

(i) The values of x for which $3x^2 - 3x - 4 = 0$

(ii) The values of x for which $3x^2 - 3x - 4 = 11$

14. Draw the graph of the function $f : x \rightarrow 4x^2 + 6x - 7$ in the domain $-3 \leqslant x \leqslant 4, x \in R$.

Find, from your graph:

(i) The values of $f(-2.8)$

(ii) The values of x for which $f(x) = -1$

15. Copy and complete the following table for the function of $f : x \rightarrow 4 - x - 2x^2$.

x	-3	-2	-2	0	1	2	25
y	-11			4			-11

Draw the graph of $y = f(x)$ in the domain $-3 \leqslant x \leqslant 2.5, x \in R$.

Use your graph to find:

(i) The value of $f(1.7)$

(ii) The values of x for which $f(x) = 0$

(iii) The values of x for which $f(x) = 1.5$

16. Draw the graph of the function $y = x^2 - 8x + 16$ in the domain $0 \leqslant x \leqslant 8, x \in R$.

The readings on the y-axis represent the speed of a car in metres per second, while the readings on the x-axis represent the time (in seconds) as the car approaches a junction.

Use your graph to find:

(i) The speed of the car after 1.3 seconds

(ii) The time that passes before the car stops

(iii) The two times at which the car's speed is 2 m/s

17. Draw the graph of the function $f : x \rightarrow x^2 - x + 4$ in the domain $-3 \leqslant x \leqslant 4, x \in R$.

The graph represents the depth of water (in metres) in a harbour, from 9 p.m. one evening until 4 a.m. the next morning (each unit on the x-axis representing one hour and zero representing midnight).

Use your graph to estimate:

(i) The depth of water at 3.30 a.m.

(ii) The time when the water was at its shallowest level

(iii) The two times when the depth was 7.8 m

18. Draw the graph of $y = x^2 + x - 18$ in the domain $0 \leqslant x \leqslant 5$.

    y represents the height in metres of a missile above (and below) sea-level. The missile is launched from a submarine and rises out of the sea into the air. x represents the time (in seconds) after the launch.

    Use your graph to estimate:

    (i) The time when the missile reaches sea-level

    (ii) The depth below sea-level after 2.3 seconds

    (iii) The height above sea-level after 4.7 seconds

19. Draw the graph of $y = 6x - x^2$ in the domain $0 \leqslant x \leqslant 6$.

    y represents the height (in metres) of a ball thrown straight up into the air from ground level. x represents the time in seconds after it is thrown.

    Use your graph to find:

    (i) The height of the ball after 1.3 seconds

    (ii) The greatest height reached

    (iii) The time which the ball spends in the air

20. Draw the graph of $y = 8 + 2x - x^2$ in the domain $-2 \leqslant x \leqslant 4$.

    y represents the height (in kilometres) of an aeroplane on a long journey. x represents the time in hours. Zero represents noon. 1, 2, 3, etc. represent 1 p.m., 2 p.m., 3 p.m., etc.

    Use your graph to find:

    (i) The time of take-off

    (ii) The length of time spent in the air

    (iii) The greatest height reached and the time at which this occurred

21. On the same piece of graph paper with the same axes and scales, draw the graphs of the two functions:

    $f : x \to x^2 - x + 1$ and $g : x \to x + 4$ in the domain $-2 \leqslant x \leqslant 4$. At what points do the graphs intersect?

22. On the same piece of graph paper with the same axes and scales, draw the graphs of the two functions:

    $f : x \to 2x^2 + x - 5$ and $g : x \to 2x + 1$ in the domain $-2 \leqslant x \leqslant 2$.

    Use the graphs to find the values of x for which:

    (i) $f(x) = 0$ (ii) $f(x) = g(x)$

23. On the same piece of graph paper with the same axes and scales, draw the graphs of the two functions:

    $f : x \to x^2 - 3x + 3$ and $g : x \to 3 - x$ in the domain $-1 \leqslant x \leqslant 4$.

    Use the graphs to find the value(s) of x for which:

    (i) $f(x) = 6$ (ii) $g(x) = 0$ (iii) $f(x) = g(x)$

24. On the same piece of graph paper with the same axes and scales, draw the graphs of the two functions:

    $f : x \to 4x - x^2$ and $g : x \to x^2 - 8x + 16$ in the domain $0 \leqslant x \leqslant 6$.

    Use the graphs to find the values of x for which:

    (i) $f(x) = 0$

    (ii) $g(x) = 0$

    (iii) $f(x) = g(x)$

Answers

Chapter 1

Exercise 1.1

1. (i) {1, 2, 3, 4, 5, 6, 7, 8} (ii) {10, 12, 14}
(iii) {4, 5, 6, 7, 8, 9, 10} (iv) {3, 5, 7} **2.** (i) {2, 3, 5, 7, 11} (ii) {1, 2, 4, 7, 14, 28} (iii) {5, 10, 15, 20, 25, 30, 35, 40, 45} (iv) {2, 3} **3.** (i) {0, 1, 4, 9, 16, 25, 36, 49, 64, 81} (ii) {1, 2, 3, 4, 6, 12} (iii) {$^2/_3$, $^2/_4$, $^3/_4$}
(iv) {99} **4.** (i) {} (ii) {30, 32, 34} (iii) {} (iv) {}
5. Yes. A contains the same elements as B. **6.** No. A does not contain the same elements as B. **7.** (i) True. 3 is in the set. (ii) False. 10 is not a factor of 24.
(iii) True. 15 is not a prime number. (iv) True. 4 is a factor of 24 and of 16. (v) True. Each set contains the same elements. **8.** (i) False. A does not contain the same elements as B. (ii) False. 2 is not an odd number.
(iii) True (iv) True (v) True **9.** (i) {a, c, e, h, i}
(ii) {d, f, g} (iii) {a, c} **10.** (i) 4 (ii) 5 (iii) 9
(iv) 1 (v) 23

Exercise 1.2

1. (i) $2 \in A$ (ii) {3, 4} $\subset$ Y (iii) $7 \notin B$
(iv) {1, 2} $\not\subset$ {3, 4, 5} **2.** (i) $p \in A$ (ii) X $\subset$ Y
(iii) $q \notin B$ (iv) M $\not\subset$ N **3.** (i) {} (ii) {2, 4, 6, 8}
(iii) No. $9 \notin C$ **4.** (i) True (ii) True (iii) False
(iv) True (v) True (vi) True **5.** (i) $2^3 = 8$ (ii) $2^4 = 16$
(iii) $2^2 = 4$ (iv) $2^1 = 2$ (v) $2^0 = 1$ **6.** (i) N = {6, 7}
(ii) 4 Subsets: {}, {6}, {7}, {6, 7} (iii) Improper: {6, 7};
Proper: {6}, {7}, $\varnothing$ **7.** (i) A = {5, 7, 9} (ii) $\varnothing$, {5},
{7}, {9}, {5, 7}, {5, 9}, {7, 9}, {5, 7, 9} **9.** (i) True
(ii) True (iii) False. Some rectangles are not squares.
(iv) False. Negative integers and zero are not natural numbers. (v) True **10.** (i) Is a subset of (ii) Is not a subset of (iii) Is a subset of (iv) Is a subset of
(v) Is a subset of

Exercise 1.3

1. (ii) {1, 2, 4, 6, 8, 10, 16} (iii) {2, 4, 8} (iv) 7
(v) 3 **2.** (ii) {1, 2, 3, 5, 7, 9, 11} (iii) {3, 5, 7}

(iv) 5 (v) 5 (vi) 3 (vii) 7 **3.** (ii) {5, 10, 15, 20, 25, 30, 40} (iii) {10, 20, 30} (iv) 7 (v) 3
4. (ii) {3, 6, 9, 12, 15, 27, 81} (iii) {3, 9}
5. (ii) {1, 2, 3, 4, 10, 100, 1000, 10000} (iii) {}
6. (ii) {1, 4, 9, 16, 64} (iii) {1, 4, 16} **7.** (ii) {1, 2, 3, 5, 11} (iii) {3} **8.** (ii) {1, 2, 3, 4, 5, 6} (iii) {3, 4}
(iv) 6 (v) 2 **9.** (i) {4, 5, 6, 7, 8, 9} = D; {2, 4, 6, 8, 10, 12, 14} = E (iii) {2, 4, 5, 6, 7, 8, 9, 10, 12, 14}
(iv) {4, 6, 8} (v) 6 (vi) 3 **10.** (ii) {1, 2, 3, 4, 5, 6, 7}
(iii) {1, 3, 5}

Exercise 1.4

1. (ii) X^1 = {1, 5, 9, 15} **2.** (b)(i) A^1 = {1, 4, 5, 6, 8, 9, 10} (ii) B^1 = {1, 3, 5, 7, 9} (iii) A\B = {3, 7}
(iv) B\A = {4, 6, 8, 10} (c) No. The elements in A not in B are not the elements in B not in A. (d)(i) 3 (ii) 5
(iii) 7 (iv) 10 (v) 14 **3.** (b)(i) {1, 3, 5, 7, 9, 11}
(ii) {1, 2, 4, 5, 7, 8, 10, 11} (iii) {2, 4, 8, 10}
(iv) {3, 9} (c)(i) 6 (ii) 4 (iii) 6 (iv) 8 (v) 4 (vi) 2
4. (i) {1, 7, 9} (ii) {1, 2, 3, 5, 7, 8, 9, 10}
(iii) {2, 8, 10} (iv) {3, 5} **5.** (i) {5} (ii) {1, 4}
(iii) {1, 4, 5} (iv) {1, 4, 5} **6.** (i) {1} (ii) {5, 6}
(iii) {1, 2, 3, 4, 5, 6} (iv) {2, 3, 4} (v) {1, 5, 6}
(vi) $\varnothing$ (vii) {1, 5, 6} (viii) {2, 3, 4, 5, 6} **7.** (a) P
(b) Q (c) P $\cap$ Q (d) P $\cup$ Q (e) P \ Q (f) Q \ P
(g) P′ (h) (P $\cup$ Q)′

Exercise 1.5

1. (ii) 5 **2.** (a) 30 (b)(i) 25 (ii) 27 (iii) 3 (iv) 20
(v) 2 **3.** (ii) 6 **4.** (ii) 2 (iii) 14 **5.** (ii) 260 (iii) 130
6. (ii) 24 (iii) 53 (iv) 71 **7.** (ii) 4 **8.** (i) 150 (ii) 100
9. (ii) 13 **10.** (i) 8 (ii) 60

Revision Exercises

1. (i) False. A does not contain the same elements as B.
(ii) False. 15 $\not\in$ C (iii) True (iv) False. 4 $\notin$ B (v) True

2. (i) {1, 2, 3, 4, 5}   (ii) {2, 4, 6, 8}   (iii) {1, 2, 3, 4, 5, 6, 7, 8, 9}   (iv) {1, 2, 3, 4, 5, 6, 8}   (v) {2, 4}
(vi) {6, 7, 8, 9}   (vii) {1, 3, 5}   (viii) {6, 8}
(ix) {1, 3, 5, 6, 7, 8, 9}   **3.** (i) True   (ii) True   (iii) True
(iv) True   (v) True   (vi) False   **4.** (i) D = {6, 7, 8, 9, 10};
E = {6, 8, 10, 12, 14, 16}   (iii) {6, 7, 8, 9, 10, 12, 14, 16}   (iv) {6, 8, 10}   **5.** (i) {1, 2, 3, 5, 7, 9, 11, 13, 15}   (ii) {3, 5, 7, 11, 13}   (iii) {1, 9, 15}   (iv) {2}
(v) {0, 2, 4, 6, 8, 10, 12, 14}   (vi) {0, 1, 4, 6, 8, 9, 10, 12, 14, 15}   (vii) {0, 1, 2, 4, 6, 8, 9, 10, 12, 14, 15}
(viii) {0, 1, 2, 4, 6, 8, 9, 10, 12, 14, 15}   (ix) {0, 4, 6, 8, 10, 12, 14}   (x) {0, 4, 6, 8, 10, 12, 14}   **6.** (i) (P ∩ Q)′
(ii) Q′   (iii) (P ∪ Q) \ (P ∩ Q)   **7.** (i) {13}   (ii) {2, 3, 4, 6, 7}   (iii) {4}   (iv) {2, 3, 4, 7, 13}   (v) {2, 13}
(vi) {2}   **8.** (b) (i) 3   (ii) 3   (iii) 1   (iv) 5   (v) 2   (vi) 2
9. (ii) 9   (iii) 19   (iv) 13   **10.** (i) 73   (ii) 39   (iii) 28
(iv) 12   **11.** (ii) 29   (iii) 16   (iv) 35

Chapter 2

Exercise 2.1

1. (i) 3   (ii) 7   (iii) 14   (iv) 15   (v) 26   (vi) 24   (vii) 19
(viii) 9   (ix) 27   (x) 12   (xi) 19   (xii) 15   (xiii) 19
(xiv) 24   (xv) 17   (xvi) 22   (xvii) 21   (xviii) 18   (xix) 8
(xx) 30   **2.** (i) 697   (ii) 810   (iii) 14,984   (iv) 11,849
(v) 33,585   (vi) 235,098   **3.** (i) 33   (ii) 676   (iii) 4,584
(iv) 1,025   (v) 14,015   (vi) 164,902   **4.** W = 24;
X = 56; Y = 40; Z = 16   **5.** (i) €109,696   (ii) €6,550
(iii) €20,250   (iv) €2,696
8. (i) 25 − 19 = 25 − 20 + ① = 6
(ii) 44 − 17 = 44 − 20 + ③ = 27
(iii) 87 − 28 = 87 − 30 + ② = 59
(iv) 57 − 29 = 57 − 30 + ① = 28
(v) 147 − 98 = 147 − 100 + ② = 49
(vi) 764 − 79 = 764 − 80 + ① = 685
9. (i) 715 − 57 = 715 − 60 + 3 = 685
(ii) 115 − 88 = 115 − 90 + 2 = 27
(iii) 964 − 69 = 964 − 70 + 1 = 895
(iv) 644 − 29 = 644 − 30 + 1 = 615
(v) 776 − 73 = 776 − 80 + 7 = 703
(vi) 533 − 21 = 533 − 30 + 9 = 512
10. (i) 55 − 19 = 55 − 20 + ① = 36
(ii) 61 − 28 = 61 − 30 + ② = 33
(iii) 48 − 37 = 48 − 40 + ③ = 11
(iv) 67 − 49 = 67 − 50 + ① = 18
(v) 81 − 57 = 81 − 60 + ③ = 24
(vi) 73 − 18 = 73 − 20 + ② = 55

Exercise 2.2

1. (i) {1, 5, 25}   (ii) {1, 2, 3, 4, 6, 8, 12, 24}
(iii) {1, 3, 9, 27}   (iv) {1, 2, 3, 4, 6, 12}   (v) {1, 2, 43, 86}   (vi) {1, 2, 19, 38}   (vii) {1, 89}   (viii) {1, 2, 3, 6, 7, 14, 21, 42}   **2.** (i) {3, 6, 9, 12, 15}   (ii) {5, 10, 15, 20, 25}   (iii) {7, 14, 21, 28, 35}   (iv) {6, 12, 18, 24, 30}   (v) {10, 20, 30, 40, 50}   (vi) {12, 24, 36, 48, 60}   (vii) {15, 30, 45, 60, 75}   (viii) {16, 32, 48, 60, 72}   **3.** (i)(a) {1, 2, 4}   (b) 7   (c) 8   (ii)(a) {1, 2, 4, 8}   (b) 15   (c) 64   (iii) (a) {1, 3, 9}   (b) 13
(c) 27   (iv)(a) {1, 2, 3, 4, 6, 8, 12, 24}   (b) 60
(c) 331,776   (v)(a) {1, 2, 3, 6, 9, 18}   (b) 39   (c) 5,832
(vi)(a) {1, 2, 4, 5, 10, 20}   (b) 42   (c) 8,000
(vii)(a) {1, 2, 4, 8, 16}   (b) 31   (c) 1,024
(viii)(a) {1, 2, 4, 7, 14, 28}   (b) 56   (c) 21,952
4. (i) HCF = 2   (ii) HCF = 5   (iii) HCF = 4
(iv) HCF = 9   (v) HCF = 2   (vi) HCF = 15
(vii) HCF = 3   (viii) HCF = 5   (ix) HCF = 2
(x) HCF = 1   **5.** (i) LCM = 12   (ii) LCM = 24
(iii) LCM = 60   (iv) LCM = 45   (v) LCM = 90
(vi) LCM = 80   (vii) LCM = 12   (viii) LCM = 20
(ix) LCM = 120   (x) LCM = 180   **6.** (i) 23 and 29
(ii) True   (iii) 3 and 5, 5 and 7, 11 and 13, 17 and 19,
29 and 31, 41 and 43, 59 and 61, 71 and 73
(iv) 92 = 89 + 3; 94 = 89 + 5; 96 = 89 + 7;
98 = 79 + 19   (v) 42 = 37 + 5; 42 = 31 + 11
(vi) 24, 25, 26, 27, 28   **7.** (i) HCF = 34; LCM = 408
(ii) HCF = 13; LCM = 1,170   (iii) HCF = 58;
LCM = 174   (iv) HCF = 15; LCM = 3,060
(v) HCF = 123; LCM = 615   (vi) HCF = 3;
LCM = 2,829   (vii) HCF = 34; LCM = 510
(viii) HCF = 1; LCM = 203,688   **8.** (i) 25 or 26 or 27
(ii) 53 or 59   (iii) 1 or 7 or 13 or 91   (iv) 8 or 16 or
24 or …   (v) 2   (vi) 12   (vii) 64   **9.** (i) 31 people
attended the party   (ii) 5   **10.** 72 girls   **11.** 28 mm
12. 42 students   **13.** Largest possible
plot = 28 m × 28 m   **14.** Step 20   **15.** 10.15 am
16. 60 seconds   **17.** 1,020 teenagers

Exercise 2.3

1. (i) 30   (ii) 20   (iii) 66   (iv) 36   (v) 20   (vi) 3
(vii) 2   (viii) 5   (ix) 10   (x) 50   **3.** (i) 15   (ii) 15
(iii) 24   (iv) 24   (v) 30   (vi) 30   (vii) 28   (viii) 28
(ix) 30   (x) 30   **4.** (i) 6,052   (ii) 4,484   (iii) 2,511
(iv) 2,064   (v) 4,650   **5.** (i) 5,488   (ii) 1,798   (iii) 3,285
(iv) 2,754   (v) 513   (vi) 7,872   (vii) 32,298
(viii) 26,208
6. (i) (132 ÷ 2) ÷ 2 = 132 ÷ 9 = 33
(ii) (144 ÷ 4) ÷ 3 = 144 ÷ 12 = 12

(iii) $(180 ÷ 5) ÷ 6 = 180 ÷ \boxed{30} = \boxed{6}$

(iv) $(140 ÷ 2) ÷ 5 = 140 ÷ \boxed{10} = \boxed{14}$

(v) $(336 ÷ 4) ÷ 7 = 336 ÷ \boxed{28} = \boxed{12}$

8. (i) 8   (ii) 32   (iii) 16   (iv) 128   (v) 32   **9.** (i) 36
(ii) 18   (iii) 18   (iv) 3   **10.** (i) 14   (ii) 60   (iii) 60
(iv) 15   (v) 28   **11.** (i) 4   (ii) 8   (iii) 9   (iv) 25   (v) 64
12. 20   **13.** 704   **14.** 24 bags   **15.** 6 times   **16.** 16
17. 800   **18.** 30 pages   **19.** 24 million   **20.** €1,050
21. €10   **22.** 13 years

Exercise 2.4

1. (i) Commutative   (ii) Associative   (iii) Commutative
(iv) Distributive   (v) Associative   (vi) Distributive
(vii) Distributive   (viii) Associative   **2.** (i) 148   (ii) 162
(iii) 186   (iv) 1,025   (v) 863   **3.** (i) 59   (ii) 59
(iii) 192   (iv) 148   (v) 100   **4.** (i) 556   (ii) 754
(iii) 857   (iv) 579   (v) 184   **5.** (i) 1,724   (ii) 1,112
(iii) 1,246   (iv) 1,123   (v) 752   **6.** (i) 1,600   (ii) 98,400
(iii) 76,500   (iv) 56,700   (v) 29,400   **7.** (i) 71,600
(ii) 18,300   (iii) 96,500   (iv) 56,700   (v) 39,400

Exercise 2.5

1. (i) 6   (ii) 0   (iii) 9   (iv) 1   (v) 27   **2.** (i) 13   (ii) 17
(iii) 25   (iv) 2   **3.** (i) 9   (ii) 100   (iii) 5   (iv) 60
4. (i) 10   (ii) 56   (iii) 162   (iv) 15   **5.** (i) 9   (ii) 23
(iii) 84   (iv) 7   (v) 2   (vi) 42   (vii) 66   (viii) 49
6. (i) 150   (ii) 101   (iii) 525   (iv) 0   **7.** (i) 1   (ii) 2
(iii) 15   (iv) 10

Revision Exercises

1. (b) 4   **2.** (a)(i) $994 - 69 = 994 - \boxed{70} + 1 = \boxed{925}$

(ii) $776 - 67 = 776 - \boxed{70} + 3 = \boxed{709}$ (b) 80 metres

3. (a)(i) Sum $= 2 \times 6$ (ii) 28 is a perfect number
(b) Small box is €7   **4.** (a)(i) 2, 3, 11, 13, 19   (ii) 48
(iii) 4, 10, 12, 21, 22   (iv) 69   (v) The sum of the
primes on the list equals the sum of the composites.
(b) 460 notes   **5.** (a)(i) HCF = 4; LCM = 48
(ii) HCF = 35; LCM = 210   (iii) HCF = 12;
LCM = 3,876   (iv) HCF = 13; LCM = 1,170
(b) 246 seats   **6.** (b) 30 is the greatest possible product.
7. (i) 26   (ii) 10   (iii) 1   (iv) 4   **8.** (a)(i) 99   (ii) 634
(iii) 86,500   (b)(i) 10 is a natural number   (ii) 6 is a
natural number   (iii) 16 is a natural number   (iv) ¼ is
not a natural number   (v) 64 is a natural number
9. (a)(i) 4   (ii) 31   (b) 32   **10.** (i) 55 points
(ii) There are five ways to score 7 points

Chapter 3

Exercise 3.1

1. Systematic: {10, 11, 12, 13, 14}   **2.** The possible
outcomes are: Red and yellow, red and blue, purple
and yellow, purple and blue, orange and yellow and
orange and blue   **3.** There are 12 possible outcomes:
H1, H2, H3, H4, H5, H6, T1, T2, T3, T4, T5 and T6
4. Possible outcomes: Vegetarian and custard, steak and
custard, fish and custard, vegetarian and pudding, steak
and pudding and fish and pudding   **6.** There are 12
possible outcomes   **7.** Systematic: {ABC, BAC, BCA,
CBA, CAB, ACB}   **9.** (ii) 1   (iii) 0   **10.** (i) 11   (ii) 5
(iii) {4,6}, {5,5}, {6,4}   (iv) 2   **11.** (ii) Even   (ii) ¾
(iv) 25%   **12.** (i) 18   (iv) $^{11}/_{18}$ (v) $^4/_9$

Exercise 3.2

1. 18   **2.** 20   **3.** 30   **4.** 21   **5.** 15   **6.** 10   **7.** 24
8. 12   **9.** 120   **10.** 150   **11.** 104   **12.** 4   **13.** 350
14. 12   **15.** (i) 720   (ii) 1,000   **16.** (i) 2,600   (ii) 2,106
17. 18   **18.** 15,600

Revision Exercises

1. (ii) 6   **2.** (i) {H, H}, {H, T}, {T, H}, {T, T}
(iv) Systematic   **3.** (ii) 4   (iv) 8   **4.** (ii) 9
5. (ii) Mandatory/Compulsory   (iii) 15
6. (ii) 4   **7.** (i) 16   (iii) 4   (iv) 14   **8.** (v) 64
9. (a)(i) 6   (ii) 3   (b)(i) Student A   (ii) No   **10.** (i) 12
(iii) 144   (iv) 2,985,984

Chapter 4

Exercise 4.1

1. (i) A = 3, B = −2, C = 6, D = −5   (ii) A = 2,
B = 0, C = 7, D = −4   (iii) A = −1, B = 4, C = −6,
D = 5   **3.** (i) {−20, −16, 0, 9, 12}   (ii) {−14, 0, 12,
16, 29}   (iii) {−21, −18, −2, 25, 29}   (iv) {−146,
−106, −47, 140, 271}   **4.** (i) {9999, 1000,
−1000, −9999}   (ii) {101, 8, 0, −8, −101}
(iii) {8530, 4530, −970, −4370, −4880, −9840}
(iv) {1000, 100, −10, −100, −1000}   **7.** 104°C
8. 1°C   **9.** (i) −3 < 2   (ii) 5 > −5   (iii) 5 > 4
(iv) 2 > −3   (v) 2 > −2   (vi) −5 < −3   (vii) 0 < 4
(viii) −4 < 0   (ix) −3 < −2   (x) 8 > −5   **10.** (ii) 13 levels
11. 10 over par

Exercise 4.2

1. (i) –1 (ii) 6 (iii) –1 (iv) –5 (v) 1 (vi) –2 (vii) –5 (viii) –2 (ix) –3 (x) 0 **3.** (i) 1 (ii) 4 (iii) –3 (iv) –5 (v) –11 (vi) –11 (vii) 4 (viii) –4 (ix) –6 (x) –6 **5.** P = –11, Q = 25, R = –17, S = 4 **6.** (i) 2 (ii) –7 (iii) 0 (iv) 2 (v) –18 (vi) 6 (vii) 0 (viii) –14 (ix) –2 (x) 0 **7.** J = 3, K = –27, L = 10, M = –18 **8.** (i) 5 + 23 = $\boxed{28}$ (ii) 3 – 22 = $\boxed{-19}$ (iii) 7 – $\boxed{2}$ = 5 (iv) –7 – 5 = $\boxed{-12}$ (v) $\boxed{3}$ – 12 = –9 (vi) –15 – $\boxed{10}$ = –25 (vii) 12 – $\boxed{5}$ + 8 = 15 (viii) –3 – 5 – $\boxed{2}$ + 12 = 2 (ix) 2 = 5 – 3 + $\boxed{0}$ (x) 15 = 8 – 7 + $\boxed{14}$

9. –€300 **10.** (i) Alice: 21 marks (ii) Bob: 31 marks (iii) Kylie: 18 marks **11.** (i) 765 (ii) 567 **12.** No. He still owes €700.

7. (i) ±456, ±465, ±546, ±564, ±645 ±654 (ii) –654, –645, –564, –546, –465, –456, 456, 465, 546, 564, 645, 654 **8.** A = –6, B = –4, C = –15, D = –17 **9.** P = –4, Q = –24, R = –2, S = 4 **10.** W = –4, X = –2, Y = –1, Z = 4

11. (i) 3 × 4 = $\boxed{12}$ (ii) 4 ÷ –2 = $\boxed{-4}$ (iii) 3 + 7 = $\boxed{10}$ (iv) 10 ÷ $\boxed{-2}$ = –5 (v) –10 ÷ $\boxed{-5}$ = 2 (vi) (3 + $\boxed{4}$)² – 9 = 40 (vii) $\boxed{-245}$ + (–3 – 2)³ = –120 (viii) 3³ + (24 – ($\boxed{51}$)) = 0 (ix) 5² + (24 – ($\boxed{49}$)) = 0

12. (i) 5 > 3 (ii) –5 < 3 (iii) –5 < –3 (iv) 5 > –3 **14.** –7°C **15.** 12 metres

Exercise 4.3

3. (i) 30 (ii) –30 (iii) –30 (iv) 30 (v) 40 (vi) –32 (vii) –56 (viii) 90 (ix) 90 (x) –150 **4.** (i) 5 (ii) –4 (iii) 3 (iv) –3 (v) 4 (vi) 3 (vii) –6 (viii) –12 (ix) 2 (x) –25 **5.** (i) 75 (ii) –96 (iii) –42 (iv) 44 (v) –5 (vi) 3 (vii) 9 (viii) –1 (ix) 11 (x) –122 **10.** (i) 4 (ii) 9 (iii) 16 (iv) 1 (v) 1 (vi) 8 (vii) 27 (viii) 25 (ix) 36 (x) 64 (xi) 1,000 (xii) 125 **11.** (i) 4 (ii) 9 (iii) 16 (iv) –8 (v) 16 (vi) –27 (vii) 36 (viii) –2 (ix) –32 (x) 64

Exercise 4.4

1. (i) –6 (ii) 14 (iii) 14 (iv) –21 **2.** (i) 29 (ii) –9 (iii) –10 (iv) 9 **3.** (i) 19 (ii) –18 (iii) 13 (iv) –45 **4.** (i) 14 (ii) 57 (iii) 48 (iv) 28 **5.** (i) 0 (ii) 6 (iii) –9 (iv) –1 (v) 9 (vi) –27 **6.** (i) 25 (ii) –33 (iii) –50 (iv) 40 **7.** (i) 9 (ii) 100 (iii) –5 (iv) 60 **8.** (i) –18 (ii) 4 (iii) –108 (iv) 5 **9.** (i) 1 (ii) 108 (iii) –42 (iv) 49 **10.** (i) –158 (ii) –95 (iii) –245 (iv) 10

Revision Exercises

1. (i) –3 (ii) 3 (iii) –3 (iv) 0 (v) –1 (vi) –1 **2.** (i) 0 (ii) 0 (iii) 18 (iv) 22 (v) 13 (vi) –6 **3.** (i) 13 (ii) 3 (iii) 13 (iv) –6 (v) –1 (vi) 24 (vii) 94 (viii) 53 **5.** A = –1, B = 4, C = –6, D = 5 **6.** (i) {–20, –24, –28, –29} (ii) {20, 24, 28, 29} (iii) {–29, –20, 24, 28} (iv) {–28, –24, 20, 29}

Chapter 5

Exercise 5.1

1. (i) $\frac{3}{8}$ (ii) $\frac{1}{4}$ (iii) $\frac{3}{16}$ (iv) $\frac{2}{5}$ (v) $\frac{1}{3}$ (vi) $\frac{3}{8}$
2. (i) $\frac{3}{8} \neq \frac{6}{8}$ (ii) $\frac{2}{8} \neq \frac{5}{16}$ **3.** (i) $\frac{3}{6}$ (ii) $\frac{6}{8}$ (iii) $\frac{56}{49}$ (iv) $\frac{30}{33}$ (v) $\frac{18}{15}$ (vi) $\frac{68}{20}$ (vii) $\frac{48}{128}$ (viii) $\frac{6}{2}$ (ix) $\frac{1}{2}$ (x) $\frac{1}{2}$ **4.** (i) $\frac{9}{2}$ (ii) $\frac{8}{5}$ (iii) $\frac{35}{8}$ (iv) $\frac{17}{3}$ (v) $\frac{55}{8}$ (vi) $\frac{94}{13}$ (vii) $\frac{53}{6}$ (viii) $\frac{102}{11}$ (ix) $\frac{117}{8}$ **5.** (i) $1\frac{1}{3}$ (ii) $1\frac{4}{5}$ (iii) $1\frac{3}{7}$ (iv) $1\frac{2}{21}$ (v) $8\frac{1}{2}$ (vi) $2\frac{1}{2}$ (vii) $4\frac{1}{2}$ (viii) $3\frac{3}{4}$ (ix) $1\frac{2}{3}$ **6.** No. If Nicole has only three books in her home while Seán has 12 books then Nicole would have two biographies, while Seán would have four. **7.** (i) $\left\{\frac{3}{15}, \frac{1}{2}, \frac{2}{3}, \frac{5}{6}\right\}$ (ii) $\left\{\frac{1}{24}, \frac{5}{12}, \frac{1}{2}, \frac{5}{6}\right\}$ (iii) $\left\{\frac{7}{10}, \frac{11}{15}, \frac{3}{4}, \frac{23}{30}\right\}$ (iv) $\left\{\frac{13}{40}, \frac{7}{20}, \frac{3}{8}, \frac{2}{5}\right\}$
8. (i) $\left\{\frac{13}{25}, \frac{1}{2}, \frac{12}{25}, \frac{23}{25}\right\}$ (ii) $\left\{\frac{21}{30}, \frac{2}{3}, \frac{1}{2}, \frac{1}{4}\right\}$ (iii) $\left\{\frac{7}{20}, \frac{3}{10}, \frac{1}{4}, \frac{1}{5}\right\}$ (iv) $\left\{\frac{77}{100}, \frac{19}{25}, \frac{3}{4}, \frac{37}{50}\right\}$
9. (i) $\frac{1}{6}$ is bigger (ii) $\frac{1}{6} = \frac{14}{84}$, $\frac{1}{7} = \frac{12}{84}$ (iii) $\frac{13}{84}$ (iv) $\frac{25}{168}$ and $\frac{27}{168}$ **10.** (i) $\frac{1}{8}$ is bigger (ii) $\frac{1}{8} = \frac{18}{144}$, $\frac{1}{9} = \frac{16}{144}$ (iii) $\frac{17}{144}$ (iv) $\frac{65}{576}$, $\frac{66}{576}$, $\frac{67}{576}$, $\frac{69}{576}$, $\frac{70}{576}$, $\frac{71}{576}$ **11.** $\frac{7}{10}$ is closer to $\frac{2}{3}$ **12.** (i) $\frac{1}{4}$ shaded, $\frac{3}{4}$ not shaded (ii) $\frac{5}{16}$ shaded, $\frac{11}{16}$ not shaded (iii) $\frac{1}{4}$ shaded, $\frac{3}{4}$ not shaded (iv) $\frac{1}{4}$ shaded, $\frac{3}{4}$ not shaded

Exercise 5.2

2. (i) $\frac{9}{10}$ (ii) $\frac{15}{16}$ (iii) $1\frac{1}{6}$ (iv) $1\frac{3}{8}$ (v) $\frac{1}{2}$ (vi) $\frac{7}{12}$ **3.** (i) $\frac{1}{6}$ (ii) $\frac{1}{4}$ (iii) $\frac{7}{15}$ (iv) $\frac{1}{8}$ (v) $\frac{1}{10}$ (vi) $\frac{1}{6}$ **4.** (i) Because LCM = 12. (ii) $\frac{11}{12}$ **5.** (i) $\frac{5}{8}$ (ii) $\frac{17}{30}$ (iii) $\frac{23}{36}$ (iv) $\frac{27}{20}$ (v) $\frac{55}{63}$ (vi) $\frac{29}{24}$ (vii) $\frac{45}{56}$ (viii) $\frac{31}{20}$ (ix) $\frac{53}{100}$ (x) $\frac{17}{64}$ **6.** (i) $\frac{7}{8}$ (ii) $\frac{7}{5}$ (iii) $\frac{16}{27}$ (iv) $\frac{31}{24}$ (v) $\frac{19}{36}$ (vi) $\frac{17}{12}$ (vii) $\frac{19}{12}$ (viii) $\frac{37}{30}$ (ix) $\frac{41}{30}$ (x) $\frac{47}{15}$ **7.** (i) $\frac{1}{8}$ (ii) $\frac{13}{30}$ (iii) $\frac{1}{130}$ (iv) $\frac{1}{120}$ (v) $\frac{32}{99}$ (vi) $\frac{1}{4}$ (vii) $\frac{1}{6}$ (viii) $\frac{1}{60}$ (ix) $\frac{18}{35}$ (x) $\frac{4}{9}$ **8.** (i) $5\frac{3}{4}$ (ii) $2\frac{5}{8}$ (iii) $11\frac{13}{24}$

(iv) $6^7/_{24}$ (v) $1^3/_4$ (vi) $1^{23}/_{30}$ (vii) $9^{13}/_{24}$ (viii) $4^3/_{10}$
(ix) $98^{11}/_{16}$ (x) $50^1/_4$ **9.** (i) A = $^1/_{16}$, B = $^1/_4$, C = $^1/_2$,
D = $^5/_8$ (ii) J = 0, K = $^1/_4$, L = $^3/_8$, M = $-^1/_4$
(iii) J = $1^1/_{36}$, K = $^3/_4$, L = $^1/_2$, M = $-^1/_4$ (iv) J = $^1/_{12}$,
K = $^1/_{12}$, L = $^5/_{24}$, M = $^1/_2$ **10.** (i) $^{13}/_{20}, ^7/_{20}$ (ii) €10.50
11. (i) $^1/_{25}$ (ii) Fine Gael   (iii) Green Party
13. $15^{11}/_{40}$ km

Exercise 5.3

1. (i) $^1/_8$ (ii) $^1/_4$ (iii) $^4/_{15}$ (iv) $^3/_{20}$ **2.** (i) $^3/_{20}$ (ii) $^3/_{10}$
(iii) $^2/_{15}$ (iv) $^1/_{12}$ **3.** (i) $^2/_9$ (ii) $^3/_{16}$ (iii) $^6/_{25}$ (iv) $^5/_{36}$
4. (i) $^2/_{15}$ (ii) $^1/_6$ (iii) $^5/_{24}$ (iv) $^{16}/_{45}$ (v) $^9/_{20}$ (vi) $^1/_5$
(vii) $^1/_6$ (viii) $^3/_{20}$ (ix) $^7/_{36}$ (x) $^1/_{10}$ **5.** (i) 7   (ii) $7^1/_2$
(iii) $^{231}/_8$ (iv) $12^1/_2$ (v) $^9/_2$ (vi) $12^1/_{12}$ (vii) 18   (viii) $^5/_2$
(ix) $^7/_2$ (x) $^{93}/_5$ **7.** 84   **8.** $38^1/_2$ hectares   **9.** $^3/_5$
10. $^9/_{20}$ **11.** $^2/_5$ of $6^1/_2$ is bigger   **12.** (i) $-^1/_6$ (ii) $-^9/_{20}$
(iii) $^5/_8$ (iv) $^9/_5$ (v) $-^{25}/_2$ (vi) $-^{135}/_4$ (vii) -7 (viii) $-^5/_{144}$

Exercise 5.4

1. (i) 5   (ii) 8   (iii) 22   (iv) 7   **2.** (i) 6   (ii) 8   (iii) 8
(iv) 6   **3.** (i) 5   (ii) 10   (iii) 9   (iv) 5   **4.** (i) 4   (ii) 2
(iii) 2   (iv) 2   **5.** (i) $^1/_4$ (ii) $^3/_8$ (iii) $2^2/_5$ (iv) $^4/_{15}$
(v) $1^1/_6$ (vi) $^1/_3$ (vii) 4   (viii) $1^1/_3$ (ix) $5^3/_5$ **6.** (i) $1^1/_3$
(ii) 4   (iii) 12   (iv) $4^1/_5$ (v) 10   (vi) $1^2/_3$ (vii) $1^{58}/_{185}$
(viii) 6   (ix) 3   **7.** 25   **8.** 13   **9.** 28   **10.** (i) 39 kg
(ii) 40 weeks   **11.** (i) 24 pieces   (ii) 48 pieces
(iii) 36 pieces

Exercise 5.5

1. (i) 1 : 3   **2.** (i) 1 : 5   (ii) 1 : 5   (iii) 2 : 3   (iv) 1 : 4
(v) 3 : 2   (vi) 17 : 2   (vii) 4 : 2 : 1   (viii) 2 : 3 : 5
(ix) 6 : 2 : 1   (x) 6 : 3 : 1   (xi) 7 : 9 : 6   (xii) 2 : 1 : 5
3. (i) 1 : 2   (ii) 3 : 5   (iii) 5 : 6   (iv) 6 : 3 :2
(v) 20 : 2 : 1   (vi) 7 : 9   (vii) 4 : 11   (viii) 5 : 7
(ix) 9 : 15   (x) 20 : 15 : 12   **4.** (i) 1 : 25   (ii) 1 : 30
(iii) 3 : 20   (iv) 4,000 : 1   (v) 1 : 2,160   (vi) 20 : 1
(vii) 3 : 650   (viii) 15 : 1   (ix) 1 : 960   **5.** 500 cm
6. 20 g : 40 g   **7.** €20,000   **8.** $^3/_8$ **9.** 40 sweets
10. (i) 10 litres   (ii) 35 litres   **11.** (i) Monica $300;
Naomi $200   (ii) Monica $275; Naomi $225

Exercise 5.6

1. (i) $-^5/_{24}$ (ii) $^{59}/_{96}$ (iii) $^{49}/_{200}$ (iv) $^1/_4$ **2.** (i) $^5/_8$ (ii) $^{13}/_{30}$
(iii) $^1/_8$ (iv) $^{23}/_{50}$ **3.** (i) $^{13}/_{72}$ (ii) $^{99}/_{400}$ (iii) $-^1/_4$ (iv) $^{57}/_{800}$
4. (i) $-^{23}/_{36}$ (ii) $-^1/_4$ (iii) 0   (iv) $-^{33}/_{80}$ **5.** (i) $^{113}/_{360}$

(ii) $^{301}/_{600}$ (iii) $^{89}/_{900}$ (iv) $^{23}/_{300}$ **6.** (i) $5^7/_{12}$ (ii) $2^9/_{16}$
(iii) $1^1/_3$ (iv) $4^7/_{18}$ **7.** (i) $^{91}/_{144}$ (ii) $^6/_{25}$ (iii) $^{35}/_{64}$
(iv) $-^{271}/_{400}$

Revision Exercises

1. (i) $^4/_5$ (ii) $^1/_2$ (iii) $^7/_9$ (iv) $^5/_8$ **2.** (i) $^{11}/_{14}$ (ii) $-^1/_{10}$
(iii) $^5/_8$ (iv) $^2/_5$ **3.** (i) $1^1/_8$ (ii) $1^1/_{10}$ (iii) $1^1/_{15}$ (iv) $^5/_8$
4. (i) $^1/_2$ (ii) $2^5/_8$ (iii) $^2/_9$ (iv) $^9/_{16}$ **5.** (i) $^7/_{16}$ (ii) $^{229}/_{400}$
(iii) $^3/_8$ (iv) $^9/_{32}$ **6.** (a) $^4/_6$, $^6/_9$, $^8/_{12}$, $^{10}/_{15}$, $^{12}/_{18}$ (b) $^3/_{10}$, $^1/_3$,
$^7/_{20}$, $^2/_5$, $^4/_9$ (c) $^9/_{10}$ is closer to $^{37}/_{40}$ **7.** (i) $1^1/_4$, $6^1/_3$, $2^2/_7$,
$1^1/_5$ (ii) $^{26}/_{150}$, $^{27}/_{150}$, $^{28}/_{150}$, $^{29}/_{150}$ (iii) 120 ml   **8.** (a)(i) $^1/_{12}$
(ii) $^1/_{15}$ (iii) $1^3/_8$ (iv) $^2/_{15}$ (b) (i) $^{31}/_{40}$ (ii) $^{13}/_{16}$ (iii) $5^5/_6$
(iv) $5^{26}/_{35}$ (C)(i) <   (ii) <   (iii) >   (iv) <   **9.** (i) 20
(ii) $^2/_5$ **10.** (i) 60   (ii) $^2/_5$ (iii) $^3/_5$ **11.** (i) $^7/_{10}$, $^3/_5$
(ii) $4^1/_4$ cm   (iii) $^1/_4$ **12.** (a) (i) $^1/_6$ (ii) $^1/_{10}$ (iii) $^6/_{25}$ (iv) $^5/_{42}$
(b) 38   (c) (i) $43^3/_8$ acres   (ii) $8^{27}/_{40}$ acres   **13.** (a) (i) 16
(ii) 20   (iii) 18   (iv) 5   (b) $1^{37}/_{75}$ (c) 40 times   **14.** (i) $3^2/_3$
(ii) $5^{49}/_{64}$ (iii) $^{21}/_{32}$ **15.** (a) 1,875 shares   (b) $^1/_{10}$
(c)(i) 6 black   (ii) 4 white

Chapter 6

Exercise 6.1

1. (i) 3.146   (ii) 76.215   (iii) 35.651   (iv) 14.678
2. (i) 2.675   (ii) 1.758   (iii) 8.567   (iv) 765.3
3. (i) $^2/_{10}$ (ii) $^2/_{100}$ (iii) $^2/_{1,000}$ (iv) $^2/_{10}$ (v) $^2/_{100}$
(vi) $^2/_{100,000}$ **4.** (i) $^9/_{100}$ (ii) $^9/_{1,000}$ (iii) $^9/_{10}$ (iv) $^9/_{10,000}$
(v) $^9/_{10}$ (vi) $^9/_{100}$ **5.** (i) $^4/_5$ (ii) $^3/_{10}$ (iii) $^9/_{100}$ (iv) $^1/_{1,000}$
(v) $2^1/_2$ (vi) $1^1/_{20}$ (vii) $^6/_{25}$ (viii) $^{213}/_{1,000}$ (ix) $^7/_{40}$
(x) $3^1/_{40}$ **6.** (i) 0.5   (ii) 0.18   (iii) 0.022   (iv) 0.8
(v) -0.005 (vi) 0.35   (vii) 1.6   (viii) -3.38 (ix) 0.035
(x) 2.75   (xi) 0.04   (xii) 0.44   (xiii) 7.05   (xiv) 12.03
(xv) 31.7   **7.** (i) 0.0425   (ii) 0.00859…   (iii) 0.0264
(iv) 0.34   (v) 0.00488…   (vi) 0.06125   (vii) 0.041875
(viii) 0.0559…   (ix) 0.8005   (x) 0.78271…   **8.** (i) 0.684
(ii) 0.0732…   (iii) 0.08625   (iv) 0.016875   (v) 0.003
(vi) 0.46   (vii) 0.0296   (viii) 0.006625   (ix) 0.00390…
(x) 0.0005

Exercise 6.2

1. (a)(i) 0.7777777777   (ii) 0.7171717171
(iii) 0.7111111111   (iv) 0.7151515151
(v) 0.7157157157   (b)(i) 0.3333333333
(ii) 0.3434343434   (iii) 0.3473473473
(iv) 0.3477777777   (v) 0.3474747474
(c) (i) 3.6222222222   (ii) 3.6262626262

(iii) 3.6242424242 (iv) 3.6246246246
(v) 3.6244444444 **2.** (i) $0.\dot{5}$ (ii) $0.3\dot{5}$ (iii) $0.4\dot{3}\dot{5}$
(iv) $0.01\dot{7}\dot{2}$ (v) $0.68\dot{2}$ (vi) $9.4\dot{1}\dot{3}$ (vii) $3.9\dot{1}$ (viii) $2.89\dot{5}\dot{7}$
(ix) $3.\dot{1}2\dot{8}$ **3.** (i) $40 = 2^3 \times 5$; 2; 5; $50 = 2 \times 5^2$;
$65 = 5 \times 13$; $400 = 2^4 \times 5^2$ (ii) $^3/_{40}$ terminates;
$^1/_2$ terminates; $^3/_5$ terminates; $^6/_{50}$ terminates;
$^9/_{65}$ recurs; $^{13}/_{400}$ terminates **4.** (i) $^1/_7 = 0.\dot{1}4285\dot{7}$
(ii) $^2/_7 = 0.\dot{2}8571\dot{4}$; $^3/_7 = 0.\dot{4}2857\dot{1}$; $^4/_7 = 0.\dot{5}7142\dot{8}$;
$^5/_7 = 0.\dot{7}1428\dot{5}$; $^6/_7 = 0.\dot{8}5714\dot{2}$ **5.** (i) $^1/_6 = 0.1\dot{6}$
(ii) $^1/_3 = 0.\dot{3}$; $^2/_3 = 0.\dot{6}$; $^5/_6 = 0.8\dot{3}$ **6.** (i) $0.\dot{0}\dot{9}$
(ii) $^2/_{11} = 0.\dot{1}\dot{8}$; $^5/_{11} = 0.\dot{4}\dot{5}$; $^7/_{11} = 0.\dot{6}\dot{3}$; $^9/_{11} = 0.\dot{8}\dot{1}$
7. (i) $^1/_{12} = 0.08\dot{3}$ (ii) $^5/_{12} = 0.41\dot{6}$; $^7/_{12} = 0.58\dot{3}$;
$^{11}/_{12} = 0.91\dot{6}$

Exercise 6.3

1. (i) 5.13 (ii) 3.86 (iii) 12.46 (iv) 1.37 (v) 5.97
2. (i) 22.3 (ii) 4.7 (iii) 1.5 (iv) 0.1 (v) 1.8 **3.** (i) 2.234
(ii) 31.290 (iii) 0.017 (iv) 0.004 (v) 1.380 **4.** (i) 30
(ii) 4 (iii) 20,000 (iv) 2,000 (v) 6,000 **5.** (i) 0.0099
(ii) 0.013 (iii) 1.0 (iv) 0.24 (v) 52 (vi) 0.0023
(vii) 0.00000079 (viii) 0.00085 (ix) 52 (x) 970,000
7. (i) 0.67 (ii) 0.64 (iii) 0.62 (iv) 0.43 **8.** (i) 4 (ii) 9
(iii) 6 (iv) 6 (v) 5.775 **9.** (i) 15 (ii) 1 (iii) 2 (iv) 7.5
(v) 8.4 **10.** (i) 4 (ii) 8 (iii) 8 (iv) 4 (v) 4.0834
11. (i) 20 (ii) 7 (iii) 3 (iv) 3 (v) 3 (vi) 3.0390625
12. (i) 4 (ii) 6 (iii) 9 (iv) 3 (v) 2 (vi) 2.2
13. (i) 46 (ii) 44.3

Exercise 6.4

1. (i) $^3/_4$ (ii) $^1/_{20}$ (iii) $^1/_5$ (iv) $^1/_4$ (v) $^9/_{10}$ (vi) $^{19}/_{50}$
(vii) $^3/_5$ (viii) $^4/_5$ (ix) $^1/_3$ (x) $^1/_8$ **2.** (i) 30% (ii) 80%
(iii) 85% (iv) 6% (v) 28% (vi) 70% (vii) 55%
(viii) 44% (ix) 2% (x) 25% **3.** (i) 12% (ii) 25%
(iii) 30% (iv) 69% (v) 42% (vi) 14.5% (vii) 41%
(viii) 51% (ix) 67% (x) 92.3% **5.** 2%, 0.03, $^1/_{30}$, 5%,
$^3/_{10}$, 0.32 **6.** $^{31}/_{100}$, 30%, 0.29, $^{36}/_{125}$, $^7/_{25}$, 0.27
7. (i) 40% (ii) 50% (iii) 40% (iv) 40% (v) $33^1/_3$%
(vi) 31.25% (vii) 25% **8.** (i) History 90%; CSPE 85%;
Maths 91%; Science 85%; English 92.5% (ii) English
9. 10% **10.** (i) 30% (ii) 20% **11.** Isaac 20%;
Albert $33^1/_3$%; Leonardo $46^2/_3$%

Exercise 6.5

1. 53% **2.** 65% **3.** (i) 8 (ii) 238 (iii) 30 (iv) 0.7
(v) 3.6 (vi) 18 **4.** (a) 1 (b) 12 kg (c) 1 km (d) €0.75
5. 0.4 m **6.** (i) 165 m (ii) 38 g (iii) 7.5 mm

(iv) 45 km (v) 36 m (vi) 31.2 cm (vii) €435
(viii) 30.6 g (ix) 32 kg (x) €18 **7.** €900 **8.** 1.2 kg
9. (i) 60% (ii) 40% (iii) 12 **10.** Subtotal: €19.00;
Service charge: €1.90; Total: €20.90

Exercise 6.6

1. 6.24% **2.** (i) €40 (ii) $26.\dot{6}$% **3.** (i) €760 (ii) $15.\dot{5}$%
4. 50% **5.** 4.30% **6.** (i) 15.38% (ii) $13.\dot{3}$%
(iii) The denominator in part (i) is smaller than that
in part (ii). As numerators are the same, part (i) gives a
larger % than part (ii). **7.** €18 **8.** 700 pupils **9.** €20
10. ≈ 13% **11.** Sinéad's mark has increased by the
greatest percentage. **12.** 5.36% **13.** 22% **14.** (i) 5.36
(ii) 0.004 (iii) 0.07% **15.** (i) 4.35 (ii) 0.002
(iii) 0.05% **16.** Fine Gael 49% increase; Fianna Fáil
75% decrease; Labour 85% increase; Green Party 100%
decrease; Sinn Féin 250% increase; Independent 350%
increase; PDs 100% decrease

Revision Exercises

1. (a)(i) $^9/_{10}$ (ii) $^9/_{100}$ (iii) $^9/_{1,000}$ (iv) 9 (v) 90
(vi) 900 (vii) 9,000 (viii) $^9/_{10,000}$ (ix) 90,000
(b)(i) 90% (ii) 9% (iii) 0.9% (iv) 80% (v) 82%
(vi) 82.5% (vii) 120% (viii) 125% (ix) 112.5%
(c)(i) 0.22 (ii) 0.65 (iii) 0.68 (iv) 0.12 (v) 0.52
(vi) $0.28\dot{3}$ (vii) 0.125 (viii) $0.\dot{3}$ (ix) 0.6
2. (a)(i) $0.0\dot{5}$ (ii) $0.2\dot{7}$ and $0.3\dot{8}$ (b) €57.50
3. (a)(i) 2.8 (ii) 5.9 (iii) 29.2 (b)(i) 13 (ii) 0.00015
(iii) 64,000 **4.** (a) 9 (b)(i) 10 (ii) 10.07142857
5. (a)(i) $^7/_{20}$ (ii) $^4/_5$ (iii) $^3/_{20}$ (iv) $^1/_{20}$ (v) $^{17}/_{100}$
(vi) $^{13}/_{50}$ (vii) $^9/_{10}$ (viii) $^3/_{25}$ (ix) $^{11}/_{20}$ (b) (i) 30%
(ii) 75% (iii) 80% (iv) 50% (v) 25% (vi) 40%
(vii) 70% (viii) 45% (ix) 44% **6.** (a) €189 (b) €2.40
7. (a) €8,450 (b) 41.43% **8.** (a)(i) $^1/_5$ (ii) 0.2 (b) 45
(c) 50% **9.** €68 **10.** €1,020 **11.** €836 **12.** (i) 168
(ii) 176 (iii) 56

Chapter 7

Exercise 7.1

1. Certain **2.** Evens **3.** Unlikely **4.** Certain
5. Impossible **6.** Impossible **7.** Unlikely **8.** Likely
9. Unlikely **10.** Evens **11.** Depends on year
12. Impossible **13.** Certain **14.** Certain **15.** Unlikely
16. Likely **17.** Impossible **18.** Evens **19.** Certain
20. Evens

Exercise 7.2

5. (a) S (b) Q (c) P (d) R (e) T

Exercise 7.3

1. 0.1 **2.** 0.2 **3.** 0.4 **4.** (i) 0.2 (ii) 0.8 **5.** (i) $^2/_3$
(ii) 0.67 **6.** (i) $^7/_8$ (ii) 0.875 **7.** (i) 0.25 (ii) 1 (iii) 6
(iv) 9 **8.** (i) 0.25, 0.1, 0, 0.2, 0.45 (ii) Friday
9. (i) 1, $^3/_4$, $^2/_3$ (ii) Mia **10.** (i) 0.3 (ii) 0.5 **11.** (i) 200
(ii) $^{47}/_{100}$ (iii) 0.135 (iv) 17%

Exercise 7.4

1. (i) 0.55 (ii) No **2.** (i) 105 (ii) 4 (iii) 6 (iv) No
3. (i) Red **6.** (i) 0.05, 0.25, 0.3, 0.15, 0.2, 0.05 **7.** (i) 14
(ii) $^7/_{15}$ (iii) $^8/_{15}$ (iv) Yes **8.** (i) 106 (ii) 0.16, 0.17,
0.17, 0.16, 0.17, 0.18 (iii) No **9.** (i) No
10. (a)(i) 0.3, 0.25, 0.45 (ii) No

Exercise 7.5

1. (i) $^1/_6$ (ii) $^1/_6$ (iii) 0 (iv) $^1/_2$ (v) $^1/_2$ (vi) $^1/_3$ (vii) 1
2. (i) 0.1 (ii) 0.1 (iii) 0 (iv) 0.5 (v) 0.5 (vi) 0.4
3. (i) $^1/_2$ (ii) $^1/_4$ (iii) $^1/_{13}$ (iv) $^1/_{52}$ (v) $^1/_{26}$ (vi) $^3/_{13}$
4. (i) 0.35 (ii) 0.2 (iii) 0.55 (iv) 0.15 (v) 0.8
5. (i) 0.4 (ii) 0.6 **6.** (i) 0.2 (ii) 0.2 (iii) 0.2 (iv) 0.8
7. (i) $^2/_7$ (ii) $^5/_7$ (iii) $^2/_7$ (iv) $^2/_7$ (v) $^3/_7$ **8.** (i) 0.125
(ii) 0.375 (iii) 0.5 (iv) 0.5 (v) 0.625 **9.** (i) 0.1
(ii) 0.3 (iii) 0.4 **10.** (i) 40% (ii) 60% **11.** (i) 0.1
(ii) 0.4 (iii) 0.3 **12.** (i) $^1/_3$ (ii) $^2/_3$ **13.** 0.006
14. (i) 0.5 (ii) $^4/_{15}$ (iii) $^7/_{30}$ (iv) 0.5 **15.** A
16. (i) $^1/_{10}$ (ii) $^2/_5$ (iii) $^{19}/_{30}$ (iv) $^1/_3$

Exercise 7.6

1. (i) 1,000 (ii) 3,000 **2.** (i) 520 (ii) 80 (iii) 20
3. 210 **4.** 150 **5.** (i) 110 (ii) 55 **6.** (i) 5 (ii) €20
(iii) Lose €25 **7.** (i) 150 (ii) Second **8.** (i) 27
(ii) 23 (iii) 54 (iv) 138 **9.** (i) 90 (ii) 180 (iii) 100
10. (i) 5 (ii) 12 (iii) 21 (iv) 26 (v) 35 (vi) 7
(vii) 700

Exercise 7.7

1. (ii) 10 (iii) 0.1 (iv) 0.1 (v) 0.1 **2.** (ii) 0.5
(iii) 0.25 (iv) 0.25 **3.** (ii) 36 (iii) $^1/_{36}$ (iv) $^1/_{36}$
(v) 0.25 (vi) $^1/_6$ (vii) $^5/_{12}$ (viii) $^2/_9$ **4.** (ii) 0.25
(iii) 0.25 **5.** (ii) $^1/_{24}$ (iii) $^1/_{24}$ (iv) 0.125 (v) 0.125

6. (ii) $^1/_9$ (iii) $^5/_{36}$ (iv) $^7/_{36}$ (v) $^2/_9$ **7.** (ii) $^1/_9$ (iii) $^2/_9$
8. (ii) $^1/_3$ (iii) $^2/_3$ **9.** (ii) $^5/_{36}$ (iii) $^5/_{12}$ (iv) $^5/_{12}$ (v) 1
(vi) $^1/_6$ (vii) 0 **10.** (b)(i) 0.25 (ii) 0.25 (iii) 0.5
(iv) 0.5

Exercise 7.8

1. 0.25 **2.** $^3/_{16}$ **3.** (i) 0.3 (ii) 0.09 **4.** $^1/_{16}$ **5.** $^9/_{64}$
6. $^{12}/_{49}$ **7.** 0.04 **8.** $^{65}/_{324}$ **9.** $^1/_{25}$ **10.** 0.16 **11.** $^1/_9$

Revision Exercises

1. (b)(i) Likely (ii) Unlikely (iii) Evens (iv) Certain
(v) Impossible (c)(i) Heads (ii) Eq ual (iii) Equal
(iv) Red card **2.** (a)(i) 0.5 (ii) 0.2 (iii) 0.3 (iv) 0.5
(v) 0.7 (b) 0.5 (c)(i) $^1/_8$ (ii) $^1/_8$ (iii) 0.25 (iv) 0.5
3. (a)(i) $^3/_{16}$ (ii) 0.125 (iii) 0.625 (iv) 0.875
(b)(i) 18, 16 (ii) $^{13}/_{34}$ (iii) $^7/_{34}$ (iv) $^{12}/_{17}$ (v) 0.5
(vi) 0.25 (c)(ii) 7 (iii) $^1/_6$ (iv) $^5/_{12}$ **4.** (a)(i) 0.25 (ii) $^1/_{13}$
(iii) $^3/_{13}$ (iv) 0.5 (v) $^1/_{52}$; 50 (b)(i) 24 (ii) 36
(iii) Yes (c)(i) $^1/_4$ (ii) 0.5 (iii) $^1/_4$ (iv) $^1/_4$ **5.** (a)(i) $^1/_{12}$
(ii) 5 (b) 400 (c)(i) 9 (ii) $^1/_9$ (iii) $^1/_9$ (iv) $^1/_9$
(v) $^1/_3$ (vi) $^2/_3$ **6.** (a)(i) $^1/_7$ (ii) $^6/_7$ (iii) $^2/_7$ (iv) $^5/_7$
(v) $^2/_7$ (b) C **7.** (b)False, True, True, True, False, True,
False, True **8.** (a)(i) 50%, 25%, 60%, 25% (ii) 37.5%
(b)(i) 0.1 (ii) 0.25 (iii) 0.5 (iv) 0.05 **9.** (a)(i) $^1/_4$,
$^1/_4$, $^1/_4$ (ii) 25 (b)(ii) No

Chapter 8

Exercise 8.1

1. (i) Circle (ii) Triangle (iii) Circle (iv) Heart
(v) Smiley face **2.** (i) Blue, Blue, Red (ii) Blue, Red,
Green (iii) Red, Red, Blue (iv) Orange, Blue, Green
3. (i) Blue (ii) Red (iii) Red **4.** (i) Circle (ii) Square
(iii) Triangle (iv) Circle **5.** (i) Red (ii) Green
(iii) 7 times **6.** (i) Square (ii) Circle (iii) Circle
(iv) 8 times **7.** (i) 9 (ii) 11 **8.** (i) Blue: 10
(ii) Red: 16 (iii) 33 (iv) Pattern 6

Exercise 8.2

2. (i) 13, 25 (ii) 27, 33 (iii) 62, 74 (iv) 79, 95, 127
(v) 24, 88, 120 (vi) −16, −2, 19 (vii) 17, 21, 25
(viii) −20, −31, −64 **3.** (i) 0, 2, 4, 6, ...
(ii) 10, 14, 18, 22, ... (iii) 200, 190, 180, 170, ...
(iv) −20, −16, −12, −8, ... (v) −80, −87, −94, −101, ...

4. (i) Start at 3, add 5 every term (ii) Start at 26, subtract 4 every term (iii) Start at 6, add 9 every term (iv) Start at 17, add 16 every term (v) Start at 75, subtract 20 every term

Exercise 8.3

1. (i)(a) 14 (b) 4 (c) $T_n = 4n + 10$ (d) $T_{10} = 50$
(ii)(a) 4 (b) 6 (c) $T_n = 6n - 2$ (d) $T_{12} = 70$
(iii)(a) 10 (b) 12 (c) $T_n = 12n - 2$ (d) $T_{18} = 214$
(iv)(a) 19 (b) 10 (c) $T_n = 10n + 9$ (d) 359
(v)(a) 0 (b) 7 (c) $T_n = 7n - 7$ (d) 693 (vi)(a) 75
(b) 9 (c) $T_n = 9n + 66$ (d) 309 (vii)(a) 22 (b) −2
(c) $T_n = 24 - 2n$ (d) −76 (viii)(a) 250 (b) 30
(c) $T_n = 30n + 220$ (d) 520 (ix)(a) 22 (b) −10
(c) $T_n = 32 - 10n$ (d) −128 (x)(a) −16 (b) −4
(c) $T_n = -12 - 4n$ (d) $T_{30} = -132$ **2.** (i) 1st = 7,
2nd = 9, 3rd = 11, 100th = 205 (ii) 1st = 2, 2nd = 6,
3rd = 10, 100th = 398 (iii) 1st = 6, 2nd = 4, 3rd = 2,
100th = −192

Exercise 8.4

1. (i)(a) 13 (b) 6 (c) 57, 83, 115 (ii)(a) 6 (b) 9
(c) 80, 121, 171 (iii)(a) 16 (b) 1 (c) 26, 31, 37
(iv)(a) 12 (b) 1 (c) 26, 32, 39 (v)(a) 15 (b) 8
(c) 95, 135, 183 (vi)(a) 8 (b) −2 (c) 8, 2, −6
(vii)(a) 5 (b) −4 (c) −25, −43, −65 (viii)(a) 1
(b) 3 (c) 7, 16, 28 **2.** (i)(a) Doubling
(b) 512, 1024, 2048 (ii)(a) Tripling
(b) 1458, 4374, 13122 (iii)(a) Tripling
(b) 8019, 24057, 72171 (iv)(a) Doubling
(b) 416, 832, 1664 (v)(a) Tripling
(b) −1215, −3645, −10935 **3.** (i) Quadratic
(as second difference is constant).
(ii) Quadratic (as second difference is constant).
(iii) Exponential (as each term is double the previous).
(iv) Exponential (as each term is triple the previous).
(v) Quadratic (as second difference is constant).

Exercise 8.5

1. €68 **2.** (i) €100 (ii) €300 **3.** 243,000
4. (i) €35 (ii) €140 **5.** (i) 8 litres (ii) 94 minutes
6. (i) 30 (ii) 180 **7.** (i) 92.5 litres (ii) 77.5 litres
(iii) $66\frac{2}{3}$ days **8.** (i) 13 (ii) 16 (iii) 46 **9.** (ii) 320 km
10. (ii) 6 hours **11.** (ii) Exponential **12.** (i) Quadratic
(ii) 9 km/hr **13.** (i) 12 metres (ii) 87 metres

Revision Exercises

1. (ii) Linear (iii) 10 (iv) 13 (v) 28
2. (i) In terms of numbers of blocks, the pattern is
quadratic. (ii) 10 (iii) 21 (iv) 210 **3.** (i) Linear
(ii) 10 (iii) 22 (iv) 34 patterns **4.** (ii) Blue (iii) Red
(iv) Orange **5.** (i) Orange (ii) Blue (iii) Blue
(iv) Blue **6.** (i)(a) 6 (b) 12 (c) 66, 78, 90
(ii)(a) 6 (b) 15 (c) 81, 96, 111 (iii)(a) 9 (b) 14
(c) 79, 93, 107 (iv)(a) 13 (b) 15 (c) 88, 103, 118
(v)(a) −5 (b) −6 (c) −35, −41, −47 **7.** (i)(a) 12
(b) 14 (c) $14n - 2$ (d) 166 (ii)(a) 15 (b) 2
(c) $2n + 13$ (d) 47 (iii)(a) 13 (b) 18 (c) $18n - 5$
(d) 445 (iv)(a) 50 (b) 27 (c) $27n + 23$ (d) 1,643
(v)(a) 326 (b) −31 (c) $357 - 31n$ (d) −356
8. (i)(a) Doubling (b) 192, 384, 768 (ii)(a) Tripling
(b) 972, 2916, 8748 (iii)(a) Doubling (b) 320, 640,
1280 (iv)(a) Tripling (b) 6561, 19683, 59049
(v)(a) Tripling (b) 364.5, 1093.5, 3280.5 **9.** (i)(a) 11
(b) 1 (c) 46, 56, 67 (ii)(a) 0 (b) 8 (c) 110, 156,
210 (iii)(a) 2 (b) 7 (c) 82, 119, 163 (iv)(a) 3
(b) −1 (c) −2, −6, −11 (v)(a) 5 (b) −4 (c) −25, −43,
−65 **10.** (i)(a) Quadratic (c) 4 (d) 3 (e) 63, 87,
115, 147, 183 (ii)(a) Exponential (d) 5 (e) 160, 320,
640, 1280, 2560 (iii)(a) Linear (b) 17 (d) 14
(e) 99, 116, 133, 150, 167 (iv)(a) Quadratic (c) 2
(d) 15 (e) 40, 51, 64, 79, 96 (v)(a) Linear (b) 13
(d) 5 (e) 70, 83, 96, 109, 122 (vi)(a) Exponential
(d) 12 (e) 2916, 8748, 26244, 78732, 236196
(vii)(a) Linear (b) 16 (d) 8 (e) 88, 104, 120, 136, 152
(viii)(a) Quadratic (c) 1 (d) 1 (e) 16, 22, 29, 37, 46
(ix)(a) Linear (b) −7 (d) −3 (e) −38, −45, −52,
−59, −66 (x)(a) Quadratic (c) +4 (d) −3 (e) 22, 39,
60, 85, 114 **11.** (ii) €25 (iii) €34 (iv) Option A is
cheaper. **12.** (ii) Start/Initial Amount (iii) Holly
13. (i) Pens: 10; Counters: 7 (ii) 13 (iii) 54 **14.** (i) 8
(ii) 16 (iii) 512 (iv) 7 (v) 11

Chapter 9

Exercise 9.1

1. (i) 3 (ii) 1 (iii) −1 (iv) 5 (v) 6 (vi) 9 (vii) −1
(viii) 10 (ix) −3 (x) −8 **2.** (i) 6 (ii) 4 (iii) −8
(iv) 8 (v) 5 **3.** (i) −1 (ii) 6 (iii) 40 (iv) −1 (v) 8
4. (i) −16 (ii) 3 (iii) −1 (iv) 16 (v) $-2\frac{1}{4}$ or $-\frac{9}{4}$
5. (i) 1 (ii) 4 (iii) −27 (iv) 2 (v) 12 (vi) 63
(vii) 2 (viii) 2 (ix) −2 (x) 72 **6.** (i) 16 (ii) 9
(iii) −12 (iv) −16 (v) 13 (vi) 33 (vii) 76 (viii) 55
(ix) 18 (x) 51 **7.** (i) 4 (ii) −12 (iii) −36 (iv) 18

(v) 18   (vi) –64   (vii) 18   (viii) 0   (ix) 1,296
(x) $11\frac{1}{4}$ or $\frac{45}{4}$

Exercise 9.2

1. (i) $2x$ (ii) x (iii) $6y$ (iv) $3a$ (v) $6b$ (vi) $4x$
(vii) $11z$ (viii) $5y$ (ix) 0   (x) $3a$ **2.** (i) $3x$
(ii) $9a + 4$ (iii) b (iv) $4c$ (v) $9x + 2$ **3.** (i) $3a + 3b$
(ii) $x + y$ (iii) $3p - 7q$ (iv) $-7m + 5n + 4$
(v) $10a - 7b$ (vi) $-p + 9q$ **4.** (i) ab (ii) $8xy$
(iii) $-2pq + 4rq$ (iv) $3mn$ (v) $6ab - 3bc$ (vi) $2xy - 10yz$
5. (i) $-x + 11y$ (ii) $5a - 5b + 2c$ (iii) $19q$
(iv) $3m + 2l$ (v) $3y - 60z$ (vi) $12a + 8b - c$
6. (i) $ab + 12bd$ (ii) $4xy - 2xz$ (iii) $-7pq + 13rq$
(iv) $6xy - 5x + 2q + 9$ (v) $2ab + 3cd + a$
(vi) $-2xy + 5xz$ **7.** (i) $3x^2$ (ii) $2a^3$ (iii) $3c^2$ (iv) $8y^3$
(v) $3a^2$ (vi) 0   (vii) $4h^4$ (viii) $7x^2 + x$ (ix) $-z^3 + 10z$
(x) $-6m^2 - m$ **8.** (i) $x^2 + 6x$ (ii) $2b^3 - 2b$
(iii) $p^3 - p^2 - 9p$ (iv) $-2r^2 + 9r - 1$ (v) $y^3 + y^2 - 3y$
(vi) $4r^2 - 10t^2$ **9.** (i) $2p^2 + q^2$ (ii) $5x^2 - 2y^2$
(iii) $3m^2 - 4n^2$ (iv) $6a^2 - 5b^2$ (v) $4p^2 - 3q^2$
(vi) $-2r^2 + 9r - 1$ (vii) $-2x^2 + 2y^2 + 11$ (viii) $7ab^2$
(ix) $x^2y - 4xy^2$ (x) $-7pq^2 + p^2q$

Exercise 9.3

1. (i) $20x$ (ii) $16y$ (iii) $50r$ (iv) $-12x$ (v) $5a^2$
2. (i) x^2 (ii) xy (iii) x^3 (iv) $-p^4$ (v) $-p^3$ **3.** (i) $8x^2$
(ii) $10y^2$ (iii) $30y^3$ (iv) $12x^5$ (v) $-10x^2$ **4.** (i) x^2y
(ii) $50x^2y$ (iii) $49x^2y^2$ (iv) $-8p^2q^3$ (v) $9m^2n$
5. (i) $-8y^3$ (ii) $24x^3$ (iii) $50m^4$ (iv) $24a^4$ (v) $-8t^3$
6. (i) $-6xy$ (ii) $-6y^3x$ (iii) $84p^2q^2$ (iv) $-48a^3b^2$
(v) $4x^3y^2$ **7.** (i) $24x^2y^2$ (ii) $2x^2y^3$ (iii) $24m^4n^2$
(iv) $-24a^4b^2$ (v) $-2p^4q^3$ **8.** (i) $4a^2b^2$ (ii) $16x^2y^2$
(iii) $4a^2b^2$ (iv) $27x^3y^6$ (v) $-64a^3b^3$

Exercise 9.4

1. $2x + 4$ (ii) $4x - 12$ (iii) $3x + 6$ (iv) $3x - 12$
(v) $8x - 64$ **2.** (i) $8y + 12$ (ii) $27y - 9$ (iii) $-8y + 12$
(iv) $35y + 10$ (v) $-4y - 5$ **3.** (i) $4a + 2b$ (ii) $12a - 8b$
(iii) $77a + 28b$ (iv) $-3a + 9b$ (v) $4b + 28a$
4. (i) $32x + 16y - 24$ (ii) $12x - 18y + 24$ (iii) $6x - 8y - 18$
(iv) $-15x - 18y - 6$ (v) $-28x + 8y + 4$ **5.** (i) $7x^2 + 7y$
(ii) $4x^2 - 28y^2$ (iii) $-3x^2 + 6y^2$ (iv) $10x^2 + 20y^2 - 15$
(v) $-x^2 + 2y^2 - 7$ **6.** (i) $7x + 11$ (ii) $8y + 7$ (iii) $-p - 16$
(iv) $5q - 2x - 5$ (v) $-4m + 2x - 12$ **7.** (i) $12x + 8$
(ii) $30x - 6$ (iii) $-22y + 21$ (iv) $a + 4$ (v) $2b - 10$
8. (i) $11x + 7y - 18$ (ii) $10a + 10b - 2$

(iii) $3m - 7n - 14$ (iv) $8y - 12z - 9$ (v) $6p + q + 17$
(vi) $-2a + 6b + 3$ (vii) $x + 2y - 14$ (viii) $-12x - 4y - 4$
9. (i) $10x^2 + 10x + 18$ (ii) $5y^2 + 11y - 10$
(iii) $5p^2 - p + 11$ (iv) $-4a^2 - 12a + 7$
(v) $m^2 - 6m - 1$ (vi) $2b^2 - 18b + 17$
(vii) $-14c^2 - 6c - 2$ (viii) $5x^2 - 8x - 7$

Exercise 9.5

1. $2x^2 + 6x$ (ii) $3y^2 + 12y$ (iii) $5p^2 + 10p$ (iv) $3r^2 - 6r$
(v) $8a^2 - 12a$ **2.** $6a^3 + 3a$ (ii) $4p^3 + 4p$ (iii) $b^3 - 3b$
(iv) $-5y^3 + 20y^2$ **3.** (i) $4x^3 - 4x$ (ii) $14a^3 + 28a$
(iii) $6p^3 + 4p$ (iv) $-3y^3 + 12y$ (v) $-6b - 2b^3$
4. (i) $5a^3 + 3a$ (ii) $5p^3 + 9p$ (iii) $4x^3 - 3x^2 + 6$
(iv) $-5y^3 - y^2 + 8y$ (v) $x^3 - 2x$ **5.** (i) $2a^3 + 3a^2 + 2a$
(ii) $10x^3 + 10x^2 + 18x$ (iii) $4p^3 - 4p^2 - 7p$
(iv) $9y^3 + 10y^2 + 4y$ (v) $m^3 - 2m^2 - m$
(vi) $4x^3 - 4x^2 + 16x$ (vii) $2y^3 - 19y^2 + 8y$
(viii) $-y^3 + 19y^2 - 2y$ (ix) $6x^4 - x^3 + 7x^2 + 9x$
6. (i) $6a^2b^2 + 10a^2b + 3ab^2 + 4ab - 2a^2$
(ii) $4x^3 - 8x^2 + 4x - 12$

Exercise 9.6

1. $x^2 + 3x + 2$ (ii) $a^2 + 7a + 12$ (iii) $b^2 + 6b + 5$
(iv) $m^2 + 8m + 7$ (v) $y^2 + 11y + 10$ **2.** (i) $x^2 - 2x - 3$
(ii) $x^2 - 4$ (iii) $a^2 - a - 6$ (iv) $r^2 - 5r - 6$
(v) $y^2 - 4y - 5$ **3.** (i) $y^2 - 6y + 8$ (ii) $y^2 - 6y + 5$
(iii) $x^2 - 5x + 6$ (iv) $p^2 - 4p + 3$ (v) $a^2 - 4a + 4$
4. $2a^2 + 4a + 2$ (ii) $4x^2 + 5x + 1$ (iii) $6x^2 + 5x - 6$
(iv) $8b^2 - 8b - 6$ (v) $6a^2 - 10a + 4$ (vi) $5x^2 + x - 4$
(vii) $12y^2 - 22y - 4$ (viii) $8x^2 - 22x + 12$
(ix) $10a^2 - 19a + 6$ (x) $-6a^2 + 14a - 4$
5. (i) $x^2 + 2x + 1$ (ii) $x^2 + 4x + 4$ (iii) $y^2 - 8y + 16$
(iv) $y^2 - 4y + 4$ (v) $4a^2 - 4a + 1$ (vi) $25a^2 - 20a + 4$
6. (i) $2x^2 + 8x + 8$ (ii) $2y^2 - 2y + 1$ (iii) $-3a + 12$

Revision Exercises

1. (a)(i) 17   (ii) 24   (iii) 8   (iv) –4   (v) 1   (vi) 25
(b)(i) –4   (ii) 10   (iii) –15   (iv) 27   (v) 5   (vi) 16
(c)(i) –3   (ii) 9   (iii) –6   (iv) –5   (v) –16   (vi) –7
(vii) 75   (viii) –45   (ix) –42   (x) 0   **2.** (a)(i) 48
(ii) 48   (iii) 48   (iv) 48   (v) 48   (vi) 50   (b)(i) 2
(ii) 4   (iii) 1   (iv) 8   (c)(i) $(x + y) < (x - y)$
(ii) $(4x + x) = (5x)$ (iii) $(10y - 3y) = (7y)$ (iv) $xy^2 > x^2y$
(v) $x^2 + y^2 > (x + y)^2$ (vi) $2x^2 < (2x)^2$
(vii) $(3xy) = (5xy - 2xy)$ (viii) $(^x/_y) < (^y/_x)$ **3.** (a)(i) $7a$
(ii) $6a$ (iii) $12a^2$ (iv) $-2x$ (v) 0   (b)(i) $9a + 2b - 2c$
(ii) $10x^2 + 4x - 11$ (iii) $3y^3 - 2y^2 - 2y + 6x^2 + 3x + 4$

(c)(i) $4x^2 - 4x - 8$ (ii) $10ab - 2xy - x^2$ (iii) $a - 3c$
(iv) $x^3 + x^2$ (v) $(2^3/_4)x + (5^1/_2)y$ **4.** (a)(i) a^9 (ii) $12y^2$
(iii) $15x^2$ (iv) $-18p^2$ (v) $12t^2$ (vi) $24x^3$ (vii) $-70y^6$
(viii) $16x^2$ (ix) $-8x^3$ (x) $8a^6$ (b)(i) $(ab^2) = (ab^2)$
(ii) $(ab)^3 = (a^3b^3)$ (iii) $(a + b)^2 > (a^2 + b^2)$
(iv) $(2a^2b)^2 > (2a^4b^2)$ (v) $(b - a)^3 < (b^3 - a^3)$ (c)(i) $5ab$
(ii) $6a^2b^2$ (iii) $-ab$ (iv) $3x + 4y$ (v) $12xy$ (vi) $3x - 4y$
(vii) $8x^2y$ (viii) $15x^4y^2$ (ix) $-2x^2y$ (x) $4x^2 + 5x$
(xi) $4x^2 + 5x$ (xii) $4x^2 - 5x$ (xiii) $6y^3$ (xiv) $5y^6$
(xv) $4y^3$ **5.** (a)(i) $6a + 2b$ (ii) $20x - 8y$ (iii) $21a + 7b$
(iv) $60a - 50b + 10c$ (v) $20a + 18b + 2c$
(b)(i) $21p + 9q$ (ii) $15x - 11y$ (iii) $a + 10b$
(iv) $-3p + 16q$ (v) $7m - n$ (c)(i) $-x^2 - 11x + 19$
(ii) $22x - 11$ (iii) $-4x + 14$ (iv) $3x^2 - 13x + 2$ (v) $x^3 - 1$
6. (a)(i) $3x^2 + 2x - 5$ (ii) $-x^2 - 4x + 3$ (iii) $-5x + 2$
(b)(i) $10k - 13t$ (ii) $8k + 38t$ (iii) 0 (c)(i) $2x^3 + 2x$
(ii) $3a^3 - 15a$ (iii) $y^3 - 7y$ (iv) $2x^3 + 14x$
(v) $3x^3 - 27x$ (vi) $10a^3 - 80a$ **7.** (a)(i) $a^2 + 12a + 20$
(ii) $x^2 + 13x + 30$ (iii) $y^2 + 8y + 12$ (iv) $a^2 + 6a + 5$
(v) $x^2 + 2x - 15$ (b)(i) $6x^2 + 5x - 4$ (ii) $6x^2 - 11x - 10$
(iii) $12x^2 - 7x + 1$ (iv) $20p^2 - 19p + 3$
(v) $6a^2 - 11ab + 4b^2$ (c)(i) $4b^2 + 28b + 49$
(ii) $x^2 + 24x + 144$ (iii) $25t^2 - 40t + 16$
(iv) $2x^2 - 24x + 72$

Chapter 10

Exercise 10.1

1. (i) $x = 5$ (ii) $x = 10$ (iii) $a = 5$ (iv) $b = 8$
(v) $c = 1$ **2.** (i) $x = -2$ (ii) $x = -9$ (iii) $a = -7$
(iv) $p = -8$ (v) $x = -8$ **3.** (i) $x = 4$ (ii) $x = 3$
(iii) $x = 3$ (iv) $x = 16$ (v) $x = 5$ **4.** (i) $x = 2$
(ii) $x = 0$ (iii) $x = -3$ (iv) $a = -4$ (v) $x = 0$

Exercise 10.2

1. (i) $x = 3$ (ii) $a = 2$ (iii) $b = 3$ (iv) $p = 6$
(v) $x = 8$ (vi) $x = 6$ (vii) $q = 5$ (viii) $r = 6$
(ix) $y = 0$ (x) $x = 6$ **2.** (i) $a = 6$ (ii) $b = -3$
(iii) $c = -8$ (iv) $d = -2$ (v) $x = 1$ (vi) $y = -3$
(vii) $z = 8$ (viii) $p = -3$ (ix) $q = -2$ (x) $r = 2$
3. (i) $x = 3$ (ii) $x = 2$ (iii) $x = -1$ (iv) $y = 6$
(v) $y = -3$ (vi) $p = -1$ (vii) $q = -1$ (viii) $x = -2$
(ix) $x = 0$ (x) $y = 0$

Exercise 10.3

1. $x = 1$ **2.** $x = 2$ **3.** $x = 6$ **4.** $x = 2$ **5.** $x = 5$
6. $y = 2$ **7.** $y = -1$ **8.** $y = 3$ **9.** $y = 14$ **10.** $y = 1$
11. $a = -1$ **12.** $x = 2$ **13.** $a = -3$ **14.** $a = -2$

15. $a = -4$ **16.** $b = 6$ **17.** $b = -3$ **18.** $b = -8$
19. $x = -6$ **20.** $b = -7$ **21.** $x = 3$ **22.** $x = 6$
23. $x = -4$ **24.** $x = -1$

Exercise 10.4

1. (i) $x = 4$ (ii) $x = 1$ (iii) $x = 7$ (iv) $x = 5$ (v) $x = -4$
(vi) $x = -11$ (vii) $x = 2$ (viii) $x = -1$ (ix) $x = 0$
(x) $x = -1$ **2.** (i) $x = -1$ (ii) $x = 11$ (iii) $x = 3$
(iv) $x = 1$ (v) $x = 5$ (vi) $x = -3$ (vii) $x = 0$
(viii) $x = -1$ (ix) $x = -4$ (x) $x = 1$ **3.** (i) $x = 8$
(ii) $x = 3$ (iii) $x = -7$ (iv) $x = 2$ (v) $x = 3$ (vi) $x = 9$
4. (i) $x = -4$ (ii) $x = 2$ (iii) $x = -1$ (iv) $x = 1$
(v) $x = -1$

Revision Exercises

1. (a)(i) $x = 6$ (ii) $x = 5$ (iii) $x = 9$ (iv) $x = 3$
(v) $x = 4$ (b)(i) $x = 7$ (ii) $x = 4$ (iii) $x = 3$
(iv) $x = 4$ (v) $x = 4$ (c)(i) $x = 5$ (ii) $x = 5$
(iii) $x = 6$ (iv) $x = 7$ (v) $x = 7$ **2.** (a)(i) $x = 19$
(ii) $x = 11$ (iii) $a = 7$ (iv) $y = 11$ (v) $p = 31$
(b)(i) $x = 4$ (ii) $x = 3$ (iii) $x = 5$ (iv) $x = 3$
(v) $x = 2$ (c)(i) $x = 11$ (ii) $x = 3$ (iii) $x = 6$
(iv) $x = 3$ (v) $x = 4$ **3.** (a)(i) $t = 30$ (ii) $x = 91$
(iii) $k = 106$ (iv) $x = 49$ (v) $n = 31$ (b)(i) $x = 11$
(ii) $x = 6$ (iii) $y = 5$ (iv) $k = 3$ (v) $x = 4$ (c)(i) $x = 9$
(ii) $x = 10$ (iii) $x = 11$ (iv) $x = 2$ (v) $x = 4$

Chapter 11

Revision Exercises

3. (i) Point (ii) Line segment (iii) Ray (iv) Line
(v) Line (vi) Point (vii) No **7.** (i) Acute: $45°$
(ii) Acute: $80°$ (iii) Obtuse: $140°$ (iv) Reflex: $325°$
(v) Reflex: $230°$ **9.** (ii) $60°, 65°$ (iii) No the angle is
determined by the rotation of the arms
10. (i) $AD \parallel DH \parallel BH \parallel GI$; $DE \parallel HG, AF \parallel BK$
(ii) $DE \perp DA, HG \perp GI$; $DE \perp GI, HG \perp AB$ **11.** (i) $62°$
(ii) $84°$ (iii) $116°$ (iv) $35°$ (v) $70°$ (vi) $320°$ (vii) $237°$
12. (b)(i) 10 (ii) 19 (iii) 23 (iv) 9 **13.** (i) $30°, 150°$
(ii) 16, 34 **14.** (i) $21°$ (ii) $34°$ (iii) $15°$ (iv) $21°$

Chapter 13

Exercise 13.1

1. (i) $\angle A$ and $\angle C$, $\angle B$ and $\angle D$ (ii) $\angle 1$ and $\angle 2$,
$\angle 3$ and $\angle 4$ (iii) $\angle ABD$ and $\angle CBE$, $\angle ABC$ and $\angle EBD$

(iv) ∠*PTQ* and ∠*STR*, ∠*PTS* and ∠*RTQ*   **2.** (i) 110°
(ii) 90°   (iii) 50°   (iv) 180°   **3.** (i) 125°, 55°
(ii) 120°, 60°   (iii) 90°, 90°   (iv) 65°, 115°
4. (i) 145°, 35°, 145°   (ii) 60°, 120°, 60°
(iii) 90°, 90°, 60°   (iv) 120°, 60°, 120°, 60°
5. (i) 60°, 60°, 120°   (ii) 40°, 160°

Exercise 13.2

2. (i) 50°, 50°   (ii) 110°, 110°   (iii) 137°, 43°   (iv) 116°, 64°
3. (i) Yes   (ii) Yes   **4.** (i) No   (ii) Yes   **5.** (i) 74°, 106°,
74°, 106°   (ii) 140°, 70°, 70°   (iii) 72°, 115°, 65°, 108°
(iv) 80°, 100°   (v) 52°, 125°, 73°

Exercise 13.3

1. (i) 40°   (ii) 60°   (iii) 50°   (iv) 65°   (v) 30°
(vi) 75°   **2.** (i) 140°   (ii) 160°   (iii) 115°   (iv) 70°
3. (i) 110°   (ii) 127.5°   (iii) 130°   (iv) 35°
4. (i) 160°, 20°   (ii) 78°, 50°   (iii) 45°, 45°, 135°
(iv) 25°, 125°   (v) 122°, 30°   **5.** (i) 95°, 44°, 41°
(ii) 85°, 30°, 85°, 30°   (iii) 54°, 44°, 82°   (iv) 115°, 115°
(v) 65°, 85°, 65°, 50°, 65°

Exercise 13.4

1. (i) 60°, 4 cm   (ii) 110°, 7 cm   (iii) 105°, 4.5
(iv) 90°, 5.6 cm   (v) 140°, 6 cm   **2.** (i) 62°, 28°
(ii) 75°, 105°   (iii) 37°, 60°   (iv) 85°, 70°   (v) 120°, 15°
(vi) 90°, 54°   **4.** (i) 7 cm   (ii) 26 cm   **5.** (i) 66°, 114°, 66°
(ii) 60°, 78°, 102°   (iii) 41°, 32°, 107°, 107°, 107°
(iv) 30°, 30°, 100°, 100°, 50°

Revision Exercises

1. (a)(i) 60°, 120°   (ii) 50°, 50°, 130°   (iii) 45°, 45°,
45°, 135°   (iv) 65°, 50°, 65°   (v) 10°, 80°, 80°
(b)(i) Vertically opposite   (ii) Corresponding
(iii) Supplementary   (iv) Alternate   (v) Corresponding
2. (a)(i) 85°   (ii) 135°   (iii) 105°, 75°   (iv) 40°, 100°
(v) 62.5°, 62.5°   (c)(i) 30°   (ii) 20°   (iii) 25°
3. (a)(i) 60°, 75°   (ii) 60°, 120°   (iii) 60°, 70°
(iv) 135°, 135°, 75°   (v) 113°, 113°, 15°   (c)(i) 100°, 45°
(ii) 136°   (iii) 48°, 50°   (iv) 67.5°, 67.5°, 35°
(v) 38°, 76°, 38°   **4.** (a)(i) 70°   (ii) 110°   (iii) 70°   (iv) 110°
(b)(i) 3 cm   (ii) 7 cm   (iii) 4 cm   (iv) 4.5 cm   (c)(i) 63°
(ii) 54°   (iii) 63°   (iv) 27°   **5.** (a)(i) 30°   (ii) 30°   (iii) 45°
(iv) 150°   (b)(i) 90°   (ii) 60°   (iii) 60°   (iv) 30°   (v) 30°
(c)(iii) 40°   (iv) 140°

Chapter 14

Exercise 14.2

1. (ii) 30   **2.** (ii) 10   (iii) 10   (iv) 10%   **3.** (ii) Walk
(iii) Rail   **4.** (i) 30   (ii) $\frac{2}{15}$ **5.** (ii) 8   (iii) $73\frac{1}{3}$%
6. (ii) 35   (iii) 7   (iv) 23   (v) 7   **7.** (ii) 36%

Exercise 14.3

4. (i) Tom   (ii) John   (iii) 16   (iv) 25%

Exercise 14.4

1. (ii) Red   (iii) Orange   (iv) 28   (v) 25%   **2.** (i) Evelyn
(ii) Derek   (iii) 17   (iv) Alan and Carol   (v) They
scored more than half of the goals.   **3.** (ii) Paula and
Tanya   (iii) $\frac{1}{9}$ **4.** (ii) 10   (iii) $\frac{1}{3}$ (iv) 6.67%
5. (i) 40   (ii) 295   (iii) 20.34%   **6.** (ii) 40,000 km²
(iv) 43%   **7.** (ii) 30   (iii) Basketball   (iv) 20%   (v) $\frac{1}{10}$
8. (i) 28   (ii) Six   (iii) 4   (iv) 25%   **9.** (i) Máire
(ii) Eoin   (iii) €26   (iv) €20   (v) Seán €1, Máire €3,
Eoin €1, Caitlin €1, Aoife €2.

Exercise 14.5

1. (i) 30°   **2.** (i) 36°   (iii) 25%   **3.** (i) 165°   **4.** (i) 126°
(ii) 180 acres   (iii) 30 acres   **5.** (i) 200   (ii) 144°
7. (ii) $16\frac{2}{3}$%   **9.** (i) 166   (iii) 45.78%   **10.** (i) 100
(iii) 45.78%

Exercise 14.6

1. (ii) 75%   **3.** (ii) $\frac{2}{5}$ **4.** (i) 40   (ii) 6   (iii) $\frac{9}{20}$ **5.** (ii) 4
(iii) 2.6   **6.** (ii) 70%   **7.** (i) 15   (ii) 20%   **8.** (i) 46
(ii) 378   (iii) 252

Exercise 14.7

3. (i) 10   (ii) 15.38%   **4.** (ii) 35   (iii) 15   **5.** (ii) 10%
7. (ii) 16   (iii) 8

Exercise 14.8

1. (i) 4   (ii) 5   (iii) 8   (iv) 4.2   (v) 5   (vi) 7   **2.** (i) 5, 5
(ii) 3, 3   (iii) 2, 2   (iv) 7, 7   (v) 0, 0   **3.** (i) 25   (ii) 38
4. (i) 43   (ii) 49   **5.** (i) {12, 12, 12, 12, 12, 13, 14, 14,
14, 15, 15, 15, 15, 16, 16, 16}   (ii) 12   (iii) 14
(iv) 13.94 years   **6.** (i) {20, 22, 22, 22, 23, 23, 24, 24,
24, 25, 25, 25, 25, 25, 25, 26}   (ii) 25   (iii) 24
(iv) 23.75 cm   **7.** (i) {0, 0, 1, 1, 1, 1, 2, 2, 2, 2, 2, 2, 2,
3, 4, 4, 5, 5, 5, 6}   (ii) 2   (iii) 2   (iv) 2.5   **8.** (i) 3.7 kg

ACTIVE MATHS 1   **539**

(ii) 4.8 kg   (iii) 5.45 kg   (iv) 5.41 kg   **9.** (ii) €3.57
10. (i) 7   (ii) 12   (iii) 3   (iv) 9   (v) 22   **11.** (i) B, B
12. (i) 168   (ii) 240   (iii) No   **13.** (a)(i) Yes
(ii) Yes   (iii) No   (b) 2, 10   **14.** {11, 13, 13, 15, 17, 21, 23}

Exercise 14.9

1. (a) Mean   (b) Mode   (c) Mean   (d) Mode   (e) Median
2. (a) Mean   (b) Mode   (c) Median   **3.** (i) Categorical
(ii) The Mode   **4.** (a) Median   (b) No   (c) Mean
5. (a) 32.89, 12, 18   (b) Median

Exercise 14.10

4. (i) 15%

Revision Exercises

2. (iii) 4   (iv) 80%   **4.** (ii) 20   (iv) 35%   **5.** (ii) 110   (iii) $^{5}/_{11}$
(iv) $18\frac{1}{3}$ **6.** (ii) 34   (iii) Bus   **7.** (ii) 20   (iv) 6   (v) 1
8. (ii) 445   (iii) 10%   (iv) 14%   **9.** (ii) 8%   **11.** (ii) 10%
12. (ii) 31.82%   **13.** (i) 5.67   (ii) 6   (iii) 6
14. (i) Categorical   (iii) B   **15.** (ii) 37 cm   (iii) 39 cm
(iv) 39.65 cm   (v) Median   (vi) 21 cm
16. (ii) 4–8 minutes   (iii) 37   **17.** (i) 41   (ii) 58
(iii) 37.8   **18.** 6.29   **19.** (iv) €2,601, €2,587.50
20. (iv) 1.73565 cm, 1.7365 cm

Chapter 15

Exercise 15.1

1. (i) 8   (ii) 27   (iii) 25   (iv) 36   (v) 1   (vi) 64   **2.** (i) 2
(ii) 4   (iii) 9   (iv) 4   (v) 16   (vi) 81   **3.** (i) 2   (ii) 3
(iii) 7   (iv) 6   (v) 12   (vi) 13   **4.** (i) 30   (ii) 28   (iii) 27
(iv) 10   (v) 2   (vi) 2   (vii) 7   (viii) 2   **7.** (i) 8,000
(ii) 50,625   (iii) 625   (iv) 59,049   (v) 117,649
(vi) 16,384   **8.** (i) 3.46   (ii) 5.29   (iii) 9.85   (iv) 11.05
(v) 22.36   (vi) 38.21   **9.** (i) 1,728   (ii) 759,375
(iii) 9,261   (iv) 130,321   (v) 289   (vi) 456,976
10. (i) 3.87   (ii) 5.39   (iii) 8.31   (iv) 11.62   (v) 30.82
(vi) 37.03   **11.** (i) $a = 2, n = 7, b = 128$ (ii) $a = 3$,
$b = 81, n = 4$ (iii) $n = 3, b = 125, a = 5$

Exercise 15.2

1. (i) 2^5 (ii) 5^6 (iii) $2^3 \times 5^2$ (iv) $2^5 \times 3^6$ (v) $2^6 \times 5^5$
(vi) $2^4 \times 3^5 \times 5^2$ **2.** (i) 4^5 (ii) $5^3 \times 2^3$ (iii) $2^2 \times 3^2 \times 5^2$
(iv) $2^4 \times 3^4 \times 5^3$ (v) $2^4 \times 3^4 \times 4^4$ (vi) $2^3 \times 3^3 \times 4^3 \times 5^2$

3. (i) x^5 (ii) y^6 (iii) $x^2 \times y^2 \times z^2$ (iv) $x^6 \times z^5$ (v) $x^6 \times y^5$
(vi) $x^4 \times y^5 \times z^2$ **4.** (i) y^5 (ii) $x^3 \times y^3$ (iii) $x \times y^2 \times z^2$
(iv) $x^6 \times y^2 \times z^3$ (v) $x^4 \times y^4 \times z^4$ (vi) $x^4 \times y^3 \times z^4$
5. (i) $2 \times 2 \times 2$ (ii) $3 \times 3 \times 3 \times 3$ (iii) 5×5
(iv) $6 \times 6 \times 6 \times 6 \times 6$ (v) $7 \times 7 \times 7 \times 7 \times 7 \times 7$
(vi) $3 \times 3 \times 3 \times 3 \times 3$ (vii) $2 \times 2 \times 2 \times 2 \times 2 \times 2$
(viii) $5 \times 5 \times 5 \times 5 \times 5$ (ix) 7×7
(x) $8 \times 8 \times 8 \times 8 \times 8 \times 8$ (xi) $x \times x \times x \times x \times x \times x \times x \times x \times x$
(xii) $y \times y \times y$ (xiii) $z \times z \times z \times z \times z$ (xiv) $a \times a$
(xv) $b \times b \times b \times b$ **6.** (i) 5   (ii) 8   (iii) 18   (iv) 7
(v) 5   **7.** (i) 3^9 (ii) 4^{11} (iii) 5^{13} (iv) 5^{18} (v) 10^9
8. (i) 5   (ii) 7   (iii) 3   (iv) 6   (v) 2   **9.** (i) 4^4 (ii) 6^3
(iii) 8^4 (iv) 2^4 (v) 10^5 **10.** (i) -3^4 (ii) -5^5 (iii) 7^7
(iv) 4^5 (v) 9^5 (vi) -2^8 (vii) 6^5 (viii) 8^7 (ix) 9^{10}
(x) -10^5 **11.** (i) -2^2 (ii) 4^2 (iii) -6^5 (iv) -6^7 (v) 5^5
(vi) -8^7 (vii) 7^7 (viii) 10^8 (ix) -3^3 (x) 1^2 **12.** (i) -4^3
(ii) 2^6 (iii) -2^4 (iv) 3^3 (v) 2^5 (vi) -3^5 (vii) -4^3
(viii) 5^2 (ix) -6^3 (x) 6^{-1}

Exercise 15.3

1. (i) $(2^3)^5$ means 5 copies of 2^3 multiplied together,
which is: $2^3 \times 2^3 \times 2^3 \times 2^3 \times 2^3$ **2.** (i) $(3^6)^3$ means 3
copies of 3^6 multiplied together, which is:
$3^6 \times 3^6 \times 3^6$ **3.** (i) $(5^5)^4 = 5^5 \times 5^5 \times 5^5 \times 5^5$ because
$(5^5)^4$ means 4 copies of 5^5 multiplied together.   **4.** (i) 12
(ii) 15   (iii) 8   (iv) 20   (v) 25   (vi) 14   (vii) 30
(viii) 4   (ix) 42   (x) 99   (xi) 15   (xii) 6   **5.** (i) 8^{12}
(ii) 7^{45} (iii) 10^{20} (iv) 5^{54} (v) 18^{40} (vi) 12^{35}
6. (i) 3^{12} (ii) 5^6 (iii) 12^3 (iv) 8^{40} (v) 16^6 (vi) 18^4
(vii) 19^5 (viii) 10^4 (ix) -3^1 (x) -5^5 (xi) 6^{12}
(xii) 12^7 **7.** (i) $32 = 2^5 = 2^2 \times 2^3 = (2^1)^5 = 2^7 \div 2^2$
(ii) $81 = 3^4 = 3^1 \times 3^3 = (3^2)^2 = 3^{11} \div 3^7$
(iii) $64 = 2^6 = 2^2 \times 2^4 = (2^2)^3 = 2^9 \div 2^3$
(iv) $625 = 5^4 = 5^2 \times 5^2 = (5^2)^2 = 5^{171} \div 5^{167}$
8. (i) -3^6 (ii) -4^{12} (iii) -2^{40} (iv) -5^{12} (v) -6^9
(vi) -4^{35} (vii) -8^{27} (viii) -11^{10} (ix) -10^{21}
(x) -12^{45} (xi) -20^{12} (xii) -3^{63}

Exercise 15.4

1. (i) 1.5×10^1 (ii) 1.5×10^2 (iii) 1.5×10^3
(iv) 1.5×10^4 (v) 1.5×10^5 (vi) 1.5×10^8
2. (i) 3.5×10^2 (ii) 5.6×10^3 (iii) 3.45×10^6
(iv) 6.3×10^8 (v) 7.89×10^4 (vi) 4.7823×10^4
3. (i) 6.8×10^2 (ii) 3.28×10^3 (iii) 6.578×10^4
(iv) 3×10^6 (v) 4.568×10^5 (vi) 6×10^0
4. (i) 1.65×10^2 (ii) 1.785×10^4 (iii) 1.5×10^6
(iv) 1.95×10^8 (v) 1.75×10^9 (vi) 7.87×10^5
5. (i) 300,000   (ii) 9,000,000   (iii) 240   (iv) 6,400
(v) 6,120   (vi) 738,000   **6.** (i) 2,000,000   (ii) 16,900

(iii) 2,480   (iv) 647,000   (v) 61.2   (vi) 8,670
7. (i) 3.6×10^1 (ii) 5.613×10^3 (iii) 3.45×10^2
(iv) 6.349×10^3 (v) 7.89×10^6 (vi) 6.8×10^4
(vii) 3.28×10^6 (viii) 6.578×10^7 (ix) 9×10^9
(x) 5.6×10^7 **8.** (i) 1,500   (ii) 25,400   (iii) 350,000
(iv) 6,670,000   (v) 815   (vi) 91,820,000   **9.** (i) 4   (ii) 6
(iii) 5   (iv) 4   (v) 2

Exercise 15.5

1. (i) $\frac{1}{2}$, $\frac{1}{4}$, $\frac{1}{6}$, $\frac{1}{8}$, $\frac{1}{10}$ (ii) 1, $\frac{1}{3}$, $\frac{1}{5}$, $\frac{1}{7}$, $\frac{1}{9}$
(iii) $\frac{1}{2}$, $\frac{1}{3}$, $\frac{1}{5}$, $\frac{1}{7}$, $\frac{1}{11}$, $\frac{1}{13}$ (iv) $\frac{1}{5}$, $\frac{1}{10}$, $\frac{1}{15}$, $\frac{1}{20}$, $\frac{1}{25}$, $\frac{1}{30}$
2. (i) 2, 4, 6, 8, 10   (ii) 3, 5, 7, 9, 11, 13
(iii) 5, 10, 15, 20, 25, 30   (iv) 23, 29, 31, 37, 41
(v) 4, 9, 16, 25, 36, 49   **3.** (i) $\frac{3}{2}$, $\frac{4}{3}$, $\frac{5}{4}$, $\frac{6}{5}$, $\frac{7}{6}$, $\frac{8}{7}$
(ii) $\frac{5}{3}$, $\frac{7}{5}$, $\frac{9}{7}$, $\frac{11}{9}$, $\frac{13}{11}$ (iii) $\frac{5}{2}$, $\frac{7}{4}$, $\frac{3}{2}$, $\frac{11}{8}$, $\frac{13}{10}$
4. (i) $\frac{2}{5}$ (ii) $\frac{3}{10}$ (iii) $\frac{4}{17}$ (iv) $\frac{5}{26}$ (v) $\frac{6}{37}$ (vi) $\frac{7}{50}$
5. (a)(i) 0.2   (ii) 0.1   (iii) 0.25   (iv) 0.05   (v) 0.25
(vi) 0.5   (b)(i) 0.191   (ii) 0.101   (iii) 0.236   (iv) 0.051
(v) 0.251   (vi) 0.407   **6.** (i) -2 (ii) $-\frac{1}{4}$ (iii) $-\frac{5}{11}$
(iv) $-\frac{10}{3}$ (v) $-\frac{5}{57}$ (vi) -8 (vii) $-\frac{7}{12}$ (viii) $-\frac{5}{6}$
(ix) $-\frac{4}{3}$ (x) $-\frac{8}{15}$

Revision Exercises

1. (a)(i) 81   (ii) 125   (iii) 64   (iv) 81   (v) -125 (vi) 64
(b)(i) 8   (ii) 12   (iii) 16   **2.** (i) 5   (ii) 2   (iii) 9   (iv) 100
(v) 1   **3.** (a)(i) 244.14   (ii) 4.21   (iii) 19,770.61
(b)(i) Mars   (ii) Mercury   (iii) 9×10^{10} **4.** (a)(i) 8.7×10^5
(ii) 3.96×10^5 (iii) 4.3076×10^6 (b)(i) 16   (ii) 18.44
5. (a) 31,400   (b) 16   (c) 1.8×10^{25} kg   **6.** (i) 2^{11} (ii) 3^{12}
(iii) 5^5 (iv) -5^{30} (v) -7^5 (vi) 4^{21} (vii) -5^{10} (viii) -7^5
7. (i) 0.38   (ii) 0.08   (iii) 0.78   (iv) 0.44   **8.** (a)(i) 31
(ii) 1   (iii) 16   (b)(i) 29.71   (ii) 0.88   (iii) 14.12
9. 7   **10.** 5   11. (a) 1.02×10^8 (b)(i) c (ii) 28
12. (i) 2^2, 2^3, 2^4 (ii) 2^{64} (iii) 7th square

Chapter 16

Exercise 16.1

1. €5,200   **2.** €5,760   **3.** (i) €4,860   (ii) €30,140
4. (i) €15,330   (ii) €61,970   **5.** (i) €7,200   (ii) €5,370
(iii) €30,630   **6.** (i) €6,800   (ii) €4,200   (iii) €29,800
7. (i) €7,986, €5,970, €30,330   **8.** €5,880
(i) €3,990, €4,290   (ii) €25,110   **9.** €7,770
(i) €5,670, €6,470   (ii) €30,530   **10.** €6,700
(i) €4,500, €5,500   (ii) €28,000   **11.** 21%   **12.** (i) €7,600
(ii) 20%   **13.** 21%

Exercise 16.2

1. (i) €1.35   (ii) €1.89   (iii) €2.43   (iv) €2.70
2. (i) €181.50   (ii) €605   (iii) €968   (iv) €2418.79
3. €6.05   **4.** €7.10   **5.** €181.50   **6.** €158.90   **7.** €24
8. €150   **9.** €1,800   **10.** €800   **11.** €252   **12.** (i) €3,375
(ii) €4,083.75

Exercise 16.3

1. A = 576; B = €14.62; C = €81.22; D = €95.84;
E = €12.94; F = €108.78   **2.** A = 137; B = 1557;
C = €10.33; D = €61.22; E = €4.31; F = €75.86;
G = €10.24; H = €86.10   **3.** Bill 1: (i) 69   (ii) €8.28
(iii) €23.02; Bill 2: (i) 1,250   (ii) €150   (iii) €183.87
Bill 3: (i) 613   (ii) €73.56   (iii) €97.11   Bill 4: (i) 658
(ii) €78.96   (iii) €103.24   **4.** Bill 1 = €67.20;
Bill 2 = €79.36; Bill 3 = €71.28; Bill 4 = €40.08
5. (i) €9   (ii) €74   (iii) €89.54   **6.** €559.14
7. (i) €29.64   (ii) €35.57   **8.** 54   **9.** 200 minutes
10. Network B is cheaper.   **11.** (i) 410   (ii) 4659 kw/hrs
(iii) €139.77   (iv) €158.64

Exercise 16.4

2. (i) €52.50   (ii) €127.20   (iii) €270   (iv) €789.75
(v) €2,610   **3.** (i) €47.50   (ii) €1,062.50   (iii) €25,500
(iv) €8,000   (v) €12,672   **4.** 20%   **5.** €11.25   **6.** €138
7. €12   **8.** (i) €900   (ii) 15%   **9.** €25

Exercise 16.5

1. (a)(i) €60   (ii) €1,140   (b)(i) €30   (ii) €170
(c)(i) €240   (ii) €1,360   (d)(i) €88   (ii) €4,312
(e)(i) €350   (ii) €1,050   (f)(i) €180   (ii) €1,320
(g)(i) €547.50   (ii) €912.50   (h)(i) €3,408   (ii) €24,992
2. (i) 5%   (ii) 6%   (iii) 15%   (iv) 16%   (v) 12%
3. (i) €4.20   (ii) €65.80   **4.** (i) €50.82   (ii) €372.68
5. €960   **6.** €418.50   **7.** (i) €15   (ii) €31.25
8. (i) Trade discount 20% = €1,480.00;
Price (ex. VAT) = €5,920.00; VAT 21% = €1,243.20;
Total due = €7,163.20   (ii) €6,805.04

Exercise 16.6

1. (i) €40.80   (ii) €0.68   **2.** (i) $469   (ii) €650
3. €17.64   **4.** €80   **5.** (i) $85.20   (ii) ¥16,780.50
(iii) £43.50   (iv) €600   (v) €75   (vi) ¥44,748 is better.

6. (i) £738   (ii) €54   (iii) €120   (iv) €797.10
(v) ¥162,000   **7.** $439.20 €240   **8.** 1,200 IDR
9. (i) $650   (ii) €515.50   **10.** (i) €110   (ii) €113.30

Exercise 16.7

1. (i) €50   (ii) €250   (iii) €36   (iv) €217.50   (v) €36
(vi) €735   (vii) €680   (viii) €200   (ix) €285   (x) €72
2. (i) €315   (ii) €1,540   (iii) €1,344   (iv) €1,437.50
(v) €101.76   (vi) €772.50   (vii) €114.40   (viii) €16.25
(ix) €7,020   (x) €98,500.05   **3.** €2,756.25   **4.** €18 €18
5. €1,297.92   **6.** €12,597.12   **7.** €2,865.24   **8.** €762
9. €204   **10.** €1,653.75   **11.** €13,492,326.75
12. €192   **13.** €46,716   **14.** €13,706,000
15. €2,622.68

Revision Exercises

1. Tadhg = €32; Helen = €44.80; Eoin = €24;
Jenny = €77.80   **2.** €22,630   **3.** 16.67%   **4.** €4,900
5. (i) €3,640   (ii) €22,360   (iii) €430   **6.** (i) €320
(ii) 25.49%   **7.** (i) €363   (ii) €21.78   (iii) €2.27
(iv) €136.2   **8.** (i) €650   (ii) €734.5   **9.** €50.40
10. Tax @ 20% = €138; Tax credit = €65;
Tax due = €73; Take-home pay = €617
11. Bill 1: (a)(i) 58 units   (ii) €6.96   (b) €21.52
Bill 2: (a)(i) 250 units   (ii) €30   (b) €47.67
Bill 3: (a)(i) 613 units   (ii) €73.56   (b) €97.11
Bill 4: (a)(i) 658 units   (ii) €78.96   (b) €103.24
12. €597.25   **13.** 236 minutes is her limit.   **15.** 150%
16. €200   **17.** (ii) €8,920.12   **18.** (i) £629   (ii) €36
(iii) €65.50   (iv) €6,500   (v) ¥57,500   **19.** €17,640
20. €73.50   **21.** €47,590.40   **22.** €44,362.23€
23. €477,422.40   **24.** €13,120

Chapter 17

Exercise 17.1

1. (i) 00:25   (ii) 15:56   (iii) 23:55   (iv) 14:26   (v) 07:28
(vi) 12:00   **2.** (i) 2.12 pm   (ii) 10.10 pm   (iii) 12.15 am
(iv) 11.46 am   (v) 6.36 pm   (vi) 8.31 pm   **3.** (i) 2 hrs 30 mins
(ii) 4 hrs 20 mins   (iii) 1 hr 12 mins   (iv) 10 hrs 50 mins
(v) 5 mins   (vi) 2 hrs 16 mins   **4.** (i) 120   (ii) 640
(iii) 7200   (iv) 13,950   (v) 129,600   **5.** (A) 12:57
(B) 14:20   (C) 11:01   (D) 23:12   (E) 01:24 (next day)
(F) 16:17   (G) 01:09 (two days later)   (H) 02:20
(I) 01:41 (next day)   (J) 08:23 (two days later)
6. (A) 11:20   (B) 05:16   (C) 11:51   (D) 14:53   (E) 00:30

(F) 06:02   (G) 23:12 (previous day)   (H) 14:01
(previous day)   (I) 16:05   (J) 10:42   **7.** (A) 1 hr 06 mins
(B) 1 hour 11 mins   (C) 57 mins   (D) 2 hrs 18 mins
(E) 1 hr 49 mins   (F) 3 hrs 46 mins   (G) 2 hrs 01 min
(H) 10 hrs 47 mins   (I) 2 hrs 21 mins   (J) 3 hrs 54 mins
8. (i) 6 hrs 45 mins   (ii) 5 hrs 45 mins   **9.** (i) 14 engines
(ii) 15 engines   **10.** 14:50   **11.** (i) 15 hrs 45 mins
(ii) 21 trains   (iii) 7 trains

Exercise 17.2

1. (i) The 1200 bus   (ii) 1 hr 30 mins   (iii) 1 hr 20 mins
(iv) 17:30   **2.** (i) 08:30   (ii) 50 mins   (iii) 09:00
(iv) 05:00   **3.** (i) The 10:00 Sunday train
(ii) The 20:50 train   (iii) 2 hrs 7 mins   (iv) Sunday, 10:00
4. (i) 3 mins   (ii) Dalkey, Killiney   (iii) 23 mins
(iv) 6 minutes   (v) 19:15   (vi) Shankill, Bray
5. (i) The 09:00 and 13:00 trains   (ii) The 09:00
and 14:00 trains   (iii) The 11:00 train (second)
(iv) 11:00 train, 46 mins   (v) 1 hour 58 mins
6. (i) 53 minutes   (ii) 10:28   (iii) Wicklow, Greystones
(iv) 20 minutes   (v) 69 minutes

Exercise 17.3

1. (A) 24 km/hr   (B) 300 km/hr   (C) $14\frac{2}{3}$ m/s
or 880 m/min   (D) $3\frac{1}{3}$ m/s   **2.** (A) 1 hr   (B) 2 hrs
(C) 50 hrs   (D) 18 hrs   (E) 88 hrs   (F) ½ hr
(G) 18.75 hrs   (H) 5.4 hrs   **3.** (A) 112.5 km
(B) 880 km   (C) 76 km   (D) 237.5 km   (E) 29.75 km
4. 40 secs   **5.** (i) 90 km   (ii) 2½ hours   **6.** 5 m/s
7. 4 km/hr   **8.** (i) $2\frac{1}{3}$ hours (2 hrs 20 mins)
(ii) 165 km   **9.** (i) 1,100 km/hr   (ii) 22:15
10. 4.5 hrs   **11.** 5 m/s   **12.** 27 km/hr   **13.** 9 km/hr
14. 500 seconds   **15.** (i) 50 km/hr   (ii) 36 km/hr
(iii) 245 km   (iv) 5.25 or 5 hrs 15 mins   (v) $46\frac{2}{3}$ km/hr
16. (i) 210 km   (ii) 5 hrs   (iii) 510 km   (iv) 9 hrs 12 mins
(v) ≈55 km/hr   **17.** (i) 37.5 km/hr   (ii) 40 mins
(iii) 60 km   (iv) 2 hrs   (v) 30 km/hr

Revision Exercises

1. (a) 7 hrs 30 mins   (b) 20   (c) 1 hr 55 mins
2. (a) 6 hrs 25 mins   (c)(i) 27 mins 12 secs
(ii) 23 mins 27 secs   (iii) 50 mins 39 secs
3. (c)(i) 13 mins   (ii) AAAA = 12:35, BBBB = 13:01,
CCCC = 13:11, DDDD = 13:07   (iii) 12:37   **4.** (a) 24
(b)(i) 30 mins   (ii) 28 mins   (iii) 85 mins   (iv) 5 hrs 50 mins
(v) 1 hr 07 mins   (vi) More than $\frac{1}{10}$ (or 0.1)

(vii) True   (c)(i) 16:15   (ii) 17:52   (iii) Needs to take the 13:05 hours   **5.** (a) 18 km/hr   (b)(i) 2 hrs 30 mins   (ii) 72 km/hr   (c)(i) Cork + Donegal   (ii) Belfast   (iii) 3 hrs   (iv) 23⅓ km/hr   (v) 14:10   (vi) 65 km/hr
6. (a)(i) 11 mins   (ii) Every 20 mins   (iii) AAAA = 15:01, BBBB = 15:37   (iv) Howth + Sutton   (v) 45 km/hr
7. (a) 3.6 km/hr   (b)(i) 3 hrs 20 mins   (ii) 224 km
(c) 5.2 km/hr   **8.** (a) 28 km/hr   (b)(i) 21:33 bus
(ii) 20:08   (iii) 24 km/hr   (c)(i) 128⅓ km
(ii) 08:35   (iii) 09:20   (iv) 75 km/hr   (v) 10:40
(vi) ≈52 km/hr

Chapter 18

Exercise 18.1

1. (i) Perimeter = 22 cm; Area = 18 cm²
(ii) Perimeter = 22 cm; Area = 28 cm²   (iii) Perimeter = 30 mm; Area = 56.25 mm²   (iv) Perimeter = 1.8 m; Area = 0.1125 m²   (v) Perimeter = 2,000 m; Area = 250,000 m²   (vi) Perimeter = 6,900 m; Area = 2,750,000 m²   (vii) Perimeter = 226 mm; Area = 3,190 mm²   (viii) Perimeter = 18.8 km; Area = 3.6 km²   **2.** (i) 16 cm²   (ii) 20 mm²
(iii) 108 m²   (iv) 4,050 mm²   (v) 2,300 mm²   (vi) 30 cm²
(vii) 63 m²   (viii) 72 cm²   **3.** (i) 31.5 cm²   (ii) 12 cm²
(iii) 2.5 cm²   (iv) 15 cm²   (v) 333.75 cm²   (vi) 0.64 m²
(vii) 1,800 mm² (18 cm²)   (viii) 20 cm²   **4.** (i) 108 cm²
(ii) 1,275 mm²   (iii) 28 cm²   (iv) 36 m²   (v) 22.75 cm²
(vi) 36 m²   (vii) 23.5 cm²   (viii) 5,625 mm²

Exercise 18.2

1. (i) Area = 113.04 cm²; Circumference = 37.68 cm
(ii) Area = 615.44 cm²; Circumference = 87.92 cm
(iii) Area = 339.6224 mm²; Circumference = 65.312 mm
(iv) Area = 706.5 m²; Circumference = 94.2 m
(v) Area = 213.71625 cm²; Circumference = 51.81 cm
(vi) Area = 123.836576 cm²; Circumference = 39.438 cm
(vii) Area = 7,850 m²; Circumference = 314 m
(viii) Area = 0.00000314 m²; Circumference = 0.00628 m
2. (i) Area = 154 cm²; Circumference = 44 cm
(ii) Area = 3,850 cm²; Circumference = 220 cm
(iii) Area = 346.5 cm²; Circumference = 66 cm
(iv) Area = 616 cm²; Circumference = 88 cm
(v) Area = 38.5 cm²; Circumference = 22 cm
(vi) Area = 0.7546 m²; Circumference = 3.08 m
(vii) Area = 5,544 mm²; Circumference = 264 mm
(viii) Area = 1³⁄₁₁ m²; Circumference = 4 m
3. (i) Area = 100π cm²; Circumference = 20π cm

(ii) Area = 16π mm²; Circumference = 8π mm
(iii) Area = 36π m²; Circumference = 12π m
(iv) Area = 0.25π cm²; Circumference = π cm
(v) Area = 625π m²; Circumference = 50π cm
(vi) Area = 1π m²; Circumference = 2π m
4. (i) Area = 12.57 cm²; Perimeter = 12.57 cm
(ii) Area = 19.63 cm²; Perimeter = 15.71 cm
5. (i) Area = 39.27 cm²; Perimeter = 25.71 cm
(ii) Area = 38.48 cm²; Perimeter = 25 cm
(iii) Area = 58.90 cm²; Perimeter = 33.56 cm
(iv) Area = 5,428.32 mm²; Perimeter = 342.83 mm
(v) Area = 5,256.64 m²; Perimeter = 325.66 m
(vi) Area = 176.71 cm²; Perimeter = 69.27 cm
(vii) Area = 84.82 cm²; Perimeter = 37.70 cm
6. (i) 3.927 m²   (ii) 48.285 cm²   (iii) 127.235 cm²
(iv) 226.195 cm²

Exercise 18.3

1. 184 tiles   **2.** (i) 10 m²   (ii) Design 2   (iii) 98,880 cm²
3. (i) 25.1 m²   (ii) €489.45   **4.** (i) 15 m²   (ii) 3 litres
(iii) €60   **5.** (i) 5.38 m²   (ii) €98.56   **6.** (i) 30.8 m
(ii) 649 turns   **7.** (a) x = 130 m; w = y = 140 m; z = 200 m
(b)(i) 9.6 hectares   (ii) 6.52 hectares   (iii) 3.08 hectares
8. (i) 116.34 m²   (ii) €5,235.30   (iii) €555.25
9. 6.28 m extra   **10.** (i) 900 pixels   (ii) 193.5 pixels
(iii) 1,024   (iv) 78.5%   **11.** (i) 7 m each   (ii) €307.58
12. Type A

Exercise 18.4

1. (i) Volume = 72 cm³; Surface area = 108 cm²
(ii) Volume = 30 cm³; Surface area = 62 cm²
(iii) Volume = 8 cm³; Surface area = 24 cm²
(iv) Volume = 140 cm³; Surface area = 208 cm²
(v) Volume = 132 cm³; Surface area = 178 cm²
2. (i) No   (ii) Yes   (iii) No   (iv) No   **3.** (i) Volume
= 160 cm³; Surface area = 184 cm²   (ii) Volume = 27 cm³;
Surface area = 54 cm²   (iii) Volume = 33,000 mm³;
Surface area = 6,700 mm²   **4.** (i) Volume = 25,000 cm³;
Surface area = 5,500 cm²   (ii) Volume = 6 m³;
Surface area = 22 m²   (iii) Volume = 105,000 mm³;
Surface area = 19,100 mm²   (iv) Volume = 216 cm³;
Surface area = 216 cm²   (v) Volume = 3.375 m³;
Surface area = 14.7 m²   (vi) Volume = 600 cm³;
Surface area = 500 cm²   (vii) Volume = 35 m³;
Surface area = 69 m²   (viii) Volume = 0.12 m³;
Surface area = 1.88 m²   **5.** (i) 150 mm³   (ii) 1.9 cm²
6. 35,500 cm²   **7.** 552   **8.** (a) (i) 1,890,000 cm³
(ii) 1,680 cm³   (b) 1,125

Exercise 18.5

1. (i) 565.2 cm³   (ii) 150.72 m³   (iii) 6,838.92 mm³
2. (i) 56.57 mm³   (ii) 0.94 m³   (iii) 10,607.14 cm³
3. (i) 325π cm³   (ii) 245π cm³   (iii) 1π m³
4. The 1ˢᵗ has more silver   **5.** (i) 22 full cups
(ii) 16 full cups   **6.** 440,000 cm³   **7.** (i) 42,390 cm³
(ii) 62,610 cm³   **8.** (i) 3.85 litres   (ii) 105 minutes
(i.e 1 hr 45 minutes)

Exercise 18.6

1. (i) 10 m   (ii) 5 m   (iii) 24 m   (iv) 18 m   **2.** (i) 1 cm
(ii) 0.55 cm   (iii) 2.4 cm   (iv) 0.08 cm   **3.** (i) 1:100
(ii) 1:200   (iii) 1:10,000   (iv) 1:100,000   **4.** (i) 3.6 km
(ii) 2.65 km   (iii) 50 cm   **5.** (ii) 170 m   **6.** (i) 3.75 m
(ii) 1.5 m   (iii) 2 cm   **8.** Building = 8.1 m;
Dinosaur = 5.1 m; Tractor = 3 m

Revision Exercises

1. (a)(i) 15 cm²   (ii) 12.8 cm²   (iii) 16.1 cm²   (iv) 9.3 cm²
(v) 29.25 cm²   (b)(i) 9 cm²   (ii) 10 cm²   (iii) 8 cm²
(iv) 12 cm²   (v) 4 cm²   (c)(i) 15 cm²   (ii) 7.5 cm²
(iii) 5 cm²   (iv) 17 cm²   (v) 7 cm²   **2.** (a)(i) 700 mm²
(ii) 1,000 mm²   (iii) 1,023 mm²   (iv) 408 mm²
(v) 2,350 mm²   (b)(i) 70 m²   (ii) €525   (c) 96 m²
3. (a)(i) 100 mm²   (ii) 10,000 cm²   (iii) 1,000,000 mm²
(b)(i) 144 units²   (ii) 41 units²   (iii) 54 units²   (c)(i) 31 m²
(ii) €434   (iii) 24 m   (iv) 72 m²   (v) €108
4. (a)(i) 31.4 cm   (ii) 44 cm   (iii)(a) 8 cm   (b) 25.12 cm
(iv)(a) 10.5 cm   (b) 66 cm   (b)(i) 1ˢᵗ = ¹⁄₄; 2ⁿᵈ = ¹⁄₂
(ii) 1ˢᵗ = 44 units; 2ⁿᵈ = 55 units   (iii) 1ˢᵗ = 616 units²;
2ⁿᵈ = 481.25 units²   (iv) 1ˢᵗ = 100 units; 2ⁿᵈ = 90 units
(c)(i) 400 m   (ii) 100 m   **5.** (a)(i) 154 cm²
(ii) 77 cm²   (iii) 157 cm²   (iv) 3.14 cm²   (v) 3,768 cm²
(b)(i) 1.256 m   (ii) 1,256 m   (iii) 2,500 times
(c)(i) 3:1   (ii) 9:1   **6.** (a)(i) 357 units²   (ii) 266 units²
(iii) 44 units²   (iv) 1,050 units²   (b)(i) 330 m
(ii) 2,400 times   (c)(i) 72 cm²   (ii) 3:4
7. (a)(i) 66 m²   (ii) €363   (b) 33 units²
(c) 10.5 units²   **8.** (a) 60 m³   (b) 7,500 cm³
(c)(i) 3 litres   (ii) 20 glasses   **9.** (a)(i) 6,000 m³
(ii) 750 boxes   (b)(i) 3.375 litres   (ii) 1,350 cm²
(c)(i) 72 litres   (ii) 8,400 cm²   **10.** (a) 3,140 cm³
(b) 3.08 litres   (c)(i) 960 cm³   (ii) 17.28 kg
(iii) 38 bracelets with 10 cm³ left over
11. (a)(i) 8 cm: 640π cm³; 4 cm: 160π cm³   (ii) 4:1
(b)(i) 88 cm³   (ii) 17,600 cm³   (iii) 200 times
(c)(i) 0.528 cm³   (ii) 2.688 cm³   (iii) 0.576 cm³

Chapter 19

Exercise 19.1

1. Correct   **2.** Correct   **3.** Not Correct   **4.** Not Correct
5. Correct   **6.** Not Correct   **7.** Correct   **8.** Not Correct
9. Correct

Exercise 19.2

1. $x = 3, y = 2$ **2.** $x = 8, y = 6$ **3.** $x = 11, y = 4$
4. $x = 14, y = 7$ **5.** $x = 5, y = 2$ **6.** $x = 4, y = 1$
7. $x = 5, y = 3$ **8.** $x = 3, y = 1$ **9.** $x = 2, y = 3$
10. $x = 5, y = 1$ **11.** $x = 3, y = 2$ **12.** $x = 4, y = 3$
13. $x = 4, y = 2$ **14.** $x = 2, y = 1$ **15.** $x = 6, y = 1$
16. $x = 4, y = 0$ **17.** $x = 1, y = 1$ **18.** $x = 3, y = 1$
19. $x = 5, y = 4$ **20.** $x = 1, y = 4$ **21.** $x = 3, y = 2$
22. $x = 2, y = 0$ **23.** $x = 4, y = 3$ **24.** $x = 8, y = 2$
25. $x = 3, y = -1$ **26.** $x = -1, y = 2$ **27.** $x = 4, y = 4$
28. $x = 6, y = -3$

Chapter 20

Exercise 20.1

1. (i) True   (ii) True   (iii) False   (iv) True   (v) True
(vi) False   (vii) True   (viii) False   (ix) False   (x) True
2. (i) $10 > 4$ (ii) $3 < 5$ (iii) $-2 < 4$ (iv) $-3 > -10$
(v) $0 > -3$ (vi) $-7 > -9$ (vii) $-4 < 0$ (viii) $-2 < 2$
(ix) $-5 < -4$ (x) $-20 < -19$

Exercise 20.2

1. (i) $x = 5, 6, 7$ (ii) $x = 10, 11, 12$ (iii) $x = -1, 0, 1$
(iv) $x = -1, 0, 1$ (v) $x = -8, -7, -6$ (vi) $x = 1, 2, 3$
(vii) $x = 1, 2$ (viii) $x = 1, 2, 3$

Exercise 20.3

1. $x > 3$ **2.** $x > 1$ **3.** $x \leqslant 7$ **4.** $x > -3$ **5.** $x \leqslant 0$
6. $x > 6$ **7.** $x > -1$ **8.** $x < -2$ **9.** $x \geqslant 7$
10. $x \leqslant -2$ **11.** $x > 4$ **12.** $x \leqslant -10$ **13.** $x > -11$
14. $x \leqslant 2$ **15.** $x \geqslant 7$ **16.** $x < -2$ **17.** $x \leqslant 2$
18. $x \leqslant -3$ **19.** $x \leqslant 4$ **20.** $x \geqslant 3$ **21.** $x < -2$
22. $x \leqslant 1$ **23.** $x > -5$ **24.** $x > -1$

Revision Exercises

1. (a)(i) $x \leqslant 4$ (ii) $x < 7$ (iii) $x < 3$ (iv) $x \geqslant 4$
(v) $x < 4$ (b)(i) $x > 3$ or $x \geqslant 4$ (ii) $x < 2$ or $x \leqslant 1$

(iii) $x \geqslant -6$ (iv) $x < 6$ (v) $x < 2$ or $x \leqslant 1$
2. (a)(i) $x \leqslant 3$ (ii) $x \geqslant 7$ (iii) $x < 6$ (iv) $x \leqslant 8$
(v) $x > 3$ (b)(i) $x > 1$ (ii) $x \leqslant 4$ (iii) $x > 3$
(iv) $x > 2$ (v) $x \geqslant 4$

Chapter 21

Exercise 21.1

1. (i) 4   (ii) 1   (iii) x (iv) x^2 (v) $10x^2$ (vi) $4x^3$ **2.** (i) 3
(ii) 9   (iii) $27x$ (iv) $3x^2$ (v) $6x^3$ (vi) $2y^2$ **3.** (i) 1   (ii) 40
(iii) $4x$ (iv) $10xy$ (v) $6x^3$ (vi) $5y^2$ **4.** (i) 5   (ii) x (iii) 1
(iv) $-2y$ (v) $-2x^2$ (vi) $6xy$ **5.** (i) 3   (ii) $6a$ (iii) 10
(iv) $-2ba$ (v) $-8a^2$ (vi) $12b^2$ **6.** (i) 4   (ii) $36y^2$ (iii) -1
(iv) x^2 (v) $3x$ (vi) $4xy^2$ **7.** (i) 2   (ii) $-4x$ (iii) -1
(iv) y (v) $5x^3$ (vi) $4xy^2$ **8.** (i) 1   (ii) 4   (iii) $2x$
(iv) $-x^2y$ (v) $4y^4$ (vi) $4x^2y$

Exercise 21.2

1. $2(3x + 5y)$ **2.** $3(3a + 2b)$ **3.** $5(5a + 7b)$
4. $7(3p + 4q)$ **5.** $3(4x - 5y)$ **6.** $20(2m + 3n)$ **7.** $x(2 + y)$
8. $a(a + b)$ **9.** $3p(4p - 1)$ **10.** $3a(3b - 5c)$ **11.** $3(2x + 3y)$
12. $2(2a + 5b)$ **13.** $7(2p + 3q)$ **14.** $5(3a + 5b)$
15. $3(4k - 5m)$ **16.** $11(2c - 3d)$ **17.** $5x(3x - 5)$
18. $2(2x - 3)$ **19.** $7(2y - 1)$ **20.** $5(d - 7e)$
21. $6p(p - 2q)$ **22.** $11x(2x - 3y)$ **23.** $8x(3y - 2z)$
24. $5b(7b - 5a)$ **25.** $a(a - 1)$ **26.** $25a(b - 3c)$
27. $x(y - z)$ **28.** $2x(x - 3)$ **29.** $3p(2 - 3q)$
30. $x^2(x - 1)$ **31.** $2x(3x + 4y)$ **32.** $8y(2x - 3y)$
33. $5a(8a - 1)$ **34.** $9t(2 + 3t)$ **35.** $25xy(3 + 4y)$
36. $22a(2a - 3)$ **37.** $4(6x - 7y + 11z)$ **38.** $5(7a - 9b - 3c)$
39. $3ab(4a^2 + 5b)$ **40.** $8ax(20x - 3x^2 - 4a^2)$ **41.** $x^3(x - 1)$
42. $x^2(2 - x)$

Exercise 21.3

1. $(p + q)(x + y)$ **2.** $(m + n)(a + b)$ **3.** $(3 + k)(a + b)$
4. $(w + 5)(x + y)$ **5.** $(c + b)(a + 3)$ **6.** $(p + 6)(x + y)$
7. $(a + 7)(x + y)$ **8.** $(c + 3)(a + b)$ **9.** $(k + 4)(a + b)$
10. $(x + 5)(1 + y)$ **11.** $(p + q)(x - y)$ **12.** $(a + y)(b - x)$
13. $(m + n)(r - s)$ **14.** $(a + b)(x - 2y)$ **15.** $(2a + b)(c - d)$
16. $(3y + 5b)(2x - a)$ **17.** $(3x + y)(5a - 2b)$
18. $(3m + n)(2x - y)$ **19.** $(p + 2x)(q - 3y)$
20. $(10x + 6a)(5b - y)$ **21.** $(a + b)(a + 3)$
22. $(x + 9)(x - w)$ **23.** $(5 + a)(1 + b)$ **24.** $(y + 8)(x - 1)$
25. $(x + a)(2x - 3y)$ **26.** $(2 + a)(5a - 4b)$
27. $(4p + 3)(5p - 4q)$ **28.** $(3x + 7z)(3x - 2y)$
29. $(7 + a)(a - 3b)$ **30.** $(x + 4k)(x - 1)$

Exercise 21.4

1. $-5a + 10b = -5(a - 2b)$ **2.** $-6x - 8y = -2(3x + 4y)$
3. $-15t + 21s = -3(5t - 7s)$ **4.** $-24a - 28b = -4(6a + 7b)$
5. $-2x - x^2 = -x(2 + x)$ **6.** $-6x + 14z = -2(3x - 7z)$
7. $-2x + 3y = -1(2x - 3y)$ **8.** $-15p + 9r - 12s$
$= -3(5p - 3r + 4s)$ **9.** $-xy - xz = -x(y + z)$
10. $-x^2 + x = -x(x - 1)$ **11.** $(a - c)(x - y)$
12. $(3 - a)(x + y)$ **13.** $(7 - k)(x - y)$ **14.** $(a - 5)(k + t)$
15. $(x - a)(x - 4)$ **16.** $(p - 9)(q + s)$ **17.** $(a - b)(b - c)$
18. $(k + t)(a - b)$ **19.** $(3a - x)(x - 2y)$ **20.** $(5y - 3)(3x - 4y)$
21. $(a + b)(k + t)$ **22.** $(2a + b)(c + d)$ **23.** $(3x - y)(a + b)$
24. $(c - 2)(5a + b)$ **25.** $(5c - 1)(2a - b)$
26. $(a + 1)(b + 3)$ **27.** $(5c + d)(3a + 2b)$
28. $(x + 7)(3y - 1)$ **29.** $(5a - 3)(7b - 2)$
30. $(2w - z)(11x - y)$ **31.** $(2a - b)(5x - y)$
32. $(b + n)(a + m)$ **33.** $(b - 1)(a - 1)$
34. $(7x + y)(x - 1)$ **35.** $(a + 7)(a - 3b)$
36. $(y^2 - 2)(a + 6)$ **37.** $(t - 1)(x - 5)$
38. $(k + 1)(a + b)$ **39.** $(1 - p)(c - a)$
40. $(1 + k)(a - b)$

Exercise 21.5

1. $(x + 1)(x + 2)$ **2.** $(x + 2)^2$ **3.** $(x + 2)(x + 5)$
4. $(x + 5)(x + 1)$ **5.** $(x + 3)(x + 4)$ **6.** $(x + 1)(x + 4)$
7. $(x + 1)(x + 11)$ **8.** $(x + 1)^2$ **9.** $(x + 15)(x + 1)$
10. $(a + 4)(a + 2)$ **11.** $(x + 10)(x + 2)$ **12.** $(x + 7)(x + 2)$
13. $(x + 4)(x + 5)$ **14.** $(x + 1)(x + 10)$ **15.** $(x + 2)^2$
16. $(x + 3)^2$ **17.** $(p + 1)(p + 7)$ **18.** $(x + 6)(x + 3)$
19. $(x + 9)(x + 2)$ **20.** $(x + 5)^2$ **21.** $(x + 3)(x + 9)$
22. $(x + 4)(x + 7)$ **23.** $(x + 4)(x + 9)$ **24.** $(x + 3)(x + 11)$
25. $(x + 2)(x + 6)$ **26.** $(x + 5)(x + 6)$ **27.** $(x + 3)(x + 10)$
28. $(x + 2)(x + 15)$ **29.** $(x + 1)(x + 30)$ **30.** $(x + 6)^2$
31. $(x + 6)(x + 7)$ **32.** $(x + 7)^2$ **33.** $(x + 4)(x + 8)$
34. $(x + 3)(x + 8)$ **35.** $(x + 5)(x + 8)$ **36.** $(x + 9)^2$
37. $(x + 4)(x + 25)$ **38.** $(x + 6)(x + 8)$ **39.** $(x + 2)(x + 25)$
40. $(x + 3)(x + 17)$

Exercise 21.6

1. $(x - 1)(x - 2)$ **2.** $(x - 2)(x - 3)$ **3.** $(x - 3)(x - 1)$
4. $(x - 2)(x - 5)$ **5.** $(x - 2)(x - 6)$ **6.** $(x - 4)(x - 5)$
7. $(x - 13)(x - 2)$ **8.** $(x - 3)(x - 7)$ **9.** $(x - 3)(x - 5)$
10. $(x - 1)(x - 4)$ **11.** $(x - 4)(x + 2)$ **12.** $(x - 10)(x + 2)$
13. $(x - 8)(x + 3)$ **14.** $(x - 5)(x + 3)$ **15.** $(x - 15)(x + 1)$
16. $(x - 3)(x + 1)$ **17.** $(x + 5)(x - 3)$ **18.** $(x - 4)(x + 3)$
19. $(x + 3)(x - 2)$ **20.** $(x - 3)(x + 2)$ **21.** $(x + 3)(x - 1)$
22. $(x + 7)(x - 1)$ **23.** $(x + 5)(x - 2)$ **24.** $(x + 8)(x - 2)$
25. $(x + 8)(x - 4)$ **26.** $(x + 7)(x - 2)$ **27.** $(x - 6)(x - 5)$
28. $(x + 6)(x + 5)$ **29.** $(x - 5)(x + 1)$ **30.** $(x - 6)(x + 5)$

31. $(x + 11)(x - 2)$ **32.** $(x - 2)^2$ **33.** $(x - 3)^2$
34. $(x + 8)(x - 3)$ **35.** $(x - 10)(x + 9)$ **36.** $(x + 9)(x - 7)$
37. $(x - 7)(x - 8)$ **38.** $(x + 7)(x - 6)$ **39.** $(x + 10)(x - 7)$
40. $(x - 6)(x - 4)$

Exercise 21.7

1. $(x - 3)(x + 3)$ **2.** $(x - 2)(x + 2)$ **3.** $(y - 6)(y + 6)$
4. $(x - 4)(x + 4)$ **5.** $(x - 5)(x + 5)$ **6.** $(x - 10)(x + 10)$
7. $(x - 8)(x + 8)$ **8.** $(p - 11)(p + 11)$ **9.** $(14 - a)(14 + a)$
10. $(x - 9)(x + 9)$ **11.** $(y - 12)(y + 12)$ **12.** $(x - 1)(x + 1)$
13. 28   **14.** 199   **15.** 200   **16.** 41   **17.** 52

Revision Exercises

1. (i) $(x - 6)(x + 6)$ (ii) $(x - 9)(x + 8)$ (iii) $(x + 7)(x - y)$
(iv) $(x - 11)(p - 2q)$ (v) $(y - 7)(y + 7)$
2. (i) $(a + p)(x + 6)$ (ii) $(x + 9)(x - 6)$ (iii) $(y - 3)(y + 3)$
(iv) $5(y - 3)(y + 3)$ (v) $(r + s)(p + q)$ **3.** (i) $(x - 6)(x - 5)$
(ii) $(x - 1)(2x - 3y)$ (iii) $3ab(a + 10b)$
(iv) $(3ab - 1)(a + 10b)$ (v) $(x - 7)(x + 6)$
4. (a) $a = 7; b = -8$ (b) $p = -16; q = 63$ (c) $k = 1; t = 2$
5. (a) $(a - 8)(a + 8)$ (b) $(x + 13)$ (c) (i) $-2a^2b(a - 2b)$
(ii) $(13 - 2a^2b)(a - 2b)$ **6.** (a)(i) $(x + 8)(x - 4)$ (ii) 0
(b)(i) $(b - 1)(a - c)$ (iii) $(x + 9)(x - 7)$ (c) 36
7. (a)(i) $(x - 2)(x + 2)$ (ii) $x(x - 4)$ (iii) $(x - 2)^2$
(b) $a = -14; b = -51$ (c)(i) $7(x - 2)(x + 2)$
(ii) $(x - 13)(x + 13)$ (iii) $x(x - 7)(x + 7)$

Chapter 22

Exercise 22.1

1. $x = 4$ or $x = 3$ **2.** $x = -6$ or $x = -2$
3. $x = 2$ or $x = -2$ **4.** $x = 10$ **5.** $x = -3$ or $x = -1$
6. $x = -1$ or $x = 7$ **7.** $x = -4$ **8.** $x = 12$ or $x = 11$
9. $x = -2$ **10.** $x = 9$ **11.** $x = 4$ **12.** $x = -3$ or $x = 7$

Exercise 22.2

1. $x = 0$ or $x = 5$ **2.** $x = 0$ or $x = 2$ **3.** $x = 0$ or $x = 3$
4. $x = 0$ or $x = -7$ **5.** $x = 0$ or $x = -4$ **6.** $x = 0$ or $x = 11$
7. $x = 0$ or $x = 1$ **8.** $x = 0$ or $x = 12$ **9.** $x = 0$ or $x = 1$
10. $x = 0$ or $x = -1$ **11.** $x = 0$ or $x = -12$
12. $x = 0$ or $x = 9$ **13.** $x = 0$ or $x = 4$
14. $x = 0$ or $x = -3$ **15.** $x = 0$ or $x = -3$
16. $x = 0$ or $x = 7$

Exercise 22.3

1. $x = \pm2$ **2.** $x = \pm11$ **3.** $y = \pm4$ **4.** $x = \pm10$
5. $x = \pm1$ **6.** $x = \pm5$ **7.** $a = \pm14$ **8.** $x = \pm8$
9. $x = \pm9$ **10.** $a = \pm15$ **11.** $x = \pm12$ **12.** $x = \pm20$
13. $x = \pm25$ **14.** $x = \pm1$

Exercise 22.4

1. $x = -3$ or $x = -1$ **2.** $x = -7$ or $x = -5$
3. $x = -3$ or $x = -4$ **4.** $x = -5$ or $x = -1$
5. $x = -4$ or $x = -7$ **6.** $x = -11$ or $x = -1$
7. $x = -1$ or $x = -2$ **8.** $x = -1$ or $x = -13$
9. $x = 5$ or $x = 3$ **10.** $x = -2$ **11.** $x = 2$
12. $x = 1$ or $x = 8$ **13.** $x = 9$ or $x = -3$
14. $x = 7$ or $x = 3$ **15.** $x = -7$ **16.** $x = -9$ or $x = -6$
17. $x = -8$ or $x = 5$ **18.** $x = -8$ or $x = 3$
19. $x = -7$ or $x = 3$ **20.** $x = -5$ or $x = 2$
21. $x = 9$ or $x = 5$ **22.** $x = -6$ **23.** $x = 6$ or $x = -2$
24. $x = 5$ or $x = 1$ **25.** $x = 9$ or $x = 7$
26. $x = 7$ or $x = -5$ **27.** $x = -7$ or $x = -2$
28. $x = 6$ or $x = 12$ **29.** $x = -7$ or $x = -6$
30. $x = 3$ or $x = -2$ **31.** $x = 6$ or $x = 7$
32. $x = 5$ or $x = -2$ **33.** $x = 15$ or $x = 3$
34. $x = 8$ or $x = -1$ **35.** $x = -7$ or $x = 3$
36. $x = 2$ or $x = 1$ **37.** $x = 8$ or $x = -3$
38. $x = -6$ or $x = 2$ **39.** $x = 2$ or $x = -6$
or $x = -6$ or $x = 2$

Revision Exercises

1. $x = 4$ or $x = -2$ **2.** $a = -5$ or $a = 2$ **3.** $b = 4$ or $b = 3$
4. $x = 4$ or $x = -3$ **5.** $x = -5$ or $x = 4$ **6.** $x = 0$ or $x = 9$
7. $x = \pm4$ **8.** $x = 8$ or $x = -5$ **9.** $x = 0$ or $x = -8$
10. $x = 7$ or $x = 4$ **11.** $x = 1$ or $x = 2$ **12.** $x = \pm2$
13. $x = 0$ or $x = 4$ **14.** $q = -7$ or $q = 3$ **15.** $x = \pm7$
16. $x = -3$ or $x = 2$ **17.** $x = 7$ or $x = -2$ **18.** $p = \pm15$
19. $x = 10$ or $x = 3$ **20.** $x = -2$ or $x = -5$
21. $x = 8$ or $x = -2$ **22.** $x = 0$ or $x = -3$
23. $x = 0$ or $x = 1$ **24.** $x = -7$ or $x = 6$
25. $x = -9$ or $x = 6$ **26.** $x = 0$ or $x = 2$
27. $x = 6$ or $x = -2$ **28.** $x = 0$ or $x = -13$
29. $x = \pm13$ **30.** $x = 10$ **31.** $x = -9$ or $x = 2$
32. $x = -1$ or $x = -2$ **33.** $x = 2$ or $x = 11$
34. $x = 8$ or $x = 2$ **35.** $x = 9$ or $x = -7$
36. $x = -1$ or $x = -9$ **37.** $x = 3$
38. $x = 7$ or $x = -2$ **39.** $x = 6$ or $x = -4$
40. $x = -6$ or $x = 5$ **41.** $x = 10$ or $x = -9$
42. $x = 7$ or $x = -4$ **43.** $x = 8$ or $x = -6$ **44.** $x = 1$
45. $x = 4$ or $x = 25$ **46.** $x = \pm2$ **47.** $x = 0$ or $x = 4$
48. $x = 13$ or $x = -1$ **49.** $x = -6$ or $x = 5$ **50.** $x = 4$

Chapter 23

Exercise 23.1

1. (i) $^5/_6$ (ii) $^1/_6$ (iii) $^{19}/_6$ (iv) $^7/_{12}$ **2.** (i) $^{47}/_{60}$ (ii) $^{79}/_{60}$
(iii) $^{-146}/_{15}$ (iv) $^{73}/_{10}$ **3.** (i) $^{19}/_{30}$ (ii) $^{-29}/_{10}$ (iii) $^{55}/_{24}$
(iv) $^{31}/_{10}$ **4.** (i) $^{11}/_6$ (ii) $^{11}/_6$ (iii) $^2/_3$ (iv) -9

Exercise 23.2

1. $\frac{7x}{12}$ **2.** $\frac{8x}{15}$ **3.** $\frac{9y}{14}$ **4.** $\frac{y+15}{5}$ **5.** $\frac{11x}{12}$ **6.** $\frac{x}{40}$

7. $\frac{13x}{10}$ **8.** $\frac{13x}{12}$ **9.** $\frac{19x}{24}$ **10.** $\frac{13x}{14}$ **11.** $\frac{2x+45}{15}$

12. $\frac{-8x+18}{9}$ **13.** $\frac{-25x+58}{30}$ **14.** $\frac{46x}{45}$ **15.** $\frac{76x-9}{24}$

16. $\frac{5x+9}{6}$ **17.** $\frac{7x+22}{10}$ **18.** $\frac{7x+43}{12}$ **19.** $\frac{9x-14}{20}$

20. $\frac{7x}{8}$ **21.** $\frac{23x-30}{12}$ **22.** $\frac{9x-4}{12}$ **23.** $\frac{8x+39}{5}$

24. $\frac{-2x-7}{10}$ **25.** $\frac{-2x-4}{15}$ **26.** $\frac{-x+12}{6}$ **27.** $\frac{16x+13}{12}$

28. $\frac{-7x-98}{20}$ **29.** $\frac{-6x-21}{5}$ **30.** $\frac{-4x-1}{3}$ **31.** $\frac{18x+25}{12}$

32. $\frac{12x-25}{24}$ **33.** $\frac{-23x+11}{28}$ **34.** $\frac{-3x-3}{5}$ **35.** $\frac{4x+15}{18}$

36. $\frac{25x+19}{6}$

Exercise 23.3

1. $x = 8$ **2.** $x = 1$ **3.** $x = 15$ **4.** $x = 8$ **5.** $x = 2$
6. $x = 4$ **7.** $x = 15$ **8.** $x = 6$ **9.** $x = 2$ **10.** $x = 5$
11. $x = 1$ **12.** $x = 15$ **13.** $x = 20$ **14.** $x = 14$
15. $x = 5$ **16.** $x = 8$ **17.** $x = 1$ **18.** $x = 7$ **19.** $x = 3$
20. $x = 1$ **21.** $x = 4$ **22.** $x = 5$ **23.** $x = 3$ **24.** $x = 5$
25. $x = 7$ **26.** $x = 3$ **27.** $x = -3$ **28.** $x = 2$
29. $x = 10$ **30.** $x = 5$

Exercise 23.4

1. $2x^2$ **2.** $9y^3$ **3.** $2x^2$ **4.** $15a$ **5.** $5x^2$ **6.** $3y^2$ **7.** 1
8. $\frac{2}{x}$ **9.** $\frac{4}{y}$ **10.** $\frac{1}{2y^2}$ **11.** $2x^2$ **12.** $\frac{5}{2}y$ **13.** $\frac{5x^2y}{4}$
14. $\frac{x^2yz}{3}$ **15.** $2a$ **16.** 3   **17.** 5   **18.** 3   **19.** 2   **20.** 5
21. x **22.** x **23.** $2x-7$ **24.** $4x$ **25.** $7x$ **26.** $x+1$
27. $x+3$ **28.** $x+5$ **29.** $x-2$ **30.** $x-2$ **31.** $x-1$
32. $x-5$ **33.** $x-3$ **34.** $4x$ **35.** $x+10$ **36.** 1

Revision Exercises

1. $\frac{7x}{10}$ **2.** $\frac{3x}{4}$ **3.** $\frac{5x}{14}$ **4.** $\frac{k}{8}$ **5.** $\frac{2x}{3}$ **6.** $\frac{4b}{7}$
7. $\frac{5x+7}{6}$ **8.** $\frac{7x+26}{10}$ **9.** $\frac{17x+10}{12}$ **10.** $\frac{24x+13}{10}$
11. $\frac{5x+13}{6}$ **12.** $\frac{7x+4}{6}$ **13.** $\frac{2y-19}{20}$ **14.** $\frac{5y-4}{14}$
15. $\frac{9x+5}{6}$ **16.** $\frac{4x-3}{6}$ **17.** $\frac{-2x+7}{10}$ **18.** $\frac{3x+25}{8}$
19. $\frac{11x+18}{10}$ **20.** $\frac{19x-7}{6}$ **21.** $x = 12$ **22.** $x = 9$
23. $x = 4$ **24.** $x = 12$ **25.** $x = 18$ **26.** $x = 30$
27. $x = 12$ **28.** $x = 11$ **29.** $x = 4$ **30.** $x = 3$
31. $x = 36$ **32.** $x = 6$ **33.** $x = 2$ **34.** $x = 2$

35. $x = 1$ **36.** $x = -1$ **37.** $x = 3$ **38.** $x = 9$
39. (i) $\frac{x-43}{10}$ (ii) $x = 3$ **40.** $3x$ **41.** $-x$
42. $4x$ **43.** $x+3$ **44.** $x-11$ **45.** x **46.** $\frac{x-7}{x}$
47. $x-20$ **48.** $\frac{1}{x-3}$

Chapter 24

Exercise 24.1

1. (i) (AB, EF), (BC, DF), (AC, ED)   (ii) (VW, SQ), (WU, QR),
(UV, RS)   (iii) (XY, VW), (YZ, WU), (XZ, VU)
(iv) (AB, LM), (BC, MK), (AC, LK)   (v) (DE, ST), (EF, TR),
(DF, SR)   **2.** (i) 8.75   (ii) 18   (iii) 12   (iv) 8   (v) 15
3. (i) $13\frac{1}{3}$ (ii) 12   (iii) 11.25   (iv) 13.75   (v) $56\frac{2}{3}$
4. (i) 9, 15   (ii) 11.8, 7.4   (iii) 17.5, $39\frac{2}{3}$ (iv) 8, 51.25
(v) 10.5, 10.95

Exercise 24.2

1. (i) Yes   (ii) No   (iii) Yes   (iv) Yes   (v) No   (vi) Yes
(vii) No   (viii) No   **2.** (i) Yes   (ii) Yes   (iii) Yes   (iv) No
(v) Yes   (vi) Yes   (vii) Yes   (viii) No   **3.** (i) 8 cm, 10 cm
(ii) Hypotenuse   **4.** (i) 8 cm, 7 cm   (ii) 60°

Exercise 24.3

1. (i) 10 cm   (ii) 17 cm   (iii) 25 cm   (iv) 15 cm
(v) 65 cm   (vi) 55 m   (vii) 29 cm   (viii) 65 mm
(ix) 97 cm   (x) 53 m   **2.** (i) 24 cm   (ii) 7 cm
(iii) 35 cm   (iv) 7.5 cm   (v) 15 cm   (vi) 132 cm
(vii) 80 m   (viii) 35 m   (ix) 60 mm   (x) 150 cm
3. (i) No   (ii) No   (iii) Yes   (iv) Yes   (v) No
4. (i) 9.49 cm   (ii) 3.87 cm   (iii) 2.83 cm   (iv) 21.35 cm
(v) 26.53 cm   (vi) 107.70 m   (vii) 92.65 cm
(viii) 48.99 km   (ix) 7.31 cm   (x) 70.10 cm   **5.** (i) Yes
(ii) No   (iii) No   (iv) Yes   (v) Yes
6. (i) $X = 20$ cm, $Y = 21$ cm   (ii) $X = 5$ cm, $Y = 12$ cm
(iii) $X = 123$ m; $Y = 22.27$ m   (iv) $X = 75$ units;
$Y = 85$ units; $Z = 132$ units

Exercise 24.4

1. (i) $\angle BAC$, [BC]   (ii) $\angle ABC$, [AC]   (iii) $\angle BAC$, [BC]
(iv) $\angle ABC$, [AC]   **2.** (i) 90°, 65°   (ii) 90°, 18°
(iii) 45°, 45°   (iv) 90°, 90°   **3.** (i) 90°, 140°   (ii) 62°, 28°
(iii) 60°, 42°   (iv) 57°, 66°   **4.** (i) 60°, 30°   (ii) 59°, 62°
(iii) 40°, 80°   (iv) 35°, 55°   **5.** (i) 24°   (ii) 24°
(iii) 26°   (iv) 114°; Yes   **6.** (i) 74°   (ii) 57°   (iii) 70°
(iv) 20°   **7.** (i) 10   (ii) 20   (iii) 14

Revision Exercises

1. (a)(i) Yes (ii) Yes (iii) Yes (iv) No (v) No (vi) Yes
2. (a)(i) 9, 9 (ii) 6.25, 11.25 (iii) 62.5, 53.125
(iv) 12, 12 (v) 28, 39.2 (b)(i) Square (v) ΔFMG,
ΔDMG, ΔDEM **3.** (a)(i) 20 cm (ii) 65 cm (iii) 7 cm
(iv) 11 cm (v) 2 (b)(i) 14.5, 21 (ii) 25, 30.1875
(iii) 10, 8 (c)(i) 160 cm, 480 cm (ii) 800 cm
(iii) 46,080,000 cm³ **4.** (a)(i), (ii) & (iv) (b)(i) 12 cm,
9 cm (ii) 21 cm, 28 cm (iii) 40 cm, 75 cm (c) 32 m
5. (a)(i) 90°, 65° (ii) 90°, 143° (iii) 55°, 35°
(iv) 55°, 35° (v) 25°, 65° (b)(i) 60°, 87° (ii) Tangent
(iii) No (c)(i) 90° (ii) 90° (iii) 108° (iv) 18°
6. (a)(i) 1.2 m (ii) 1.73 m (b) Laneway (c)(i) 15 m
(ii) €802 **7.** (a)(i) 600 km (ii) 232 km/hr (b) 283 m
(c)(i) 1.5 m (ii) 4.56 m **8.** (a) 58 cm; 55 cm
(b) The second and third designs fulfil the condition.
(c) Linesman: ≈23 m from ball; Referee: ≈21 m
from ball.

Chapter 25

Exercise 25.3

7. Isosceles

Exercise 25.4

5. 5.2 cm **6.** 4.6 cm **7.** 6.3 cm **8.** 4.4 cm **9.** 6.9 cm

Revision Exercises

4. (ii) 10 cm, 6.7 cm **5.** (ii) 25 mm **6.** (iv) 12 cm²
7. (ii) 85°, 8 cm (iv) $|\angle JKL| = 90°$, $|JL| = 10$ cm
9. (v) 3.5 cm **10.** (ii) 360° **12.** (ii) 8 cm
(iii) Right-angled **13.** (ii) Isosceles (iii) $|\angle MNO| = 52°$,
$|\angle NMO| = 52°$, $|\angle MON| = 76°$ (v) $|\angle RST| = 52°$,
$|\angle SRT| = 52°$, $|\angle RTS| = 76°$ **14.** 3.4 m
15. (iv) Diameter **17.** ≈51 m **18.** ≈4.1 cm
19. (ii) ≈710 cm (iii) ≈50 m² (iv) 12 m²
20. (ii) ≈10 km

Chapter 26

Exercise 26.1

4. $B(-3,0)$ = x-axis, $C(2,0)$ = x-axis, $D(0,-2)$ = y-axis,
$E(4,0)$ = x-axis **5.** $W(-3,-2)$ = 3rd, $X(2,-5)$ = 4th,
$Y(3,2)$ = 1st, $Z(-5,-2)$ = 3rd **7.** (i) Yes
(ii) $\angle XYV$ or $\angle YVW$ or $\angle WXY$ or $\angle VWX$ **8.** (i) 4, 5
(ii) 20 **10.** 18

Exercise 26.2

1. (i) 5 (ii) 13 (iii) 2 (iv) 4 **2.** (i) $\sqrt{26}$ (ii) $\sqrt{29}$
(iii) $\sqrt{52}$ (iv) $\sqrt{80}$ **3.** (i) $\sqrt{40}$ (ii) 4 (iii) $\sqrt{13}$
(iv) $\sqrt{170}$ **4.** (ii) 3 (iii) $\sqrt{18}$ **5.** (ii) $\sqrt{20}$ (iii) 5
(iv) 5 units **7.** (i) C **10.** $\sqrt{20}$ **11.** Yes
12. (ii) 5, $\sqrt{5}$, $\sqrt{20}$

Exercise 26.3

1. (i) (4,3) (ii) (4,4) (iii) (4,8) (iv) (3,4) **2.** (i) (2,5)
(ii) (2,0) (iii) (2,−2) (iv) (−1,−4) **3.** (i) (2,−1) (ii) (1,−2)
(iii) (3.5,2) (iv) (2.5,1.5) **4.** (2,3) **5.** (112.5,125)
6. (1,−1) **7.** (i) (3.5,−0.5) **8.** (i) (3,−2) **9.** (i) (2,0)
(ii) (2,3), (2,−3) (iii) (−1,0), (5,0) **10.** (i) (4,−12)
(ii) (9,−2) (iii) (−2,1) (iv) (−8,−15) **11.** (i) (2,2)
(ii) (3,−1) (iii) $\sqrt{10}$ (iv) $2\sqrt{10}$

Exercise 26.4

1. (i) 3 (ii) −2 (ii) 0 (iv) 4 (v) ⅕ (vi) −⅔
2. (i) −⁴⁄₃ (ii) −⁴⁄₉ (iii) −3 (iv) 0 (v) ⁴⁄₃ (vi) ¹¹⁄₈
3. 1, 0, −1, −⁵⁄₂, ⁵⁄₂, −³⁄₂, −1, −1, ³⁄₂, −²⁄₅, ⁵⁄₃, 0
8. (4,2.5)

Exercise 26.5

4. (5,2) **5.** (−1,−2) **6.** (iii) 2 (iv) Yes **7.** (iii) −⅓
(iv) Yes **8.** (iii) 1 (iv) No **9.** 13 **10.** 9 **11.** 7
12. 4 **13.** 7

Exercise 26.6

1. (i) 3 (ii) 1 (iii) 4 (iv) ½ **2.** (i) 3 (ii) ⅔
(iii) −5 (iv) −⁶⁄₅ **3.** (i) (0,2) (ii) (0,−2)
(iii) (0,5) (iv) (0,−⅓) **4.** (i) (0,−8) (ii) (0,−2)
(iii) (0,−9) (iv) (0,−²⁄₅) **9.** (i) (−2,0) (ii) (2,0)
(iii) (−2,0) (iv) (3,0) **10.** (i) (0,6) (ii) (0,−2)
(iii) (0,−8) (iv) (0,−15) **11.** (i) (6,0), (0,6)
(ii) (5,0), (0,2.5) (iii) (2,0), (0,4) (iv) (4,0), (0,−12)
(v) (3,0), (0,5) **12.** (i) (4,0), (0,4) (ii) (5,0), (0,1)
(iii) (2,0), (0,−1) (iv) (4,0), (0,−3) (v) (10,0), (0,5)

Exercise 26.7

1. (i) $x - y = 0$ (ii) $x + y - 1 = 0$ (iii) $4x + y - 22 = 0$
(iv) $x - 2y - 10 = 0$ (v) $x + 3y + 20 = 0$
(vi) $x + 4y + 32 = 0$ **2.** (i) $x - 2y + 6 = 0$
(ii) $4x + 3y + 7 = 0$ (iii) $2x - 3y + 16 = 0$
(iv) $x + 2y - 8 = 0$ (v) $2x + 5y + 23 = 0$
(vi) $2x - 7y + 46 = 0$ **3.** (i) $x - y = 0$
(ii) $x - 3y + 10 = 0$ (iii) $5x - 4y + 1 = 0$

(iv) $3x + 2y - 5 = 0$ (v) $8x - 3y + 1 = 0$
(vi) $x + y - 3 = 0$ **4.** (i) $x + y - 1 = 0$
(ii) $x + 3y - 13 = 0$ (iii) $5x + 4y - 5 = 0$
(iv) $3x - 2y + 7 = 0$ (v) $8x + 3y - 4 = 0$ (vi) $x - y = 0$
5. $x - y - 2 = 0$, $2x + y + 3 = 0$, $y - 2 = 0$
6. $y + 2 = 0$, $2x + y - 1 = 0$, $2x - y - 3 = 0$
7. (i) $x = 1$ (ii) $x = -1$ (iii) $x = -5$ (iv) $y = 4$ (v) $y = 3$
(vi) $y = -2$ **8.** (i) $x = 5$ (ii) $y = 4$ (iii) $x = -5$
(iv) $y = 5$ (v) $y = -2$ (vi) $y = -1$ **9.** $x + 8y - 11 = 0$
10. $2x - 3y - 1 = 0$ **11.** $2x + 5y = 11$

Revision Exercises

1. (c) Rectangle **2.** (a) $A(0,3)$, $B(4,0)$ (b) 5 units
(c) $|OA| = 3$ units, $|OB| = 4$ units (d) 5 units
3. (ii) $(-1,3)$ (iv) $x + y - 2 = 0$ (v) $(2,0)$
4. (ii) $(2.5,2.5)$ (iii) -1 (iv) $x + y - 5 = 0$ (v) $(0,5)$
(vi) 14 **5.** (ii) $5/7$ (iii) $5x - 7y + 32 = 0$ (iv) $(0,{}^{32}/_7)$
(v) $y = \frac{5}{7}x + \frac{32}{7}$ **6.** (i) 450 g (ii) 7.1 ounces (iii) ${}^{225}/_8$
(iv) $y = \frac{225}{8}x$ (v) 1406.25 g **7.** (ii) 6 (iv) -3 (v) -3
8. $13x + 20y - 65 = 0$ **9.** (iii) 20 (v) Right-angled
10. (i) $|OA| = 5$ units, $|OB| = 12$ units (ii) 13 units
(iii) $(6,2.5)$ (iv) $3x - 4y - 8 = 0$ **11.** (a) $(3,4)$
(b) $E = (6,7)$ (c) Bee 2 has travelled the shorter distance.
12. (a)(i) $4\sqrt{2}$ km (ii) $\sqrt{10}$ km (iii) $\sqrt{2}$ km
(iv) $2\sqrt{10}$ km (b) ≈ 17 km (c) Incorrect

Chapter 27

Exercise 27.2

1. (i) S (ii) R (iii) $[TS]$ (iv) $[PQ]$ (v) Triangle C (vi) q
(vii) Triangle A (viii) Image 1 (ix) Image 3 **2.** (i) Image 3
(ii) Image 4 (iii) Image 2 (iv) Image 3 (v) Image 1
(vi) Image 3 (vii) Image 2 **4.** (i) One, none
(ii) None, one (iii) Three, none **5.** (i) Image 4
(ii) Image 1 (iii) Image 1 (iv) Image 1 (v) Image 3
6. (i) Axial symmetry in y-axis (ii) Axial symmetry in y-axis
(iii) Central symmetry (iv) Axial symmetry in x-axis
7. (i) **A** Central symmetry **B** Axial symmetry
C Translation (ii) **A** Axial symmetry **B** Translation
C Central symmetry (iii) **A** Translation
B Central Symmetry **C** Axial symmetry

Chapter 28

Exercise 28.1

1. (i) 5 (ii) 13 (iii) 24 (iv) 29 (v) 3 (vi) 96
2. (i) $\sqrt{2}$ (ii) $\sqrt{10}$ (iii) $\sqrt{11}$ (iv) $\sqrt{34}$ **3.** 6 m

4. (i) 3 (ii) 2 **5.** (i) 10, 24 (ii) 96, 4 (iii) 5, 12
(iv) 12 cm, 13 cm **6.** 5.66 m **7.** 100 cm **8.** Yes
9. Yes **10.** 4.83 m

Exercise 28.2

1. (i) $\frac{21}{29}, \frac{20}{29}, \frac{21}{20}$ (ii) $\frac{5}{13}, \frac{12}{13}, \frac{5}{12}$ (iii) $\frac{8}{17}, \frac{15}{17}, \frac{8}{15}$
2. (i) $\frac{1}{\sqrt{5}}, \frac{2}{\sqrt{5}}, \frac{1}{2}, \frac{2}{\sqrt{5}}, \frac{1}{\sqrt{5}}, 2$ (ii) $\frac{20}{29}, \frac{21}{29}, \frac{20}{21}, \frac{21}{29}, \frac{20}{29}, \frac{21}{20}$
(iii) $\frac{3}{\sqrt{13}}, \frac{1}{\sqrt{5}}, \frac{2}{3}, \frac{2}{\sqrt{13}}, \frac{3}{\sqrt{13}}, \frac{3}{2}$ **3.** (i) 0.9659 (ii) 0.8660
(iii) 0.2558 (iv) 0.2419 (v) 0.6691 (vi) 0.9962
(vii) 0.2126 (viii) 0.5774 (ix) 5.6713 (x) 0.3420
(xi) 0.4067 (xii) 0.9657 **4.** (i) 0.1736 (ii) 0.9397
(iii) 0.7660 (iv) 0.8660 (v) 0.2588 **5.** (i) $65°$
(ii) $48°$ (iii) $35°$ (iv) $8°$ (v) $90° - x°$

Exercise 28.3

1. (i) 8 (ii) 6.34 (iii) 11.47 (iv) 17.10 (v) 10.32
(vi) 24.59 (vii) 5 (viii) 28.28 (ix) 8.66
2. (a) (i) 8.57 (ii) 5.00 (iii) 4.37 (iv) 28.28
(v) 14.74 (vi) 6.93 (vii) 16.71 (viii) 5 (ix) 5.77
(b) (i) 10.46 (ii) 9.43 (iii) 8.25 (iv) 28.29
(v) 12.73 (vi) 13.86 (vii) 19.92 (viii) 8.66
(ix) 11.55 **3.** 64.28, 11.33 **4.** 3.58, 4.67, 12.13

Exercise 28.4

1. (i) $20°$ (ii) $40°$ (iii) $29°$ (iv) $27°$ (v) $49°$
(vi) $25°$ (vii) $50°$ (viii) $33°$ (ix) $42°$ (x) $9°$ (xi) $70°$
(xii) $24°$ **2.** (i) $15°$ (ii) $17°$ (iii) $37°$ (iv) $7°$ (v) $67°$
(vi) $41°$ (vii) $7°$ (viii) $64°$ (ix) $28°$ (x) $40°$
3. (a)(i) $53°$ (ii) $67°$ (iii) $53°$ (b)(i) 5 (ii) 12
(iii) 6 **4.** (i) $58°, 32°$ (ii) $53°, 37°$ (iii) $31°, 59°$
5. (a)(i) $56°$ (ii) $23°$ (iii) $24°$ (b)(i) 1.66 (ii) 5
(iii) 22.91 **6.** (i) $23°$ (ii) $23°$ (iii) $53°$

Exercise 28.5

1. 170 cm **2.** 46 m **3.** 231 cm **4.** (i) 16.9 km
(ii) 8.5 km/hr (iii) 270 km **5.** 113.43 m **6.** 346.41 m
7. (i) 16 m (ii) 18 m **8.** 527 m **9.** 4.95 m **10.** 5.8
11. 300 m

Revision Exercises

1. (i) 7 (ii) 15 (iii) 37 (iv) 25 **2.** (i) 0.8090 (ii) 0.3746
(iii) 0.2679 (iv) 0.8660 (v) 0.9397 (vi) 11.4301

(vii) 1.000 (viii) 0.7071 (ix) 0.7071 (x) 0.9397
3. (i) $\sin A = {}^{77}/_{85}$; $\cos A = {}^{36}/_{85}$; $\tan A = {}^{77}/_{36}$; $\sin B = {}^{36}/_{85}$;
$\cos B = {}^{77}/_{85}$; $\tan B = {}^{36}/_{77}$ (ii) $\sin A = {}^{39}/_{89}$; $\cos A = {}^{80}/_{89}$;
$\tan A = {}^{39}/_{80}$; $\sin B = {}^{80}/_{89}$; $\cos B = {}^{39}/_{87}$; $\tan B = {}^{80}/_{39}$
(iii) $\sin A = {}^{48}/_{73}$; $\cos A = {}^{55}/_{73}$; $\tan A = {}^{48}/_{55}$; $\sin B = {}^{55}/_{73}$;
$\cos B = {}^{48}/_{73}$; $\tan B = {}^{55}/_{48}$; (iv) $\sin A = {}^{65}/_{97}$; $\cos A = {}^{72}/_{97}$;
$\tan A = {}^{65}/_{72}$; $\sin B = {}^{72}/_{97}$; $\cos B = {}^{65}/_{97}$; $\tan B = {}^{72}/_{65}$
4. (i) 61.2° (ii) 9.7° (iii) 22.9° (iv) 43.1° (v) 59.1°
(vi) 18.3° (vii) 15.6° (viii) 55.6° (ix) 70.3° (x) 58.6°
5. (i) 44° (ii) $\sin A = 0.3746$, $\sin B = 0.6947$ (iii) No
6. (a) 70° (b) 8 (c) 6 **7.** (i)(a) 0.78 (b) 0.47
(ii) 9.04, 11.63 **8.** (i) $^4/_5$ (ii) 28.56 m **9.** (i) 10, $^5/_{13}$
(ii) 7.4 **10.** 18 m **11.** 40 km **12.** 42.26 m
13. (i) 37°, 53°, 25 (ii) 110.79 cm² **14.** (i) 2.89 m
(ii) 7.9 m **15.** 173.21 m²

Chapter 29

Exercise 29.1

1. $x + 2$ **2.** $x - 3$ **3.** Paul: $\$x + 5$, Paul's wife: $\$2x - 5$
4. (i) 13, 14 (ii) $n + 1, n + 2$ **5.** $15 - y$ **6.** $14 - x$
7. $25 - 2x$ **8.** (i) $14x - 6$ (ii) $10x^2 - 15x$ **9.** (i) $600x$ cm²
(ii) $500x$ cm² **10.** (i) 22, 24 (ii) $m + 2, m + 4$
11. (i) Area $= 2x^2 + 6x$, Perimeter $= 6x + 6$
(ii) Area: $2x^2 + 5x + 2$, Perimeter $= 6x + 6$
(iii) Area $= 9x^2 - 12x + 4$, Perimeter $= 12x - 8$
(iv) Area $= \frac{3x^2}{2}$ or $1.5x^2$, Perimeter $= 4x + 6$
12. (i) $x^2 + 4x + 3$ (ii) $x^2 + 14x + 40$ (iii) $2x^2 + 7x + 3$
(iv) $6x^2 + 17x + 12$ **13.** (i) $x + 3$ (ii) $3x + 6$
(iii) $84 - 3x$ **14.** (i) 48 (ii) 240 (iii) $24x$ **15.** $80 - 5x$
16. (i) 12 (ii) 24 (iii) $12y$ **17.** $3x$ points, $4x + 5$ points
18. Total score: $10x - 10$ **19.** $4x + 10$
20. (i) Perimeter $= 4x + 16$ (ii) Perimeter $= 4x + 10$
(iii) Perimeter $= 4x + 8$

Exercise 29.2

1. $x = 11$ **2.** $x = 11$ **3.** $x = 3$ **4.** $x = 9$ **5.** $x = 2$
6. $x = 30$ **7.** $a = 4, b = 3$ **8.** Harry: 12, Fred: 14
9. Paul: 36, Yousef: 37 **10.** 10, 11 **11.** 21, 22
12. Emer: 14, Nishi: 17 **13.** 19, 20 **14.** 10, 11, 12
15. Barry: 12, Colm: 24, Dave: 21 **16.** $x = 11$
17. (i) $x = 3, y = 2$ (ii) $x = 3, y = 9$
18. (i) $9x + 25$ (ii) $-10x + 6$ (iii) $x = -1$ **19.** $x = 30$
20. 7 years **21.** 6, 8, 10, 12 **22.** 10, 11, 12
23. Peter: 10, Kristin: 2 **24.** Rabbits: 7, Gerbils: 13
25. 5 **26.** Minibuses: 5, Buses: 3 **27.** 5 Packets
28. Jane: 3, Father: 15, Mother: 19 **29.** 11 years
30. $x = 8$

Exercise 29.3

1. Pen: 10 cents, Marker: 20 cents **2.** Apple: 15 cents,
Orange: 12 cents **3.** Win: 5 points, Draw: 2 points
4. Adults: 5, Children: 7 **5.** Chickens: 11, Pigs: 4
6. $x = 2, y = 3$ **7.** $x = 3, y = 11$ **8.** Adult: €5,
Child: €3 **9.** Coach: €200, Minibuses: €100
10. Short: 25, Long: 75 **11.** $x = 10, y = 4$ **12.** €30
tickets: 650, €40 tickets: 350 **13.** Wheat: 80 hectares,
Vegetables: 20 hectares **14.** 500 minutes

Exercise 29.4

1. $x = -5$ or $x = 3$ **2.** $y = -6$ or $y = 2$ **3.** $x = 5$
4. $x = 4$ or $x = 2$ **5.** 4, 5 **6.** Length $= 4$ m, Breadth $= 7$ m
7. $x = 9$ or $x = -4$ **8.** 2, 6 **9.** $x = 2$ or $x = 5$ **10.** $x = 3$
11. $-12, -8$ or 8, 12 **12.** $x = -10$ or $x = 4$ **13.** $n = 3$
14. 8, 10 **15.** (i) $12 - x$ (ii) $x^2 - 12x + 32 = 0$ (iii) 4, 8
16. $x = 3$ **17.** 3, 11 **18.** 3, 4, 5 **19.** (i) $y = 10 - x$
(ii) 3 m and 7 m **20.** 3, 5, 7 **21.** (i) $x^2 + 10x + 24$
(ii) 6 m and 8 m (iii) 44 m²

Revision Exercises

1. $4x$ **2.** $8 - x$ **3.** $20 - x$ **4.** (i) 16, 17 (ii) $a + 1, a + 2$
(iii) 17, 19 (iv) $a + 2, a + 4$ **5.** $x = 6$
6. $2(5 - x) = 10 - 2x$ **7.** (i) 180 minutes (ii) 265 minutes
(iii) $60x$ minutes (iv) $60x + y$ minutes **9.** 4 **10.** 12
11. John: 15, Simon: 16 **12.** Roberta: 12, Patricia: 16
13. 22, 23 **14.** 60, 61 **15.** Alan: 7 cents,
Bertie: 21 cents, Carol: 23 cents **16.** 17, 18, 19
17. 8 years old **18.** 7, 8 **19.** 5, 6, 7 **20.** 3 years old
21. Peter: 17 cents, Quentin: 23 cents, **22.** Part 1: 10,
Part 2: 7 **23.** 60 **24.** 9 **25.** Pen: 20 cents,
Pencil: 12 cents **26.** Cone: 45 cents, Ice-pop: 15 cents
27. $x = 10, y = 14$ **28.** Paper: 85, Hardback: 35
29. $x = 5, y = 5$ **30.** Orange: 5, Blue: 3 **31.** 4, 7
32. $x = 1$

Chapter 30

Exercise 30.1

3. (i) (4,4) (ii) (−2,1) (iii) (2,−4) (iv) (0,−3) **4.** (i) (6,2)
(ii) (2,4) (iii) (6,6) (iv) (−4,−5) (v) (4,2) (vi) (7,18)
(vii) (1,2) (viii) (−2,3) (ix) (3,2) (x) (4,3) **5.** (i) No
(ii) Yes (iii) Yes (iv) No

Exercise 30.2

1. (i) €180   (ii) €60   (iii) 550 km   (iv) $y = 0.2x + 20$
(v) €264   **2.** (i) €11   (ii) €9   (iii) $4\frac{1}{2}$ km   (iv) $y = 2x + 3$
(v) €23   **3.** (i) €136   (ii) €175   (iii) 900 units
(iv) €268.12   **4.** (i) €40   (ii) €55   (iii) 400 units
(iv) $y = 0.1x + 20$ (v) €100   **5.** (ii) 32°F   (iii) 5°C
(iv) 212°F   **6.** (i) €100   (ii) €220   (iii) 270 people
(iv) $y = 0.6x + 100$ (v) €310   **7.** (i) €20,000
(ii) €12,800   (iii) €8,000   (iv) $y = -2,400x + 20,000$
(v) €5,600   **8.** (i) €84,000   (ii) €92,000   (iii) 2013
(iv) Yes

Exercise 30.3

1. (ii) €370   (iii) €480   **2.** (iii) No. The line does not
pass through (0,0).   (iv) €200   (v) €290
3. (ii) Linear pattern   (iii) 77   **4.** (ii) 50 cm
(iii) Linear pattern   (iv) 95 cm   (v) 10 weeks
5. (ii) Linear pattern   **6.** (iii) €2,250   (iv) 16
7. (iii) After Day 3   (iv) €330,000   (v) €70,000 profit
8. (iii) 5   (iv) 18 days   **9.** (ii) 40 weeks
11. (iii) €27,000   (v) Mad Printers

Exercise 30.4

1. (ii) 159 km   (iii) 1 minute 24 seconds
2. (ii) Exponential   (iii) 8.96 km²   **3.** (i) 17,000
(ii) Quadratic   (iii) 12,000   (iv) 10 a.m.
4. (i) Quadratic   (ii) Month 11   (iii) Month 5
(iv) ≈56⅔ km²   (v) Months 9, 10 and 11   **5.** (ii) 6 cm
(iii) Day 4 and 5   (iv) Day 0 and Day 1   (v) 27 cm

Exercise 30.5

1. (i) 140 km   (ii) 13:00   (iii) Along the line segment
[*DE*]   **4.** Fig A → Statement 5, Fig B → Statement 4,
Fig C → Statement 2, Fig D → Statement 1,
Fig E → Statement 3   **5.** (ii) 2.7 secs   (iii) 45 m/s

Revision Exercises

1. (i) (−1,6)   (ii) (−1,2)   (iii) (3,2)   (iv) (12,12)
2. (i) 8   (ii) €8 per hour   (iii) €32   (iv) €64
3. (ii) Initial set-up costs   (iii) €19   (iv) €75
4. (iii) More than 6 months   **5.** (ii) $y = 20x + 50$
(iii) Call-out charge   (iv) Additional cost per hour
(v) €220   **6.** (i) 18:30   (ii) Between 18:45 and 19:00

(iii) 34.29 km/hr   **7.** (i) Yes   (ii) No   (iii) Yes   (iv) No
8. (i) About 9 m   (ii) The train travels slowly for the
first 20 seconds. Its speed then increases from around
25 seconds into the journey.   (iii) It is a train leaving
a station.   **10.** (i) 450 grams   (ii) 7 ounces   (iii) $200/7$
(iv) $y = \frac{200}{7}x$ (v) 1428.6 grams   **11.** (ii) Quadratic
(iii) Days 4 and 5   (iv) Day 6: 66, Day 7: 90
12. (ii) It is constant.   (iii) ≈26.4 cm   (iv) ≈13.6 cm
13. (i) €120   (ii) €400   (iv) Cheaper Vans
(v) Vans R Us: €1,800, Cheaper Vans: €1,150
14. (i) Exponential   (iii) Day 12: 16,384
15. (ii) Quadratic   (iii) 6.25 m   (iv) The bird had landed
and is now taking off again.   **16.** (ii) 196 cans   (iii) 84 cm

Chapter 31

Exercise 31.1

1. 17   **2.** 13   **3.** 73   **4.** 20   **6.** $a = 17, b = -11, c = 4$
7. $p = 5, q = 0, r = -2, s = 8$ **8.** {3, 8, 13}   **9.** (i) 4
(ii) {4, 3, 2, 1, 0, −1}   **10.** {1, 2, 5}   **11.** {14, 17, 20}
12. {−10, −3, 4, 11}   **13.** {4, 29}   **14.** (i) 18   (ii) 50
(iii) 200   **15.** {7, 22, 43, 70}   **16.** {7, 37, 87}
17. (i) 27   (ii) −43   (iii) 5   (iv) 2   **18.** (i) 5, 13, 21
(ii) No   (iii) 25   **19.** 19, −86, 10   **20.** 21, 3, −3
21. (i) {1, 3, 5}   (ii) {0, 1, 2, 3, 4, 5}   **22.** (i) {2, 3}
(ii) {0, 1, 2, 3}   **23.** 38   **24.** (i) 50   (ii) 2   (iii) 92
25. 0 and 0   **26.** (i) 18   (ii) 0   (iii) 0   **27.** (i) 10   (ii) 0
(iii) 0   **28.** (i) 2   (ii) 1½   **29.** 10   **30.** (i) 3   (ii) $x \leqslant 3$

Exercise 31.2

3. (ii) 6.9   **4.** (b)(i) 6   (ii) 2.5   **5.** (b)(i) 1.7   (ii) −0.4
6. (b)(i) 3.4   (ii) 2.3   **7.** (b)(i) −4.2   (ii) 2.75   **8.** (ii) (2,1)
9. (ii) (1,−2)   **10.** (ii) (−1,1)   **11.** (ii) (4,−1)   **12.** (3,−1)
13. (c)(i) 250 mins   (ii) 3.75 kg   **14.** (c)(i) 63°   (ii) 28°
15. (c)(i) 26   (ii) 18

Exercise 31.3

1. (i) 3.3   (ii) 1,3   **2.** (i) 4.3   (ii) 1.6,4.4   **3.** (i) 2.75
(ii) −1,4   (iii) −0.6,3.6   **4.** (i) −8.25   (ii) −4,3
(iii) −3.4,2.4   **5.** (i) −3.6   (ii) −1.8,2.8   (iii) −2.5,3.5
6. (i) 4.25   (ii) −0.4,2.4   (iii) −2   **7.** (i) −1.25
(ii) −1,4   (iii) 0.4,2.6   **8.** (i) −2.75   (ii) −3.2,1.2
(iii) −5,−1   **9.** (i) 1.3   (ii) −4,0   (iii) −3.4,−0.6
(iv) −4,−2   **10.** (i) −4   (ii) −2.45,+2.45

(iii) −3.3,+3.3　**11.** (i) 2.25°　(ii) −4° at 3 a.m.
(iii) 1 a.m. and 5 a.m.　**12.** (i) −6　(ii) −1.3,2.8
13. (i) −0.7,1.7　(ii) −1.8,2.8　**14.** (i) 7.5
(ii) −2.2,0.6　**15.** (i) −3.5　(ii) −1.7,1.2
(iii) x = −1.4,0.9　**16.** (i) 7.3 m/s　(ii) 4 s
(iii) 2.6 and 5.4 seconds　**17.** (i) 12.75　(ii) 00.30 a.m.

(iii) 10.30 p.m. and 2.30 a.m.　**18.** (i) 3.8　(ii) 10.4 metres
(iii) 8.8 metres　**19.** (i) 6.1 m　(ii) 9 m　(iii) 6 seconds
20. (i) 10 a.m.　(ii) 6 hours　(iii) 9 km; 1 p.m.
21. (−1,3) and (3,7)　**22.** (i) −1.85,1.35　(ii) −1.5,2
23. (i) −0.8,3.8　(ii) 3　(iii) 0,2　**24.** (i) 0,4
(ii) 4　(iii) 2,4

Theorems

1. Vertically opposite angles are equal in measure.